Reviewer Acclaim for *Debugging Microsoft .NET 2.0 Applications*

"*Debugging Microsoft .NET 2.0 Applications* is the missing manual for so many great debugging and development tools and techniques—and that's not even half of it. You'll get exact details on how to approach very tricky problems, as well as advice on engineering practices that will keep you from having those bugs to solve in the first place. John Robbins writes in an engaging style and provides many helpful references, including a treasure chest of useful tools and code so you can start using his suggestions immediately (and you'll want to)."
—Maria Blees, Software Development Engineer, Microsoft Corporation

"*Debugging Microsoft .NET 2.0 Applications* is the definitive book on debugging .NET. I think that I learned something new on every page and couldn't wait to get a peek at the next chapter. This book will be required reading for our development team."
—Jeff Lewis, Senior Developer, Xactware Inc.

"Since we can't eliminate bugs, we have to be able to deal with them effectively. It's a multi faceted problem involving attitude, thinking skills, planning, and tools. John Robbins gives us in depth coverage of everything: how to keep the bugs out in the first place, how to methodically attack bugs, and how to make best use of all the tools available to us. *Debugging Microsoft .NET 2.0 Applications* will save your bacon!"
—David Douglass, Technologies Consultant II, ADP, Inc.

"*Debugging Microsoft .NET 2.0 Applications* is simply a great resource. Not only do you get a whole heap of killer tricks to help you debug smarter and faster but also John's passion for explaining the techniques make sure you'll be writing great code, eliminating bugs before they happen."
—Jim McGregor, HBOS Plc

"After reading *Debugging Microsoft .NET 2.0 Applications*, I can only say that had John been around 300 years ago he surely would have been burned as a witch."
—Dave Montgomery, Triant

"John is the master code pest exterminator, and *Debugging Microsoft .NET 2.0 Applications* is one of the few that every .NET developer *must* have on the bookshelf! It's an intense read, but the book covers debugging from the most superficial step-through techniques in Visual Studio through the gnarly low-level .NET-Windows interaction bug. Best of all, the book is filled with the sage wisdom that John has developed over his many years of helping developers find and eradicate the worst, most pernicious, bugs."
—Don Keily, Senior Technical Consultant

"John Robbins has once again written an engaging and very practical book on debugging. With the latest techniques for .NET 2.0, in-depth discussions on how to make the most of the IDE, compilers and debuggers, and heaps of source code for his ever-useful tools, John continues to share his depth of experience with us. *Debugging Microsoft .NET 2.0 Applications* has saved countless hours of debugging by providing the right tools, methods, and pointers to quickly stamp out and even completely avoid bugs."
—**Thomas Fejes**, Independent Consultant, DeltaFusion Pty Ltd

"For software engineers gaining enough debugging skills to save a project can be a great career move. Reading *Debugging Microsoft .NET 2.0 Applications* is a major step toward gaining those skills. There is something in this book for all experience levels. Once you have read it you may find yourself wishing that you had more bugs to track down, just so that you put what you have learnt to good use."
—**Mark Bartosik**, *www.leakbrowser.com*

"Software developers can spend up to half their development time debugging code. John Robbins' *Debugging Microsoft .NET 2.0 Applications* will help anyone developing programs for .NET to learn proactive debugging skills that will help them find bugs quicker and with far less frustration. One of the 'must have' books for .NET developers."
—**Roger Orr**, OR/2.

"If you think you are a Debugging Guru and there is nothing more to learn about debugging, think twice before skipping John Robbins' *Debugging Microsoft .NET 2.0 Applications*. The tips, tools, and amount of information about bug hunting is impressive and sufficient to help you hunting the toughest and scariest bugs hidden somewhere inside the internals of some application. Definitely a must!"
—**Roberto A. Farah**, Escalation Engineer, Microsoft

Debugging Microsoft® .NET 2.0 Applications

John Robbins

Wintellect®
Know how.

PUBLISHED BY
Microsoft Press
A Division of Microsoft Corporation
One Microsoft Way
Redmond, Washington 98052-6399

ISBN-13: 978-0-7356-2202-9
ISBN-10: 0-7356-2202-7
Library of Congress Control Number 2006932078

Printed and bound in the United States of America.

1 2 3 4 5 6 7 8 9   QWT   1 0 9 8 7 6

Distributed in Canada by H.B. Fenn and Company Ltd.

Microsoft Press books are available through booksellers and distributors worldwide. For further information about international editions, contact your local Microsoft Corporation office or contact Microsoft Press International directly at fax (425) 936-7329. Visit our Web site at www.microsoft.com/mspress. Send comments to mspinput@microsoft.com.

Acquisitions Editor: Ben Ryan
Project Editor: Valerie Woolley
Technical Editor: Christophe Nasarre; Technical Review services provided by Content Master, a member of CM Group, Ltd.
Copy Editor: Joel Rosenthal
Indexer: Brenda Miller

Body Part No. X11-97539

To three of the most important people in my life.

*My parents, Rob and Doris Robbins, for giving me
a wonderful childhood full of adventure that
can only be described as growing up in a
National Geographic special. Your love
and support mean the world to me.*

*My sister, Deborah Matthews. Someday
I hope to be as sharp, as funny,
and as brave as you are.*

Contents at a Glance

Table of Contents

Part III   Power Tools

Acknowledgments

If you have read the first two editions of this book, any of my Bugslayer columns, or heard me speak a conference or in a class, I can't thank you enough! Your continued interest in debugging and writing better code is what kept me slogging through all the tough times writing another edition. I greatly appreciate the e-mail exchanges and discussions we've had. You've taught me a great deal. Thank you.

Three extraordinary people have made this book happen, and I can't thank them enough: Valerie Woolley (project editor), Christophe Nasarre (technical editor), Joel Rosenthal (copy editor), and Ben Ryan (acquisition editor). They took my incoherent ramblings and made them into the book you have in your hands. The effort they put in was simply stupendous.

As with the previous editions, a great group of people have my eternal gratitude–my "Review Crew." These brave souls put up with my complete lack of English skills and still suggested many absolutely amazing debugging tricks. They represent the best in the business today. Here's the lineup: Mark Bartosik, Maria Blees, Derek Cooke, Chad Coon, Stoyan Damov, David Douglass, Richard Dutton, Roberto Farah, Thomas Fejes, Moishe Halibard, Don Kiely, Martin Kulov, Jeff Lewis, Spencer Low, Jim McGregor, Dave Montgomery, Roger Orr, Osiris Pedroso, Jeff Scanlon, Austin Thompson, and Jalil Vaidya. A very special thanks to Maria Blees, her impact on this book is immeasurable.

I am honored and humbled to be associated with my fellow Wintellectuals who contributed to this book in countless ways: Cara Allison, Jim Austin, Jim Bail, Paula Daniels, Sam Easterby, Sara Faatz, Todd Fine, Lewis Frazer, Bethany Jones, Steve Porter, Jeff Prosise, Jeffrey Richter, Kenn Scribner, David Shoots, Justin Smith, and Gregory Young.

Finally, the biggest thank you of all goes, as always, to my wife, Pam. She sacrificed a lot of evenings and weekends while I was working on this book. Honey, it's done. You can have your husband back.

Introduction

Bugs suck. Period. Bugs are the reason you're subjected to death-march projects with missed deadlines, late nights, and grouchy coworkers. Bugs can truly make your life miserable because if enough of them creep into your software, customers might stop using your product, and you could lose your job. Bugs are serious business.

Many times, people in our industry portray bugs simply as annoyances. Nothing could be further from the truth. All engineers can point to projects with runaway bug counts and even to companies that have folded because they released software so full of bugs that the product was unusable. As I was writing the first edition of this book, NASA lost a Mars space probe because of a bug that snuck in during the requirements and design phase. While I was writing the second edition, a bomb was dropped on American Special Forces soldiers instead of the intended target because batteries were changed in GPS software, causing a programming error. The week before I wrote this introduction to the third edition, Microsoft released a software patch for a software patch that introduced a huge buffer-overrun vulnerability in Microsoft Internet Explorer 6. Although software bugs are starting to get more of their due, there's still a very long way to go until we have a development culture in which bugs are taken super seriously instead of as minor problems that just happen as a part of development.

My hope is that the information in this book will help you learn how to write your applications with fewer bugs in the first place—and that when you're required to debug, you can do it much faster. Without realizing it, most teams spend an average of 50 percent of their development cycle debugging. If you start debugging properly, you can drastically reduce that amount of time, which means that you'll ship your products faster. You can't cut corners when it comes to requirements gathering and design, but you can certainly learn to debug much smarter. This book takes a holistic approach to debugging. I don't consider debugging a separate step, but an integral part of the entire product cycle. I believe you need to start debugging in the requirements phase and continue through to the final release to manufacturing.

Two issues make debugging in the Microsoft .NET environment difficult and time consuming. The first issue is that debugging has always been a self-taught skill—you've basically been on your own to figure it out. Even if you have a computer science degree, I'm willing to bet that you never took a single college class dedicated to debugging. Other than some esoteric subjects such as devising automatic program verification for languages that no one uses, or developing debuggers for wildly optimistic, massively parallel-processing computers, the science of debugging as it applies to commercial software doesn't seem to be popular with the educational establishment. Some professors point out that you shouldn't be writing code with bugs in the first place. Although that's an excellent point and an ideal we should all strive for, reality is a little different. Learning systematic, proven techniques for debugging won't prevent you from ever writing another bug, but following the practices in this book will help you limit the number of bugs you add to your code and to track down more quickly those bugs that do occur.

The second issue is that although many excellent books on specific .NET technologies are available, none of them cover debugging in enough depth to be useful. To debug any technology effectively, you have to know far more than a book focused on a specific technology provides. It's one thing to know how to write a Microsoft ASP.NET control that plugs into your ASP.NET page, but it's another thing entirely to be able to debug that ASP.NET control. To debug that ASP.NET control, you'll have to know the ins and outs of .NET and ASP.NET, how DLLs are put in the ASP.NET temporary cache, and how ASP.NET goes about finding those controls in the first place. Some books make it look easy to implement sophisticated features, such as remote database connections, by using the hot technology du jour, but when "db.Connect ("Foo")" fails in your program—and it eventually will—you're on your own to find and mend the broken link in the technology chain. Moreover, although a few books on project management do discuss debugging, they tend to focus on managerial and administrative issues rather than on developers' concerns. Those books might include fine information about how to plan for debugging, but they don't help much when you're staring at a corrupted database or a constantly restarting ASP.NET worker process.

The idea for this book came out of my trials and tribulations as a developer and manager trying to ship high-quality products on time, and as a consultant trying to help others ship on time. Over the years, I've learned skills and techniques that I use to deal with each of the two issues that help make developing Microsoft Windows–based applications a challenge. To address the lack of formal debugging training, I wrote the first part of this book to give you a crash course in debugging—with a decided slant toward commercial development. As for the second issue—the need for a book specifically on debugging .NET—I think I've provided a book that bridges the gap between specific technologies and nitty-gritty, real-world debugging techniques.

I've been extremely fortunate to have had the opportunity to focus on debugging almost exclusively for the last eleven years. A few experiences have helped shape my unique perspective on the subject of debugging. The first experience was at NuMega Technologies (now Compuware), where I was one of the first engineers working on cool projects such as BoundsChecker, TrueTime, TrueCoverage, and SoftICE. While working at NuMega, I started writing the "Bugslayer" column in MSDN Magazine, and then I eventually left to write the first edition of this book. The fantastic e-mail exchanges and interactions I've had with engineers developing every type of application imaginable teaches me even more about the issues that engineers face today when shipping products.

Finally, the most important experience of all in shaping my view has been forming Wintellect, which gives me the chance to go out and help solve those amazing problems for companies all over the world. Imagine that you're sitting in some office at 2 A.M., you're out of ideas, and the client's going to go out of business if you don't solve the bug—this scenario can be scary, but it also gets your adrenaline flowing. Working with the best engineers at such companies as Microsoft, eBay, Intuit, and many others, is the best way I know to learn all sorts of great tricks and techniques for solving bugs.

Who Should Read This Book?

I wrote this book for developers who are tired of spending late nights at work debugging and want to improve the quality of their code and their organizations. I also wrote this book for managers and team leaders who want to develop more efficient and effective teams.

From a technical perspective, the ideal reader is someone who has one to three years of experience developing on the .NET or Windows platform. I also expect the reader to have been a member of a real-world development team and to have shipped at least one product. Although I don't care for the term, the software industry labels developers with this level of experience *intermediate developers*.

Advanced developers will probably learn a great deal as well. Many of the most enthusiastic e-mail messages I received about the previous editions were from advanced developers who didn't expect to learn anything. I was thrilled that the book was able to give them tools they could add to their toolboxes. Again, as in the previous editions, a wonderful group of friends named the Review Crew reviewed and critiqued the chapters before I submitted them to Microsoft Press. These engineers, who are listed in the Acknowledgments section of this book, are the crème de la crème of developers, and they made sure that everyone reading the book would learn something.

How to Read This Book and What's New in the Third Edition

The first edition focused on Microsoft Visual Studio 6 and Microsoft Win32 debugging. The second focused on Microsoft Visual Studio .NET 2003 and a completely new programming paradigm, .NET, along with native Windows development. This edition of the book focuses completely on .NET 2.0 and Microsoft Visual Studio 2005. For those of you still doing mostly native development, there will be another version of this book in the future that focuses entirely on native C++ development.

The first edition contained 512 pages just for native development, the second had around 850 for both native and .NET, and this edition consists of approximately 480 pages just for .NET. When I embarked on this .NET-only edition, I thought it was only going to be a partial rewrite, but it turned into at least an 80 percent rewrite. In Chapter 6, "WinDBG, SOS, and ADPlus" (the longest chapter in the book), the total shared text amounted to four paragraphs between the editions. Narrowing the book's focus and all the major changes in .NET 2.0 and Visual Studio 2005 caused a lot of the change. However, a major reason was all the wonderful e-mails and discussions I had with readers of the second edition and their excellent criticisms and suggestions on how to make the book better.

Code Samples

In the previous editions, the huge amount of code and utilities included with the book were something that everyone liked. The first edition had 2.5 MB of text source code, and the second edition had 6.9 MB. Even though the page count dropped with the .NET focus, Windows Explorer tells me that there's more than 9.7 MB of code for this edition! Remember, that's just *text* and supporting files, not compiled binaries. Several of the Review Crew said that the included code is bigger than most entire development books out there today. By the way, all of the code is brand new so it can take advantage of the .NET 2.0 features.

In the book I refer to source files that are part of the code samples with a ".\" in front of the directory. For example, when discussing the Connect.cs file in the WhoAmI add-in, which is in the WhoAmI directory where you install the source code, I show the file reference as .\WhoAmI\Connect.cs. Because of the many code references in the book's text, this saves having to read *Book_Source_Code_Installation_Directory*\WhoAmI\Connect.cs for each one.

Organization of This Book

I divided the book into three distinct parts. You should read the first two parts (Chapters 1 through 6) in order, because I build the information in a logical progression.

In the first part of the book, "The Gestalt of Debugging" (Chapters 1 through 4), I define the different types of bugs and develop a process for debugging that all great developers follow. I also discuss the infrastructure requirements necessary for proper team debugging. I strongly suggest that you pay particular attention to the discussion on setting up Symbol Servers and setting up Source Servers in Chapter 2, "Preparing for Debugging." Because you can (and should) do a tremendous amount of debugging during the coding phase, I cover how you can proactively debug as you're writing your code. The discussion on assertions in Chapter 3, "Debugging During Coding," should be the final word on the subject for .NET. To help you achieve the breadth and depth necessary to be a good debugger, in Chapter 4, "Common .NET Debugging Questions," I answer all the common debugging questions I've gotten since I wrote the last edition. I also included tricks on how to work around problems in Visual Studio so you won't pull your hair out wrestling with the tool.

In the second part of the book, "Power Debugging" (Chapters 5 and 6), I dive deep into all aspects of the two main debuggers you'll use in .NET development: Visual Studio and WinDBG. Visual Studio has undergone a substantial transformation compared to previous editions, and the power at your fingertips is astounding. Fortunately for me, the documentation does not do all the features justice, so I was able to dig deep and show you all sorts of amazing tricks for smarter and faster debugging with this wonderful tool. WinDBG, the Son of Strike (SOS) extension, and ADPlus are the tools that you'll use for the nastiest of production-only bugs. In Chapter 6, I've done my best to provide you with the direction you'll need to effectively use these tools even if you've never seen them before.

One thing I learned while working with developers from across the industry—from the inexperienced to the very experienced—was that they were using only a tiny fraction of the power of the Visual Studio debugger and almost none of WinDBG, SOS, and ADPlus. Although this sentiment might sound odd coming from an author of a book about debugging, I want to keep you out of the debugger as much as possible. As you read this book, you'll see that much of my goal for you isn't just to learn how to fix bugs and crashes but how to avoid them in the first place. I also want to teach you to use the debuggers to their maximum effectiveness because there will be times when you're forced to use them.

The last section, "Power Tools" (Chapters 7 and 8), discusses extending Visual Studio 2005 and building Code Analysis/FxCop rules. In the previous edition of this book, the Settings Master add-in proved hugely popular and I rewrote it to be even more powerful so you can apply project settings changes to all your projects at the click of a button. It's even easier to create new settings files, so making wholesale changes to your build is trivial. Additionally, I provide a new add-in, Hidden Settings, which exposes undocumented settings in the IDE so you can easily change their values. In Chapter 8, I tackled extending the undocumented Code Analysis /FxCop rules and came up with numerous rules that I felt should be part of any design guidelines.

In the previous editions, I offered a few sidebars about various debugging war stories I'd seen. I've added a few more war stories in this edition that I think you'll enjoy. I hope that by sharing with you some of the really "good" bugs I've helped solve (and some I've helped write!), you'll see the practical application of the approaches and techniques I recommend. I also want to help you avoid the mistakes that I've made.

System Requirements

To use this book, you'll need the following:

- Microsoft Windows 2000 SP4 or later, Microsoft Windows XP Professional, Windows XP Tablet PC Edition, Windows Server 2003, Windows XP Professional x64 Edition, Windows Server 2003 x64 Edition, or Windows Vista. There is no native code in the book's source code, so it should run on Windows XP Professional IA64 Edition and Windows Server 2003 IA64 Edition, but I did not have access to an Itanium-based machine for testing.

- For full functionality, you'll need Microsoft Visual Studio 2005 Team Developer Edition or Microsoft Visual Studio 2005 Team Suite. If you only have Visual Studio 2005 Professional, you will be able to build the utilities but not build or run any of the test code. The Visual Studio Express editions may be able to build the code, but I did not do any testing against them. Also, because the Visual Studio Express editions do not support any extensibility, they will not be able to use any of the macros or add-ins from Chapter 7.

What Comes with This Book's Sample Files?

As I've already mentioned, there's 9.7 MB of source files, and you can download the latest version at *http://dtt.wintellect.com*. Because the only way I know how to develop is to treat every project as a commercial project, I treated all the code as a library you would purchase (which in essence you've done by purchasing the book), so you have a full install and Readme.chm as you would expect. The tools and utilities that plug into Visual Studio 2005 also have a full installation. At Wintellect, we've been using this code in all our projects, and so have our clients. For example, several million lines of .NET code have been run through the Code Analysis/FxCop rules from Chapter 8, "Writing Code Analysis Rules" If you find this code good enough to use in your applications, I'm deeply honored.

The main installation file, Debugging.msi, runs in accounts with limited privileges so anyone can install it. The default installation location is the user's My Documents directory, but you can change that if you like. For more detailed information on building the projects, the change log, and links to all Web sites referred to in the book, read Readme.chm in the directory where you installed the program. Once you've done the main install, you can install WintellectToolsInstall.msi from an account with administrator privileges so you can include all the Visual Studio add-ins and tools for all users on the machine.

READ THIS! Running with Least Privileges

The first common question I answer in Chapter 4 is about why developers need to use only accounts that have user privileges. Let me make it simple: if you're logging on with administrator privileges, that's wrong! All the code in this book was developed and tested as a pure user under all the operating systems. Naturally, I also tested the code running with administrator privileges, just to be sure everything worked. If you are logged on with administrator privileges, some of the test code will fail because it assumes that you don't have access to items like the C:\Windows directory and other protected areas on the computer.

Feedback

I'm very interested in knowing what you think of this book. If you have questions—or your own debugging war stories—I'd love to hear them! Please don't hesitate to send e-mail to *john@wintellect.com*. Please keep in mind that I travel quite a bit and get a lot of e-mail, so you might not get an immediate response, but I will answer your e-mail messages. You will also want to subscribe to the Wintellog at *http://www.wintellect.com/Weblogs/* because that's where I'll post notices about code updates and the like.

Thanks for reading, and happy debugging!

John Robbins
September 2006
Hollis, New Hampshire
Bob in 2020

Microsoft Press Support Information

Every effort has been made to ensure the accuracy of the book. Microsoft Press provides corrections for books through the World Wide Web at:

http://www.microsoft.com/learning/support/books

To connect directly to the Microsoft Press Knowledge Base and enter a query regarding a question or issue that you may have, go to:

http://www.microsoft.com/mspress/support/search.asp

If you have comments, questions, or ideas regarding the book or the CD-ROM or questions that are not answered by querying the Knowledge Base, please send them to Microsoft Press via e-mail to:

mspinput@microsoft.com

or via postal mail to:

Microsoft Press
Attn: Debugging Microsoft .NET 2.0 Applications Editor
One Microsoft Way
Redmond, WA 98052-6399

Please note that Microsoft software product support is not offered through the above addresses.

Part I
The Gestalt of Debugging

Chapter 1
Bugs: Where They Come From and How You Solve Them

Debugging is a fascinating topic no matter what language or platform you're using. It's the only part of software development in which engineers kick, scream at, or even throw their computers. For a normally reticent, introverted group, this degree of emotion is extraordinary. Debugging is also the part of software development that's famous for causing you to pull all-nighters. I've yet to run into an engineer who has called his or her partner to say, "Honey, I can't come home because we're having so much fun doing our UML diagrams that we want to pull an all-nighter!" However, I've run into plenty of engineers who have called their partner with the lament, "Honey, I can't come home because we've run into a whopper of a bug."

Bugs and Debugging

Bugs are cool! They help you learn the most about how things work. We all got into this business because we like to learn, and tracking down bugs is the ultimate learning experience. I don't know how many times I've had nearly every programming book I own open and spread out across my office looking for a good bug. It feels just plain great to find and fix those bugs! Of course, the coolest bugs are those that you find before the customer sees your product. That means that you have to do your job to find those bugs before your customers do. Having your customers find them is extremely uncool.

Compared with other engineering fields, software engineering is an anomaly in two ways. First, software engineering is a new and somewhat immature branch of engineering compared with other forms of engineering that have been around for a while, such as structural and electrical engineering. Second, users have come to accept bugs in our products, particularly in PC software. Although they grudgingly resign themselves to bugs on PCs, they're still not happy when they find them. Interestingly enough, those same customers would never tolerate a bug in a nuclear reactor design or a piece of medical hardware. With PC software becoming more a part of people's lives, the free ride that the software engineering field has enjoyed is nearly over. I don't doubt that the liability laws that apply to other engineering disciplines will eventually cover software engineering also.

You need to care about bugs because ultimately, they are costly to your business. In the short term, customers contact you for help, forcing you to spend your time and money sustaining the current product while your competitors work on their next versions. In the long term, the invisible hand of economics kicks in, and customers just start buying alternatives to your buggy product. Software is now more of a service than a capital investment, so the pressure for higher-quality software will increase. With every application supporting Extensible Markup Language (XML) for input and output, your users are almost able to switch among software products from various vendors just by moving from one Web site to another. This boon for users will mean less job security for you and me if our products are buggy and more incentive to create high-quality products. Let me phrase this another way: the buggier your product, the more likely you are to have to look for a new job. If there's anything that engineers hate, it's going through the job-hunting process.

What Are Bugs?

Before you can start debugging, you need a definition of "bugs." My definition of a bug is "anything that causes a user pain." I classify bugs into the following categories:

- Crashes and hangs
- Poor performance and scalability
- Incorrect results
- Security exploits
- Inconsistent user interfaces
- Unmet expectations

Crashes and Hangs

Crashes and hangs are what most developers and users think of when they think of a bug. Users might be able to work around other types of bugs I'll be describing, but obviously, crashes and hangs stop them dead, which is why the majority of this book concentrates on solving these extreme problems and finding ways to test them out of your code. As we all know, some of these bugs are easy to solve, and others are almost impossible. The main point to remember about crashes and hang bugs is that you should never ship a product if you know it has one of these bugs in it. Some may argue that you can ship with that rare crash or hang problem, but if you know about it and can duplicate it, even if it's hard to duplicate, you need to fix it.

Fortunately, Microsoft .NET eliminates many of the nasty and bizarre crash problems we all spent countless late nights tracking down when developing the native code. Of course, if you're using native components in your application, they still have the power to reach up and scramble the Common Language Runtime (CLR) internals at any time, so we are not free of crashes yet. In the .NET world, unhandled exceptions are the bane of the end-user existence. With the wonderful *Exception* class as the root of all errors, we have a clean way to figure out where the problem originated, and with a small bit of code that I'll discuss later in the book, you can easily build a super-smart error reporting system much like Microsoft's Windows Error Reporting, which has contributed magnificently to improving Microsoft Windows and Microsoft Office.

Poor Performance and Scalability

Users are very frustrated by bugs that cause the application to slow down when it encounters real-world data. Invariably, improper testing is the root of all poor performance bugs—however great the application might have looked in development, the team failed to test it with anything approaching real-world volumes or scenarios. One project I worked on years ago, NuMega's BoundsChecker 3.0, had this bug with its original FinalCheck technology. That version of FinalCheck inserted additional debugging and contextual information directly into the source code so that BoundsChecker could better report errors. Unfortunately, we failed to sufficiently test the FinalCheck code on larger real-world applications before we released BoundsChecker 3.0. As a result, more users than we cared to admit couldn't use that feature. We completely rewrote the FinalCheck feature in subsequent releases, but because of the performance problems in the original version, many users never tried it again, even though it was one of the product's most powerful and useful features. Interestingly enough, we released BoundsChecker 3.0 in 1995 and I still have people eleven years later—at least four eons in Internet time—telling me that they still hadn't used FinalCheck because of one bad experience!

From the project management level, a major change of thinking needs to take place when it comes to performance. Performance can never be an afterthought; it's a feature in its own right. A major mistake I've seen in my consulting work is that very few developers have performance numbers that they have to meet. By having those numbers, you have a goal to meet to avoid the poor performance pitfall. If you don't have a performance number, I'll give you a patented, guaranteed way of setting a level of performance: don't make it any slower than the last version. Now the question is all about what that number is for the current version, so you'll have to go out and determine it. If you're working on new development, you'll need to start with those numbers from the requirements phase.

Once you have some performance numbers, you have to work at monitoring them. If your application starts missing those numbers by 10 percent or more, you need to stop and determine why your performance dropped and take steps to correct the problem. Also, make sure that you test your applications against scenarios that are as close to the real world as possible—and do this as early in the development cycle as you can.

Here's one common question I continually get from developers: "Where can I get those real-world data sets so that I can do performance testing?" The answer is to talk to your customers. It never hurts to ask whether you can get their data sets so that you can do your testing. If a customer is concerned about privacy issues, take a look at writing a program that will change sensitive information. You can let the customer run that program and ensure that the changes hide sufficient sensitive information so that the customer feels comfortable giving you the data.

A good friend of mine related a story about the time she was working for a company doing financial data applications for private banking companies. When the development team asked the major client for some real-world data to test against, they got quite a shock. The data was live and completely unobfuscated! Her initial thought was to start doing some data mining for all men under 30 years old worth over $10 million. She immediately deleted all instances of the data and asked the client for obfuscated data.

It should come as no shock to anyone reading this book, but in the modern world of .NET, performance problems can be a major part of your debugging challenges. Although .NET does a great job of eliminating much of the annoying development challenges we faced in the native C++ days, the cost of the ease is that it's harder to see into the "black box" of the Common Language Runtime (CLR) itself.

Incorrect Results

This type of bug is very subtle and potentially malicious. If you're working on an application for a bank, a bad calculation in the middle of a huge set of data can have a ripple effect that can lead to data that looks correct but costs the bank serious money. Although we have debuggers and performance tools to track down crashes and data corruption, there's very little in the way of tools for finding incorrect result problems. To find incorrect results, you're going to need to write code that checks the results.

A perfect example of double-checking all results is the Microsoft Office Excel recalculation engine. In debug builds, the normal, highly optimized calculation engine does its work, and after it finishes, a second debugging-only engine checks that all values are correct from the first engine. You need to have that test code because the alternative is to manually check all the outputs from your code. If you thought writing some of the code was tedious, spend weeks manually calculating data!

Security Exploits

You almost can't look at the news these days without seeing another story about data theft or a security hole in some company's Web site. Everyone in an organization from the receptionist on to the CEO has security at the top of his or her worry list. No matter how great your application performs or looks, a single SQL injection attack can change you from hero to loser in fifteen seconds.

Just like performance and scalability, security can't be an afterthought; it has to be treated as a full feature right from the requirements phase. You have to have someone on the team who's responsible for the security of the product. However, don't make the mistake of randomly assigning someone as the security czar for the project on top of his or her other duties. This role has to have the time to plan security testing and threat modeling for the project as a whole. As Michael Howard and David LeBlanc say in the seminal *Writing Secure Code, 2nd Edition* (Microsoft Press, 2003), "Secure products are quality products."

Inconsistent User Interfaces

Inconsistent user interfaces, though not the most serious type of bug, are annoying. One reason for the success of the Windows operating system is that all Windows-based applications generally behave the same way. When an application deviates from the Windows standard, it becomes a burden for the user. An excellent example of this nonstandard, irksome behavior is in the Find accelerators in Microsoft Office Outlook. In every other English-language Windows-based application on the planet, Ctrl+F brings up the Find dialog box so that you can find text in the current window. In Office Outlook, however, Ctrl+F forwards the open message, which I consider a bug. Even after many years of using Outlook, I can never remember to use the F4 key to find text in the currently open message. Maybe if we all file bug reports about the incorrect accelerator key, Microsoft will finally fix this glaring problem.

With client applications, it's easy to solve problems with inconsistent user interfaces by following the recommendations in the Windows Vista User Experience Guidelines, available at *http://msdn.microsoft.com/windowsvista/building/ux/default.aspx*. If that book doesn't address a particular issue, look for another Microsoft application that does something similar to what you're trying to achieve and follow its model. Microsoft seems to have infinite resources and unlimited time; if you take advantage of their extensive research, solving consistency problems won't be so expensive.

If you're working on Web front ends, life is much more difficult because there's no standard for user interface display. As we've all experienced from the user perspective, it's quite difficult to get a good user interface (UI) in a Web browser. For developing strong Web client UIs, I can recommend two books. The first is the standard bible on Web design, Jacob Nielsen's *Designing Web Usability: The Practice of Simplicity* (New Riders Press, 2000). The second is an outstanding small book that you should give to any self-styled usability experts on your team who couldn't design their way out of a wet paper bag (such as any executive who wants to do the UI but has never used a computer): Steve Krug's *Don't Make Me Think! A Common Sense Approach to Web Usability* (New Riders Press, 2000). Whatever you do for your Web UI, keep in mind that not all your users will have 100-MB-per-second pipes for their browsers, so keep your UI simple and avoid lots of fluff that takes forever to download. When doing research on great Web clients, User Interface Engineering (*www.uie.com*) found that approaches, such as the UI on *CNN.com*, worked best with all users. A simple set of clean links with information groups under clean sections lets users find what they are looking better than anything else.

Another excellent way to handle usability testing comes from the excellent mind of Joel Spolskey, whose blog all software developers absolutely must subscribe to. In his "The Joel Test: 12 Steps to Better Code" entry (*http://www.joelonsoftware.com/articles/fog0000000043.html*), his

Step 12 is "Do you do hallway usability testing?" The idea is to grab five people walking down the hall and force them to use the code you just wrote. According to Joel, you'll find 95 percent of your usability problems immediately.

Unmet Expectations

Not meeting the user's expectations is one of the hardest bugs to solve. This bug usually occurs right at the beginning of a project when the company doesn't do sufficient research on what the real customer needs. In both types of shops—shrinkwrap (those writing software for sale) and Information Technology (or IT, which are those writing in-house applications)—the cause of this bug comes down to communication problems.

In general, development teams don't communicate directly with their product's customers, so they aren't learning what the users need. Ideally, all members of the engineering team should be visiting customer sites so that they can see how the customers use their product. Watching over a customer's shoulder as your product is being used can be an eye-opening experience. Additionally, this experience will give you the insight you need to properly interpret what customers are asking your product to do. If you do get to talk to customers, make sure you speak with as many as possible so that you can get input from across a wide spectrum. In fact, I would strongly recommend that you stop reading right now and go schedule a customer meeting. I can't say it strongly enough: the more you talk with customers, the better an engineer you'll be.

In addition to customer visits, another good idea is to have the engineering team review the support call summaries and support e-mail messages. This feedback will allow the engineering team to see the problems that the users are having without any filtering applied. These visits can lead to all sorts of interesting ideas in addition to tools to help diagnose problems.

Another aspect of this kind of bug is the situation in which the user's level of expectation has been raised higher than the product can deliver. This inflation of user expectations is the classic result of too much hype, and you must resist misrepresenting your product's capabilities at all costs. When users don't get what they anticipated from a product, they tend to feel that the product is even buggier than it really is. The rule for avoiding this situation is to never promise what you can't deliver and to always deliver what you promise.

Process Bugs and Solutions

Although shipping software without bugs is theoretically possible—provided you give enough attention to detail and almost infinite time—I've shipped enough products to know that most companies would go out of business if they tried that. Bugs are a fact of life in this business, even at places like the National Aeronautics and Space Administration (NASA) Software Engineering Laboratory, which is considered the most bug-free development shop in the world. However, you can minimize the number of bugs your applications have. That is what teams that ship high-quality products—and there are many out there—do. The reasons for bugs generally fall into the following process categories:

- Short or impossible deadlines
- The "Code First, Think Later" approach
- Misunderstood requirements
- Engineer ignorance or improper training
- Lack of commitment to quality

Short or Impossible Deadlines

We've all been part of development teams for which "management" has set a deadline that was determined by either a tarot card reader or, if that was too expensive, throwing a dart at the calendar. Although we'd like to believe that managers are responsible for most unrealistic schedules, more often than not, they aren't to blame. Engineers' work estimates are usually the basis of the schedule, and sometimes engineers underestimate how long it will take them to develop a solid product. Engineers are funny people. They are introverted but almost always very positive thinkers. Given a task, they believe down to their bones that they can make the computer stand up and dance. If their manager comes to them and says that they have to add an XML transform to the application, the average engineer says "Sure, boss! It'll be three days." Of course, that engineer might not even know how to spell "XML," but he'll know it'll take three days. The big problem is that engineers and managers don't take into account the learning time necessary to make a feature happen. In the section "Scheduling Time for Building Debugging Systems" in Chapter 2, I'll cover some of the rules that you should take into account when scheduling. Whether an unrealistic ship date is the fault of management or engineering or both, the bottom line is that a schedule that's impossible to meet leads to cut corners and a lower-quality product.

I've been fortunate enough to work on several teams that have shipped software on time. In each case, the development team truly owned the schedule, and we were good at determining realistic ship dates. To figure out realistic ship dates, we based our dates on a feature set. If the company found the proposed ship date unacceptable, we cut features to move up the date. In addition, everyone on the development team agreed to the schedule before we presented it to management. That way, the team's credibility was on the line to finish the product on time. Interestingly, besides shipping on time, these products were some of the highest-quality products I've ever worked on.

The "Code First, Think Later" Approach

My friend Peter Ierardi coined the term "Code First, Think Later" to describe the all-too-common situation in which an engineering team starts programming before they start thinking. Every one of us is guilty of this approach to an extent. Playing with compilers, writing code, and debugging is the fun stuff; it's why we got interested in this business in the first place. Very few of us like to sit down and write documents with UML diagrams that describe what we're going to do.

If you don't write these documents, however, you'll start to run into bugs. Instead of stopping and thinking about how to avoid bugs in the first place, you'll start tweaking the code as you go along to work around the bugs. As you might imagine, this tactic will compound the problem because you'll introduce more and more bugs into an already unstable code base. The company I work for goes around the world helping debug the nastiest problems that developers encounter. Unfortunately, many times we are brought in to help solve corruption or performance problems, and there's nothing we can do because the problems are fundamentally architectural. When we bring the problems to the management who hired us and tell them it's going to take a partial rewrite to fix the problems, we sometimes hear, "We've got too big an investment in this code base to change it now." That's a sure sign of a company that has fallen into the "Code First, Think Later" problem. When reporting on a client, we simply report "CFTL" as the reason we were unsuccessful when helping them.

Fortunately, the solution to this problem is simple: plan your projects. Some very good books have been written about requirement gathering and project planning. Although it is not every engineer's idea of a good time and is generally a little painful, up-front planning is vital to eliminating bugs.

One of the big complaints I got on previous versions of this book was that I recommended that you plan your projects but didn't tell you how to do it. That complaint is perfectly valid, and I want to make sure that I address it now. The only problem is that I really don't know how because I'm certainly not a project management guru. Now you're wondering if I'm doing the bad author thing and leaving it as an exercise to the reader. Read on, and I'll tell you what planning tactics have worked for me as an engineer and frontline manager. You'll still want to read books and articles on project management, but I hope my tactics provide you with some ideas to handle the battles all us engineers face when planning software.

If you read my bio at the end of the book, you'll notice that I didn't get started in the software business until I was in my late 20s and that it's really my second career. My first career was to jump out of airplanes and hunt down the enemy, as I was a paratrooper and Green Beret in the United States Army. If that's not preparation for the software business, I don't know what is! Of course, if you meet me now, you'll see just a short fat guy with a pasty green glow—a result of sitting in front of a monitor too much. However, I really used to be a man. I really did!

Being a Green Beret taught me how to plan. When you're planning a special operations mission and the odds are fairly high that you could die, you are extremely motivated to do the best planning possible. When planning one of those operations, the Army puts the whole team in isolation. At Fort Bragg, North Carolina, the home of Special Forces, there are special areas where they actually lock the team away to plan the mission. The whole key during the planning was called "what if-ing yourself to death." We'd sit around and think about scenarios. What happens if we're supposed to parachute in and we pass the point of no return and the Air

Force can't find the drop zone? What happens if we have casualties before we jump? What happens if we hit the ground and can't find the guerilla commander we're supposed to meet? What happens if the guerilla commander we're supposed to meet has more people with him than he's supposed to? What happens if we're ambushed? We'd spend forever thinking up questions and devising the answers to these questions before ever leaving isolation. The idea was to have every contingency planned out so that nothing was left to chance. Trust me: when there's a good chance you might die when doing your job, you want to know all the variables and account for them. I tell this story to illustrate the truth of the statement I heard long ago in the Army: *Plans are worthless, but planning is everything.* We worked so hard to look at the problem for every conceivable angle that we were able to quickly adapt when the unexpected happened.

When I got into the software business, that's the kind of planning I was accustomed to doing. The first time I sat in a meeting and said, "What if Bob dies before we get through the requirements phase?" everyone got quite nervous, so now I phrase questions with a less morbid spin, like "What if Bob wins the lottery and calls in rich before we get through the requirements phase?" However, the idea is still the same. Find all the areas of doubt and confusion in your plans and address them. It's not easy to do and will drive weaker engineers crazy, but the key issues will always pop out if you drill down enough. For example, in the requirements phase, you'll be asking questions such as, "What if our requirements aren't what the user wants?" Such questions will prompt you to budget time and money to find out if those requirements are what you need to be addressing. In the design phase, you'll be asking questions like, "What if our performance isn't good enough?" Such questions will make you remember to sit down and set your performance goals and start planning how you're going to achieve those goals by testing against real-world scenarios. Planning is much easier if you can get all the issues on the table. Just be thankful that your life doesn't depend on shipping software on time!

If you've ever done some reading on risk analysis, the "what if" approach might sound very familiar because risk analysis is the fancy work for my "what if" approach. In risk analysis, you're trying to find all the issues and, more importantly, assign levels to those risks so you can determine the possibilities of those issues coming back to hurt you. By finding the issues that will cost the most or have the highest probability, you can deal with them before they blow up in your face. Every project has its own peculiar risk issues, but unless you have an idea of what they are, you're never going to get the job done.

Debugging War Story
Severe CFTL

The Battle

A client called us in because they had a big performance problem and the ship date was fast approaching. One of the first things we ask for when we start on these emergency problems is a 15-minute architectural overview so that we can get up to speed on the terminology and get an idea of how the project fits together. The client hustled in one of the architects, and he started the explanation on the whiteboard.

Normally, these circle-and-arrow sessions take 10 to 15 minutes. However, this architect was still going strong 45 minutes later, and I was getting confused because I needed more than a roadmap to keep up. I finally admitted that I was totally lost and asked again for the 10-minute system overview. I didn't need to know everything; I just needed to know the high points. The architect started again and in 15 minutes was only about 25 percent through the system!

The Outcome

This was a large COM system, and at about this point I started to figure out what the performance problem was. Evidently, some architect on the team had become enamored with COM. He didn't just sip from a glass of COM Kool-Aid; he immediately started guzzling from the 55-gallon drum of COM. In what I later guessed was a system that needed 8 to 10 main objects, this team had over 80! To give you an idea how ridiculous this was, it was as if every character in a string was a COM object. This thing was over-engineered and completely under-thought. It was the classic case in which the architects had zero hands-on experience.

After about a half a day, I finally got the manager off to the side and said that there wasn't much we could do for performance because the overhead of COM itself was the problem. He was none too happy to hear this and immediately blurted out this infamous phrase: "We've got too big an investment in this code to change now!" Unfortunately, with their existing architecture, we couldn't do much to effect a performance boost.

The Lesson

This project suffered from several major problems right from the beginning. First, team members handed over the complete design to non-implementers. Second, they immediately started coding when the plan came down from on high. There was absolutely no thought other than to code this thing up and code it up now. It was the classic "Code First, Think Later" problem preceded by "No-Thought Design." I can't stress this enough: you have to get realistic technology assessments and plan your development before you ever turn on the computer.

Misunderstood Requirements

Proper planning also minimizes one of the biggest bug causers in development: feature creep. Feature creep—the tacking on of features not originally planned—is a symptom of poor planning and inadequate requirements gathering. Adding last-minute features, whether in response to competitive pressure, as a developer's pet feature, or on the whim of management, causes more bugs in software than almost anything else.

Software engineering is an extremely detail-oriented business. The more details you hash out and solve before you start coding, the fewer you leave to chance. The only way to achieve proper attention to detail is to plan your milestones and the implementation for your projects.

Of course, this doesn't mean that you need to go completely overboard and generate thousands of pages of documentation describing what you're going to do.

One of the best design documents I ever created for a product was simply a series of paper drawings, or paper prototypes, of the user interface. Based on research and on the teachings of Jared Spool and his company, User Interface Engineering, my team drew the user interface and worked through each user scenario completely. In doing so, we had to focus on the requirements for the product and figure out exactly how the users were going to perform their tasks. In the end, we knew exactly what we were going to deliver, and more importantly, so did everyone else in the company. If a question about what was supposed to happen in a given scenario arose, we pulled out the paper prototypes and worked through the scenario again.

Even though you might do all the planning in the world, you have to really understand your product's requirements to implement them properly. At one company where I worked—mercifully, for less than a year—the requirements for the product seemed very simple and straightforward. As it turned out, however, most of the team members didn't understand the customers' needs well enough to figure out what the product was supposed to do. The company made the classic mistake of drastically increasing the number of engineers but failing to train the new engineers sufficiently. Consequently, even though the team planned everything to extremes, the product shipped several years late, and the market rejected it.

There were two large mistakes on this project. The first was that the company wasn't willing to take the time to thoroughly explain the customers' needs to the engineers who were new to the problem domain, even though some of us begged for the training. The second mistake was that many of the engineers, both old and new, didn't care to learn more about the problem domain. As a result, the team kept changing direction each time marketing and sales reexplained the requirements. The code base was so unstable that it took months to get even the simplest user scenarios to work without crashing.

Very few companies train their engineers in their problem domain at all. Although many of us have college degrees in engineering, we generally don't know much about how customers will use our products. If companies spent adequate time up front helping their engineers understand the problem domain, they could eliminate many bugs caused by misunderstood requirements.

The fault isn't just with the companies, though. Engineers must also make the commitment to learn the problem domain. Some engineers like to think that they're building tools that enable a solution so that they can maintain their separation from the problem domain. As engineers, we're responsible for solving the problem, not merely enabling a solution!

An example of enabling a solution is a situation in which you design a user interface that technically works but doesn't match the way the user works. Another example of enabling a solution is building your application in such a way that it solves the user's short-term problem but doesn't move forward to accommodate the user's changing business needs.

When solving the user's problem rather than just enabling a solution, you, as the engineer, become as knowledgeable as you can about the problem domain so that your software product becomes an extension of the user. The best engineers are not those who can twiddle bits but those who can solve a user's problem.

Engineer Ignorance or Improper Training

Another significant cause of bugs results from developers who don't understand the operating system, the language, or the technology their projects use. Unfortunately, few engineers are willing to admit this deficiency and seek training. Instead, they cover up their lack of knowledge and, unintentionally, introduce avoidable bugs.

In many cases, however, this ignorance isn't a personal failing so much as a fact of life in modern software development. So many layers and interdependencies are involved in developing software these days that no one person can be expected to know the ins and outs of every operating system, language, and technology. There's nothing wrong with admitting that you don't know something. It's not a sign of weakness, and it won't take you out of the running to be the office's alpha geek. In fact, if a team is healthy, acknowledging the strengths and limitations of each member works to the team's advantage. By cataloging the skills their developers have and don't have, the team can get the maximum advantage from their training dollars. By strengthening every developer's weaknesses, the team will better be able to adjust to unforeseen circumstances and, in turn, broaden the whole team's skill set. The team can also schedule development time more accurately when team members are willing to admit what they don't know. You can build in time for learning and create a much more realistic schedule if team members are candid about the gaps in their knowledge.

The best way to learn about a technology is to do something with that technology. Years ago, when NuMega sent me off to learn about Microsoft Visual Basic so that we could write products for Visual Basic developers, I laid out a schedule for what I was going to learn, and my boss was thrilled. The idea was to develop an application that insulted you, appropriately called "The Insulter." Version 1 was a simple form with a single button that, when pressed, popped up a random insult from the list of hard-coded insults. The second version read insults from a database and allowed you to add new insults by using a form. The third version connected to the company's Microsoft Exchange server and allowed you to e-mail insults to others in the company. My manager was very happy to see how and what I was going to do to learn the technology. All your manager really cares about is being able to tell his boss what you're doing day to day. If you give your manager that information, you'll be his favorite employee. When I had my first encounter with Microsoft .NET, I simply dusted off the Insulter idea, and it became Insulter .NET!

I'll have more to say about what skills and knowledge are critical for developers to have in the section "Prerequisites to Debugging" later in this chapter.

Lack of Commitment to Quality

The final reason that bugs exist in projects is, in my opinion, the most serious. Every company and every engineer I've ever talked to has claimed to be committed to quality. Unfortunately, some companies and engineers lack the real commitment that quality requires. If you've ever worked at a company that was committed to quality or with an engineer who was, you certainly know it. They both exude a deep pride in what they are producing and are willing to spend the effort on all parts of development, not on just the sexy parts. For example, instead of getting all wrapped up in the minutia of an algorithm, they pick a simpler algorithm and spend their time working on how best to test that algorithm. The customer doesn't buy algorithms, after all; the customer buys high-quality products. Companies and individuals with a real commitment to quality exhibit many of the same characteristics: careful up-front planning, personal accountability, solid quality control, and excellent communication abilities. Many companies and individuals go through the motions of the big software development tasks (that is, scheduling, coding, and so on), but only those who pay attention to the details ship high-quality products on time.

A good example of a commitment to quality is when I had my first monthly review at NuMega. First off, I was astounded that I was getting a review that quickly when normally you have to beg for any feedback from your managers. One of the key parts of the review was to record how many bugs I had logged against the product. I was stunned to discover that NuMega would evaluate this statistic as part of my performance review, however, because even though tracking bugs is a vital part of maintaining a product's quality, no other company I had worked at had ever checked something so obvious. The developers know where the bugs are, but they must be given an incentive to enter those bugs into the bug tracking system. NuMega found the trick. When I learned about the bug count entry part of my review, you'd better believe that I logged everything I found, no matter how trivial. With all the technical writers, quality engineers, development engineers, and managers engaged in healthy competition to log the most bugs, few surprise bugs slipped through the cracks. More important, we had a realistic idea of where we stood on a project at any given time.

Two additional examples from the engineering side come from the first two editions of this book. The first edition's companion CD has over 2.5 MB of source code. The second edition, which covers both native and .NET debugging, has over 6.9 MB of source code (and that wasn't compiled code, it was just the source code!). That's a huge amount of code, and I'm happy to say many times more than what you get with most books. What many people don't realize is that I spent nearly 60 percent of the time on both books just testing the code. People get really excited when they find a bug in the Bugslayer's code, and the last thing I want is one of those "Gotcha! I found a bug in the Bugslayer!" e-mails.

In both books, I failed in my goal of zero bugs. In the first edition, I have five, and the second edition had 13 reported. With the phenomenal testing tools that are part of Microsoft Visual Studio 2005, I'm striving extremely hard for zero bugs in this edition. The classic software book, *Software Reliability: Measurement, Prediction, Application*, by John D. Musa, Anthony Iannino, and Kazuhira Okumoto (McGraw-Hill Book Company, 1987), states that the average code contains one bug per ten lines of code. What's the secret to producing that much code and keeping the bug counts down? It's simple: testing the heck out of it. In fact, it's such a big topic that I'm dedicating an entire book on testing to follow this one, called, appropriately enough, Testing .NET 2.0 Applications.

As a development manager, I follow a ritual that I'm sure fosters a commitment to quality: each team member has to agree that the product is ready to go at every milestone. If any person on the team doesn't feel that the product is ready, it doesn't ship. I'd rather fix a minor bug and suffer through another complete day of testing than send out something the team wasn't proud of. Not only does this ritual ensure that everyone on the team believes the quality was there, but it also gives everyone on the team a stake in the outcome. An interesting phenomenon I noticed was that team members never stop the release for someone else's bug; the bug's owner always beats them to it.

A company's commitment to quality sets the tone for the entire development effort. That commitment starts with the hiring process and extends through the final quality assurance on the release candidate. Every company says that it wants to hire the best people, but few companies are willing to offer salaries and benefits that will draw them. In addition, some companies aren't willing to provide the tools and equipment that engineers need to produce high-quality products. Unfortunately, too many companies resist spending $500 on a tool that will solve a nasty crash bug in minutes but are willing to spend many thousands of dollars to pay their developers to flounder around for weeks trying to solve that same bug.

A company also shows its commitment to quality when it does the hardest thing to do in business—fire people who are not living up to the standards the organization set. When building a great team full of people on the right side of the bell curve, you have to work to keep them there. We've all seen the person whose chief job seems to be stealing oxygen but who keeps getting raises and bonuses like yours even though you're killing yourself and working late nights and sometimes weekends to make the product happen. The result is good people quickly realizing that the effort isn't worth it. They start slacking off or, worse yet, looking for other jobs.

When I was a project manager on one project, I dreaded doing it, but I fired someone two days before Christmas. I knew that people on the team were feeling that this one individual wasn't working up to standards. If they came back from the Christmas holiday with that person still there, I'd start losing the team we had worked so hard to build. I had been documenting the person's poor performance for quite a while, so I had the proper reasons for proceeding. Trust me, I would rather have been shot at again in the Army than fire that person. It would have been much easier to let it ride, but my commitment was to my team and to the company to do the quality job I had been hired to do. It was better to go through that upheaval than to have anyone turn off and stop performing. I agonized over every firing, but I had to do it. A commitment to quality is extremely difficult and will mean that you'll have to do things that will keep you up at night, but that's what it takes to ship great software and take care of your people.

If you do find yourself in an organization that suffers from a lack of commitment to quality, you'll find that there's no easy way to turn a company into a quality-conscious organization overnight. If you're a manager, you can set the direction and tone for the engineers working for you and work with upper management to lobby for extending a commitment to quality across the organization. If you're an engineer, you can work to make your code the most robust and extensible on the project so that you set an example for others.

Planning for Debugging

Now that we've gone over the types and origins of bugs, and you have some ideas about how to avoid or solve them, it's time to start thinking about the process of debugging. Although many people start thinking about debugging only when they have a crash during the coding phase, you should think about it right from the beginning, in the requirements phase. The more you plan your projects up front, the less time—and money—you'll spend debugging them later.

As I mentioned earlier in the chapter, feature creep can be a bane to your project. More often than not, unplanned features introduce bugs and wreak havoc on a product. This doesn't mean that your plans must be cast in stone, however. Sometimes you must change or add a feature to a product to be competitive or to better meet the user's needs. The key point to remember is that before you change your code, you need to determine—and plan for—exactly what will change. And keep in mind that adding a feature doesn't affect only the code; it also affects testing, documentation, and sometimes even marketing messages. When revising your production schedule, a general rule to follow is that the time it takes to add or remove a feature grows exponentially the further along the production cycle you are.

In Steve McConnell's excellent book, *Code Complete, 2nd Edition* (Microsoft Press, 2004, pp. 29–30), he discusses the costs of fixing a bug. To fix a bug during the requirements and planning phases costs very little. As the product progresses, however, the cost of fixing a bug rises exponentially as does the cost of debugging—much the same as if you add or remove features along the way.

Planning for debugging goes together with planning for testing. As you plan, you need to look for different ways to speed up and improve both processes. One of the best precautions you can take is to write file data dumpers and validators for internal data structures and for binary files, if appropriate. If your project reads and writes data to a binary file, you should automatically assign someone to write a testing program that dumps the data in a readable format to a text file. The dumper should also validate the data and check all interdependencies in the binary file. This step will make both your testing and your debugging easier.

By properly planning for debugging, you minimize the time spent in your debugger, which is your goal. You might think such advice sounds strange coming from a book on debugging, but the idea is to try to avoid bugs in the first place. If you build sufficient debugging code into your applications, that code—not the debugger—should tell you where the bugs are. I'll cover the issues concerning debugging code more in Chapter 3.

Prerequisites to Debugging

Before we get into the meat of debugging, I want to cover what you must know to be a good debugger. The first quality that all expert debuggers have in common is being good developers, too. You simply can't be a good debugger without being a good developer, and vice versa.

The Skill Set

Good debuggers and good developers all have strong problem-solving skills that are particular to software. Fortunately, you can learn and hone those skills. What sets great debuggers/developers apart from good debuggers/developers is that in addition to having basic problem-solving skills, great debuggers/developers understand how all the parts of a project relate to the project as a whole.

What you're building with the skill set is one of the most important debugging traits of all: intuition. The better your mental model of how things work, the faster you can start eliminating false leads and getting down to the real root issue of the problem. We've all worked with that one developer who just seems to know everything that's going on. I'll let you in on the secret: that developer doesn't, but he or she does know the logical progression of the key skill-set items and thus can get at the answer faster than you can.

The following list contains the areas in which you need to be proficient to become a great—or at least a better—debugger/developer:

- Your project
- Your language
- Your technology/tools
- Your operating system/environment

Know Your Project

Knowing your project is the first line of defense for user interface, logic, and performance bugs. By knowing how and where features are implemented in the various source files, you can quickly narrow down who is doing what to whom.

Unfortunately, because each project is different, the only way to learn your project is to read the design documents (if they exist), and to walk through the code in the debugger. If you have Visual Studio 2005 Team Edition for Software Architects or Visual Studio 2005 Team Suite, you can use the class diagramming tools to initiate that higher-level overview. It will never replace a solid model that shows data relationships between classes, but it will be more than enough to get you started.

One thing I've found very interesting in Wintellect's debugging business is how few companies have anything approaching design documents. As I described earlier in the Debugging War Story: Severe CFTL, we need to get that 15-minute overview from the Vice President of Circles and Arrows so we have an idea about the big picture. Invariably, the drawing will appear on the whiteboard and someone will exclaim in a loud voice, "Wow! I've never seen this before!" Immediately after that outburst, someone will run out of the room and grab a digital camera to start taking pictures of the first documentation he or she has ever had on the project.

If you don't have good documentation on the big picture of your project, get the senior developers to spend those 15 minutes to draw their version of the system. You can scan those drawings into Microsoft Office Word and drop them into your version control system. It's a cheap way to get at least the start of your application documented.

Know Your Language

Knowing the language (or languages) your project uses is more difficult than it sounds. I'm referring to knowing what your language is doing behind the scenes in addition to knowing how to program in it. For example, Microsoft Visual Basic developers have the very-easy-to-use On Error Goto construct for error handling. As that's how Visual Basic 6.0 did error handling; many Visual Basic developers are still using it. However, compared to structured exception handling in .NET, On Error Goto is a million times slower. In fact, On Error Goto should be renamed to On Error Goto Hell. We tracked down a performance problem in a client's application to the huge amount of code generated by a single On Error Goto statement being called in a loop. Many bugs, especially those that cause performance problems, are the result of language misuse, so it's well worth the effort to spend some time reading up on the idiosyncrasies of the programming languages you use.

Know Your Technology/Tools

Getting a handle on the technologies you're using is the first big step to tackling the more difficult bugs. For example, if you have an idea of what COM does to instantiate a COM object and return an interface, you'll have a much easier time tracking down why a specific interface request failed. The same goes for paying very close attention to something like your XML manipulation. The .NET Base Class Library (BCL) offers many ways of reading, writing, and manipulating XML data. As everything is XML-based these days, you need to have an idea of the differences as to why you'd want to use an *XmlReader* versus an *XmlDocument* class. I'm not saying that you need to quote files and lines from the source code or a book. Rather, I'm saying that you should have at least a general understanding of the technologies you're using and, more important, you should know exactly where you can find more detailed information if you need it.

In addition to knowing the technology, it's vital to know the tools you're using. A big portion of this book is spent discussing advanced usage of the debugger, but many other tools are out there, such as those distributed with the Platform SDK. The Visual Studio 2005 Team Editions come with more tools than some operating systems. You need to spend several days playing with the different windows in Visual Studio but also with open source and commercial tools. You never want to be in the situation of working on the showstopper bug from Hell and trying to learn the tools at the same time. A great deal of debugging is just having an idea of the capabilities of the tools because you can apply them faster to solve the problem.

Know Your Operating System/Environment

Knowing the basics of how your operating system or operating environment goes about doing its work can make the biggest difference between solving a bug and just floundering around. Every developer should be able to answer questions such as the following: What is a dynamic-link library (DLL)? How does an image loader work? How does the registry work? For managed code, you should know answers to questions such as: How does Microsoft ASP.NET find the components that a page is using? When do finalizers get called? What's the difference between an application domain and an assembly? Many of the worst bugs appear when you misuse the operating system or environment. My friend Matt Pietrek, who taught me a great deal about debugging, maintains that knowing the operating system/environment and the CPU is what separates the debugging gods from mere mortals.

Learning the Skill Set

With any job that regularly deals with technology, you have to study continually just to keep up, let alone get better and advance.

Besides reading books and magazines on debugging, you should also write utilities, any kind of utilities. The ultimate way to learn is by doing, and in this business, coding and debugging are what you need to do. Not only will you enhance your hard skills, such as coding and debugging, but if you treat these utilities as real projects (that is, by completing them on time and with high quality), you'll also enhance your soft skills, such as project planning and schedule estimating.

To give you some incentive to complete your utilities, consider this: completed utilities are excellent show-and-tell items to bring to job interviews. Although very few engineers bring their own code to demonstrate their skills to interviewers, companies consider those candidates who do well before those candidates who don't. Bringing a portfolio of the work you did on your own time at home shows that you can complete work independently and that you have a passion for software engineering, and it will almost immediately put you in the top 20 percent of engineers.

Another practice that has helped me a great deal, especially when it comes to learning more about languages, technologies, and the operating system, is to look at other engineers' code.

As you probably know, a great deal of code that you can look at is floating around on the Internet. By running different programs under the debugger, you can see how someone else tackles bugs. If you're having trouble coming up with a utility you'd like to write, you can simply add a feature to one of the utilities you find.

Some of the most productive time you can spend with the Microsoft .NET Framework is simply looking through the Framework Class Library (FCL) source code. The great news is that even though we don't have that source code, we have the next best thing: Lutz Roeder's Reflector (*http://www.aisto.com/roeder/dotnet*). With a full decompiler and analysis tools to tell you who calls what, Reflector can teach you a tremendous amount of .NET development just by reading the Framework source code. Some of the most productive time I've ever spent has been just sitting around with Reflector asking myself how things work.

Reading books and magazines, writing utilities, reviewing other engineers' code, and doing reverse engineering are all great ways to improve your debugging skills. However, your greatest resources are your engineering friends and coworkers. Never be afraid to ask them how they did something or how something works; unless they are in the middle of a deadline crunch, they should be happy to help. I enjoy it when people ask me questions because I end up learning more than the individuals who ask the questions! Programming newsgroups are also excellent places to pose questions. I read them all the time because their responses are so good, especially from those folks Microsoft has designated MVPs (Most Valuable Professionals).

The Debugging Process

Finally, let's start talking about hands-on debugging by discussing the debugging process. Determining a process that works for all bugs, even "freak" bugs (bugs that come out of the blue and don't make any sense), was a bit challenging. But by drawing on my own experiences and by talking to my colleagues and clients about their experiences, I eventually came up with a debugging approach that all great developers intuitively follow but that less experienced (or just less-skilled) developers often don't find obvious.

As you'll see, this debugging process doesn't take a rocket scientist to implement. The hard part is ensuring that you start with this process every time you debug. Here are the nine steps involved in the debugging approach that I recommend:

- Step 1: Duplicate the bug.
- Step 2: Describe the bug.
- Step 3: Always assume that the bug is yours.
- Step 4: Divide and conquer.
- Step 5: Think creatively.
- Step 6: Utilize tools.
- Step 7: Start heavy debugging.

- Step 8: Verify that the bug is fixed.
- Step 9: Learn and share.

Depending on your bug, you can skip some steps entirely because the problem and the location of the problem are entirely obvious. You must always start with Step 1 and get through Step 2. At any point between Steps 3 and 7, however, you might figure out the solution and be able to fix the bug. In those cases, after you fix the bug, skip to Step 8 to verify and test the fix. Figure 1-1 illustrates the steps of the debugging process.

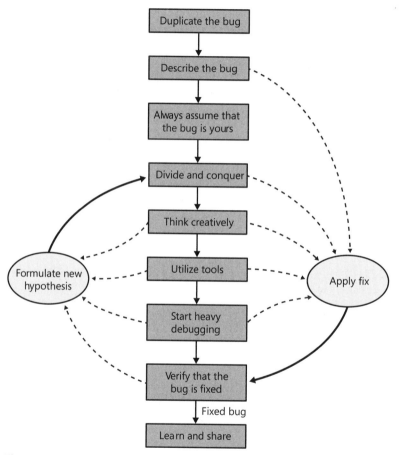

Figure 1-1   Leverage tools should say Utilize tools.

Step 1: Duplicate the Bug

The most critical step in the debugging process is the first one: duplicating the bug. This is sometimes difficult, or even impossible, but if you can't duplicate a bug, you probably can't eliminate it. When trying to duplicate a bug, you might need to go to extremes. I had one bug in my code that I couldn't duplicate just by running the program. I had an idea of the data conditions that might cause it, however, so I ran the program under the debugger and entered the data I needed to duplicate the bug directly into memory. It worked. If you're dealing with a synchronization problem, you might need to take steps, such as loading the same tasks so that you can duplicate the state in which the bug occurred.

At this point you're probably thinking, "Well, duh! Of course the first thing you do is duplicate the bug. If I could duplicate it all the time, I wouldn't need your book!" It all depends on your definition of "duplicatability." My definition is duplicating the bug on a single machine once in a 24-hour period. That's sufficient for my company to come in to work on it. Why? Simple. If you can get it on one machine, you can throw 30 machines at it and get the bug duplicated 30 times. The big mistake people make with duplicating the bug is to not get as many machines as possible into the mix. If you have 30 people to manually punch keys for you, that's great. However, a valuable effort would be to automate the user interface to drive the bug out into the open. You can use either the excellent testing tools that are part of Visual Studio 2005 or another commercial product if you need user interface automation.

Once you've duplicated the bug by using one general set of steps, you should determine whether you can duplicate the bug through a different set of steps. You can get to some bugs via one code path only, but you can get to other bugs through multiple paths. The idea is to try to see the behavior from all possible angles. By duplicating the bug from multiple paths, you have a much better sense of the data and boundary conditions that are causing the problems. Additionally, as we all know, some bugs can mask other bugs. The more ways you can find to duplicate a bug, the better off you'll be.

Even if you can't duplicate the bug, you should still log it into your bug tracking system. If I have a bug that I can't duplicate, I always log it into the system anyway, but I leave a note that says that I couldn't duplicate it. That way, if another engineer is responsible for that section of the code, that engineer at least has an idea that something is amiss. When logging a bug that you can't duplicate, you need to be as descriptive as possible. If the description is good enough, it might be sufficient for you or another engineer to solve the problem eventually. A good description is especially important because you can correlate various non-reproducible bug reports, enabling you to start seeing patterns in the bug's behavior.

The last thing I want to discuss about duplicating the bug is that it's very rare you get the bug duplicated on your development machine. That's because you have different tools and processes on the development machine than on the running machine, or worse yet, you're logged in with Administrator rights. With both Microsoft and VMWare giving away their virtualization environments, there are no excuses for you to not have a virtualized version of the runtime environment on your machine set up with remote debugging. You should work at duplicating your bugs in the virtual machine so you have a better chance of finding the exact pattern that works.

Step 2: Describe the Bug

If you were a typical engineering student in college, you probably concentrated on your math and engineering classes and barely passed your writing classes. In the real world, your writing skills are almost more important than your engineering skills because you need to be able to describe your bugs, both verbally and in writing. When faced with a tough bug, you should always stop right after you duplicate it and describe it. Ideally, you do this in your bug-tracking system, even if it's your responsibility to debug the bug, but talking it out is also useful. The main reason for describing the bug is that doing so often helps you fix it. I can't remember how many times another engineer's description helped me look at a bug in a different way.

Step 3: Always Assume That the Bug Is Yours

In all the years that I've been in software development, only a minuscule percentage of the bugs I've seen were the result of the compiler or the operating environment. If you have a bug, the odds are excellent that it's your fault, and you should always assume and hope that it is. If the bug is in your code, at least you can fix it; if it's in your compiler or the operating environment, you have bigger problems. You should eliminate any possibility that the bug is in your code before spending time looking for it elsewhere.

To reinforce the need to assume that the bug is yours, we've found a very interesting statistic at Wintellect. Over the last six years, we've worked on thousands of bugs for our clients. Of all of those bugs, only four were not in our client's code. I can't stress enough: always assume it's your bug, because it is.

Step 4: Divide and Conquer

If you've duplicated your bug and described it well, you have started a hypothesis about the bug and have an idea of where it's hiding. In this step, you start firming and testing your hypothesis. The important thing to remember here is the paraphrased line from the movie *Star Wars*: "Use the source, Luke!" Read the source code, and desk-check what you think is happening with what the code really does. Reading the code will force you to take the extra time to look at the problem. Starting with the state of the machine at the time of the crash or problem, work through the various scenarios that could cause you to get to that section of code. If your hypothesis of what went wrong doesn't pan out, stop for a moment and reassess the situation. You've learned a little more about the bug, so now you can reevaluate your hypothesis and try again.

Debugging is like a binary search algorithm. You're trying to find the bug, and with each iteration through your different hypotheses, you are, hopefully, eliminating the sections of the programs where the bug is not. As you continue to look, you eliminate more and more of the program until you can box the bug into a section of code. As you continue to develop your hypothesis and learn more about the bug, you can update your bug description to reflect the new information. When I'm in this step, I generally try out three to five solid hypotheses before moving on to the next step. If you think you're getting close, you can do a little light debugging in this step to do final verification of the hypothesis. By *light*, I mean double-checking states and variable values, not slogging through looking at everything.

Everything you do in this step is strictly evidence-based. Don't go down a path because it feels right. I'm not saying to ignore your hunches, but back up that hunch with actual data that helps confirm or deny that hunch. I've seen many developers, myself included, waste too much time on a wild goose chase with no solid evidence. Errors in software are a cause-and-effect situation, so keep your eyes on finding that cause.

Step 5: Think Creatively

If the bug you're trying to eliminate is one of those nasty ones that happens only on certain machines or is hard to duplicate, start looking at the bug from different perspectives. This is the step in which you should start thinking about version mismatches, operating system differences, problems with your program's binaries or its installation, and other external factors.

When I'm teaching a training class on debugging, I ask how many people have been working on a bug all day long and solve it on the drive home. Nearly all the hands in the room go up. What's even wilder is when I ask how many of us have woken up in the middle of the night with the exact solution for a bug. While it's a sign of our sleep deprivation, at least 40 percent of the hands always go up. It's all about seeing the forest for the trees. Your subconscious knows exactly where to look, so set it free on the bug.

My big hint here is the "two-hour rule." After working on a bug for two hours, you have to do an honest assessment: are you making progress or not? If you're not, just stop working on the particular problem because you're wasting your time. Of course, if this is the one bug holding up shipment, telling your boss that you've worked the two hours and are going to work on something else might be a career-limiting move.

When you are at that two-hour wall and need to get the creative juices going, the secret is "Bug Talk," which at several companies I've worked at, is the highest priority interrupt possible. That means that you are totally stumped and need to talk the bug over with someone. The idea is that you can walk into a person's office and present the problem on a whiteboard. I don't know how many times I've walked into someone's office, uncapped the marker, literally just touched the marker on the board, and solved my problem without even saying a word. Just getting your mind prepared to present the problem helps you get past the individual tree you're staring at and lets you see the whole forest. When you choose a person to do a Bug Talk with, you should not pick someone you're working very closely with on the same section of the project. That way, you can increase the likelihood that your Bug Talk partner isn't making the same assumptions you are about the problem.

What's interesting is that the "someone" doesn't even have to be a human. My cats, as it turns out, are excellent debuggers, and they have helped me solve a number of really nasty bugs. After rounding them up, I draw the problem out on my whiteboard and let them work their magic. Of course, one time I was doing this when I hadn't taken a shower and was wearing nothing but shorts—that was a little difficult to explain to the United Parcel Service (UPS) delivery guy standing at my door.

The one person you should always avoid doing Bug Talks with is your spouse or significant other. For some reason, the fact that you're having a relationship with that person means that there's a built-in problem. Of course, you've probably already seen this when you try to describe that bug and the person's eyes glaze over, and he or she nearly passes out.

Step 6: Utilize Tools

I've never understood why some companies let their engineers spend weeks searching for a bug when spending a thousand dollars for error detection, performance, and code-coverage tools would help them find the current bug—and bugs they will encounter in the future—in minutes.

I've run into several clients now that will provide the Visual Studio 2005 Professional Edition only for their developers. Say what you want about the Developer Division's crazy marketing, but there's nothing "professional" about that version. It lacks the real tools you need to do your job. The Team Editions of Visual Studio, specifically Visual Studio 2005 Team Edition for Software Developers or the ultimate, Visual Studio 2005 Team Suite (which includes all the flavors of Visual Studio Team Editions), are the minimum that developers need to do their job.

I realize that what I'm advocating is not cheap. At the time I wrote this, a brand new purchase of Visual Studio 2005 Team Edition for Software Developers costs $5,469.00 USD when paired with an MSDN Subscription. The Visual Studio 2005 Team Suite is an eye-watering and knee-buckling $10,939.00 USD. Personally, I think Microsoft is absolutely insane to overcharge their developer base like this, but it's the cost of making real things happen on the .NET platform. While it's not much good news, if you are buying multiple copies or upgrading, you can force the price down considerably.

The reason you need at least Visual Studio 2005 Team Edition for Software Developers is because of the extra tools. The static analysis portion, which used to be called FxCop, looks over your code to ensure that you're following rules as promulgated by the outstanding book, *Framework Design Guidelines : Conventions, Idioms, and Patterns for Reusable .NET Libraries* by Krzysztof Cwalina and Brad Abrams (Addison Wesley, 2004). The code analysis tool will help ensure that everyone is following a consistent usage for all public-facing interfaces and classes.

Also included are the performance and coverage tools in the Visual Studio 2005 Team Edition for Software Developers. As you can guess, the performance tool is an excellent profiler that helps you find the bottlenecks in your code. As you'll see throughout this book, code coverage is a major passion of mine when it comes to debugging. The information that you're looking for from a code coverage tool are the lines you haven't executed. Any time you have more than 15 percent of your code not executed, you're going to experience extreme pain when testers get a hold of your code.

If you're at a startup company where money is tight, or you just have a cheap boss, not having Visual Studio 2005 Team Suite doesn't mean the end of your .NET development days. With a combination of open source and commercial tools, some of which are much better than their counterparts in Visual Studio, you can get some great debugging, testing, and tuning done.

For unit testing, NUnit (*www.nunit.org*) combined with the TestDriven.NET add-in (*www.testdriven.net*) is an excellent replacement for the unit testing tools in Visual Studio Team Developer Edition. FxCop (*www.gotdotnet.com/team/fxcop/*) is the standalone version of the integrated Code Analysis tools and offers a few extra checks, such as checking spelling using the Microsoft Office spelling engine. For profiling, Red Gate's ANT and SciTech Software's .NET Memory Profiler (*www.memprofiler.com*), along with the free CLRProfiler (*www.microsoft.com /downloads/*) from Microsoft, will handle all your profiling and tuning needs. You also have complete suites of .NET developer tools from Rational-IBM and Compuware.

Step 7: Start Heavy Debugging

I differentiate heavy debugging from the light debugging I mentioned in Step 4 by what you're doing in the debugger. When you're doing light debugging, you're just looking at a few states and a couple of variables. In contrast, when you're doing heavy debugging, you're spending a good deal of time exploring your program's operation. It is during the heavy debugging stage that you want to use the debugger's advanced features. Your goal is to let the debugger do as much of the heavy lifting as possible. Chapter 5 discusses the Visual Studio debuggers' advanced features.

Just as when you're doing light debugging, when you're doing heavy debugging, you should have an idea of where you think your bug is before you start using the debugger and then use the debugger to prove or disprove your hypothesis. Never sit in the debugger and just poke around. In fact, I strongly encourage you to actually write out your hypothesis before you ever fire up the debugger. That will help you keep completely focused on exactly what you're trying to accomplish.

Also, when you're doing heavy debugging, remember to regularly review changes you made to fix the bug in the debugger. I like to have two machines set up side-by-side at this stage. That way I can work at fixing the bug on one machine and use the other machine to run the same code with normal condition cases. The idea is to always double-check and triple-check any changes so that you're not destabilizing the normal operation of your product. Here's some career advice: your boss really dislikes it when you check in code to fix a bug and your product handles only weird boundary conditions and no longer handles the normal operation case.

If you set up your project correctly and follow the debugging steps in this chapter and the recommendations in Chapter 2, you hopefully won't have to spend much time doing heavy debugging.

Step 8: Verify That the Bug Is Fixed

When you think that you've finally fixed the bug, the next step in the debugging process is to test, test, and retest the fix. Did I also mention that you need to test the fix? If the bug is in an isolated module on a line of code called once, testing the fix is easy. However, if the fix is in a core module, especially one that handles your data structures and the like, you need to be very careful that your fix doesn't cause problems or have side effects in other parts of the project.

When testing your fix, especially in critical code, you should verify that it works with all data conditions, good and bad. Nothing is worse than a fix for one bug that causes two other bugs. If you do make a change in a critical module, you should let the rest of the team know that you made the change. That way, they can also be on the lookout for any ripple effects.

The only way I've found to know that you have the right level of testing is to ensure that you've executed the code. With the excellent code coverage tools built into Visual Studio Team Developer and Team Tester Editions, you have no excuse for not showing that you've thoroughly tested the change code. Code coverage is not the end all and be all of testing, but it's an excellent benchmark to ensure that you're getting your job done.

Debugging War Story
Where did the integration go?

The Battle

One of the developers I worked with at NuMega thought he'd found a great bug in NuMega's Visual C++ Integrated Development Environment (VC IDE) integration because it didn't work on his machine. For those of you who are unfamiliar with NuMega's VC IDE integration, let me provide a little background information. NuMega's software products integrate with the VC IDE—and have for a number of years. This integration allows NuMega's windows, toolbars, and menus to appear seamlessly inside the VC IDE.

The Outcome

This developer spent a couple of hours using SoftICE, a kernel debugger, exploring the bug. After awhile, he had set breakpoints all over the operating system. Finally, he found his "bug." He noticed that when he started the VC IDE, *CreateProcess* was being called with the \\R2D2\VSCommon\MSDev98\Bin\MSDEV.EXE path instead of the C:\VSCommon\MSDev98\Bin\MSDEV.EXE path he thought it should be called with. In other words, instead of running the VC IDE from his local machine (C:\VSCommon\ MSDev98\Bin\MSDEV.EXE), he was running it from his old machine (\\R2D2\ VSCommon\MSDev98\Bin\MSDEV.EXE). How did this happen?

The developer had just gotten a new machine and had installed the full NuMega VC IDE integration for the products. To get it set up faster, he copied his desktop shortcuts (.lnk files) from his old machine, which were installed without VC IDE integration, to his new machine by dragging them with the mouse. When you drag shortcuts, the internal paths update to reflect the location of the original target. Since he was always starting the VC IDE from his desktop shortcut, which was pointing to his old machine, he'd been running the VC IDE on his old machine all along.

> **The Lesson**
>
> The developer went about debugging the problem in the wrong way by just jumping right in with a kernel debugging instead of attempting to duplicate the problem in multiple ways. In Step 1 of the debugging process, "Duplicate the Bug," I recommended that you try to duplicate the bug in multiple ways so that you can be assured that you're looking at the right bug, not just multiple bugs masking and compounding one another. If this developer had followed Step 5, "Think Creatively," he would have been better off because he would have thought about the problem first instead of plunging right in.
>
> As an alternative, the developer could have used Step 6, "Utilize Tools," and seen if there were any tools that could have helped. In this case, a quick run of Sysinternal's excellent FileMon (*www.sysinternals.com/Utilities/Filemon.html*), which watches all file accesses on your machine, would have shown that the file reads were coming off a network path instead of a local machine.

Step 9: Learn and Share

Each time you fix a nasty bug, you should take the time to quickly summarize what you learned. I like to record my good bugs in a journal so that I can later see what I did right in finding and fixing the problem. More important, I also want to learn what I did wrong so that I can learn to avoid dead ends when debugging and solve bugs faster. You learn the most about development when you're debugging, so you should take every opportunity to learn from it.

One of the most important steps that you can take after fixing a good bug is to share with your colleagues the information you learned while fixing the bug, especially if the bug is project-specific. This information will help your coworkers the next time they need to eliminate a similar bug. For example, the SQL Team at Microsoft has set up an internal e-mail alias called "SQL Dev Debugging Discussion," and that's where fantastic war stories can be shared across the team. Alternatively, you could set up an internal blog or wiki where everyone could post those stories.

If you're worried about no one contributing to these areas, there's a simple solution. Make it part of their performance review. It's an easy matter to make it part of everyone's goals to achieve the company's goals. It will take some thought on the manager's part to work out the details, but if a developer's pay is based on it, you can get the contributions you need.

Final Debugging Process Secret

I'd like to share one final debugging secret with you: the debugger can answer all your debugging questions as long as you ask it the right ones. Again, I'm suggesting that you need to have a hypothesis in mind—something you want to prove or disprove—before the debugger can help you. As I recommended earlier in Step 7, I write out my hypothesis before I ever touch the debugger to ensure that I have a purpose each time I use it.

Remember that the debugger is just a tool, like a screwdriver. It does only what you tell it to do. The real debugger is the software in your hardware cranium.

Summary

This chapter started out defining bugs and describing process problems that contribute to bugs. Then it discussed what you should know before you start debugging. Finally, it presented a debugging process that you should follow when you debug your code.

The best way to debug is to avoid bugs in the first place. If you plan your projects properly, have a real commitment to quality, and learn about how your products fit with their technologies, the operating environment, and the CPU, you can minimize the time you spend debugging.

The key thought I want to leave you with is this: while debugging is difficult and can sometimes make you feel overwhelmed when faced with an impossible problem, it's only a temporary solution. What makes debugging hard is that almost none of us have had any education in debugging, so we've all learned it on the job piecemeal. In fact, when I was in college getting my bachelor's degree in Computer Science, I asked about debugging, and my entire debugging training consisted of the following: "Don't write bugs in the first place." You can learn to debug better, and I hope this chapter has started you on your way.

Chapter 2
Preparing for Debugging

In this chapter, I'll introduce some important infrastructure tools and requirements that will contribute to your debugging success over the lifetime of your application. Some of the tools involve the engineering process, and others are software utilities. What they all have in common is that they allow you to see the progress of your project on a daily basis. I believe this daily monitoring is the key to getting your product out the door on time—with quality. Projects don't slip massively in one day; they slip a little each day along the way.

All the ideas presented here and in Chapter 3, "Debugging During Coding," come from my experience in shipping real-world software products in addition to my work as a consultant with some of the best development shops in the world. I can't imagine developing without these tools and techniques. I've learned some lessons the hard way and watched others learn the same lessons, and I hope to save you time and pain by sharing with you what these lessons have taught me. You might think that some of these ideas don't apply to you because you're on a two-person or three-person team. Don't worry, they do. Even when I'm working alone, I still approach a project in the same way. I've worked on projects of every size I can think of, so I know that the recommendations I make scale from the tiniest to the largest teams.

Track Changes Until You Throw Away the Project

Version control and bug tracking systems are two of the most important infrastructure tools you have because they give you the history of your project. Although the developers might say that they can keep everything in their heads, the company needs to have some record of what's been accomplished on the project in case the entire development team wins the lottery and everyone quits the next day. Because most teams don't adequately maintain their requirements and design documents throughout the life of a project, the only real documentation becomes the audit trail in the version control and bug tracking systems.

I hope I'm preaching to the converted. Unfortunately, I keep running into teams that haven't yet started using these tools, especially bug tracking systems. As someone interested in history, I feel that you have to know where you've been to know where you're going. Putting these two types of tools to use is the only sure way to learn that lesson. By monitoring the outstanding bugs and bug fix rates in the bug tracking system, you can better predict when your product will be ready to ship. With the version control system, you'll get an idea of your "code churn," or the volume of changes, so that you can see how much additional testing needs to be done. Additionally, these tools are the only effective way to judge whether you're getting any results from changes you implement in your development cycle.

When you bring a new developer to your team, these tools can pay for themselves in a single day. When the new developer starts, have her sit down with the version control and bug tracking software and begin working her way through the changes. Good design documents are ideal, but if they aren't available, the version control and bug tracking systems at least provide a record of the code evolution and highlight any trouble areas.

I'm talking about these two tools in the same breath because they are inseparable. The bug tracking system captures all the events that might have driven changes to your master sources. The version control system captures every change. Ideally, you want to maintain the relationship between reported problems and actual changes in the master sources. By correlating the relationship, you can see your cause and effect for bug fixes. If you don't track the relationship, you're left wondering why certain changes to the code occurred. Invariably, in later versions of the product, you have to find the developer who made the change and hope he remembers the reason for the change.

Some products are integrated and automatically track the relationship of the master source change to the bug report, but if your current systems don't, you'll need to maintain the relationship manually. You can track the relationship by including the bug number in the comments that describe the fix. When you check the file back into version control, you'll need to identify the bug number you're fixing in the check-in comment for the file. Also, in the bug tracking system, you should identify the version of the file the fix for the bug was in. That way you can complete correlation between the two variables: the bug item and the source file.

Version Control Systems

The version control system isn't just for your project's master sources. Anything and everything related to the project—including all test plans, automated tests, the help system, and design documents—needs to go into the version control system. Some companies even include the build tools (that is, the compiler, linker, include files, and libraries), which allow them to completely re-create the shipped version of their products. If you have any question about whether something should go in version control, ask yourself whether maintenance programmers could use the information in a couple of years. If you think they could, that information belongs in the version control system.

A version control system can easily tell you what changed, but knowing the reason for the change is the key. Whenever you check in a source file, you need to have a clear, lucid explanation of what and why you were changing the source file. We've all seen the check-in comment that says *Fixed a bug* somewhere in our careers. It makes you want to contemplate inflicting serious bodily harm to the developer because there's no information there. As a product manager, I will go through the check-in comments and immediately apply counseling to anyone who's not writing clear enough check-in comments. Those comments are as important as the source code.

The Importance of Including Unit Tests

Even though I just said to check in everything that could be of use, one of the biggest problems I've seen in development shop after development shop is not including the unit tests in the version control system. In case you're not familiar with the term *unit test*, I'll briefly describe it here: A *unit test* is the piece of code that drives portions of your main program code. (It's sometimes also referred to as *test apps* or *test harness*.) It's the testing code created by the developer that allows the developer to do *glass box*, or *white box*, testing to ensure that the basic operations take place. For a complete definition of unit tests, see Chapter 22, "Developer Testing," of Steve McConnell's book *Code Complete, 2nd Edition* (Microsoft Press, 2004).

Including the unit tests in version control accomplishes two key objectives. First, you make the job of maintenance developers infinitely easier. So many times, the maintenance developer, who could easily turn out to be you, has to reinvent the wheel when upgrading or fixing the code. Doing so is not only a huge waste of effort but is also a real morale killer. Second, you make general testing for QA teams trivial so that those teams can focus on the important testing areas, such as performance and scalability, in addition to fit and finish. One sign of a seasoned professional is that she always has her unit tests checked in.

Of course, checking in your unit tests requires you to keep them up to date with code changes. Yes, that's going to be additional work on your behalf. Nothing is worse than having a maintenance developer tracking you down and screaming at you because the unit tests no longer work. Having outdated unit tests is worse than having no unit tests in the version control system.

If you look at the source code for this book, you'll notice that all my unit tests are included as part of the code. In fact, my builds build all unit tests at the same time. I'm not about to recommend anything in this book that I don't do myself.

Some readers might be thinking that implementing the unit test discipline I advocate is going to take a lot more work. In reality, it's not going to take that much longer because most developers (I hope!) are already conducting unit tests, especially now that the testing tools are built into Microsoft Visual Studio Team Editions. The big differences I'm suggesting are keeping those tests based on a well-known framework checked in and up to date in addition to building them. The time you'll save by following the proper procedures will be huge. For example, for most of this book, I did my development on a machine with Microsoft Windows XP Professional x64 Edition installed. To turn around and do immediate testing on my computers running Microsoft Windows Server 2003 or Windows Vista, I simply had to get the code from version control and do the build scripts. Many developers do a one-off unit test, so testing on other operating systems is difficult because they have no easy way to get the unit tests over to the other machines and have them built and executed. If everyone is making unit tests part of the code, you can shave many weeks off your schedules.

Controlling Changes

Tracking changes is vital; however, having a good bug tracking system in place doesn't mean that developers should be allowed to make wholesale changes to the master sources whenever they want. Such freedom would make all the tracking pointless. The idea is to control the changes during development, restricting certain types of changes to certain stages of the project so that you can have an idea of the state of the master sources on a day-to-day basis. The best scheme I've heard of for controlling changes comes from my friend Steve Munyan, and he calls it "Green, Yellow, and Red Times." In Green Time, anyone can check in anything to the master sources. The earliest parts of the project are usually fully in Green Time because at this point, the team is working on new features.

Yellow Time is when the product is in a bug fix phase or nearing a code freeze. The only code changes allowed are for bug fixes—and *only* bug fixes. No new features or other changes are permitted. Before a developer can check in a bug fix, a technical lead or a development manager must approve it. The developer making the bug fix must describe the bug fix he's making and what section of code it affects. In essence, this process is a mini-code review for every single bug fix. The important item to remember when conducting that code review is to utilize the version control product's differencing utility to ensure exactly which changes occurred so that extraneous changes don't sneak in. On some teams I've been on, the product was in Yellow Time from day one because the team liked the code review aspects of this stage. We did loosen the approval requirements so that any other developer could approve changes. The interesting outcome was that because of the constant code reviews, the developers caught many bugs before they checked the code into the master sources.

Red Time occurs when you're in a code freeze or near a key milestone and all code changes require the product manager's approval. When I am a product manager (the person on the team responsible for the code as a whole), I go to the extent of changing the permissions in the version control system so that the team has read-only access. I take this step mainly because I understand what the developers are almost certainly thinking: "This is just a little change; it will fix this bug, and it won't hurt anything else." The developers' intentions were good, but that one little change could mean that the entire team would have to restart the test plan from the beginning.

The product manager must strictly enforce Red Time. If the product has a reproducible crash or data corruption, the decision to make the change is essentially automatic because you just do it. In most cases, however, deciding whether to fix a particular bug is less black and white. To help me decide how critical a bug fix is, I always ask the following questions with the company's needs in mind:

- How many people does this problem affect?

- Is the change in a core or a peripheral part of the product?

- If the change is made, what parts of the application will need to be retested?

The answers to these questions provide the criteria I need to allow or disallow the change. Let me put some concrete numbers behind this list and give you my general rules for the beta phases: If the bug is serious, such as a painting or drawing problem, but not a case of a crash or data corruption showstopper, and it's going to affect greater than 15 percent of our external testers, the bug must be fixed. If the bug will result in a change to a data file, I go ahead and fix it so that we don't have to change file formats later in the development process and so that beta testers can consequently get larger data sets for subsequent betas.

The Importance of Labeling

One of the most important commands that you can learn to use in your version control system is its label command. Microsoft Visual SourceSafe and SourceGear's Vault call it a *label*, and Visual Studio Team Foundation calls it a *changeset*. Different version control systems might refer to the label command in different ways, but whatever it's called, a label marks a particular set of master sources. A label allows you to retrieve a specific version of your master sources in the future. If you make a labeling mistake, you might never be able to retrieve the exact master sources used for a particular version. That could mean that you might not be able to discover why a particular version is crashing.

When deciding what to label, I've always followed these five hard-and-fast rules:

- Label all internal milestones.

- Label any transitions from Green, Yellow, or Red development times.

- Label any build sent to someone outside the team.

- Label any time you branch a development tree in the version control software.

- Label after the daily build and smoke tests complete successfully. (Smoke tests are discussed in the "Smoke Tests" section later in this chapter.)

    In all cases, I follow a scheme of <Project Name> <Milestone/Reason> <Date> so that the label names are descriptive.

The third labeling rule is one that many people forget. Your quality engineers are usually working with the milestone or daily build, so when they report a problem, they do so against a particular version of the master sources. Because developers can change code quickly, you want to make it simple for them to get back to the exact version of the files they need to reproduce the bug, and next, to ensure that it is fixed in a clear versioned build that quality engineers can identify.

Bug Tracking Systems

In addition to tracking your bugs, the bug tracking system makes an excellent vehicle for jotting down reminders and keeping a to-do list, especially when you're in the process of developing code. Some developers like to keep notes and to-do lists in notebooks, but essential information often gets lost between random hexadecimal number streams from a debugging session and the pages and pages of doodling that you used to keep yourself awake in the last management status meeting. By putting these notes into the bug tracking system and assigning them to yourself, you consolidate them in one place, making them easier to find. Additionally, although you probably like to think that you own the code you work on, you really don't—it belongs to the team and on a larger scale to the company. With your to-do list in the bug tracking system, other team members who have to work with your code can check your list to see what you have or haven't done. Another benefit of including to-do lists and notes in the bug tracking system is that fewer details fall through the cracks at the last minute as a result of your forgetting about a problem or because of another issue. I always find myself running the bug tracking system so that I can quickly jot down important notes and tasks to perform right when I think about them.

I like to reserve the lowest priority bug code in the system for notes and to-do lists. Flagging notes and to-do lists as lowest-priority bugs makes it easier to keep them separate from the real bugs, but at the same time, you can quickly raise their priority if you need to. You should also structure your bug metrics reports so that they don't include the lowest-priority bug code because it will skew your results.

Don't be afraid to peruse the bug tracking data either. All the unvarnished truths about your products are there. When you're planning an update, run through the bug tracking system, and find those modules or features that had the most bugs reported against them. Consider adding some time in your schedule to allow team members to go back and strengthen those sections.

When deploying your bug tracking system, make sure that everyone who needs it has it. At a minimum, everyone on the development team and the technical support team needs access to it. If your bug tracking system supports different levels of access, you might also want to think about allowing others, such as sales engineers (technical experts who are part of the sales organization and help the salespeople as needed when they're selling a complicated product) and marketing representatives, to have access as appropriate. For example, you might want to allow certain sales and marketing people to enter bugs and feature requests but not to view existing bugs. These two groups are generally out talking to customers more than your typical engineers are, and the customer feedback they can supply can be invaluable. Of course, this means that you're going to have to give sales and marketing folks classes on how to fill out bug reports. They're more than happy to help, but you need to give them the guidance so that they can do it properly. Having these groups log their feature requests and bug reports in the same system that everyone else uses is efficient and practical. The idea is to have one central place where all problems and feature requests reside. If you store this information in multiple locations, such as in the product manager's e-mail inbox, in engineers' paper notebooks, and in the bug tracking system, you're more likely to lose track of it.

Choosing the Right Systems for You

Numerous version control systems are available. Some might be easier to use than others or offer more features, but the real issue in choosing the best version control system comes down to your specific requirements. Obviously, if you're in a shop that has high-end requirements, such as multiple platform support, you're going to need to look at one of the commercial systems, such as Perforce, or possibly an open source solution, such as CVS or Subversion. If you're a small team targeting just Windows development, however, you can consider some of the Windows-only products, such as Team Foundation System or SourceGear's SourceVault. Make sure that you spend some time doing some hard evaluation of the system you're thinking about implementing, especially in trying to predict what you'll need in the future. You're going to be living with your version control system for a while, so make sure it will grow with you. And keep in mind that just as important as choosing the right version control system is using a version control system in the first place; any system is better than no system.

As for bug tracking systems, I've seen many people try to limp along with a homegrown system. Although doing a project with a homemade system is possible, I strongly recommend investing in a commercial product or utilizing an open source solution. The information in the bug tracking system is too vital to put into an application that you don't have the time to support and that can't grow to meet your needs six months or a year into the project. Additionally, developers avoid wasting time on internal tools and work instead on revenue-producing products. If you work at a company where the managers won't consider a commercial system, there are some excellent open source bug tracking systems. I've seen numerous companies have great luck with Bugzilla (*http://www.bugzilla.org/*).

The same criteria apply for choosing a bug tracking system as for choosing a version control system. Once, as a product manager, I decided on a bug tracking system without spending enough time looking at the most important part, reporting bugs. The product was easy enough to set up and use. Unfortunately, its reporting capabilities were so limited that we ended up transferring all our existing bugs to another product right after we hit our first external code milestone. I was rather embarrassed for not having evaluated the product as thoroughly as I should have.

As I mentioned earlier in the chapter, you should definitely consider a bug tracking product that offers integration with a version control product. In the Windows marketplace, most version control systems support the Microsoft Source Code Control Interface (MSSCCI). If your bug tracking system also supports MSSCCI, you can coordinate the bug fixes with particular file versions.

Some people have described code as the lifeblood of a development team. If that description is accurate, the version control and bug tracking systems are the arteries. They keep the lifeblood flowing and moving in the right direction. Don't develop without them.

Schedule Time for Building Debugging Systems

As you're doing the design and initial scheduling for your project, make sure to add in time for building your debugging systems. You need to decide up front how you're going to implement your crash handlers, file data dumpers, and other tools you'll need to help you reproduce problems reported from the field. I've always liked to treat the error handling systems as if they were a product feature. That way, others in the company can see how you're going to handle bugs proactively when they come up.

When it comes to .NET development, choosing how to handle error conditions is simple: use exceptions. The beauty of .NET is that, unlike native code, there's a standard exception class, *System.Exception*, which all other exceptions derive from. The one drawback to .NET exceptions is that you still have to rely on the developer documenting those exceptions being thrown by the method because it is not done at the language or .NET runtime level. However, I'll discuss some analysis tools later in this chapter that can force developers to provide that documentation.

Build All Builds with Debugging Symbols

Some of the debugging system recommendations that I do make aren't that controversial. I've been harping on my first recommendation for years: build all builds, including release builds, with full debugging symbols. Debugging symbols are the data that let the debugger show you source and line information, variable names, and data type information for your program. All that information is stored in a Program Database (PDB) file associated with your modules. If you're paid by the hour, spending forever at the assembly language level could do wonders for paying your mortgage. Unfortunately, the rest of us don't have the luxury of infinite time, so speedily finding those bugs is a priority.

There's a bit of confusion when it comes to turning on PDB file creation, mainly because there are numerous extra options to the /DEBUG switch, and the documentation on those switches appears to be wrong. The documentation says that the /DEBUG, /DEBUG+, and /DEBUG:FULL switches all produce full debugging symbols and have the compiler produce a *DebuggableAttribute* on the assembly to inform the JIT compiler that debugging information is available. This allows the application to be debugged if it's started under the debugger or attached to by the debugger. The documentation also lists a different switch, /DEBUG:PDBONLY, which it says will not generate the *DebuggableAttribute*, which is better for release builds. Again, according to the documentation, the drawback is that specifying

/DEBUG:PDBONLY means that you can debug the program only if you start it under the debugger. Given that the inability to do source debugging after attaching to an application makes debugging infinitely harder, my eyes almost popped out of my head when I read that. I determined from doing several experiments that using /DEBUG:PDBONLY allows you to both start and attach to applications to debug to your heart's content. The main difference is that /DEBUG:FULL turns off inlining, which is putting the code for a method inside another method instead of making a call to a function. Because inlining helps with performance, I set all my Release builds to /DEBUG:PDBONLY and my Debug builds to /DEBUG:FULL.

Turning on debug symbols for a release build is quite easy, mainly because it is turned on by default for assembly-based wizard-generated projects. An assembly-based project is one in which the output is a .NET assembly, such as a class library or console application. For a C# normal assembly-based project, right click the project in Solution Explorer and select Properties. In the Project window, click the Build tab. Set the Configuration drop-down list box to Release. At the bottom of the page, click Advanced to get to the Advanced Build Settings dialog box. Set the Debug Info combo box to *pdbonly*. For Debug builds, you will set it to full. Figure 2-1 shows the Advanced Build Settings dialog box all set up to properly build with debugging symbols. Of course, don't get me started about why this option is buried in such an out-of-the-way dialog box when it should be in the General section of the Build property page.

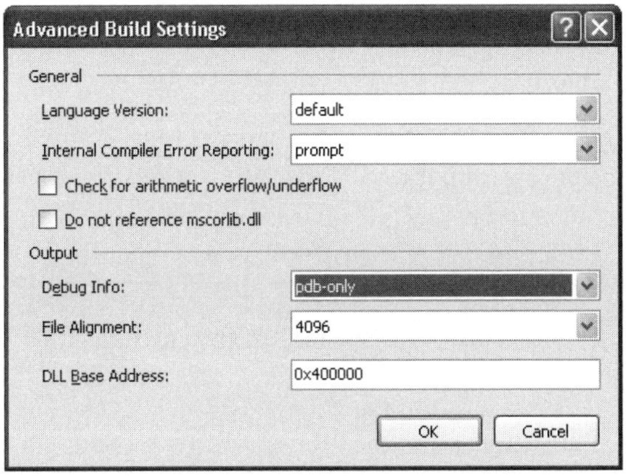

Figure 2-1   Generating debugging information for a normal C# assembly-based project

For reasons that I still can't quite fathom, the Microsoft Visual Basic assembly-based project property pages are different from the one for C# projects, but the compiler switch is still the same. I guess differences such as this, which make it more confusing for everyone, are the result of language teams that obviously don't speak to one another. Figure 2-2 shows setting a release build that produces full debug symbols for an assembly-based project in Visual Basic. Right-click the project in Solution Explorer and click Properties. In the Project window, click the Compile tab. Set the Configuration drop-down list box to Release. Near the top of the page, click Advanced Compile Options to get to the Advanced Compiler Settings dialog box. Set the Generate debug info combo box to *pdb-only*. For Debug builds, you will set it to *full*.

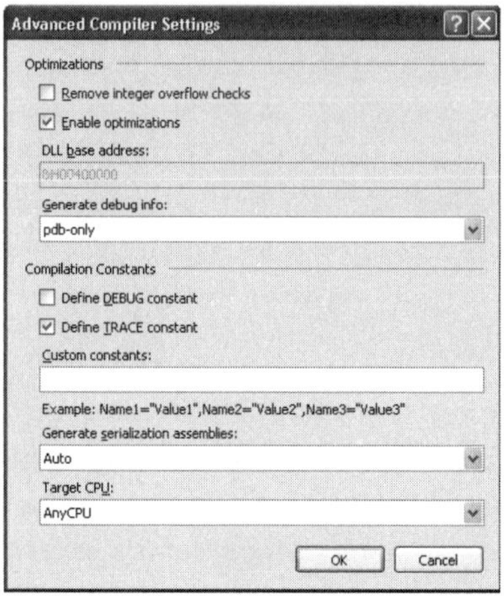

Figure 2-2   Generating debugging information for an assembly-based Visual Basic project

For Microsoft ASP.NET applications, the only time you can debug you page code is by setting *compilation* element, *debug* attribute to *true* in Web.config. By setting the *debug* attribute to *true*, you are telling the development environment to add the *−D* switch to Aspnet_compiler.exe, which is what actually builds your pages. The *−D* switch in turn calls the language compiler with the /DEBUG+ switch, which is the equivalent to /DEBUG:FULL. Additionally, using /D with Aspnet_compiler.exe turns off all optimizations because your language compiler is spawned with the /OPTIMIZE switch.

Since I'm talking about setting ASP.NET compiler options, it's a good time for me to mention how you can set additional compiler options for your ASP.NET applications other than setting the *debug* element to *true*. The barely discussed *<compilers>* element in Web.config is where you can configure the *<compiler>* element for each of the compilers you're going to use. This is where Aspnet_compiler.exe picks up the settings from when it calls the appropriate language compiler. The following shows how to set options for both C# and Visual Basic:

```
<configuration>
  <system.codedom>
  <compilers>
     <compiler language="c#;cs;csharp"
               extension=".cs"

               type="Microsoft.CSharp.CSharpCodeProvider, System,
                     Version=2.0.0.0, Cuture=neutral,
                     PublicKeyToken=b77a5c561934e089"
               compilerOptions="/d:TRACE /warnaserror+ /checked+"
               warningLevel="4" />
     <compiler language="VB"
               extension=".vb"
               compilerOptions="/d:Trace=true"
               type="Microsoft.VisualBasic.VBCodeProvider, SystemVersion=2.0.0.0,
                     Cuture=neutral,  PublicKeyToken=b77a5c561934e089"
               compilerOptions="/d:TRACE /warnaserror+"
   </compilers>
  </system.codedom>
</configuration>
```

If the thought of manually changing your project's settings for your 200 projects to build with debug symbols in addition to the rest of the proper build switches has you dreading the work, don't worry—there's hope. For Chapter 7, "Extending the Visual Studio IDE," I wrote an extremely cool add-in, SettingsMaster, that takes all the work out of changing project settings. SettingsMaster's defaults are to set up your projects by using the settings recommended in this chapter.

Treat Warnings as Errors

If you've written anything more than *Hello World!* in managed code, you've certainly noticed that the compilers don't let much slide as far as compiler errors are concerned. For those of you coming from a C++ background and who are new to .NET, you are probably amazed at how much tighter everything feels; in C++, you could cast values to almost anything, and the compiler would blindly go on its merry way. In addition to ensuring that data types are explicit, the managed code compilers can do much more to help you with errors if you let them. As usual, the trick to debugging smarter is not one big gesture, but taking advantage of lots of small steps along the way. Making your tools as smart as possible is one of those steps.

In the Visual Studio documentation, if you browse the Contents pane and navigate to Development Tools and Languages\Visual Studio\Visual C#\C# Reference\C# Compiler Options \C# Compiler Errors (or go to *http://msdn2.microsoft.com/en-us/library/ms228296.aspx*), you'll see all the compiler errors for C#. (The Visual Basic compiler errors are also included in the Index pane if you start typing *BC20*, but amazingly, the compiler errors aren't indexed in the Contents pane.) As you scroll down the list of C# errors, you'll notice that some say Compiler Warning and indicate a level, for example, Compiler Warning (level 3) CS0168. If you keep scrolling down the list, you'll find warning levels from 1 through 4. When you have a warning, the compiler indicates that the construct at that location in the source code is syntactically correct but might not be contextually correct.

A perfect example is CS0168, which is "The variable 'var' is declared but never used." If you've ever had to maintain code, nothing is more frustrating than spending 20 minutes pounding through a 300-line poorly written method looking for what uses a particular variable, only to discover that nothing does. One of my favorite warnings is CS1591, "Missing XML comment for publicly visible type or member 'Type_or_Member'." That wonderful warning ensures that you're documenting all your code!

Given that the compiler can inform you of all sorts of wonderful contextual problems such as this, doesn't it make sense to fix these problems? I don't like to call the problems *warnings* because they are really errors. If you've ever had the opportunity to learn about compiler construction, particularly parsing, you probably walked away with two thoughts: parsing is extremely difficult, and people who write compilers are different from the rest of us. (Whether that's a good different or bad different, I'll let you decide.) If the compiler writers go to tremendous trouble to report a warning, they are telling you something they obviously feel is quite important and is probably a bug. When a client asks us to help with a bug, the first thing we do is verify with them that the code compiles with no warnings. If it doesn't, I tell them that I'll be glad to help but not until their code compiles cleanly.

Fortunately, Visual Studio generates projects with the appropriate warning levels by default, so you shouldn't have to set the warning levels manually. If you're building your C# project manually, you'll want to set the /WARN switch to /WARN:4. For Visual Basic manual compiles, warnings are on by default, so you specifically have to turn them off.

Although the warning levels are appropriately set by Visual Studio, the default for treating warnings as errors is not set correctly. Cleanly compiling code is a great thing, so you'll want to get the /WARNASERROR+ switch set for both the C# and Visual Basic compilers. That way you can't even begin to start debugging until the code is perfect. For C# projects, navigate to the Build tab of the project's property page as discussed in the "Build All Builds with Debugging Symbols" section earlier in the chapter. In the "Treat Warnings as Errors" group box, select the All option. As usual, you'll want to do this for both Debug and Release builds. For Visual Basic projects, on the Compile tab of the project's property page, select the Treat All Warnings As Errors check box (near the bottom of the page).

For C# projects in particular, treating warnings as errors will stop the build on all sorts of problems that you would normally not halt the build, such as CS0649 ("Field 'field' is never assigned to, and will always have its default value 'value'"), which indicates that you have a class member that is uninitialized. However, other messages, such as CS1573 ("Parameter 'parameter' has no matching param tag in XML comment (but other parameters do)"), might seem so annoying that you'll be tempted to turn off treating warnings as errors. I strongly suggest that you don't.

In the case of CS1573, you're using the phenomenal /DOC switch to generate the XML documentation for your assembly. This is a warning that should be an error because if you're using XML documentation, someone else on your team is probably going to be reading that documentation, and if you aren't documenting everything you assume with parameters, or anything else for that matter, you're doing everyone on your team a disservice.

Both the C# and Visual Basic compilers have a switch you should never use: /NOWARN. It allows you to ignore a specific warning. The whole point of using /WARNASERROR+ is to have the compiler do as much heavy lifting as possible so that you don't have to waste those late hours debugging something when you could have been sleeping. Never do anything at run time that you can do at compile time.

Know Where Your Assemblies Load

In the mean world of native C++ development, you have to carefully watch where your DLLs load into memory. Because of the way native code works, there are many hard-coded addresses embedded into the actual assembly language generated by the compiler. In a perfect world, this allows Windows to map the code section into memory and all hard coded addresses are correct with no extra work required.

In an imperfect world, if your native DLL loads into an address different from the one it was compiled to assume, major problems occur. The resulting activity is called *relocation* when the operating system has to run through the assembly language code for the DLL and find all the hard-coded offsets and update them. If there were only four or five offsets, that would be very quick on modern computers. Unfortunately, the number is always much higher than you ever expect, and it's not uncommon to see 100,000 or more hard-coded offsets in native code. That causes a major slowdown in DLL (and so application) loading.

As the operating system is updating the addresses, it's changing the actual in-memory code pages for the DLL. That means that your process can't take advantage of tricks that the operating system plays to share those code pages in memory across all processes using that DLL. Because the memory is changed just for your process, you are charged for that memory, significantly increasing your overall memory usage.

The last problem is the worst for native code. You have no idea where that DLL loads if relocation occurs. Even two machines with identical hardware and drivers will load the DLL into different places. The end result is that if your code crashes in that DLL, the user will report a crash address, and you'll be left explaining to the boss that that address means nothing to you and you can't solve the problem. That's always a career-limiting move!

As you can see, controlling where a DLL loads into memory can have a major impact on memory consumption and performance of your applications. The good news is that it's not difficult to get right, as we'll see in a few paragraphs. Before I jump into discussing the addressing situation in .NET applications, this is a perfect spot to show you how easily you can see if you have relocations in your application. The first way is to turn on mixed mode (both managed and native debugging at the same time). (I'll discuss how to turn on mixed mode debugging in the "Mixed-Mode Debugging" section of Chapter 5, "Advanced Debugger Usage with Visual Studio.") Run your application in Visual Studio and display the Modules window, which is accessible from the Windows submenu of the Debug menu or by pressing Ctrl+Alt+U with the default keyboard mapping. If a module has been relocated, its icon is partially covered by a red ball with an exclamation point. Additionally, the load address for the module has an asterisk (*) after the address range. Figure 2-3 shows where DllA.dll and DllC.dll were relocated in the debugging session.

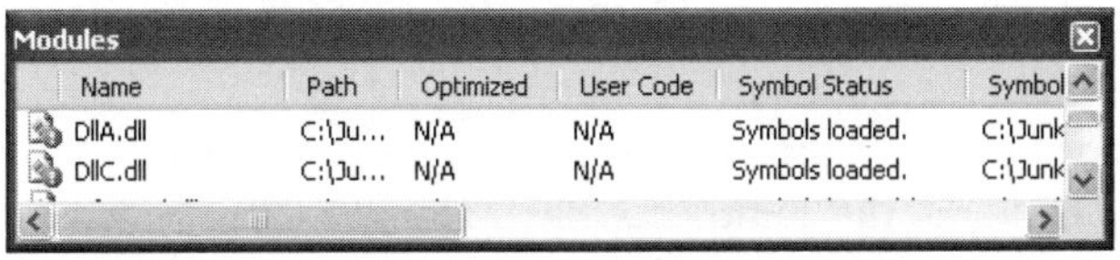

Figure 2-3   The Visual Studio debugger Modules window with relocated DLLs

The second way is to download the free Process Explorer, written by my good friend Mark Russinovich, from Sysinternals (*www.sysinternals.com*). Process Explorer, as its name implies, shows you all sorts of information about your processes, for example, loaded DLLs and all open handles. It's such a useful tool that if you don't have it on your machines right now, stop immediately and download it! Also, make sure to read Chapter 4, "Common .NET Debugging Questions" for additional hints and tricks you can use to make debugging easier with Process Explorer.

Seeing whether you have relocated DLLs is very easy. Just follow the next procedure. Figure 2-4 shows what it looks like to have relocated DLLs in a process.

1. Start Process Explorer and select your process.

2. Select View DLLs from the View menu.

3. Select your process in the upper half of the main window.

If any DLLs show up highlighted in yellow, they have been relocated.

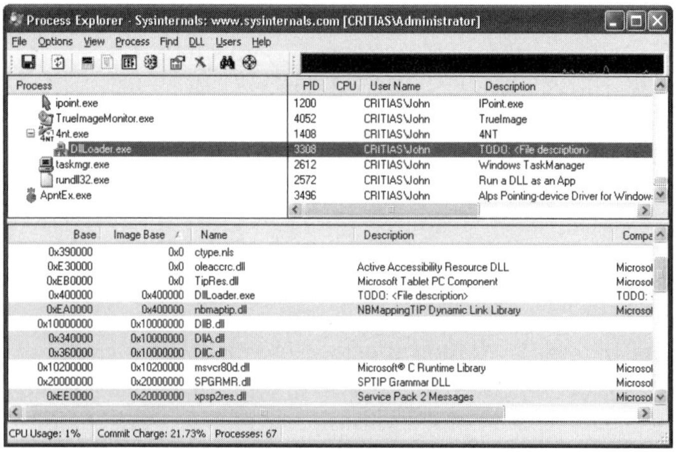

Figure 2-4   Process Explorer showing relocated DLLs

Another excellent tool that will show relocated DLLs with not only the relocated address but also the original address is ProcessSpy from Christophe Nasarre's excellent "Escape from DLL Hell with Custom Debugging and Instrumentation Tools and Utilities, Part 2" in the August 2002 edition of MSDN Magazine (*http://msdn.microsoft.com/msdnmag/issues/02/08 /escapefromdllhell/*). Process Explorer and ProcessSpy are similar utilities, but ProcessSpy comes with source code so that you can see how all the magic happens.

At this point, you're probably thinking that since managed components are compiled to DLLs, you might want to set their load location also. This is also referred to as setting the base address or *rebasing*. If you've explored the compiler switches for the C# and Visual Basic compilers, you might have seen the /BASEADDRESS switch for setting the base address. Well, when it comes to managed code, things are quite a bit different. If you really look at a managed DLL with Link.exe DUMP, the Portable Executable (PE) dumper from Visual Studio C++, or with Matt Pietrek's much better PEDUMP (MSDN Magazine, February 2002, *http://msdn.microsoft.com/msdnmag/issues/02/02/PE/default.aspx*), you'll notice a single imported function, *_CorDllMain* from MScoree.dll, and a single relocation entry.

Thinking that there might be actual executable code in managed DLLs, I disassembled a few, and everything in the module code section looked like data. I looked a bit more and noticed something very interesting. The entry point of the module, which is the place where execution starts, happens to be the same address as the imported *_CorDllMain*. That helped confirm that there's no native executable code.

Even though you might think that you don't have to worry about the DLL base address because managed code does not have any actual CPU-specific assembly language in them by default, you still will want to do it. This is especially important if you are running NGen on your binaries and installing them in the Global Assembly Cache (GAC). NGen is the tool that will pre-Just-In-Time (JIT) compile your .NET Intermediate Language (IL) and save the assembly language as part of the binary. When you NGen a binary, you can pay the same performance hit that you would if it were a native C++ DLL. Even if you aren't running NGen on your assemblies, and you have the relocation, the operating system will still have to go down the extra code paths to do the relocation. In fact, two recent articles in MSDN Magazine by members of the .NET team specifically addressed the performance issues with relocations, and they are worth looking at because they discuss how the team found and addressed relocation errors. The first article is "Winning Forms: Practical Tips For Boosting The Performance Of Windows Forms Apps" by Milena Salman, the performance lead on the Windows Form team in the March 2006 issue of MSDN Magazine (*http://msdn.microsoft.com/msdnmag/issues/06/03/WindowsFormsPerformance/*). The second is the February 2006 CLR Inside Out column by Claudio Caldato, a Program Manager for Performance and Garbage Collection on the CLR Team (*http://msdn.microsoft.com/msdnmag/issues/06/02/CLRInsideOut/*).

There are two ways to rebase the DLLs in your application. The first method is to use the Rebase.exe utility that comes with Visual Studio. Rebase.exe has many different options, but your best bet is to call it using the /b command-line switch with the starting base address and place the appropriate DLLs on the command line. The good news is that once you do the rebasing, you'll almost never have to touch those DLLs again.

There's one small drawback to using Rebase.exe: if you've strongly named your DLL, as you always should, you can't use Rebase.exe. The same applies if you've digitally signed the DLL. The problem is that Rebase.exe works by physically changing the binary on the disk. When strongly named DLLs or digitally signed DLLs are physically changed, they can no longer be loaded and will cause an unhandled *AssemblyLoadException* in your application. If you do want to use Rebase.exe, you'll have to rely on delayed signing.

Table 2-1 shows a table from the Visual Studio documentation for rebasing your DLLs. As you can see, the recommended format is to use an alphabetical scheme. I generally follow this scheme because it's simple. The operating system DLLs load from 0x70000000 to 0x78000000, even on 64-bit operating systems, so using the range in Table 2-1 will keep you from conflicting with the operating system. Of course, you should always look in your application's address space by using Process Explorer or ProcessSpy to see whether any DLLs are already loaded at the address you want to use.

Table 2-1   DLL Rebasing Scheme

DLL first letter	Starting address
A–C	0x60000000
D–F	0x61000000
G–I	0x62000000
J–L	0x63000000
M–O	0x64000000
P–R	0x65000000
S–U	0x66000000
V–X	0x67000000
Y–Z	0x68000000

If you have four DLLs in your application, Apple.dll, Dumpling dll, Ginger.dll, and Gooseberries.dll, you run Rebase.exe three times to get all the DLLs rebased appropriately. The following three commands show how to run Rebase.exe with those DLLs:

```
REBASE /b 0x60000000 APPLE.DLL
REBASE /b 0x61000000 DUMPLING.DLL
REBASE /b 0x62000000 GINGER.DLL GOOSEBERRIES.DLL
```

If multiple DLLs are passed on the Rebase.exe command line, as shown here with Ginger.dll and Gooseberries.dll, Rebase.exe will rebase the DLLs so that they are loaded back to back starting at the specified starting address.

There's an easier way than wrestling with the Rebase.exe program. You'll change your build to use the /BASEADDRESS switch. For both C# and Visual Basic, you'll need to get to the Advanced Build Settings or Advanced Compiler Settings dialog boxes, respectively. Refer to the "Build All Builds with Debugging Symbols" section earlier in the chapter. Each of those dialog boxes has a DLL Base Address edit box in which you can manually type in the address you want. As always, set the same base address for both Debug and Release builds.

Although you can use Rebase.exe to automatically handle setting multiple DLL load addresses at a time, you have to be slightly more careful when setting the load address at link time. If you set the load addresses of multiple DLLs too close together, you'll see the relocated DLL in the debugger's Modules window. The trick is to set the load addresses far enough apart that you never have to worry about them after you set them.

Using the same DLLs from the Rebase.exe example, I'd set their load address to the following:

```
APPLE.DLL          0x60000000
DUMPLING.DLL       0x61000000
GINGER.DLL         0x62000000
GOOSEBERRIES.DLL   0x62100000
```

The important two DLLs are Ginger.dll and Gooseberries.dll because they begin with the same character. When that happens, I use the third-highest digit to differentiate the load addresses. If I were to add another DLL that started with *G*, its load address would be 0x62200000.

One of the big questions I get when I tell people to rebase their files is, "What files am I supposed to rebase?" The rule of thumb is simple: if you or someone on your team wrote the code, rebase it. Otherwise, leave it alone. If you're using third-party components, your binaries will have to fit around them.

Always Build with Code Analysis Turned On

Many years ago I read an old Digital Equipment Corporation manual that had the phrase *Never do at run time what you can do at compile time* in the introduction. That's something that's always stayed with me because it's such a salient point when it comes to software. Though the /WARNASERRORS switch is quite useful, as I have already mentioned, Microsoft developed an internal set of best practices, called the Design Guidelines, to ensure the best .NET code possible. Fortunately, Brad Abrams and Krzysztof Cwalina brought them out in a book, *Framework Design Guidelines: Conventions, Idioms, and Patterns for Reusable .NET Libraries* (Addison-Wesley, 2005), which should be required reading for all .NET developers.

The one problem with any form of development guidelines is that unless you are going to manually review the code, there's no possible way for you to ensure that you're going to catch all the violations. That prompted the Common Language Runtime (CLR) team to invest in a tool that would try to automate finding as many of those errors as possible. Originally, this tool was released as FxCop, but it is now fully integrated into Visual Studio Team Developer Edition and Visual Studio Team Suite and has been renamed *Code Analysis*. The stand-alone FxCop is still available at *http://www.gotdotnet.com/team/FxCop/* and I'll talk soon about why you still want to use it.

What's surprised me over the last few years is how few teams are running either Code Analysis or FxCop on their code. The main reason most teams don't run it is because the first time they run the analysis on their code, they are confronted with a large number of very picky naming convention and capitalization errors, so most folks immediately discount the tool. The idea behind the naming convention and capitalization rules is to ensure consistency across all .NET development, so the idea of the rule is good. And by tossing out the tool, you're missing a huge opportunity to catch many tough errors in your code that you'll have to debug at run time.

For example, look closely at the following snippet of code to see if you can see the error:

```
int ret = ExpandEnvironmentStrings ( environmentVariable ,
                                      expandedVariable ,
                                      expandedVariable.Capacity ) ;
Debug.Assert ( ret != 0 , "ret != 0" );
if ( Marshal.GetLastWin32Error ( ) != 0 )
```

It's a very subtle error, and this is one I had in some of my code. Code Analysis immediately finds that the error is the fact that the code is relying on the last error value from *Expand-EnvironmentStrings* (the Windows API) but calling *Debug.Assert* in between the PInvoke call and the use of the last error value. *Debug.Assert* may cause a message box to appear, which could destroy the last error and lead to code that behaves differently between debug and release build. The specific error reported by Code Analysis is CA2122. Sharp-eyed readers might also notice the other Code Analysis error in the above code snippet: instead of calling the Windows API, Code Analysis reports that the code should use the *Environment.Expand-EnvironmentVariables* .NET method.

If that example doesn't convince you that Code Analysis is the cure to bad code, look at this code snippet and try to spot the error:

```
someConnection = new SqlConnection ( connection );
someCommand = new SqlCommand ( );
someCommand.Connection = someConnection;

someCommand.CommandText = "SELECT AccountNumber FROM Users " +
    "WHERE Username='" + name +
    "' AND Password='" + password + "'";

someConnection.Open ( );
accountNumber = someCommand.ExecuteScalar ( );
```

At first glance you may not see it, but you're looking at a classic case of leaving yourself open to an SQL Injection Attack. Code Analysis reports this as a CA2100 error and even tells you exactly what's wrong in the code:

```
Microsoft.Security : Review if the query string "SELECT AccountNumber FROM Users WHERE Usern
ame='____' AND Password='____'", passed to DbCommand.set_CommandText(String):Void in DemoCla
ss.UnsafeQuery(String, String, String):Object, accepts any user input. If so, consider using
 a parameterized Sql query instead of building up the query via string concatenations.
```

It's a great idea to read through all the rules that Code Analysis supports by searching the help index for CA1000 to access the list of rules. What's great about the documentation is that it shows you examples of each of the errors in addition to solid suggestions for fixing the errors.

Amazingly, for assembly-based projects, enabling Code Analysis is done the same way for C# as it is for Visual Basic. Navigate to the project's property sheet, click the Code Analysis tab, and then select the Enable Code Analysis (Defines CODE_ANALYSIS Constant) check box. This property page is where you can set warnings to errors and disable specific Code Analysis rules. For ASP.NET projects, you can turn on Code Analysis by selecting Code Analysis Configuration from the Website menu. Also, with all types of projects, you can right-click the project in Solution Explorer and select the option to run Code Analysis at any time.

My rule for Code Analysis best practices are that you always turn it on for both Debug and Release builds. That way it's always part of the compile, and you can fix any reported problems as soon as they occur. I also recommend that you never turn off any of the rules in Code

Analysis on your deliverable modules/projects. I know it's tempting to turn them off, especially the first time you run Code Analysis, for the purpose of eliminating capitalization and naming errors, on a set of code that's never been run through Code Analysis before. Another reason to fix those errors is so that your code looks like and is named consistently with the Framework Class Library in addition to all the code that everyone else is writing.

My final recommendation when it comes to Code Analysis is that you always set all rules to report errors so that the build stops if there's any problem. If you leave the default, which is to show warnings of errors, you'll never pay attention to problems found by Code Analysis. As I mentioned in the "Treat Warnings as Errors" section earlier in this chapter, you have to make builds stop on problems to force developers to address them.

Of course, the second time I had to manually change the Debug and Release builds on a project to have all Code Analysis rules treated as errors, I realized that was a task that needed to be automated. As part of the SettingsMaster add-in I wrote in Chapter 7, "Extending the Visual Studio IDE," I made sure it had the functionality to easily control all your Code Analysis settings. If you use the SettingsMaster Update Solution toolbar button, SettingsMaster will set all Code Analysis rules to errors.

Stand-Alone FxCop

Although there's quite a bit of overlap between Code Analysis and the stand-alone FxCop, the main difference is that FxCop offers spelling rules. It will use the Microsoft Office spelling engine to do the work of ensuring that you're spelling all your variables and natural parts of names correctly. If you're spelling-challenged as I am, the stand-alone FxCop can keep you from looking like an idiot when people are using your public APIs.

Although you can manually add all of your unique spellings to the Office spelling dictionary, a better way to tell FxCop about your spellings is through the CustomDictionary.xml file. This file resides in the same directory as the .FxCop project you'll save with your assemblies loaded. Listing 2-1 shows the CustomDictionary.xml file used by my code, which you can find in the .\FxCop directory of the book's source code.

Listing 2-1   Example CustomDictionary.xml File

```
<Dictionary>
  <Words>
   <Recognized>
    <Word>Wintellect</Word>
    <Word>Unboxing</Word>
    <Word>cref</Word>
    <Word>Visualizers</Word>
    <Word>Perf</Word>
    <Word>nologo</Word>
    <Word>nosymlocals</Word>
    <Word>pid</Word>
    <Word>Hhc</Word>
    <Word>Plugin</Word>
    <Word>plugin</Word>
```

```
        <Word>minidump</Word>
        <Word>Automator</Word>
        <Word>Validators</Word>
        <Word>Visualizers</Word>
        <Word>Visualizer</Word>
        <Word>Switches</Word>
      </Recognized>
      <Deprecated/>
      <Inappropriate/>
    </Words>
    <Acronyms>
      <CasingExceptions>
      </CasingExceptions>
    </Acronyms>
  </Dictionary>
```

Custom Code Analysis Rules

As soon as I saw Code Analysis, I immediately wanted to write some custom rules. In Chapter 8, "Writing Code Analysis Rules," I'll give you all the details, because rule development is undocumented. However, it's appropriate to discuss using the rules in this section.

I've provided three rules files, Wintellect.FxCop.DesignRules.DLL, Wintellect.FxCop.PerformanceRules.DLL, and Wintellect.FxCop.UsageRules.DLL. You can use the supplied WintellectToolsInstall.MSI to install my rules into your copy of Visual Studio Team Developer Edition or Visual Studio Team Suite Edition. Once you've installed my Code Analysis Rules, they automatically show up in the Code Analysis project properties. If you're using FxCop, my rules compiled against FxCop 1.35, the latest version at the time I wrote this, are in the .\FxCop directory where you installed the book's source code.

The rule in Wintellect.FxCop.PerformanceRules.DLL is AvoidBoxingAndUnboxingInLoops. The first thing everyone hears about .NET development is that you're supposed to avoid BOX and UNBOX instructions. A BOX instruction is generated when you are passing a value type to a method that takes only objects. An UNBOX instruction extracts the value type from the object. The problem with these two instructions is that they are very slow and put pressure on the managed heap, so you don't want them in your code.

Because it's so hard to spot the value types by code inspection, I guess you could disassemble all your binaries to Intermediate Language files and manually look for the offending instructions if they appear in a looping construct. It's completely impractical to manually look for these instructions, and having one inside a loop can destroy performance. Consequently, I wrote this rule to warn you if you have that condition in your code.

The Wintellect.FxCop.Design.DLL file contains numerous interesting rules. Although Code Analysis has a rule to ensure that you've set the assembly version number, I wanted a set of rules that would look for other key assembly attributes, such as the company name, copyright values, descriptions, and titles. Those rules aren't very exciting, but they ensure that your assemblies are identifiable.

The more interesting rules deal with XML Doc Comments. The first, AssembliesHaveXmlDoc-CommentFiles, ensures that you're building valid XML documentation files with your assemblies. The other two rules, ExceptionDocumentationInvalidRule and ExceptionDocumentation MissingRule, require a little background discussion as to why they are important.

The most important data in your XML Doc Comments are the exceptions directly thrown by a method. A direct throw is one that has a physical *throw* statement in the method. A caller is much more interested in potentially handling a direct throw in a method because they are specifically expected. Although other methods called by the target method could certainly throw exceptions from deep in a call chain, it's those direct *throw* statements that everyone's interested in and that everyone needs to see documented with the wonderful *<exception>* tag.

The ExceptionDocumentationMissingRule rule looks through the instructions in the method and finds all direct throws and compares them to the actual XML Doc Comment file. If the documentation is missing, a Code Analysis error is the result. ExceptionDocumentationInvalidRule is the opposite of ExceptionDocumentationMissingRule in that if it finds a documented exception that's not actually thrown, the rule generates the error.

The first two rules in Wintellect.FxCop.UsageRules.DLL are DoNotUseTraceAssertRule and CallAssertMethodsWithMessageParametersRule. As you can deduce from the rule names, they are to warn you when you're calling *Trace.Assert* and the *Debug.Assert* overload without a message parameter. In the Assertions in .NET section, I go through the numerous reasons why these two methods should be avoided.

In Chapter 24 of his *CLR via C#, Second Edition* (Microsoft Press, 2005), Jeffrey Richter goes through a litany of problems that can occur in your synchronization using SyncBlocks and Monitors. Jeffrey's rules were screaming to be put into Code Analysis rules, so I created the four rules DoNotLockOnPublicFields, DoNotLockOnThisOrMe, DoNotLockOnTypes, and DoNotUseMethodImplAttributeWithSynchronized to ensure that you have your synchronization implemented correctly.

Frequent Builds and Smoke Tests Are Mandatory

Two of the most important pieces of your infrastructure are your build system and your smoke test suite. The *build system* is what compiles and links your product, and the *smoke test* suite comprises tests that run your program and verify that it works. Jim McCarthy, in his book, *Dynamics of Software Development* (Microsoft Press, 1995), called the daily build and smoke test the heartbeat of the product.

Frequent Builds

Your project has to be built every day. That process is the heartbeat of the team, and if you're not building, your project is dead. Many people tell me that they have absolutely huge projects that can't be built every day. Does that mean that those people have projects that are even larger than the 50 million lines of code in the Windows Vista source code tree? Windows Vista is the largest commercial software project in existence, and it builds every day. So there's no excuse for not building every day. Not only must you build every day, but you must have a build that is completely automated.

When building your product, you must build both release and debug versions at the same time. As you'll see later in the chapter, the debug builds are critical. Breaking the build must be treated as a sin. If developers check in code that doesn't compile, they need to pay some sort of penalty to right the wrong. A public flogging might be a little harsh (though not by much), but what has always worked on the teams I've been on is penance in the form of supplying doughnuts to the team and publicly acknowledging the crime. If you're on a team that doesn't have a full-time release engineer, you can punish the build breaker by making him or her responsible for taking care of the build until the next build breaker comes along.

One of the best daily-build practices I've used is to notify the team via e-mail when the build is finished. With an automated nightly build, the first message everyone can look for in the morning is the indication of whether the build failed; if it did, the team can take immediate action to correct it.

To avoid problems with the build, everyone must have the same versions of all build tools and parts. As I mentioned earlier, some teams like to keep the build system in version control to enforce this practice. If you have team members on different versions of the tools, including the service pack levels, you have room for error in the build. Unless there is a compelling reason to have someone using a different version of the compiler, no developer should be upgrading on his or her own. Additionally, everybody must be using the same build script as the build machine to do their builds. That way there's a valid relationship between what developers are developing and what the testers are testing.

Your build system will be pulling the latest master sources from your version control system each time you do a build. Ideally, the developers should also be pulling from version control every day. If it's a large project, developers should be able to get the daily compiled binaries easily to avoid big compilation times on their machines. Nothing is worse than spending time trying to fix a nasty problem only to find out that the problem is related to an older version of a file on a developer's machine. Another advantage of developers pulling frequently is that it helps enforce the mantra of "no build breaks." By pulling frequently, any problem with the master build automatically becomes a problem with every developer's local build. Whereas managers get annoyed when the daily build breaks, developers go ballistic when you break their local build. With the knowledge that breaking the master build means breaking the build for every individual developer, the pressure is on everyone to check only clean code into the master sources.

Wonderful MSBuild

One of the most exciting parts of .NET 2.0 is the inclusion of the fantastic MSBuild system. It's in every install of .NET itself, and with all Visual Studio projects being MSBuild files, we finally have a situation in which you can do exactly the same build script in the IDE as you do on the build server. Having built several industrial-strength build systems in the past, I can only applaud Microsoft for getting it mostly right in the first version. Once we have direct native C++ building and per-CPU builds in MSBuild, we'll have the ultimate in build technology.

With MSBuild a vital tool in your life, you cannot afford to be ignorant of the technology. Some good resources include the MSBuild team blog at *http://blogs.msdn.com/msbuild/* and the Channel 9 MSBuild Wiki at *http://channel9.msdn.com/wiki/default.aspx/MSBuild.HomePage*. For the following discussion, I'm assuming that you've at least read the MSBuild documentation and are familiar with MSBuild terminology.

As part of this book's source code, I put together numerous build tasks that you might find useful in your own development. All the code is in the highly secretive name of Wintellect.Build.Tasks.DLL. Numerous parts of the book's code build with that DLL , so you can look at the main build project for the book's source code in .\Build\Build.proj to get an idea of real usage.

The first set of tasks I built was to handle build versioning. Having done build number versioning on every project I've ever worked on, I wanted to get it done for the last time. I wanted a task that would read in a file, figure out the build number, increment it, and write the file back out. The *IncrementBuildNumberTask* handles the build numbering. I also threw in the ability to choose between straight incrementing build numbers or to have the build number use the Microsoft Developer Division format of integers (<year><month><day>.<revision>). The .\Shared directory contains the SharedVersion.xml file I used for all the source code.

Having a file that contains a version is nice, but you want to get that version number into your source files through the *AssemblyFileVersionAttribute*. That's the job of the *GenerateAssembly-FileVersionTask*. It reads in the version XML file and spits out C#, Visual Basic, and C++/CLI source files that you can include in your projects. All my projects include a linked file called SharedAssemblyFileVersion.CS or SharedAssemblyFileVersion.VB to have the code applied. In the .\Build\Versions.targets, I included a wrapper task, *UpdateBuildAndSharedFiles* that calls the two tasks to do the work. To use the versioning tasks, you'll need only to create the XML file to hold your version and set up a project file to use Versions.targets.

As I was doing the two versioning tasks, I realized that having the version information could be handy in other tasks also. For example, numerous tools that use a preprocessor approach allow you to override a variable or property on the command line with a different value. For those cases, I wanted to be ready to plug in the version number to apply versioning to projects that don't use .NET source files.

The *VersionAwareTask* lets you define a property, *VersionCommandLinePart*, with which you can specify the usual .NET formatting code, {0}, where you want the version information to be plugged in to the tool's command line. You can't use the *VersionAwareTask* on its own because it's an abstract class.

There are several tasks to help with building installations. The *WixCandleTask* and *WixLight-Task* are there to run the tools from the Windows Installer XML Tool Set. If you look at the WiX binaries, you'll see that it comes with their own MSBuild tasks, but I started using it before the "Release of the Primes" version when they first appeared. I'll discuss WiX in more detail later in Chapter 4.

One trick that's unique about my WiX tasks is that they are derived from *VersionAwareTask*. If you look in .\Build\WiX.targets, you'll see that I define a property, *WiXVersionCommandLine*, that's preset to -dInstallVersion={0}. In your .wxs install files, you can set the *Product* element, *Version* attribute to *Version="$(var.InstallVersion)"* to get the build version directly into your resulting .msi file. For an example, look at either of the installs in .\Installs\directory.

If you've ever heard me speak at a conference, you know I'm a huge fan of the new performance and coverage tools in Visual Studio Team Developer Edition and Visual Studio Team Suite Editions. What many people don't realize is that both the coverage and performance tools offer a complete set of command-line tools, so you can do everything without the IDE. In many cases, especially for automated testing, using the command-line tools is much more useful. To make it easier for everyone, I put together several tasks so that you could perform those runs from MSBuild scripts.

The first target, *CodeCoverageInstrumentTarget*, is a simple wrapper around the command-line instrumentation tool, Vsinstr.exe. The code is all in Coverage.targets and handles instrumenting a binary for code coverage. The target makes it easy to pass in a whole list of assemblies that you want to instrument. In addition, if you define a *StrongName* property, the *CodeCoverageInstrumentTarget* will automatically re-sign the instrumented assemblies so that they run. Remember, if a strongly named assembly is changed, it will not run. However, if you re-sign the assembly with Sn.exe, the strong naming utility, that will fix up the signing so the binary will load and execute.

The other two targets in *Coverage.targets*, *StartCoverageMonitorTarget* and *StopCoverageMonitor-Target*, are used to start and stop the code coverage monitor, which is used to collect data from instrumented binaries as they run. The idea of these targets is that you can use them in an automated way to build an automated smoke test that's an integral part of your MSBuild build.

In the two monitor targets, the task that does all of the heavy lifting is *VSPerfMonTask*, exported from Wintellect.Build.Tasks.DLL. My original intent was to have a simple wrapper target around the Vsperfcmd.exe program. However, whenever I started the program with the built in *Exec* task, MSBuild hung completely. After quite a bit of head scratching, I finally realized that Vsperfcmd.exe, the control program for performance and coverage data collection, spawns off another program, Vsperfmon.exe, with inherited handles set to true. I quickly whipped up two sample programs the same way and found that the hang on inherited handles is a problem with MSBuild itself.

When I changed my approach to have my simple target start Vsperfmon.exe directly, I was still hanging in Msbuild.exe because Vsperfmon.exe shuts down only when you call Vsperfcmd.exe with the shutdown command. I'm not exactly sure why the coverage and performance monitors are going through all these odd gyrations, but that's how they work.

It finally dawned on me that I was going to have to write some code to work around the hanging from inherited handles and to figure out a way to get Vsperfmon.exe started but allow MSBuild to continue execution. My *VSPerfMonTask* tricks MSBuild by starting Vsperfcmd.exe, which avoids the inherited handles problem. Since Vsperfcmd.exe can start Vsperfmon.exe, I'm also skipping the hang waiting for the Vsperfmon.exe process. It's a little roundabout, but I met my goal of having targets that allow you to get code coverage information as part of a build.

If having a way to instrument your binaries in addition to starting the coverage monitor is nice, there needed to be a way to run the tests that use those instrumented binaries from an MSBuild project. The Visual Studio Team Developer Edition, Visual Studio Team Tester Edition, and Visual Studio Team Suite Editions, come with a very nice tool called MSTest.exe, which can execute all test types from the command line.

The first of the two testing-related tasks in Wintellect.Build.Tasks.DLL is a task called *MSTestTask*, which wraps the MSTest.exe so you can easily use if from your MSBuild projects. There's quite a bit of work inside *MSTestTask* to handle an odd issue in MSTest.exe related to the output file-naming scheme because it can be changed by a run configuration file even if you specify a specific name. Consequently, I had to do more work than necessary to have *MSTestTask* figure out file names to keep the same behavior.

The better part of the testing execution code I've provided is in .\Build\RunTests.targets. The Microsoft testing tools are nice, but they assume that you're going to manually update a file containing your lists of tests (a .vsmdi file) whenever you add a new test. As we all know, any time you have to ask a developer to do something manually, there is a chance it won't get done. What I wanted was an automatic MSBuild project that would start at a specific directory, automatically find all the test code, and then execute any tests in them. That's what RunTest.targets is designed to do. You can look at the RunTests.targets file itself for how to use it. It's also a nice example of how you can use the very powerful files searching with exclude items in MSBuild to control exactly what files are found in a search.

The next set of MSBuild tasks are all about version control. As I started this book, Microsoft had not released the Team Foundation System, so I started with Visual SourceSafe as my version control tool. The *SourceSafeTask* derives from *VersionAwareTask* and is a thin wrapper around Ss.exe, the Visual SourceSafe command-line tool. You can look at .\Build\Source-Safe.targets and .\Build\Build.proj to see how I used it to check out and check in the shared version files automatically. The main functionality provided by these SourceSafe tasks are to check in and out my version number files in addition to providing automatic labeling.

The more interesting set of version control tasks are the *SourceIndexTask* and the *VssSourceIndexTask*. Later in this chapter, I'll be discussing in depth the great importance of source indexing with the Source Server. Because Source Indexing is a build-time activity, automating it is a perfect candidate for a set of MSBuild tasks. I'll discuss these two tasks in detail in the "Set Up a Source Server" section near the end of this chapter because they make sense only if you know the details of the Source Server tools.

Finally, there are a couple of other interesting tasks and targets that are part of the source code. To build the ReadMe.chm file, I wrote HhcTask to make running the HTML Help Compiler easy from a build. In .\Build\CleanUp.targets, there are three useful targets to keep your source trees clean and sanitary. *CorrectClean* is intended as a replacement for the standard *Clean* target supplied by Microsoft. The problem with Microsoft's *Clean* target is that it not only removes the intermediate files, it also removes all the output files. In the normal development world, that's what's called *Really Clean*—that has been the name of that type of clean since before I started working with software. My *CorrectClean* will remove all the intermediate files but keep the output files. Because I want to be able to install the compiled binaries as part of my installation but not install all the temporary files in those OBJ directories, *CorrectClean* is a big help.

To clean up all the extraneous files created by running Code Analysis and programs such as the *.Vshosts.exe files, you can use the *CrudCleaner* task. The last scrubber task in .\Build\CleanUp.targets is *RemoveAllDevelopmentTests*, which removes all the directories and files created when using the Visual Studio testing tools inside the IDE to run your unit tests. When doing Test Driven Development with the Visual Studio testing tools, the run files can chew up a considerable amount of disk space. If you have saved off the key test results, you can use the *RemoveAllDevelopmentTests* to get rid of all the unnecessary run files in a single statement in an MSBuild project file.

In addition to the MSBuild tasks, there are two other collections of tasks that will definitely make your life easier. The first is the open source MSBuild Community Tasks Project at *http://msbuildtasks.tigris.org/*, which offers complete tasks for Subversion among other things. The second is the huge Microsoft Services (UK) Enterprise Solutions Build Framework collection put together by Andy Reeves and friends. It has tasks to create a Microsoft Active Directory account, control SQL Server 2005, and configure a Microsoft BizTalk Server. You can find the SDC collection at *http://www.gotdotnet.com/codegallery/codegallery .aspx?id=b4d6499f-0020-4771-a305-c156498db75e*.

Writing Your Own MSBuild Tasks

You should never hesitate to look at writing a custom task or target for any tools you have. Of course, a good Google search might locate the code to the task you need, so use existing code first. However, every company I've ever worked for or consulted for had several special tools that had to run as part of their build. Now that .NET is starting to standardize on MSBuild, your tasks can be utilized by others in your company or team very easily.

If you don't want to write any .NET code, you can use the *Exec* task to wrap the call to your tool. The *Exec* task provides a property, *ExitCode,* which you set to indicate proper tool execution so you can wrap nearly any command-line tool. The drawback to the *Exec* task is that you can't gather output from the tool and parse it up to provide better error or warning messages. If you want to look at an example of using the *Exec* task, look at *CodeCoverageInstrumentTarget* in .\Build\Coverage.targets, where I use the *Exec* task to start the Vsinstr.exe program to perform coverage instrumentation.

The next step to maximizing your use of MSBuild is to write your tasks in the .NET language of your choice. The MSBuild documentation is quite good, and there are a sufficient number of useful samples available on the Internet to get you going. Regrettably, I haven't seen any discussion of one of the better tricks I've found in writing MSBuild tasks, deriving your task from the excellent *ToolTask* class from Microsoft.Build.Utilities.dll, which is in the Framework directory. The *ToolTask* wraps up much of the common functionality every task will do, so you don't have to derive directly from the *ITask* interface.

ToolTask is an abstract class, and the two methods you must always provide are *ToolName,* which returns the program name of the tool, and *GenerateFullPathToTool.* Nothing in the documentation on building your own tasks discusses the fact that Msbuild.exe absolutely has to have the full path to your tool. Even if your tool is in the path, Msbuild.exe will still fail the task because it does no path searching. You'll provide an implementation of the *GenerateFullPathToTool* method to give that information to Msbuild.exe.

One item missing from the Framework Class Library (FCL) is the wrapper around *SearchPath,* the Windows API that does all the work of finding a file given the PATH environment variable. You'll need to make the PInvoke call to the method yourself. Copy the Native Methods.CS file from my .\Wintellect.Build.Tasks directory, and you'll have the code you need to find that program.

Another area that will trip up your task is the 32-bit/64-bit divide. One of the first tasks I wrote was the *HhcTask,* which handles the HTML Help Compiler. Because the HTML Help Compiler is installed by Visual Studio into a fixed directory, C:\Program Files\HTML Help Workshop, I blindly assumed that if I simply drop the hard-coded path into my task, I'd be successful. In fact, the HhcTask worked great on the 32-bit machine I was testing.

If you've ever looked at a 64-bit machine, you might have noticed there is something odd when you look for the Program Files directory; there are actually two. There's C:\Program

Files, but there's also C:\Program Files (x86). The "(x86)" should be the giveaway that this directory has something to do with 32-bit programs, and that's where the system does put all 32-bit programs. All 64-bit programs go into C:\Program Files. If the tool that you're working with has both 32-bit and 64-bit variants, and it's always installed into the C:\Program Files directory, you'll have no trouble hard-coding the path.

Alas, in the case of the HTML Help Compiler, there's no 64-bit variety, so the first time I ran my build using my *HhcTask* on a 64-bit system, I got an error indicating that it couldn't find the program to execute. Consequently, you can look at the code for *HhcTask* and see that I'm checking first in the C:\Program Files directory, and if I don't find Hhc.exe, I look in the C:\Program Files (x86) directory.

In the case of HTML Help Workshop, you can get away with the hard-coded path because you have no choice about where the help compiler is installed. For the *MSTestTask*, I faced a different problem. Because you *do* have a choice where Visual Studio is installed, I can't hard-code C:\Program Files\Microsoft Visual Studio*and_the_40-level_deep_directory_structure*\Mstest.exe. My hunt brings up the second issue with the 32/64 divide: the registry.

As I've mentioned, 32-bit applications that install on Win64 will go to a different Program Files directory, but their registry keys also go to a different place. For example, to find where Visual Studio is installed, on a 32-bit machine, you look in the HKEY_LOCAL_MACHINE \SOFTWARE\Microsoft\VisualStudio\8.0 registry key. In addition, if on a Win64 machine, you execute the 64-bit version of Msbuild.exe, your registry lookup works just fine. However, if your task runs under the 32-bit version of Msbuild.exe, the registry key is actually HKEY_LOCAL_MACHINE\SOFTWARE\Wow6432Node\Microsoft\VisualStudio\8.0. Notice the *Wow6432Node* in the middle of the key.

Neither of these two issues is major, but I wanted to mention them to aid you in creating tasks that successfully find the executable files that you need to run. Look at my *MSTestTask* for an example of properly looking for registry values that will work no matter what operating system your task runs on.

What makes the *ToolTask* so nice is that it already knows how to do the tool execution, and it has a very well-thought-out API that you can take advantage of so that it's even easier to write your task. With most tools, you'll want to provide some sort of parameter validation, and that's what the virtual *ToolTask.ValidateParameters* method is all about. If you return *false* from your override, MSBuild will report a failure, and the build will be stopped.

In addition to controlling the execution, you'll want to take advantage of the excellent internationalization support in *ToolTask* (inherited from the Task base class) by setting the *TaskResources* property to your own *ResourceManager*. That way you can use the *Log* property on ToolTask to get the corresponding *TaskLoggingHelper* instance and call its *LogErrorFromResources* to properly report any error. There are numerous other methods on the *TaskLoggingHelper* returned by the *Log* property so that you can report all sorts of information based on the logging level and your particular desires.

To build the command lines to tools, Microsoft.Build.Utilities.dll has a very nice public class called *CommandLineBuilder*. It's a smart wrapper around a *StringBuilder* that will append the particular switch only if its value is *null/Nothing*. The *CommandLineBuilder* class is a bit rudimentary, so I extended it with the *ExtendedCommandLineBuilder* in Wintellect.Build.Tasks .DLL to add even more smarts. The idea is that no matter which particular switch you want to use, you can simply use the *ExtendedCommandLineBuilder* and one of its methods without resorting to fancy parsing or analysis.

In your *ToolTask* derived class, you have *GenerateCommandLines*, which is the perfect method to build your command lines. That's where you'll use the *ExtendedCommandLineBuilder* to do all the major work. The *ToolTask* also supports methods to build response files, which are commands in a text file, so you have the ultimate in flexibility for getting options passed to the tool you're wrapping.

I've already mentioned the *Execute* method, which as you can guess, starts the tool. What's great about the *ToolTask.Execute* method is that it calls the *ValidateParameters* and *Generate-CommandLineCommands* methods, so you need only build up the tool command line. The only time you'll need to override *Execute* is when you do special processing. For example, any time you deal with the Visual SourceSafe command-line tool, Ss.exe, you need to set the SSDIR environment variable to point to the database to use. For what must be insane historical reasons, Visual SourceSafe will not let you specify the database to use on the Ss.exe command line. In tasks such as *VssSourceIndex*, I overrode *Execute* to let me set the SSDIR environment variable before calling the base *Execute* class.

The final method from ToolTask that I want to mention is the excellent *LogEventsFromTextOutput*. When writing tasks for a tool, you usually need to look at the output to determine if any errors occurred. If you were writing your tasks directly from the raw *ITask* interface, you could provide an *Execute* method that redirects output to a file and perform some tough parsing to determine if there's an error.

The *ToolTask.LogEventsFromTextOutput* method is the result of *ToolTask* handling all tool output line by line and calling this method on each line. By overriding the *LogEventsFromTextOutput* method, you can grab the output as it's coming through and determine if there have been any problems. For an excellent example of making your life drastically simpler by overriding *LogEventsFromTextOutput*, see the *SourceIndexTask* in Wintellect.Build.Tasks.DLL.

Now that you have a good idea of the possibilities of MSBuild and how easy it is to write tasks, go forth and task away! You can easily automate your entire build from the physical build all the way through smoke testing. To see an example, look at the work done in the book's main build file in .\Build\Build.proj. I think it's a testament to the skill of the developers who designed MSBuild as to how easy it was for me to put together that complicated of a build with just a little bit of work.

Smoke Tests

In case you're not familiar with the term, a *smoke test* is a test that checks your product's basic functionality. The term comes from the electronics industry. At some point in a product's life cycle, electronics engineers would plug in their product to see whether it smoked (literally). If it didn't smoke, or worse, catch fire, they were making progress. In most software situations, a smoke test is simply a run-through of the product to see whether it runs and is therefore good enough to start testing seriously. A smoke test is your gauge of the baseline health of the code.

Your smoke test is just a checklist of items that your release build program can handle. Initially, start out small: install the application, start it, and shut it down. As you progress through the development cycle, your smoke test needs to grow to exercise new features of the product. The best rule of thumb is that the smoke test should contain at least one test for every feature and major component of the product. If you are in a shrink-wrap company, that means testing each feature that appears in a bullet point for your advertisements. In an IT shop, that means testing each of the major features you promised the CIO and your client. Keep in mind that your smoke test doesn't need to exhaustively test every code path in your program, but you do want it to judge whether you can handle the basics. Once your program passes the smoke test, the quality engineers can start doing the hard work of trying to break the program in new and unique ways.

One vital component of your smoke test is some sort of performance benchmark. Many people forget to include these and pay the price later in the development cycle. If you have an established benchmark for an operation (for example, how long the last version of the product took to run), you can define failure as a current run that is 10 percent or more over or under your benchmark. I'm always amazed by how many times a small change in an innocuous place can have a detrimental impact on performance. By monitoring performance throughout the development cycle, you can fix performance problems before they get out of hand.

The ideal situation for a smoke test is one in which your program is automated so that it can run without requiring any user interaction. The tool you use to automate the input and operations on your application is called a *regression*-testing tool. Unfortunately, you can't always automate every feature, especially when the user interface is in a state of flux. If you have Visual Studio Team Tester Edition or Visual Studio Team Suite, you can use the excellent WebTest test type to automate and validate any HTTP-based application.

For automating rich client applications, such as a Windows Forms–based product, you'll need to turn to a user interface automation tool, such as Mercury WinRunner (*http://www.mercury .com/us/products/quality-center/functional-testing/winrunner/*). Another alternative is IBM's Rational Robot (*http://www-306.ibm.com/software/awdtools/tester/robot/index.html*). Unfortunately, these industrial-strength user interface automation tools are extremely expensive. If you are doing Windows Forms applications, James McCaffrey offered up a quick way to automate the user interface in his January 2003 Test column in MSDN Magazine (*http://msdn.microsoft.com/msdnmag/issues/03/01/UITestAutomation/*).

Breaking the smoke test should be as serious a crime as breaking the build. It takes more effort to create a smoke test, and no developer should treat it lightly. Because the smoke test is what tells your QA team that they have a build that's good enough to work on, keeping the smoke test running is mandatory. If you have an automated smoke test, you should also consider having the smoke test available for the developers so that they can use it also to help automate their testing. Additionally, with an automated smoke test, you should have the daily build start the smoke test so that you can immediately gauge the health of the build. As with the daily build, you should notify the team via e-mail to let them know whether the smoke test succeeded or failed.

Build the Installation Program Immediately

Begin developing the installation program immediately after you start developing your project. The installation program is the first part of your product that your users see. Too many products give a poor first impression, showing that the installation program was left to the last minute. By getting the installation program started as early as possible, you have sufficient time to test and debug it. If the installation program is done early, you can also incorporate it into your smoke test. This way, you're always testing it, and your tests will be one step closer to simulating how the users will be running your program.

Earlier in the chapter, I recommended that you should build both release and debug versions of your product. You also need to have an installation program that allows you to install either version. Even though managed applications are supposed to support XCOPY installation, that's only for toy programs. Real-world managed applications are going to have to initialize databases, put assemblies in the global assembly cache, and handle other operations that just can't be done with a simple copy. By having a debug build installation program, developers can easily get a debug version on a machine so that they can quickly start debugging a problem.

One extra benefit of having the installation program done as early as possible is that others in your company can start testing your program that much sooner. With the installation program done, the technical support engineers can start using your program and providing you with feedback early enough in the cycle so that you can actually do something about the problems they find.

Back in the "Wonderful MSBuild" section, I mentioned several tasks for using the Windows Installer XML Tool Set (*http://wix.sourceforge.net/*). It is Microsoft's first big open source project and is an excellent tool for building setup applications. Like many open source projects, it lacks great documentation, but if you can work your way through it, you'll be rewarded with an installation that becomes part of your development process. If you're worried about the scalability of WiX, rest assured that it can handle anything you throw at it. For example, WiX builds the Microsoft Office and Microsoft SQL Server 2005 installations.

I strongly suggest that you give WiX a very hard look for your particular applications, no matter what type of development you are doing. You can look at my installation program, which is built using WiX as an example. If you're brand new to WiX, the best place to start is with the outstanding WiX Tutorial from Gábor Deák Jahn at *http://www.tramontana.co.hu/wix/*.

QA Must Test with Debug Builds

If you follow my recommendations in Chapter 3, you'll have some excellent diagnostics in your code base. The problem is that, generally, only the developers benefit from the diagnostics. To better help debug problems, the quality engineers need to be using the debug builds as well. You'll be amazed at how many problems you'll find and fix when the quality assurance (QA) folks do their testing with debug builds.

One key point is that any assertions you add to the code can have their UI output disabled but still report errors in a log file so that they do not mess up any automated tests the QA department runs. In the next chapter, I discuss assertions for managed code and how important they are. My SUPERASSERT.NET, which is a much-improved user interface for assertions over the standard .NET Framework message box, has ways of turning off any pop-up message boxes or other interrupting output that causes automated tests to fail.

In the initial stages of the product cycle, the quality engineers should be alternating between debug and release builds. As the product progresses, they should gradually start concentrating more on the release builds. Until you reach the alpha release milestone, at which point you have enough of the features implemented to show customers the product, you should have the quality engineers use the debug build two to three days a week. As you approach beta 1, they should drop to two days a week. After beta 2, when all features and major bugs are fixed, they should drop to one day a week. After the release candidate milestone, they should be on the release build exclusively.

Set Up a Symbol Store

As anyone who has spent more than 5 minutes of development time on Windows knows, getting the correct symbols lined up is the secret to debugging faster. Whereas managed code has only the source and line information and local variable names in the PDB file, if you have problems where native code is involved, you may be completely out of luck. Native code puts much more information into a PDB. The most important piece is the frame pointer omission (FPO) data. That's the information that allows you to walk native stacks back into your managed code. Without FPO, you are in serious trouble when it comes to debugging.

If you think *you* have trouble getting everyone on your team and in the company to work with the correct symbols, think about how bad the operating system team at Microsoft has it. They build every day and can have thousands of different builds of the operating system running at any time across the world. Suddenly, your symbol challenges seem quite small—even if you think you're on a big project, your project is nothing compared to that much symbol pain!

In addition to the challenge of getting the symbols lined up, Microsoft was also facing the problem of getting the binaries lined up. One technology that Microsoft introduced to help them debug crashes better is called a *minidump*, or a *crash dump*. These are files that contain the state of the application at the time of the crash. For some of you coming from other operating systems, you might refer to these as *core dumps*. The beauty of a minidump is that by having the state of the application, you can load it up into the debugger so it's almost as if you were sitting there at the time of the crash. I'll discuss the mechanics of creating your own minidumps, in addition to how to read them in the debuggers, in subsequent chapters. The big issue with minidumps is getting the correct binaries loaded. You might be developing on a post–Windows Vista operating system, but the customer's minidump could have been written on Windows Server 2003 with only Service Pack 1 applied. Like the case with the symbols, if you can't get the exact binaries loaded that were in the address space when the minidump was written, you're completely out of luck if you think you can solve the bug easily with the minidump.

The developers at Microsoft realized they had to do something to make their lives easier. We folks outside Microsoft also had been complaining for a long time that our debugging experiences were a few steps short of abysmal because of the lack of operating system symbols and binaries that matched the myriad of hot fixes on any machine. The concept of Symbol Servers is simple: store all the public builds symbols and binaries in a known location, and make the debuggers smarter so that they load the correct symbols and binaries for every module loaded into a process—regardless of whether that module is loaded from your code or from the operating system—without any user interaction at all. The beauty is that the reality is nearly this simple! There are a few small issues that I'll point out in this section, but with the Symbol Server properly set up, no one on your team or in your company should ever lack the correct symbols or binaries regardless of whether you're doing managed, native, or both styles of development, or you're using Visual Studio or WinDBG as your debugger. Even better, I've supplied a tool that will take all the thinking work out of ensuring that you have the perfect symbols and binaries for the operating system and for your products.

Compared to previous versions, Visual Studio 2005 introduces a much improved way of accessing Symbol Servers for debugging. Sadly, the documentation still doesn't discuss the most important idea, which is getting *your* symbols and binaries into the Symbol Server. Because that's where the huge benefit to using the Symbol Server lies, I next describe how to set up an effective Symbol Server.

The steps for getting a server machine that everyone in your company who is executing your projects can access are quite simple. You'll probably want to name this server \\SYMBOLS to identify it easily. For the rest of this discussion, I'll assume that's the name of the server. This machine doesn't have to have much horsepower; it's simply going to act as a file server. One thing you'll definitely want is a lot of disk space on that server. At least 80 GB should be a good start. Once the server software's installed, create two shared directories named OSSYM-BOLS and PRODUCTSYMBOLS. Allow everyone in development read and write access to OSSYMBOLS. For PRODUCTSYMBOLS, developers and QA need only read access, but the account that does your builds needs write access. As you can tell by the share names, one directory is for the operating system symbols and binaries, and the other is for your product's symbols and binaries. You'll want to keep them separate for ease of management. Of course, it's quite easy for me to assume that you can get a server in your organization. I'll leave all the political battles of getting that server as an exercise for the reader.

The next step is to either download and install the latest version of Debugging Tools for Windows from *http://www.microsoft.com/whdc/devtools/debugging/default.mspx*, because the Symbol Server binaries are developed by the Windows team, not the Visual Studio team. Make sure to install the correct version matching the "bitness" of the operating system you're using in order to debug applications correctly. You'll want to check back for updated versions of Debugging Tools for Windows; the team seems to update the tools frequently. After installing Debugging Tools for Windows, add the installation directory to the system's PATH environment variable. The four key binaries, Symsrv.dll, Dbghelp.dll, Symchk.exe, and Symstore.exe, must be able to read from and write to your Symbol Servers.

For those of you who are working behind proxy servers that require you to log in each time you access the Internet, you have my sympathies. Fortunately, the Windows team does feel your pain. Debugging Tools for Windows and Visual Studio 2005 ship with a version of Symsrv.dll that will work for companies that monitor all your Internet packets. You'll want to read the Debugging Tools for Windows documentation that discusses proxy and firewalls under the topic, "Using Symbol Servers and Symbol Stores." In there, you'll see how to set up the _NT_SYMBOL_PROXY environment variable to download symbols without requiring you to type your user name and password with each request.

You'll also want to look for new versions of Debugging Tools for Windows. Since the Windows team is always improving the Symbol Server binaries, you should look for new releases. In most cases, the team releases new versions in January and July. However, the team has snuck in releases at other times. Read the Wintellect Blog at *http://www.wintellect.com/WEBLOGS/* because I always try to alert everyone when the team ships a new Debugging Tools for Windows.

Once you have Debugging Tools for Windows installed, it's time to set up both debuggers to use it. For WinDBG, it's best to use two environment variables in the system settings to tell the debugger where the symbol servers reside. To access this area in Windows XP and Windows Server 2003, right-click My Computer and select Properties from the shortcut menu. Click the Advanced tab, and at the bottom of the System Properties dialog box, click Environment Variables. Figure 2-5 shows the Environment Variables dialog box. You'll want to create two new environment variables, _NT_SYMBOL_PATH and _NT_EXECUTABLE_IMAGE_PATH, and I'll show you the values in a moment. As you can guess from the names, the first environment variable is where WinDBG will look up PDB files, and WinDBG uses the second to look up the binaries from minidumps. The value for _NT_SYMBOL_PATH is as follows (note that the following code is all supposed to be entered on one line, and you'll put your path to the Visual Studio installation directory in place of *Visual_Studio_installation_directory*).

```
SRV*c:\symbols*\\Symbols\OSSymbols*\\Symbols\ProductSymbols*
http://msdl.microsoft.com/download/symbols;
<VS install directory>\SDK\v2.0\symbols;
<VS install directory>\SDK \v2.0 64bit\symbols;
```

The value for _NT_EXECUTABLE_IMAGE_PATH is very similar:

```
SRV*c:\symbols*\\Symbols\OSSymbols*\\Symbols\ProductSymbols
```

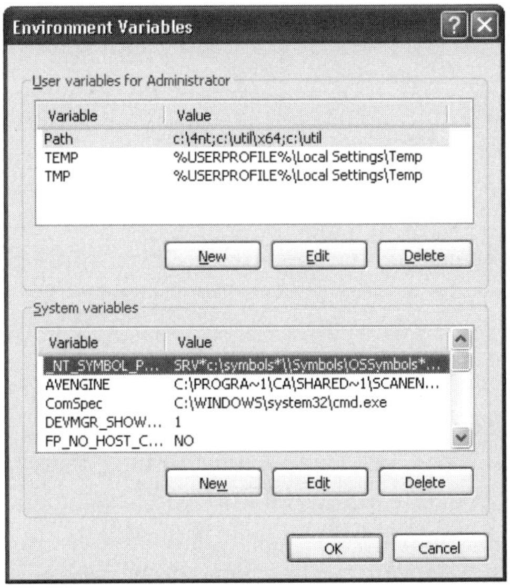

Figure 2-5   The Environment Variables dialog box

To explain the details of the symbol path, it's good to learn how a debugger goes about looking up symbols. The key values are all in the PDB file and the GUID. When you compile source code to a Portable Executable (PE) file and produce a PDB file, the compiler/linker puts in what's called a *debug* section. In that section, it lists the complete path to the PDB file built in addition to a GUID. That same GUID is also written to the PDB file. By having the unique GUID in both places, the debugger does not have to rely on error-prone timestamps to ensure that it's looking at the matching PDB file for a binary.

When the debugger goes to load a PDB, the first place it looks is in the debug section of the binary for the full path to the PDB file built. If the matching PDB file is there, the debugger opens that PDB file, and you're debugging with symbols. If you've ever wondered why you can build a binary on a machine and move the binary to a different drive and directory, but the debugger seems to magically know where to find symbols, this is why.

If the debugger can't find the matching PDB file from the path embedded in the binary, it looks in the directory where the binary was loaded. If the matching symbols are there, they are loaded and life is good. Now you know why you can copy a binary and PDB file to a different machine and symbols properly show up.

If the PDB file is not in the binary load directory, and you have the _NT_SYMBOL_PATH environment variable set, your symbol search embarks on a slightly different quest. Originally, _NT_SYMBOL_PATH was intended to contain the list of paths to search separated by semicolons. The debugger would parse out the paths and look for the matching name and GUID and if found, that PDB file was loaded.

When the Symbol Server sees the path start with SRV, that's the signal to start working the symbol-finding magic. By the way, if you set the environment variable and you are still not getting any Symbol Server support, I can almost guarantee that you have swapped the R and the V in SRV. The first asterisk (*) following the SRV is the spot called the *download cache*.

If the debugger looks through the various Symbol Servers you've set, and if it finds the PDB file, it copies the file to your download cache. When the debugger looks there and finds the matching PDB file, it will open that one and stop looking through the rest of the Symbol Server path. The download cache means that you don't experience the network performance hit of accessing the PDB file over the network every time you debug. If you're running out of disk space, all you have to do is delete everything in the C:\SYMBOLS directory the next time you debug, and the debugger will automatically repopulate with the matching PDB files.

If the PDB file is not found in the download cache, the debugger looks for the Symbol Servers delineated by subsequent asterisks in the environment variable. In the value for _NT_SYMBOL_PATH above, the first place searched will be your operating system Symbol Server, \\Symbols\OSSymbols. A little later in this section, I'll show you how to populate your operating system Symbol Server with a minimum of pain. If the PDB file is found in your operating system Symbol Server, the PDB file is copied to the download cache, so you aren't required to set up the network access on the matching PDB file again. As you can guess, the \\Symbols\ProductSymbols Symbol Server contains your product symbols. You'll also learn how to get all your builds into your product Symbol Server in this chapter so you never go without symbols again.

The last Symbol Server specified, *http://msdl.microsoft.com/download/symbols*, is the most interesting of all. If the debugger can't find the symbols in your company's Symbol Servers, it will ask Microsoft's public Symbol Server for the matching PDB file. Why this is so wonderful is that for all versions of Windows operating systems from Microsoft Windows 2000 forward, including all service packs and hot fixes, you'll get the operating system symbols automatically. If you come into work on Wednesday after "Patch Tuesday," which is the second Tuesday of the month when Microsoft releases the latest hot fixes, you'll immediately get all the updated operating system symbols as a matter of course.

If you can't guess, this is a huge boon for productivity, and being able to walk the stack out of the middle of native code is fantastic. The symbol download applies regardless if you're debugging your unit test on your machine or on a minidump from a customer. The right PDB files just appear.

In the case of your company Symbol Servers set up on \\SYMBOLS, you will have the PDB files in addition to the appropriate binaries necessary for minidump debugging. The Microsoft public Symbol Server has only the PDB files on it. That still might cause some issues on certain minidumps, but the debuggers will go to heroic efforts to allow the debugging to work. The last point about the public Symbol Server is that the symbol files up there are not the full native PDB files, but they're stripped so they contain only public functions and the all-important FPO data to walk the stacks.

After all the Symbol Servers in the environment variable value shown earlier come two semi-colon-deliniated paths: *Visual_Studio_installation_directory*\SDK\v2.0\symbols and *Visual_Studio_installation_directory* \SDK\v2.0 64bit\symbols. If you believe me that your Symbol Servers combined with the Microsoft Public Symbol Server are awesome, you might be wondering why I'm recommending that you add the Framework SDK symbols directories to your path. In most cases, the Visual Studio installation automatically installs the Framework SDK, though you can opt not to install it, which I would not recommend.

The Framework SDK symbols directory has the PDB files for the core DLLs from the Common Language Runtime (CLR). A few of the Son of Strike (SOS) WinDBG extension commands that you'll be using for the most hard-core problems need access to the PDB files to do their work. In the rare situation in which you don't have the files already in your cache and you lose your connection to the Internet, having those paths in your environment variables can make the difference when it comes to solving the problem.

Now that you know about the steps that the debugger goes through for symbols, you can see the same process for the _NT_EXECUTABLE_IMAGE_PATH environment variable for binaries. Because the binary files are not in the Microsoft Public Symbol Server, you're telling WinDBG to search only your internal Symbol Servers. The one difference is that WinDBG will look for the binaries on your machine first. For example, if the minidump has a record of a binary in the C:\Foo directory, that's where WinDBG will look first before going through the steps of searching the Symbol Server.

In WinDBG, it can be a bit difficult to see if you have the _NT_SYMBOL_PATH set correctly. Because this is a WinDBG issue, in the "Symbol Server Setup" section in Chapter 6, "WinDBG, SOS, and ADPlus," I go over the steps necessary for ensuring that WinDBG is properly loading symbols.

Visual Studio 2005 will use the _NT_SYMBOL_PATH and _NT_EXECUTABLE_IMAGE_PATH environment variables, but you can set the exact same values in the IDE. What's even better about the way Visual Studio sets the symbol and binary paths is that once you set it, you can export and import those settings to other installations very easily. It is a good idea to have a team-wide set of settings that everyone can import when setting up a new machine and immediately be ready to start debugging.

In Visual Studio 2005, in the Options dialog box, click the Debugging node and then the Symbols node. The property page there is where you'll type the paths directly. In the setup I'm advocating, you'd type the paths in the following order:

1. \\Symbols\OSSymbols

2. \\Symbols\ProductSymbols

3. http://msdl.microsoft.com/download/symbols

4. *Visual_Studio_installation_directory* \SDK\v2.0\symbols

5. *Visual_Studio_installation_directory* \SDK\v2.0 64bit\symbols

Additionally, you will set the cache directory to C:\SYMBOLS to share the cache file between the two debuggers. Figure 2-6 shows the Options dialog box with all the values properly filled out.

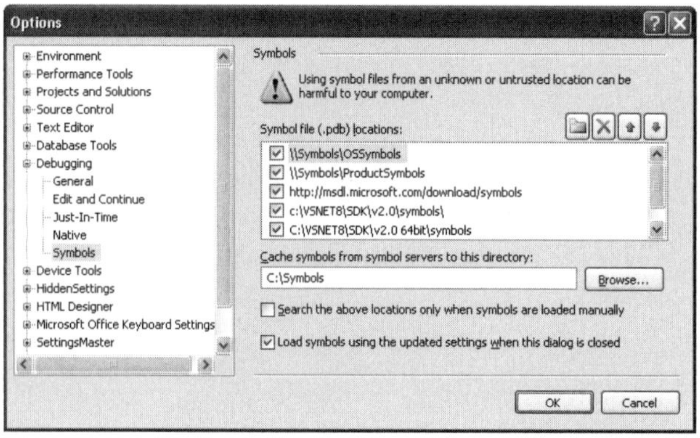

Figure 2-6 The Visual Studio debugging symbols setup

What makes the Visual Studio method superior to the WinDBG environment variable approach is that Visual Studio automatically handles Symbol Servers just by putting the *server_name**share_name* in the symbols setup. This is a major improvement compared to previous versions and will make your debugging considerably easier.

The symbol store itself is nothing very exciting. It's simply a database that happens to use the file system to find the files. Figure 2-7 shows a partial listing from Windows Explorer of the tree for the Symbol Server on my Symbol Server computer. The root directory is OSSymbols, and each different symbol file, such as Advapi32.pdb, is listed at the first level. Under each symbol's file name is a directory that corresponds to the GUID to recognize a particular version of that symbol file. Keep in mind that if you have multiple versions of a file, such as Advapi32.pdb for different operating system builds, you'll have multiple directories under Advapi32.pdb for each unique version you have accessed. In the signature directory, you'll most likely have the particular symbol file for that version. Figure 2-7 shows two GUID values under the Advapi32.pdb directory. If you happen to see a directory name that's shorter than a GUID, which will be the timestamp that will indicate that you were debugging symbols from

Windows 2000. Compilers prior to Visual Studio 2005 did not embed a GUID, so they used the Portable Executable (PE) file checksum as the unique identifying characteristic.

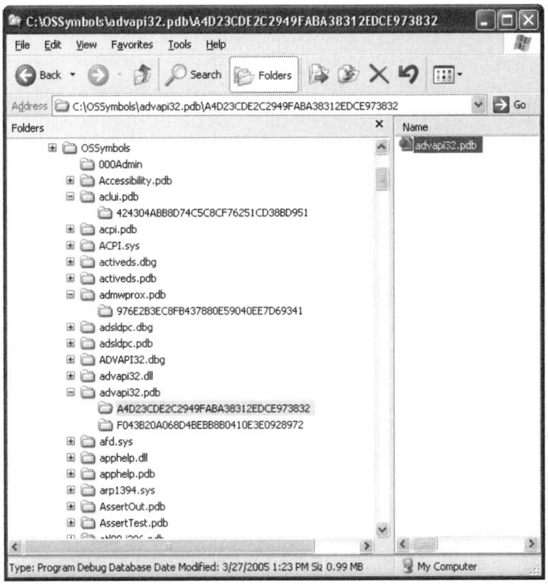

Figure 2-7   An example of the Symbol Server database

Although getting the symbols downloaded while you're debugging is great, it does nothing for getting the operating system binaries into your Symbol Server. Additionally, instead of relying on developers' debugging applications to get the symbols, you might want to pre-populate your Symbol Servers with all the operating system binaries and symbols for all versions you are supporting. That way, you'll be able to handle any minidumps coming in from the field in addition to any debugging challenges you'll encounter in your development shop.

The Debugging Tools for Windows (which includes WinDBG) includes two tools that do the bulk of the work. The first, Symbol Checker (Symchk.exe), takes care of getting the symbols from Microsoft into your Symbol Server. The second, Symbol Store (Symstore.exe), takes care of getting the binaries into the symbol store. Since I realized that I'd have to run both tools to get my operating system Symbol Server fully populated with symbols and binaries for all OS versions I wanted to support, I decided to automate the process. I wanted to quickly build up my operating system Symbol Server and keep it filled with the latest binaries and symbols with essentially no work at all.

When you're setting up your initial operating system Symbol Server, you'll install the first version of the operating system without any service packs or hot fixes. You'll install the Debugging Tools for Windows, and you'll probably want to add its installation directory to your path. To get the binaries and symbols for that operating system, you'll run my Ossyms.js file, which I'll discuss in a moment. After Ossyms.js finishes, you'll install the first service pack and reexecute Ossyms.js. After you've gotten all service packs loaded and their binaries and symbols copied, you'll finally apply any hot fixes recommended by the Windows Update feature of Windows XP, Windows Vista, and Windows Server 2003 and run Ossyms.js one last time. Once you run through this process for all operating systems you need to support, you'll just have to run Ossyms.js whenever you install a hot fix or a new service pack to keep your Symbol Server up to date. For planning purposes, I've found that it takes a little less than a gigabyte for each operating system and approximately the same for each service pack.

Before you run Ossyms.js, you'll want to change the program that executes Windows Script Hosting files, from the default Wscript.exe to Cscript.exe. Wscript.exe will do all output through message boxes, and with scripts such as Ossyms.js, or any other script for that matter, you'll go nuts clicking OK. Open a command prompt with administrator privileges and execute the following command to set Cscript.exe as the Windows Script Hosting executing program:

```
cscript //H:CScript to set
```

While you might think that Ossyms.js is just a simple wrapper around executing Symchk.exe and Symstore.exe, it's actually a pretty nice wrapper. If you look at the command-line options for both programs, you'll definitely want help automating them because it's very easy to mess up their usage. If you execute Ossyms.js without any command-line parameters, you'll see the following output showing you all the options:

```
OSsyms - Version 2.0 - Copyright 2002-2006 by John Robbins
   Debugging Microsoft .NET 2.0 Applications

   Fills your Symbol Server with the OS binaries and symbols.
   Run this each time you apply a service pack/hotfix to get perfect
   symbols while debugging and for minidumps.
   SYMSTORE.EXE and SYMCHK.EXE must be in the path.

Usage : OSsyms <Symbol Server> [-e|-b|-s|-d]

   <Symbol Server> - Symbol server in \\server\share or drive:\dir format.
   -e              - Do EXEs as well as DLLs.
   -d              - Debug the script. (Shows what would execute.)
   -b              - Don't add the binaries to the symbol store.
   -s              - Don't add the symbols to the symbol store.
                     (Not recommended)
```

The only required parameter is the Symbol Server in *server**share* format. Ossyms.js runs through and recursively adds all DLL binaries from the operating system directory (%SYSTEMROOT%). After the binary files are copied, Ossyms.js calls Symchk.exe to automatically download all the symbols it can for those DLLs. If you would like to also add all EXE binaries and associated symbols, add the -e command-line option to Ossyms.js after the Symbol Server parameter.

To see what binaries and symbols were added or ignored (including the reasons why), check out the two text files, DllBinLog.txt and DllSymLog.txt, which show the binary add results and the symbol add results, respectively. For EXE files, the two files are ExeBinLog.txt and ExeSymLog.txt.

Keep in mind that Ossyms.js can take quite awhile to run. Copying the binaries onto your Symbol Server will be very fast, but downloading the symbols can take a lot of time. If you download both DLL and EXE operating system symbols, you probably have somewhere around 400 MB of data to download. One thing you'll want to avoid is having multiple computers adding binaries to the Symbol Server simultaneously. That's because the Symstore.exe program uses the file system and a text file as its database, so it has no transactional capabilities. Symchk.exe doesn't access the Symstore.exe text file database, so it's perfectly fine to have multiple developers adding symbols only.

Microsoft is putting more of its products' symbols on their public symbol server all the time. Ossyms.js is flexible enough that you can easily add different directories where you'd like to have binaries in addition to symbols installed into your Symbol Server. To add your new binaries, search for the *g_AdditionalWork*, a global variable near the top of the file. The Ossyms.js file has *g_AdditionalWork* set to *null* so it's not processed in the *main* routine. To add a new set of files, allocate an *Array* type, and add a *SymbolsToProcess* class as the element. The following code snippet shows how to add processing to add all the DLLs that appear in the Program Files directory. Note that the first element isn't necessarily required to be an environment variable; it could have been a specific directory, such as "C:\ Program Files." However, by using a common system environment variable, you'll avoid hard-coded drives.

```
var g_AdditionalWork = new Array
(
    new SymbolsToProcess ( "%ProgramFiles%"    ,   // Start directory.
                           "*.dll"             ,   // Searching wildcard.
                           "PFDllBinLog.TXT"   ,   // Binary logging file.
                           "PFDllSymLog.TXT"   )   // Symbol logging file.
) ;
```

Now that you've seen how to get your operating system symbols and binaries, let's turn to getting *your* product symbols into the symbol store with Symstore.exe. Symstore.exe has a number of command-line switches. I show the important switches in Table 2-2.

Table 2-2   Symstore.exe Important Command-Line Options

Switch	Explanation
Add	Adds files to a symbol store
Del	Deletes the files added in a particular set
/f *File*	Adds a particular file or directory
/r	Adds files or directories recursively
/s *Store*	The root directory of the symbol store
/t *Product*	The name of the product
/v *Version*	The product version
/c	Additional comment

Table 2-2   Symstore.exe Important Command-Line Options

Switch	Explanation
/o	Verbose output helpful for debugging
/i ID	The ID from history.txt to delete
/?	Help output

The best way to use Symstore.exe is to have it automatically add your build tree's EXEs, DLLs, and PDBs at the end of every daily build (after the smoke test verifies that the product works), after each milestone, and for any builds sent outside the engineering team. You probably don't want to have developers adding their local builds unless you're really into using up tons of disk space. For example, the following command stores all PDB and binary files in your symbol store for all directories found under D:\BUILD (inclusive):

```
symstore add /r /f d:\build\*.* /s \\Symbols\ProductSymbols
    /t "MyApp" /v "Build 632" /c "01/22/06 Daily Build"
```

Although the /t (Product) option is always required when adding files, unfortunately, /v (Version) and /c (Comment) are not. I strongly recommend that you always use /v and /c because you can never have too much information about what files are in your product Symbol Server. This becomes extremely important as your product Symbol Server fills up. Even though the symbols placed in your operating system Symbol Server are smaller because they are stripped of all private symbols and types, your product's symbols are larger and can lead to quite a bit of wasted disk space on a six-month project.

You'll always want to leave milestone builds and builds sent outside the engineering team in your Symbol Server. I also like to keep no more than the last four weeks' daily build symbols and binaries in my symbol store. As you saw in Table 2-2, Symstore.exe does support deleting files.

To ensure that you're deleting the correct files, you'll need to look at a special directory, 000admin, under your shared Symbol Server directory. In there is the History.txt file, which contains the history of all transactions that occurred in this Symbol Server and, if you've added files to the Symbol Server, a set of numbered files that contain the list of actual files added as part of a transaction.

History.txt is a comma separated value (CSV) file whose fields are shown in Table 2-3 (for adding files) and Table 2-4 (for deleting files).

Table 2-3   History.txt CSV Fields When Adding Files

Field	Explanation
ID	The transaction number. This is a 10-digit number, so you can have 9,999,999,999 total transactions in your Symbol Server.
Add	When adding files, this field will always say *add*.
File or Ptr	Indicates whether a file (*file*) or a pointer to a file in another location (*ptr*) was added.

Table 2-3   History.txt CSV Fields When Adding Files

Field	Explanation
Date	The date of the transaction.
Time	The time the transaction started.
Product	The product text from the /t switch.
Version	The version text from the /v switch (optional).
Comment	The comment text from the /c switch (optional).
Unused	An unused field for future use.

Table 2-4   History.txt CSV Fields When Deleting Files

Field	Explanation
ID	The transaction number.
Del	When deleting files, this field will always say *del*.
Deleted Transaction	The 10-digit number of the deleted transaction.

Once you've located the transaction ID you want to delete, it's a simple matter to tell Symstore.exe to do the work.

```
symstore del /i 0000000009 /s \\Symbols\ProductSymbols
```

One thing I've noticed that's a little odd about deleting from your Symbol Server is that you don't get any output telling you if the deletion succeeded. In fact, if you forget a vital command-line option, such as the Symbol Server itself, you're not warned at all and you might mistakenly think that the deletion happened. After doing a deletion, I always check the History.txt file to ensure that the deletion actually took place.

If you're looking for a nice project, what you might consider doing is writing a form-based application to manage the symbols in your symbol store. Manually looking to see what's in the server in addition to deleting old versions of your product symbols is rather tedious. By showing the dates the files were added in addition to showing the names of the files added, you could make the delete a one-click option.

Set Up a Source Server

Setting up a Symbol Server will help get call stacks out of native code back into your managed code, but if you don't know the source version, you're still debugging at the assembly language level. No matter how vigilant your team is with the version-control system, there are those times where you're debugging a build and just don't know what version you need. Although you might get close, the one change you need to see isn't in the particular version you guessed it was, and you don't solve the problem.

Wouldn't it be great if there were a way for the debugger to already have the knowledge about the source code version and automatically have the right version in the Source window? Even better would be if the debugger would get the source code without any prompting or input on your part? I don't know about you, but that just about sounds like debugging perfection to me! That's exactly what the Source Server tools are all about.

Before we jump into setting up and using the Source Server, I have to warn you that it can be an adventure to get it working. The Source Server has a few foibles and lacks documentation. However, I think I've teased out all the oddities and issues you'll run into, which took me a solid week of experimentation, so I'll help you skip the parts where you'll be wondering what its doing.

The Zen of Source Server

As you've seen, the Symbol Server is really a database using the file system. When you go to load Foo.pdb, the debugger builds up a directory path starting with your cache directory, appends to the file to open, and finishes with the GUID uniquely identifying that particular version of the file. In that directory path is the actual PDB file the debugger needs.

Although it has *Server* in the name, the Source Server doesn't actually store your source code as the Symbol Server does with PDBs. A PDB file created with any of the recent compilers has in it the full path for each of the source files used to create the binary. When you run the Source Server programs on your binaries, they add a section to the PDB file where it embeds the exact version control system–reported version of the file. Moreover, it also embeds the actual version control commands to get that file out of the version control system. The process of running the Source Server tools and embedding this information in the PDB files is called *indexing* the source code. Once you've indexed the version and commands to extract from the version control system into the PDB, no matter where you are in the company, as long as you have access to the version control system, the debuggers will ask the version control system for the correct version of the file as necessary. I'll show you how you can see this information in the PDB files later in the chapter.

Because the Source Server is using your version control system, it has to support the particular version control you are using. When you install the latest Source Server binaries, it has support for Perforce, *http://subversion.tigris.org/Subversion*, and, of course, the ubiquitous Visual SourceSafe. Support for additional version control systems, including Microsoft Team Foundation System, will be available shortly. If you're using an unsupported version control system, the good news is that the Source Server tools are extensible, and as long as your system supports a command-line tool to get version information and retrieve source files, you can write your own module to coordinate and use your system. See the Srcsrv.doc file in the Source Server installation directory on what you will need to do to create that module and integrate it into the tools.

From the highest level, the Source Server workflow is straightforward. The first step is obviously to build both the debug and release builds of your application. After you've run your automated smoke tests to ensure that you have a build worth keeping, you'll use the Source Server programs to index the PDB files with the version control information. The final step will be to store those indexed PDB files into your Symbol Server so that everyone can benefit.

For this chapter, I used Visual SourceSafe because it's the most common version control system used by developers on Windows. However, the way Source Server is written, there are few differences between the various products, so the concepts are almost identical. No matter what version control system you are using, I strongly recommend that you set up a little practice spot so you can practice and become proficient with Source Server.

When I refer to the Source Server binaries, I refer to those programs do the actual source indexing. The debuggers already have the Srcsrv.dll that knows how to execute the version control system embedded into your PDB files. The Source Server binaries are part of the Debugging Tools for Windows package, which you can download free from Microsoft at *http://microsoft.com/whdc/devtools/debugging/default.mspx*. If you are going to be running your code on a 64-bit system, you can use the appropriate 64-bit debugger package tools, but the 32-bit versions will work on x64 also.

The only problem is that a default Debugging Tools for Windows installation does not install the necessary Source Server binaries by default. You'll need to do a custom installation of the Debugging Tools for Windows and select the SDK portion to install. That will add an SDK directory under the Debugging Tools for Windows directory. Inside the SDK directory is a SRCSRV directory that contains all the appropriate programs. You can leave that directory there and point your path to it, or you can copy it somewhere else. In any event, the directory that contains the tools has to be in your path.

After installing the custom Debugging Tools for Windows, you'll need to install Perl 5.6 or greater if you don't already have it on your machine. I've been using Perl 5.8.7, which you can download from *http://www.cpan.org/*.

When you look at the files in the Source Server directory, you'll see that most of the work in Source Server tools is in Perl code. The Ssindex.cmd file, which is the core batch file, just calls Perl.exe and passes the Perl code in through standard input. The .pm files are the Perl modules that know how to talk to the individual version control systems, and Ssindex.cmd loads them and calls through a standard interface to isolate the system differences. The other .cmd files, such as VSsindex.cmd, are wrappers that make it easier to use a specific version control system because Ssindex.cmd needs the version control system on the command line. The Pdbstr.exe and Srctool.exe files in the SRCSRV directory read and write to PDB files. The Vssdump.exe program is a helper for the Visual SourceSafe integration; it's installed only with the x86 version of the Debugging Tools for Windows package.

When you run Ssindex.cmd, after validating parameters, it asks the version control system for the list of all source files and associated version numbers in the target version control project and all child projects. The next step is to start looking for PDB files recursively. For each PDB file found, the Perl code calls Srctool.exe to extract the list of source file names out of the PDB. The code looks through the source file names in the PDB and sees if they match any of those stored earlier from the version control search, and if so, saves that file information into a temporary file. Once the code has looked at all the source files, it's time to call Pdbstr.exe to write the index stream, appropriately called SRCSRV, to the PDB file. (Note that the stream is not an NTFS file system stream, but a section in the PDB file). When debugging, the debugger looks for that stream, and if it finds it, it knows that there's a Source Server involved and calls into Srcsrv.dll to execute the version control system to get the right file.

I just wanted to provide you a general overview of what happens when you index source code. If you're more interested in what's going on in Ssindex.cmd, you can look at the code or Src-srv.doc. As I mentioned earlier, if the Source Server does not support your version control system out of the box; you'll just need to write the Perl module that conforms to the interface specified in Srcsrv.doc.

Basic Indexing

To walk you through the steps of manually using the Source Server, I'll use a very simple source tree that comprises two console applications, CppApp and NetApp, which reside in appropriately named directories: D:\Dev\CppApp and D:\Dev\NetApp. CppApp is a native C++ application, and NetApp was written in C#. I want to show native code also because many of you are still supporting C++ applications. Both tools build their Debug builds to D:\Dev\Debug. The Visual SourceSafe version control is on the share, \\Timon\Source, with CppApp and NetApp as projects of $/ (which is the root project in Visual SourceSafe). Note that to index source files with Visual SourceSafe, you are required to set the working directories on the project. I've also applied the version control label "First Version" to the project. Finally, I built both projects. Now they're ready for indexing.

The first step is to ensure that the Visual SourceSafe command line-program (Ss.exe), Perl, and the Source Server programs are all in the path for the command shell you are using. If they are not, nothing will work. Where it gets confusing is when you start debugging. If the version control program is not in the path, the source file fetch silently fails, and you have no idea why you are looking at the Disassembly window.

Another note of caution regarding the Source Server Visual SourceSafe code: although the Source Server Help says that you can specify the server to use on the command line, for Visual SourceSafe, that doesn't work. You'll need to set the SSDIR environment variable to the Visual SourceSafe database. In the case of my example, I'll issue the following command in the command prompt before continuing:

```
set SSDIR=\\Timon\Source\
```

Another problem with Visual SourceSafe is the concept of current project, which is the project selected when you end the SourceSafe Explorer GUI. The source indexing for Visual Source-Safe "respects" the current project, which means that it assumes that the current project is the one you want to work on. If you have a single project in your version control system, that's fine, but no one actually does. In order to get the Visual SourceSafe indexing to work, you'll need to set the Visual SourceSafe current project to the project you are about to index. For indexing at the command line, you can set it with the Ss.exe cp option. In my example, I'd run the following command because I'm working with the root project:

```
ss cp $/
```

The second step is to set up Srcsrv.ini for use when indexing, which consists of defining a logical name for the server and the server path itself. The example Srcsrv.ini that is in the C:\Program Files\Debugging Tools for Windows\SDK\SRCSRV directory has more documentation that you'll want to read. In the case of my Visual SourceSafe database, my Srcsrv.ini will look like the following (in the case of Visual SourceSafe, the value to the right of the equal sign must exactly match the value in the SSDIR environment variable, including the trailing backslash):

```
[variables]
BOOKSRC=\\Timon\Source\
```

In almost all instances, you'll need only the Srcsrv.ini file during the indexing phase. It will store the BOOKSRC logical name and the actual location for the server in the PDB files processed. However, if the machine TIMON dies and you need to move the version control to a different machine, you can put an Srcsrv.ini file in the same directory as the debugger's Srcsrv.dll, and the settings in that file will override what source file indexing embedded in the PDB file. Thus, you wouldn't need to reindex the PDB files.

Another use for the Srcsrv.ini file during debugging is to have the debugger use a mirrored version control system that provides only read-only access. This allows you to share source indexed PDB files across teams and departments in a large company without requiring each team to have direct access to the real version control systems for other teams. Also note that it's perfectly acceptable to include all your company's version control systems in the Srcsrv.ini under the [variables] section and share that file across the company. When I get to the "Debugging with Source Servers" section later in the chapter, I'll discuss the [trusted commands] section of Srcsrv.ini.

When indexing, there are several places where the Srcsrv.ini file can reside. If you've copied the Source Server code directory to its own location on the machine, you can put your version there, and the source indexing tools will pick it up automatically. Alternatively, you can put it in the current directory where you execute the indexing commands. Finally, you can also tell the tools where to find it by using a command-line option or set the SRCSRV_INI environment variable to point to it. In my case, I'll put it in the root directory for my source code (D:\Dev) and run all my indexing commands from there.

To start the indexing, most of you will set command-line options to tell the tools where to find sources, symbols, and the like, so it's important to discuss those command-line options. Since I'm using Visual SourceSafe, I'll run Vssindex.cmd to do my indexing. I could also run the identical Ssindex.cmd /System=VSS. There are two help command-line options, -? and -??; two question marks show you more help than one. If you look at the Help, you'll see there are all sorts of switches and environment variable combinations that you can set to tell the tools what to do.

There are four command-line options of real importance and a fifth necessary for Visual SourceSafe. The first is /Ini, which specifies the Srcsrv.ini file to use. As I mentioned, the file can be placed in numerous spots and automatically be found, but if you want to be specific, you can use /Ini to set it. The /Source switch tells the indexing tools where the source code root starts. The default is the current directory. The indexing script will attempt to correlate any source file found in and below the specified directory with files in the version control system. The /Symbols switch indicates the root directory that will be recursed looking for PDB files; like the source, this directory defaults to the current directory. If the PDB file contains one or more source code files from the version control system, the PDB file will be indexed with the *srcsrv stream*, which I'll show you later.

For Visual SourceSafe only, the /Label command is required. Because of limitations in Visual SourceSafe, the source indexing cannot figure out the version of a source file in a given directory. Thus, you need to first set a label on the root of the project with Visual SourceSafe and pass that same name to the source indexing tools. Because you should always be labeling your builds for good version control hygiene, that should not be too onerous.

The last command-line option, /Debug, is the most important of all. One major problem with the source indexing tools is if there are any problems and no PDB files are indexed, they give you no notification at all, so you think life is grand until you start debugging and nothing works. You must always run the indexing commands with /Debug so you can see what worked and what didn't.

Given the brief tour of command-line switches, it's time to do some indexing. I have a command prompt open, and my current directory is D:\Dev. Since that's the root of both my source code and symbols, I don't have to set those command-line options. My Srcsrv.ini file is in that directory also, so there is no need to set that command-line value either. I've applied the label "First Version" in SourceSafe already. Lastly, I've set the SSDIR environment variable to set the server to use. Executing the command VSSINDEX /Label="First Version"/Debug produces the output shown in Listing 2-2.

Listing 2-2   Initial Source Indexing Output

```
[D:\Dev]vssindex /Label="First Version" /debug
-----------------------------------------------------------------------------

SSIndex.cmd [STATUS] : Server ini file: D:\Dev\srcsrv.ini
SSIndex.cmd [STATUS] : Source root     : D:\Dev
SSIndex.cmd [STATUS] : Symbols root    : D:\Dev
SSIndex.cmd [STATUS] : Control system : VSS
SSIndex.cmd [STATUS] : VSS Server      : \\Timon\Source\
SSIndex.cmd [STATUS] : VSS Client Root: D:\Dev
SSIndex.cmd [STATUS] : VSS Project     : $/
SSIndex.cmd [STATUS] : VSS Label       : First Version
-----------------------------------------------------------------------------

SSIndex.cmd [STATUS] : Running... this will take some time...
SSIndex.cmd [STATUS] : Processing ss.exe properties output ...
SSIndex.cmd [INFO  ] : ... indexing D:\Dev\CppApp\Debug\vc80.pdb
SSIndex.cmd [INFO  ] : ... zero source files found ...
```

```
SSIndex.cmd [INFO  ] : ... indexing D:\Dev\debug\CppApp.pdb
SSIndex.cmd [INFO  ] : ... wrote C:\DOCUME~1\john\LOCALS~1\Temp\indexD9F8.stream
 to D:\Dev\debug\CppApp.pdb ...
SSIndex.cmd [INFO  ] : ... indexing D:\Dev\debug\NetApp.pdb
SSIndex.cmd [INFO  ] : ... wrote C:\DOCUME~1\john\LOCALS~1\Temp\index18A3B.stream
 to D:\Dev\debug\NetApp.pdb ...
SSIndex.cmd [INFO  ] : ... indexing D:\Dev\NetApp\obj\Debug\NetApp.pdb
SSIndex.cmd [INFO  ] : ... wrote C:\DOCUME~1\john\LOCALS~1\Temp\index19DD.stream
 to D:\Dev\NetApp\obj\Debug\NetApp.pdb ...
```

As you can see in the output, Vssindex.cmd found some PDB files and wrote streams to them, which is how you'll know the tools have indexed a PDB file. Technically, this all worked, but I want to point out some issues in the output. First, scan down until you find the line containing VC80.PDB, which is a PDB file produced by the native C++ build. The line after it says "zero source files found". In the case of any Vc?0.pdb files, that's normal because those are the throwaway type information files, and you don't need them. However, if you see that one of your PDB files reports zero source files, that's a very serious problem, but the indexing tools do not stop on indexing errors. That means that you must very carefully read the output and double-check that your PDB files are all properly indexed. If you did not specify the /debug option, you would not see those lines with [INFO], and you'd have no idea that indexing actually failed.

If you look carefully at the output in Listing 2-2, you might see another problem. Though not very serious, it can slow down your overall indexing performance. I left the /Symbols switch to the default, which treats the current directory as the root for all PDB files. The last PDB file indexed was the file D:\Dev\NetApp\obj\Debug\NetApp.pdb, which for .NET applications is the spot where MSBuild actually builds your application. MSBuild copies them to the output directory you specified as the last step of the build. If you index those files in the Obj directory, you'll be doubling the time it takes to index your sources.

Best practices in general dictate that you build your applications to a central directory or directory tree for easier maintenance. In the case of my example here, everything builds to the D:\Dev\Debug directory. Therefore, if I use the command line:

```
vssindex /Label= "First Version" /debug /symbols=.\Debug
```

Vssindex will index only the PDB files I'm going to put in my Symbol Server next.

I've purposely put my source code in the D:\Dev directory to work around a major problem in the indexing code. If all your source directories are directly off the drive root directory, source indexing will not work at all. When I first tried Source Indexing, I had my directories set to D:\CppApp, D:\NetApp, and D:\Debug, and I went absolutely nuts trying to work around this bug. If your build is set up so that all source directories are off the root directory, to work around the bug, you'll need to switch to each source code directory and run the indexing commands. For example, you'd switch to the D:\CppApp directory and run the command:

```
vssindex /debug /symbols=..\Debug /Ini=..\srcsrv.ini /Project=CppApp
```

Note that the /Project option is Visual SourceSafe–specific. Other version controls systems use a different value to specify the version control project.

If you have more than source code directories at the root, running multiple indexing commands will quickly become painful. You'll be much better off changing your build to be in a directory down from root. That way, you'll have to run the command just once, and the command will automatically pick up all new directories you add without your having to do it manually.

The next surprise with indexing will be if the version control project you want to index is a subproject in your version control system, for example, if my Visual SourceSafe contained one root project, $/Happy, which had two subprojects, $/Happy/Foo and $Happy/Bar. Under the two subprojects to $/Happy were all the subprojects necessary for those pieces of code. If I were responsible only for source indexing $/Happy/Foo, and if the working directory was D:\Dev\Happy\Foo, if I ran the indexing command:

```
vssindex /debug /Symbols=.\Debug
```

The indexing would report that zero source code files were indexed.

It took an hour or so for the idea to pop up in my head as to why source indexing wasn't working, but it finally did. The issue is that the default project for source indexing is the root of the version control system. My bad assumption was that the source indexing commands considered the current directory and matched the version control projects appropriately, but they don't. Keep in mind that all my testing is with Visual SourceSafe. If you are using a different version control system, you will need to practice all the scenarios I've discussed to see if there are any foibles in your particular system.

What you need to do to get everything working is to tell the source indexing code which Visual SourceSafe version control project you want to work with using the /Project command-line option. In the example I'm discussing, the command line that will get everything properly indexed is:

```
vssindex /debug /Symbols=.\Debug /Project=Happy/Foo
```

The Visual SourceSafe source indexing code will put in the leading "$/" necessary for Ss.exe. It's a very good idea to get in the habit of always specifying the /Project command-line option, even if it is the root, which would be /Project=/. I can't stress enough that you need to manually test various scenarios to see what works and doesn't work in your environment.

In the output of the indexing command, seeing the output that a .stream file was written to the PDB file is enough to rest assured that life is good. If you want to verify the stream, the Pdbstr.exe program allows you to look at what's in that stream. Pdbstr.exe is a little persnickety, so you'll have to get the command-line options just right; otherwise, the output looks like no stream is in the PDB. The first parameter must be -r to indicate you want to read the PDB. The second parameter is -p:*file_name*.pdb for the PDB you want to look at. The last parameter is the stream you want to see, which is always -s:srcsrv. Listing 2-3 shows the output of running Pdbstr.exe on Netapp.pdb.

Listing 2-3   Pdbstr.exe Output

```
[D:\Dev\debug]pdbstr -r -p:NetApp.pdb -s:srcsrv
SRCSRV: ini ------------------------------------------------
VERSION=1
INDEXVERSION=2
VERCTRL=Visual Source Safe
DATETIME=Thu Aug 31 15:35:43 2006
SRCSRV: variables ------------------------------------------
SSDIR=\\Timon\Source\
SRCSRVENV=SSDIR=%BOOKSRC%
VSSTRGDIR=%targ%\%var2%\%fnbksl%(%var3%)\%var4%
VSS_EXTRACT_CMD=ss.exe get -GL"%vsstrgdir%" -GF- -I-Y -W "$/%var3%" -V"%var4%"
VSS_EXTRACT_TARGET=%targ%\%var2%\%fnbksl%(%var3%)\%var4%\%fnfile%(%var1%)
BOOKSRC=\\Timon\Source\
SRCSRVTRG=%VSS_extract_target%
SRCSRVCMD=%VSS_extract_cmd%
SRCSRV: source files --------------------------------------
d:\Dev\NetApp\Program.cs*BOOKSRC*NetApp/Program.cs*First Version
SRCSRV: end -----------------------------------------------
```

The ini section of the stream tells the tale of the source-indexing version, version control system used, and the time you did the indexing. The variables section shows variables that are used by the debuggers to do the work. The debuggers look for the SRCSRVCMD value and treat values surrounded by percent signs as variables to build up. In Listing 2-3, the VSS_EXTRACT_CMD contains the actual command line that Srcsrv.dll builds up to call the version control system with the appropriate file and extraction directory. The last section, the source files, shows the values that will be filled in as part of the variables. Each line contains the data for a single source file, delineated by asterisks. The first value is the path to the source file as it came from the PDB. The second value, in this case BOOKSRC, indicates the version control database to use. The third field is the version control project, and the last field is the file version in version control. If you want to see a great example of exactly how the data is built up, see the Srcsvr.doc file.

Because of all the niggling surprises I kept running into when I started playing with Source Server, I put together a quick checklist that lists all the issues you need to ensure are set up to achieve Source Server nirvana. That checklist is in Table 2-5. Let's now turn to using the Source Server in the debuggers, the moment you've been waiting for!

Table 2-5   The Source Server Indexing Checklist

Source Server Indexing Checklist
Is your source tree in a directory below the root?
Have you built both debug and release builds?
Have you built all binaries and PDBs to inhabit a logical directory structure?

Table 2-5   The Source Server Indexing Checklist

Source Server Indexing Checklist
Did you add your version control logical name(s) to Srcsrv.ini?
Is Srcsrv.ini in the tools directory, the SRCSRV_INI environment variable, or the current directory, or specified with the /Ini switch?
Is your version control system command-line tool in the path?
For Visual SourceSafe, have you set the SSDIR environment variable?
For Visual SourceSafe, is the working directory set for each project?
For Visual SourceSafe, have you applied a label to the project?
Is Perl 5.0 or greater installed and in the path?
Are the Source Server tools and scripts in the path?

Debugging with Source Servers

Turning on Source Server support in WinDBG or its console-based siblings, Ntsd.exe or Cdb.exe, is similar to turning on the Symbol Server support. To turn it on globally for all WinDBG sessions, you have two options: The first is to start WinDBG with no debuggee open and select Source File Path from the File menu to get to the Source Search Path dialog box. The second way is to set the _NT_SOURCE_PATH environment variable. In both cases, you'll want the value to be SRV*c:\symbols;.

The SRV, much like its counterpart in Symbol Servers, tells the debugger that you're expecting to use a Source Server. After the asterisks comes the directory that you want to use as the local cache for all the files. If you don't specify a download cache, which I don't recommend, the sources will be pulled to the Debugging Tools for Windows\Src directory. As the default directory is in Program Files, the pull will abort if you're correctly running in a Least User Access (LUA) environment. In addition to setting source paths globally, you can always set it during a debugging session by running the .srcpath command.

In my development, I like to set the Source Server cache directory to my Symbol Server cache directory. That way, all my caches are in the same place, and if I need to reclaim disk space, I can wipe everything out and immediately start again.

Once you start debugging in WinDBG and perform any operation in which you need source code, the dialog box shown in Figure 2-8 will pop up. This is your sign that everything's starting out great for your Source Server adventure. The upper part of the dialog box shows you the command to run. The set of option buttons allow you to determine how you want Source Server to proceed in the future. If you select Perform This Action Each Time From Now On, that will assign "off" to the Default value in HKEY_CURRENT_USER\Software\Microsoft \Source Server\Warning so you never see the Microsoft Source Server Security Alert dialog box again.

Figure 2-8   WinDBG Source Server Security dialog box

In many cases, you'll want to turn off the security warning and always have WinDBG jump directly to executing the version control command to get the source. However, if you use the Source Server, that's the first place the debugger will look for the source. Even if you have the source on the machine and it's in the exact same directories as embedded in the PDB file, the Source Server execution will be first. If you have a very fast version control system, that might not be any problem, but not everyone does.

An alternative way of disabling the security dialog box is to put a copy of Srcsrv.ini in the Debugging Tools for Windows program directory. That's where Srcsrv.dll resides, and it knows to look for the file there. If Srcsrv.ini has the version control system in the [trusted commands] section, it will not display the security dialog box. For each trusted command, you'll specify on the left side the base name of your version control system command-line program. On the right side, you'll specify the full path to the version control system command-line program. On my machines, my [trusted commands] section looks like the following:

```
[trusted commands]
ss.exe=C:\VSNET8\Microsoft Visual SourceSafe\ss.exe
```

In the example I'm showing in Figure 2-8, I used a source path of SRV*c:\symbols for demonstration purposes. If you look carefully enough at Figure 2-8, you'll see the whole path where the version control will extract the file, C:\symbols\BOOKSRC\ CppApp\CppApp.cpp\First Version. The C:\symbols is obvious, but the rest of the string is how it uniquely identifies the particular source file. The BOOKSRC lines up with the version control identifier specified in Srcsrv.ini when indexing the PDBs. The CppApp directory identifies the version control project, and the CppApp.cpp directory identifies the source file. In the example I'm showing, the file label version is "First Version," which explains why that is the last directory. If I used a version control system that understood file versions, the last directory would be the version number. Like the symbol server, the Source Server uses the file system as a database to uniquely identify the exact version of the file you need. The beauty of this system is that if the Source Server code in Srcsrv.dll sees that the file already exists in the extract directory, it will load the source file from there without querying the version control system for the file.

Once you click Yes in the Microsoft Source Server Security Alert dialog box, if everything has been done correctly, WinDBG displays the source code, and you'll cheer. If you're having trouble with your Source Server in WinDBG, use the .srcnoisy WinDBG command to see the verbose output from Srcsrv.dll. In nearly all cases, that will show you what the problem is.

Setting up Source Server debugging in Visual Studio 2005 is nearly as simple as it is in WinDBG. Instead of using an environment variable, the magic is in the Options dialog box. Once you get to the Options dialog box, navigate to the General node under the Debugging node. In there, as shown in Figure 2-9, you'll see the Enable Source Server Support check box. Select that check box and the indented one below it, Print Source Server Diagnostic Messages To The Output Window. When you click OK, you'll be notified that using the Source Server is a potential security problem, because you're asking the debugger to execute a program in the path. Click Yes, and you're on your way to Source Server heaven.

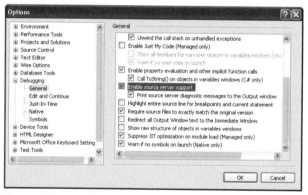

Figure 2-9   Turning on Source Server in Visual Studio

When you start debugging with Visual Studio, you'll see a slightly different security dialog box, as shown in Figure 2-10. Like WinDBG, it's warning you that you're about to execute a program, and it's giving you a chance to say no. Unfortunately, there's no option that says, "I trust the Symbol Server; I don't want to see this dialog box ever again." That means that for every source file, you'll be prompted with this dialog box, which can get tedious to say the least. As I discussed with WinDBG, you can put a Srcsrv.ini file that defines your [trusted commands] section with your version control system into the *Visual_Studio_Install Directory*\Common7\IDE and never see the security dialog box again.

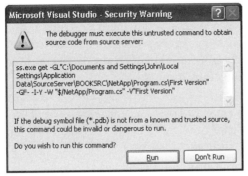

Figure 2-10   Visual Studio Source Server Security dialog box

Although it's great that Visual Studio doesn't require a weird SRV* thing in an environment variable to get the source server running, the quiz question is where does Visual Studio put the Source Server download cache? The default location is C:\Documents and Settings*user_name* \Local Settings\Application Data\SourceServer. That's great from a security standpoint because with proper security in place, only the logged-in user can see that directory. However, I do want to share the Source Server cache directory so I can share the source between the debuggers. Although you can change the WinDBG source path to SRV*C:\Documents and Settings *user_name*\Local Settings\Application Data\SourceServer, I like keeping the source files under my Symbol Server directory as I mentioned earlier.

That began my quest to figure out where Visual Studio sets the cache directory. Poking through each property page accessible from the Options dialog box does not show anything that can set the Source Server cache directory. Looking at the registry, you'll eventually find the SourceServerExtractToDirectory under HKEY_CURRENT_USER\Software\Microsoft \VisualStudio\8.0\Debugger, which is where the cache directory setting resides.

Since I don't relish manually changing registry keys because of the great potential for error, I wrote an add-in, HiddenSettings, in Chapter 7, which exposes this key in an Options property page along with a few other undocumented and hidden settings in Visual Studio. The great news here is that the Import and Export Settings Wizard in Visual Studio will properly export and import the settings between machines. One word of caution is that if you import the settings to a new machine where the cache directory does not exist, the Source Server file pull will silently fail, and you'll be left wondering what happened. Always make sure the cache directory exists.

If you are having troubles with the Source Server with Visual Studio, make sure to look at the Output window. There you'll see the reports of any problems with the Source Server. That's the first place you'll go whenever there's anything odd going on with it. In addition, you can verify where the source file is located by moving the mouse cursor over the source file tab in Visual Studio. The tooltip will show you the full path to the open files. Finally, like WinDBG, Visual Studio will grab the source code through the Source Server before it will search the raw paths in the PDB file.

The last tip I want to mention about debugging with Visual Studio 2005 is about Srcsrv.dll file versions. WinDBG generally has two public releases a year, while Visual Studio has less than that. The WinDBG team is working hard making bug fixes and performance improvements to Srcsrv.dll, thus the version with the latest version of WinDBG is always an improvement over the version that shipped with Visual Studio 2005. It's up to you, but I always copy the latest x86 version of Srcsrv.dll to the *Visual_Studio_Install_Directory*\Common7\IDE directory to ensure that Visual Studio 2005 is always using the latest and greatest version. Even if you're using only 64-bit versions of Windows, Visual Studio 2005 is a 32-bit x86 program, so that's why you need the 32-bit version. Given your newfound Source Server debugging prowess, I want to turn to a much-improved source-indexing tool.

Better and Easier Source Server Indexing

Up to this point, I've covered all the painful manual steps you need to apply Source Server in your development shop. However, if you're like me, you quickly realized that manually executing a batch file to do your source indexing and manually reading its output to see if everything worked is a complete waste of time. As soon as you have more than five binaries in your project, your eyes will glaze over, and you'll miss that one binary you need source indexed, to the detriment of everyone on your team.

As I mentioned back in the "Wonderful MSBuild" section, I set up a couple of tasks to make indexing your source code easier. Because Source Server is so vital to better debugging, I want to spend some time going over the requirements and the task specifics so you can better apply these tasks to your development shop.

My requirements for a good source indexing task are pretty simple: if there's any problem indexing source files, generate an error to stop MSBuild. Those problems can occur if

- There's any kind of [ERROR] output from Ssindex.cmd.

- There's any PDB file indexing that reports zero source files found.

- There are no source files indexed at all.

The last error is particularly insidious with source indexing because it reports no errors at all, so you think that life is great.

Given those requirements, my plan was to build a reusable base task, *SourceIndexTask*, that all version control product-specific tasks could inherit from. Additionally, I wanted to do the *VssSourceIndexTask* because so many of you are using Visual SourceSafe, and it has the additional required items I discussed earlier. If you do write a task for a Source Server–supported version control system, please send it to me, and I'll include it in Wintellect.Build.Tasks.DLL and post the code for everyone's use.

To keep life slightly simpler, I did make a couple of assumptions about the Source Server tools and your directory setup. My tasks assume that you have the Source Indexing tools in the path. The base *SourceIndexTask* will hunt the tools down in the path because MSBuild will not run unless the full path to the tools is present. The second assumption is that your directory setup matches your version control project names. While the various product-specific indexing scripts allow you to set project and client parameters, it's much better if directory names align with project names. That way, you can run the indexing script at the top directory, and everything just works. If there are mismatches, you'll have to run the source indexing separately on each directory, which is a major pain.

The *SourceIndexTask* has three required properties that you must set in your .proj files. The first is Symbols, which defines the directory where your PDB files are located and can be a relative path from your .proj file. The second is *Sources*. I had to make Sources required, because the source indexing commands work best if I have the task switch to the sources directory before executing the commands.

The last required parameter is *VersionControlSystem*, which defines the version control system. This parameter is not marked with *RequiredAttribute* because I didn't want derived classes, such as *VssSourceIndexTask*, to require redundantly specifying the version control system all over again. However, if *VersionControlSystem* is not defined, the task will report an error as though it were required.

The first of the optional properties to *SourceIndexTask* is *IniFile*, and you can use that property in case you want to explicitly specify the location of your Srcsrv.ini file. The *AdditionalCommand-LineOptions* property lets you add any additional commands not covered by derived types. It's also very useful if you are using a version control system that does not have its own task class and you want to get started with indexing immediately. You can add the version control–specific files to the *AdditionalCommandLineOptions* and be up and running. Obviously, there's no error checking on the values inside *AdditionalCommandLineOptions*.

The last of the optional properties is *IgnorePdbFiles*. This *ITaskItem* array is where you can put PDB files on which you don't care if source indexing reports an error while processing. This can happen on automatically generated binaries and items, such as the Vc?0.pdb type files I described earlier. The SourceIndexTask already knows to ignore Vc60.pdb, Vc70.pdb, and Vc80.pdb, but this property gives you the place to add any additional PDBs on which you don't want error checking performed.

The *VssSourceIndexTask*, which is the task that handles Visual SourceSafe, defines two required parameters. The first, *Server*, holds the version control system server name. The second required parameter is *Label* because Visual SourceSafe cannot be indexed without a version label. The task does the right thing and sets the SSDIR environment variable before executing the indexing commands to work around the bug in the Visual SourceSafe processing.

The *Project* optional parameter deserves some explanation. As I described earlier, if you are indexing source code from a project that's below the top level in Visual SourceSafe, the indexing will not work. If you do not set the *Project* property, the *VssSourceIndexTask* will take the *Source* property, expand it to the full path, and convert that path to the Visual SourceSafe project. If your Visual SourceSafe projects map to your file directories, this will automatically set the /Project option with no effort on your part. If you do set the *Project* property, that value is sacred and not changed by the task, so *VssSourceIndexTask* passes it directly to the source indexing tools.

The one small issue here with the *Project* property occurs if you are working with projects directly off $/ (the Visual SourceSafe root). In that case, you need to manually set the Project property to / in your MSBuild project to keep everything straight. I've wracked my brain on how to best handle subproject indexing, and this is the best I've come up with. If you have a better idea, please don't hesitate to contact me!

To see all the magic in action, look at the MSBuild project, SourceServerIndex.proj, in the .\Build directory. This project indexes the source code for everything in the book. Yes, there's nothing like dogfooding yourself.

From an implementation standpoint, there's not much hacking and excitement in the code. The most interesting challenge was figuring out how I was going to handle looking for errors in the source indexing output. I originally thought I'd redirect the output to a file and use my super regular expression skills to parse up all the problems. However, I found the power of the *ToolTask.LogEventsFromTextOutput* method to process each of the lines as they came in. I set up a simple state machine so I could report any possible problems when it comes to indexing.

Summary

This chapter covered vital infrastructure requirements necessary to help you minimize your debugging time. They run the gamut from version control and bug tracking systems to the compiler and linker settings you need, to the benefits of daily builds and smoke tests, to the importance of symbols.

Although you might need additional infrastructure requirements for your unique environment, you'll find that the ones covered in this chapter are generic across all environments. And they are the ones that I've seen make a great deal of difference in real-world development. If you don't have one or more of these infrastructure tools or techniques set up at your development shop, I strongly encourage you to implement them immediately. They will save you literally hundreds of hours of debugging time.

Chapter 3
Debugging During Coding

In Chapter 2, "Preparing for Debugging," I laid the groundwork for the project-wide infrastructure needed to enable engineers to work more efficiently. In this chapter, we'll turn to what you need to do to make debugging easier while you are at the stage of writing your code. Most people refer to this process as defensive programming, but I like to think of it as something broader and deeper: proactive programming or debugging during coding. To me, defensive programming is the error-handling code that tells you an error occurred. Proactive programming tells you why the error occurred.

Coding defensively is only part of the battle of fixing and solving bugs. Engineers generally attempt to make the obvious defensive maneuvers—for example, verifying that a string isn't *null* or *Nothing*—but they often don't take the extra step that proactive programming would require: checking that same parameter to ensure that it's not an empty string. Proactive programming means doing everything possible to avoid ever having to use the debugger and instead making the code tell you where the problems are. The debugger can be one of the biggest time drains in the world, and the way to avoid it is to have the code tell you exactly when something isn't perfect. Whenever you type a line of code, you need to stop and review what you're assuming is the good-case scenario and determine how you're going to verify that exact state is met every time that line of code executes.

It's a simple fact: bugs don't just magically appear in code. The "secret" is that you and I put them in as we're writing the code, and those pesky bugs can come from myriad sources. As Edsger Dijkstra, the great computer scientist who invented structured programming, said, "If debugging is the process of removing bugs, then programming must be the process of putting them in." Those bugs that you're entering can be the result of a problem as critical as a design flaw in your application or as simple as a typographical error. Although some bugs are easy to fix, others are nearly impossible to solve without major rewrites. It would be nice to blame the bugs in your code on gremlins, but you need to accept the fact that you and your coworkers are the ones putting the bugs in the code. (If you're reading this book, it has to be mainly your coworkers putting the bugs in.)

Because you and the other developers are responsible for any bugs in the code, the issue becomes one of finding ways to create a system of checks and balances that lets you catch bugs as you go. I've always referred to this approach as "trust, but verify," which is the late United States President Ronald Reagan's famous quote about how the United States was going to enforce one of the nuclear arms limitation treaties with the former Soviet Union. I trust that my colleagues and I will use my code correctly. To avoid bugs, however, I verify everything. I verify the data that others pass into my code, I verify my code's internal manipulations, I verify every assumption I make in my code, I verify data my code passes to others, and I verify data coming back from calls my code makes. If there's something to verify, I verify it. This obsessive verification is nothing personal against my coworkers, and I don't have any psychological problems (to speak of). It's just that I know where the bugs come from; I also know that you can't let anything by without checking it if you want to catch your bugs as early as you can. By checking everything, you also make maintenance and code evolution drastically easier because you'll know immediately when there's anything that doesn't match the original set of assumptions.

Before we go any further, I need to stress one key tenet of my development philosophy: code quality is the sole responsibility of the development engineers, not the test engineers, technical writers, or managers. You and I are the ones designing, implementing, and fixing the code, so we're the only ones who can take meaningful measures to ensure the code we write is as bug free as possible.

As a consultant, one of the most surprising attitudes I encounter in many organizations is that developers should only develop and testers only test. The prevailing problem with this approach is that developers write a bunch of code and ever so briefly decide whether it executes the good condition before throwing it over the wall to the testers. It goes without saying that you're asking for schedule slippage in addition to a poor-quality product when developers don't take responsibility for testing their code.

In my opinion, a developer is a tester is a developer. I can't stress this enough: *if a developer isn't spending at least 40 to 50 percent of his development time testing his code, he is not developing.* A tester's job is to focus on issues such as regression testing, stress testing, and performance testing. Finding a crash or unhandled exception should be an extremely rare occurrence for a tester. If the code does crash, it reflects directly on the development engineer's competence. The key to developer testing is the unit test. Your goal is to execute as much of your code as possible to ensure that it doesn't crash and properly meets established specifications and requirements. Armed with solid unit test results, the test engineers can look for integration issues and systemwide test issues.

Assert, Assert, Assert, and Assert

I hope most of you already know what an assertion is, because it's the most important proactive programming tool in your debugging arsenal. For those who are unfamiliar with the term, here's a brief definition: an *assertion* declares that a certain condition must be true at a specific point in a program. The assertion is said to *fail* if the condition is false. You use assertions in addition to normal error checking. Traditionally, assertions are functions or macros that execute only in debug builds and bring up a message box or log into a file telling you what condition failed. I extend the definition of assertions to include conditionally compiled code that checks conditions and assumptions that are too complex for a general assertion function or macro to handle. Assertions are a key component of proactive programming because they help developers and test engineers determine not just that bugs are present but also why the errors are happening.

Even if you've heard of assertions and drop them in your code occasionally, you might not be familiar enough with them to use them effectively. Development engineers can never be too rich or too thin—or use too many assertions. The rule of thumb I've always followed to judge whether I've used enough assertions is simple: I have enough assertions when my junior coworkers complain that they get multiple assertion failure reports whenever they call into my code with invalid information or assumptions.

If used sufficiently, assertions will tell you most of the information you need to diagnose a problem at the first sign of trouble. Without assertions, you'll spend considerable time in the debugger working backward from the crash searching for where things started to go wrong. A good assertion will tell you where and why a condition was invalid. A good assertion will also let you get into the debugger after a condition fails so that you can see the complete state of the program at the point of failure. A bad assertion tells you something's wrong, but not what, why, or where.

A side benefit of using plenty of assertions is that they serve as outstanding additional documentation in your code. What assertions capture is your intent. I'm sure you go well out of your way to keep your design documents perfectly up to date, but I'm just as sure that a few random projects let their design documents slip through the cracks. By having good assertions throughout your code, the maintenance developer can see exactly what value ranges you expected for a parameter or what you anticipated would fail in a normal course of operation versus a major failure condition. Assertions will never replace proper comments, but by using them to capture the elusive "here's what I meant, which is not what the documents say," you can save a great deal of time later in the project.

Before we go any further, I want to rebut what some of you are thinking right now: "I don't need to read this chapter on assertions; if I have a problem in my code, I'll just throw an exception." The problem is that once you throw that exception, you've lost the state! Look at the result of an unhandled exception such as the following (note that I wrapped some of the lines for readability):

```
Unhandled Exception: System.ComponentModel.Win32Exception: Only part of a
        ReadProcessMemory or WriteProcessMemory request was completed
    at System.Diagnostics.NtProcessManager.GetModuleInfos(Int32 processId,
                                     Boolean firstModuleOnly)
    at System.Diagnostics.Process.get_Modules()
    at DiagnosticHelper.StackWriter.IsDotNetInProcess() in c:\Bar\StackWriter.cs:line 343
    at DiagnosticHelper.StackWriter.Execute() in c:\Bar\StackWriter.cs:line 58
    at DiagnosticHelper.Program.Main(String[] args) in c:\Bar\Program.cs:line 79
```

While you can detect a memory reading problem in the *Process.get_Modules* method, can you tell me exactly which module loaded was causing the problem? Is the value of *firstModuleOnly* true or false? What were the local variables in the *Execute* method?

The problem with Microsoft .NET is that you get very little of the information you need to diagnose problems in an exception. The call stack tells you where it started, but it says nothing about your local variables and parameters even in the function that caused the state to be bad. Without an assertion, you are going to spend far more time debugging than with one.

The key with assertions is that good assertion code, such as that in .NET, allows you to get the debugger attached before the *state* is lost. With the debugger, you'll be able to see all the data you can't see in an exception, so you now have the information to solve the problem faster. You'll still throw the exception as part of your normal error handling, but by adding the assertion, you'll spend less time on the problem and have more time for more interesting tasks.

Some of you may be thinking that you can still do without assertions because if you set the debugger to stop instantly when an exception is thrown, you'll achieve the same effect. That's true, but you'd have to start your application from the debugger every time you run it. Although that may be the only way you run the application, I can assure you that testers, your coworkers, or even your manager are not starting those debug builds from the debugger. The assertions are always there ready to trigger the instant anything is amiss so you can decide how you want to proceed from the problem.

How and What to Assert

My stock answer when asked what to assert is to assert everything. I would love to say that for every line of code you should have an assertion, but it's an unrealistic albeit admirable goal. You should assert any condition because it might be the one you need to solve a nasty bug in the future. Don't worry that putting in too many assertions will hamper your program's performance—assertions are active only in debug builds, and the bug-finding opportunities created outweigh any performance hit.

Assertions should never change any variables or states of a program. Treat all data you check in assertions as read-only. Because assertions are active only in debug builds, if you do change data by using an assertion, you'll have different behavior between debug and release builds, and tracking down the differences will be extremely difficult.

In this section, I want to concentrate on how to use assertions and what to assert. I'll do this by showing code examples. For .NET, all your assertions start with *Debug.Assert* methods from the *System.Diagnostic* namespace. There are three overloaded *Assert* methods. All three take a *Boolean* value as their first or only parameter, and if the value is *false*, the assertion is triggered. As shown in the following examples in which I used *Debug.Assert,* one of the methods takes a second parameter of type *string*, which is shown as a message in the output. The final overloaded *Assert* method takes a third parameter of type *string*, which provides even more information when the assertion triggers. In my experience, the two-parameter approach is the easiest to use because I simply copy the condition checked in the first parameter and paste it in as a string. Of course, now that the assertion requiring the conditional expression is in quotes, make it part of your code reviews to verify that the string value always matches the real condition. As I mentioned in the Custom Code Analysis Rules section in Chapter 2, using the one parameter *Debug.Assert* is not good because the assertion output does not tell you why you're asserting. That's why I wrote the Code Analysis rule to report an error if you're using it. The following code shows all three *Assert* methods in action:

```
Debug.Assert ( i > 3 ) ;
Debug.Assert ( i > 3 , "i > 3" ) ;
Debug.Assert ( i > 3 , "i > 3" , "This means I got a bad parameter") ;
```

Debugging War Story
A Career-Limiting Move

The Battle

A long, long time ago in the C++ days, I worked at a company whose software product had serious stability problems. As the senior Microsoft Windows engineer on this behemoth project, I found that many of the issues affecting the project resulted from a lack of understanding about why calls made to others' modules failed. I wrote a memo advising the same practices I promote in this chapter, telling project members why and when they were supposed to use assertions, in addition to requiring everyone to use a C++ macro, *ASSERT,* to do their assertions. I had a little bit of power, so I also made it part of the code review criteria to look for proper assertion usage.

After sending out the memo, I answered a few questions people had about assertions and thought everything was fine. Three days later, my boss came into my office and started screaming at me about how I screwed everyone up, and he ordered me to rescind my assertion memo. I was stunned, and we proceeded to get into an extremely heated argument about my assertion recommendations. I couldn't quite understand what my boss was arguing about, but it had something to do with making the product much more unstable. After five minutes of yelling at each other, I finally challenged my boss to prove that people were using assertions incorrectly. He handed me a code printout that looked like the following:

```
BOOL DoSomeWork ( HMODULE * pModArray , int iCount , LPCTSTR szBuff )
{
    ASSERT ( if ( ( pModArray == NULL ) &&
               ( IsBadWritePtr ( pModArray ,
                                ( sizeof ( HMODULE ) * iCount ) ) &&
               ( iCount != 0 ) &&
             ( szBuff != NULL ) ) )
             {
                 return ( FALSE ) ;
             }
           ) ;
    for ( int i = 0 ; i < iCount ; i++ )
```

```
        {
            pModArray[ i ] = m_pDataMods[ i ] ;
        }
    ...
}
```

The Outcome

I should also mention here that my boss and I generally didn't get along. He thought I was a young whippersnapper who hadn't paid his dues and didn't know a thing, and I thought he was a completely clueless PHB who couldn't engineer his way out of a wet paper bag. As I read over the code, my eyes nearly popped completely out of my head! The person who had coded this example had completely misunderstood the purpose of assertions and was simply going through and wrapping all the normal error handling in an assertion macro. Since assertions disappear in release builds, the person who wrote the code was removing *all* error checking in release builds!

By this point, I was livid and screamed at the top of my lungs, "Whoever wrote this needs to be fired! I can't believe we have an engineer on our staff who is this incredibly and completely stupid!" My boss got very quiet, grabbed the paper out of my hands, and quietly said, "That's my code." My career-limiting move was to start laughing hysterically as my boss walked away.

The Lesson

I can't stress this enough: use assertions *in addition* to normal error handling, never as a replacement for it. If you have an assertion, you need to have some sort of error handling near it in the code. As for my boss, when I went into his office a few weeks later to resign because I had accepted a job at a better company, I was treated to a grown man dancing on his desk and singing that it was the best day of his life.

How to Assert

The first rule when using assertions is to check one item at a time. If you check multiple conditions with just one assertion, you have no way of knowing which condition caused the failure. In the following example, I show the same function with two assertion checks. Although the assertion in the first function will catch a bad parameter, the assertion won't tell you which condition failed or even which of the three parameters is the offending one. Your first assertion goal is to check each condition *atomically*.

```
// The wrong way to write an assertion. Which parameter was bad?
string FillData ( char[] array , int offset , int length )
{
    Debug.Assert ( ( null != array ) &&
                ( offset > 0 )    &&
                ( ( length > 0 && ( length < 100 ) ) ) ) ;
    ...
}
```

```
// The proper way. Each parameter is checked individually so that you
// can see which one failed.
string FillData ( char[] array , int offset , int length )
{
    Debug.Assert ( null != array , "null != array") ;
    Debug.Assert ( offset > 0 , "offset > 0") ;
    Debug.Assert ( ( length > 0 ) && ( length < 100 ) ,
                   " ( length > 0 ) && ( length < 100 )" ) ;
    ...
}
```

In looking at the fixed *FillData* example above, you may think that I'm breaking my own rules by checking that the *length* parameter is between 0 and 100. Because I'm checking against a constrained range, that check is atomic enough. There's no need to break apart the expression into two separate *Debug.Assert* calls.

When you assert a condition, you need to strive to check the condition *completely*. For example, if your .NET method takes a string as a parameter and you expect the string to have something in it, checking against *null* checks only part of the error condition.

```
// An example of checking only a part of the error condition
bool LookupCustomerName ( string customerName )
{
    Debug.Assert ( null != customerName , "null != customerName") ;
    ...
}
```

You can check the full condition by also checking to see whether the string is empty.

```
// An example of completely checking the error condition
bool LookupCustomerName ( string customerName )
{
    Debug.Assert ( false == string.IsNullOrEmpty ( customerName ),
                   "false == string.IsNullOrEmpty ( customerName )" );
    ...
}
```

Another step I always take is to ensure that I'm asserting against specific values so I'm asserting *correctly*. The following example shows first how to check for a value incorrectly and then how to check for it correctly:

```
// Example of a poorly written assertion.  What happens if count is negative?
Function UpdateListEntries ( ByVal count As Integer) As Integer
    Debug.Assert ( count <> 0 , "count <> 0" )
    ...
End Function

// A proper assertion that explicitly checks against what the value
// is supposed to be
Function UpdateListEntries ( ByVal count As Integer) As Integer
    Debug.Assert ( count > 0 , "count > 0" )
    ...
End Function
```

The incorrect sample essentially checks only whether *count* isn't 0, which is just half of the information that needs to be asserted. By explicitly checking the acceptable values, you guarantee that your assertion is self-documenting, and you also ensure that your assertion catches corrupted data.

What to Assert

Now that you're armed with an idea of how to assert, we can turn to exactly what you need to be asserting throughout your code. If you haven't guessed from the examples I've presented so far, let me clarify that the first mandatory items to assert are the parameters coming into the method or property setter. Asserting parameters is especially critical with module interfaces and class methods that others on your team call. Because those gateway functions are the entry points into your code, you want to make sure that each parameter and assumption is valid. As I pointed out in the debugging war story earlier in this chapter, "A Career-Limiting Move," assertions always work hand in hand with normal error handling.

As you move inside your module, the parameters of the module's private methods might not require as much checking, depending mainly on where the parameters originated. Much of the decision about which parameters to validate comes down to a judgment call. It doesn't hurt to assert every parameter of every method, but if a parameter comes from outside the module, and if you fully asserted it once, you might not need to again. By asserting each parameter on every function, however, you might catch some errors inside your module.

I sit right in the middle of the two extremes. Deciding how many parameter assertions are right for you just takes some experience. As you get a feel for where you typically encounter problems in your code, you'll figure out where and when you need to assert parameters internal to your module. One safeguard I've learned to use is to add parameter assertions whenever a bad parameter blows up my code. That way, the mistake won't get repeated, because the assertion will catch it.

Another area that's mandatory for assertions is API and COM return values because the return values tell you whether the API succeeded or failed. One of the biggest problems I see in debugging other developers' code is that they simply call API functions without ever checking the return value. I have seen so many cases in which I've looked for a bug only to find out that some method early on in the code failed but no one bothered to check its return value. Of course, by the time you discover the culprit, the bug is manifested, so the program dies or corrupts data some 20 minutes later. By asserting API return values appropriately, you at least know about a problem when it happens. Of course, you will still perform regular error handling on those API return values.

Keep in mind that I'm not advocating asserting on every single possible failure. Some failures are expected in code, and you should handle them appropriately. Having an assertion fire each time a lookup in the database fails will likely drive everyone to disabling assertions in the project. Be smart about it, and assert on return values when it's something serious. Handling good data throughout your program should never cause an assertion to trigger.

Another area in which you'll have assertions is when you verify the state of the object. For example, if you have a private method that assumes that the object hasn't been disposed, you'd have an assertion to ensure that the method call happens with the correct state. The big idea behind proactive programming is that you leave nothing to chance and never leave an assumption unquestioned.

Finally, I recommend that you use assertions when you need to check an assumption. For example, if the specifications for a class require 3 MB of disk space, you should assert this assumption with conditional inside the class to ensure that the callers are upholding their end of the deal. Here's another example: if your code is supposed to access a database, you should have a check to see whether the required tables actually exist in the database. That way you'll know immediately what's wrong instead of wondering why you're getting weird return values from other methods in the class.

In both of the preceding examples, as with most assumption assertions, you can't check the assumptions in a general assertion method. In these situations, the conditional compilation technique that I indicated in the last paragraph should be part of your assertion toolkit. Because the code executed in the conditional compilation works on live data, you must take extra precautions to ensure that you don't change the state of the program. To avoid the serious problems that can be created by introducing code that has side effects, I prefer to implement these types of assertions in separate methods, if possible. By doing so, you avoid changing any local variables inside the original method. Additionally, the conditionally compiled assertion methods can come in handy in the Watch window, as you'll see in Chapter 5, "Advanced Debugger Usage with Visual Studio," when we talk about the Microsoft Visual Studio 2005 debugger. Listing 3-1 shows a conditionally compiled method that checks whether a table exists so that you'll get the assertion before you start any significant access. Note that this test method assumes that you've already validated the connection string and can fully access the database. *AssertTableExists* ensures that the table exists so that you can validate this assumption instead of looking at an odd failure message from deep inside your code.

Listing 3-1   *AssertTableExists* checks whether a table exists

```
[Conditional ( "DEBUG" )]
static public void AssertTableExists ( string connStr ,
                                       string tableName )
{
#if DEBUG
    SqlConnection conn = new SqlConnection ( connStr );

    StringBuilder buildCmd = new StringBuilder ( );

    buildCmd.Append ( "select * from dbo.sysobjects where " );
    buildCmd.Append ( "id = object_id('" );
    buildCmd.Append ( tableName );
    buildCmd.Append ( "') and xtype = 'U'" );

    // Make the command.
    SqlCommand cmd = new SqlCommand ( buildCmd.ToString ( ) , conn );
    SqlDataAdapter tableDataAdapter = null;
    try
```

```
    {

        // Open the database.
        conn.Open ( );

        // Create a dataset to fill.
        DataSet tableSet = new DataSet ( );
        tableSet.Locale = Thread.CurrentThread.CurrentUICulture;

         // Create the data adapter.
        tableDataAdapter = new SqlDataAdapter ( );

        // Set the command to do the select.
        tableDataAdapter.SelectCommand = cmd;

        // Fill the dataset from the adapter.
        tableDataAdapter.Fill ( tableSet );

        // If anything showed up, the table exists.
        if ( 0 == tableSet.Tables [ 0 ].Rows.Count )
        {
            String sMsg = "Table : '" + tableName +
                            "' does not exist!\r\n";
            Debug.Assert ( false , sMsg );
        }
    }
    catch ( SqlException e )
    {
        Debug.Assert ( false , e.Message );
    }
    finally
    {
        if ( null != tableDataAdapter )
        {
            tableDataAdapter.Dispose ( );
        }
        if ( null != cmd )
        {
            cmd.Dispose ( );
        }
        if ( null != conn )
        {
            conn.Close ( );
        }
    }
#endif
}
```

Assertions in .NET

Before I get into the gritty details of .NET assertions, I want to mention one key mistake I've seen in almost all .NET code written, especially in many of the samples from which developers are lifting code to build their applications. Everyone forgets that it's entirely possible to have an object parameter passed as *null* (or *Nothing* in Visual Basic). Even when developers are using assertions, the code looks like the following:

```
void DoSomeWork ( string name )
{
    Debug.Assert ( name.Length > 0 ) ;
...
```

Instead of triggering the assertion, if *name* is *null*, calling the *Length* property causes a *System.NullReferenceException* exception in your application, effectively crashing it. This is a horrible case in which the assertion is causing a nasty side effect, thus breaking the cardinal rule of assertions. Of course, it logically follows that if developers aren't checking for *null* objects in their assertions, they aren't checking for them in their normal parameter checking. Do yourself a huge favor and start checking objects for *null*.

The fact that .NET applications don't have to worry about pointers and memory pointers and manual memory management means that at least 60 percent of the assertions we were used to handling in the C++ days just went away. On the assertion front, the .NET team added as part of the *System.Diagnostic* namespace two objects, *Debug* and *Trace*, which are active only if you defined *DEBUG* or *TRACE*, respectively, when compiling your application. Both of these conditional compilation symbols can be specified as part of the Build tab in the project property pages dialog box. Visual Studio–created projects always define *TRACE* for both debug and release builds, so if you're doing manual projects, make sure to add it to your build options. As you've seen, the *Assert* is the method that handles assertions in .NET. Interestingly enough, both *Debug* and *Trace* have identical methods, including an *Assert* method. I find it a little confusing to have two possible assertions that are conditionally compiled differently. Consequently, because assertions should be active only in debug builds, I use only *Debug.Assert* for assertions. Doing so prevents surprise phone calls from end users asking about a weird dialog box or message telling them that something went bad. I strongly suggest that you do the same so that you contribute to some consistency in the world of assertions. If you use the Code Analysis rules provided with the book's source code, I have a rule that will tell you that you are using *Trace.Assert* so you can remove it from your code.

The .NET *Debug* class is intriguing because you can see the output in multiple ways. The output for the *Debug* class—and the *Trace* class for that matter—goes through another class, named a *TraceListener*. Classes derived from *TraceListener* can be added to the *Debug* class's *Listeners* collection property. The beauty of the *TraceListener* approach is that each time an assertion fails, the *Debug* class runs through the *Listeners* collection and calls each *TraceListener* object in turn. This convenient functionality means that even when new and improved ways of reporting assertions surface, you won't have to make major code changes to benefit from them. Even better, in the next section, I'll show you how you can add new *TraceListener* objects without changing your code at all, which makes for ultimate extensibility!

The initial *TraceListener* in the *Listeners* collection, appropriately named *DefaultTraceListener*, sends the output to two different places, the most visible of which is the assertion message box shown in Figure 3-1. As you can see in the figure, the bulk of the message box is taken up with the stack walk and parameter types in addition to the source and line for each item. The top lines of the message box report the string values you passed to *Debug.Assert*. In the case of Figure 3-1, I just passed *"Debug.Assert assertion"* as the second parameter to *Debug.Assert*.

The result of clicking each button is described in the title bar for the message box. The only interesting button is Retry. If you're running under a debugger, you simply drop into the debugger at the line directly after the assertion. If you're not running under a debugger, clicking Retry triggers a special exception and then launches the Just In Time debugger selector to allow you to select the registered debugger you'd like to use to debug the assertion.

In addition to the message box output, *Debug.Assert* also sends all the output through *Output-DebugString*, the Windows API tracing function, so the attached debugger will get the output. The output has a nearly identical format, shown in the following code. Since the *DefaultTrace-Listener* does the *OutputDebugString* output, you can always use Mark Russinovich's excellent DebugView (*www.sysinternals.com/utilities/debugview.html*) to view the output even when you're not running under a debugger. I'll discuss this in more detail later in the chapter.

```
---- DEBUG ASSERTION FAILED ----
---- Assert Short Message ----
Debug.Assert assertion
---- Assert Long Message ----


    at HappyAppy.Fum()  D:\AssertExample\Class1.cs(11)
    at HappyAppy.Fo(StringBuilder sb)  D:\AssertExample\Class1.cs(16)
    at HappyAppy.Fi(IntPtr p)  D:\AssertExample\Class1.cs(20)
    at HappyAppy.Fee(String Blah)  D:\AssertExample\Class1.cs(25)
    at HappyAppy.Baz(Double d)  D:\AssertExample\Class1.cs(30)
    at HappyAppy.Bar(Object o)  D:\AssertExample\Class1.cs(35)
    at HappyAppy.Foo(Int32 i)  D:\AssertExample\Class1.cs(42)
    at HappyAppy.Main()  D:\AssertExample\Class1.cs(48)
```

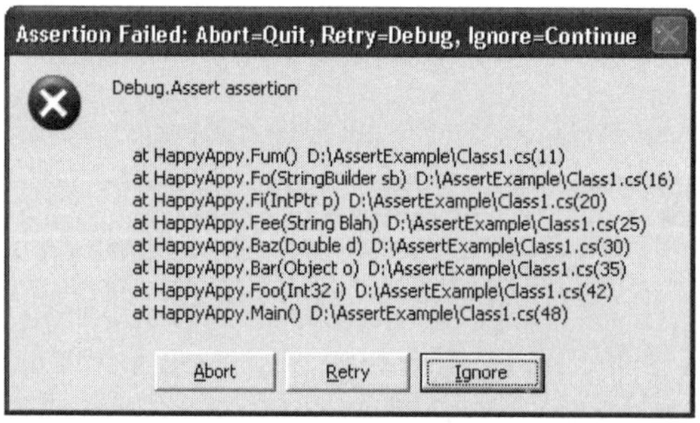

Figure 3-1   The DefaultTraceListener message box

Armed with the information supplied by *Debug.Assert*, you should never again have to wonder how you got into the assertion condition! The .NET Framework also supplies numerous other

TraceListener-derived classes. To write the output to a text file, use the *TextWriterTraceListener* class. To write the output to the event log, use the *EventLogTraceListener* class. The other *TraceListener*-derived classes, *DelimitedListTraceListener*, *ConsoleTraceListener*, and *XmlWriterTrace-Listener* are used more in pure tracing, so I'll discuss them in the "Trace, Trace, Trace, and Trace" section later in the chapter.

Unfortunately, the *TextWriterTraceListener* and *EventLogTraceListener* classes are essentially worthless because they log only the message fields to your assertions and not the stack trace at all. The good news is that implementing your own *TraceListener* objects is fairly trivial, so as part of Wintellect.Diagnostics.dll, I went ahead and wrote the correct versions for *TextWriter-TraceListener* and *EventLogTraceListener* for you: *FixedTextWriterTraceListener* and *FixedEvent-LogTraceListener*, respectively.

Neither *FixedTextWriterTraceListener* nor *FixedEventLogTraceListener* are very exciting classes. *FixedTextWriterTraceListener* is derived directly from *TextWriterTraceListener*, so all it does is override the *Fail* method, which is what *Debug.Assert* calls to do the output. Keep in mind that when using *FixedTextWriterTraceListener* or *TextWriterTraceListener*, the associated text file for the output isn't flushed unless you set the *trace* element *autoflush* attribute to *true* in the application configuration file, explicitly call *Close* on the stream or file, or set *Debug.AutoFlush* to *true* so that each write causes a flush to disk. Alternatively, you can also set these values to *true* in the configuration files, which I'll show in a moment.

For some bizarre reason, the *EventLogTraceListener* class is sealed, so I couldn't derive directly from it and had to derive from the abstract *TraceListener* class directly. However, I did retrieve the stack trace by using the standard *StackTrace* class that's been around since .NET 1.0. One nice feature in .NET 2.0 is that you no longer have to manually work through reflection to find the source and line of each method on the stack. If you want the full stack with source and line, use one of the *StackTrace* constructors that take a *Boolean* value and pass *true*. Since I'm talking about the source and line, I should mention that the .NET *StackTrace* class source lookup will look only at .pdb files in the same directory as the binary. It will not look in your Symbol Server.

Controlling the *TraceListener* Property with Configuration Files

For the most part, *DefaultTraceListener* should serve most of your needs. However, having a message box that pops up every once in a while can wreak havoc on any automated test scripts you might have. Also if you use a third-party component in a Win32 service, which was not tested running under a service but has calls to *Debug.Assert* in it, the debug build of that component could cause message box popups using *DefaultTraceListener,* which would hang your service. In both of these cases, you want to be able to shut off the message box generated by *DefaultTraceListener*. You could add code to remove the *DefaultTraceListener* instance from the *Debug.Listeners* property, but it is also possible to remove it even without touching the code.

Any .NET executable can have an external XML configuration file associated with it. This file resides in the same directory as the binary file and is the name of the executable with ".Config" appended to the end. For example, the configuration file for Example.exe is Example.exe.Config. You can easily add a configuration file to your project in Visual Studio by adding a new XML file named App.Config. That file will automatically be copied to the output directory and named to match the binary. For Microsoft ASP.NET applications, the configuration file is always named Web.Config.

In the XML configuration file, the *assert* element under *system.diagnostics* has two attributes. If you set the first attribute, *assertuienabled*, to *false*, .NET doesn't display message boxes, and the output still goes through *OutputDebugString*. The second attribute, *logfilename*, allows you to specify a file you want any assertion output written to. Interestingly, when you specify a file in the *logfilename* attribute, any trace statements will also appear in the file. A minimal configuration file is shown in the next code snippet, and you can see how easy it is to shut off the assertion message boxes. Don't forget that the master configuration file Machine.Config, which is stored in the *%SystemRoot%*\Microsoft.NET\Framework64*FrameworkVersion*\Config directory, has the same settings as the EXE configuration file, so you can optionally turn off message boxes on the whole machine by using the same settings, as follows:

```
<?xml version="1.0" encoding="UTF-8" ?>
<configuration>
    <system.diagnostics>
        <assert assertuienabled="false"
                logfilename="tracelog.txt" />
    </system.diagnostics>
</configuration>
```

As I mentioned earlier, you can add and remove listeners without touching the code, and as you probably guessed, the configuration file has something to do with it. This file looks straightforward in the documentation, but the documentation at the time I am writing this book is not correct. After a little experimentation, I figured out all the tricks necessary to control your listeners correctly without changing the code.

All the action happens under the *trace* element of the configuration. The *trace* element happens to have one very important optional attribute you should always set to *true* in your configuration-files: *autoflush*. By setting *autoflush* to *true*, you force the output buffer to be flushed each time a write operation occurs. If you don't set *autoflush*, you'll have to add calls to your code to get the output saved onto the disk. Note that *autoflush* is *false* by default, and this could be the reason why you don't get any trace after your application crashes: the last output was not saved on disk before the crash occurs.

Underneath *trace* is the *listeners* element, containing the list of the *TraceListener*-derived objects that will be added to or removed from the *Debug.Listeners* property at run time. Removing a *TraceListener* object is very simple. Specify the *remove* element, and set the *name* attribute to the string name of the desired *TraceListener* class. If you define your own *TraceListener*-derived class, don't forget to either override the get accessor of its *Name* property or, in the constructor, call the base constructor with your own specific name; this is how your class will be identified within configuration files. The complete configuration file necessary to remove *DefaultTrace-Listener* is as follows:

```xml
<?xml version="1.0" encoding="UTF-8" ?>
<configuration>
    <system.diagnostics>
      <trace autoflush="true" indentsize="0">
          <listeners>
            <remove name="Default" />
          </listeners>
      </trace>
    </system.diagnostics>
</configuration>
```

The *add* element has two required attributes. The *name* attribute is a string that specifies the name of the *TraceListener* object set into the *TraceListener.Name* property when the instance is created. The second attribute, *type*, specifies the .NET type you want to load and associate with the given *name*. The one optional attribute, *initializeData*, is the string passed to the constructor of the *TraceListener* object. The documentation shows only adding a type that is in the global assembly cache (GAC) and implies that that's where all assemblies must be in order to load, which is not the case.

To add a *TraceListener* object that's in the GAC, the *type* element can consist of two different forms. The usual is the fully qualified type name, which specifies the type, assembly, version, culture, and public key token. You'll want to use this form in most cases to specify the exact type you want to load. An undocumented feature will allow you to specify just the type name, and .NET will load the first type found in the GAC. In the case of the Microsoft-supplied *TraceListener* classes, this works fine.

If you want to add your custom *TraceListener* class that doesn't reside in the GAC, your options become a little more involved. The easy case is when your *TraceListener* resides in the same directory where the EXE for your process loads from. In that case, to add the derived *Trace-Listener* object, you specify the full type name, a comma, and the name of the assembly. You can enter the fully qualified type name, but because you can have only a single named DLL in the directory at one time, the extra typing is overkill. The following shows how to add *Fixed-TextWriterTraceListener* from Wintellect.Diagnostics.dll:

```xml
<?xml version="1.0" encoding="UTF-8" ?>
<configuration>
    <system.diagnostics>
      <trace autoflush="true" indentsize="0">
          <listeners>
            <add name="AGoodListener"
                 type=
"Wintellect.Diagnostics.FixedTextWriterTraceListener,Wintellect.Diagnostics"
                 initializeData="HappyGoLucky.log"/>
          </listeners>
      </trace>
    </system.diagnostics>
</configuration>
```

In adding *TraceListeners* from configuration files, there has been a change concerning where .NET creates the output files for *TraceListeners*. In .NET 2.0, the output file is relative to the App.Config/Web.Config. For the example above, the HappyGoLucky.log file will be written to the same directory as App.Config. In .NET 1.x, the output file was always created relative to the application. In the case of the ASP.NET worker process, this was usually a major problem because the worker process is down deep in *%SystemRoot%*\system32\INETSRV directory, where your application probably does not have write permissions.

If you'd like to keep the assembly containing your *TraceListener* type in a different directory, you have two choices. Using the *probing* element in the App.Config/Web.Config, you can set the *privatePath* attribute to the private assembly search path to a directory below the application directory. The following example configuration file shows adding *FixedTextWriter-TraceListener* and telling the runtime to look both in the directories Happy and Joyful for the assembly. I've found that it works best to use the fully qualified type name of the assembly when utilizing the *probing* element.

```xml
<?xml version="1.0" encoding="utf-8" ?>
<configuration>
    <runtime>
        <assemblyBinding xmlns="urn:schemas-microsoft-com:asm.v1">
            <probing privatePath="Happy;Joyful"/>
        </assemblyBinding>
    </runtime>
    <system.diagnostics>
        <trace autoflush="true" indentsize="0">
            <listeners>
                <add name="CoolListener"
                    type="Wintellect.Diagnostics.FixedTextWriterTraceListener,
                        Wintellect.Diagnostics,
                        Version=2.0.0.0,
                        Culture=neutral,
                        PublicKeyToken=f54122dc856f9575"
                    initializeData="MyConfigEventLog"/>
            </listeners>
        </trace>
    </system.diagnostics>
</configuration>
```

The final way of specifying the assembly to load is the most flexible because the *TraceListener* can be anywhere, but it requires a little more typing. The trick is to tell .NET where to look by using the *<dependentAssembly>* elements in the configuration to have the assembly loader look for a specific assembly in a different location. In the following example, I'll specify the three assemblies needed to load *FixedTextWriterTraceListener*. The *assemblyIdentity* elements specify the exact name, culture, and public key token for the assembly, and the *codeBase* element indicates the version and points to a directory where the assembly will be loaded from. Interestingly, the *href* attribute in *codeBase* takes a Uniform Resource Identifier (URI), so you could also specify a Web site with an http:// location.

```
<configuration>
    <runtime>
        <assemblyBinding xmlns="urn:schemas-microsoft-com:asm.v1">
            <dependentAssembly>
                <assemblyIdentity name="Wintellect.Diagnostics"
                                  culture="neutral"
                                  publicKeyToken="f54122dc856f9575"/>
                <codeBase version="2.0.0.0"
                        href="file://c:/Listeners/Wintellect.Diagnostics.dll"/>
            </dependentAssembly>
            <dependentAssembly>
                <assemblyIdentity name="Wintellect.Utility"
                                  culture="neutral"
                                  publicKeyToken="f54122dc856f9575"/>
                <codeBase version="1.0.0.0"
                        href="file://c:/Listeners/Wintellect.Utility.DLL"/>
            </dependentAssembly>
            <dependentAssembly>
                <assemblyIdentity name="Caudal.Windows.Forms"
                                  culture="neutral"
                                  publicKeyToken="f54122dc856f9575"/>
                <codeBase version="1.0.0.0"
                        href="file://c:/Listeners/Caudal.Windows.Forms.dll"/>
            </dependentAssembly>
        </assemblyBinding>
    </runtime>
    <system.diagnostics>
        <trace autoflush="true" indentsize="0">
            <listeners>
                <add name="CoolListener"
                    type="Wintellect.Diagnostics.FixedTextWriterTraceListener,
                        Wintellect.Diagnostics,
                        Version=2.0.0.0,
                        Culture=neutral,
                        PublicKeyToken=f54122dc856f9575"
                    initializeData="MyOutputFile.txt"/>
            </listeners>
        </trace>
    </system.diagnostics>
</configuration>
```

Assertions in ASP.NET

Up to this point, if you're doing primarily ASP.NET development, you're thinking that what I've talked about applies only to Windows Forms or console applications. In the mean old .NET 1.1 days, you would have been right. There was zero support for *Debug.Assert* in ASP.NET, but at least the message box didn't pop up on some hidden desktop and wipe out the ASP.NET worker process. Without assertions, you might as well not program! In the previous edition of this book, I had a bunch of code that developed assertion handling for ASP.NET, but I'm not including it in this version.

The great news with .NET 2.0 is the Web Development Server ultimately makes ASP.NET applications nothing more than regular user mode programs that just happen to run through the browser. If you have an assertion in your code, you get to see the exact same message box shown in Figure 3-1. I personally am thrilled that we now have a single way to assert across all types of .NET development.

When your application is running under Internet Information Services (IIS) instead of the Web Development Server, your calls to *Debug.Assert* behave slightly differently. You'll still see the message box from *DefaultTraceListener* if you are logged into the physical server or are connected with Remote Desktop Program (Mstsc.exe) with /console specified at the command prompt. As you would expect, clicking the Ignore button ignores the assertion, and your application continues what it was doing. Clicking the Abort button unceremoniously terminates the ASP.NET worker process just as it does for any console application. Clicking the Retry button gets a little more interesting.

In the Web Development Server, clicking the Retry button calls *Debugger.Launch*, which brings up the Visual Studio Just-In-Time Debugger dialog box, in which you can choose the debugger with which you want to debug the application. When running under IIS, the Retry button does not trigger the debugger dialog box. While I wish we still had the option to see the dialog box, it does expose a security hole to have the debugger dialog box pop up when the logged-in user might not be someone you want debugging applications.

Fortunately, it's easy enough to start the debugger and attach it to the ASP.NET worker process that's showing the assertion. Once you've attached the debugger, clicking the Retry button will break inside the debugger, and you'll be on your way to assertion nirvana. The last point I need to make about assertions in ASP.NET applications is that you must have the compilation element, *debug* attribute in Web.Config set to *true* for any calls made in your ASP.NET code to be compiled in through conditional compilation. With the *debug* attribute set to *false*, Aspnet_Compiler.exe compiles your binary on the fly without the /define:DEBUG switch passed to CSC.exe or VBC.exe.

Debugging War Story
Disappearing Files and Threads

The Battle

Many years ago, while working on a version of NuMega's BoundsChecker, we had incredible difficulty with random crashes that were almost impossible to duplicate. The only clues we had were that file handles and thread handles occasionally became invalid, which meant that files were randomly closing and thread synchronization was sometimes breaking. The user-interface developers were also experiencing occasional crashes, but only when running under the debugger. These problems plagued us throughout development, finally escalating to the point when all developers on the team stopped what they were doing and started trying to solve these bugs.

The Outcome

The team nearly dipped me in tar and covered me with feathers because the problem turned out to be my fault. I was responsible for the debug loop in BoundsChecker. In the debug loop, you use the Windows debugging API to start and control another process, the debuggee, and to respond to debug events that the operating system generates. Being a conscientious programmer, I saw that the *WaitForDebugEvent* function was returning handle values for some of the debugging event notifications. For example, when a process started under a debugger, the debugger would get a structure that contained a handle to the process and the initial thread for that process.

Because I'm so careful, I knew that if an API gave you a handle to some object and you no longer needed the object, you called *CloseHandle* to free the underlying memory for that object. Therefore, whenever the debugging API gave me a handle, I closed that handle as soon as I finished using it. That seemed like the reasonable thing to do.

However, much to my chagrin, I hadn't read the fine print in the debugging API documentation, which says that the debugging API itself closes any process and thread handles it generates. What was happening was that I was holding some of the handles returned by the debugging API until I needed them, but I was closing those same handles after I finished using them—after the debugging API had already closed them.

To understand how this situation led to our problem, you need to know that when you close a handle, the operating system marks that handle value as available. Microsoft Windows NT 4.0, the operating system we were using at the time, is particularly aggressive about recycling handle values. (Windows 2000 and Windows XP exhibit the same aggressive behavior toward handle values.) Our UI portions, which were heavily multithreaded and opened many files, were creating and using new handles all the time. Because the debugging API was closing my handles and the operating system was recycling them, sometimes the UI portions would get one of the handles that I was saving. As I closed my copies of the handles later, I was actually closing the UI's threads and file handles!

I was barely able to avoid the tar and feathers by showing that this bug was also in the debug loop of previous versions of BoundsChecker. We'd just been lucky before. What had changed was that the version we were working on had a new-and-improved UI that was doing much more with files and threads, so the conditions were ripe for my bug to do more damage.

The Lesson

I could have avoided this problem if I'd read the fine print in the debugging API documentation. Additionally—and this is the big lesson—I learned that you always check the return values to *CloseHandle*. Although you can't do much when you close an invalid handle, the operating system does tell you when you're doing something wrong, and you should pay attention.

As a side note, I want to mention that if you attempt to double-close a handle or pass a bad value to *CloseHandle*, and you're doing native debugging, Windows operating systems will report an "Invalid Handle" exception (0xC0000008) when running under a debugger. When you see that exception value, you can stop to investigate why it occurred.

I also learned that it really helps to be able to out-sprint your coworkers when they're chasing you with a pot of tar and bags of feathers.

SUPERASSERT.NET

In the previous edition of this book, which covered both .NET and native C++ debugging, I presented what I'd like to think was the ultimate in native C++ assertions, SUPERASSERT. Many people liked it, and I've lost track of the number of companies that had integrated the code into their applications. Nothing is better than when I'm working on a super-difficult bug for a client and run across some of my own code in their application. It's happened many times, and it's still an amazing thrill for me to see that someone found my code good enough to use.

When we all started turning to .NET development, many people kept asking for a version of SUPERASSERT that worked with .NET. After a lot of thinking, I came up with a version that I first published in my "Bugslayer" column for the November 2005 issue of "MSDN Magazine" (*http://msdn.microsoft.com/msdnmag/issues/05/11/Bugslayer/default.aspx*). Many people liked it, but that version always bothered me because it just wasn't as useful as the native C++ version. After even more thought, I have finally come up with a worthy successor to the native SUPERASSERT.

SUPERASSERT.NET Requirements

As with any project, you need a good set of requirements so you know what to develop and if you're meeting your goals. Based on the success of the native SUPERASSERT, the idea of a user interface much better than a message box is mandatory to present even more information and, most importantly, allow you to debug deeper without starting a debugger. You'll see some screenshots of the dialog box in a few pages. The user interface is nothing fancy, but it allows you to see the key information quickly and efficiently.

The primary mission of the user interface is to offer better assertion-ignoring capabilities. For example, with the *DefaultTraceListener*, if you had a misplaced assertion that triggered every time through a loop counting to 1,000, you'd see 1,000 message boxes, which would drive you to distraction. With SUPERASSERT.NET, I wanted the option to mark an assertion as ignored for a specific number of times it's triggered. Additionally, I wanted to be able to completely disable a particular assertion for the remainder of the application's instance. Finally, I wanted to be able to turn off all assertions at any time.

As you'll see when I start talking about Son of Strike (SOS) and WinDBG in Chapter 6, "WinDBG, SOS, and ADPlus," minidump files of your application are critical to solving the toughest problems. By getting that snapshot of all the memory currently in use, you can start looking at the tough problems, such as why a particular object is in Generation 2 and who's referencing it. When it comes to .NET assertions, you need that ability to write the minidump file to be able to look at the state of the application after the fact, so I wanted to include that functionality in SUPERASSERT.NET.

I had two requirements under "getting the information out of an assertion." The first was the ability to copy all the data in the assertion dialog box onto the clipboard. Because SUPER-ASSERT.NET shows much more data than *DefaultTraceListener*, I wanted to be able to get all that data to the clipboard. Because I'm talking about the clipboard, I'll toss in here one of my favorite undocumented tricks in Windows: In any application that calls the standard Windows message box, you can press CTRL+C to copy the entire contents to the clipboard, title, text, and even button text. This isn't a screenshot, but the text values of everything in the message box. I have no idea why Microsoft has never documented this wonderful message box shortcut.

The second informational requirement is to be able to e-mail the assertion to the developer. This is especially important in testing environments so the tester can get as much information to the developer as quickly as possible. While some of you might be shuddering in horror right now, I assure you that this is an extremely valuable feature. If you're getting the same assertion messages in your inbox repeatedly, that's a very good sign that you need to look at why this particular assertion is popping up all the time.

Although Visual Studio is an outstanding debugger, there are times when you need to look at a process with SOS and WinDBG, or its close cousin, the console-based CDB. With *Default-TraceListener* supporting only managed debugger attaching, I wanted the option to get more debuggers on the process. Additionally, I wanted WinDBG and CDB to have SOS loaded and ready to rock when they attached.

The final two features are the big ones. I wanted SUPERASSERT.NET to run perfectly on all operating systems and CPUs that .NET supports. That means handling 32-bit and 64-bit versions in addition to the specific CPU differences. The last requirement sounds simple, but in practice, is extremely difficult: I want to be able to see call stacks from all the threads in the application in addition to all the parameters and local variables.

If you look carefully at Figure 3-1, which shows the *DefaultTraceListener* message box, it's wonderful that you get to see the call stack, but do you see anything that shows the parameter or local values? There's no way to get those values, because if you could, you would break all the security in .NET. For example, if your code is used in a secure context and you can crawl up the stack to look at local variables, you could steal secrets. The same goes for looking at the call stacks of other managed threads in your application. Even though you can get the *Process* class instance that represents your process and can even enumerate the threads as *ProcessThreads*, there's no way to get at the call stack.

However, when you're debugging, all the information that the great .NET security hides from you is exactly what you need to see. I wanted my code to get that information because the more you can see in an assertion, the less need you'll have for the debugger to do, thus your work will get done faster. Of course, working around the .NET security to show the good stuff is something you'll want to have enabled only in the development shop—not for the customer. Finally, I felt that without the ability to see the other stacks and all their variables, there was no way I was going to be able to call my assertion SUPERASSERT.NET. I know you're dying to see the implementation details to see if I was able to fulfill all the requirements, but I need to show you how to use SUPERASSERT.NET first.

Using SUPERASSERT.NET

SUPERASSERT.NET is composed of three assemblies that you'll need to incorporate with your application: Caudal.Windows.Forms.dll, Wintellect.Diagnostics.dll, and Wintellect.Utility.dll. Three other applications, DiagnosticHelper-AMD64.exe, DiagnosticHelper-i386.exe, and DiagnosticHelper-IA64. exe, must be in the path on the machine. If you want to e-mail assertions through Microsoft Office Outlook, you'll also need to include Wintellect.Diagnostics.Mail. Outlook.dll. Note that Wintellect.Diagnostics.Mail.Outlook.dll is not built by default because it relies on the Office Primary Interop Assemblies (PIA) and there's no way for me to know which version of Office is on your computer. You can find the main binaries in the .\Debug or .\Release directories in the directory where you installed the book's source code. In the implementation section, I'll describe what each of the assemblies does.

With any development tool, there's always the implied requirement that the tool be easy to use. To accomplish that, I derived the *SuperAssertTraceListener* class in Wintellect.Diagnostics.dll directly from the *DefaultTraceListener* class, so all the same rules about adding and loading *TraceListener* classes through code or configuration files apply just the same. Because it's derived from *DefaultTraceListener*, SUPERASSERT.NET properly pays attention to the *assert* element's *assertuienabled* attribute in App.Config or Machine.Config and won't pop up if you don't want it to.

Once you have SUPERASSERT.NET integrated into your application, and you encounter an assertion, you'll see the dialog box in Figure 3-2. The text box control at the top of the window shows the message and detailed message parameters you passed to *Debug.Assert*. You also see the module, source, and line where the assertion occurred. So far, it's the same information you'd see in the standard *DefaultTraceListener*.

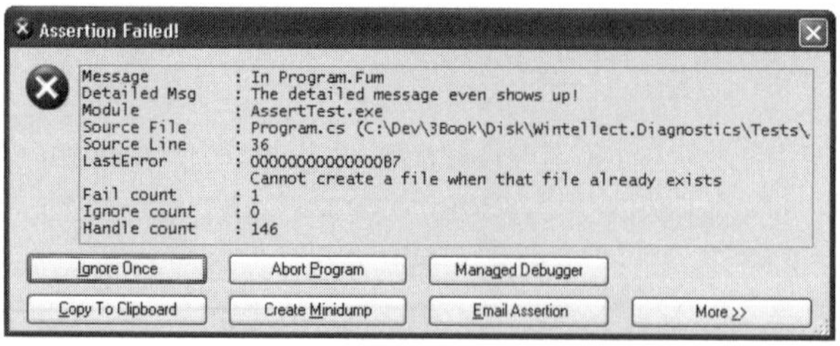

Figure 3-2   SUPERASSERT.NET's main dialog box

The LastError value shows you the last native Windows error as reported by *GetLastError*, which can be helpful, especially if you're doing lots of interop. Note that the value displayed here might not have anything to do with the assertion you're seeing. My code saves off the last error value as soon as it's called. However, the last error value could have been changed by a previous *TraceListener* in the *Listeners* collection.

After the last error value comes the number of times this particular *Debug.Assert* failed. The penultimate value is the number of times this particular assertion has been ignored. The last value in the edit control is the number of native Windows handles your process currently has open. Leaking handles is a huge problem in both native and managed code. So seeing the total number of handles can, in fact, help you detect potential problems.

I'm sure that you can guess what the Ignore Once button does for the current assertion. The Abort Program button is a true death button, as it will call the *GetCurrentProcess().Kill()* method to rip the process completely out of memory. To save accidental clicks on this button, you'll always be prompted to ensure that this is what you want to do.

The Managed Debugger button triggers the managed debugger. If you are debugging the process, it will call *Debugger.Break* to stop in the debugger. If there is no debugger present, SUPERASSERT.NET will call *Debugger.Launch* to start the Just-In-Time debugger process so that you can choose the debugger to use. As you would expect, you need to have sufficient operating system privileges to debug the process.

The Copy To Clipboard button does exactly what you'd expect and copies all the text values in the dialog box to the clipboard. The Create Minidump button brings up the standard file Save dialog box in which you can specify the name of the minidump file you want to write. If you look at the code, you'll see that I had to do the interop to call the native Windows *GetSave-FileName* function in order to show the Save dialog box. The reason is that the standard .NET *SaveFileDialog* class uses COM, so it's not safe to use without an Single Threaded Apartment (STA) main thread, which is an onerous requirement just to use an assertion.

The minidump files that I created are the appropriate full-memory minidump files, which means that you can fully use SOS on them and really see what's going on in your application. That also means that minidump files can get huge. For the simple test program, I created full-memory minidump files on Windows XP Professional x64 Edition that were 421 MB!

The Email Assertion button allows you to e-mail the assertion to a developer. By default, the To e-mail address will be blank, but a very small change to your code can make it easier for the user. The *CodeOwner* attribute from the *Wintellect.Diagnostics* namespace in Wintellect. Diagnostics.dll allows you to specify the e-mail address. Add it to your classes, as shown in the following snippet:

```
[CodeOwner ( "Assertion Report" , "assertreport@mycompany.com" )]
class Program
...
```

SUPERASSERT.NET will look up the stack of the assertion for the first class with the *Code-Owner* attribute and use that e-mail address as the To field for the message. When using the *CodeOwner* attribute, you probably don't want to include an actual developer name as that address because your binary has the address embedded in it. You'll want to set up a separate account for receiving all assertions or use conditional compilation so that the *CodeOwner* attribute appears only in debug builds.

As I mentioned earlier, if you include the Wintellect.Diagnostics.Mail.Outlook.dll with the code, you could also use Office Outlook to send the message. To choose the e-mail program to use, in the SUPERASSERT.NET dialog box, select Options from the System menu, which you access by clicking the icon in the dialog box's caption bar. On the Mail tab, select the e-mail program to use.

Figure 3-3 shows the Options dialog box. As you can see in the dialog box, there are other tabs to set such as the path to CDB.exe, stack walking options, and other options, such as if you want SUPERASSERT.NET to play a sound when it pops up on the screen. Any settings are stored for the user in the appropriate *%SystemDrive%*\Documents and Settings*user_name*\Local Settings\Application Data\Wintellect\SUPERASSERT.NET*version* directory. This allows settings that are global for the current Windows user.

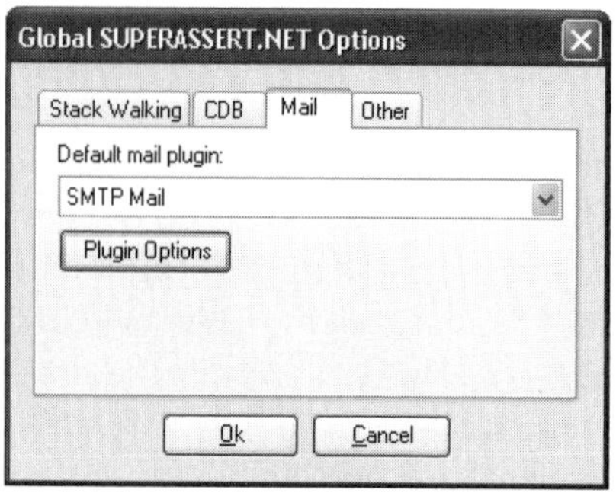

Figure 3-3   SUPERASSERT.NET Options dialog box

If you've chosen to use the SMTP mail option, SUPERASSERT.NET will assume initially that the appropriate settings are in the App.Config/Web.Config as described in the *SmtpClient* class. You can change the SMTP settings in the Options dialog box by selecting SMTP Mail as the Default mail plugin and clicking the Plugin Options button. You can also set the same settings when sending a message.

If you've chosen Office Outlook to send the messages, things are a little more annoying because the only way to access Office Outlook across all operating systems is through COM. That means that you'll get all the scary dialog boxes about an application accessing your e-mail and have to navigate the timeout dialog boxes. It's enough to make you want to find a virus writer and smack him silly. I strongly suggest that you always use the SMTP e-mail, but depending on how draconian your network administrators are, getting SMTP e-mail set up in your environment may be very difficult. If you can't set it up, you can always use Google's Gmail because it is free and fully supports SMTP sending. It's what I used to test the SUPER-ASSERT.NET code.

Once you click the Email Assertion button, you'll see the dialog box in Figure 3-4, which is the simple e-mail dialog box in which you can type in additional data about the bug. If the user enters her own SMTP settings, she will be prompted for a password when sending messages. No password is stored in any of the SUPERASSERT.NET settings.

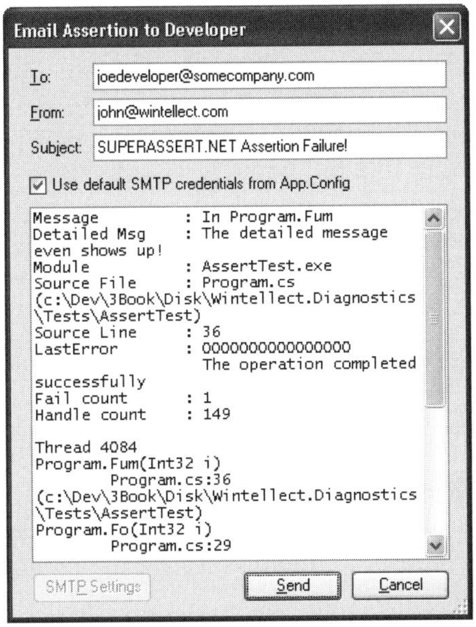

Figure 3-4   Sending the assertion by e-mail

The More button in the SUPERASSERT.NET dialog box is where the excitement is. Because I don't do much UI programming, I expect you to oooh and aaah every time you click it. The expanded SUPERASSERT.NET dialog box, shown in Figure 3-5, has all sorts of interesting information in it. The Ignore group contains advanced options for disabling specific assertions or even all assertions and should be used with care. Make sure to read the section "A Word About Ignoring Assertions" later in this chapter.

The Native Debuggers for SOS section allows you to choose which debugger you want to spawn to look at the process with SOS. When you start one of the native debuggers, SUPER-ASSERT.NET automatically loads SOS in the native debugger, so you're all set to start exploring to your heart's content. When you are finished poking at the process, use the *qd* command to detach and quit the debugger to return to the asserting process.

Looking at the dialog box in Figure 3-5, you can see that the stack walk shown looks identical to what you'd see in regular *DefaultTraceListener*, and you're wondering what the excitement is all about. The magic begins when you click the Walk Stacks button. The edit control that contained the stack turns into a tree control, and as you start clicking the plus signs, or right-clicking and selecting Expand All, a big smile will appear on your face. I almost didn't include a screen shot here because the effect the first time you see it is quite amazing! Since a picture is worth a thousand words, I need to include one so I can explain what's going on.

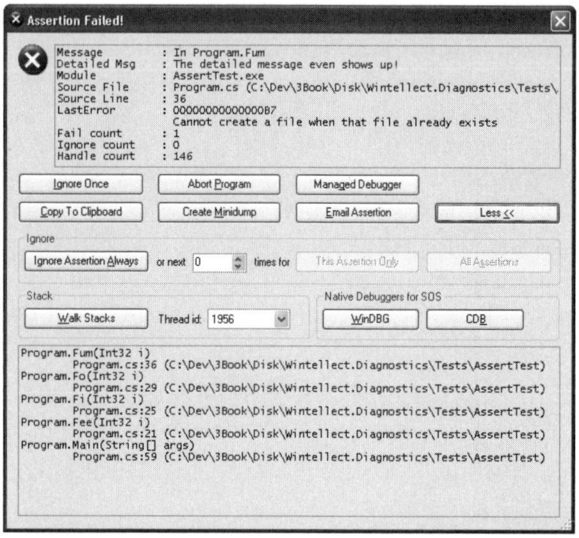

Figure 3-5   The expanded SUPERASSERT.NET dialog box

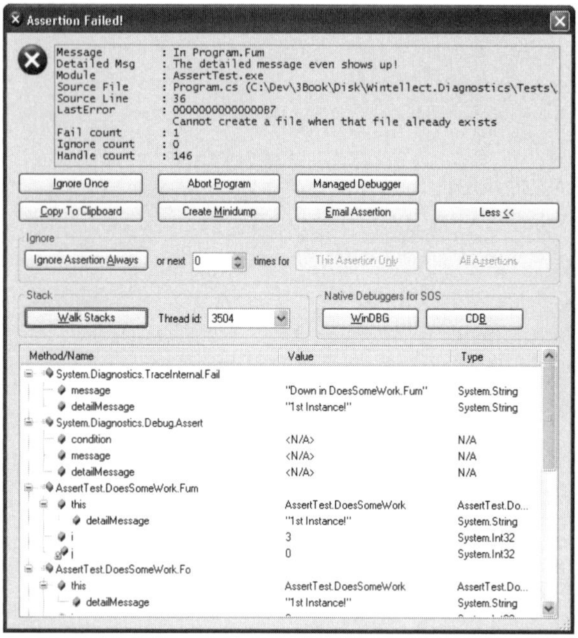

Figure 3-6   The amazing SUPERASSERT.NET!

What you're seeing in the tree control are all the methods on the stack, their parameters, and their locals, and you have the ability to expand objects to show all the field values. The blue icons with the lock next to them denote local variables. What I can't show in the book text is clicking the Thread id combo box and showing you that you'd be looking at the call stacks with full detail for any other managed thread in your application. Of course, if you do show the cool stack display, all the call stack data is copied to the clipboard and any e-mail messages you send from SUPERASSERT.NET, just as you would expect.

The object expansion defaults to a single level, so you'll see parameter and local object fields. If you need to drill down more, go into the SUPERASSERT.NET Option dialog box, and on the Stack Walking tab, set the Stack variable expansion up-down control to the level you want. You can also elect to have arrays expanded in the display. After changing the values and closing the dialog box, click Walk Stacks again in the main dialog box to see the changed expansion. Because SUPERASSERT.NET has to gather all the thread detail at once, you'll want to be careful about expanding too far because you'll use a ton of memory and it will take quite a while to generate the data.

Console and Windows Forms applications in addition to any ASP.NET applications running under the development Web server will now have all the glory of SUPERASSERT.NET to help keep you out of the debugger more than ever. Of course, things are a little different if you're running an ASP.NET application under Internet Information Services (IIS). The rules are different there, and there's no clean way to show Windows Forms or spawn applications because both would potentially open security holes. Consequently, SUPERASSERT.NET degrades gracefully by falling back to the *DefaultTraceListener* to generate the output. It's not ideal, but it's better than changing the account IIS runs under and having it interact with the desktop. If you are going to those extremes, that's exactly what the development Web server is all about.

A Word About Ignoring Assertions

It's always a bad moment when another developer or tester drags you over to his machine to blame your code for a crash. It's even worse when you start diagnosing the problem by asking him if he clicked the Ignore button on an assertion that popped up. Many times he'll swear to you that he didn't, but you know that there's no way that crash could have occurred without a particular assertion trigger. When you finally pin him down and force him to admit that he did click that Ignore button, you're on the verge of ripping his head off. If he had reported that assertion, you could have easily solved the problem!

The Ignore button, if you haven't already guessed, is a potentially very dangerous option because people are so tempted to click it! Although it might have been a little draconian, I seriously considered not putting an Ignore button on *SUPERASSERT.NET* to force users to deal with the assertion and its underlying cause. I specifically added the ignore count to the upper text box to ensure an easy way to check whether a specific assertion has been ignored. This allows you to see at a glance if the Ignore button has been clicked before wasting your time looking at the crash.

What you might want to consider adding to the *Debug.Listeners* collection is a second listener, such as the *FixedTextWriterTraceListener*, so you have complete logging of all assertions that are triggered. That way you'd automatically have a running total of the number of Ignore values clicked by users, allowing you to validate the user actions that led to the crash. Some companies automatically log assertions to a central database so that they can keep track of assertion frequencies and determine whether developers and testers are improperly using the Ignore button.

Since I've talked about protecting yourself against the user's reflex reaction of clicking the Ignore button, it's only fair that I mention that you might be doing it, too. Assertions should never pop up in normal operation–only when something is amiss. Here's a perfect example of an improperly used assertion that I encountered while helping debug an application. When I chose an item on the most recently used menu that didn't have a target item, an assertion fired before the normal error handling. In such a case, the normal error handling was more than sufficient. If you're getting complaints that assertions are firing too much, you need to carefully analyze whether those assertions really need to be there.

Debugging War Story
Assertions Save the Day!

The Battle

A friend of mine related the following story: Our current Service Oriented Architecture sets up a bank of Web services, which provide the business services to our client-side applications. The first of these was a Windows Forms application performing a wide variety of user operations using all of the different areas of the services provided. Like many projects, it started out small with a proof of concept and as a result used a workstation on my desk as the development server. The development team would all refresh the references from this server each time the code set changed.

As the project grew, more developers came online and more servers were added to create the different levels of testing environments we needed. This meant that a sturdier beast replaced the original development server. The different server configurations were handled with changes to the configuration file, which was updated by the installer to ensure that the correct servers were being used for the correct environment, and the original development server became my test deployment server.

The Web services were grouped so that the application required five different Web references, all of which had to point at the correct server or server cluster for the correct environment.

Our release cycles are fairly rigid, and therefore, when something reaches the final stages of testing, there's not much that can be done—the cycle faces a series of go/nogo decisions, but no fixes are applied because the testing processes would need to be restarted. As our application went into its last phase of testing, I was scheduled to move to a different desk, so I powered down all of my machines.

The Outcome

A few minutes after turning off all my computers, we got a frantic call from the preproduction test environment team because all of the tests had started failing with strange timeout messages saying that some services were not responding. Oddly, all of the servers running the Web services seemed to be fine, processing messages and with almost no resource utilization.

After a lot of head scratching and some network tracing, we finally figured out that for some reason, one of the sets of Web services was routing back to the original development server, the same one that was now turned off ready to be moved. After a quick hunt through the code, we finally discovered that one of the Web references had not been set to dynamic because of a file being read-only when the Web reference was refreshed. As a result, the Web reference had always been routing through the server on my desk. Because I had always kept the code up to date and the Web reference was to some services that were not heavily used, no one had ever noticed that the application routed through my workstation—we were all convinced it would have gone live if it weren't for a desk move!

The Lesson

At around the same time as this, I was having difficulty conveying to the development team why assertions are so important. When we almost deployed a major business application running on one of my desktops, we modified the code to include an assertion checking the Web reference URL against the config file to see if we had mistakenly configured it to be static. Suddenly, the whole team understood why assertions are so important, and this helped justify usage of assertions tremendously.

SUPERASSERT.NET Implementation

I do have to admit that I had a great time developing SUPERASSERT.NET. In the end, I wrote four different versions of the core code to achieve the results. While I was able to achieve my ultimate goal, I also learned a good bit of .NET along the way. Most of the assertion code is in the Wintellect.Diagnostics.dll assembly, so you might want to open that project to follow along as I describe some of the initial interesting highlights.

As I mentioned, SUPERASSERT.NET starts out as a *TraceListener*, *SuperAssertTraceListener*, derived from *DefaultTraceListener*. All of the work takes place in the overridden *Fail* method. The first challenge I had to tackle was trying to figure out how to uniquely identify the spot where the assertion occurred so I could keep track of the assertion count. Because the *Stack-Trace* class always returns a stack starting at the location where it's created, I had to walk the frames back to the point before the call to *Debug.Assert* so I would not be showing a call stack starting inside *SuperAssertTraceListener*. Realizing that I now had the location where the call occurred, I could use the *StackFrame* class for that location to build up a unique key because it has the class, method, and module name, along with the IL offset into the module making the call to *Debug.Assert*. That meant that I could just toss all the assertions I saw into a hash table so I could keep track of the number of times triggered, and I could ignore counts easily.

If the assertion is not ignored, the next challenge in *SuperAssertTraceListener.Fail* is to figure out if it's safe to show the assertion dialog. Because I wanted to respect the *DefaultTraceListener assertuienabled* attribute, I started looking at how I was going to read App.Config and Machine.Config to determine if they were set. It was looking as if it were going to be quite hard to do the configuration parsing because the configuration classes provided by the Framework Class Library (FCL) were returning an internal-only class, *SystemDiagnosticsSection*, which was causing all sorts of *InvalidCastExceptions* when I'd try to access it. Thinking I was going to have to do my own XML parsing, I was getting a little desperate when I saw the *DefaultTraceListener. AssertUiEnabled* property, which does all the work I needed. There's nothing like trying to completely reinvent the wheel.

Checking if the user interface is enabled is only the first check I needed to make before I could bring up the dialog box. In order to play well in a limited-rights settings, I demand unrestricted *UIPermission* rights. The *DefaultTraceListener* does not need full rights, but my dialog box is doing much more than a message box, so I need full *UIPermission* to have any hope of it to work. If the configuration settings are for no user interface or there are insufficient rights to show a full user interface, I'll call the *DefaultTraceListener.WriteLine* method to at least log that an assertion occurred. See the *SuperAssertTraceListener.UiPermission* property for how I demand the appropriate permissions.

The final check is the usual *SystemInformation.UserInteractive* to see if the process is running in user interactive mode. *Form.ShowDialog* makes the same check and will throw an *InvalidOperation-Exception* if you call it without checking first. If I can't show my dialog box in this case, I'll try calling the *DefaultTraceListener.Fail* method because it will just show a message box and, as I explained earlier, you'll at least see that with ASP.NET under IIS.

If you are familiar with my native SUPERASSERT, you know that it has a very cool feature that would suspend all the other threads in the application other than the one with the assertion. This allowed the assertion to have as minimal an impact on the application as possible. In showing the new SUPERASSERT.NET to numerous developers, they asked if I kept that excellent feature. If you think about it for a moment, that would be a very bad idea in the .NET world. What's one of the most important threads in .NET? The garbage collector thread! Because SUPERASSERT.NET uses .NET, I'd end up deadlocking or terminating the process if I suspended all other threads, which would not make my assertion very useful.

The assertion dialog box itself, which is in AssertDialog.cs, is derived from *Wintellect.Utility.System-MenuForm,* which allows me to easily add the Options and Center on Screen commands to the system menu. If you're interested in how to make your own folding dialog boxes, you can search for the Folding/Unfolding Handling region, which shows how it's done.

There are only two key items about the user interface I wanted to point out. The first is that clicking the Abort Program button calls *Process.GetCurrentProcess ( ).Kill ( )*, which is identical to calling the *TerminateProcess* API. I originally started to call the .NET *Application.Exit* method, but looking at what it does with Lutz Roeder's Reflector (*http://www.aisto.com/roeder /dotnet/*), it is a little too kind in how it asks the windows and threads in your application to shut down. Because an assertion is indicating that you have a bad state, I felt that it was safer to have this button do the death kill to avoid partial transactions or race conditions.

The last interesting thing in the user interface was getting the clipboard to always work. Like the *OpenFileDialog*, the *ClipBoard* class in .NET relies on COM to do some of its work. While we would all love for COM to finally die the hard death it deserves, we're stuck with it and its nasty Single Threaded Apartment (STA) model. In order for it to work, the clipboard code requires that your thread be marked with the *STAThreadAttribute*. I wanted to solve this because that is an onerous requirement and because copying the assertion data is so important.

I was all set to do the interop work to directly call the Windows clipboard API functions when I ran across a cool trick from Jeff Atwood (*http://www.codinghorror.com/blog/archives /000429.html*): spawn your own thread, set its state to STA, and do the clipboard operation in that thread. I wrapped up Jeff's idea in the *Wintellect.Utility.SmartClipboard* class so you could reuse it.

The first major hurdle I wanted to tackle was getting a minidump file of the process written. It's simple enough to make a call to *MiniDumpWriteDump*, the Windows API that does all the work, but that minidump file won't be readable by any debugger. The problem is that the API is designed for writing dumps of other processes, not for being called from your own process. In the native version of SUPERASSERT, I used inline assembly language to simulate making the call to *MiniDumpWriteDump* and allow you to write a perfect minidump file from inside your own process.

Even though there's no inline IL in .NET applications, which is a scary thought all on its own, I figured there had to be a way I could do some Ninja hacking and get *MiniDumpWriteDump* working inside the process. Alas, no amount of sneaking around the code in a black suit worked. I tried everything to get this working inside the process with just .NET code. The only way I was able to write a minidump file from inside the process was to write a native C++ DLL that mimicked the way I had done the writing in the native version of SUPERASSERT. Given the fact that I was then going to have to support three separate DLLs, one for each CPU type .NET runs on, that was going to be a mess to manage.

However, I could get good minidump files from *MiniDumpWriteDump* when using it to write dumps of other processes. That meant that to keep the code all .NET, I was going to have to write a process that my assertion would spawn. The assertion code would pass on its process ID or name on the command line to this other program to tell it what to dump, which is basically the same thing as writing the dump from inside my own process. Although it's not exactly how I wanted the code to be, the DiagnosticHelper executables achieves the desired result of a minidump file that SOS can process.

The big feature of course, is getting all the thread's call stacks and variables. As you can guess, that one was the hardest to get working. At the initial glance, I thought it might be relatively easy because I'd noticed in the .NET Framework 2.0 documentation that the *StackTrace* class has a new constructor that takes a *Thread* object. The idea is that you can pass in any *Thread* object and get that thread's stack. That gave me some hope of enumerating the threads from inside the application and getting their corresponding *Thread* objects.

You may have noticed that the *Process.Threads* property is a *ProcessThreadCollection* that contains the *ProcessThread* objects for all the native threads in the process. Thinking that there might be a way to convert those *ProcessThread* objects into the equivalent *Thread* object, I spent some serious quality time with the compiler and Reflector trying and looking at ideas. Alas, there's absolutely no way to get the list of *Thread* objects that I could in turn pass to *StackTrace*. Even if I could, that would still not achieve the goal of getting the locals and parameters.

What I really wanted was a way that I could work around the whole security system in .NET so I could get those locals and parameters. Although the security protections are a great feature of .NET, they can sometimes get in the way of fun tools. If given enough time, I probably could find some way to wander the stack and extract the locals, but I certainly wouldn't be doing it from straight .NET code. That meant that I had to do some serious thinking and look at the big picture.

As we all know, a debugger can see everything inside a process. My thinking was that there was nothing stopping me from spawning off a debugger on myself. That would definitely work and get me the information that I wanted to present. Because I already had the dialog box set up to spawn off CDB, I couldn't see any reason why I couldn't tell CDB to load SOS and gather all the data for me.

When I presented the first version of SUPERASSERT.NET in my Bugslayer column, that's exactly what I did. I created a temporary file with the commands to execute and passed that on the CDB command line. Those commands loaded SOS, opened up a logging file I specified, and ran the SOS *!clrstack* command to perform the magic. The bad news was that the *!clrstack* command is essentially broken and doesn't always return the parameters and locals correctly. The other problem with this approach is that you're required to install the Debugging Tools for Windows on every machine to have access to CDB.

To get what I wanted, I turned next to the CLR Debugging API, which you can read about at *http://msdn2.microsoft.com/en-us/library/ms404520(VS.80).aspx*. This certainly looked like the way to go, but with approximately 102 COM interfaces, I certainly wasn't looking forward to grinding through writing a native C++ EXE to be a debugger. Just as I was starting to sketch out exactly what I was going to have to do, the CLR Debugging Team handed all of us a major present: the CLR Managed Debugger Sample, also known as *MDBG*. You can download MDBG at *http://www.microsoft.com/downloads/details.aspx?familyid=38449a42-6b7a-4e28-80ce-c55645ab1310&displaylang=en*.

As part of their internal testing of the debugging APIs, the CLR Debugging Team had written a test system completely in .NET that wrapped the entire COM-based API. This eventually evolved into MDBG, and they released it as source code so others could write debugging tools without grinding through the mind-numbing COM interfaces. The CLR Debugging Team did a major service to the community by releasing this code and certainly made my life a heck of a lot easier! This meant that I could do a complete .NET solution for the debugger portion.

From a high level, the idea is to spawn the debugger and have it attach back to the process with the assertion. Once attached, it will open up a file where it can write data. The debugger will enumerate the threads and walk the stack for each thread. In each stack frame, it will dump the parameters and locals. The code I wrote turns out to be almost as easy as that description.

Listing 3-2 shows the .\DiagnosticHelper\StackWriter.cs file that does the work to do all the CLR debugger work and stack writing. As you can see, most of the code is concerned with writing out the XML file. If the code looks a bit familiar, that's because it's based on a blog entry by Mike Stall, *http://blogs.gotdotnet.com/jmstall/archive/2005/11/28/snapshot.aspx.* Mike is a developer on the CLR Debugging Team, and you definitely need to subscribe to his blog because there are all sorts of interesting tips about debugging and using the CLR Debugging API.

Listing 3-2   StackWriter.cs

```
/*----------------------------------------------------------------------------
 * Debugging Microsoft .NET 2.0 Applications
 * Copyright © 1997-2006 John Robbins -- All rights reserved.
 ----------------------------------------------------------------------------*/
using System;
using System.Diagnostics;
using System.Collections.Generic;
using System.Text;
using System.IO;
using System.Xml;
using System.Globalization;
using Microsoft.Samples.Debugging.MdbgEngine;
using System.Reflection;


namespace DiagnosticHelper
{
    /// <summary>
    /// The class that will walk the stack of a specific process and write the
    /// output to an XML file.
    /// </summary>
    internal class StackWriter
    {
        // The process Id we're to work on.
        private Int32 processId;
        // The XML output filename.
        private String fileName;
        // The number of levels to expand objects.
        private Int32 levels;
        // The flag that if true has this class show locals even if source is
        // not available.
        private Boolean noSymLocals;
        // Flag to indicate if arrays are supposed to be expanded also.
        private Boolean showArrays;

        /// <summary>
        /// Initializes a new instance of the <see cref="StackWriter"/> class.
```

```
/// </summary>
/// <param name="processId">
/// The process id to dump the stack on.
/// </param>
/// <param name="fileName">
/// The name of the output file to write.
/// </param>
/// <param name="levels">
/// How many levels deep to display object fields.
/// </param>
/// <param name="noSymLocals">
/// If set to <c>true</c> will show locals for methods that don't have
/// source.
/// </param>
/// <param name="showArrays">
/// if set to <c>true</c> expands array values.
/// </param>
public StackWriter ( Int32 processId ,
                     String fileName ,
                     Int32 levels ,
                     Boolean noSymLocals ,
                     Boolean showArrays )
{
    // Check the parameters.
    Debug.Assert ( 0 != processId , "0 != processId" );
    if ( 0 == processId )
    {
        throw new ArgumentException ( Constants.InvalidParameter ,
                                      "processId" );
    }
    Debug.Assert ( false == String.IsNullOrEmpty ( fileName ) ,
                   "false == String.IsNullOrEmpty ( fileName )" );
    if ( true == String.IsNullOrEmpty ( fileName ) )
    {
        throw new ArgumentException ( Constants.InvalidParameter ,
                                      "fileName" );
    }
    this.processId = processId;
    this.fileName = fileName;
    this.levels = levels;
    this.noSymLocals = noSymLocals;
    this.showArrays = showArrays;
    errorMessage = String.Empty;
}

private String errorMessage;
/// <summary>
/// Gets the error message for error returns.
/// </summary>
/// <value>
/// The error message.
/// </value>
public String ErrorMessage
{
    get { return ( errorMessage ); }
}
```

```
// The XmlWriter used everywhere.
private XmlWriter xw;
// The process name we're snapping.  This is set in the
// IsDotNetInProcess method.
private String processName;
// The process we'll be debugging.
private MDbgProcess proc;

/// <summary>
/// Does the work to walk the stack and write to a file.
/// </summary>
/// <returns>
/// One of the <see cref="ReturnCodes"/> enumerations.
/// </returns>
public Int32 Execute ( )
{
    // The value we'll be eventually returning.
    Int32 retValue = (Int32)ReturnCodes.ERROR_SUCCESS;

    // Before we get too far into the code, let's see if .NET is in the
    // process.  If not, jump out immediately.
    if ( false == IsDotNetInProcess ( ) )
    {
        errorMessage = Constants.DotNetNotInProcess;
        return ( (Int32)ReturnCodes.ERROR_NO_DOTNET_IN_PROCESS );
    }

    try
    {
        // Create us a debugger!
        MDbgEngine debugger = new MDbgEngine ( );

        // Create the XML file.
        xw = XmlWriter.Create ( fileName );
        try
        {
            // Do the attach.
            proc = debugger.Attach ( processId );
            // Drain all events until we have completed the attach.
            DrainAttachEvents ( debugger , proc );

            // Start with ye olde process.
            xw.WriteStartElement ( "process" ,
    "http://schemas.wintellect.com/diagnostics/SuperAssertStackDump" );
            // Poke on a few attributes.
            WriteProcessElementAttributes ( );
            // Hu Ra!  Let's go!
            DumpAllThreads ( );

        }
        finally
        {
            // Make sure to always detach or the process is dead.
            if ( null != proc )
            {
```

```
                        proc.Detach ( ).WaitOne ( );
                }
                // Close off the XML files.
                if ( null != xw )
                {
                    xw.WriteEndDocument ( );
                    xw.Flush ( );
                    xw.Close ( );
                }
            }
        }
        // Means we weren't able to write the XML file.
        catch ( UnauthorizedAccessException ex )
        {
            retValue = (Int32)ReturnCodes.E_ACCESSDENIED;
            errorMessage = ex.Message;
        }
        return ( retValue );
    }

    private void DumpAllThreads ( )
    {
        // Grab all the threads.
        MDbgThreadCollection tc = proc.Threads;
        foreach ( MDbgThread t in tc )
        {
            // Write out the thread only if there's actually something on
            // the stack.
            if ( true == t.HaveCurrentFrame )
            {
                try
                {
                    xw.WriteStartElement ( "thread" );
                    xw.WriteAttributeString ( "tid" ,
                        t.Id.ToString ( CultureInfo.InvariantCulture ) );

                    xw.WriteStartElement ( "callstack" );
                    foreach ( MDbgFrame f in t.Frames )
                    {
                        DumpFrame ( f );
                    }
                }
                finally
                {
                    // Finish off call stack.
                    xw.WriteEndElement ( );
                    // Finish off thread.
                    xw.WriteEndElement ( );
                }
            }
        }
    }

    private void DumpFrame ( MDbgFrame f )
    {
```

```
        // Skip the managed/native transitions stuff.
        if ( false == f.IsInfoOnly )
        {
            try
            {
                xw.WriteStartElement ( "frame" );
                WriteFrameElementAttributes ( f );

                // Let's start with the arguments.
                try
                {
                    xw.WriteStartElement ( "arguments" );
                    foreach ( MDbgValue v in f.Function.GetArguments ( f ) )
                    {
                        DumpValue ( v );
                    }
                }
                finally
                {
                    // Close of <arguments>.
                    xw.WriteEndElement ( );
                }
                // Party on the locals.
                try
                {
                    xw.WriteStartElement ( "locals" );
                    // Write out only the actual values if there's source
                    // or the user is telling me to do it anyway.
                    if ( ( null != f.SourcePosition ) ||
                         ( true == noSymLocals ) )
                    {
                        foreach ( MDbgValue v in
                                    f.Function.GetActiveLocalVars ( f ) )
                        {
                            DumpValue ( v );
                        }
                    }
                }
                finally
                {
                    xw.WriteEndElement ( );
                }

            }
            finally
            {
                // Close off <frame>.
                xw.WriteEndElement ( );
            }
        }
}

private void DumpValue ( MDbgValue v )
{
    DumpValueWorker ( v , levels );
}
```

```
private void DumpValueWorker ( MDbgValue v , Int32 depth )
{
    // Take a quick look at the name.  If it's one of those auto created
    // things, skip it.
    if ( true == IsCompilerCreatedVariable ( v.Name ) )
    {
        return;
    }

    try
    {
        xw.WriteStartElement ( "value" );
        xw.WriteAttributeString ( "name" , v.Name );
        xw.WriteAttributeString ( "type" , v.TypeName );
        // Always show the value for the item.
        String val = v.GetStringValue ( 0 , true );
        // Special case empty values coming from GetStringValue.
        if ( val == "'\0'" )
        {
            val = "\\0";
        }
        xw.WriteAttributeString ( "val" , val );

        // Is it recursion time!?
        if ( depth >= 1 )
        {
            // Dump sub items.
            if ( true == v.IsComplexType )
            {
                MDbgValue [] fields = SafeGetFields ( v );
                if ( ( null != fields ) && ( fields.Length > 0 ) )
                {
                    try
                    {
                        xw.WriteStartElement ( "fields" );
                        foreach ( MDbgValue v2 in fields )
                        {
                            DumpValueWorker ( v2 , depth - 1 );
                        }
                    }
                    finally
                    {
                        // Close off <fields>.
                        xw.WriteEndElement ( );
                    }
                }
            }
            else if ( ( true == v.IsArrayType ) &&
                      ( true == showArrays ) )
            {
                MDbgValue [] items = v.GetArrayItems ( );
                if ( ( null != items ) && ( items.Length > 0 ) )
                {
                    try
                    {
```

```
                        xw.WriteStartElement ( "fields" );
                        foreach ( MDbgValue v2 in items )
                        {
                            DumpValueWorker ( v2 , depth - 1 );
                        }
                    }
                    finally
                    {
                        // Close off <fields>.
                        xw.WriteEndElement ( );
                    }
                }
            }
        }
    }
    finally
    {
        // Close off <value>.
        xw.WriteEndElement ( );
    }
}

// I've seen cases in Visual Basic apps where calling GetFields has
// NullReferenceException problems.
private static MDbgValue [] SafeGetFields ( MDbgValue v )
{
    MDbgValue [] fields;
    try
    {
        fields = v.GetFields ( );
    }
    catch ( NullReferenceException )
    {
        fields = null;
    }
    return ( fields );
}

private static Boolean IsCompilerCreatedVariable ( String name )
{
    return ( name.StartsWith ( "CS$" ,
                      StringComparison.InvariantCultureIgnoreCase ) );
}

private void WriteFrameElementAttributes ( MDbgFrame f )
{
    String func = f.Function.FullName;
    String moduleName = f.Function.Module.CorModule.Name;
    xw.WriteAttributeString ( "function" , func );
    xw.WriteAttributeString ( "module" , moduleName );

    if ( null != f.SourcePosition )
    {
        String source = f.SourcePosition.Path;
        String line = f.SourcePosition.Line.ToString (
                                    CultureInfo.InvariantCulture );
```

```
        xw.WriteAttributeString ( "source" , source );
        xw.WriteAttributeString ( "line" , line );
    }
}

private void WriteProcessElementAttributes ( )
{
    // We'll add a few attributes for each identification.
    xw.WriteAttributeString ( "name" , processName );
    xw.WriteAttributeString ( "timestamp" ,
            DateTime.Now.ToString ( CultureInfo.InvariantCulture ) );
}

// The MDBG API does the right thing when you attach to a process that
// doesn't have .NET loaded, it waits until .NET shows up.
// Unfortunately, for a stack-n-go app like this, that's not an ideal
// situation. I'll cheat a bit and look to see if MSCORWKS.DLL is
// loaded in the process, which means .NET is there. Note that this is
// a change from .NET 1.1 to .NET 2.0. There's only one garbage
// collector DLL, MSCORWKS.DLL for both workstation and server.
private Boolean IsDotNetInProcess ( )
{
    Process targetProc = Process.GetProcessById ( processId );
    for ( int i = 0 ; i < targetProc.Modules.Count ; i++ )
    {
        // Get the filename.
        string currModName =
                Path.GetFileName ( targetProc.Modules [ i ].ModuleName );
        // Save off the process name.
        if ( i == 0 )
        {
            processName = currModName;
        }
        // I've only got to look for MSCORWKS.DLL as that's the only
        // CLR DLL for both workstation and servers in .NET 2.0.
        if ( 0 == String.Compare ( currModName ,
                            "mscorwks.dll" ,
                        StringComparison.InvariantCultureIgnoreCase ) )
        {
            // Good enough.
            return ( true );
        }
    }
    return ( false );
}

// Once you first attach to a process, you need to drain a bunch of fake
// startup events for thread-create, module-load, etc.
// Lifted right from Mike Stall's samples.
private static void DrainAttachEvents ( MDbgEngine debugger ,
                                        MDbgProcess proc )
{
    bool fOldStatus = debugger.Options.StopOnNewThread;
    // Skip while waiting for AttachComplete
    debugger.Options.StopOnNewThread = false;
```

```
        proc.Go ( ).WaitOne ( );
        Debug.Assert ( proc.StopReason is AttachCompleteStopReason );
        if ( !( proc.StopReason is AttachCompleteStopReason ) )
        {
            throw new InvalidOperationException (
                                        Constants.InvalidDebugAttach );
        }
        // Needed for attach
        debugger.Options.StopOnNewThread = true;

        // Drain the rest of the thread create events.
        while ( proc.CorProcess.HasQueuedCallbacks ( null ) )
        {
            proc.Go ( ).WaitOne ( );
            Debug.Assert ( proc.StopReason is ThreadCreatedStopReason );
            if ( !( proc.StopReason is ThreadCreatedStopReason ) )
            {
                throw new InvalidOperationException (
                                        Constants.InvalidDebugAttach );
            }
        }
        debugger.Options.StopOnNewThread = fOldStatus;
    }
  }
}}
```

As you read Listing 3-2, you can see how trivial it actually is to attach a debugger to the process. You create an instance of *MDbgEngine* and call its *Attach* method. Right after you attach, in a regular debugger, you'd ask for notifications for all thread creates, module loads, and other interesting events, because that's the CLR Debugging API telling you what's in the process. In the case for my code, I don't care about those, so I'm going to drain all of those off events in the *DrainAttachEvents* method at the bottom of the file.

The CLR Debugging API is interesting because of the fact that if you attach to a process that has no .NET in it, the CLR Debugging API will wait in the process until the hosted runtime shows up. In my case, I want only to do the actual debugging attach if .NET is already loaded and running in the process. Consequently, before I call *Attach*, I take a quick peek to ensure that MScorwks.dll is loaded in the process. If it's not, I'll report that there's no .NET in the process. If SUPERASSERT.NET spawns the DiagnosticHelper code, .NET is there and running. However, there's nothing stopping someone from executing the DiagnosticHelper executable from a command prompt. I wanted to handle the case in which .NET wasn't loaded. The reason is that the DiagnosticHelper code will just sit there until .NET loads. If you accidentally attach to Notepad.exe, you're going to be waiting a very long time for .NET to load.

The *DumpAllThreads* and *DumpFrame* methods take care of enumerating the threads and call stacks respectively. While I could have chosen to show threads that had native code or managed-native transitions, I chose to limit the dumping to only the managed code parts. If you would like to extend SUPERASSERT.NET, it would be nice to offer the option to show all the data.

The *DumpFrame* method is also where the key work of dumping out the parameters and locals occurs. In .NET applications, you'll always have the parameter values because that information is part of the metadata in the assembly itself. The locals are part of the .pdb files, so unless they are found by the CLR Debugging API, you won't see them. The .pdb files are loaded only locally, not out of your Symbol Server, so they must be next to the binaries in the file system. I don't know about you, but it amazes me that 388 lines of code, including comments, can do that much work.

Whereas it's easy to use the CLR Debugging API, integrating it into your application is a completely different matter. Originally, I had my DiagnosticHelper executable linking against the MDBGCore.dll that shipped as part of the Framework SDK. In a meeting with the CLR Debugging Team, they pointed out two issues with that version of MDBGCore.dll. The first was that there were numerous bugs fixed in the released MDBG source code, so I'd be much better off with that version. The second was that the licensing agreement would not allow me to redistribute that DLL.

When I started linking my code against the MDBG source code versions, I found that parts of the MDBGCore.dll had been pulled out into separate DLLs, MDBGEng.dll, Corapi.dll, and Corapi2.dll. Because I didn't want to add three more DLLs to what you had to distribute, I started looking for a way to combine the code for those DLLs into the actual DiagnosticHelper executable.

My initial thought was that I could use Michael Barnett's excellent ILMerge utility (*http://research.microsoft.com/~mbarnett/ilmerge.aspx*) to combine the binaries together. ILMerge will take separate .NET assemblies and mash them together into a single assembly. The .NET 2.0 version also merges the .pdb files together so you'll have full source debugging. Initially, this approach worked, and I was very happy to have a single DiagnosticHelper.exe that took care of minidump file writing in addition to the stack walking.

Regrettably, I ran into a problem with my DiagnosticHelper.exe. I had a utility that did a ton of interop, and I recompiled it to run under .NET 2.0 so I could take advantage of the better startup performance and working set tuning. Because I didn't want to tackle the many P/Invoke declarations to ensure that it worked with 64-bit, I took the easy route and set the compiler's /platform switch to x86 to force the utility to run with the 32-bit version of the CLR when running on my x64 machine.

Being the good developer I think I am, I added SUPERASSERT.NET through the App.Config file so I could get the killer assertion dialog box. On the first assertion in my utility, I clicked the Walk Stacks button and was looking at a crash dialog box from the spawned off Diagnostic-Helper.exe. The unhandled exception follows and is wrapped for readability:

```
Unhandled Exception: System.ComponentModel.Win32Exception:
    Only part of a ReadProcessMemory or WriteProcessMemory request was completed
    at System.Diagnostics.NtProcessManager.GetModuleInfos(Int32 processId,
                                            Boolean firstModuleOnly)
    at System.Diagnostics.Process.get_Modules()
```

```
at DiagnosticHelper.StackWriter.IsDotNetInProcess() in
                C:\Dev\3Book\Disk\DiagnosticHelper\StackWriter.cs:line 343
at DiagnosticHelper.StackWriter.Execute() in
                C:\Dev\3Book\Disk\DiagnosticHelper\StackWriter.cs:line 58
at DiagnosticHelper.Program.Main(String[] args) in
                C:\Dev\3Book\Disk\DiagnosticHelper\Program.cs:line 79
```

The exception is occurring at the for loop in *IsDotNetInProcess* where I'm calling *targetProc.
Modules.Count* to get the module count. I was quite stumped when I ran the AssertTest.exe
program, which is the unit test for the whole SUPERASSERT.NET code, and was able to manually
execute the exact same DiagnosticHelper.exe and get the correct stack output. Whenever I ran
DiagnosticHelper.exe against my utility, I always had the unhandled *Win32Exception*.

That's when it dawned on me that what was happening was as I described in Chapter 2; the
default on Win64 systems is for the .NET application to run as a 64-bit binary. My 32-bit utility
was asking a 64-bit binary to walk its stack, and the CLR Debugging API does not support that.
I thought that all I would have to do is build the DiagnosticHelper.exe code, set the */platform*
switch to the three CPUs that .NET runs on, run ILMerge on each of those to jam in the three
MDBG DLLs, and I'd be set. The first run of ILMerge gave me an error stating that it did not
support merging assemblies that had different PE architectures set, so the only step left was to
bring the source code for the three MDBG DLLs I needed into DiagnosticHelper and build it
three different ways. I was already going to have three separate DiagnosticHelper-*CPU*.exe
programs, and I didn't want a total of three separate MDBG DLLs just to run ILMerge on them.

Of course, I would immediately run into a doozy of a problem bringing the code together:
Corapi2.dll is written entirely in IL. That's the DLL that has all the P/Invoke marshalling
definitions in it. I'm not sure why it's all written in IL when it could have accomplished the
same thing in C#. However, I was certainly not looking forward to the prospect of manually
converting all the IL to C# to bring it into the DiagnosticHelper project.

Fortunately, I'm a man armed with tools and wouldn't let the piddling problem of different
languages stop me. I took the compiled Corapi2.dll, loaded it into the amazing Reflector,
loaded Denis Bauer's fantastic Reflector.FileDisassembler add-in (*http://www.denisbauer.com
/NETTools/FileDisassembler.aspx*), and decompiled the IL directly to C#. I threw the output files
together into the DiagnosticHelper project along with the C# source code for MDBGEng.dll and
Corapi.dll and had everything compiling together in no time. In the .\DiagnosticHelper
directory are the three different projects that all contain the same source files but compile to
the three CPU-specific versions.

I also updated the AssertDialog.cs file, where Diagnostic-*CPU*.exe is started, to look at the
ImageFileMachine type of MScorlib.dll because that has CPU-specific code in it so it always will
reflect the type of runtime you're actually executing under. The *Wintellect.Utility.RuntimeInfo*
class does the actual work, and you can look at that code if you're curious.

The DiagnosticHelper-*CPU*.exe utility might be something you want to consider using on its
own because it can generate minidump files and call-stack XML files any time you need them.

I've found it much easier to use in ASP.NET test systems than messing with WinDBG or CDB to simply snap a minidump file. Run the CPU-specific version you need at a command prompt to look at all the options you can pass to the program to output the dumps or call stacks any way you want.

To display the cool tree list view, I used an article from the always excellent Code Project by Thomas Caudal (*http://www.codeproject.com/cs/miscctrl/treelistview.asp*). The code was written for .NET 1.0 and was three years old when I looked at it. I ported the code over to .NET 2.0 and tweaked the code to work on all Microsoft operating systems. Note that I concentrated only on the parts of the code I needed for SUPERASSERT.NET, so not every-thing's been tested under .NET 2.0. I greatly appreciate Thomas's letting me use his code.

In the .\Caudal.Windows.Forms\Test\StackReader directory is a standalone test program that will let you view DiagnosticHelper-*CPU*.exe–produced stack walks. It was the unit test for the control, but it's there if you need it. It's not built as part of the normal book code build, so you'll need to build it on your own.

Trace, Trace, Trace, and Trace

Assertions might be the best proactive programming trick you can learn, but trace statements, if used correctly with assertions, will truly allow you to debug your application without the debugger. For some of you old programmers out there, trace statements are essentially *printf*-style debugging. You should never underestimate the power of *printf*-style debugging because that's how most applications were debugged before interactive debuggers were invented. Tracing in the .NET world is intriguing because when Microsoft first mentioned .NET publicly, the key benefits were not for developers but rather for network administrators and IT workers responsible for deploying the applications developers write. One of the critical new benefits Microsoft listed was the ability of IT workers to easily turn on tracing to help find problems in applica-tions! I was quite stunned when I read that because it showed Microsoft responding to the pain our end users experience when dealing with buggy software.

The trick to tracing is analyzing how much information you need for solving problems on machines that don't have the development environment installed. If you log too much, you get large files that are a real pain to slog through. If you log too little, you can't solve your problem. The balancing act requires having just enough logged to avoid a last-minute, 5,000-mile plane trip to a customer who just duplicated that one nasty bug—a plane trip in which you have to sit in the middle seat between a crying baby and a sick person. In general, good logging balance means that you need two levels of tracing: one level to give you the basic flow through the soft-ware so that you can see what's being called when and another level to add key data to the file so that you can look for data-stream–dependent problems.

Unfortunately, each application is different, so I can't give you an exact number of trace statements or other data marks that would be sufficient for your log. One of the better approaches I've seen is giving some of the newer folks on the team a sample log and asking whether they can get enough of a clue from it to start tracking down the problem. If they give up in disgust after an hour or two, you probably don't have enough information. If after an hour or two they can get a general idea of where the application was at the time of the corruption or crash, you've got a good sign that your log contains the right amount of information.

The problem of having too much tracing output, while not as common as having too little, is bad also. When there's too much tracing, you have two problems. The first is that the tracing does slow down your application. On one consulting job we worked on, the tracing overhead on a production box made it impossible to turn on tracing for peak usage times. Too much tracing also makes it much harder to find the problems because you're wading through tens of pages to find that one special nugget of information you need. When you use your trace logs to do the debugging and you find yourself skipping lots of output, you need to question seriously if that data is necessary and if it's not, remove those traces.

As I mentioned in Chapter 2, you must have a team-wide logging system. Part of that logging system design has to consider the format of the tracing, especially so that debug build tracing is easier to deal with. Without that format, tracing effectiveness quickly vanishes because no one will want to wade through a ton of text that constantly repeats worthless data. The good news for .NET applications is that Microsoft did quite a bit of work to make controlling the output easier.

Before I jump into the different platform-specific issues, I want to mention one extremely cool tool you always need to have on your development machines: DebugView. My former neighbor Mark Russinovich wrote DebugView and many other outstanding tools that you can download from Sysinternals (*www.sysinternals.com/utilities/debugview.html*). The price is right (free!), and Mark's tools solve some very difficult problems, so you should subscribe to the Sysinternals RSS feed to be notified immediately where there are new tools or versions available. While you're there, you should also subscribe to Mark's blog if you want to read some of the best writing on hard-core system-level debugging in the world. DebugView monitors any calls to the user mode *OutputDebugString* or the kernel mode *DbgPrint*, so you can see any debug output when your application isn't running under a debugger. What makes DebugView even more useful is that it can burrow its way across machines, so you can monitor from a single machine all the machines that are part of a distributed system.

Basic Tracing

As I mentioned earlier, Microsoft made some marketing noise about tracing in .NET applications. In general, they did a good job creating a clean architecture that better controls tracing in real-world development. I already mentioned the *Trace* object during the assertion discussion, which is designed to use for your own tracing. Like the *Debug* object, the *Trace* object uses the concept of *TraceListeners* to handle the output. In your development, you'll want your assertion code to do the same thing. The *Trace* object's method calls are active only if *TRACE* is defined. The default for both debug and release build projects created by Visual Studio is to have *TRACE* defined, so the methods are probably already active.

The *Trace* object has four overloaded methods to output trace information: *Write, WriteIf, WriteLine,* and *WriteLineIf.* You can probably guess the difference between *Write* and *WriteLine,* but understanding the **If* methods is a little more challenging: they allow for conditional tracing. If the first parameter to the **If* method evaluates to *true,* the trace happens; evaluating to *false* means it doesn't. That's quite convenient, but it possibly could lead to some big performance problems if you're not careful. For example, if you write code like that shown in the first portion of the next snippet, you will incur the overhead of the string concatenation every time the line executes because the determination for doing the actual tracing occurs inside the *Trace.WriteLineIf* call. You're much better off following the second method in the next snippet, in which you use an *if* statement to make the call to *Trace.WriteLine* only when you need to, minimizing how often you must incur the string concatenation overhead.

```
// Paying the overhead every time
Trace.WriteLineIf ( bShowTrace , "Parameters: x=" + x + "y =" + y ) ;

// Causing the concatenation only when necessary
if ( true == bShowTrace )
{
    Trace.WriteLine ("Parameters: x=" + x + " y =" + y ) ;
}
```

I think the .NET designers did us all a favor when they added the *TraceSwitch* class. With the **If* methods for the *Trace* object allowing for conditional compilation, it took only a small step to define a class that provided for multiple levels of tracing and a consistent way to set them. The most important part of *TraceSwitch* is the name it's given in the first parameter of the constructor. (The second parameter is a descriptive name.) The name enables you to control the switch from outside the application, which I'll talk about in a moment. *TraceSwitch* objects wrap a tracing level. The levels are shown in Table 3-1. To check whether *TraceSwitch* matches a particular level, you use a set of properties, such as *TraceError,* that returns *true* if the switch condition is met. Combined with the **If* methods, using *TraceSwitch* objects is quite straight-forward.

```
public static void Main ( )
{
    TraceSwitch TheSwitch = new TraceSwitch ( "SwitchyTheSwitch",
                                              "Example Switch" );
    TheSwitch.Level = TraceLevel.Info ;
    Trace.WriteLineIf ( TheSwitch.TraceError ,
                        "Error tracing is on!" ) ;
    Trace.WriteLineIf ( TheSwitch.TraceWarning ,
                        "Warning tracing is on!" ) ;
    Trace.WriteLineIf ( TheSwitch.TraceInfo ,
                        "Info tracing is on!" ) ;
    Trace.WriteLineIf ( TheSwitch.TraceVerbose ,
                        "VerboseSwitching is on!" ) ;
}
```

Table 3-1   *TraceSwitch* Levels

Trace Level	Value
Off	0
Error	1
Warnings (and errors)	2
Info (warnings and errors)	3
Verbose (everything)	4

The real magic of *TraceSwitch* objects is that they allow you to easily set them from outside the application in the ubiquitous .Config file. The *switches* element under the *system.diagnostics* element is where you specify the *add* elements to add and set the name and level. A complete configuration file for an application follows this paragraph. Ideally, you have a separate *TraceSwitch* object for each assembly in your application. Keep in mind that the *TraceSwitch* settings can also be applied to the global Machine.Config.

```
<?xml version="1.0" encoding="UTF-8" ?>
<configuration>
    <system.diagnostics>
        <switches>
            <add name="Wintellect.ScheduleJob" value="4" />
            <add name="Wintellect.DataAccess" value="0" />
        </switches>
    </system.diagnostics>
</configuration>
```

The number-one sentiment about tracing is that it's very cool to set a *TraceSwitch* externally in the .config file, but getting the *TraceSwitch* to reread the .config file while the app is running is a big concern. In the .NET Framework 1.x, you have to do all the work yourself manually. But in the .NET Framework 2.0, the *Trace* object has a static method, *Refresh*, that will force a reread of the configuration files and update any trace switches as appropriate.

Instead of everyone writing their own file change watcher, I wrote a little class called *Wintellect. Diagnostics.ConfigTraceSwitchWatcher*, which you can instantiate in your apps to get the *TraceSwitch* updates easily. The class sets a *FileSystemWatcher* on the directory that contains your application .config file, and when it changes, *ConfigTraceSwitchWatcher* will automatically call the *Trace.Refresh* method to automatically update all *TraceSwitches*. The only interesting part of the implementation was ensuring the correct name of the App.Config when running under the special debugging helper, *.vshost.exe, for Windows Forms and Console applications.

Back in the Assert, Assert, Assert, and Assert sections, I discussed two of the *TraceListener*s included with the Framework Class Library (FCL): *TextWriterTraceListener* and *Event-LogTraceListener*. Whereas those two have the problem that they don't show the stack traces for assertions, they will show everything from one of the *Trace.Write** calls. In .NET 2.0, Microsoft has added several other *TraceListener*-derived classes that you may find useful.

The *FileLogTraceListener* class from the *Microsoft.VisualBasic.Logging* namespace is a great new listener because it automatically handles log file rollover on a per-date or per-week basis. Additionally, the class has options to limit disk space usage and to specify the file output directory. If you've been doing any .NET server development, you've probably already written your own version of the *FileLogTraceListener* class. It's nice to see this functionality incorporated into the FCL.

I've already mentioned a couple of the others: *ConsoleTraceListener*, *DelimitedListTraceListener*, and *XmlWriterTraceListener*. All three of those are derived from *TextWriterTraceListener*, and you can tell by the names what they do with their output. However, I need to explain some of the issues with the *XmlWriterTraceListener*. The following code snippet shows manually creating and writing to an *XmlWriterTraceListener*, and Listing 3-3 shows the example output.

Listing 3-3   Example *XmlWriterTraceListener* output

```
XmlWriterTraceListener xwtl = new XmlWriterTraceListener ( "Foo.xml" );
Trace.Listeners.Add ( xwtl );
Trace.WriteLine ( "Hello there, XmlWriterTraceListener!" );
Trace.WriteLine ( "Nice to have you as part of .NET 2.0" );
xwtl.Flush ( );
xwtl.Close ( );

<E2ETraceEvent xmlns="http://schemas.microsoft.com/2004/06/E2ETraceEvent">
    <System xmlns="http://schemas.microsoft.com/2004/06/windows/eventlog/system">
        <EventID>0</EventID>
        <Type>3</Type>
        <SubType Name="Information">0</SubType>
        <Level>8</Level>
        <TimeCreated SystemTime="2006-03-06T14:55:42.6553629-05:00" />
        <Source Name="Trace" />
        <Correlation ActivityID={00000000-0000-0000-0000-000000000000}" />
        <Execution ProcessName="ConsoleApplication1.vshost"
                   ProcessID="3100"
                   ThreadID="10" />
        <Channel/>
        <Computer>TIMON</Computer>
    </System>
    <ApplicationData>Hello there, XmlWriterTraceListener!</ApplicationData>
</E2ETraceEvent>
<E2ETraceEvent xmlns="http://schemas.microsoft.com/2004/06/E2ETraceEvent">
    <System xmlns="http://schemas.microsoft.com/2004/06/windows/eventlog/system">
        <EventID>0</EventID>
        <Type>3</Type>
        <SubType Name="Information">0</SubType>
        <Level>8</Level>
        <TimeCreated SystemTime="2006-03-06T14:55:42.8272379-05:00" />
        <Source Name="Trace" />
        <Correlation ActivityID="{00000000-0000-0000-0000-000000000000}" />
        <Execution ProcessName="ConsoleApplication1.vshost"
                   ProcessID="3100"
                   ThreadID="10" />
        <Channel/>
        <Computer>TIMON</Computer>
```

```
    </System>
    <ApplicationData>Nice to have you as part of .NET 2.0</ApplicationData>
</E2ETraceEvent>
```

As you read the Listing 3-3 XML output, you can see the first problem is that there's a ton of stuff written on each trace statement. When I get to the *TraceSource* discussions later in the chapter, I'll explain why the *XmlWriterTraceListener* is doing the heavy writing. Suffice it to say, you won't be doing massive detailed tracing with the *XmlWriterTraceListener*, but it's perfect for general tracing in your application. The subsequent, and bigger, issues with the output might be difficult to see in the book, but if you opened this file with the XML editor in Visual Studio 2005, the second E2ETraceEvent node has a squiggly red line under it indicating the error: "XML document cannot contain multiple root level elements."

As a wise developer once told me: there are two types of XML, well formed and garbage. Some have argued that the *XmlWriterTraceListener* does not output valid XML for performance reasons. That may be the case, but if I'm turning on super-heavy tracing, I'm probably not going to want to spew that much data for a single trace anyway. Whatever the reason, it's what we have to deal with.

Any discussion of basic tracing wouldn't be complete if I didn't mention the open source log4net project you can find at *http://logging.apache.org/log4net/*. It's a derivation of the Java log4j project and offers many ways of controlling exactly what type of tracing output your heart desires. In our consulting business we've run into many projects using log4net that have excellent results.

Tracing in ASP.NET Applications and XML Web Services

In the .NET 1.1 days, ASP.NET tracing used a completely different system than everything else in .NET. The old way is still supported for backwards compatibility, so I do want to discuss it. However, at the end of this section, I'll describe how to easily merge both tracing systems into one so that everything's consistent across your Web interface in addition to your business logic pieces.

The *System.Web.UI.Page* class has its own *Trace* property that returns an instance of type *System.Web.TraceContext* based on the *HttpContext* of the page. The two key methods for *TraceContext* are *Write* and *Warn*. Both handle tracing output, but the *Warn* method writes the output in red. Each method has three overloads, and both take the same parameters: the usual message and category with message overload, but also one that takes the category, message, and *System.Exception*. That last overload writes out the exception message and callstack. To avoid extra overhead processing when tracing isn't enabled, check whether the *IsEnabled* property is *true*.

The easiest way to turn on tracing is to set the *Trace* attribute to *true* inside the *@Page* directive at the top of your .aspx files.

```
<%@ Page Trace="true" %>
```

That magic little directive turns on a ton of tracing information that appears directly at the bottom of the page, which is convenient, but it will be seen by both you and the users. In fact, there's so much tracing information that I really wish it were divided into several levels. Although seeing the Cookies and Headers Collections in addition to the Server Variables is nice, most of the time you don't need them. All sections are self-explanatory, but I want to point out the Trace Information section because any calls you make to *TraceContext* appear here. Even if you don't call *TraceContext.Warn/Write*, you'll still see output in the Trace Information section because ASP.NET reports when several of its methods have been called. This section is also where the red text appears when you call *TraceContext.Warn*.

Setting the *Trace* attribute at the top of each page in your application is tedious, so the ASP.NET designers put a section in Web.Config that allows you to control tracing. This tracing section, named, appropriately enough, *trace* element, is shown here:

```xml
<?xml version="1.0" encoding="utf-8" ?>
<configuration>
    <system.web>
        <trace
            enabled="false"
            requestLimit="10"
            mostRecent="true"
            pageOutput="false"
            traceMode="SortByTime"
            localOnly="true"
        />
    </system.web>
</configuration>
```

The *enabled* attribute dictates whether tracing is turned on for this application. The *request-Limit* attribute indicates how many trace requests to cache in memory on a per-application basis. (In just a moment, I'll discuss how to view these cached traces.) The new-to-.NET 2.0 *mostRecent* attribute, tells ASP.NET to keep the most recent *requestLimit* traces. If *mostRecent* is *false*, your tracing will match the .NET 1.1 way, which was to stop tracing after the *requestLimit* count was met. The *pageOutput* element tells ASP.NET where to show the trace output. If *pageOutput* is set to *true*, the output appears on the page just as it would if you set the *Trace* attribute in the *Page* directive. You probably won't want to change the *traceMode* element so that the Trace Information section in the trace is sorted by time. If you do want to see the sort-by category, you can set *traceMode* to *SortByCategory*. The final attribute, *localOnly*, tells ASP.NET whether the output should be visible only on the local machine or visible to any client applications.

To see cached traces when *pageOutput* is false, append the HTTP handler, *Trace.axd*, to the application directory, which will show a page that allows you to choose the stored trace you'd like to see. For example, if your directory is *http://www.wintellect.com/schedules*, to see the stored traces, the path would be *http://www.wintellect.com/schedules/trace.axd*.

As you can see, if you're not careful with tracing, your end users will be looking at them, which is always a little scary since developers are notorious for trace statements that could be career limiting if the output fell into the wrong hands. Luckily, setting *localOnly* to *true* keeps the trace viewing only on the local server, even when accessing the trace log through the Trace.axd HTTP handler. To view your application trace logs, you'll simply have to use the greatest piece of software known to humankind, Terminal Services, so that you can access the server directly from your office and don't even have to get up from your desk. You'll want to update the *customErrors* section of Web.Config so that you have a *defaultRedirect* page, preventing your end users from seeing the ASP.NET "Server Error in '*AppName*' Application" error if they try to access *Trace.axd* from a remote machine. You'll also want to log that someone tried to access *Trace.axd*, especially because an attempted access is probably an indication of a hacker.

You've probably guessed the limitation of the old ASP.NET means of tracing. Your user interface tracing goes to one location, and all your class libraries are sending theirs through *Trace.WriteLine*, so they go to a different location. In the previous edition of this book, I had to write a *TraceListener* that would take care of mapping the *System.Diagnostic.Trace* object to the ASP.NET page so you could see them. Fortunately, with .NET 2.0, Microsoft now provides that code inside the FCL in the form of the *WebPageTraceListener*. The only problem is that ASP.NET does not automatically add it to the *Trace.Listeners* collection. You will need to include the following lines in all your Web.Config files to ensure that you have all your tracing going through *TraceContext* so you can see it:

```
<system.diagnostics>
        <trace autoflush="true" indentsize="4">
           <listeners>
                <add name="webListener"
                    type="System.Web.WebPageTraceListener,
                    System.Web,
                    Version=2.0.0.0,
                    Culture=neutral,
                    PublicKeyToken=b03f5f7f11d50a3a"/>
           </listeners>
        </trace>
    </system.diagnostics>
```

Advanced Tracing

The tracing system consisting of the *Trace* object is quite good and will generally suffice for all small- and medium-sized applications as is. However, the *Trace* object is not perfect and can lead to some issues. The main problem is that there's only one *Trace* object global to the application domain. As you move into larger industrial-strength applications, the global, one-size-fits-all nature of the *Trace* object becomes a hindrance because all threads in the application domain must go through the bottleneck of the single tracing object. In heavily multithreaded applications, your goal is to use as much of the time-slice given to your thread as possible. If you are artificially giving up your time slice because of synchronization, you're slowing down your application.

The second problem with a single *Trace* object is that everyone sharing the same object can quickly overload you with data. Although you can use *TraceSwitch* options to control output, you can become overwhelmed when you have to turn on tracing for multiple pieces of a large application. You'll be sorting through lots of potential output you don't really want to see in many cases.

Another problem with the existing *Trace* object in larger applications is that the output is limited to just the string passed to *Trace.Write**. In real-world apps, many times, such as when tracing into error handling code, you want to add lots of additional output, such as the call stack, process information, thread information, and so on. While you could programmatically add that data into every place where you think you might need it in your trace output, it would be much better if you could dynamically change the data output in the configuration file.

To rectify these problems, Microsoft added several new features to the FCL. The biggest is the *TraceSource* class, which is a *Trace* object you can instantiate. The idea is that you'll instantiate a *TraceSource* for each of your major subsystems so you can avoid blocking across them. Microsoft also extended the existing *TraceListener* class with all sorts of new output options. To take advantage of the new output options, they've added a *SourceSwitch*, which is like a *TraceSwitch* on steroids. Finally, they've also added a *TraceFilter* class to allow better filtering of output.

Because code and pictures are worth a thousand words, the best way for me to show how the new enhancements work is to show some code and a picture of how things work. Listing 3-4 is a simple program that shows using a *TraceSource* along with the other options now available for large application tracing control. Read over the code because it wasn't until I wrote the code that I started seeing the amazing power of the new tracing functionality.

Listing 3-4   The TraceSource, TraceListener, and TraceFilter features

```
using System;
using System.Collections.Generic;
using System.Text;
using System.Diagnostics;

namespace TraceSourceExample
{
    class Program
    {
        static void ShowAllTraceMethods ( TraceSource trc )
        {
            // The simplest method. Notice that it takes parameters, which is a
            // big improvement over the Trace object.
            trc.TraceInformation ( "The simplest trace method with {0}{1}" ,
                                   "params" , "!" );

            // The method to trace an event based on the TraceEventType enum.
            trc.TraceEvent ( TraceEventType.Error , 100 , "Pretend error!" );

            // The method to make dumping out data easy.
            trc.TraceData ( TraceEventType.Information ,
                      50 , "Some" , "pretend" , "data." );
```

```csharp
            // The method to record a transfer. This method is primarily for
            // the XmlWriterTraceListener. See the text for more discussion.
            trc.TraceTransfer ( 75 , "What was transferred?" ,
                new Guid ( "7b5fcdbc-913e-43bd-8e39-ee13c062ecc3" ) );
        }

    static void Main ( string [] args )
    {
            // Create the TraceSource for this program. Like the Trace
            // object, the TraceSource.Listeners collection starts out with
            // the DefaultTraceListener.
            TraceSource trc = new TraceSource ( "HappySource" );

            // Set the switch level for this TraceSource instance so
            // everything is shown. The default for TraceSource is to *not*
            // trace. The default name of the switch is the same as the
            // TraceSource. You'll probably want to be sharing Switches across
            // TraceSources in your development.
            trc.Switch.Level = SourceLevels.All;

            // Trace to show the default output.
            ShowAllTraceMethods ( trc );

            // The TraceListener class has a very interesting new property,
            // TraceOutputOptions, which tells the TraceListener the additional
            // data to automatically display.
            trc.Listeners [ "Default" ].TraceOutputOptions =
                TraceOptions.Callstack | TraceOptions.DateTime |
                TraceOptions.ProcessId | TraceOptions.ThreadId |
                TraceOptions.Timestamp;

            // Now all the trace calls in the Debug Output window will show
            // all the data included in the TraceOutputOptions.

            ShowAllTraceMethods ( trc );

            // Filtering allows you to apply a limiter to the TraceListener
            // directly. That way you can turn on tracing, but apply more
            // smarts to the actual output so you can better separate the
            // wheat from the chaff on a production system.
            EventTypeFilter evtFilt =
                new EventTypeFilter ( SourceLevels.Error );

            // Apply the filter to the DefaultTraceListener.
            trc.Listeners [ "Default" ].Filter = evtFilt;

            // The only output in the Debug Output window will be from the
            // TraceEvent method call in ShowAllTraceMethods.
            ShowAllTraceMethods ( trc );

            trc.Flush ( );
            trc.Close ( );
        }
    }
}
```

After I'd written that code, I ran across a wonderful blog entry from Mike Rousos (*http://blogs.msdn.com/bclteam/archive/2005/03/15/396431.aspx*), a member of the Base Class Library Team, talking about the *TraceSource*. The blog had a graphic that showed where the various classes fit together. For those of you who are graphical thinkers, I took Mike's idea and expanded it so you could see how a trace flows through the new tracing system.

Figure 3-7 shows three different *TraceSource* instances in use by an app. When a *Trace** method is called, it checks the *Switch*-derived class in the *TraceSource.Switch* property to see if the condition on the *Trace** method matches. If the condition doesn't match, nothing is traced. Notice that a *Switch* class can be shared between *TraceSource* instances (see B and C in the diagram). If the *Switch*-derived condition is met, the *TraceSource* loops through its *Listeners* collection calling the appropriate *TraceListener.Trace** method. (In the .NET Framework 2.0 documentation, you'll see that the *TraceListener* class has numerous new properties and methods.)

If the individual *TraceListener* class has a *TraceFilter* instance in the *TraceListener.Filter* property, before any output is sent, the *TraceListener* checks to see if *TraceFilter.ShouldTrace* returns *true*. If it does not, no output is sent. If *ShouldTrace* returns *true*, the output is sent to that *TraceListener*'s internal writing method.

In Figure 3-7, *TraceSource* instance B has a single *TraceListener* instance called X1 set in its *TraceListeners* collection, and *TraceSource* C has a single *TraceListener* called Y1. However, the *TraceSource* objects are sharing a *Switch 2*, so any initial matching on the *TraceSource.Trace** methods for B or C will be filtered identically. In the case of the two *TraceListeners*, they both share a filter, *Filter 2*, so any filtering will apply to both.

At the top of Listing 3-4, the *ShowAllTraceMethods* calls each of the methods in a *TraceSource* instance dedicated to tracing. The first method, *TraceInformation*, is for the simplest tracing, and after I talk about the other methods, you probably won't want to use it for your tracing because it has no flexibility for controlling output externally. The main method you'll want to use is *TraceEvent* because it allows you to assign a *TraceEventType* enumeration to indicate the level of tracing. The second parameter is the numeric identifier for the trace. With that parameter, you either uniquely identify tracing or assign a specific value to a class to help identify tracing output at a glance. There are three overloads to *TraceEvent*, but the big news is that one takes variable-length parameters so you can pass a formatting string and get your data displayed nicely in the trace.

The *TraceData* method also accepts the trace identifier, but its main purpose is to allow you to pass either an object array or multiple parameters so the trace output shows them separated by commas. If you are dealing with data objects whose *ToString* method does the heavy lifting, the *TraceData* call can be your dependable friend. In general, you'll nearly always use *TraceEvent*.

The final method, *TraceTransfer*, was designed to work hand in glove with the *XmlWriterTrace-Listener*. If you look back at the output of *XmlWriterTraceListener* in Listing 3-3, you might have noticed a *Correlation* element with an *ActivityID* attribute that looks like a GUID. *TraceTransfer* sets the internal GUID that the *XmlWriterTraceListener* will use until the next time a call to

TraceTransfer sets a new GUID. You can assign a GUID to major activities in your application, such as login handling, so you can quickly scan the *XmlWriterTraceListener* output looking for logical operations in your tracing.

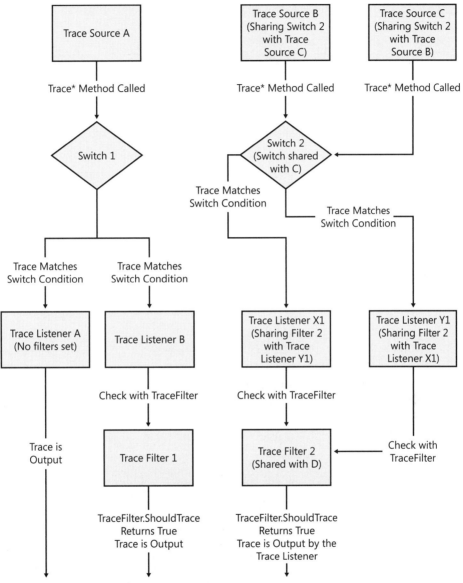

Figure 3-7 Data flow of TraceSource to output

I'm willing to bet that only the largest applications will use *TraceTransfer* and the *ActivityID*. That's because the first parameter of both the *TraceEvent* and *TraceData* methods is a *TraceEvent-Type*, and it's worth mentioning how much this has grown in the .NET Framework 2.0. In the .NET Framework 1.x, you were limited to *Error*, *Warning*, *Info*, and *Verbose* with a *TraceSwitch*.

Table 3-2 shows all the values of the *TraceEventType* enum and what they are for. As you can see, *Start*, *Stop*, *Resume*, and *Transfer* are all called activity types. Since one of the primary uses of tracing is to determine which operations occurred and the order in which they occurred, these new tracing events make that extremely easy. To see just the activity tracing, you can set the *TraceSource.Switch.Level* to *SourceLevels.ActivityTracing*.

Table 3-2   *TraceEventType* Values

***TraceEventType* Value**	**Usage**
Critical	Unrecoverable errors and exceptions in the application
Error	Recoverable errors the application handled, such as invalid logins
Warning	Unusual activity that may need exploration, such as data not being in the proper format
Information	Normal operation information, such as a user logging in or out
Verbose	Debugging information, such as entering and exiting a method
Start	The activity type indicating a logical operation started
Stop	The activity type indicating that a logical operation stopped
Suspend	The activity type indicating that a logical operation was suspended
Resume	The activity type indicating that a logical operation was restarted
Transfer	The activity type indicating that a change in the correlation ID (that is, a call to *TraceTransfer*)

While programmatically manipulating *TraceSource* instances is possible, as shown back in Listing 3-4, the real action is in manipulating the tracing from the application's configuration file. Listing 3-5 shows the App.Config file of a program that has two *TraceSource* instances, *HappySource* and *GiddySource*. (Remember, anything you can put in App.Config you can put in Web.Config.) The *sources* element is where you configure the individual *TraceSource* instances in a *source* element for each instance you want to configure. The two required attributes to the *source* element are the self-explanatory *name* and *switchName*. By associating a *Switch* instance with the *TraceSource*, you can control the output for the *TraceSource* instance. Keep in mind that *Switch* instances can be shared across multiple *TraceSource* instances.

Underneath the *source* element, you can specify any *TraceListeners* you want to associate with that *TraceSource*. You can add and remove any items from the *TraceSource.Listeners* property and dynamically create new *TraceListeners* directly from the configuration file, just as you can in the .NET Framework 1.x.

What's most interesting in Listing 3-5 is the *sharedListeners* element with which you can create *TraceListener* instances that are shareable across all *TraceSource* instances in the application. As you can see in the listing, you will still need to add the shared instance to the individual *Trace-Sources*. In the *XmlWriterTraceListener* added in Listing 3-5, I also show how to apply a *Trace-Filter* to a *TraceListener*. The new *traceOutputOptions* attribute allows you to specify the *TraceOptions* you want applied to the *TraceListener*. Whereas I added that filter to the *TraceListener* being shared across all *TraceSource* instances, you can also add those *TraceFilters* to *TraceListeners* that you add to an individual *TraceSource* instance.

The last piece of Listing 3-5 is the *switches* element, with which you configure individual *Switch* instances. The only difference in the *switches* element in the .NET Framework 2.0 from the .NET Framework 1.x is that the *value* attribute can now take string values that are passed to the switch constructor to set the value instead of numbers like the original *TraceSwitch* class.

As you can see, the amount of control that you have over your tracing in the configuration with the .NET Framework 2.0 is simply amazing. The icing on the cake is the new ability in the .NET Framework 2.0 to tell you the exact line in the configuration file that's not correct, so those of us who have spent hours pulling our hair out looking for problems in our configuration file can now start growing some of it back.

Listing 3-5   Example App.Config setting *HappySource* and *GiddySource*

```xml
<?xml version="1.0" encoding="utf-8"?>
<configuration>
    <system.diagnostics>
        <!-- The <sources> is where you configure the TraceSource instances in
             your application. -->
        <sources>
            <!-- Configure the HappySource TraceSource instance.  The
                 switchName attribute associates the Switch-derived class with
                 the TraceSource.  The Switch classes are configured in the
                 <switches> section below, reminiscent of the TraceSwitch
                 classes in .NET 1.1.
            -->
            <source name="HappySource" switchName="HappySwitch">
                <listeners>
                    <!-- Add a TextWriterTraceListener just to the individual
                         TraceSource called HappyName. -->
                    <add name="myTextListener"
                         type="System.Diagnostics.TextWriterTraceListener"
                         initializeData="TextWriterOutput.txt"/>
                    <!-- Remove the DefaultTraceListener from just
                         HappySource. -->
                    <remove name="Default"/>
                    <!-- Add the shared listener. -->
                    <add name="myXmlListener"/>
                </listeners>
            </source>
            <source name="GiddySource" switchName="GiddySwitch">
                <listeners>
                    <!-- Add a ConsoleTraceListener just to Giddy. -->
                    <add name="myConsoleListener"
                         type="System.Diagnostics.ConsoleTraceListener"/>
                    <!-- Remove the DefaultTraceListener. -->
                    <remove name="Default"/>
                    <!-- Add the shared listener. -->
                    <add name="myXmlListener"/>
                </listeners>
            </source>
        </sources>
        <!-- In <sharedListeners> you can add trace listeners to ALL
             TraceSource instances in your application at once.  Note that you
```

```
                    may *add* only TraceListeners here. You cannot remove them.  If
                    you want to remove the DefaultTraceListener, you must do what I
                    did above. -->
            <sharedListeners>
                <!-- I'll add an XmlWriterTraceListener and set the output options
                    as well as a filter.  You can do these same operations for an
                    individual TraceSource as well. -->
                <!-- Notice the traceOutputOptions attribute.  The values come from
                    the TraceOption enumeration.-->
                <add name="myXmlListener"
                    type="System.Diagnostics.XmlWriterTraceListener"
                    initializeData="SharedOutput.XML"
                    traceOutputOptions="DateTime, Timestamp, Callstack">
                    <!-- Apply a brand new filter to this trace listener.  This
                        will filter everything but SourceLevels.Warning and
                        higher. -->
                    <filter type="System.Diagnostics.EventTypeFilter"
                            initializeData="Warning"/>

                </add>
            </sharedListeners>
            <switches>
                <!-- Have HappySwitch report everything. -->
                <add name="HappySwitch" value="All" />
                <!-- Have GiddySwitch list only errors. -->
                <add name="GiddySwitch" value="Error"/>
            </switches>
        </system.diagnostics>
    </configuration>
```

Comment, Comment, Comment, and Comment

One day, my friend François Poulin, who was working full-time on maintaining some code that someone else wrote, came in wearing a button that said, "Code as if whoever maintains your code is a violent psychopath who knows where you live." François is by no means a psychopath, but he did have a very good point. Although you might think your code is the model of clarity and completely obvious, without descriptive comments, it is as bad as raw assembly language to the maintenance developers. The irony is that the maintenance developer for your code can easily turn out to be you! Not too long before I started writing the second edition of this book, I received an e-mail message from a company I had worked for nearly 13 years ago asking me whether I could update a project I had written for them. It was an amazing experience to look at code I wrote that long ago! I was also amazed at how bad my commenting was. Remember François's button every time you write a line of code.

Our job as engineers is twofold: develop a solution for the user, and make that solution maintainable for the future. The only way to make your code maintainable is to comment it. By "comment it," I don't mean simply writing comments that duplicate what the code is doing; I mean documenting your assumptions, your approach, and your reasons for choosing the approach you did. You also need to keep your comments coordinated with the code. Normally mild-mannered maintenance programmers can turn into raving lunatics when they're trying to update code that does something different from what the comments say it's supposed to do. As Norm Schryer, a researcher at AT&T, so wonderfully said: "If the code and the comments disagree, then both are probably wrong."

I use the following approach to commenting:

- Each function or method needs a sentence or two that clarifies the following information:
  - ❏ What the routine does
  - ❏ What assumptions the method makes
  - ❏ What each input parameter is expected to contain
  - ❏ What each output parameter is expected to contain on success and failure
  - ❏ Each possible return value
  - ❏ Each exception directly thrown by the method
- Each part of the function that isn't completely obvious from the code needs a sentence or two that explains what it's doing.
- Any interesting algorithm deserves a complete description.
- Any nontrivial bugs you've fixed in the code need to be commented with the bug number and a description of what you fixed.
- Well-placed trace statements, assertions, and good naming conventions can also serve as good comments and provide excellent context to the code.
- Comment as if you were going to be the one maintaining the code in five years.
- Avoid keeping dead code commented out in source modules whenever possible. It's never really clear to other developers whether the commented-out code was meant to be removed permanently or removed only temporarily for testing. Your version control system is there to help you revert to areas of code that no longer exist in current versions.
- If you find yourself saying, "This is a big hack" or "This is really tricky stuff," you probably need to rewrite the function instead of commenting it.

Proper and complete documentation in the code marks the difference between a serious, professional developer and someone who is playing at it. Donald Knuth, author of the seminal *The Art of Computer Programming* series of books, once observed that you should be able to read a well-written program just as you read a well-written book. Although I don't see myself curling up by the fire with a copy of the TeX source code, I strongly agree with Dr. Knuth's sentiment.

I recommend that you study Chapter 32, "Self-Documenting Code," of Steve McConnell's phenomenal book, *Code Complete, 2nd Edition* (Microsoft Press, 2005). I learned to write comments by reading this chapter. If you comment correctly, even if your maintenance programmer turns out to be a psychopath, you know you'll be safe.

Some of you may be questioning the earlier line in which I say that you need to document each exception directly thrown by the method. As I discussed back in the "Custom Code Analysis Rules" section in Chapter 2, the exceptions that are directly thrown by the method are the ones that the programmer is much more interested in handling. If you start documenting every possible exception value that can be thrown by every method your code calls, you'll end up listing every exception in the entire Framework Class Library (FCL). It's reasonable to document an exception thrown by a private helper method for a public method because that's just common sense code separation. However, documenting exceptions that can be thrown deep inside the FCL will just confuse all the users of your API.

Since I'm discussing comments, I need to mention how much I love the XML documentation comments, especially now that they are supported by all languages from Microsoft. The main reason is that those XML files produced by the compiler are what's used to build your Intellisense. That alone should be reason enough to produce them religiously.

You can read the help documentation for the specifics, but as I pointed out in Chapter 2, the *<exception>* tag is one of the most important but one that everyone forgets. That's why I wrote the Code Analysis rule to flag errors when you're not using it. Another tag that everyone forgets is the *<permission>* tag, with which you can document the permissions you demand for your code to run.

I like the XML documentation comments so much, I built a moderately complicated macro, *CommenTater*, in Chapter 7 Extending the Visual Studio IDE, that takes care of adding and keeping your XML documentation comments current in addition to ensuring that you're adding them. Although my macro is useful, Roland Weigelt's outstanding GhostDoc add-in (*http://www.roland-weigelt.de/ghostdoc/*) is what you really want. It's one of those tools that you'll wonder how you can live without.

For example, I had a method called *Initialize*, which took a path string. Right-clicking the method and selecting Document This from the menu automatically filled in the following documentation:

```
/// <summary>
/// Initializes the specified path.
/// </summary>
/// <param name="path">The path.</param>
void Initialize ( String path )
{
    ...
}
```

The beauty of GhostDoc is that it has some serious smarts built in and does an excellent job of figuring out what a big chunk of text should be. You can also add your own rules and analysis in the configuration. It can greatly cut down on a huge chunk of tedious typing for all those simple methods.

The part of GhostDoc that will make you say *Whoa!* is when you ask it to document an inherited method that you're overloading. It automatically pulls in the base class's documentation, thus saving you a huge amount of time. Of course, it is still your job to ensure that the documentation is the best possible, but I'm all in favor of any helping hand to speed up the process.

Once you have that excellent XML documentation file being produced by the compiler, you'll want to turn to using it to produce your documentation. In the .NET 1.x days, we all used the open source NDOC program, but alas, NDOC is no more. Fortunately, Microsoft is, at the time I write this, working on releasing their internal tool to produce help files, SandCastle. The tool looks very promising and is actively under development. You can find more information on SandCastle at *www.sandcastledocs.com*. A Community Technical Preview (CTP) was available at the time I wrote this, but SandCastle was undergoing quite a bit of change so I wasn't able to use it in time for the book's release. As soon as SandCastle releases, I will integrated it into the book's source code to produce appropriate help files and release the changes.

If you are serious about producing help files from your XML documentation comments, you'll need to turn to a nice product from Innovasys, Document! X (*http://www.innovasys.com/products /documentx.asp*). It will not only produce help that makes it easy to integrate that help into the Visual Studio Help system, Innovasys will give you the Dynamic Help capability free. Its integration the IDE is excellent, so you can edit your comments in a WYSIWYG editor so you'll know exactly what the output will look like. Additionally, Document! X supports documenting databases, XSD Schemas, and other code documentation.

Summary

This chapter presented the best proactive programming techniques you can use to debug during coding. The best technique is to use assertions everywhere so that you gain control whenever a problem occurs. The SUPERASSERT.NET assertion code in Wintellect.Diagnostics.dll should help you narrow down problems without needing to get into a debugger at all. In addition to assertions, proper tracing and comments can make maintaining and debugging your code much easier for you and others. The more time you spend debugging your code during development, the less time you'll have to spend debugging it later and the better the quality of the final product.

Chapter 4
Common .NET Debugging Questions

The best part about writing books and articles, in addition to speaking at conferences, is getting the questions from developers about debugging and .NET in general. Although I do get a few "my application doesn't run–what do I do?" e-mails, most of the questions are well thought out and make me look at areas of .NET I normally don't get a chance to work with– it's a great learning experience for me. In fact, I enjoy the questions so much I will feel lonely if I don't get an e-mail question from each of you who purchase the book.

Since the last edition of this book, I've been keeping a list of all the questions I've been asked, and I want to answer the most common of those. Obviously, many of them apply to debugging .NET applications, but having gotten many questions about other aspects of development, I wanted to answer those also. Because of the breadth and depth of .NET development, I may not answer your particular burning question in this chapter, but I can guarantee you'll learn something.

Process- and Infrastructure-Related Questions

Many questions I've gotten are about debugging and process-related issues. Although I've done my best to make Chapter 1, "Bugs: Where They Come From and How You Solve Them," and Chapter 2, "Preparing for Debugging," which discussed those issues, as complete as possible, I still get many questions about those issues. Additionally, some common questions are even about the nature of using computers.

Why must you *always* develop as a non-admin?

If you are logging on to your computer using an account with administrator privileges, you need to raise your right hand and repeat after me: "I do solemnly swear that by the time I get to the end of this question's answer, I will put this book down and immediately correct the situation. Additionally, I will make all my coworkers do the same." *There is absolutely no reason at all for logging in with administrator rights to develop software!* The only time you need to use an account with administrator rights is if you are debugging across user accounts. Fortunately, it's easy to start individual processes with greater rights so you can do the debugging.

One of the most important features of Microsoft Windows Vista is User Account Control (UAC), which defaults users to less privileged accounts and prompts for required credentials whenever a process tries to do something that needs higher privileges. Even with the release of Windows Vista imminent, we will realistically be developing on and using Microsoft Windows XP and Microsoft Windows Server 2003 for many years before we have most of our development teams using the new operating system. That doesn't even consider the end-user or corporate-user scenario, which will take even longer to migrate over.

The most important reason you need to be developing without administrator rights, in other words using a limited user account, is to ensure that your application works correctly on a less privileged account. As someone who's been developing as a limited user for years, it's hugely frustrating to run an application and see it crash or have an unhandled exception because the developers assumed that everyone runs with administrator rights. This is a completely preventable bug that tells the user that the developers are lazy and certainly aren't doing their job.

The good news is that on Windows XP and Windows Server 2003, it's easy to find all the tricks because there's now an excellent Web site that will get you started: Jonathan Hardwick's *http://nonadmin.editme.com*. Many of the links and articles on the Web site point to Aaron Margosis's blog (*http://blogs.msdn.com/aaron_margosis*)—he's done the best writing on the subject. Both Web sites are excellent and are part of your required reading.

The main idea behind using your computer without administrator rights is that you'll use the Runas.exe program that comes with Windows to start particular processes as a user with administrator rights on that machine. For example, if you wanted to debug a Microsoft ASP.NET application running inside Internet Information Services (IIS), the debugger would need administrator rights to debug across the user accounts (your account to Local Service), so you would run the following command (assuming that Microsoft Visual Studio is in the path and the account you want to use is Administrator):

```
runas /u:Administrator devenv.exe
```

The runas command will prompt you for the Administrator account password, and after you type it, Visual Studio will start. From the new instance of Visual Studio, you can now debug the IIS-based application without exposing your whole system to viruses and spyware because you logged in as an administrator. Note that you can also use Mark Russinovich's excellent Psexec.exe program (*http://www.sysinternals.com/Utilities/PsExec.html*), which even allows you to start programs on other machines.

The last thing I want to mention about runas is that when you start a program with it, the program is using the profile from a different user, not the logged-in user. You probably already guessed that, but I've seen people get tripped up with setting an environment variable in their logged in account and wonder why their program started with runas doesn't see the environment variable.

If you're still not convinced that running with a non-administrator account is worthwhile, you should read the wonderful study done by Andrew Garcia in the magazine eWeek, "Is System Lockdown the Secret Weapon?" (*http://www.eweek.com/article2/0,1759,1891447,00.asp*). He took two fully patched systems, one running Microsoft Windows 2000 Professional SP4 and the other running Windows XP Professional SP2, and surfed some not-so-good Web sites using Administrator, Power User, and User accounts. After each surfing session, he ran spyware scans. On Windows XP, the Administrator and Power User accounts had 16 total threats! In setting up my friends' and family members' machines so they all run as a limited user, I've eliminated nearly all the spyware and virus calls I used to get.

The *http://nonadmin.editme.com* site does a great job of getting you started, but I wanted to share some of my tips about running and developing in a limited user account to help you make the transition. The Runas program is great from the command line, but there's a hidden feature with shortcuts (.lnk files) that I like to use to automatically be prompted for the user account to run in when clicking the shortcut. After you've created the .lnk file, right-click its icon and select Properties from the shortcut menu. On the Shortcut tab, click Advanced to open the Advanced Properties dialog box. If you select the first check box, Run With Different Credentials, now whenever you double-click the shortcut, you'll be prompted with the Run As dialog box, shown in Figure 4-1, in which you can specify the user name and password to run the application.

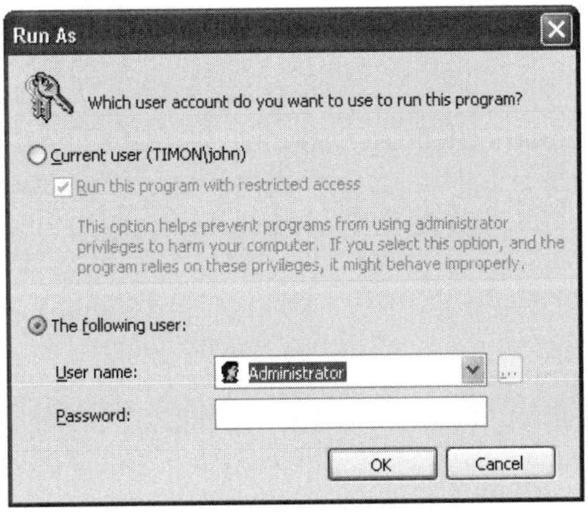

Figure 4-1 Shortcut prompt for user account

This is a very convenient way to start applications such as Visual Studio. However, there seems to be a bug in saving the shortcut, because if you change other values in the .lnk file properties, Windows Explorer randomly forgets that you selected the Run With Different Credentials check box. To work around this bug, make all the other changes to the shortcut and save those changes. Go back into the Properties dialog box for the shortcut and select the Run With Different Credentials check box as the last change.

One shortcut I like to set up with Run With Different Credentials is one to a Command Prompt. If the Command Prompt is running with administrator privileges, any applications you start from it are also under the same account. If you need to run multiple items with administrator privileges, this trick is very convenient. I even change the icon for that link to be a pirate skull and bones so it appears when pressing Alt+Tab thus helping me find it quickly.

When logged on with limited privileges, you sometimes need to access to Windows Explorer to set security on a directory or set up a share. To allow you to run Windows Explorer for another account, you'll first need to log on to that account and then set Windows Explorer to use separate instances. On the Tools menu, select Folder Options, click the View tab, and in the Advanced Settings box, scroll down and select the Launch Folder Windows In A Separate Process check box. It is a very good idea to enable this setting in general because each Explorer window is in a separate process—if one hangs, you don't hang the desktop, the taskbar, and everything else on the machine.

From your limited user account, you can now use Runas.exe or the shortcut trick I just discussed to start Windows Explorer for the account with administrator privileges. The only problem is that now you'll have trouble telling your limited account's Explorer windows from your administrator privilege account's windows. Fortunately, that's easy to fix with a bitmap and a registry key; the technique works with all Windows operating systems and CPUs. For the account with administrator privileges you want to use, set the HKEY_CURRENT_USER \Software\Microsoft\Internet Explorer\Toolbar key, BackBitmap string value to the complete file name of a bitmap file you want displayed behind the Microsoft Internet Explorer and Windows Explorer toolbars. I use a solid red 32 x32 pixel bitmap to make it completely obvious which windows have administrator privileges.

There's a fairly nasty bug you're going to run into running Windows Explorer in an account with administrator privileges when logged on with limited privileges. The UI of the Explorer instance running with administrator privileges does not properly refresh. When you delete a file, it's deleted, but the UI doesn't reflect the change. Just get in the habit of pressing F5 after each operation to force the refresh.

One of the greatest contributions that Aaron Margosis made in his quest to having everyone running in limited privileges accounts is a deceptively simple batch file that solves the hardest problem: temporarily grant your limited account administrator privileges. His script is called MakeMeAdmin (*http://blogs.msdn.com/aaron_margosis/archive/2004/07/24/193721.aspx*).

Now you can log on with your domain account as a limited privilege account on your development computer, but if you need to run something that needs both network access and administrator privileges on the computer, you're in business.

Using your computer as a limited user works great until you need to access something in Control Panel. You've had great luck with Runas to install applications and perform other tasks that require administrator privileges, but you'll eventually run into the wall with Control Panel. When you attempt to start Control.exe from Runas.exe, you will find that no window appears. This is incredibly frustrating and means you have to start Windows Explorer with administrator privileges and browse to My Computer\ Control Panel in Explorer's folder view so you can click the particular item you want.

Fortunately, there's an easy workaround, but it appears to be undocumented. Go ahead and start Control Panel from your limited privilege account. You may have noticed that in Explorer, if you right-click an executable, one of the menu items is Run As, which brings up the same dialog box shown in Figure 4-1 so you can type the user credentials. If you right-click a Control Panel application, you see Open, but no Run As. However, if you hold down the Shift key and right-click, the elusive Run As command will appear so you can start that individual Control Panel application with different credentials!

From a debugging standpoint, the only difference is if you need to debug across accounts, you'll need to start the debugger to run with administrator privileges. If you want to debug a process that's running under your limited account, you can run Visual Studio in your limited account and debug all day long. Not only is saving yourself from viruses and spyware always worthwhile, but if there's any chance that your application could be run in limited accounts, you are developing and testing the application in the same usage scenarios as those of your application's users.

Now that you've read this whole question, I'll remind you of your promise to put the book down and go set up your development machines so your main account has limited privileges. Some of you might be grumbling that running as a limited user isn't worth the pain, but I hope I've proven to you that it's well worth it. You have no excuse not to do the right thing. The book will wait; your customers and users will not.

What's the secret to debugging?

In my consulting work, everyone asks if there is a single key to debugging better to produce great code. I'll sum up the secret in two words: code coverage. *Code coverage* is simply the percentage of lines (or blocks) you've executed in your module. If 100 lines are in your module and you execute 85, you have 85 percent code coverage. The simple fact is that a line not executed is a line waiting to crash. I'm to the point now at which I enter "religion mode" because I believe in code coverage so much. If you were standing in front of me right now, I'd be jumping up and down and extolling the virtues of code coverage with evangelical fervor. Many developers tell me that taking my advice and trying to get good code coverage has paid off with huge improvements in code quality. It works, and is the only secret there is.

You can get code-coverage statistics in two ways. The first way is the hard way and involves using the debugger and setting a breakpoint on every single line in your module. As your module executes a line, clear the breakpoint. Continue running your code until you've cleared all the breakpoints, and you have 100 percent coverage. With .NET, there are far easier ways. If you have either Visual Studio Team Developer Edition, Visual Studio Tester Edition, or Visual Studio Team Suite Edition, you have an excellent code-coverage product built right in. Alternatively, you can use the free NCover (*http://www.ncover.net*). There are other tools out there, but those are the two I use. Personally, I don't check in any code to the master sources until I've executed at least 85 to 90 percent of the lines in my code. I know some of you are groaning right now. Yes, getting good code coverage can be time consuming. Sometimes you need to do far more testing than you ever considered, and it can take awhile. Getting the best coverage possible means that you need to run your application in the debugger and change data variables to execute code paths that are hard to hit though normal execution. Your job is to write solid code, however, and in my opinion, code coverage is about the only way you'll get it during the unit test phase.

Granted, I don't expect developers to test on every flavor of the operating system that customers might be using. However, if engineers can get 90 percent coverage on at least one operating system, the team wins 66 percent of the battle for quality. If you're not using a code-coverage tool, you're cheating yourself on quality. When it comes to debugging, you can't debug code that isn't executing. By driving the code coverage during your unit tests to high levels, you're doing the most effective debugging possible: executing the code!

What sort of development methodology should I use?

A Google search for "software development methodologies" yields 82,600,000 different links (at the time I wrote this) expounding on all sorts of wild-sounding names: Adaptive Software Development, Scrum XP (Extreme Programming, not the operating system), Context Driven Testing, Test Driven Development (TDD), and many more. It gets even more confusing when you realize that there are 10 to 15 different versions of *Agile* development. In addition, people are extremely passionate about their chosen methodology. The last thing you want to do is get caught in the middle of a rumble between Chrystal and Scrum supporters. It's just like the Capulets and the Montagues, but without the sexy iambic pentameter.

I very much like the ideas of Agile development because they've done a good bit to help focus developers on quality, and I try to use the appropriate form of Agile development on all my projects. However, like most things in software, you just can't walk in to the office one day and say, "We're going to be a Scrum shop!" What you need to do is have everyone, including upper management, do a complete dump on what went right and wrong on the last few development cycles. You can use that as a base to start your research into the pros and cons of different methodologies. You'll be looking for the one that best matches the type of development you are doing.

This is a major undertaking in which you have to have absolute full support from management to do the experimenting and learning to change how your shop works. The ideal situation is to try to pilot different methodologies on smaller pieces of the development. The goal is to try to get an apples-to-apples comparison on what will work best in your development shop.

I'd also strongly recommend getting real training for managers and developers in the methodologies you are interested in. It's one thing to read a book on how to use the Windows Presentation Foundation, but a whole other problem to tackle the fuzziness of software development methodologies that way. The whole team has to go to this training, not just one or two members, so you can practice as a team, and most importantly, think about the ramifications of the ideas as they relate to your company.

When it comes down to the level of developers with their day-to-day work, I'm a firm believer in the precepts of Test Driven Development (TDD)—the idea of developing test cases right along with your code. I'm not a zealot who goes off and blindly follows the extreme view of writing all the tests before I ever tackle a line of the actual code. For me it's an iterative approach. For example, I'll write the parameter checking for a method and then write the tests to call the method with all the good and bad conditions. If you look at the code for the book, you'll also see that my tests are always compiled with the main application code so that no unit tests are ever out of date.

Should we do code reviews?

Absolutely! Unfortunately, many companies go about them in completely the wrong way. One company I worked for required formal code reviews that were straight out of one of those only-in-fantasyland software engineering textbooks I had in college. Everything was role-based: there was a Recorder for recording comments, a Secretary for keeping the meeting moving, a Door Keeper to open the door, a Leader to suck oxygen, and so on. All that you really had, however, were 40 people in a room, none of whom had read the code. It was a huge waste of time.

The kind of code reviews I like are the one-on-one informal kind. You simply sit down with a printout of the code and read it line by line with the developer. As you read it, you're keeping track of all the input and output so that you can see what's happening in the code. Think about what I just wrote. If that sounds perilously close to debugging the code, you're exactly right. Focus on what the code does—that's the purpose of a code review.

One of the wonderful members of the Review Crew, who reviewed this book as I was writing it, pointed out that on one project he was on, the management dictated that these informal code reviews be done before checking in any code. His reaction was, "This is absolutely nuts, and they won't accomplish anything!" As he was forced to go through with the reviews, he was pleasantly surprised at how much good advice and bug fixes came out of the review. Even better, the overhead was so much lower than that from actual debugging.

Another trick for ensuring that your code reviews are worthwhile is to have the junior developers review the senior developer's code. Not only does that teach the less-experienced developers that their contribution is valuable, but it's also a fine way to teach them about the product and show them great programming tips and tricks.

When you're doing these code reviews, your focus is on finding logic errors and bugs and making performance tweaks. The first step is to do a very quick read-through after the developer has given a verbal presentation on his requirements and a general description of how he went about solving the problem. What you're looking for here is if the developer is meeting the requirements. The reviewer has already read the code, but this gives the developer the chance to explain the reason why the developer picked certain implementations and handled situations the way they did. These reviews are also where the reviewer asks the general questions he composed during the initial reading.

The next step is the bulk of the review: reading through the code with the developer. In this stage, you're manually executing the code. When I do this, I like to sit down, start with good data passed into the module, and follow the flowthrough. As I'm reading, I'm asking the developer who wrote the code the detail questions I came up with in my prior reading.

The key to this process is that confrontation is absolutely not allowed. I know it's sometimes very hard to avoid offending people when reading their code, but it's not the job of the reviewer to show any superiority, only to make suggestions. The one way to prevent confrontation is by keeping the two or three folks doing the code reviews together so they are very aware that if they get out of line, their turn in the review seat is next and their reviews will be done by the person whose code they are currently reviewing.

What do we do if we're having trouble reproducing builds sent to others outside the team?

Every time you do a build for someone outside the team, you should make a complete copy of the project build directory on CD/DVD or tape. This copy will include all your source files, the intermediate files, the symbol files, and the final output. Also include the installation kit that you sent the customer. CD/DVDs and tapes are inexpensive insurance against future problems.

Even when I've done everything possible to preserve a particular build in version control, I've still experienced cases in which a rebuild produced a binary that differed from the original. By having the complete build tree archived, you can debug the user's problem with exactly the same binaries that you sent.

What additional C# compiler options will help me with my proactive debugging of managed code?

Although managed code eliminates many of the most common errors that plagued us with native code, certain errors can still affect your code. Fortunately, there are some fine command-line options to help find some of those errors. The good news about Microsoft Visual

Basic is that it has all the appropriate defaults, so no additional compiler switches are necessary. If you don't want to set all of these manually, the SettingsMaster add-in from Chapter 7, "Extending the Visual Studio IDE," will do the work for you.

/checked+ (Check Integer Arithmetic)

You can specify the checked keyword around potential problem areas, but it's something you have to remember to do as you're typing the code. The /checked+ command-line option will turn on integer underflow and overflow checking for the whole program. If a result is outside the range of the data type, the code will automatically throw a run-time exception. This switch will cause quite a bit of extra code generation, so I like to leave it on in debug builds and look for the places in code where I would need to use the checked keyword for explicit checking in release builds. To turn this switch on, in the project Properties, select the Build tab and click Advanced. In the Advanced Build Settings dialog box, select the Check For Arithmetic Underflow/Overflow check box.

/noconfig (Ignore Csc.rsp)

Interestingly, you can't set this switch in Visual Studio. However, it's worth knowing what the switch can allow you to do if you want to build from the command line. By default, the C# compiler reads in the Csc.rsp file to set default command-line options before it processes the command line. You can set any valid command-line options in that file you want to be globally applied. In fact, the default supplied Csc.rsp file includes a slew of /REFERENCE command-line options to common assemblies that we all use over and over. If you've ever wondered why you don't need to specifically reference something like System.XML.dll, it's because System.XML.dll is included in Csc.rsp with the /r: System.XML.dll switch. Csc.rsp is located in the .NET Framework version directory, *%SystemRoot%*\Microsoft.NET\Framework*Framework_Version*.

What CPU should I set my build to?

The default for .NET applications is anycpu, and you should leave it at that. That enables what I think is one of the most interesting features in .NET: *automatic bitness*. What that means is that your application automatically becomes a full-fledged 64-bit application on 64-bit machines. I think it's amazing that for the price of a single compile, you have a binary that will run as a natural binary on 32-bit CPUs, 64-bit CPUs, and even the 64-bit Itanium.

The automatic bitness can, though, come back to hurt you. If your code relies on an in-process DLL, either through COM or straight Platform Invoke (PInvoke), you might be in for a shock the first time you run on a 64-bit system. Since your program is loaded and automatically switches to being a 64-bit application, what do you think happens when you go to load that 32-bit dependency you have? Suddenly, your application is no longer happy, and you're dealing with an unexpected unhandled exception.

If you are dependent on a 32-bit native DLL, you'll want to look at building your application with the /platform:x86 switch to ensure that your code will run on all .NET platforms.

The 64-bit version of the .NET Framework also installs the 32-bit version, so your code will still run just fine. This does not excuse you from testing on 64-bit operating systems at all. Consider this the perfect excuse to justify an x64 box in your office.

As I mentioned in Chapter 2, I did much of the development for this book on Windows XP Professional x64 Edition. What's been interesting about being an early adopter of 64-bit technology is finding out how much code is still making bad pointer-size assumptions. This is especially prevalent on PInvoke declarations. Even if your code does not knowingly rely on any 32-bit DLLs, you can still cause havoc with incorrectly sized structures.

The one structure I've seen consistently wrong is the NMHDR structure, which is the basis of the shell notifications for all the common controls. The problem is that the MSDN documentation shows the wrong structure, not the one that's actually in the headers. The documentation says that the second field is a UINT (unsigned integer), but the actual type is UINT_PTR (unsigned integer pointer) If you're hand-crafting PInvoke declarations, go directly to the headers and verify exactly what the native types are. The correct C# declaration is as follows:

```
[StructLayout(LayoutKind.Sequential)]
public struct NMHDR
{
    public IntPtr hwndFrom;
    public IntPtr idFrom;
    public int code;
}
```

Even if you get your structure declarations from the wonderful *http://www.PInvoke.net*, double-check them anyway. I updated the NMHDR definition on the site, but I'm sure there are others that don't properly account for 64-bit variants.

When should I freeze upgrades to the compiler and other tools?

Once you've hit feature complete, also known as beta 1, you should definitely not upgrade any tools. You can't afford the risk of a new compiler optimization scheme, no matter how well thought out, changing your code. By the time you hit beta 1, you've already done some significant testing, and if you change the tools, you'll need to restart your testing from zero.

Is there anything I can do to speed up the Source Server when I first debug a program?

The Source Server support in Srcsrv.dll executes your version-control system to pull files one at a time. If your version-control software or network isn't the fastest in the world, you may start dreading bouncing around the stack while debugging because you'll be waiting for the file to show up. Fortunately, there's a way to pre-pull the source code versions in a binary—by using the Srctool.exe program.

When I described in Chapter 2 how Source Server performed the source indexing, I mentioned that the Source Server code uses Srctool.exe to extract the names of the source files in a PDB.

The developers added many more capabilities to the tool, which you can see by passing ? on the command line. The -x and -d options are the interesting options: -x tells Srctool.exe to do an extraction operation on a specified PDB file, and -d is followed by the destination directory of the extraction. Note that all the -x switch does is extract all the source files indexed in the PDB file.

There's a small bug in the Srctool.exe directory parsing that you need to be aware of. If you specify C:\Symbols\Source, the actual directory will be C:\Symbols\Source\Src because Srctool.exe appends the SRC no matter what. What I do is extract the files to a temporary directory and copy the directories under the SRC file to my cache directory to work around the bug.

How does *ConditionalAttribute* work?

There's a good bit of confusion and misinformation about *ConditionalAttribute* and conditional compilation, so I want to clear up exactly what happens in both. Because code is worth a million words of prose, I'll use the following program to show exactly what's happening:

```
using System;
using System.Collections.Generic;
using System.Text;
using System.Diagnostics;

namespace CondComp
{
    class Program
    {
        [Conditional ( "DEBUG" )]
        static void ConditionalWriteALine ( String data )
        {
            Console.WriteLine ( data );
        }

#if DEBUG
        static void IfDefWriteALine ( String data )
        {
            Console.WriteLine ( data );
        }
#endif

        static String ReturnData ( String data )
        {
            return ( data );
        }
        static void Main ( string [] args )
        {
            ConditionalWriteALine ( ReturnData ( "Hello from " ) +
                                ReturnData ( "ConditionalWriteALine" ));
#if DEBUG
            IfDefWriteALine ( ReturnData ( "Hello from " ) +
                            ReturnData ( "IfDefWriteALine" ));
#endif
        }
    }
}
```

By applying *ConditionalAttribute* to a method, which can have only a *void* return value because of the way *ConditionalAttribute* is declared, you're telling the compiler to not generate any calls to that method if the defined value is not specified with the /define: compiler switch. The compilers are also smart enough to look at the calls to the method with *ConditionalAttribute* specified, and if the attributed method has any method calls as parameters, as shown in *Main* with *ConditionalWriteALine* in the example above, those calls to *ReturnData* are also removed. If you look at the release build of the above code with ILDASM, where *DEBUG* is not defined, *Main* shows the following intermediate language (IL):

```
.method private hidebysig static void  Main(string[] args) cil managed
{
  .entrypoint
  // Code size       1 (0x1)
  .maxstack  8
  IL_0000:  ret
} // end of method Program::Main
```

As you can see, neither the calls to the *ConditionalWriteALine* or *IfDefWriteALine* methods appear, nor do any of the calls to the return *ReturnData* method in the parameter lists. Where things are a little more interesting with *ConditionalAttribute* is that the definition of the *ConditionalWriteALine* method is still in the IL for the whole program. That means that a nefarious person who has physical access to your assembly can load it through reflection and call that method you meant only to be called in a debug build because the method is still there in a release build. Depending on your application, that could potentially open up a security hole.

As you saw in the IL snippet, the method that uses the *#if DEBUG...#endif* conditional compilation is not called either by *Main*. The advantage to conditional compilation is that the method definition is stripped from the program, so in the example above, the *IfDefWriteALine* method doesn't appear in the release build. Of course, the drawback of conditional compilation is shown in the C# code at the beginning of this question: you'll have to surround every call to that method with conditional compilation to avoid compiler errors.

Spencer Low, one of the excellent Review Crew members, suggested a workaround with which you can get the benefit of *ConditionalAttribute* without letting any debug-only code slide into your released bits. You'll use *ConditionalAttribute* on the method, but use conditional compilation inside the method as in the following:

```
[Conditional ( "DEBUG" )]
static void ConditionalWriteALine ( string data )
{
#if DEBUG
    Console.WriteLine ( data );
#endif
}
```

With Spencer's trick, you won't have to litter your code with conditional compilation around all the callers.

Why do you always put the constants on the left side of conditional statements?

As you look through my code, you'll notice that I always use statements such as *if (0 == processId)*" instead of "*if (processId == 0)*. The reason I use this style is that I'm an ancient C programmer from a bygone era. In the old days, it was very easy to forget one of the equal signs, and unlike the latter statement, using the former syntax will yield a compiler error if you do forget the second equal sign. The C# compiler is good enough that it will produce a warning if you forget an equal sign on the latter. Having been burned so many times in the old days with the insidious bug of doing an assignment in a conditional statement, it's ingrained in my DNA to always put the constant on the left side.

By trying to assign to a constant, this becomes a compiler error instead of a warning, thus stopping all builds no matter what the compiler settings are. I've found that it's a lot easier to fix compiler warnings and errors than to fix bugs in the debugger.

Some developers have complained, sometimes vociferously, that the way I write conditional statements makes the code more confusing to read. I don't agree. My conditional statements take only a second longer to read and translate. I'm willing to give up that second to avoid wasting huge amounts of time later.

What's the difference between a .NET debug and release binary?

Much like native C++, it's all about the optimizations. From a physical standpoint, a debug build has less optimized IL instructions, so more IL instructions mean more CPU instructions when JIT compiling. The main reason for the additional IL instructions is to increase debuggability. For example, the release build code for the *ExtendedTask.ToolLocation* property in Wintellect.Build.Tasks.DLL consists of three straightforward instructions to return a private field:

```
.method public hidebysig specialname instance string
        get_ToolLocation() cil managed
{
  // Code size       7 (0x7)
  .maxstack  8
  IL_0000:  ldarg.0
  IL_0001:  ldfld string Wintellect.Build.Tasks.ExtendedTask::toolLocation
  IL_0006:  ret
} // end of method ExtendedTask::get_ToolLocation
```

The debug build, on the other hand, has seven instructions and introduces a compiler-generated local variable:

```
.method public hidebysig specialname instance string
        get_ToolLocation() cil managed
{
  // Code size       12 (0xc)
  .maxstack  1
```

```
.locals init ([0] string CS$1$0000)
IL_0000:  nop
IL_0001:  ldarg.0
IL_0002:  ldfld  string Wintellect.Build.Tasks.ExtendedTask::toolLocation
IL_0007:  stloc.0
IL_0008:  br.s        IL_000a
IL_000a:  ldloc.0
IL_000b:  ret
} // end of method ExtendedTask::get_ToolLocation
```

The first instruction in the bug build is a *NOP*, which just like the x86 instruction with the same mnemonic, means *no operation*. The C# and Visual Basic compilers put these in for debug builds so that you can set breakpoints at the beginning of a basic block. A *basic block* is a section of code with exactly one entry and one exit.

Another major difference between a debug and release build is the *DebuggableAttribute* value. As you can see from the name, this has something to do with debuggability and is what the JIT compiler looks for to determine how to compile the IL. *DebuggableAttribute* is initialized with the OR'd values from the *DebuggingModes* structure shown here:

```
public enum DebuggingModes
{
    // Fields
    Default = 1,
    DisableOptimizations = 0x100,
    EnableEditAndContinue = 4,
    IgnoreSymbolStoreSequencePoints = 2,
    None = 0
}
```

In a debug build, the compiler sets all the flags in the *DebuggerAttribute* constructor. Obviously, the *DebuggingModes.DisableOptimizations* value does what the name says and tells the JIT compiler to do no optimizations. The *DebugggingModes.IgnoreSymbolStoreSequencePoints*, if set, tells the debugger to use the implicit sequence points in the IL itself instead of the PDB file. The sequence points tell the debugger where a source line maps to an IL instruction. Rick Byers, a developer on the CLR debugging team, has an excellent blog post that describes exactly why you always want to set the *DebugggingModes.IgnoreSymbolStoreSequencePoints* if you are a compiler writer or using *Reflection.Emit* at *http://blogs.msdn.com/rmbyers/archive /2005/09/08/462676.aspx*. In essence, by using the implicit sequence points in the IL, the debugger doesn't have to read the PDB file, thus producing a large performance boost.

In the "Build All Builds with Debugging Symbols" section in Chapter 2, I mentioned that you want to use /debug:pdbonly when compiling your release builds instead of /debug. As far as the *DebuggerAttribute* constructor is concerned, the difference is that with /debug, the *DebuggingModes* value is *Default* and *IgnoreSymbolStoreSequencePoints* OR'd together. The *Default* is present for backwards compatibility with .NET 1.1, so the debugger runs .NET 2.0 binaries the same way they were run in .NET 1.1. The new .NET 2.0 /debug:pdbonly compilation switch specifies only *IgnoreSymbolStoreSequencePoints*.

Visual Studio Bugs

As we all know, no piece of software is perfect, Visual Studio included. However, there are a few bugs in Visual Studio that have tripped many people up, so I want to show you how to recover from them so you don't destroy your keyboard or monitor out of complete frustration.

Visual Studio crashes when I load a specific project or when I press F5, won't debug at all, or won't hit any breakpoints. What's going on?

Welcome to .suo hell. Sitting beside your .sln solution files is a hidden file with the same name as your solution except for the .suo file name extension. The .suo file gets corrupted simply by your breathing. If you see any flakiness with Visual Studio, immediately delete the .suo file associated with your solution, and it will usually clear up the problems you are having.

The .suo file contains the open file list for the project, all your breakpoints, and the contents of your Watch windows. For my sanity, every couple of days, I open a command prompt and execute the following command at the root of my project source code to delete any .suo files.

```
del /f /a:h /s *.suo
```

What annoys me so much about the corrupt .suo file bug is that it's been a bug in Visual Studio since Microsoft Visual C++ 2.0, which Microsoft shipped in 1994, when some of you reading were in elementary school. Sadly, the day after the release to manufacturing (RTM) for Visual Studio 2005, I was using my freshly installed RTM bits and I had yet another perfectly reproducible .suo corruption problem with one of my projects. It's enough to drive you insane.

Suddenly, a specific key doesn't work in the editor. I've tried uninstalling and reinstalling, but I still can't use the key. How can I get my key back?

When you uninstall Visual Studio, it does not remove your settings, which are stored in C:\Documents and Settings*User_Name*\Application Data\Microsoft\VisualStudio\8.0. In that directory is a file, Current.vsk, that contains your current keyboard settings. Move that file to a different directory, and then restart Visual Studio. That should clear up the missing key problem. Obviously, you'll lose any custom keyboard mappings with this workaround, so you'll need to recreate them.

What happened to the Debug menu (or some other major UI portion)?

One particularly odd problem that I've experienced on a few machines is that selecting Windows on the Debug menu shows only 5 items instead of the 14 items that are supposed to be there when you are debugging. Additionally, the Debug toolbar will be missing the Step Into and Step Out buttons. Even if you use the command Devenv.exe /ResetSettings, which is supposed to return everything to the raw defaults, you'll never get all the Windows menu items under Debug menu or toolbar back to what they were.

The trick is to select Import and Export Settings on the Tools menu, and in the Import and Export Settings Wizard, click Reset All Settings. Once you click Next and go through a couple of pages asking if you want to save the settings, you'll get to a page where you can select the Default Collection Of Settings. (I use the General Development settings.) After clicking Finish, everything will be reset, and your Windows sub-menus under Debug will have the correct screen elements on it.

Designing for Debugging

Having a consistent plan for exception and error handling is critical to ensuring that you'll be able to debug problems in production environments. Additionally, many developers are confused about when to use finalization, so I wanted to give you the concise rules to finalization.

How should you implement exception handling?

Even though Microsoft cleaned up the exception handling story considerably in .NET, compared to other environments, it's still the one area people have the biggest problem getting right. Two books show you the background of exception handling and the best practices that everyone needs to follow. The first is Jeffrey Richter's *CLR via C#* (Microsoft Press, 2006), and the second is *Framework Design Guidelines: Conventions, Idioms, and Patterns for Reusable .NET Libraries,* by Krzysztof Cwalina and Brad Abrams (Addison Wesley, 2006). If you're doing .NET development without having read those books' sections on exception handling, you're wasting your time.

Both books mention the idea that you should let the applications crash instead of trying to recover from exceptions. Continually in my consulting work, I find that developers will go to great lengths to attempt to recover from unknown exceptions, and this is exactly the wrong approach to take. If you have an unknown exception occurring in your application, and you attempt to recover, you'll be running with unpredictable behavior and opening yourself up to security vulnerabilities.

Additionally, if you try to recover from an unknown exception, you will end up causing an exception later in the application and mask off the root cause of the original exception. You could cause a different exception anywhere from a millisecond or less to two weeks later or more depending on the application and exception. By letting the application crash, you'll have a direct correlation between the root cause and the crash so you'll be able to fix the application more quickly.

How can I log unhandled exceptions in my applications?

As I described in the last question, you want to let your application crash if there's an unhandled exception, but you will want to at least log that there's been an unhandled exception. For ASP.NET applications, you can look for unhandled exceptions in two places. If you want to get those errors on a per page basis, provide a *Page_Error* method for the page. For application-wide unhandled exceptions, add a global application class (in Global.asax) to the project, and put your logging in the *Application_Error* method.

No matter which method is logging your ASP.NET unhandled exceptions, you'll be getting the actual *Exception*-derived unhandled exception by using the *Server.GetLastError* method. After carefully logging the error in your *Page_Error* or *Application_Error* method, you need to decide how to report the error to the user. If you call *Server.ClearError*, the error propagation through the rest of ASP.NET will not happen. If you do not call *Server.ClearError*, the error will be reported to the user through the settings in the *<customErrors>* section of Web.Config.

The one limitation of the *<customErrors>* section is that the *defaultRedirect* attribute and *<error>* elements, where you can specify HTTP error redirects caused by your ASP.NET code, is that you can redirect only to static HTML pages. What I prefer doing in my *Application_Error* is to put the unhandled exception into the session state and redirect to an ASPX page so I can do better logging and display to the user. I'll still keep my *<customErrors>* section for the HTTP errors. The following shows an example *Application_Error* performing the redirect.

```
void Application_Error(object sender, EventArgs e)
{
    // Get the exception and stuff it into a session state variable.
    // If you call Server.GetLastError in the redirect page, it will
    // return null.
    Exception ex = Server.GetLastError ( );
    Session.Add ( "UnhandledException" , ex );
    // Redirect to the error page.
    Response.Redirect ( "ErrorReportingPage.aspx" , false );
    // You have to clear the error or it will go through the
    // <customErrors> section.
    Server.ClearError ( );
}
```

For console applications, all unhandled exceptions by any thread in your application are reported on a per-AppDomain basis through the *AppDomain.UnhandledException* event. A breaking change between .NET 1.1 and .NET 2.0 is that in .NET 2.0, unhandled exceptions on all threads terminate the application. In .NET 1.1, only an exception on the main thread terminates the application. Having your application continue on its merry way after a pool thread disappears was completely wrong, and the old behavior was a bug in .NET itself.

Even with the improved unhandled exception behavior in console applications, there's still a small problem. If you have an unhandled exception in a pool thread or a finalizer thread, you get the standard crash message, which provides an opportunity to debug the application.

However, the main application thread is still running while the dialog is displayed, so your application can end before you get a chance to attach the debugger. I have no idea why pool threads and finalizer threads are treated this way, but I certainly hope that by the time the next version of the CLR ships, when one thread crashes, all threads will stop in unhandled exception scenarios.

Windows Forms applications add another twist to the unhandled exception mix. For background, pool, and finalizer threads, unhandled exceptions are reported through the *AppDomain .UnhandledException* event. As with the console application case, the main thread continues to run as you're handling the event. If the unhandled exception is in the main thread, you'll need to set the *Application.ThreadException* event in order to receive the notification. The good news is that setting the *Application.ThreadException* will disable the standard Windows Forms exception notification dialog box.

Since I'm talking about Windows Forms applications, instead of writing your own exception-reporting user interface, you should take a look at the Microsoft Exception Message Box, which is part of Feature Pack for Microsoft SQL Server 2005 - April 2006 and can be downloaded from *http://www.microsoft.com/downloads/details.aspx?FamilyID=df0ba5aa-b4bd-4705-aa0a-b477ba72a9cb&DisplayLang=en*. If you've ever seen an error in any of the SQL Server 2005 graphical tools, this is the same message box but in a redistributable package. The message box supports copying all the exception data to the clipboard in addition to showing the detailed data about the assertion. You can find more information on the features and usage of the Microsoft Exception Message Box at *http://msdn2.microsoft.com/en-us/library /ms166343.aspx*.

If you control the computers and network your application is running on, you can simply log any unhandled exception information to a file or database in a shared location. However, if you are providing software that runs outside your company, things get a little more interesting. You may want to develop with a Web service you can call with all the exception information from the user's application. If you don't have a server that can run your Web service, you may want to take a look at the Shareware Starter Kit that Microsoft put together to help shareware authors provide program registration, buy-now functionality, and, most importantly, a Web service to record your unhandled exceptions. You can find the source code and more information about the Shareware Software Starter Kit at *http://sharewarestarterkit.com*.

The last item I want to mention about unhandled exceptions is how you can send errors your users report to Microsoft. When the crash dialog box (which is in Figure 4-2, in case you've never seen it before) appears, the user can send the error information to Microsoft. To get all your company's errors, all you have to do is register for Windows Error Reporting at *http://msdn.microsoft.com/isv/resources/wer/default.aspx*. The only cost to you is for the purchase of a digital certificate.

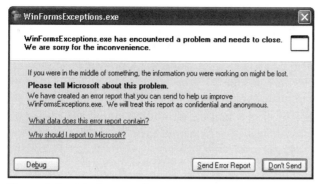

Figure 4-2   Windows application error message

I'd strongly recommend that you sign up for Windows Error Reporting so you can get those crash reports. Even if you set up your logging to upload the data directly through a Web service right into your bug-tracking database, you never know when that interop problem will kill some memory inside the CLR and cause it to have a native crash. Although not everyone clicks the Send button, enough will for you to quickly see which errors are causing the most pain for end users.

When do I put a finalizer on my class?

Almost never. Finalization offers a way for a class to clean up resources before the object is garbage collected in memory. The idea was that if you were holding onto a native resource, such as a native Windows file handle, you'd have a method that allowed you to get the handle closed. The problem is that with C#, a finalizer method is denoted with a "~" in front of a method that's the same name as the class.

It was a mistake to use "~," because many developers coming from a C++ background thought that meant the method was a destructor and the object would be cleaned up when you set the object instance to *null* or when the reference goes out of scope. The garbage collector is a nondeterministic system, so you have no idea when the object is actually freed and its finalizer called. This can lead to situations in which you're holding onto native resources far longer than you expect.

To alleviate the problems on developers inadvertently using finalizers, .NET 2.0 introduces the *SafeHandle* class in the *System.Runtime.InteropServices* namespace. If you have a native resource, you'll wrap the native resource and only the native resource in a *SafeHandle*-derived class and override the abstract *ReleaseHandle* and *IsInvalid* get property. In those two methods, you'll handle cleaning up your native resource and returning if the handle you're wrapping is invalid. By using a *SafeHandle*-derived class, which is derived from *CritialFinalizerObject* class, you're telling the runtime to pay extra attention to this class to ensure that it truly gets cleaned up.

Having seen numerous problems with finalizers, I wanted to make sure I mentioned what you need to be doing instead. In code reviews, I specifically look for finalizers on classes and flag them as errors so the developer can get rid of them. A good article by Steve Toub, "Keep Your Code Running with the Reliability Features of the .NET Framework," in the October 2005 MSDN Magazine, discusses *SafeHandle* classes and reliability in more depth (*http://msdn.microsoft.com/msdnmag/issues/05/10/Reliability/*). A blog entry by Joe Duffy, "Never write a finalizer again (well, almost never)," also offers another discussion of the topic (*http://www.bluebytesoftware.com/blog/PermaLink.aspx?guid=86c71425-57bc-4fcb-b34b-3262812f12cf*).

Debugger Questions

Although Chapter 5, "Advanced Debugger Usage with Visual Studio," covers the amazing .NET debugger in Visual Studio, a few common questions fall outside the realm of pure .NET. I want to answer those questions here. Some of these are discussed in the Visual Studio documentation but are scattered around, so many developers aren't aware of the answers.

I need a debugger on a production system. Do I have to purchase an additional copy of Visual Studio for that machine?

The Visual Studio Express editions are free, but the Visual Web Developer edition does not support debugging inside Internet Information Services (IIS), so that doesn't work. The good news is that the Framework SDK includes the Microsoft CLR Debugger (DBGCLR) as part of its installation. DBGCLR is essentially the Visual Studio main frame with nothing but the managed debugging packages, which means that the memory footprint is almost trivial when compared to the full version of Visual Studio. The Framework SDK is also free, and you can download it from *http://msdn.microsoft.com/netframework/*. When you install the Framework SDK, make sure to select Custom Installation, and install only the tools portion to get just what you need.

What is that VSHOST thing?

In Windows, process creation is a relatively slow operation. Consequently, for .NET 2.0, the debugger team took advantage of the fact that there's no difference between EXEs and DLLs in the .NET world. The debugger keeps *AppName*.vshost.exe running as you're developing, and when you start debugging, they communicate to it to load your actual EXE into a separate AppDomain and execute all your code there.

There's a noticeable speed increase with the Vshost approach, and in almost all instances, you won't have any problems running in the default scenario. However, if you rely on certain Framework APIs, such as *AppDomain.CurrentsDomain.FriendlyName* and *Assembly.GetCalling-Assembly().FullName*, which obviously return different values if you're running under the *AppName*.vshosts.exe process. If your code absolutely relies on the running application, you can always resort to debugging the binary directly by going into the project properties, and on the Debug tab, clearing Enable The Visual Studio Hosting Process check box.

Can you debug SQL stored procedures by using Visual Studio?

Absolutely! You can debug all the SQL Server 2000 and SQL Server 2005 stored procedures you want by using Visual Studio because the support has been drastically improved. The one thing the documentation fails to mention is that you need to be a sysadmin for the SQL Server instances you'll want to debug. SQL Server 2005 is ready for debugging automatically, but for SQL Server 2000, you'll need to enable Visual Studio debugging each time it starts by executing the following statement in SQL Analyzer: *exec sp_sdidebug 'legacy_on'*.

The Server Explorer tool window in Visual Studio is where you can create your data connections to the particular database you want to use. Once you've established the connection, you can manipulate the database to your heart's content. To execute or debug any stored procedure in the database, right-click the stored procedure, and then select either Execute or Step Into Stored Procedure as appropriate. If the stored procedure requires parameters, Visual Studio will prompt you for them.

Single-stepping stored procedures is just like debugging any other type of code you'd debug in Visual Studio, so to see parameters and locals, use the Locals and Watch windows. You won't get to see temporary tables you create, but the convenience factor of using a single environment is wonderful.

A known problem prevents you from stepping into stored procedures on some systems when you could do so on those systems in the past. To work around this bug, delete the database connections and re-create them. That should clear up the problem. While I'm talking about issues, I should mention that it's an excellent idea *not* to use the Server Explorer default of always being shown on the left side of the IDE with auto-hide enabled. If you have an invalid data connection in Server Explorer, and you move your pointer over the Server Explorer tab, the IDE will refresh the window right before showing it. Because the connection to the server is done on the UI thread, the whole IDE will hang for a minute or more. By the way, the same UI hang on network access occurs with the Team Explorer window used to view your Team Foundation System servers.

In addition to stepping into stored procedures from Server Explorer, you can set up your projects so that you debug the stored procedures as your C# or Visual Basic code executes them. For console and Windows Forms applications, go into the project properties, and on the Debug tab at the bottom, select the Enable SQL Server Debugging check box. For ASP.NET projects, on the Web site menu, click Start Options, and in the Debuggers section of the Properties dialog box, select the SQL Server check box. In all cases, you'll need to open the stored procedure code from Server Explorer and set your breakpoints in the stored procedure before that stored procedure executes. Now you can step from your C# or Visual Basic code to the stored procedure and back.

How do you debug script by using Visual Studio?

Given the massive interest in all things AJAX, scripting with JavaScript and Microsoft Visual Basic, Scripting Edition (VBScript) are about to become quite important in your future. As is the case with SQL stored-procedure debugging, Visual Studio handles script debugging, but there are a few more twists along the way. Before debugging script in Microsoft Internet Explorer, you need to go into the Internet Options dialog box, and then on the Advanced tab, under the Browsing node, clear the Disable Script Debugging (Internet Explorer) check box. Note that if you want to debug scripts running with the HTML control in other applications, such as Microsoft Office Outlook, you'll also need to clear the Disable Script Debugging (Other) check box.

In all ASP.NET scenarios, using the JavaScript *debugger* or VBScript *Stop* keywords will always break into the debugger. However, the danger is that you'll accidentally check in the source code with the breaking keywords still there, which most development teams frown on. It's much better to use the built-in script-debugging support in your ASP.NET projects if you can. However, the way you set your breakpoints depends on the type of page you're working with.

If the page is an .html/.htm static HTML page, you can set your breakpoints in the *<script>* tags any time you like, and they will be hit. If the script is in an ASP.NET .aspx page, if you try to set a breakpoint, the IDE will complain that "This is not a valid location for a breakpoint." Even if you start debugging and you see the .aspx page loaded, you still won't be able to set a breakpoint. To solve this problem when you start debugging, on the Debug menu, click Windows, and then select Script Explorer to open the Script Explorer window. In the Script Explorer window, double-click the page that contains the script you want to debug. That will shift focus to the .aspx file, and you can set your breakpoints. One annoying problem with the ASP.NET script-debugging support is that none of the breakpoints you set in the script code is saved between debugging runs. That means that you'll have to manually set the script breakpoints each time.

If you want to debug any client-side script running in an instance of Internet Explorer, on the Tools menu, click Attach to Process to open the Attach To Process dialog box. In the Available Process section at the bottom of the dialog box, you'll select the instance of IExplore.exe you want to debug. If you leave the Attach To options set to Automatic, Visual Studio will assume that you want to debug script. After you click the Attach button, the Script Explorer window should appear. If it does not, on the Debug menu, click Windows, and then select Script Explorer. Double-click the script item in the Script Explorer window. The source opens, and now you can set breakpoints.

If you have to support a traditional ASP application, sometimes referred to as ASP.OLD, you're in luck with Visual Studio 2005. There's sufficient support in the script-debugging portion to make it relatively easy. All the steps are listed at *http://msdn.microsoft.com/library/default.asp?url=/library/en-us/vsdebug/html/vxtskaspscriptdebugging.asp?frame=true*. It's a little convoluted to set up, but it keeps you from installing an older version of Visual Studio just for ASP.OLD debugging.

For Windows Script Host (WSH) files and stand-alone .js and .vbs files, the JavaScript *debugger* or VBScript *Stop* keywords will break into the debugger. You can also start both wscript.exe and cscript.exe with the //X command-line option to trigger the script debugger so you can debug from the first executable line of script code.

How can I debug with a different Code Access Security (CAS) level?

Although you can debug across Windows accounts by starting the program in one account and running the debugger from an account with administrator privileges, debugging your code from the IDE running in a partially trusted zone, such as the Internet zone, was impossible until Visual Studio 2005. In .NET 1.1, you had to go to the CAS settings in the .NET Configuration Microsoft Management Console and manually change the process settings.

To play with your code in any CAS situation from the Visual Studio 2005 debugger, go into the project properties' Security tab, and then select the Enable ClickOnce Security Settings check box. That will enable you to select the execution zone and grant or deny specific permissions. Figure 4-3 shows where I've set custom CAS settings to deny *FileIOPermission* for the process.

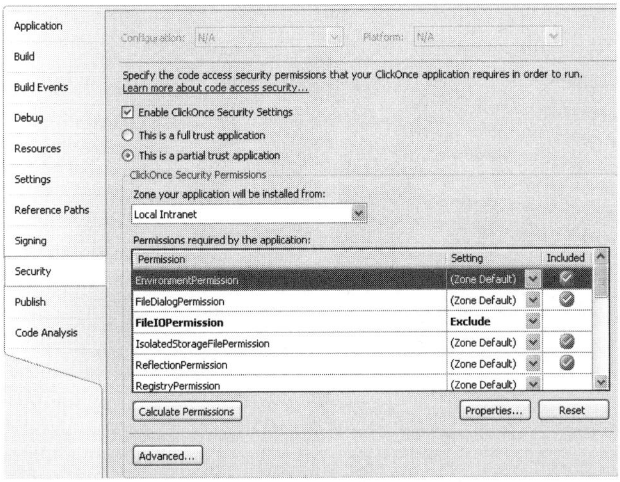

Figure 4-3   Setting the Code Access Security for the debuggee

Why do I sometimes get that annoying context switch deadlock exception when stopped in the debugger too long on Windows Forms applications? What are Managed Debugging Assistants?

Even though my friend Don Box likes to say, "Windows is the device driver," it's not quite to that point yet. We all have legacy C DLLs and COM/COM+ objects that we still need to use in our development. (By the way, am I the only one who thinks it odd that the COM specification reached only version 0.9? Does that mean that COM never made it to 1.0? Microsoft no longer has the COM Specification document posted, but see *http://www.sei.cmu.edu/str /descriptions/com_body.html* for the version number.)

When Microsoft was planning .NET 2.0, they looked at all the areas where developers were having trouble in their .NET applications, and PInvoking to both C DLLs and COM/COM+ components was at the top of the list. To rectify that, they added a very nice feature to the CLR runtime called Managed Debugging Assistants (MDAs), which do extra checking on that PInvoke boundary to ensure that you're not inadvertently causing yourself a major problem.

A perfect example of a seriously nasty problem to debug is if you pass a delegate to native code in order for the native code to be able to call back into your managed code. If, on the managed side, you release all references to the delegate, the delegate is eligible for garbage collection. However, the native code knows nothing about the garbage collector, so it's holding onto the delegate to call it when necessary. You can probably guess that what's going to happen is that a garbage collection is going to occur and clean up the actual delegate, and later, the native code will call the delegate, and you'll crash spectacularly.

There are 42 MDAs to assist you, although some are for logging purposes. You can read all about the MDAs at *http://msdn2.microsoft.com/en-us/library/d21c150d.aspx*. Additionally, Steve Toub wrote an excellent article on using them at *http://msdn.microsoft.com/msdnmag /issues/06/05/BugBash/*. The one thing I do want to specifically address is why some MDA errors cause you to stop in the debugger.

In the Exception dialog box, accessible from the Debug menu, if you expand the Managed Debugging Assistants node, you'll see that some items are selected by default, such as CallbackOnCollectedDelegate and ContextSwitchDeadlock. When running under a debugger, those selected MDAs cause the CLR to break into the debugger when one of those items triggers. Because the ContextSwitchDeadlock MDA is selected by default, you probably have seen the error when you have stopped in the debugger for longer than 60 seconds. Technically, the error reported by the ContextSwitchDeadlock MDA is a bug, but I wish it weren't.

Because Microsoft obviously put so much work into the MDA architecture, and MDA reports such good bugs, I like to occasionally run my applications with all MDA options selected when under the debugger. That way I get the best checking possible. You can also turn on all the MDA checking when running outside the debugger by setting an environment variable, COMPLUS_MDA. You can also turn on MDA checking with a registry key, but that is global to all processes, and it's better to set only the environment variable for specific processes.

If you set the COMPLUS_MDA to 1, the runtime will look for a file called *AppName*.exe .mda.config and read the settings you want for that program. The following shows an example file that turns on several interesting MDAs. I've discussed CallbackOnCollectedDelegate already. LoadFromContext tells you when the code calls *Assembly.LoadFrom*, which can lead to problems in serialization, casting, and dependency resolution because *Assembly.LoadFrom* does less proper checking than *Assembly.Load*. PInvokeStackImbalance checks that the native methods you are calling are properly declared and do not corrupt the stack. Finally,

StreamWriterBufferDataLost looks for the case in which a Stream object is being garbage collected before you have closed the stream. Even though all the MDA names start with an upper case letter, you specify them in *AppName*.exe.mda.config with an initial lower case:

```xml
<?xml version="1.0" encoding="UTF-8" ?>
<mdaConfig>
  <assistants>
    <callbackOnCollectedDelegate />
    <loadFromContext />
    <pInvokeStackImbalance />
    <streamWriterBufferedDataLost />
  </assistants>
</mdaConfig>
```

So you don't have to hand-write a configuration file every time, you can also set the COMPLUS_MDA environment variable to the MDA values you want to use. The following shows how to turn on the first two MDAs from the previous configuration file:

```
set COMPLUS_MDA=callbackOnCollectedDelegate;loadFromContext
```

Because the MDA checking is so important, I put a batch file in the code .\MDA\Ultimate-MDAEnv.CMD, which turns on all the error-checking MDA values. Now you can have your test environments running with a higher level of checking to find those errors before your customers do. What's even better is that the MDA settings work with your release build code so you could use them to monitor production systems if you absolutely had to.

Debugging War Story
The Garbage Collector Ate My Lunch

The Battle

In the middle of demonstrating the very cool SUPERASSERT.NET from Chapter 3, "Debugging During Coding," to a group of people, I was showing how to create a mini-dump at the assertion when the DiagnosticHelper-i386.exe program failed and returned the error code: D000000D. After the shock of showing a bug to the world wore off, I did have to laugh at the error code because it sounds like something my 16-year-old nephew would say. I wasn't laughing when I couldn't find anything on the Web that said anything about code returning an error code of D000000D.

What turned out to be even odder was that I could see this error on only a single machine. I tried all sorts of combinations of physical and virtual machines, but I'd get the error only on that one machine and, as always, it wasn't consistent. Just the kind of bug that screams that your life is going to be completely miserable for the next three days.

The error was occurring when SUPERASSERT.NET spawned the DiagnosticHelper-i386.exe program, so I left the assertion dialog box up and tried manually running Diag-nosticHelper-i386.exe from the command line to see if I could duplicate the behavior.

That's when I found something very interesting. If I passed the *-n process name* option, I didn't see any error, but if I used *-p process id,* I not only got the D000000D error, I was getting the standard Windows error message that a handle was invalid. Interestingly, when starting DiagnosticHelper-i386.exe from SUPERASSERT.NET, I saw the invalid handle error only once, and all the rest were D000000D. Another interesting find was that when D000000D was returned, a corrupt minidump file was left on the disk.

Obviously, the *MiniDumpWriteDump* Windows API call was failing, and seeing the invalid handle error was a major hint. *MiniDumpWriteDump* takes two handles, one for the process to write and the other for the file to write. One of the two was bad, but which one?

The Outcome

This one turned out to be a whopper of a bug! I flipped a coin and decided to look at the process handle first. Inside *Main*, my code was calling *Process.GetProcesses* and iterating through the returned array looking for the *Process* object matching the process ID from the p command-line option. Once I found the *Process* object, I called *Process.Handle* to get the handle to the process. After creating the stream to write to and a few other set-up items, I passed that handle value to the native *MiniDumpWriteDump* API.

If a handle is invalid, that means that some code had to call *CloseHandle* on it somewhere along the chain. That closing had to occur between getting the handle in *Main* and the eventual call to *MiniDumpWriteDump*. Therefore, I started the process under the debugger and set a breakpoint on the code that called *Process.Handle* and the call to *MiniDump-WriteDump*. I checked the handle value at the first breakpoint and started Process Explorer, which I'll discuss later in this chapter, and verified it was a valid handle. I ran to the breakpoint on *MiniDumpWriteDump* and was shocked to see that the handle value was no longer in Process Explorer's handle view! No wonder I was getting those invalid handle return values.

My next step was to open the teller of all truth, Reflector, and look at the code for *Process.Handle* to see how it worked:

```
public IntPtr Handle
{
    get
    {
        this.EnsureState(Process.State.Associated);
        return this.OpenProcessHandle().DangerousGetHandle();
    }
}
```

That *DangerousGetHandle* freaked me a bit when I read the following in the documentation: "...if the handle has been marked as invalid with *SetHandleAsInvalid, Dangerous-GetHandle* still returns the original, potentially stale handle value. The returned handle can also be recycled at any point." "... recycled at any point" screamed garbage collection!

My hypothesis at this point was that the *Process* object I was calling *Process.Handle* on was being garbage collected and so the process handle I was using was invalid. Using the coolest debugger trick of all, Make Object ID, which I'll discuss in the next chapter, I verified that that was indeed the case. Using WinDBG, discussed in Chapter 6, "WinDBG, SOS, and ADPlus," I set a breakpoint on the *CloseHandle* API, looked up the parameter on the native stack, and verified that the handle value I got on the call to *Process.Handle* was passed to *CloseHandle*, and that was occurring before my code called *MiniDumpWriteDump*.

Because the *Process* class does not have a finalizer on it, the *CloseHandle* call wasn't happening there. However, the process handle is stored in an internal class, *ProcessSafe-Handle*, so something in there was calling *CloseHandle*. I was just thrilled that I had a duplicatable case on a single machine so I could track the problem down.

I fixed the code by doing all the process-handle opening myself to ensure that the process handle wasn't eaten by the garbage collector. You can see all the code in the .\DiagnosticHelper\NativeMethod.cs file. The other lesson I learned was to not trust the return value from *Process.Handle* at all.

Debugging Scenario Questions

In this section, I want to talk about some of those very cool tricks in my debugging arsenal that come in handy in specific scenarios. Some of these techniques appear in the documentation, but they are so obscure that you may have never heard of them.

How do I debug assembles in the Global Assembly Cache (GAC)?

If you have a situation in which your assembly can reside only in the GAC, debugging can get a little interesting because getting PDB files loaded can be a pain. If you're working on the machine on which the assembly was built, the embedded path in the binary will find the PDB file, but if you're on a different machine, you may not find it. You could also go to the trouble of creating a mini Symbol Server, as I discussed in Chapter 2, in order to get the symbols. The good news is that there's an easier way.

The technique is to use the DEVPATH environment variable. By enabling DEVPATH, you're telling the assembly loader to look in the specified directory before looking at the GAC or the application directories. Additionally, although name, culture, public key token and processor architecture checking is done on the assembly, no version checking is done at all. This means that you can potentially have a situation in which the application runs differently on your development machine than in test or production. Interestingly, the lack of version checking can be valuable if you want to see how your application will work with a newer version of the assembly without having to remove the old one from the GAC.

> **Warning**   Note that this is only for development and test machines and should never be employed in production environments.

To enable DEVPATH, you must turn it on in the *<runtime>* section of Machine.Config, which you can find in *%SystemRoot%*\Microsoft.NET\Framework*versison*\CONFIG. The following shows what you would add:

```
<configuration>
    <runtime>
        <developmentMode developerInstallation="true"/>
    </runtime>
</configuration>
```

Once you have the *<developmentMode>* section set, you need to set the DEVPATH environment variable to the drive and directory where you want the runtime to look first. For .NET 2.0, you can specify only a single directory in the DEVPATH environment variable. If you leave the PDB file for the assembly in the DEVPATH specified directory, the debugger will load the PDB file from that directory. For more information about DEVPATH, see Junfeng Zhang's blog entry on DEVPATH at *http://blogs.msdn.com/junfeng/archive/2005/12/13/503059.aspx*.

How can I debug the startup code for a Windows service written in .NET?

Whereas you can easily attach to your service with Visual Studio once your Windows service is running and debug to your heart's content, debugging the startup code is an adventure. Because the Service Control Manager (SCM) is what has to call the *CreateProcess* API to get the service started, you can't start from the debugger. The traditional way of debugging service startup is through the Image File Execution Options registry key, and if your service is written in a managed language, you can still use the Image File Execution options.

The Image File Execution Options registry key (HKEY_LOCAL_MACHINE\SOFTWARE \Microsoft\Windows NT\CurrentVersion\Image File Execution Options) is where the operating system reads special values for setting global flags in the process. Additionally, you can also set a debugger so that no matter how you start the application, it always starts under a debugger. Keep in mind that the instructions I'm about to discuss apply only to 32-bit Windows systems. The reason is that the debugger program I'll show you in this trick is 32-bit only, so it can't debug 64-bit programs.

If you're feeling hard core and looking for adventure, you'll manually go into the Image File Execution Options key and start adding the appropriate entries. If that thought scares you, you can do what us normal people do, use GFlags.exe, which comes with the Debugging Tools for Windows package. Since the Image File Execution Options key is in HKEY_LOCAL_MACHINE, you'll have to run GFlags.exe from an account with administrator privileges.

Before we go any further, I have to scream, *You can make your machine unbootable and unusable with GFlags!* When you start GFlags, the first two tabs, System Registry and Kernel Flags, will change system-wide settings you don't want to change unless you work at Microsoft on the Windows kernel team and have full source code access. For you and me, as soon as you start GFlags, you want to click the Image File tab as fast as possible. In the Image File tab, you'll be limited to screwing up just the individual process.

On the Image File tab, in the edit control next to the Image: (TAB to refresh) label, type in only the name of your service with no path. In other words, if your service were happyserv.exe, that's exactly what you'd type. To enable the rest of the UI in Image File tab, press the Tab key after typing the name of your application. The Debugging Tools for Windows help file, Debugger.chm, documents all of the various check boxes for a process. As you can guess from the names of the fields, all of them are for native memory debugging.

For debugging your service startup, the two items of interest are the Debugger check box and text box. After selecting the Debugger check box, the text box becomes available, and you can specify the debugger you want to use. You won't type Devenv.exe here (the Visual Studio program name), but you'll type VsJITDebugger.exe, which is the Visual Studio Just-In-Time Debugger. There's no need to specify the path because the debugger is installed into the %SystemRoot%\System32 directory. Figure 4-4 shows a properly filled out GFlags screen shot.

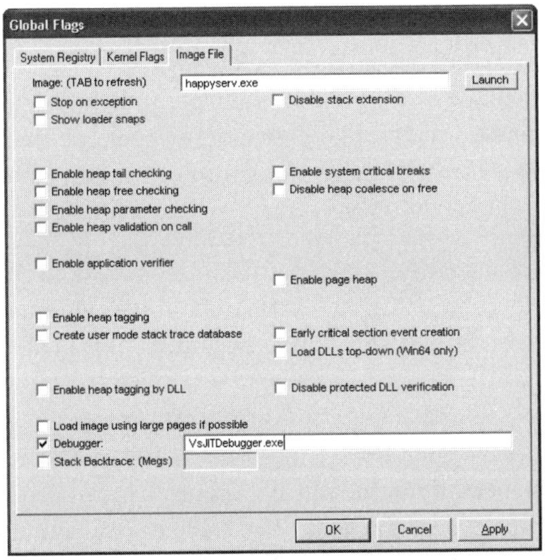

Figure 4-4   Setting the Image File Execution Options debugger value

When your service or any other program you specify starts, the operating system passes the program and any command-line arguments to VsJITDebugger.exe so you'll see the usual Visual Studio Just-In-Time Debugger dialog box asking you which debugger to use on the process. What's interesting about the undocumented behavior of VsJITDebugger.exe is that it sees your process is a managed process and enables mixed-mode (both managed and native) debugging.

As I mentioned, this trick won't work on x64 systems, so if you have to debug service startup on the wide bits, set the debugger to Windbg.exe. Because WinDBG is a native-only debugger and doesn't support .NET debugging, you'll have to use the SOS extension to debug your startup. Chapter 6 discusses WinDBG and SOS in detail. Although painful, it is doable but not something you want to do every day.

Even if you haven't done Windows service development before, you're probably aware that there's a startup timeout when starting a service. If your service does not call back into the SCM within 30 seconds of starting, the SCM will terminate the service. This isn't a lot of time to let Visual Studio start up and load all the symbols let alone for you to single-step through the service startup.

Fortunately, there's another barely documented registry tweak in which we can set the time-out value: In the HKEY_LOCAL_MACHINE\SYSTEM\CurrentControlSet\Control key, create a new DWORD value called ServicesPipeTimeout, and set the number of milliseconds you want the SCM to wait for service startup. After you set this value, you'll need to reboot the computer for the change to take effect. Obviously, you want to set the Services-PipeTimeout value on a production server because it's global to all services.

My boss is sending me so much e-mail that I can't get anything done. Is there any way I can slow down the dreaded PHB e-mail?

Although many of your bosses mean well, their incessant e-mail messages can become distracting and keep you from the real work you need to do. Fortunately, there's a simple solution that works quite well and will give you a week or so of wonderful peace so that you can work at hitting your deadlines. The less-technically proficient your boss and network administrators are, the more time you'll get.

In the previous section, I talked about the Image File Execution Options section of the registry and the fact that whenever you set a process's Debugger value, that process automatically starts under that debugger. The trick to ending the PHB (pointy haired boss) mail is the following:

1. Walk into your boss's office.

2. Open Regedit.exe. If your boss is currently in the office, explain that you need to run a utility on his machine so that he can access the XML Web services you're building. (It doesn't really matter whether you're creating XML Web services—the buzzwords alone will cause your boss to readily let you mess with his machine.)

3. In the Image File Execution Options section, create a key called Outlook.exe. (Substitute the executable name of your e-mail program if you don't use Outlook.) Tell your boss that you're doing this to allow him to have e-mail access to XML Web services.

4. Create the Debugger value and set the string to Sol.exe. Indicate to your boss that Sol is to allow your XML Web services to access Sun Solaris machines, so it's necessary for you use it.

5. Close Regedit.

6. Tell your boss that he's all set and can now start accessing XML Web services. The real trick at this point is to keep a straight face while walking out of your boss's office.

Avoiding laughter during this experiment is much more difficult than it sounds, so you might want to practice these steps with a few coworkers first.

What you've just set up is a situation in which every time your boss starts Outlook, Solitaire runs instead. (Since most bosses spend their days playing Solitaire anyway, your boss will be sidetracked for a couple of games before he realizes that he meant to start Outlook.) Eventually, he'll continue to click the Outlook icon until so many copies of Solitaire are running that he'll run out of virtual memory and have to reboot his machine. After a couple of days of this click-a-million-times-and-reboot cycle, your boss will eventually have a network administrator come in and look at his machine.

The admin will get all excited because she has a problem that is a little more interesting than helping the folks in accounts receivable reset their passwords. The admin will play with the machine for at least a day in your boss's office, thus keeping your boss from even being close to a machine. If anyone asks your opinion, the stock answer is, "I've heard of strange interaction problems between EJB and NTFS across the DCOM substrata architecture necessary to access the MFT using the binary least squares sort algorithm." The admin will take your boss's machine back to her office and continue to play with it for a couple of days. Eventually, the admin will repave the hard disk and reinstall everything on the machine, which will take another day or so. By the time your boss gets his machine back, he'll have four days of e-mail to get through, so it will be at least a day before he gets out from under all that mail, and you can safely ignore those messages for another day or two. If the PHB mail starts getting thick again, simply repeat the steps.

 Warning   Use this technique at your own career-limiting risk.

What strategies do you have for debugging deadlocks?

Without a doubt, some of the hardest problems to solve in modern software development are deadlocks. In fact, I spend a considerable amount of time showing you how to find them in Chapter 6, and I even wrote Code Analysis/FxCop rules in Chapter 8, "Writing Code Analysis Rules," to help ensure that you're following proper multithreading in managed code. However, even if you think you can plan for every situation, your multithreaded application can stop dead when you least expect it. The biggest obstacle to debugging multi-threaded deadlocks is that by the time your application is deadlocked, it's almost too late to start debugging.

As I've been emphasizing throughout this book, one of the keys to debugging is up-front planning. With multithreaded programming, up-front planning is the only way you can avoid the dreaded deadlocks. I break down the necessary planning for multithreaded applications into the following categories:

- Don't do it.
- Don't overdo it.
- Multithread only small, discrete pieces.
- Synchronize at the lowest level.
- Review the code—and review the code again.
- Test on multiprocessor machines.

Don't Do It

This first tip might seem a little facetious, but I'm absolutely serious. Make sure there's no other way you can structure your program before you decide to incorporate multithreading into your application. When you include multithreading in your application, you're easily adding a minimum of an extra month of development and testing to your schedule.

If you're coding thick-client applications and you need your program to do some lightweight background processing, check to see whether the work can be handled with a background periodic timer event. With a little creative thinking, you can probably find a way to avoid multithreading and the headaches that go with it.

Don't Overdo It

When it comes to server-based applications, you also have to be extremely careful not to create too many threads. One common mistake we've all seen is that some developers end up with a server application in which each connection runs on its own thread. The average development team is doing well to get 10 concurrent connections during their heaviest testing, and it looks like their code works fine. The code might work fine when first deployed, but as soon as business picks up, the server starts bogging down because it's not scalable.

When working on server applications, you'll definitely want to take advantage of the excellent support .NET has for thread pooling with the *ThreadPool* class from the *System.Threading* namespace. If used properly, you can get some wonderful throughput in your application. However, it's much easier to deadlock with misused thread pools than you can ever imagine. For more information on using the *ThreadPool* class, see Chapter 23, "Performing Asynchronous Operations," in *CLR via C#, 2nd Edition*.

Multithread Only Small, Discrete Pieces

If you must multithread, try to keep it to small, discrete pieces. With thick-client applications, you should stick to small pieces of work that are generally devoid of any user interface (UI) elements. For example, printing in the background is a smart use of multithreading because your application's UI will be able to accept input while data is printing.

In server applications, it's slightly different in that you need to judge whether the overhead of thread creation and work will actually speed up your application. Although threads are much more lightweight than processes, they still take quite a bit of overhead. Consequently, you'll want to make sure that the benefit of cranking up that thread will be worth the effort. For example, many server applications have to transfer data back and forth between some type of database. The cost of waiting for the write to that database can potentially be high. If you have a situation in which you don't need to do transactional recording, you can plop parts of the database write into a thread pool object and let it complete on its own time, and thus continue your processing. That way you'll be more responsive to the calling process and get more work done.

Synchronize at the Lowest Level

In my travels, I've seen this rule broken almost more than the rule that says curly braces go below the *if* statement. In .NET, it's trivial to use a *lock* statement on a field and grab it at the top of your method so you protect the whole method, when in reality; you need to protect just a single field access. Whenever you grab a lock or other synchronization object, you're causing other threads to block when they try to access that object. Your job as a developer using multithreading is to keep your threads running as much as possible and never block. It's far better to do three or four synchronization object grabs in a method instead of doing a single overall grab.

Review the Code—and Review the Code Again

If you really do need to multithread your application, you must allow plenty of time to walk through your multithreaded code in full code reviews. The trick is to assign one person to each thread in your code and one person to each synchronization object. In many ways, the code review in multithreaded programming is really a "multithreaded" review.

When you review the code, pretend that each thread is running at real-time priority on its own dedicated CPU and that the thread is never interrupted. Each "thread person" walks through the code, paying attention only to the particular code that his thread is supposed to be executing. When the thread person is ready to acquire a synchronization object, the "object person" literally moves behind the thread person. When the thread person releases a synchronization object, the object person goes to a neutral corner of the room. In addition to the thread and object representatives, you should have some developers who are monitoring the overall thread activity so that they can assess the program's flow and help determine the points at which different threads deadlock.

Test on Multiprocessor Machines

As I mentioned, a multithreaded application requires a much higher level of testing than a single-threaded one. The most important tip I have for testing your multithreaded application is to test it thoroughly on multiprocessor machines. And I don't mean simply running your application through a few paces; I mean continually testing your program in all possible scenarios. Even if your application runs perfectly on single-processor machines, a multiprocessor machine will expose deadlocks you never thought possible.

The best approach to this kind of testing is to have the team's developers run the application on multiprocessor machines every day. If you're a manager and you don't have any multiprocessor machines in your shop, stop reading right now and immediately equip your developers and QA testers with multiprocessor machines! If you're a developer without a multiprocessor machine, show this chapter to your manager and demand the proper equipment to do your job! Several people have written me and mentioned that showing this section really did help them get a multiprocessor machine, so don't hesitate to tell your manager that John Robbins said the company owed you one.

How do you debug design-time assemblies? How do you debug add-ins?

No matter if you're developing the world's greatest ASP.NET component or the world's best add-in, debugging those items is exactly the same. Anything loading into Visual Studio means that you'll be debugging Visual Studio itself. For your assembly, go into the project properties, Debug tab, and then click Start External Program. In the text box, you'll specify the path and directory to Devenv.exe. If Devenv.exe is in your PATH environment variable, which I would highly recommend, all you need to add is Devenv.

To debug your design-time components or add-ins, open the source file you want to debug and set a breakpoint. Whenever your assembly is loaded, Visual Studio will load the symbols and match up the source and line information from the breakpoint you've set. If it's a valid breakpoint, you'll break at the location.

To make it easier to set up debugging, the SettingsMaster add-in I discuss in Chapter 7, "Extending the Visual Studio IDE," makes it trivial to set up a .SettingsMaster file with your common debugging settings so you can apply those settings with a click of the mouse.

How do you debug assembly-loading issues?

In the native C++ days, it was straightforward to find out why a *LoadLibrary* could not find a particular DLL. However, in the .NET world, things are a little bit different because we have things such as the GAC, satellite assemblies, *<probing>* elements, and *<dependentAssembly>* elements; it can become quite tricky to figure out exactly where an assembly is supposed to be loaded from when you're staring at a *FileLoadException*. Fortunately, a mostly hidden utility that ships with the Framework SDK, the Assembly Binding Log Viewer, Fuslogvw.exe, can show you everything about assembly loading. The "Fus" in the program name stands for *Fusion*, which was the code name for the assembly loading portion of the CLR runtime.

If you want to see assembly load details for any .NET program on a machine, start Fuslogvw.exe from an account with administrator rights and click the Settings button on the UI. One strange bug with Fuslogvw.exe is that unless you specify a custom logging directory, the logging won't work. In the Settings dialog box, select the Enable Custom Path check box, and in the text box, specify a directory on the disk. The rest of the Settings dialog box lets you specify if you want to disable logging, log exception text, log binding failures, and log all binding. It's quite eye-opening to look at how your application is going through the gyrations of loading assemblies, so I'd recommend that you click Log All Binds To Disk.

Once your application starts, you can double-click any of the entries in the main window to see exactly how and what the .NET runtime was doing to look for the assemblies your program loaded. In the entries, you'll see exactly what was going on and where the runtime was looking for particular items so you can narrow down the assembly-loading problems.

How can I always get the source and line information in any unhandled exception?

You may have noticed that on your development machine when you're running your application, the unhandled exception stack walk shows the source and line of all items on the stack. If you would like the same information on your production systems, and you control those machines, all you need to do is include the PDB files in the same directory as the binary, and the .NET *StackWalk* class will automatically pick them up.

As I described in Chapter 2, there are no secrets in NET PDB files like those in native code. They contain only the source and line information and the names of local variables. If you're having trouble seeing exactly where an unhandled exception is coming from, dropping the PDB files into the same directory as the binary will give you the exact location where the exception is originating without giving up too much information.

What Tools Do You Use?

When I do a presentation at a conference or a company, the most common question I get is: "What tools do you use?" As someone who's spent a major portion of his career writing software development tools, everyone is interested in what I'm using. As a tool freak, I'm more than happy to share. I'll use any tool that can save me five minutes because time is truly money.

Throughout this book, I've been discussing various tools as they come up in the discussion. In this portion of the chapter, I want to list some of the tools that I haven't discussed or that require a more detailed explanation. If you're looking for general documentation and usage tools, see Chapter 2. For add-ins and macros, see Chapter 7.

Everything from SysInternals!

All through the book, I've referred to particular tools from Bryce Cogswell and Mark Russinovich at *www.sysinternals.com*, but anything at the Web site will be a lifesaver. All the tools there are free, so the price is certainly right! While you might not have heard of Bryce before, you've definitely heard of Mark. He's the coauthor, along with David Solomon, of *Windows Internals, 4th Edition* (Microsoft Press, 2005), the book on how Windows works. In addition to Mark's writing, he's the developer that broke the Sony rootkit story, which you can read about at *http://www.sysinternals.com/blog/2005/10/sony-rootkits-and-digital-rights.html*. As I was writing this book, both SysInternals and Winternals, Bryce and Mark's commercial software companies, were acquired by Microsoft. Even with all that, Mark's real claim to fame is that he used to be my neighbor in New Hampshire.

Process Explorer

Simply put, Process Explorer is what TaskManager hopes to be when it grows up. If you want to see anything about running processes on your computer, Process Explorer is the tool. In the "Know Where Your Assemblies Load" section in Chapter 2, I discussed the simple steps on how to use Process Explorer to view your relocated DLLs in your address space. Although that's a great trick, there's much more to Process Explorer that I want to cover here.

One of Process Explorer's fortes is that it lets you look at the open handles for a process. In the upper window, select your process and press Ctrl+H to cause the lower window to show you all the handles. It can't get much simpler than that. By default, Process Explorer shows you only the named handles. To see the unnamed handles, select Show Unnamed Handles And Mappings from the View menu. I will discuss why you want to name your handles and the strategies for doing so in the "The *!handle* Command" section of Chapter 6.

Because Process Explorer will update the Handle View as the process creates and deletes handles, you can see the exact state at any time. A great debugging trick is to sort by name in the Handle View by clicking on the Name column. If you see the same name repeatedly, you're looking at a handle leak, and by naming your handles, you've made it trivial to find exactly which one is being leaked. I've found countless handle-leak problems in our clients' applications by using nothing more than the Handle View window in Process Explorer.

By double-clicking any handle in the Handle View, you can see the detailed information about that handle. For example, if the handle is an Event, you can see its type and signaled state. This information is invaluable for looking at your handle state and potentially looking at deadlocks based on synchronization handles. Right-clicking a handle will show two menu items, the Properties and Close Handle commands. When I asked Mark why he put that feature in, he said, "Because I could." When I laughed and said that it was pretty dangerous, he said it was my job to come up with a reason for having it. The key reason for randomly closing handles in Process Explorer is so you can sneak into your manager's office and close half the handles in Outlook to keep him from sending you annoying e-mail. I figure that's a plenty good enough reason.

The upper window in Process Explorer, the Process View, is where you can see all sorts of very important information about the process itself. If you press the Delete key after highlighting a process, that is a true death kill. If you've ever run into the issue of which Task Manager won't terminate a process, you'll find that Process Explorer is the true process assassin and will kill any type of process you have rights to. Make sure that you have the Confirm Kill command on the Options menu selected so you don't accidentally start terminating important processes, such as Csrss.exe (Client Server Runtime Subsystem) or Lsass.exe (Local Security Authority Service). Of course, if you kill either of those two processes, you'll actually know about it because Windows will stop running.

Double-clicking a process or right-clicking and selecting Properties from the shortcut menu will get you the Properties dialog box for the process. The numerous tabs are self-explanatory, but I want to mention a couple highlights of which you might not be aware. The first is in the Performance Graph tab on which you see the process CPU utilization, Private Bytes history, and I/O Bytes history.

The CPU utilization and I/O Bytes history are self-explanatory, but Private Bytes deserves elaboration. The working set for a process, which is the Mem Usage column in the Processes tab in TaskManager, is all the physical memory the process needs at the current moment to execute. That's a nice number, but it includes all the modules and files mapped into the address space along with all allocated memory. The Private Bytes are just the allocated memory for the process. Thus, if you see the Private Bytes increasing over time, you may be looking at a memory leak. If Private Bytes, which is a standard performance counter, are increasing at the same rate as the .NET CLR memory counter # Bytes in All Heaps, the memory being used is .NET memory. If the Private Bytes are increasing at a sharper rate than the # Bytes in All Heaps, that's a sign of a potential native code memory leak.

The Threads tab in the process Property page will show you the native call stacks for the threads in your process. However, to get the best call stacks, you'll first need to tell Process Explorer about your Symbol Server. Select Configure Symbols from the Options menu, and in the Configure Symbols dialog box that pops up, the first text box, Dbghelp.dll path, needs to point to the latest version of Dbghelp.dll from your WinDBG installation. Make sure to point at the proper "bitness" and CPU version when specifying the location. In the Symbols Path text box, type the same value you set for the _NT_SYMBOL_PATH environment variable I discussed in "Set Up a Symbol Store" in Chapter 2.

What makes Process Explorer's stack walking so interesting is that it will show you the call stack from user mode through to kernel mode. Without running a kernel debugger, Process Explorer is the only tool that shows you the real stack in your application. As with closing handles, the Threads tab in the process Properties dialog box allows you to kill a thread. I guess this is another one of those "because I can" moments for Mark.

One nice trick of the Process View is that it will place a background color on the process based on key information. If you go into the Configure Highlighting dialog box, you'll see the legend for all the colors. I do want to point out that if you're on a 64-bit machine, processes that contain .NET will be highlighted in the default yellow only if they are 64-bit processes. In other words, 32-bit processes, such as Visual Studio or those compiled as 32-bit, running in Windows on Windows (WoW), will not have the highlighting. However, if you select the process and look for MSCoree.dll in the DLL View, you can check if .NET is running in that process.

Have you ever tried to delete a file and received the dreaded message, "Error Deleting File or Folder, Cannot delete Foo: Access is denied. Make sure the disk is not full or write-protected"? You know you have access to the file, so it's not a security error, but some process has the file open and you have no idea which one. Process Explorer comes to the rescue with the Process Explorer Search dialog box accessible by pressing Ctrl+F. In the dialog box, type in the partial name of the file you want to delete, and the Process Explorer Search dialog box will show you all DLLs and handles with that name. Select the handle, and the main Process Explorer window will jump to show you that handle in the process that has it open. Right-click the handle in the main Process Explorer window and select Close Handle. Now you can delete the file. Of course, you may end up crashing the application that had it open, so alternatively, you can choose to kill the whole process instead.

Using the Process Explorer Search dialog box is also an easy way to see which of the many ASP.NET worker processes is hosting a particular ASP.NET site. Simply type in the name of the site in the Process Explorer Search dialog box, and you'll find the instance immediately.

I've already mentioned a few hints for configuring Process Explorer, but the best new feature in the 10.0 version was the ability to set up column groups. Choosing Select Columns from the View menu brings up the dialog box in which you can select the columns that appear in the various list views in Process Explorer. The Process Image, Process Performance, and .NET tabs of the Select Columns dialog box are interesting because those contain the columns you can select for the Process View.

One weakness of Process Explorer is that there's no way to export the column groups from one machine to the rest of your computers. Mark may add that feature in a future version, but a little poking around in the registry and a hint from Mark showed me where they were stored. In the .\ProcessExplorer\ ProcessExplorerColumnSets.reg file that installs with the book's source code, are my column settings for Process Explorer. I've listed the column groups in Tables 4-1 and 4-2 so you can see the most important performance counters at a glance and why I have them turned on. Because Process Explorer sets up the column sets with accelerator keys, it's trivial to switch between them. If you chose to use my .reg file, it will remove your first four existing column sets and replace them with mine.

Table 4-1 lists the columns I have turned on for Process Explorer Column Sets. Table 4-2 shows the unique values for each particular Column Set. Only the checked items are used; all other check-box items in the Select Column dialog tabs are clear.

Table 4-1   Process Explorer Options for All Column Sets

Select Column Dialog Tab	Checked Items
Process Image	User Name
	Description
	Image Type (64 vs. 32 bit) *if applicable on x64/IA64 systems*
	Integrity Level *if applicable on Windows Vista systems*
Process Performance	CPU Usage

Table 4-2   Custom Column Sets for Process Explorer

Column Set Name	Description	Select Column Dialog BoxTab	Checked Items
Private Bytes	Used to monitor allocated memory in the process	Process Memory	Private Bytes
			Private Bytes History
			Working Set Size
.NET GC Data	To watch all garbage collection usage for .NET processes	.NET	Gen 0 Collections
			Gen 1 Collections
			Gen 2 Collections
			% Time in GC
Handle Data	Looking for handle-based memory leaks	Process Performance	Thread
			Handle Count
		Process Memory	GDI Objects
			USER Objects
I/O Data	Looking for disk or other I/O hogs	Process Performance	I/O Reads
			I/O Writes
			I/O Other
			I/O History

One major question I've gotten many times about Process Explorer is how a single binary manages to run natively on Windows 9*x* (yes, Mark still supports Windows 95!), 32-bit versions of Windows 2000, Windows XP, Windows Vista, and Windows Server 2003, and the x64 and IA64 versions of Windows XP, Windows Vista, and Windows Server 2003? When you consider that Process Explorer is loading a device driver, which has to be CPU specific, it's obviously performing a little magic to get a single EXE to run without an installation.

The magic is all done through binary resources in the resources for the main binary. Procexp.exe is the 32-bit native application. When Procexp.exe runs on an x64 operating system, it detects the operating system and extracts from the 32-bit resources the x64 version of Process Explorer, called, appropriately enough, Procexpx64.exe. The x64 EXE is written to the disk, and Procexp.exe starts Procexpx64.exe. You can see this by looking at the Process Explorer Process View on an x64 machine. You'll see the hierarchy of Procexp.exe starting Procexpx64.exe. As you can probably guess, the device driver Process Explorer uses is also embedded as a binary resource and is extracted and loaded when the appropriate bit version starts.

Process Monitor

For years, we've been using FileMon (*http://www.sysinternals.com/utilities/filemon.html*) and RegMon (*http://www.sysinternals.com/utilities/regmon.html*) from SysInternals to look at all the file and registry accesses on our computers. Mark and Bryce were looking at the state of their tools and decided to combine FileMon and RegMon and add more process-related activity; thus Process Monitor was born. Like all SysInternals tools, it runs on all 32-bit and 64-bit based Windows operating systems from Windows 2000 forward.

What makes Process Monitor so interesting is that the filtering has taken a major jump in improvement. Prior tools did destructive filtering, which actually didn't collect data when filters were applied, but Process Monitor keeps the data so you don't lose what's already been monitored. Additionally, the filters are drastically improved so you can narrow down the display on anything you want. My favorite filtering enhancement is that when creating filters, instead of relying on your typing the names for a process, the filters' drop-down list will include all the processes currently running on the computer. Additionally, you can filter the output on items directly from the list view by right-clicking and selecting the item you want to filter on from the possible values.

Process Monitor allows you to save your particular filters so you can apply them again. This is incredibly convenient when you want to monitor multiple processes that make up a solution. The list of items that you can filter on contains all the different data items Process Monitor collects. If you want to filter on all *RegRenameKey* API calls, you can do so.

In addition to the great new filtering, another new feature I'm sure everyone will find useful is the ability to see the full stack on any of the events collected. As does Process Explorer, the Process Monitor call stacks show you both the user-mode and kernel-mode sides. It's so trivial to see that your process is querying for a file or registry key over and over again that even a manager can figure out that doing that isn't a good idea.

Reflector by Lutz Roeder

If it weren't for Reflector (*http://www.aisto.com/roeder/dotnet/*), no one could do any .NET development at all. With this tool, we have the source code to the Framework Class Library (FCL) in addition to any other .NET code you want to look at. I've referred to Reflector all through the book because I used it to figure out all sorts of interesting problems, especially in Chapter 8, in which I used it to figure out how to write Code Analysis/FxCop rules even though rule development is completely undocumented.

What many people aren't aware of is that Reflector offers a plug-in architecture so developers can extend its functionality. Lutz keeps a running list of new Reflector add-ins on his blog at *http://www.aisto.com/roeder/Frontier/*. There are lots of add-ins up there, including one to decompile to the Boo programming language if you're feeling scary.

What I want to do is to show you the add-ins that I find most useful. Keep in mind that Lutz doesn't worry too hard about backwards compatibility with add-ins, so if you get a new version of Reflector, your add-ins may break. You'll want to keep the add-ins you rely on in your browser's favorites list so you can check if an updated version that works with the latest and greatest Reflector has been released.

The first add-in is probably the most useful: Denis Bauer Reflector.FileDisassembler (*http://www.denisbauer.com/NETTools/FileDisassembler.aspx*). Whereas Reflector does a great job decompiling individual methods, what happens if you want to decompile a complete assembly? I guess you could manually copy and paste each method into a code editor, but by the time you finish, .NET will be out of style. With Reflector.FileDisassembler, you'll select the assembly in Reflector's tree control and then choose the File Disassembler from the View menu.

Reflector.FileDisassembler asks you which directory you want to decompile the assembly to and what project type it is. What makes Reflector.FileDisassembler so amazingly cool is that it will also produce a Visual Studio .NET 2003 project, which will open with a quick conversion in Visual Studio 2005, so you can compile the source directly.

Another add-in I like quite a bit is Reflector Diff AddIn by Sean Hederman at *http://www.codingsanity.com/diff.htm*. If you have two compiled assemblies you want to compare, this is the add-in for you. If you've ever experienced a situation in which you had a computer crash and you lost the source code for an assembly, this add-in will save your life (not that that's happened to me)!

The final add-in I like is Kevin Dente's Running Assembly Reflector Add-in from *http://Weblogs.asp.net/kdente/articles/438539.aspx*. It's so nice to be able to select Open Running Assembly from the File menu and select directly an assembly from the application it is running in instead of wandering through a thousand directories.

The last point I want to address related to Reflector is protecting your intellectual property. Because you can see anything and everything with Reflector, your company managers and lawyers will twist themselves into knots if you show them Reflector. If you have intellectual property you need to protect, consider using an obfuscator. There are numerous obfuscators on the market, but the one I like the best is Brent Rector's Demeaner (*http://www.wiseowl.com/*). Don't take my word for it—what do you think Lutz Roeder uses to protect Reflector?

When using an obfuscator, it's a one-way street. Once you've obfuscated the Intermediate Language (IL), you can no longer debug the code because the binary no longer matches the PDB file. However, if you have a key algorithm you must protect, you have to do something. If you are going down the obfuscation route, you need to make sure that you've tested your application completely, because once it goes through the obfuscator, it's a black box. Some obfuscators, such as Demeaner, offer tools to help with stack trace decoding, but there's no way to load the obfuscated process into the debugger and start debugging.

Sells Brothers' RegexDesigner.NET

Chris Sell's RegexDesigner.NET (*http://www.sellsbrothers.com/tools/#regexd*) has saved me thousands of hours. As a regular expression aficionado, having an IDE to test all your regular expressions interactively is a wonderful thing. Additionally, once you finish the regular expression, pressing Ctrl+G will generate the code you can paste into your application. You can find other regular expression testers on the Internet, but I find myself using RegexDesigner.NET far more than any of the others. In fact, several of the directories in the source code for the book contain .rep files for the regular expressions used in the code.

Regular expressions have always been one of the black art areas of software, but a single book, *Mastering Regular Expressions, Third Edition* (O'Reilly, 2006), by Jeffrey E. F. Friedl, will show you the way. It's one of those books that every time I pick it up I learn something. You certainly won't learn anything about regular expressions from the Microsoft documentation, so you need this book.

To continue your learning about regular expressions, spend some quality time at the Regular Expression Library Web site (*http://www.regexlib.com*). There are many excellent examples of regular expressions that numerous people have contributed. Although you might not find the regular expression that does exactly what you need, you'll probably find something quite close that you can tweak. Make sure to look at regular expressions contributed by Michael Ash and Steven Smith because they've both posted some quite complicated examples that show the real power of regular expressions.

Windows Installer XML (WiX)

Microsoft likes to say that .NET installations are outdated and we'll all be doing XCOPY deployment from now on. I don't know about you, but the only XCOPY deployment I've ever seen was HelloWorld.exe. You simply can't copy real applications because there are database connections, registry settings, and all the pieces necessary to be a modern application. When I started the development for the book's code, I wanted a good installation to handle the code in addition to all the add-ins and Visual Studio extensions that I had planned.

After trying a few different tools, I settled on the Windows Installer XML (WiX), the free installer product from Microsoft available at *http://wix.sourceforge.net*. Having never built a modern installer before, I was able to architect the installation quite quickly with Gábor Deák Jahn's excellent WiX tutorial at *http://www.tramontana.co.hu/wix/*. Additionally, I received answers to my few remaining questions as a result of subscribing to the WiX-Users mailing list. For searching the archive, use *http://www.mail-archive.com/wix-users@lists.source-forge.net/* because it's better than the SourceForge mailing list viewer.

What I like so much about WiX is that it makes the developers responsible for installation by making the installation files themselves easy-to-edit XML files. You don't need expensive licenses for special tools. Now if there's a new file the developer needs to have installed, she simply adds it to the XML file. When I added a new directory to the book's code, I could integrate it into the setup in about three minutes total. When I tried this with other tools, it was far more difficult than I felt it should have been.

You can look at the source code to see how I did the installation. The .\Install\MainInstall directory contains the installation for the initial .msi file you'll install to get the book's code on your computer. Each top-level directory has a .wxs file that lists that directory's files. The main install is built to include all the .wxs files that MSBUILD finds in the code directories minus those dedicated to the WintellectToolsInstall.MSI. If you look at .\Install\MainInstall\Debugging.wxs, you'll see the steps in comments to incorporate a new top-level directory into the main install.

To see a slightly more complicated installation, the .\Install\WintellectTools directory contains the installation code for WintellectToolsInstall.MSI. One of the advanced items I needed to perform in WintellectToolsInstall.MSI was to determine the version of Visual Studio installed. If the Visual Studio Team Developer or Visual Studio Team Suite is not on the machine, I disable the option to install the Code Analysis Rules. There are plenty of comments in the file, so you can see how it all fits together.

To give you an idea how powerful WiX is, consider that Microsoft Office, Visual Studio, SQL Server 2005, and almost everything else coming out of Microsoft these days is using WiX. It's a great toolset and one you definitely want to get familiar with. The faster you push installation tasks down to the developer level, the better install experience you will have for your applications.

Other Tools

Although there are numerous tools on my hard disk, as does any developer, I use some tools far more than others, so I want to give those tools their due here. One tool that I'm constantly using is the free Notepad2 from Florian Balmer (*http://www.flos-freeware.ch/notepad2.html*). With syntax highlighting supplied by the excellent Scintilla editing library (*http://www.scintilla.org/*), it starts up approximately a million times faster than Visual Studio. Of course it doesn't have Microsoft IntelliSense or tooltips, but when you want to look at a source file quickly, it's the perfect tool.

Because I started developing on PCs with Microsoft DOS 3.2 (I think I just showed my age!), the command line is part of my DNA. The default cmd.exe that comes with Windows is quite weak compared to JPSoft's excellent 4NT (*http://www.jpsoft.com*). It's a commercial product, but the time savings you get with its superb command line and extra commands will more than pay for itself within a month. Throw on the enhancements to the batch language and the batch file debugger, and you'll wonder how you ever lived without it.

The new Windows PowerShell (*http://www.microsoft.com/windowsserver2003/technologies /management/powershell/default.mspx*) appears to be very interesting, but I haven't fully gotten into it. The learning curve can be a bit steep, but it's lacking some of the basic command-line behaviors from 4NT and cmd.exe that I'm finding very hard to break. However, I'm willing to bet that by this time next year, I'll be doing quite a bit of work in the PowerShell.

If your primary focus is ASP.NET applications or Web Services, seeing the data going back and forth between IIS and the browser is a great way to learn how things work. Additionally, sometimes you want to change the data to test hard to test scenarios. To see every byte running across a system, there's always WireShark (*http://www.wireshark.org/*), which is the complete network protocol analyzer. It's simply amazing what you can see with WireShark.

Since most of us are interested in more the HTTP traffic with our ASP.NET applications, another tool, Fiddler (*http://www.fiddlertool.com/fiddler/*) is a HTTP Debugging Proxy. With Fiddler, you can change any of the HTTP data easily. There are many features in Fiddler to break on specific data and customize it extensively. My favorite feature of Fiddler is that you can export a .WebTest project directly from it so your logging can be played back with the Visual Studio testing tools.

The final tool I want to mention is one of those tools that looks like magic to me. I've written commercial profilers and looked extremely hard at the .NET Profiling API, but I can't figure out how the incredible developers at SciTech were able to make their .NET Memory Profiler (*http://memprofiler.com/*) so amazingly fast. If you have ever wondered which object is in which garbage-collected generation, this is the tool for you.

You can look at your memory in almost any way you want and do it fast. It has overhead, but it's lower than that of any of the other .NET memory-tracking tools. If you have an application that's using a bit too much memory, now you can easily find exactly which objects are bubbling up to generation 2 but being released. Since generation 2 garbage collections don't come around that often, you can end up in situations in which you're using more memory than you need, so you start paging and thrashing as memory is swapped in and out of the paging file.

My favorite view of all in .NET Memory Profiler is the real-time view. You can watch your memory usage and see when garbage collections trigger certain operations. Add in comment calls to the .NET Memory Profiler API, and you'll be able to see exactly who's doing what to whom and what memory you're using. The real-time view is worth the price of the entire tool!

Summary

My plan for this chapter was to provide answers to all those questions I've gotten from developers over the last few years. Additionally, I wanted to prepare you for some of the upcoming chapters in which we're going to dive deep into the debuggers and extend Visual Studio. I hope I was able to answer some of those questions about debugging and development floating around in your head.

Finally, don't be afraid to ask questions of others. One of the big problems I've seen in my years of development is that many developers don't want to ask questions because they feel it's a sign of weakness that will prevent them from achieving Alpha Geek status. Nothing could be further from the truth! All the great developers I have ever worked with asked more questions than you could ever imagine. However, when they do ask a question, they first do their research and prepare in order to ask intelligent questions to not waste anyone's time. Asking good questions is what makes a developer an Alpha Geek.

Part II
Power Debugging

Chapter 5
Advanced Debugger Usage with Visual Studio

No matter how much great diagnostics code you use and how much planning you do, occasionally you need to run the debugger. As I've mentioned many times in this book, the whole key to debugging effectively is to have a purpose every time you start the debugger. Now I know that most of you will be in the debugger to fix your coworkers' code, not your own (because the code you write is undoubtedly perfect). I want to make sure that when you must resort to the debugger, you're able to get the most out of it and fix problems as quickly as possible.

Before we talk about any debugger usage, I have to mention that debuggers prove the existence of black holes. If you get in the debugger prematurely, the debugger will suck all the time out of the room. The trick to using the debugger effectively is to ensure that you have a solid hypothesis *written down* before you ever start. Without that hypothesis, you'll have nothing giving you that road to follow. Since all computer geeks have seen the movie "Finding Nemo," you know that Dori the Fish had an attention span of a gnat on crack and that even a bright light would distract her. The last thing you want to do in the debugger is be Dori the Debugger wandering around going "Oh, look at the shiny variable!" and being distracted from the task.

With a hypothesis written down, you'll keep focused on the potential problem turned up by source code inspection. As you find interesting information, be sure to write it down, but follow that hypothesis to its conclusion so that you prove or disprove it. When I see one of my developers in the debugger, I always ask to see his hypothesis. You need this focus to avoid the huge time drain using a debugger can be.

In this chapter, I'll talk about how to take advantage of the wonderful Microsoft Visual Studio debugger. If you've been developing for Microsoft platforms for a long time as I have, you can certainly see a marked progression of debugger improvements over the years. In my opinion, Visual Studio 2005 represents a huge jump in progress and is the state-of-the-art debugging tool. The team has done an outstanding job of combining an extremely easy-to-use user interface (UI) with power to spare for the really difficult problems. The fact that Microsoft Windows developers now have one debugger that handles JavaScript/VBScript, Microsoft ASP.NET, .NET, XML Web Services, native code, and SQL debugging in a single debugger UI is amazing.

If you're new to the Visual Studio debugger, I suggest that you read the documentation before continuing. I won't be covering the basics of the debugger in this chapter; I'll assume that you'll study the documentation if you need to. The debugger is discussed in the Visual Studio documentation under Development Tools and Languages\Visual Studio\Integrated Development Environment for Visual Studio\Building Debugging and Testing\Debugging in Visual Studio (*http://msdn2.microsoft.com/en-us/library/sc65sadd(VS.80).aspx*).

Before you read any further, there are two assumptions I'm making in this chapter: The first is that you've followed all the best practices I laid out in Chapter 2, "Preparing for Debugging," and, most importantly, you have set up a Symbol Server. No matter whether you're developing .NET or native applications, getting perfect symbols automatically loaded means that you'll always have an advantage in solving your debugging problems.

The second assumption is that you've turned off a "feature" of Visual Studio debugging, Just My Code. The idea behind Just My Code is vaguely interesting as the documentation says, "This feature enables you to focus on only the code you have written, and ignore code you are not interested in." However, the correct name for Just My Code is "Hide Everything From Me So I Can't Debug." This "feature" sets the debugger so you can debug only if you have symbols and the code is not optimized. Yes, you read that right, it makes it nearly impossible to debug into optimized code, and I can't see why anyone would consider this a feature of a debugger. Countless developers have asked me about problems in the debugger that come down to the fact that Just My Code is turned on by default. To turn off Just My Code, in the Options dialog box, expand the Debugging node, and on the General page, clear the Enable Just My Code (Managed Only) check box.

On a brighter note, I wanted to mention that all of the core tricks of Visual Studio's debugger that I discuss also work in Dbgclr.exe, the free GUI debugger installed as part of the Framework Software Development Kit (SDK). That's because Dbgclr.exe is made up of the same managed debugging binaries as Visual Studio.

Advanced Breakpoints and How to Use Them

Setting a breakpoint on a source line in the Visual Studio debugger is simple. Just load the source file, put the cursor on the line you want to stop on, and then press the default breakpoint key, F9. Alternatively, you can click in the left margin next to the line. Setting a breakpoint on a source line this way is called *setting a location breakpoint*. When the code for such a line executes, the debugger will stop at that location. The ease of setting a location breakpoint belies its importance; the location breakpoint on a specific source code line is what separates the modern age of debugging from the debugging dark ages.

In the early days of computing, breakpoints simply didn't exist. Your only "strategy" for finding a bug was to run your program until it crashed and then look for the problem by wading through page after page of hexadecimal core-dump printouts of the state of memory. The only debuggers in the debugging dark ages were trace statements and faith. In the renaissance age of debugging, made possible by the introduction of higher-level languages, developers could set breakpoints but had to debug only at the assembly-language level. The higher-level languages still had no provisions for viewing local variables or seeing a program in source form. As the languages evolved into more sophisticated tools, the modern debugging age began, and developers were able to set a breakpoint on a line of source code and see their variables in a display that interpreted the variables' values into the exact types they specified. This simple location breakpoint is still extremely powerful, and by using just it alone, my guess is that you can solve 99.46 percent of your debugging problems.

However wonderful, though, location breakpoints can get tedious very quickly. What would happen if you set the breakpoint on a line inside a *for* loop that executed from 1 through 10,000, and the bug turned up on the 10,000th iteration? Not only would you wear your index finger down to a nub from pressing the F5 key assigned to the Go command, but you would also spend hours waiting to get to the iteration that produced the bug. Wouldn't it be nice if there were some way to tell the debugger that you want the breakpoint to execute 9,999 times before stopping?

Fortunately, there is a way: welcome to the realm of advanced breakpoints. In essence, advanced breakpoints allow you to program some smarts into breakpoints, letting the debugger handle the menial chores involved in tracking down bugs and minimizing the time and effort you have to spend in the debugger. A couple of conditions you can add with advanced breakpoints are having the breakpoint skip for a certain count and break when an expression is true. The advanced breakpoint capabilities have finally moved debuggers solidly into the modern age, allowing developers to do in minutes what used to take hours with simple location breakpoints.

Developers coming from a native C++ background invariably ask if they can still set data breakpoints in .NET. Unfortunately, data breakpoints are a native-only feature. Data breakpoints work by using the CPU debug registers to tell the CPU to watch a physical address and when that address comes on the memory bus, trigger a single step exception. Although technically you could still write code to put the address of a .NET object into the debug register, the fact that we are now working with a garbage-collected system means that the address where you think the object resides will move when the heap is compacted. Thus, the debug register would still trigger, but you'd be looking at a completely different address if you stopped in the debugger.

In native C++, we needed data breakpoints because there was no protection stopping you from reaching out and writing to any memory address randomly, which is also known as a *wild write*. With .NET, we have the memory protection, so there is no possibility of a .NET code doing a wild write into other objects. When developers are asking for data breakpoints in .NET, they are really asking to know when a field is changing. If you have public fields in your class, which is a horrible practice, there's no way for you to find those changes other than searching for all accesses of that field across all your source code and setting a location breakpoint.

If you have a property setter on your field, you could set a location breakpoint on the property, and you'll know all the accesses. When it comes to fields, you should never access them directly even inside your class; you should always go through the accessor just to know when they are being changed. If you have several fields that you want to watch, it can get tedious to manually set breakpoints on all of them. Part of the Wintellect.VSMacros file, included with the book's source code, is a module, *BreakPointHelper*, which contains *SetBreakpointsOnDoc-Methods*. That will run through the active document and set a breakpoint on the entry point of each method. What's nice about the macro is that it uses the *Breakpoint* object's *Tag* property to identify the breakpoints set by the macro. If you want to clear the breakpoints with *Remove-BreakpointsOnDocMethods*, only those breakpoints set with *SetBreakpointsOnDocMethods* are cleared, so your other breakpoints are not lost.

Since .vsmacro files are binary files, you'll have to load it into your copy of Visual Studio by going to the Tools menu, pointing to Macros, and then selecting Macro Explorer to bring up the Macro Explorer window. Right-click the Macros parent node and select Load Macro Project to load .\Macros\Wintellect.vsmacros.

Breakpoint Tips

Before we jump into advanced breakpoints, I just want to quickly mention four things you might not have been aware of when setting breakpoints. The first is that when setting advanced breakpoints, before you set them, it's always best if you start debugging with a single-step command. When you aren't debugging, the debugger uses Microsoft IntelliSense to set advanced breakpoints. However, when you start debugging, you also get the actual Program Database (PDB) debugging symbols in addition to the IntelliSense to help set your breakpoints.

As you've probably realized with .NET, having completely self-describing objects in the assembly itself means that the debugger uses that metadata to find the type information about an object. Type data used to make up the bulk of the data in the native binary's PDB files, but simply disappears in .NET; which is the reason why .NET PDB files are so much smaller. In a .NET PDB file, the two main pieces of data are the source and line information (so you can do the single-step debugging) and the names of the local variables.

One recommendation I have is that you should ensure that your Breakpoints window—the view that shows which breakpoints are set—isn't docked. Sometimes when you're setting breakpoints, Visual Studio will set them, and you'll wonder why they aren't triggered. By having the Breakpoints window as a full-fledged window, you'll be able to find it among all the other thousands of dockable windows in the Visual Studio IDE. I don't know about you, but running Visual Studio makes me long for a dual 35-inch monitor setup. To view the Breakpoints window, press Ctrl+Alt+B with the default keyboard mappings. Right-click the Breakpoints window title bar, or tab and select Tabbed Document on the shortcut menu. You'll need to do this for both the normal editing mode and the debugging mode. Once you have the Breakpoint window set as a full-fledged window, drag its tab over to the first position so that you can always find it.

The Breakpoints window shows various glyphs that indicate whether the breakpoint was set. Table 5-1 shows all the codes you'll see. Unlike Visual Studio .NET 2003, which featured only flat red circles to indicate breakpoints, Visual Studio 2005 now shows new and improved three-dimensional spheres! That's certainly one of the key reasons for upgrading. Additionally, Visual Studio 2005 introduces *tracepoints*, which are really breakpoints with additional capabilities. Tracepoints are shown as three-dimensional diamonds. I'll discuss tracepoints in depth in the "Tracepoints" section later in this chapter.

The Warning breakpoint/tracepoint, the empty circle or triangle with the yellow warning sign, needs some extra explanation. In your normal debugging, you'll see the Warning glyph when you set a location breakpoint in a source file whose module has not been loaded yet, so the breakpoint is in essence an unresolved breakpoint. Since I recommend that you start debugging before you set advanced breakpoints, if you see the Warning glyph in the Breakpoints window, you have a sign that the breakpoint wasn't set correctly.

Table 5-1   Breakpoint Window Codes

Glyph	Meaning
	Normal breakpoint in the enabled and disabled states.
	Advanced breakpoint (hit count, condition, and/or filter) property set.
	Mapped breakpoint in an ASP/ASP.NET HTML page.
	Normal tracepoint in the enabled and disabled states.
	Advanced tracepoint (hit count, condition, and/or filter) property set.

Table 5-1   Breakpoint Window Codes

Glyph	Meaning
	Mapped tracepoint in an ASP/ASP.NET HTML page.
	Breakpoint or tracepoint error. The breakpoint or tracepoint will never be set.
	Breakpoint or tracepoint warning. Generally means the source location is not currently in any loaded module.

Although you might never have realized it, you can set breakpoints in the Call Stack window except when doing SQL debugging. This capability is extremely helpful when trying to get stopped on recursion or deeply nested stacks. All you need to do is highlight the call you want to stop on and either press F9 or right-click on the line and select Insert Breakpoint from the shortcut menu. Even nicer, just as with margin breakpoints, you can right-click any breakpoint in the Call Stack window to enable, disable, or set the properties of that breakpoint.

Another much-underused feature for setting breakpoints is the Run To Cursor option for setting one-shot breakpoints. You can set them in source edit windows by right-clicking on the line and selecting the Run To Cursor option from the menu, which is available both when debugging and editing, and which will start debugging. For the default keyboard layout, pressing Ctrl+F10 will do the same thing. As with breakpoints, right-clicking in the magical Call Stack window opens the shortcut menu, which also has a Run To Cursor command. If you hit a breakpoint before execution takes place on the Run To Cursor line, the debugger stops on that breakpoint and discards your Run To Cursor one-shot breakpoint.

Finally, subexpression breakpoints are supported in managed code. For example, if you have this expression

```
for ( int i = 0 , m = 0 ; i < 10 ; i++ , m-- )
{
}
```

when you are debugging, and you click in the margin next to the line, the red highlight extends only on the $i = 0$, $m = 0$ or on the initializer's portion of the expression. If you wanted to stop on the iterator's subexpression (in which the increment and decrement take place), place the cursor anywhere in the $i++$, $m--$ portion of the statement, and press F9. In this statement, you can have up to three breakpoints on the line. You can differentiate them in the Breakpoints window because each will indicate the line and character position. There will be only a single red dot in the margin indicating the breakpoints. To clear all breakpoints at once, click the red dot in the left margin.

Quickly Breaking on Any Function

The starting point for any advanced breakpoint is the New Breakpoint dialog box, which is accessible by pressing Ctrl+B in the default keyboard mapping. In many ways, the New Breakpoint dialog box is simply a front end to the IntelliSense system. IntelliSense is extremely helpful for writing your code, but it's also used to help set breakpoints. If you clear the Use IntelliSense To Verify The Function Name check box in the New Breakpoint dialog box, you'll be relying on the PDB file to set the breakpoint, which has only a portion of the information you need. Finally, you'll get only IntelliSense breakpoints if you have a project with source code open.

By using IntelliSense, you get a very powerful breakpoint-setting feature that can save you a tremendous amount of time. In the midst of my debugging battles, if I know the name of the class and method I want to break on, I can type it directly into the Function edit control in the New Breakpoint dialog box. The Line and Character fields in the New Breakpoint dialog box seem to indicate that you can specify spots inside the function, but if you try any values in those fields other than 1, you'll get the ever-helpful error: "The breakpoint cannot be set. Function breakpoints are only supported on the first line." The last field in the New Breakpoint dialog box is the language list. If you have a monolingual project, it will default to the appropriate language. If your project is multilingual, select the language for the class and method you want to set the breakpoint in. I've looked over the shoulder of countless developers who know the name of the method but spend 20 minutes wandering all over the project opening files just so they can move the cursor to the line and press F9.

An additional benefit of setting breakpoints by using the New Breakpoint dialog box is that the Breakpoints window, which shows the breakpoints you have set, shows the fully qualified name of the method in the Name column. Setting a margin breakpoint will show the source file and line number, which isn't nearly as descriptive. When dealing with lots of breakpoints spread out across a large application, seeing the fully qualified name is extremely helpful.

Numerous things can happen when you try to set a breakpoint on a function by using the Breakpoint dialog box. I want to go through the possible outcomes you'll see and explain how to work around any problems you might encounter. What you might want to do so that you can see the outcomes yourself is open up one of your projects and try to set a few breakpoints with the New Breakpoint dialog box as I go through this discussion.

The first case of quickly setting a breakpoint that I'll discuss is when you want to set the breakpoint on a class and method. For example, I have a Visual Basic class named *MainForm* with a method named *SuperDuperThreader*. When I open the New Breakpoint dialog box by pressing Ctrl+B, all I have to type in is *mainform.superduperthreader* (remember that Visual Basic is a case-insensitive language) and click OK. Figure 5-1 shows the filled-out Breakpoint dialog box using the Visual Basic example. If you aren't currently debugging when you set the breakpoint, the breakpoint dot appears in the margin, but the red highlight doesn't appear on the *Public Sub SuperDuperThreader* because the breakpoint still must be resolved. Once you start debugging, *Public Sub SuperDuperThreader* is highlighted in red. If you're currently debugging, the breakpoint will be fully resolved by showing a filled-in red dot in the Breakpoints window, and you'll see that the *Public Sub SuperDuperThreader* is highlighted in red.

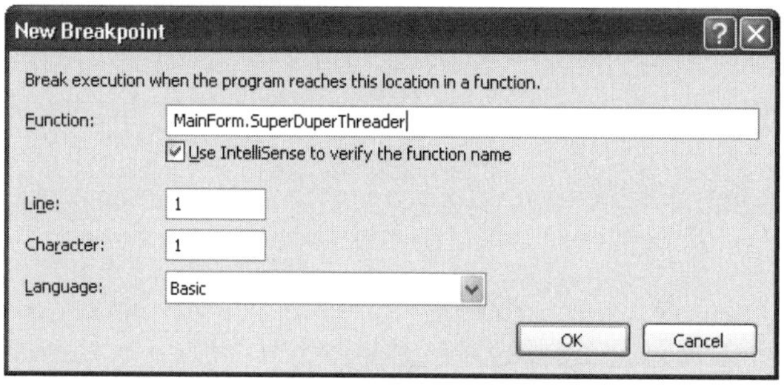

Figure 5-1   Breakpoint dialog box about to set a quick breakpoint on a function

If the class and method name you specify in the Breakpoint dialog box is incorrect, you'll see a message box that says, "IntelliSense could not find the specified location. Do you still want to set the breakpoint?" If you go ahead and set the breakpoint on the nonexistent method, the Breakpoints window shows one of two glyphs because of a bug. If you are already debugging and you set a breakpoint on an invalid location, the breakpoint glyph is incorrectly set to the red circle. However, if you see the invalid breakpoint before you start debugging, the yellow glyph is properly shown in the Breakpoints window because the breakpoint can't be resolved.

Because setting a breakpoint by specifying the class and method works well, I had to experiment with attempting to set a breakpoint in the Breakpoint dialog box by just specifying the method name. If the method name is unique in the application, the debugger will set a breakpoint on the method just as if you typed in the complete class and method.

Since setting a breakpoint with just the method name works quite well and will save you time debugging, you might be wondering what would happen if you had a large project and you wanted to set a breakpoint on a common method name or an overloaded method. For example, suppose you have the Wintellect.Diagnostics solution open and you want to set a breakpoint on the *Fail* method used anywhere in the solution. If you type *Fail* in the Breakpoint dialog box and click OK, something wonderfully interesting happens and is shown in Figure 5-2.

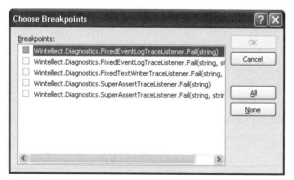

Figure 5-2   The Choose Breakpoints dialog box

What you see in Figure 5-2 is the IntelliSense listing from all classes in the Wintellect.Diagnostics project that have *Fail* as a method. I don't know about you, but I think this is an outstanding feature—especially because you can see that clicking the All button allows you to set breakpoints on all those methods all at once! The Choose Breakpoints dialog box also appears for overloaded methods in the same class. I don't know how many times I've gone to set a breakpoint and the Choose Breakpoints dialog box reminded me that I should consider stopping on other methods also.

If you know the parameter types or names of the overloaded method, you can type those also in the New Breakpoints dialog box to skip the Choose Breakpoints dialog box entirely. For example, the *Wintellect.Windows.Forms.GlobalMessageBox* class has six overloaded *Show* methods. If I wanted to set the breakpoint only on the method that takes types of a *Control* and two *Strings* as parameters, I'd type *Show(Control,String,String)* to set the one breakpoint I wanted. If I wanted to use parameter names, for the *Show* overloaded method whose parameter names are *control* and *text*, I'd type *Show(control,text)* to enable that breakpoint.

Of course, as soon as I saw that the Choose Breakpoints dialog box appeared on overloaded methods, I set about trying to find if I could get it to show me all the methods in the class. No matter what I've tried, the New Breakpoint dialog box won't show all the methods in the class for managed code. Interestingly, it will for native C++ code if you type in *classname::**. Given that all the IntelliSense information is available to add-ins, if you're looking for a fun project, you should write that add-in.

I'm simply amazed that the ability to select from multiple methods in your application when setting a breakpoint in the debugger isn't pointed out in big, bold type as a killer feature of Visual Studio. In fact, there's only a passing reference to the Choose Breakpoints dialog box in the MSDN documentation. We all owe the debugger team a big thanks for this feature.

If you're debugging when you want to set a quick breakpoint, things get a little more interesting than what I've already discussed because there is some very interesting power in the New Breakpoint dialog box. During a brain cramp one day while debugging, I typed in the name of a class and method in the Microsoft .NET Framework class library instead of the class and method from my project, and a whole bunch of really weird-looking breakpoints popped up in the Breakpoints window. Let's say that I have a C# console application that calls *Console.WriteLine*, and while debugging, you type *Console.WriteLine* into the Breakpoint dialog box. You'll get the usual message about IntelliSense not knowing what to do. If you click Yes and go to your Breakpoints window, you'll see something that looks like Figure 5-3. (You might have to expand the top tree node, and you'll need to have Just My Code turned off as I described at the beginning of the chapter.)

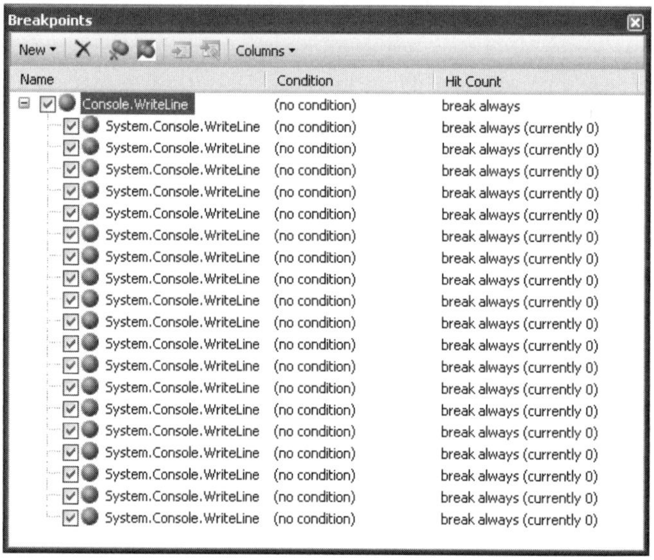

Figure 5-3   Child breakpoints in the Breakpoints window

What you're looking at in Figure 5-3 are child breakpoints. Basically, the Visual Studio documentation says that they exist and that's it. For example, the documentation says child breakpoints occur when you set breakpoints on overloaded functions, because they'll show you the method name at the root level, and the child elements refer to the specific locations. You can also see child breakpoints when you're debugging multiple executables, both programs load the same control into their AppDomain/address spaces, and you set breakpoints in the same spot in that control in both programs. What's wild is that the Breakpoints window in Figure 5-3 is showing you a single program that's currently running in which I set a breakpoint on *Console.WriteLine.*

If you right-click a child breakpoint while debugging and select Go To Disassembly, the Disassembly window displays the disassembly code. However, you'll get a clue as to what's happening if in the Breakpoints window you add the Address column to the display by selecting it from the Columns button. Figure 5-4 shows that all but one of the child breakpoints is set on the first instruction of *Console.WriteLine.* The screen shot in Figure 5-4 is from Windows XP Professional x64 Edition, and if you try the same breakpoint on a 32-bit operating system, the offsets will be different. I haven't found the pattern as to why the offsets are different values for some methods.

If that's not clear enough, you can always execute your program and notice that you stop deep down in the assembly language. If you pull up the Call Stack window, you'll see that you're stopped inside a call to *Console.WriteLine,* and you'll even see the parameter(s) passed. The beauty of this undocumented means of handling a breakpoint is that you'll always be able to get your applications stopped at a known point of execution.

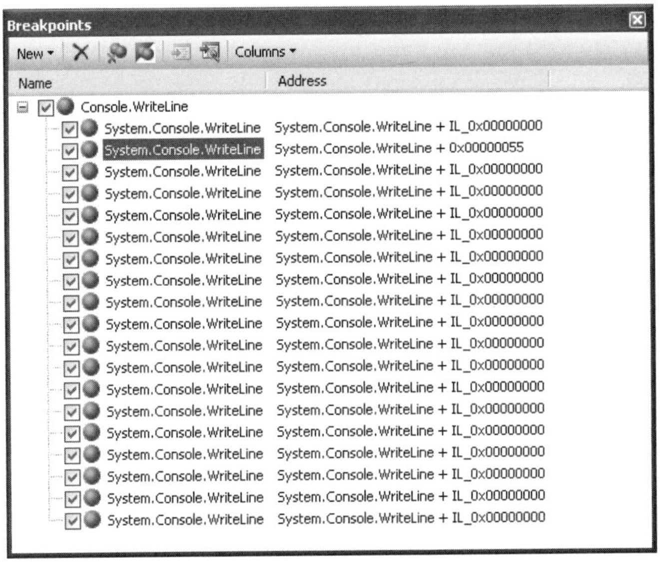

Figure 5-4   Breakpoint on any call to Console.WriteLine

Although I made only a single call to *Console.WriteLine* in my program, the Breakpoints window shows 19 child breakpoints, as shown in Figure 5-3. Based on some trial and error, I discovered that the child breakpoints count is the number of overloaded methods. In other words, setting breakpoints by typing in the .NET Framework class and method name or typing where you don't have source code will set a breakpoint on all overloaded methods.

The ability to stop on a method that's called anywhere in my AppDomain is amazingly cool. I've learned quite a bit about how the .NET Framework class library fits together by choosing to stop at specific .NET Framework class library methods. Although I've been using a static method as an example, this technique works perfectly well on instance methods in addition to properties as long as those methods or properties are called in your AppDomain. Keep in mind that to set breakpoints on a property, you'll need to prefix the property with *get_* or *set_*, depending on what you want to break on because a property is really just a method. For example, to set a breakpoint on the *Console.In* property, you'd specify *Console.get_In*. Also, the language selected in the New Breakpoint dialog box is still important. For C# applications you can leave the language set to C#, and they work fine. For Visual Basic applications, you'll need to set the Language combo box to Unknown for this undocumented trick to work.

In setting these breakpoints deep in the .NET Framework, I need to mention three final items. The first is that the development environment now saves them across debugging sessions. In prior versions of Visual Studio, you'd have to set these breakpoints each time you restarted debugging. The second is that you'll need to watch the New Breakpoint dialog box carefully after setting these breakpoints. The debugger has a tendency to clear the Use IntelliSense To Verify The Function Name check box in the New Breakpoint dialog box.

The third item is that these breakpoints are per AppDomain. If my example had two App-Domains that both called *Console.WriteLine*, you would have seen 38 total child breakpoints. That's because each AppDomain is getting its own set of breakpoints. A .NET AppDomain is equivalent to a process, and you can have as many as you want in a single Windows EXE.

Although you might think that I've beaten the topic of setting quick location breakpoints to death, there's still one completely non-obvious but extremely powerful place to set location breakpoints. Figure 5-5 shows the Find combo box on the Standard toolbar. If a source file is active in the main window and you type the name of the class and method you want to break on in that combo box and press F9, a breakpoint on that method is set if that method exists. If you specify an overloaded method, the system will automatically set breakpoints on all the overloaded methods. The Find combo box is a little more discriminating in that if it can't set the breakpoint, it won't.

Figure 5-5   The Find combo box

That little Find combo box has two other hidden secrets. For the default keyboard layout, if you type in the name of a project file or an include file in the INCLUDE environment variable and press Ctrl+Shift+G, the Find combo box opens the file ready for editing. Finally, if you like the Command window in Visual Studio, try this: in the Find combo box, type the greater than symbol (>), and see the window turn into a mini Command window with its own IntelliSense. With all this undocumented magic in the Find combo box, I often wonder if I could type in "Fix my bugs!" and with a magic keystroke have it do just that.

Location Breakpoint Modifiers

Now that you know how to set location breakpoints anywhere with aplomb, I can turn to some of the scenarios discussed in the opening section on breakpoints. The whole idea is to add some real smarts to breakpoints so that you can use the debugger even more efficiently. The vehicles for these smarts are hit counts and conditional expressions.

Hit Counts

The simplest modifier applicable to location breakpoints is a *hit count*, also sometimes referred to as a *skip count*. A hit count tells the debugger that it should put the breakpoint in but not stop on it until the line of code executes a specific number of times. With this modifier, breaking inside loops at the appropriate time is trivial.

Adding a hit count to a location breakpoint is easy. First, set a regular location breakpoint either on a line or a subexpression of the line. Right-click the red dot for the location breakpoint, and select Hit Count from the context menu. Alternatively, you could also select the breakpoint in the Breakpoints window and select Hit Count. No matter how you do it, you'll end up in the Breakpoint Hit Count dialog box.

In the Breakpoint Hit Count dialog box, you'll see that Microsoft improved the hit-count options from previous debuggers. In the When The Breakpoint Is Hit drop-down list, you can choose how you want the hit count calculated in four different ways, as shown in Table 5-2. After choosing the evaluation you want, type the hit-count number in the edit box next to the drop-down list.

Table 5-2   Hit-Count Evaluations

Hit-Count Evaluation	Description
Break always	Stop every time this location is executed.
Break when the hit count is equal to	Stop only when the exact number of executions of this location has occurred. Note that the count is a 1-based count.
Break when the hit count is a multiple of	Break every x number of executions.
Break when the hit count is greater than or equal to	Skip all executions of this location until the hit count is reached and break every execution thereafter. This was the only hit count in previous editions of Microsoft debuggers.

What makes hit counts so useful is that when you're stopped in the debugger, the debugger tells you how many times the breakpoint has executed. If you have a loop that's crashing or corrupting data, but you don't know which iteration is causing the problem, add a location breakpoint to a line in the loop and add a hit-count modifier that is larger than the total number of loop iterations. When your program crashes or the corruption occurs, bring up the Breakpoints window, and in the Hit Count column for that breakpoint, you'll see in parentheses the number of times that loop executed. The Breakpoints window shown in Figure 5-6 shows that the breakpoint has been hit 17 times so far.

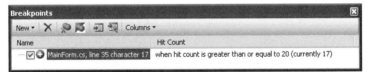

Figure 5-6   An example of remaining hit-count breakpoint expressions

Hit counts are also fantastic when you're trying to see what's executing in an application. When we go into debugging someone else's code, we rarely have any idea of how everything fits together. What we'll do is set many breakpoints all over the application across the major subsystems and set the hit counts to 100,000. That way we can exercise the application without stopping in the debugger on one of those breakpoints. After a while, we'll break into the application and look at the execution counts. That gives you an excellent idea of which parts of the application are executing the most based on the data running through the system. When it comes to finding that needle in a haystack, hit-count modifiers can get you pointed in the right direction. Keep in mind that the remaining count works only when your program is running at full speed. Single-stepping over a breakpoint doesn't update the hit count because the single step takes precedence over a breakpoint in the debugger's internal state machine.

You can reset the count back to zero at any time by right-clicking the breakpoint and selecting Hit Count from the shortcut menu. In the Breakpoint Hit Count dialog box, click the Reset button to set the execution count back to zero. One additional nice feature is that you can change the hit-count evaluation at any time or the hit-count number without changing the current hit count.

Conditional Expressions

The second modifier for location breakpoints—and the one that if used correctly saves you more time than any other type of breakpoint—is a *conditional expression*. A location breakpoint that has a conditional expression triggers only if its expression evaluates to true or changes from the last time it was evaluated. A conditional expression is a powerful weapon for gaining control exactly when you need it. The debugger can handle just about any expression you throw at it. To add a conditional expression to your breakpoint, right-click a location break-point and select Condition from the shortcut menu, which brings up the Breakpoint Condition dialog box. In the Condition edit box, enter the condition you want to check and click OK to set your condition.

You can think of conditional modifiers like this: "What's in the parentheses of an *if* statement that I'd enter on the breakpoint line?" You have full access to local and global variables because they are evaluated in the context of the currently executing scope. The conditional expression breakpoint modifier is extremely powerful because it allows you to directly test the specific hypothesis that you're out to prove or disprove. The important point to remember is that the expression syntax must follow the same rules as the language in which the break-point is set, so remember to mind your *And*'s and | |'s as appropriate.

The default condition handling breaks into the debugger if the conditional expression you enter evaluates to true. However, if you want to break when the condition changes value, you can change the option button selection from Is True to Has Changed. One thing that can be confusing but makes sense after some thought is that the expression isn't evaluated when you enter the condition. The first time it's evaluated is when the associated location breakpoint is hit. Because the condition has never been evaluated, the debugger sees no value stored in the internal expression result field, so it saves off the value and continues execution. Thus it can possibly take two executions of that location before the debugger stops.

What's extra nice about the Has Changed evaluation is that the condition you enter doesn't have to be an actual condition. You can also enter a variable that is accessible from the scope of the location breakpoint, and the debugger evaluates and stores the result of that variable so that you can stop when it changes.

The expressions that the debugger can handle are quite interesting. Given the following C# source code:

```
for ( i = 0 ; i < 20 ; i++ )
{
    Console.WriteLine ( "i = {0}" , i );
}
```

What would happen if I set a breakpoint on the call to *Console.WriteLine* and set the conditional modifier to *i=3* (notice that I used only a single equal sign instead of the double equal)? My first thought would have been that you would get an error in the Breakpoint Conditional dialog box telling you that the expression was incorrect. The expression is accepted, and when the debugger hits the location breakpoint, you'd just see *i = 3* continually streaming to the console window. When I first saw this, I actually did a little victory dance around my office because I saw that the conditional modifier was doing more than calling methods; it supports full expression evaluation.

Although you probably don't want to see me dancing, the fact the debugger supports full expression evaluation is very exciting because it means you can call a function from a location breakpoint conditional expression modifier. Calling functions or methods from conditional expressions opens up all sorts of excellent debugging capabilities, but as you can imagine, the side effects can make debugging almost impossible if you don't pay careful attention. In case you're wondering, the Common Language Runtime (CLR) Debugging API has this functionality built right in and fully documented. The magic is through the *ICorDebugEval* interface, and the technique of calling a function in the debugger is called *func-eval*.

When I first started learning .NET, I didn't realize that this extra power in conditional expressions existed because the functionality seemed natural. For example, I was using expressions such as *userName.Length* == 7, thinking the debugger was reaching into the debuggee and getting the length value by reading memory directly just as it does in native debugging. After using an expression that called a more interesting property get accessor that did more work, I started experimenting to see everything I could do. Essentially, I figured out that I could make any valid calls I wanted except to Web methods.

Probably the best way to show you the process of calling methods from conditional expressions is through an example. Listing 5-1 is a simple program, ConditionalBP, which has a class, *TestO*, which keeps track of the number of times a method is called.

Listing 5-1   Conditional breakpoint modifier example

```
using System;

namespace ConditionalBP
{
    class TestO
    {
        public TestO ( )
```

```
        {
            callCount = 0;
            toggleValue = false;
        }

        private Int32 callCount;

        public Int32 CondTest ( )
        {
            callCount++;
            return ( callCount );
        }

        private Boolean toggleValue;

        public Boolean Toggle ( )
        {
            toggleValue = !toggleValue;
            return ( toggleValue );
        }
    }

class App
{
    static void Main ( string [] args )
    {
        Test0 x = new Test0 ( );

        for ( Int32 i = 0 ; i < 10 ; i++ )
        {
            // Set BP: (x.Toggle() == true) || (x.CondTest() == 0)
            Console.WriteLine ( "{0}" , i );
        }
    }
}
}
```

Set a conditional breakpoint on *Console.WriteLine* in *Main* with the expression (*x.Toggle()* ==
true) || (*x.CondTest()* == 0), and think about what occurs when the breakpoint is executed.
After pressing F5 for the first time, you'll stop when *i* equals 0. If you put *z* in the Watch window and expand it, you'd see that the value of the *callCount* field is 0 and the *toggleValue* field
is *true*. That shows that the *Toggle* method has executed once. Since C# supports short circuit
evaluation, the *CondTest* method was not executed. Pressing F5 again, will stop when the
value if *i* is now 2. Looking at the fields of the *x* object in the Watch window, *callCount* is 1, and
the *toggleValue* field is again *true*. What this is proving is that the methods are being called
from the breakpoint.

In the Condition edit box, when you type in the class and enter the period after an instance,
you'll be greeted with a new surprise built into the debugger: full IntelliSense! That makes it
trivial to call those methods from breakpoints because you'll see exactly what you can and
can't call. The debugger team *wants* you to start calling methods from your conditional breakpoints, so they made it easy.

Before you start slinging any property or method calls in your location breakpoint conditional expression modifiers, you should probably take a good look at what the property or method does. If it happens to copy a 3-GB database or otherwise changes state, you probably don't want to call it. What's also interesting about how the debugger evaluates the methods and properties you call is that the 20-second timeout that applies to the Watch window doesn't apply to calling methods from a conditional expression. If you have a method that happens to take days to evaluate, the debugger will merrily wait for the expression to finish. Fortunately, the Visual Studio user interface (UI) isn't frozen, so pressing Ctrl+Alt+Break or selecting Break All from the Debug menu will immediately stop the debuggee.

In Visual Studio .NET 2003, the debugger had a giant bug with which if you set the conditional modifier incorrectly after you started debugging, the debugger would report the problem but would not stop at the location. The development team fixed that problem and now when you enter an invalid expression, the Breakpoint Condition dialog box warns you immediately. Also, in C#, the expression evaluator now properly evaluates *null* so you use it in your conditional modifier expressions.

Before I leave the conditional modifier, I want to show you one of my favorite debugging tricks. Because you can call a method from a conditional modifier, that essentially gives us method injection on the fly. This is especially important because this gives you assertions on the fly. For example, Listing 5-2 shows a class with an *IsNameNull* method that returns true if the private field *name* is *null*.

Listing 5-2   Example of a debug-only method used in breakpoint condition modifiers

```
using System;
using System.Diagnostics;

namespace AssertExample
{
    class AssertExample
    {
        public AssertExample ( String inputString )
        {
            name = inputString;
        }

        private String name = null;

        public String Name
        {
            get
            {
                return ( name );
            }
            set
            {
                name = value;
            }
        }
    }
```

```
              // Can't use [Conditional("DEBUG")] here because it applies only to
              // void return values.
       #if DEBUG
              public bool IsNameNull ( )
              {
                  if ( null == name )
                  {
                      return ( true );
                  }
                  return ( false );
              }
       #endif
          }

          class Program
          {
              static void Main ( string [] args )
              {
                  AssertExample a = new AssertExample ( "Pam" );

                  // Set BP: a.IsNameNull()
                  Trace.WriteLine ( a.Name );

                  a.Name = null;

                  // Set BP: a.IsNameNull()
                  Trace.WriteLine ( a.Name );
              }
          }
      }
```

Because the *IsNameNull* method returns *true* or *false*, you can use it in any location breakpoint conditional modifier in which you want to ensure that the *name* field is properly set. For example, you could set breakpoints class methods themselves by using the expression *this.IsName-Null()* as the conditional modifier. As those location breakpoints execute, you'd get checking of the currently executing instance. If you wanted to check outside the class, you'd use the specific variable name in the expression. I'm amazed at how much I rely on the debugger to do those additional assertions on the fly.

Tracepoints

A new feature of the debugger in Visual Studio 2005 is tracepoints, which are really just another custom action on breakpoints, such as a conditional or hit-count modifier. From the name, you can guess that it has something to do with tracing. The original impetus with tracepoints was to have the option to do logging of some sort as part of a breakpoint. What confuses most developers when they want to insert a tracepoint is that there are no user interface options for setting one. All tracepoints start life as a breakpoint.

Once you have your breakpoint set, right-click the red circle in the margin and select When Hit from the shortcut menu. That will bring up the When Breakpoint Is Hit dialog box, which gives you two options for action when the breakpoint triggers: printing a message and running a macro. Selecting the Continue Execution check box at the bottom of the dialog box turns your breakpoint into a tracepoint, and you'll get the fancy diamond in the margin instead of the old boring sphere.

If you choose to print a message, you can print any variable value to the Output window by surrounding it in curly braces ({}). The ability to jam in that trace statement on the fly is a very welcome addition to your debugging arsenal. To make life even better, there's a set of special keywords that you can use in the trace message to get even more information. They are all listed in Table 5-3.

Table 5-3   Tracepoint Message Codes

Tracepoint Special Variable	Meaning
$ADDRESS	Current instruction address
$CALLER	Previous function caller by name
$CALLSTACK	The call stack at the current location
$FUNCTION	Current function name
$PID	Process ID
$PNAME	Process name
$TID	Current thread ID
$TNAME	Current thread name

What I especially appreciate is that the $CALLSTACK special variable shows you the mixed native-managed stack if you have turned on both managed and native debugging in the same process, which I'll discuss how to do in the "Mixed-Mode Debugging" section later in this chapter. However, it does not show you the method parameters or their values. The one bit of frustration with the trace statement is that you are limited to a single line. There's no way you can get a carriage return or linefeed to split the trace message apart to make it easier to read. Tracing from a tracepoint was designed to handle those quick and small pieces of data you need to see during debugging. If you want to change the default message the When Breakpoint Is Hit dialog box shows, you can edit the DefaultTracepointMessage value under the HKEY_CURRENT_USER \Software\Microsoft\VisualStudio\8.0\Debugger registry key.

To get better formatting from a tracepoint, you can take advantage of the second option at a tracepoint, specifying a macro to run. Because a Visual Studio macro has full access to the debugger object, you can do all the formatting you could ever want in the macro. Because I wanted to see the parameters and their values at a tracepoint, I wrote the *DumpTheCallstack* macro you can find in the Wintellect.VSMacros file, *TracePointMacros* module. It's an excellent example of the type of macro tracepoints were designed to call.

When I first saw the ability to call macros from tracepoints, I was very excited because I thought that we would now be able to do seriously programmed breakpoints. For example, I once worked on a heavy parsing system on which we needed to stop only when there were at least 1,000 items on the call stack. Because nearly everything you could ever want from the debugger is exposed in the Visual Studio automation model, I would now be able to write a macro that verified that you were debugging and grabbed the current thread, and if the stack frame count was greater than 1,000, I could stop.

As you start thinking about it, you can come up with many super programmable breakpoint options calling a macro can offer. For example, what about breakpoints when a file on the disk is a specific size? How about a breakpoint that will cause you to stop only when a registry key exists or has a certain value in it? The possibilities become endless and can really go a long way to doing some amazing power debugging.

Sadly, macros at breakpoints don't work as expected. When I wrote my first macro to be executed at a tracepoint, I called the *Debugger.Break* method to have the macro stop in the debugger. When the tracepoint with my macro executed, I got a message box with the following text: "A macro called a debugger action which is not allowed while responding to an event or while being run because a breakpoint was hit." Sadly, the debugger does not support stopping from a macro directly, which bothered me because I think being able to stop from a macro is a highly valuable feature.

My next attempt was in the When Breakpoint Is Hit dialog box. I cleared Continue Execution and rewrote my macro to call *Debugger.Go* when my condition was not met. I figured that although it was an extra step, at least I'd get my super-programmable breakpoints. Alas, calling *Debugger.Go* triggers the same annoying message, so that plan didn't work either. I was stumped trying to figure this out and was swapping mail with Shahar Prish, a developer on the Microsoft Office Excel Server team whose blog is at *http://blogs.msdn.com/cumgranosalis /default.aspx*, in which we were lamenting that this feature didn't work the way anyone wanted. Shahar kept fiddling around and came up with an excellent workaround.

There seems to be an issue from having the macro control the debugger from the thread the debugger is running on. Shahar's trick is to have the macro continue execution by calling *Debugger.Go* on another thread. Of course, this trick may break in the next release of the debugger, but at least it lets us use more powerful breakpoints today.

In the When Breakpoint Is Hit dialog box, you'll clear Continue Execution so the debugger thinks it's going to stop. In the Run a macro list, you'll select your macro as normal. Inside your macro is where you'll take advantage of Shahar's workaround. The following code shows a macro, *StopOnCallstackBiggerThanFive*, that will continue execution by calling *Deferred-ContinueExecution* if the stack has fewer than five items in it. The magic is using a *ThreadPool* thread to do the work of continuing execution. All of this code is in the Wintellect.VSMacros file *TracePointMacros* module, so you can try it out.

```
' Shahar Prish's cool trick
Private Sub DeferredContinueExecution()
        ThreadPool.QueueUserWorkItem(New _
                        Threading.WaitCallback(AddressOf ContinueExecution))
End Sub

Private Sub ContinueExecution(ByVal o As Object)
    DTE.Debugger.Go()
End Sub

Public Sub StopOnCallstackBiggerThanFive()
    Dim dbg As EnvDTE.Debugger = DTE.Debugger
    If (dbg.CurrentProgram IsNot Nothing) Then
        Dim thread As EnvDTE.Thread = dbg.CurrentThread
        If (thread.StackFrames.Count <= 5) Then
            DeferredContinueExecution()
        End If
    End If
End Sub
```

Filters

The last breakpoint modifier I want to discuss is the new Filter modifier. In prior versions of Visual Studio, setting a per-thread breakpoint was an adventure. The only way to do it in .NET code was to either remember to set the thread name in your code or rely on a private variable called *DONT_USE_InternalThread* on the thread. Neither trick allows you to set that per-thread breakpoint on something as simple as the thread ID as listed in the Thread window.

The idea behind filter breakpoint modifiers is that in today's multithreaded machine world, you need a consistent way to easily set a breakpoint on a specific thread, process, or machine. After you've set the location breakpoint, right-click the red dot and select Filter to get to the Breakpoint Filter dialog box. As you'll see in the dialog box, you can set a conditional style breakpoint by using machines, threads, and processes. Although it's not mentioned in the dialog box, the C# == operator is fully supported.

The Watch Window

If I had to give an Academy Award for technical achievement and overall usefulness in Visual Studio, the Watch window would win hands down. One idea that companies creating development tools for other environments and operating systems haven't figured out at all is that if developers can easily develop and debug their applications, they'll more likely flock to that environment or platform. In previous versions of Visual Studio, the power offered by the Watch window and its related cousins, the QuickWatch dialog box, Autos window, Locals window, This window, and Me window, has been legendary. With Visual Studio 2005, the new power of DataTips, Visualizers, and the Immediate window is something that will have developers debugging faster than ever before.

I want to make sure to point out that you can use any of the related Watch windows to change a variable's value. Unfortunately, many developers coming over from other environments, and a few who have been doing Windows development for many years, aren't aware of the capabilities. Let's take the Autos window as an example. You just select the variable or the child variable you want to change, and click once on the value field for that variable. Simply type in the new value and you've changed the variable.

Many developers treat the Watch window as a read-only place in which they drop their variables and watch. What makes the Watch window exciting is that it has a complete expression evaluator built in. If you want to see something as an integer that's not an integer, simply cast or convert it in the same way you would if you were programming in the currently active programming language. Here's a simple example: Suppose *CurrVal* is declared as an integer and you want to see what it evaluates to as a Boolean. In the Name column of the Watch window, in C# enter *(bool)CurrVal*, or for Visual Basic, enter *CBool(CurrVal)*. The value is displayed as true or false as appropriate.

Changing an integer to a Boolean might not be that exciting, but the ability of the Watch window to evaluate expressions gives you the ultimate code-testing trick. As I discussed in the "What's the secret to debugging?" section of Chapter 4, code coverage is one of the goals you need to strive for when doing your unit testing. If, for example, you have a conditional expression inside a function, and it's difficult to see at a glance what it evaluates to so that you can step into the true or false branch as appropriate, the Watch window becomes your savior. Because there's a full expression evaluator built in, you can simply drag the expression in question down to the Watch window and see what it evaluates to. Granted, there are some restrictions. If your expression calls all sorts of functions instead of using variables, you could be in trouble. If you look at my code, I use only local variables in conditions that I can see the result of the expression in the Watch window. Some of you might be truth table geniuses and be able to see how those expressions evaluate off the top of your heads, but I certainly am not one.

To make this clearer, let's use the next expression as an example. You can highlight everything inside the outer parentheses and drag it to the Watch window. However, because it's on three lines, the Watch window interprets it as three separate lines in its display. I still do that so that I can copy and paste the two lines into the first one and thus build my final expression without too much typing. Once the expression is entered on one line in the Watch window, the value column is either true or false, depending on the values in the variables.

```
if ( ( RunningState.eRunning == currentState   ) ||
     ( RunningState.eException == currentState  ) &&
     ( true == seenInitialCall )   )
```

The next step is to put each of the variables that make up a part of the expression in their own entries in the Watch window. The really cool part is that you can start changing the values of the individual variables and see that the full expression on the first line automatically changes based on the changing subexpressions. I absolutely love this feature because it helps you see the data coverage you need to generate in your unit tests.

Format Specifiers and Property Evaluation

If you're coming from a C++ background, you'll remember the, *code* values, called *format specifiers*, that you could use to influence exactly how you wanted the data to be displayed. If you're a C# developer, some of those format specifiers have reappeared to make your life easier. For example, if you have a variable *i* and you type *i,h* in the Watch window, the number will be displayed as hexadecimal instead of the decimal default. By the way, you can force the default Watch window display to hexadecimal by right-clicking in the Watch window and selecting Hexadecimal Display from the shortcut menu. If you have set the default display to Hexadecimal, you can specify the *,d* format specifier to display the data as decimal. The *,raw* formatting code is used when *DebuggerTypeProxyAttributes* have been applied to a class, which I will explain more in detail in the "Expanding Your Own Types" section later in the chapter.

The *,nq* formatting code is especially handy because to make the string more readable, it will display a string without the escaped quotes. For example, if you have the XML element, the default view of the inner text would show the string like the following: "*<book genre=\"novel\" ISBN=\"1-861001-57-5\" misc=\"sale item\"/>*." After you add the *,nq* on the end of the string property, the display changes to "*<book genre="novel" ISBN="1-861001-57-5" misc="sale item"/>*" that is much easier to read. Personally, I wish the Watch window would default to the non-quoted string display.

If you have Just My Code enabled, and you want to see the private members of an object, you'd specify the *,hidden* code after the variable name. Note that the Visual Studio documentation is incorrect and calls this formatting code *,private*.

The last format specifier I want to mention is *,ac*, which exists to force expression evaluation. The documentation lists this format specifier with a capital A, which is incorrect. In order to talk about the *,ac* specifier, I have to talk about implicit property evaluation. Whereas the format specifiers are annoyingly C# only, implicit property evaluation applies to all .NET languages, and it's important that you understand the ramifications.

For .NET developers, it's second nature to see the values of properties on objects in any of the Watch window family of windows. What the debugger's doing is actually calling the property's *get* method in the context of debuggee. In most cases, there's no trouble at all having the debugger help you out that way. Occasionally, a property evaluation inside the debugger can cause a side effect that causes a great deal of trouble. If there is a property getter that makes a database query that changes data, the property evaluation in the debugger will certainly be changing the state of your application. I know no one reading this would ever have a property getter changing data, but you can't always force your coworkers to follow best practices.

If there's any hint that the debugger property evaluation will cause you problems, you'll want to turn it off by going to the Options dialog box, clicking the Debugging node, General property page, and clearing the Enable Property Evaluation and Other Implicit Function Calls check box. You can toggle this option all you want during a debugging session to control the debugger behavior. Although I would prefer a menu command or a toolbar button to control the option, it's not too onerous to toggle it. You'll know that implicit property evaluation is turned off when you start debugging because you'll see "Property evaluation is disabled in debugger windows. Check your settings in Tools.Options.Debugging.General." for Visual Basic and "Implicit function evaluation is turned off by user." for C#. Interestingly, turning off property evaluation does not disable calling properties and methods on conditional breakpoint modifiers.

In previous versions of the debugger, once you turned off implicit property evaluation, there was no way to see those property values without turning it fully back on. Fortunately, the Visual Studio 2005 debugger is much more forgiving, and you have various ways to evaluate specific properties. For all languages, the easiest thing to do is to click the green refresh button on the right side of the Value column. Figure 5-7 shows the Watch window with the refresh buttons called out. As you can see, you can click the refresh button for the entire object so all properties in the class are shown, or you can do just the one property you're interested in seeing.

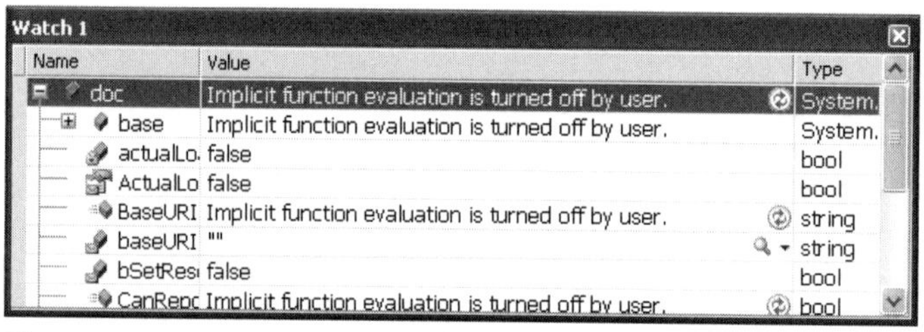

Figure 5-7   Controlling debugger-implicit property evaluation

If you're debugging a C# application, you can add the *,ac* format specifier to that property or the class as a whole. This will tell the debugger that you always want to evaluate the specific property or all properties on the object every time you stop the debugger.

One interesting item I noticed with implicit property evaluation turned off is that when you add an object to the Watch window, the Watch window will evaluate all the properties on that object so you can see their values. It's intuitively what you would expect, but if you drag and drop that one object with a nasty-side-effect property, you've just caused it to execute. Just keep that in mind when you are adding scary objects to the Watch window. What you'll want to do instead is stop in another scope where the variable is not defined and add the value you want to watch there. That way it's in the Watch window when you stop, so the debugger won't evaluate the properties when it stops in the real location.

Before I jump to my favorite new feature in the Watch window, I wanted to mention two pseudo variables you can display in the Watch window. If you've turned off the Exception

Assistant, the window that shows the unhandled exception, the C#-only $exception pseudo variable will be automatically added to the Locals window so you can see the unhandled exception. The new pseudo value, $user, will display the account information for the current thread and indicate if it's impersonating.

Make Object ID

Very few C# developers (yes, this is a C#-only feature) have bothered to right-click in the Watch window family. If you have in the past, you might think that nothing changed because the shortcut menu still has the options for toggling the display between hexadecimal and decimal display in addition to the usual copy and paste. Depending on where you click, one of the most important but least mentioned of the new debugger tricks shows up in the middle of the menu: *Make Object ID*. You'll see this only when right-clicking on a value that's live, which means it's either in a local variable, parameter, or an object field, in the current scope.

After you've selected *Make Object ID*, it doesn't look like much happened, but if you look closely at the Value field, you might see something interesting. Figure 5-8 shows the results of selecting *Make Object ID* in an Autos window.

Figure 5-8   Result of selecting Make Object ID from the shortcut menu

Although you still see the object type in curly braces, you now also see a *{1#}*. That signifies the object ID assigned to that object instance. That might not sound that exciting, but if you go over to the Watch window and enter *1#*, as I've done in Figure 5-9, you'll start to get an inkling of the power you just unleashed.

Figure 5-9   Using an object ID in the Watch window

The object ID is where a managed debugger can keep an eye on an object anywhere in the garbage-collected heap regardless of scope. Therefore, if you want to watch a local variable from a method twenty items up the stack, create an object ID for that object, and you'll see it live no matter where you are. You can even have object IDs for values that are in other threads. Even better, you'll see this object no matter what generation it bounces to, and if it's collected, the display for that object ID will be unavailable.

I don't know how many times I've added a temporary static field to a class so I can keep track of a particular value or set of values. Now with the amazingly cool *Make Object ID* value, you can keep track of those objects using the debugger and not have to change your code.

The only drawbacks are that you have no control over the naming so if you create twenty or thirty object IDs, you'll have to write down what each number means in order to remember them. Alternatively, you could develop a photographic memory to avoid keeping track of them manually.

As I mentioned at the beginning of this section, this is a C#-only feature, although it also works in Microsoft Visual J#. I cannot understand why this amazingly useful feature isn't present in Visual Basic applications. Sometimes I have to wonder if the Visual C# and Visual Basic teams work at the same company. It's as if the Visual Basic team is from Venus and the Visual C# team is from Mars. My hope is that when the next version of Visual Studio ships, the teams will learn how to communicate so we have the same features no matter what .NET language we're using.

DataTips

One of the sexiest items of any Visual Studio 2005 demo is the new DataTips in the debugger. As we've all seen, they've grown way past being simple tool tips into a complete Watch window jammed into an automatic pop-up message box. I had to debug a .NET 1.1 problem with Visual Studio .NET 2003 the other day and realized just how amazing the new DataTips are when you don't have them.

Although most of us have played with the DataTips, I want to mention a few cool tricks that you might not be aware of. The first is that any time a DataTip appears, you can press the Ctrl key to make it go to nearly transparent. Because DataTips can expand to cover the entire screen, this little trick works great to see the code you're working on while still enabling you to keep the expanded DateTip available.

Although the only way to get a DataTip up is to move the mouse over it, once a DataTip is active, it does support a number of keyboard options. Page Up and Page Down scroll through the available items as does the mouse wheel. The up and down arrows move through the list, and if you are on an item that's expandable, the right arrow key will expand the child items. Once you are finished with the expanded display, the left arrow will collapse the opened values.

Because the DataTips are the complete Watch window in a tool tip, you can also edit values directly in the DataTip itself. You can either click in the value area to the right of the value or press the F2 key if you've highlighted the item with the Up and Down arrow keys. Obviously, the DataTip won't let you edit read-only values. If you have doubts on what you can edit, right-click the item in the DataTip, and if the Edit Value command is unavailable, it's read-only. If the Edit Value item is available, it's the third way to enable editing in a DataTip.

The shortcut menu on a DataTip has nearly the same items as present in a normal Watch window, so you can do the magical Make Object ID (C# only) any time you need it. In addition to being able to add a value to the Watch window from the DataTip, it also has the Copy Expression menu item, which copies only the *variable/class.field* name and Copy Value, which copies only the value of the highlighted item.

Expanding Your Own Types

Although the Watch window family does an excellent job of displaying data, it doesn't always display the data in the most concise form. This isn't the fault of the debugger; it's just that there's no way the debugger knows what the key data for every class is. Every class has those two or three items that at a glance tell you everything you need to know so you don't have to expand the class and wade through thirty fields to find those items.

Fortunately, the improved debugger in Visual Studio 2005 offers a much better way to show key data than before. Past versions relied on a file called MCEE_CS.dat hidden down deep in the Visual Studio installation directory—that file worked only for C#. By keeping these special expansions separate from the classes themselves, unless you were hyper-vigilant with version control, other developers couldn't take advantage of your helpful expansions.

C# developers will get the first of these new expansions simply by overriding *ToString*, which in many cases shows nearly all the key data you need at a glance. Now instead of seeing the type in the Value field of the Watch window family or the DataTip, you'll see the result of the debugger calling *ToString* on the instance. If you've wondered how the debugger could always show you the current string in a *StringBuilder* class, this is exactly what's happening.

If having the *ToString* called on your objects is causing side effects, the evaluation will be turned off when in the Options dialog box, Debugger node, General page, you clear Call ToString() on objects in variables windows (C# only). Because that option is under Enable property evaluation and other implicit function calls, disabling the parent option will disable all *ToString* calls also.

To automatically have the debugger display the key data about your classes, you'll apply the new *DebuggerDisplayAttribute* to the class where you'll specify the data to display in the Value column when viewing the data in the Watch window family. For example, the *ComplexNumber* class in Listing 5-3 shows applying the *DebuggerDisplayAttribute* to a class. As you can see in the listing, the expression "{_Real}.{_Imaginary}i" will evaluate the _Real and _Imaginary fields whenever an instance of the class is evaluated by the debugger because any value in curly braces is assumed to be a field in the instance. Any value outside of curly braces is assumed to be hard-coded text, which is why an *i* will always follow the evaluations of the two fields in this example. Being able to see *3.4i* at a glance is so much faster than clicking and expanding the class to look at the individual field values.

Listing 5-3   *DebuggerDisplayAttribute* Example

```
<DebuggerDisplay("{_Real}.{_Imaginary}i")> _
Public Class ComplexNumber
    ' Setting the state to Never tells the debugger to hide
    ' this field in any display. Since there's a Real
    ' property, hiding this internal field makes the display
    ' easier to deal with.
    <DebuggerBrowsable(DebuggerBrowsableState.Never)> _
    Private _Real As Integer
```

```vbnet
    ' The debugger will show this value with the Imaginary property.
    <DebuggerBrowsable(DebuggerBrowsableState.Never)> _
    Private _Imaginary As Integer

    Public Sub New(ByVal Real As Integer, ByVal Imaginary As Integer)
        _Real = Real
        _Imaginary = Imaginary
    End Sub

    Public Sub New()
        _Real = 0
        _Imaginary = 0
    End Sub

    Public Property Real() As Integer
        Get
            Return (_Real)
        End Get
        Set(ByVal value As Integer)
            _Real = value
        End Set
    End Property

    Public Property Imaginary() As Integer
        Get
            Return (_Imaginary)
        End Get
        Set(ByVal value As Integer)
            _Imaginary = value
        End Set
    End Property

    Public Shared Operator +(ByVal right As ComplexNumber, _
                             ByVal left As ComplexNumber) As ComplexNumber
        Dim ret As ComplexNumber = New ComplexNumber(right.Real + left.Real, _
                                       right.Imaginary + left.Imaginary)
        Return (ret)
    End Operator

    Public Overrides Function ToString() As String
        Return (String.Format("{0}.{1}i", _
            Real.ToString(), _
            Imaginary.ToString()))
    End Function

End Class
```

As soon as I saw that the *DebuggerDisplayAttribute* can process fields, I had to try a test in which I tried a method call in the passed-in expression to see what the debugger is able to handle. Using a C# version of the *ComplexNumber* class, I tried setting the *DebuggerDisplay-Attribute* expression to "*ToString()*" because that method was doing the same thing as the expression evaluating the string directly. That worked great in the C# driver program. However, when I tried the same expression in the Visual Basic version of *ComplexNumber*, I didn't see the string I expected. Only the type appeared in the Value column of the Watch window, as though I didn't have any *DebuggerDisplayAttribute* at all. Interestingly, using the properties in the expression for the Visual Basic example, "*{Real}.{Imaginary}i*" (notice the lack of underscores) shows that the properties are being executed by the debugger. With a little more exploration, it turns out that Visual Basic expression evaluator used with the *DebuggerDisplayAttribute* will not call any methods with parenthesis.

Because of the limitations in the Visual Basic evaluation, to ensure that the appropriate expression appears, you'll want to limit yourself to only fields and properties in your *DebuggerDisplayAttribute* values no matter what language you program in. Even given that minor limitation, I'm thrilled with *DebuggerDisplayAttribute* because the super-quick debugger display now stays with the class, and the debugger automatically uses it. Even more exciting is that if you have a class that is derived from a class that has a *DebuggerDisplayAttribute* defined, the derived class will automatically get the benefit because the debugger will scoot down the class derivation chain and use the *DebuggerDisplayAttribute* that was found.

If you're looking for a good project, you might want to consider writing a Code Analysis rule that will look to see if a public class does not have a *DebuggerDisplayAttribute* defined. If not, you could report an error. I will give you extra credit if you have the rule look up the class derivation chain and not report the error if a base class has a *DebuggerDisplayAttribute* defined. For more information on writing Code Analysis rules, see Chapter 8, "Writing Code Analysis Rules."

Listing 5-3 also shows the *DebuggerBrowsableAttribute*, which allows you to control how the Watch window expands and displays a type. In the example, I've applied the *DebuggerBrowsableAttribute* with the *DebuggerBrowsableState* set to *Never* to the two fields in the class. Because properties expose those two field values, the actual fields will not be displayed if you expand a *ComplexNumber* type. By condensing the data display, without hiding any actual data, you'll see the important data more quickly, which is especially important in DataTips.

Back in the "Format Specifiers and Property Evaluation" section of this chapter, I discussed how the implicit property evaluation could cause side effects because the debugger is executing the property. Although you should avoid property getters that have side effects, in some cases you can't. If you're faced with that conundrum, you could apply the *DebuggerBrowsableAttribute* with the *DebuggerBrowsableState* set to *Never*, and the debugger will never execute the property. Now you won't have to worry about the debugger executing that particular property. Of course, any time you apply a *DebuggerBrowsableAttribute*, you need to have a comment as to why you're applying it so maintenance developers and coworkers know why you're hiding an item from the debugger.

The *DebuggerBrowsableState.Never* state will usually be what you pass to *DebuggerBrowsableAttribute*. However, if you have a collection or array and want to hide the variable name but expand the data, you can specify *DebuggerBrowsableState.RootHidden*. This enumeration is used in conjunction with the *DebuggerTypeProxyAttribute*, which I'll discuss in a moment.

The last of the *DebuggerBrowsableState* trio is *Collapsed*, which you'll never use because that's the default state for any type displayed in the Watch window family. The last thing I want to mention about the *DebuggerBrowsableAttribute* is that numerous places in the Visual Studio documentation say that Visual Basic debugging does not support the *DebuggerBrowsable-Attribute*, which is incorrect.

If you want even more control over how the debugger displays your type, you can tell the debugger that you have a class that should be used by the debugger to show its fields and properties instead of your real type with the *DebuggerTypeProxyAttribute*. This jumps into the realm of the super-advanced, but if you need it, you'll thank the debugger team for adding the capability. To see how *DebuggerTypeProxyAttribute* works, see the code in Listing 5-4, which is an excellent example that Habib Heydarian, the Program Manager for the Visual Studio debugger, showed me for using *DebuggerTypeProxyAttribute*.

The constructor for *DebuggerTypeProxyAttribute* takes either a type or a string or both, which is the class the debugger will instantiate to do the display. Traditionally, the class used to display is an *internal* or *Friend* class nested inside the main class in order to allow easy access to private members. However, there is nothing stopping you from having the display class be anywhere in the module. The only requirement of the display class passed to *DebuggerTypeProxyAttribute* is that the constructor on the class must have the type to display as a parameter. Inside the display class, you can have as many properties or fields as necessary to be shown by the debugger.

Before you look at Listing 5-4, which works with *SecureString* types, it's worth showing you what the default display looks like in the debugger. Figure 5-10 shows a *SecureString*, and as you can see, there's no way you can find the real string at all.

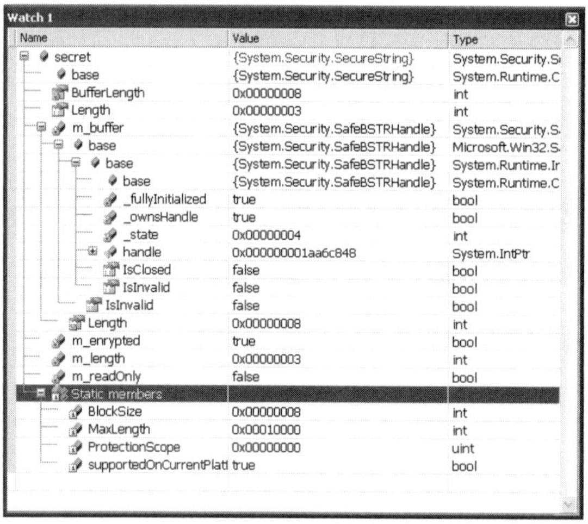

Figure 5-10   Default display for *SecureString*

The code in Listing 5-4 is not a full program, and I will discuss a bit more about where it's loaded and how it's executed in the "Adding *DebuggerDisplayAttribute* without Source Code" section later in this chapter.

Listing 5-4   *DebuggerTypeProxyAttribute* example

```
[assembly: DebuggerTypeProxy ( typeof ( Example.SecureStringDebuggerProxy ) ,
                                Target = typeof ( SecureString ) )]

namespace Example
{
    public class SecureStringDebuggerProxy
    {
        private string m_value;

        public SecureStringDebuggerProxy ( System.Security.SecureString s )
        {
            IntPtr ptr = Marshal.SecureStringToBSTR ( s );
            this.m_value = Marshal.PtrToStringBSTR ( ptr );
            Marshal.FreeBSTR ( ptr );
        }

        public string Value
        {
            get
            {
                return m_value;
            }
        }
    }
}
```

When the code in Listing 5-4 is used, the display looks like that in Figure 5-11. As you can see, there are a lot fewer items, and the *Value* field shows the string, which is the exact same one shown in Figure 5-10. Even a manager can figure out that Figure 5-11 is much easier to understand.

Figure 5-11   DebuggerTypeProxyAttribute display for SecureString

The Raw View element is a C#-only feature that allows you explicit access to the actual instance data. This is very helpful if you suspect that the *DebuggerTypeProxyAttribute* has a bug or may be hiding data from you. If you want to force off the *DebuggerTypeProxyAttribute* for a class, you can add the *,raw* formatting specifier after the variable name in the Watch window.

Adding *DebuggerDisplayAttribute* Without Source Code

I was working on a bug in a Visual Basic application that used a ton of *StringBuilder* classes, and I was lamenting the automatic C# *ToString* expansion so I could see the strings automatically as they were built up. After I was done with the debugging job, I set out to see if it were possible to provide my own expansions for classes where I didn't have the source code. The great news is that I found the undocumented way of accomplishing the goal, and it turned out to be extremely easy.

As with any reverse engineering in .NET, it always starts with Reflector from Lutz Roeder. I'd noticed that items like *WebControls.Button* and any *Exception* derived type showed custom text in the Value column so they must have had a *DebuggerDisplayAttribute* on them. Checking with Reflector showed that they didn't have any *DebuggerDisplayAttribute*. In fact, almost no classes in the Framework Class Library (FCL) have *DebuggerDisplayAttribute* on them. About the only ones that do are those in the *System.Collections.Generic* namespace.

I looked at the debugger binaries but didn't see that they had any hard-coded values in them that would show custom values for known types. Maundering through the debugger binaries, I thought I'd look in the directories where debugger visualizers, which I'll talk about later in the chapter, were loaded. In the C:\Documents and Settings*user_name*\My Documents \Visual Studio 2005\Visualizers directory are two files, AutoExp.cs and AutoExp.dll. Being that the old C++ expansion file was called AutoExp.dat, I figured I was on to something, and a quick look in AutoExp.cs showed that that is the file that contains the code for the *Debugger-DisplayAttributes* and is compiled into AutoExp.dll, which is what the debugger loads to show the custom values.

The trick to specify a *DebuggerDisplayAttribute* where you don't have source code is to specify it as an assembly-level attribute and use the Target parameter to specify the type. For example, the default AutoExp.cs (and compiled DLL) shows the following custom expansion for a *Point* structure:

```
[assembly: DebuggerDisplay(@"\{X = {x} Y = {y}}", Target = typeof(Point))]
```

Thus, to solve my problem in which I wanted to see the current string in a *StringBuilder* instance at a glance, I just needed to add the following expression to AutoExp.cs and recompile the source code into AutoExp.dll so the debugger would show it.

```
[assembly: DebuggerDisplay ( "{m_StringValue}" , Target = typeof ( StringBuilder ) )]
```

Given how easy it is to add display for types where you don't have source code, I immediately wanted to start adding numerous values to the default AutoExp.cs. However, that would work only for the current user, and I wanted to see if I could get something working globally on the machine so that all accounts using Visual Studio would get the enhanced debugging capability.

A couple of tests later, I saw that every new user account that starts Visual Studio gets the default AutoExp.cs and accompanying AutoExp.dll. Additionally, if there's an AutoExp.dll in the system-wide visualizer directory, *Visual_Studio_Install_Directory*\Common7\Packages \Debugger\Visualizers, the debugger will aggregate the one in that directory with the default in the C:\Documents and Settings*user_name*\My Documents\Visual Studio 2005\Visualizers directory.

My goal for the book's source code was to provide a new AutoExp.dll that would add all the *DebuggerDisplayAttribute* values I thought were missing from the FCL. Listing 5-5 shows the values that I thought were missing from the default AutoExp.cs file. This file contains the excellent example of *DebuggerTypeProxyAttribute* usage for the *SecureString* type I showed in Listing 5-4. Now you'll be able to see the values of those secure strings right inside the debugger!

Listing 5-5   AutoExp.cs from the book's source code

```
/*-------------------------------------------------------------------------------
 * Debugging Microsoft .NET 2.0 Applications
 * Copyright © 1997-2006 John Robbins -- All rights reserved.
 -------------------------------------------------------------------------------*/
using System;
using System.Diagnostics;
using System.Text;
using System.Text.RegularExpressions;
using System.Globalization;
using System.Runtime.InteropServices;
using System.Threading;
using System.IO;
using System.Security;
using System.Xml;
// For Code Analysis/FxCop Rule development.
using Microsoft.Cci;

using Web = System.Web;
using WebCaching = System.Web.Caching;

// System.
[assembly:
  DebuggerDisplay ( "IsAlive={IsAlive} TrackResurrection={TrackResurrection}" ,
                   Target = typeof ( WeakReference ) )]

// System.Diagnostics
[assembly: DebuggerDisplay ( "Count={Count}" ,
                            Target = typeof ( TraceListenerCollection ) )]
[assembly: DebuggerDisplay ( "Name={Name}" ,
                            Target = typeof ( TraceListener ) )]
[assembly: DebuggerDisplay ( "CounterName={CounterName}" ,
                            Target = typeof ( PerformanceCounter ) )]
[assembly: DebuggerDisplay ( "Count={Count}" ,
                            Target = typeof ( ProcessModuleCollection ) )]
[assembly: DebuggerDisplay ( "Arguments={Arguments}" ,
                            Target = typeof ( ProcessStartInfo ) )]
[assembly: DebuggerDisplay ( "Count={Count}" ,
                            Target = typeof ( ProcessThreadCollection ) )]
```

```
[assembly: DebuggerDisplay ( "Id={Id}" ,
                             Target = typeof ( ProcessThread ) )]
[assembly: DebuggerDisplay ( "DisplayName={DisplayName} Level={Level}" ,
                             Target = typeof ( SourceSwitch ) )]
[assembly: DebuggerDisplay ( "Source={Source}" ,
                             Target = typeof ( SourceFilter ) )]
[assembly: DebuggerDisplay ( "IsRunning={IsRunning}" ,
                             Target = typeof ( Stopwatch ) )]
// System.Globalization
[assembly: DebuggerDisplay ( "Name={Name} ({DisplayName})" ,
                             Target = typeof ( CultureInfo ) )]


// System.IO
[assembly: DebuggerDisplay ( "Name={Name} Position={Position} Length={Length}" ,
                             Target = typeof ( FileStream ) )]


[assembly: DebuggerDisplay ( "Encoding={CurrentEncoding.EncodingName} " +
                             "EOF={EndOfStream}" ,
                             Target = typeof ( StreamReader ) )]


// System.Text
[assembly: DebuggerDisplay ( "{m_StringValue}" ,
                             Target = typeof ( StringBuilder ) )]


// System.Text.RegularExpression
[assembly: DebuggerDisplay ( "Group Count={Groups.Count}, Text={Value}" ,
                             Target = typeof ( Match ) )]


// System.Threading
[assembly: DebuggerDisplay ( "Name={Name}, Id={ManagedThreadId} " +
                             "AptState={ApartmentState}" ,
                             Target = typeof ( Thread ) )]
[assembly: DebuggerDisplay ( "IsReaderLockHeld={IsReaderLockHeld} " +
                             "IsWriterLockHeld={IsWriterLockHeld}" ,
                             Target = typeof ( ReaderWriterLock ) )]


// System.Runtime.InteropServices
[assembly:
 DebuggerDisplay ( "handle={handle} IsClosed={IsClosed} IsInvalid={IsInvalid}" ,
                   Target = typeof ( SafeHandle ) )]
// System.Web
[assembly: DebuggerDisplay ( "IsEnabled={IsEnabled} TraceMode={TraceMode}" ,
                             Target = typeof ( Web.TraceContext ) )]


// System.Web.Caching
[assembly: DebuggerDisplay ( "Count={Count}" ,
                             Target = typeof ( WebCaching.Cache ) )]
[assembly: DebuggerDisplay ( "UtcLastModified={UtcLastModified}" ,
                             Target = typeof ( WebCaching.CacheDependency ) )]


// System.Xml
[assembly: DebuggerDisplay ( "Count={Count}" ,
                             Target = typeof ( XmlAttributeCollection ) )]
```

```
[assembly: DebuggerDisplay ( "Count={Count}" ,
                             Target = typeof ( XmlNodeList ) )]


// Code Analysis/FxCop helpers. Thanks to Jim McGregor for most of these.
[assembly: DebuggerDisplay ( "Length={Length}" ,
                             Target = typeof ( AttributeList ) )]
[assembly: DebuggerDisplay ( "{Type.FullName} ExpLength={Expressions.Length} " +
                             "Expressions[0]={Expressions[0]}" ,
                             Target = typeof ( AttributeNode ) )]


[assembly: DebuggerDisplay ( "Value={Value}" ,
                             Target = typeof ( Literal ) )]


[assembly: DebuggerDisplay ( "Name={Name} Value={Value}" ,
                             Target = typeof ( NamedArgument ) )]
[assembly: DebuggerDisplay ( "Type={Type.FullName}" ,
                             Target = typeof ( AttributeNode ) )]
[assembly: DebuggerDisplay ( "Name={Name} in {Location}" ,
                             Target = typeof ( AssemblyNode ) )]
[assembly: DebuggerDisplay ( "OpCode={OpCode}" ,
                             Target = typeof ( Instruction ) )]


[assembly: DebuggerDisplay ( "Count={Count}" ,
                             Target = typeof ( TrivialHashtable ))]
[assembly: DebuggerDisplay ( "Length={Length}" ,
                             Target = typeof ( AssemblyNodeList ) )]
[assembly: DebuggerDisplay ( "Length={Length}" ,
                             Target = typeof ( AssemblyReferenceList ) )]
[assembly: DebuggerDisplay ( "Length={Length}" ,
                             Target = typeof ( AttributeList ) )]
[assembly: DebuggerDisplay ( "Length={Length}" ,
                             Target = typeof ( ExceptionHandlerList ) )]
[assembly: DebuggerDisplay ( "Length={Length}" ,
                             Target = typeof ( ExpressionList ) )]
[assembly: DebuggerDisplay ( "Length={Length}" ,
                             Target = typeof ( FieldList ) )]
[assembly: DebuggerDisplay ( "Length={Length}" ,
                             Target = typeof ( InstructionList ) )]
[assembly: DebuggerDisplay ( "Length={Length}" ,
                             Target = typeof ( InterfaceList ) )]
[assembly: DebuggerDisplay ( "Length={Length}" ,
                             Target = typeof ( MemberList ) )]
[assembly: DebuggerDisplay ( "Length={Length}" ,
                             Target = typeof ( MethodList ) )]
[assembly: DebuggerDisplay ( "Length={Length}" ,
                             Target = typeof ( ParameterList ) )]
[assembly: DebuggerDisplay ( "Length={Length}" ,
                             Target = typeof ( PropertyList ) )]
[assembly: DebuggerDisplay ( "Length={Length}" ,
                             Target = typeof ( ResourceList ) )]
[assembly: DebuggerDisplay ( "Length={Length}" ,
                             Target = typeof ( SecurityAttributeList ) )]
[assembly: DebuggerDisplay ( "Length={Length}" ,
                             Target = typeof ( StatementList ) )]
```

```
[assembly: DebuggerDisplay ( "Length={Length}" ,
                             Target = typeof ( TypeNodeList ) )]

// Handles Microsoft.Cci.Local and Microsoft.Cci.Parameter.
[assembly: DebuggerDisplay ( "Name={Name}" ,
                             Target = typeof ( Variable ) )]
// Handles the following Microsoft.Cci types: ArrayType, BoxedTypeExpression,
// Class, DelegateNode, EnumNode, FlexArrayTypeExpression, Interface,
// InvariantTypeExpression, NonEmptyStreamType, NonNullableTypeExpression,
// NonNullTypeExpression, OptionalModifierTypeExrpression, Pointer, Reference,
// RequiredModifierType, StreamTypeExpression, Struct, TypeExpression,
// TypeIntersectionExpression, TypeModifier, and TypeUnionExpression.
[assembly: DebuggerDisplay ( "Name={FullName}" ,
                             Target = typeof ( TypeNode ) )]
// Handles the following Microsoft.Cci types: Event, Field, Method, Namespace,
// Property, TypeMemberSnippet, TypeNode.
[assembly: DebuggerDisplay ( "Name={Name}" ,
                             Target = typeof ( Member ) )]


// System.Security
[assembly: DebuggerTypeProxy ( typeof ( AutoExp.SecureStringDebuggerProxy ) ,
                               Target = typeof ( SecureString ) )]

// Thanks to Habib Haydarien for this.
namespace AutoExp
{
    public class SecureStringDebuggerProxy
    {
        private string m_value;

        public SecureStringDebuggerProxy ( System.Security.SecureString s )
        {
            IntPtr ptr = Marshal.SecureStringToBSTR ( s );
            this.m_value = Marshal.PtrToStringBSTR ( ptr );
            Marshal.FreeBSTR ( ptr );
        }

        public string Value
        {
            get
            {
                return m_value;
            }
        }
    }
}
```

Although having a new AutoExp.dll is good, I wanted to find a way to install my version as part of WintellectToolsInstall.MSI, included as part of the book's code, without overwriting any customizations you might have done. Because each user had the default version of the file, I thought that that was where someone would have added his own values. Because the global directory visualizer directory does not have an AutoExp.dll in it, I thought that was where

I could install my version. However, I didn't want my installation to put my version in that directory and potentially overwrite any existing AutoExp.dll. Consequently, the Wintellect-ToolsInstall.MSI performs a check, and if there is an AutoExp.dll in the global visualizer location, I won't install my version. If you do have your own AutoExp.dll, all you'll need to do is copy my definitions out of AutoExp.cs, put them into your own version, and recompile.

Debugger Visualizers

Although the *DebuggerDisplayAttribute* and friends will go a long way to making your debugging easier, they still have some limitations. Looking at XML data in the Watch window family is something of a pain in the neck. The debugger team heard our cries of lament and created debugger visualizers to help us see our data in a natural form. I know the first time I clicked the magnifying glass next to an XML string and saw the XML data in a natural form was a bit thrilling. If you think I lead a boring life, keep in mind that the first time I demonstrated the XML display at a conference, the audience gave a resounding cheer, and half even gave it a standing ovation!

The default string visualizers for strings, XML, and HTML also provide a way to fix one of the more subtle issues in the Watch window: the value column supports only strings that are 250 characters in length. You'll be able to see unlimited string lengths now.

In addition to the string visualizers, Microsoft also included a very nice database visualizer, the DataSet Visualizer, that handles DataViewManager, DataView, DataTable, and DataSet types. Figure 5-12 shows the viewer with a DataSet. What most developers don't realize about the DataSet Visualizer is that it supports editing the data directly in the visualizer. This is perfect for all sorts of testing while you are debugging. Like any DataGrid, click in the particular cell and start editing away.

Figure 5-12   The DataSet Visualizer

Writing Custom Visualizers

If the *String* and *DataSet* visualizers weren't enough, the busy folks on the debugger team did some outstanding work that allows us to write our own visualizers. For years, I've wanted ways to see my application's data in a natural form. Although you can look at an *Image* type in the Watch window and see all sorts of data, such as the actual pixel format, it'd be much faster if you could simply look at the bitmap in its graphical form.

The debugger team really sat down and thought about how they could make the process as painless as possible, which is actually the most impressive feature about custom visualizers. When it comes to development tools, you can provide all the extensibility you want, but if it's going to take a developer more than fifteen minutes to get started, she'll continue to do the task manually. Whenever you are working on a data structure that's more complicated than one of the collection classes, you need to plan time to write a custom visualizer if it makes sense. Custom visualizers give the debugger an alternative view of the data in an appropriate user interface. The great news is that all you as a visualizer developer have to worry about is the user interface. The debugger will take care of getting the data from the debuggee into the debugger process.

Visualizers are loaded from two directories: the first is the global location in *Visual_Studio_ Install_Directory*\Common7\Packages\Debugger\Visualizers, and the second is the per-user location in C:\Documents and Settings*user_name*\My Documents\Visual Studio 2005 \Visualizers. How the debugger knows that an assembly contains a visualizer is if the assembly has at least one assembly-level *DebuggerVisualizerAttribute*. This attribute tells the debugger the name of the visualizer class itself, the class responsible for marshalling the data from the debuggee to the debugger, the type whose content will be shown, and the description of the visualizer to display in the Watch window. An assembly can have as many custom visualizers in it as you would like.

A visualizer is a simple class derived from the abstract class, *DialogDebuggerVisualizer*. Your visualizer needs to provide only the *Show* method implementation that shows your Windows Form with the custom data in it. Passed as parameters to the *Show* method are the means of retrieving the data from the debugger in addition to a debugger service responsible for coordinating your modal form with the IDE main window.

As the Watch window family is displaying a type, if there's a visualizer for that type, it displays the small magnifying glass icon in the value column. When the user clicks the magnifying glass, the debugger chooses the last visualizer used for that class. As you've seen with the *String* class visualizer, you can have multiple visualizers per type. Clicking the down arrow next to the magnifying glass lets you pick among the various visualizers for that type.

The description I've just provided is almost as simple as the code. Listing 5-6 shows the code for the *StringVisualizer* I provide in Wintellect.Visualizers.DLL. Although the built-in String visualizers are excellent for viewing data as a string, XML, or HTML, they don't support editing the data in the form. Because there are many times when I've needed to change a string longer than 250 characters, I needed this visualizer.

Listing 5-6   StringVisualizer.cs

```
/*----------------------------------------------------------------------------
 * Debugging, Testing, and Tuning Microsoft .NET Applications
 * Copyright © 1997-2006 John Robbins -- All rights reserved.
 ----------------------------------------------------------------------------*/
using System;
using System.Diagnostics;
using System.Collections.Generic;
using System.Text;
using System.Windows.Forms;
using System.Drawing;
using Microsoft.VisualStudio.DebuggerVisualizers;
using System.Runtime.InteropServices;

[assembly: DebuggerVisualizer (
                       typeof ( Wintellect.Visualizers.StringVisualizer ) ,
                       typeof ( VisualizerObjectSource ) ,
                       Target = typeof ( System.String ) ,
                       Description = "Wintellect String Visualizer" )]


namespace Wintellect.Visualizers
{
    /// <summary>
    /// A visualizer for <see cref="String"/> classes that provides full editing
    /// support.
    /// </summary>
    public class StringVisualizer : DialogDebuggerVisualizer
    {
        /// <summary>
        /// Shows the form for the <see cref="String"/> visualizer.
        /// </summary>
        /// <param name="windowService">
        /// An object of type <see cref="IDialogVisualizerService"/>
        /// that provides methods your visualizer can use to display Windows
        /// Forms, controls, and dialog boxes.
        /// </param>
        /// <param name="objectProvider">
        /// An object of type <see cref="IVisualizerObjectProvider"/>. This
        /// object provides communication from the debugger side of the
        /// visualizer to the object source
        /// (<see cref="VisualizerObjectSource"/>) on the debuggee side.
        /// </param>
        protected override void Show ( IDialogVisualizerService windowService ,
                                       IVisualizerObjectProvider objectProvider )
        {
            // Marshall the string.
            String dataString = (String)objectProvider.GetObject ( );
            Debug.Assert ( null != dataString );
            if ( null != dataString )
            {
                using ( StringVisualizerForm form =
                    new StringVisualizerForm ( dataString ,
                                        objectProvider.IsObjectReplaceable ))
```

```
                    {
                        if ( DialogResult.OK == windowService.ShowDialog ( form ) )
                        {
                            // Just a double check to ensure that the data is
                            // replaceable.
                            if ( true == objectProvider.IsObjectReplaceable )
                            {
                                // Grab the new data from the form.
                                String data = form.StringData;
                                // Replace it!
                                objectProvider.ReplaceObject ( data );
                            }
                        }
                    }
                }
            }

            /// <summary>
            /// Static method for testing the <see cref="StringVisualizer"/>.
            /// </summary>
            /// <param name="itemToVisualize">
            /// The <see cref="String"/> object to view.
            /// </param>
            public static void TestStringVisualizer ( String itemToVisualize )
            {
                VisualizerDevelopmentHost visualizerHost =
                        new VisualizerDevelopmentHost ( itemToVisualize ,
                                                typeof ( StringVisualizer ) );
                visualizerHost.ShowVisualizer ( );
            }
        }
    }
```

If you've never looked at the code for a custom visualizer before, you're probably wondering where all the hard work is. Granted, although the code does not show the actual dialog box, what you're seeing is everything you need to do in order to be a visualizer. I told you the debugger team did a great job!

At the top of the file is the assembly-level *DebuggerVisualizerAttribute* the debugger looks for when it loads a visualizer. The only interesting parameter is the second, which defines the class you want to use for serialization support. As I mentioned a moment ago, I've never found a need to use anything other than the default *VisualizerObjectSource* class.

The *StringVisualizer.Show* method is where the most interesting work is for a custom visualizer. The first line that calls the *IVisualizerObjectProvider.GetSource* method is all that it takes to get your data from the debuggee to the debugger. If you've ever wrestled with any sort of custom marshalling back in the nasty COM days, that single line might have made you want to cry. Once you cast the return value, you're manipulating the object.

After creating the form and showing it through the supplied *IDialogVisualizerService* interface, I check if the data is replaceable, in other words, changeable just as you were in the Watch window. If the data is replaceable, I get the value from the form and call the *IVisualizerObject-Provider.ReplaceObject* to change the data in the debuggee. Very little has been mentioned about the fact you can replace data from a custom visualizer, but you can see how trivial it is to do.

As you should deduce from the name of the last method in Listing 5-6, *TestStringVisualizer*, it has something to do with testing. The two lines of code in there are all that it takes to test a custom visualizer. If you've ever debugged an add-in, you know how painful that can be, but debugging a debugger that's debugging a dialog box is a major pain. The Visual Studio debugger developers correctly realized that they needed a simple way to quickly test a visualizer, so they came up with the *VisualizerDevelopmentHost*, and those two code lines are all it takes. You can paste the code for the *TestStringVisualizer* into your custom visualizers, change the name, and change the two parameters to the constructor of *VisualizerDevelopmentHost*, and you are finished. I think the debugger team deserves a huge round of applause for making visualizer debugging and testing so trivial.

In addition to the *StringVisualizer* in Wintellect.Visualizers.DLL, I've also included *Image-Visualizer* that will show you any *System.Drawing.Image* derived types. Several developers have written open source or free visualizers that I know you'll find extremely helpful. The first is Brett Johnson's outstanding ASP.NET Cache Visualizer, which you can download at *http://blog.bretts.net/?p=11*. Now you can see what's in your cache and even remove items. I'm so jealous that Brett thought of doing the Cache visualizer before I did. If you do a lot of regular expressions as I do, you'll find that Roy Osherove's RegEx Kit (*http://regex.osherove.com /Articles/RegexKit.html*) makes looking at the regular expression *Match*, *MatchCollection*, and *RegEx* classes much more informative.

Calling Methods in the Watch Window Family

Something I've found relatively amusing about some developers who have moved to Windows and .NET development from those UNIX operating systems is that they insist that UNIX is better. When I ask why, they indignantly respond in their suspender-wearing glory, "In GDB, you can call a function in the debuggee from the debugger!" I was amazed to learn that operating system evaluations revolved around an arcane debugger feature. Of course, those suspenders snap pretty quickly when I tell them that we've been able to call functions from Microsoft debuggers for years. You might wonder what's so desirable about that. If you think like a debugging guru, however, you'll realize that being able to execute a function within the debugger allows you to fully customize your debugging environment. For example, instead of spending 10 minutes looking at 10 different data structures to ensure data coherency, you can write a function that verifies the data and then call it when you need it most—when your application is stopped in the debugger.

Let me give you two examples of code in which I've written methods that I called only from the Watch window. The first example is when I had a data structure that was expandable in the Watch window, but to see all of it I would have been expanding the little plus signs halfway to the planet Eris. By having the debugger-only method, I could more easily see the complete data structure. The second example was when I inherited some code that (don't laugh) had nodes that were shared between a linked list and a binary tree. The code was fragile, and I had to be doubly sure I didn't screw up anything. By having the debugger-only method, I was in essence able to have an assertion function I could use at will.

As you've seen, evaluating, in other words *executing*, managed code properties is automatic. Calling methods on your object instances or static methods in the Watch window is just like calling them from your code. If the method doesn't take any parameters, simply type the method name and add the open and close parentheses. For example, if your debugging method is *MyClass.MyDataCheck ( )*, you'd call it in the Watch window with *MyClass.MyDataCheck ( )*. If your debugging method takes parameters, which you see with the IntelliSense now in the Watch window, just pass them as if you're calling the function normally. If your debugging method returns a value, the Value column in the Watch window displays the return value.

A few rules apply when calling methods from the Watch window. The first rule is that the method should execute in less than 20 seconds because the debugger UI stops responding until the method finishes. After 20 seconds, the Watch window shows "Function evaluation timed out". The good news is that your threads will continue to execute. Once a method has timed out, the debugger correctly remembers that fact for the debugging session and won't reexecute the method unless you click the reevaluate button.

The Watch window isn't the only place where you can call a method; you can also call methods in the Immediate window. Finding the Immediate window is a bit tricky because it's not activated on the View menu as is nearly every other window. It's on the Debug menu, Windows submenu. Alternatively, you can also type *immed* in the Command window to activate it.

Once in the Immediate window, the one trick you'll have to remember is that to see the value of a variable, you'll need to prefix it with a *?* to have the value printed. The *?* is just an alias for the *Debug.Print* command, and it saves you from typing ten characters over and over. Also, the documentation talks about some Immediate window–only commands, such as *.K* to show the stack, but those commands are not available in managed-only debugging.

Calling a method in the Immediate window is nearly identical to how you'd do it in the Watch window, except to see the return value, you'd start the expression with *?*. For example, if you type *? this.*, you'll see the same IntelliSense. Once you type the closing parenthesis and press Enter, you've executed the method. It appears so far that the Watch and Immediate windows are doing the same operation when executing a method, but the Immediate window actually has some amazing functionality that's not documented clearly.

If you set a breakpoint in a method and call that method from the Immediate window, you'll see something very interesting: the debugger stops at the breakpoint. For those of you who loved being able to debug a method from the Immediate window, your favorite feature finally came back. This little trick is great for doing a quick test on the code. You'll know that you're in the middle of function evaluation by looking at the Call Stack window because it will show *Evaluation of: class.method* so you can see where you are in the debuggee. Another neat trick is that if you are not debugging, and the method you want to execute is a static method, you can start the program by calling it in the Watch window.

As if being able to call methods from the Watch and Immediate windows wasn't enough, there's yet another place, which is documented, but I'm willing to bet you've never seen it, the Object Test Bench. This intriguing window is available only at design time, not while debugging. The basic idea of the Object Test Bench window is that it will hold object instances you've created so you can call methods and manipulate them. Debugging a single method called from the Immediate window is useful, but the Object Test Bench allows you to create multiple object scenarios and debug their interactions. Although you won't do the bulk of your testing with the Object Test Bench, it's excellent for those what-if cases in which you want to try something out but don't want to have to write a bunch of code.

To use the Object Test Bench, you first have to create an object. In the Immediate window, you can enter in the appropriate C# or Visual Basic source line you want to execute. For example, executing the following line will open Object Test Bench window as shown in Figure 5-13:

```
SomethingToDo exampleObject = new SomethingToDo();
```

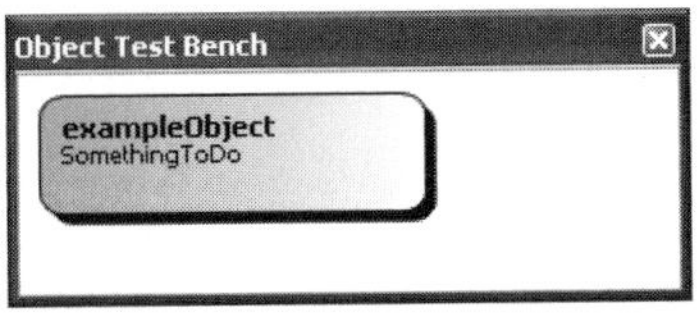

Figure 5-13   Object Test Bench window

Once the object is in the Object Test Bench window, right-click the object and select Invoke Method from the shortcut menu. If the method takes parameters, that will bring up the Invoke Method dialog box, into which you'll type the parameters. If the method you're calling has XML documentation comments, you'll even see those in the Invoke Method dialog box. If you've created additional objects shown in the Object Test Bench window, you can pass those instances if they are the valid type. Once you click OK, your method is executed. Just as in the immediate window, if you have a breakpoint set, you'll stop at the breakpoint.

What's especially nice about invoking methods is if the method returns a value, the Object Test Bench shows the Method Call Result dialog box. In the dialog box is a check box, Save Return Value, which allows you to save the value so it appears in the Object Test Bench. Although you might not be able to completely run a large ASP.NET application from the Object Test Bench, you'll be able to do quite a bit of exploration with no code at all.

Once an object is in the Object Test Bench window, you can manipulate the fields in the object through the Immediate window or through a DataTip. Keep in mind that because the Object Test Bench window is available only in design mode, there's no Watch window, or Quick Watch for that matter.

There are two other places where you can create objects for the Object Test Bench window. The first is in the Class View window. If you right-click the class name, the shortcut menu will show two submenus: Create Instance and Invoke Static Method. The Create Instance menu will show all the constructors for the class so you can pick the one you want to use. After selecting the constructor you want to use, the Create Instance dialog box appears so you can assign a name to the instance and fill in the parameters. The Invoke Static Method is analogous, but as the name says, it's only for static methods. The second place is in a Class Diagram for the solution. Because the Class Diagram is just a graphical display of the Class View, the same creation and execution options appear when you right-click the object diagram.

Advanced Tips and Tricks

In this section, I want to discuss the features that the debugger has up its sleeve to make debugging easier. Half of the debugging process is knowing how to use your tools better, and Visual Studio is filled with features to help you solve your problems quickly and efficiently.

The *Set Next Statement* Command

One of the coolest hidden features in the Visual Studio debugger is the *Set Next Statement* command. It is accessible in both source windows and the Disassembly window on the shortcut menu or by pressing Ctrl+Shift+F10 (using the default keyboard layout), but only when you're debugging. What the *Set Next Statement* command lets you do is change the instruction pointer to a different place in the program. Changing what the program executes is a fantastic debugging technique when you're trying to track down a bug or when you're unit testing and want to test your error handlers.

A perfect example of when to use *Set Next Statement* is manually filling a data structure. You single-step over the method that does the data insertion, change any values passed to the function, and use *Set Next Statement* to force the execution of that call again. Thus, you fill the data structure by changing the execution code.

I guess I should mention that changing the instruction pointer can easily crash your program if you're not extremely careful. For .NET applications, it's safe enough to use *Set Next Statement* at the source code level for both debug and release builds. However, if you skip over a variable initialization to a spot where that variable is used, you'll cause a *NullReferenceException* in your code.

If I'm looking for a bug, and my hypothesis is that said bug might be in a certain code path, I set a breakpoint in the debugger before the offending method or methods. I check the data and the parameters going into the methods, and I single-step over the methods. If the problem isn't duplicated, I use the *Set Next Statement* command to set the execution point back to the breakpoint and change the data going into the methods. This tactic allows me to test several hypotheses in one debugging session, thus saving time in the end. As you can imagine, you can't use this technique in all cases because once you execute some code in your program, executing it again can destroy the state. *Set Next Statement* works best on code that doesn't change the state too much.

As I mentioned earlier, the *Set Next Statement* command comes in handy during unit testing. For example, *Set Next Statement* is useful when you want to test error handlers. Say that you have an *if* statement and you want to test what happens when the condition fails. All you need to do is let the condition execute and use *Set Next Statement* to move the execution point down to the failure case. In addition to *Set Next Statement*, the Run To Cursor menu option, also available on the shortcut menu in a source code window when debugging, allows you to set a one-shot breakpoint. I also use Run To Cursor quite a bit in testing, and it is especially useful to skip long loops without creating a breakpoint that might trigger afterwards and disturb your mind from the workflow you are interested in.

Filling data structures, especially lists and arrays, is another excellent use of *Set Next Statement* when you're testing or debugging. If you have some code that fills a data structure and adds the data structure to a list, you can use *Set Next Statement* to add some additional items to the list so that you can see how your code handles those cases. This use of *Set Next Statement* is especially handy when you need to set up difficult-to-duplicate data conditions when you're debugging.

You can get quite creative with *Set Next Statement*. In one debugging battle, we needed to look at a file the debuggee had opened with no sharing. I used *Set Next Statement* to move the instruction pointer to the *Close* method call, single stepped over the *Close*, and therefore was able to look at the file because the sharing lock was removed and could even modify the contents of the file. After I was finished looking at the data, I used *Set Next Statement* back to the line that opened the file and reset the state of the application.

Mixed-Mode Debugging

For those of you doing interop to native code, which includes most .NET developers, one of the major improvements with .NET 2.0 and Visual Studio 2005 is the massive performance boost for mixed-mode debugging, which allows you to debug both the managed and native parts at the same time. In prior versions of Visual Studio, the mixed mode debugging performance was so abysmal that you were far better off debugging both sides of the application by themselves. In some cases with Visual Studio 2005, I've turned on mixed-mode debugging and forgotten for weeks that it's on. My only complaint is that mixed-mode debugging works only on 32-bit operating systems. For 64-bit systems, you'll need to debug each side of the application separately.

Part of the confusion of mixed-mode debugging is getting it turned on because the option location is different depending on the type of project you're working on. For console and Windows Forms applications, you'll go into the project properties, select the Debug property page, and at the bottom of the page, select the Enable Unmanaged Code Debugging check box. Figure 5-14 shows the location.

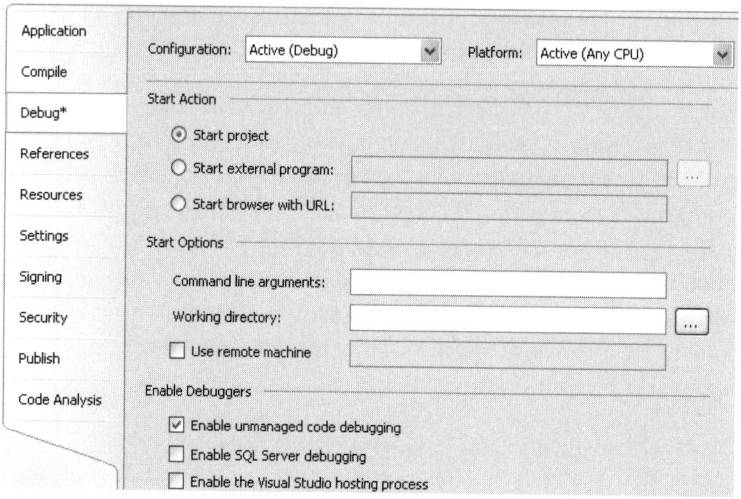

Figure 5-14   Enabling unmanaged debugging in a Console or Windows Forms application

For ASP.NET applications, the option for turning on unmanaged debugging is hidden in the Start Options property page, which you can get to by right-clicking the Web site and selecting Properties. In the ensuing Web Site Property Pages dialog box, select Start Options, and at the bottom of the property page is the Debuggers section. Selecting the Native Code check box turns on unmanaged debugging. Figure 5-15 shows the location.

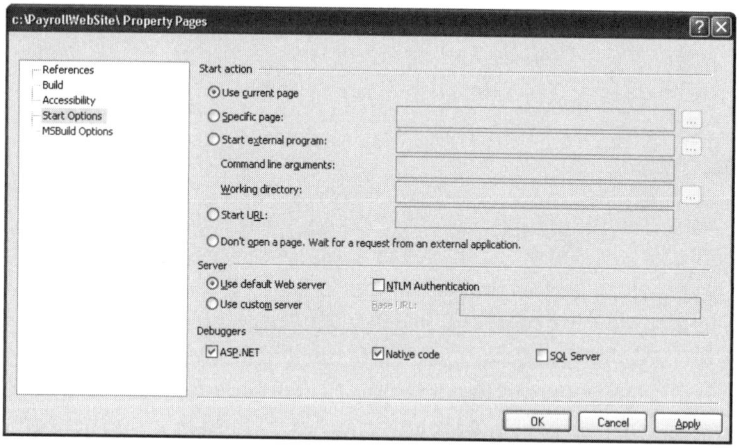

Figure 5-15   Enabling unmanaged debugging in an ASP.NET application

Debugging .NET assemblies that load into native processes can be a bit confusing. For example, if you're developing Microsoft Management Console (MMC) snap-ins in C#, the confusion can occur because although MMC.exe is a native application, it can host the .NET runtime if your assembly implements the snap-ins COM interface. If the hosting executable can be started by the debugger, like MMC.exe, you'll go into the Debug property page and set the name of the process to run in the Start external process edit control. The Visual Studio debugger will behave as expected, and you'll be debugging your C# code with the managed debugger. To turn on both managed and native debugging, you'll select the Enable Unmanaged Debugging check box as I described earlier.

If you've opened the native hosting EXE by going to File, Open, and Project/Solution, life gets a little more interesting if you want to do both native and managed debugging. When opening an EXE outside of a solution, the IDE defaults to a C++ project. That means when you press any of the debugging keys to start debugging, the debugger inspects the binary, and if it's a native binary, it does only native debugging. Conversely, if it's a managed binary, the debugger does only managed debugging. To ensure that you get the exact type of debugging you want, right-click the EXE in Solution Explorer and select Properties from the shortcut menu. In the Property Page dialog box, the only option is the Debugging property page. In the Debugger Type field, the default is Auto, which uses the EXE type to determine the type of debugging to do. To do both native and managed debugging, in the Debugger Type list, select Mixed as shown in Figure 5-16.

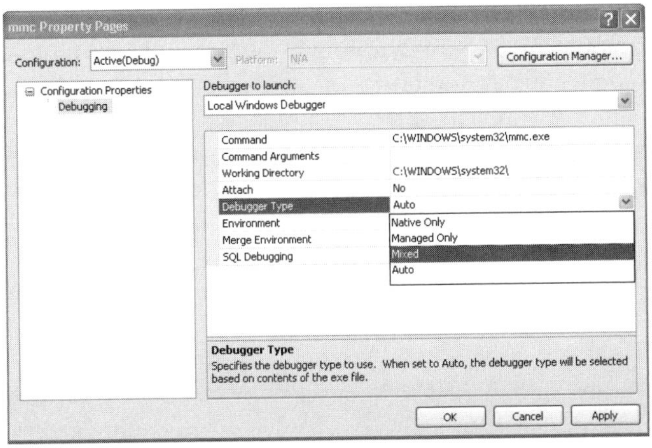

Figure 5-16   Enabling mixed-mode debugging when debugging a stand-alone EXE

The final way you can enable mixed-mode debugging is when you attach to an existing process. In the Attach To Processes dialog box, accessible by selecting Attach To Processes from the Debug menu, the debugger, as it does when opening up just an EXE, attempts to determine the type of debugging you'll want to do. In order to change the default, click Select, and in the Select Code Type dialog box, select the Debug These Code Types option button, and then select both Managed and Native check boxes. Keep in mind that no matter how you turn on mixed-mode debugging, it can be turned on only when you first start or attach to the process. Unfortunately, there's no way to toggle mixed-mode debugging.

Once you are doing mixed-mode debugging, a new feature sneaks into the Debug menu when you break into the debugger: the ability to write minidumps while debugging, which you do by selecting the Save Dump As menu item. For this reason alone, you may want to consider always running mixed-mode debugging as writing out a dump so you can look at your application state after you finish debugging.

After you've selected the new menu item, the Save Dump As dialog box appears, and, unfortunately, always defaults to saving your dump in your *user_name*\Application Data directory. Personally, I wish the dialog box would remember the last directory where you saved a mini-dump file. One key item in the Save Dump As dialog box is the Save As Type drop-down list. It offers two types of dump: Minidump and Minidump with Heap. The straight Minidump type is what I refer to as a basic minidump. It contains the list of loaded modules, their load addresses, and just enough information to walk the native stack. Those minidumps are nice and small, but they sadly don't have sufficient information in them to see the managed side of your application.

A Minidump with Heap contains everything in a basic minidump, but it also contains all the actual memory for the program. As you can guess, those minidumps don't have anything mini about them, because they are the complete address space for the process. However, the Minidump with Heap is what you'll need to look at your managed portions.

Opening minidumps is almost as easy as creating them. You'll start a new instance of Visual Studio, and on the File menu, select Open, and then Project/Solution. In the Open Project dialog box, navigate to the directory where your minidump file is located and double-click it. That will create a new solution with your minidump the only item in it. Once the minidump is open, you'll press debugging keys, such as F5, to start debugging. Visual Studio will open the minidump and allow you to look at the native side of the application at the moment you wrote the minidump. To see the managed side, you'll have to load the Son of Strike (SOS) extension into the Immediate window and use it from there. Chapter 6, "WinDBG, SOS, and ADPlus" goes into the hard-core usage of SOS.

Debugging Exceptions

When developing, it's always an excellent idea to know exactly what code is throwing and catching exceptions. Fortunately, Visual Studio makes debugging exceptions quite easy. On the Debug menu, selecting Exceptions brings up the Exceptions dialog box in which you can tell the debugger exactly what to do when your code throws any exception. Figure 5-17 shows the Exceptions dialog box with some of the Common Language Runtime (CLR) Exceptions expanded.

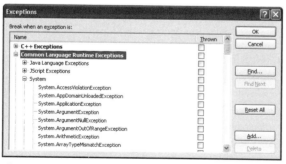

Figure 5-17   Exceptions dialog box

The debugger team has drastically simplified the Exceptions dialog box compared to the one in previous releases. If you want to stop whenever your application throws a *System.Argument-NullException*, for example, you would expand the Common Language Runtime Exceptions node and the System node, and then put a checkmark in the Thrown column next to *System.ArgumentNullException*. When your application and any assembly it is using now throws this error, you'll stop in the debugger with the Exception pop-up message, before any catch block is searched.

Once you're at the code that threw the exception, if you press the Step Into key (F11 on the default keyboard layout), you'll single-step to the exact catch block that's handling that particular exception. Because numerous bugs I've looked at involved overzealously catching exceptions, I know that gaining insight into exactly what code is handling particular exceptions can avoid those problems completely. What I like to do many times when debugging is place a check mark in the Thrown statement next to the Common Language Runtime Exceptions node. That way I'll stop in the debugger whenever I've had any type of exception so I can assure that the handlers are not too generic and are only handling just the exceptions they are supposed to handle.

The one drawback to the approach I just outlined is that you will now be stopping on exceptions that occur anywhere in the address space, including from the CLR and FCL itself. That can get to be a little tedious if you are just trying to see the exceptions your code throws. The reason is that I strongly recommended in the beginning of the chapter to turn off the Just My Code feature. However, this is one time where Just My Code does help you out. If it's turned on, and you set the Exceptions dialog box to stop on all thrown exceptions, you'll stop only inside your code. Personally, I never turn on Just My Code, because I do want to see every possible exception thrown anywhere in my application, but when you're working on very large applications, turning it on trying to look at your exceptions can speed you up.

The last trick with .NET exceptions I want to mention is something that's incorrectly documented in the Visual Studio documentation. If you read the documentation page, "Continuing Execution After an Exception," it says for managed code, "the Exception Assistant unwinds the call stack to the point where the exception was thrown." As anyone who's seen the Exception Assistant knows, that's not the case. The Exception Assistant shows you the location after the throw occurred. Fortunately, there's a nifty little trick to get the state of the application right back to the instruction causing the throw.

After you dismiss the Exception Assistant, go to the Call Stack window in the debugger. Right-click on the first line in the call stack, and the shortcut menu will have an additional menu item on it, Unwind To This Frame. It is active only if you're stopped because of a throw. Selecting Unwind To This Frame will reset the stack to the instruction and state at the time of the throw. This little trick will allow you to change parameters or locals in the debugger to avoid the exception in the first place.

Debugging Multiple Threads and Processes

Life would be so much simpler if we allowed only one thread in a process, but that's not the reality of modern development. Visual Studio has a fine Threads window, which, like all debugger windows, is accessible by selecting Debug on the Windows menu. When stopped in the debugger, the Threads window shows you the Windows thread ID, the name of the thread, its current location, the current priority, and the suspend count. Note that through .NET 2.0, a native thread backs each managed thread. That may change in future versions of .NET.

The most important trick for debugging multiple threads is to set the *Thread.Name* property so you'll see that name in the Threads window Name column. That makes identifying the threads much easier. Keep in mind that you can set the *Thread.Name* property only once because it generates an *InvalidOperationException* when you try to change the name. You'll want to always set those threads you create yourself, but you'll want to be very careful with *ThreadPool* threads in checking first if this property is null before setting it. Also, if you're worried about exposing too much of your internal details by naming a thread, you can use conditional compilation so you name only the threads in debug builds.

Of course, if you forget to name your threads in your code, because you all now know the secrets of the Watch window masters, you can simply name the threads by using the Watch window. Type *System.Threading.Thread.CurrentThread.Name* into the Watch window, and if the name value is *null* or *Nothing*, you can set it to whatever you want. If the name is already set, you'll generate an *InvalidOperationException* trying to set the name because it can be set only once.

One nice trick you have in the Threads window is that you can suspend threads by right-clicking them and selecting Freeze from the shortcut menu. Those threads will be marked with double blue bars in the first column of the Threads window and will have their suspend count incremented by one. Figure 5-18 shows two threads manually frozen in the Threads window. One trick with freezing threads I haven't seen mentioned is that you can select multiple threads and freeze them all with a single right-click. Thawing threads is as simple as right-clicking the frozen threads and selecting Thaw from the shortcut menu.

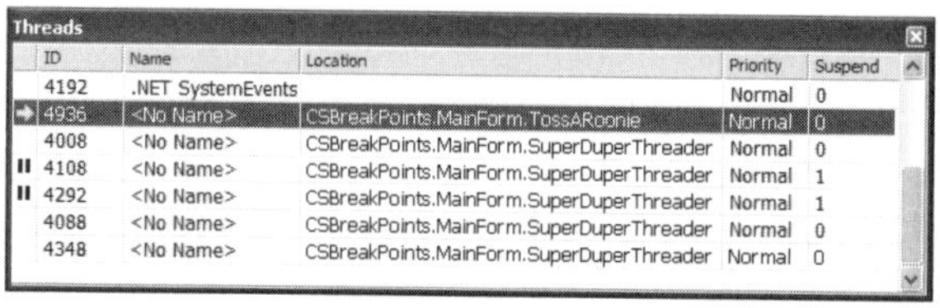

Figure 5-18 Frozen threads in the Threads window

As you can imagine, wantonly freezing your threads can cause a few issues in your application if you're not careful. However, it's a nice trick if you want to follow a single connection in an ASP.NET application through to completion. If you're doing mixed-mode debugging, you'll also want to be extra careful about which threads you freeze. If you freeze the finalizer thread, you'll cause a major problem for your application. In Chapter 6, you'll learn how to identify the finalizer thread with SOS.

The new Processes window, which was sorely missing in previous versions of Visual Studio, makes debugging multiple processes much easier. As with any of the debugging windows, you can access the Processes window by selecting Windows on the Debug menu once a debugging session is started. By default, when one process you are debugging breaks, all processes being debugged will stop in the debugger as well. That way if you have multiple processes talking to one another, all of them will stop at the same time. However, if you go into the IDE Options dialog box, Debugging General node, the second item down is Break All Processes When One Process Breaks. If you clear that option, you'll break only on the individual process that you have chosen to break into or on a process encountering a breakpoint or exception.

The great news is that you can toggle this option on and off all you want when debugging. If the Process window shows a green go button and a blue pause button as the first two buttons, you'll know that the option to break independently is active. Although you probably won't enable this option very much, it's nice that the debugger team made it an option for those times when you are debugging multiple disparate programs.

Summary

Visual Studio is the state-of-the-art debugger on the market today. Microsoft listened to developers and produced a debugger that makes some extremely difficult problems much easier to debug. This chapter introduced all the tricks for setting advanced breakpoints and using the amazing Watch window in managed code, especially concentrating on those new options introduced with Visual Studio 2005. As you've seen, the debugger can do a considerable amount of work for you if you know how to utilize it effectively. You should strive to make the most of the Visual Studio debugger so that you can minimize the time you spend in it.

Advanced breakpoints help you avoid tedious debugging sessions by allowing you to specify the exact conditions under which a breakpoint triggers. The location breakpoint modifiers, hit counts, and condition expressions are your best friends, mainly because the breakpoint modifiers will save you a huge amount of time since they'll allow you to use the debugger more efficiently. I strongly encourage you to play with them a bit so that you can see what you can and can't do, thus avoiding having to learn their idiosyncrasies under extreme pressure.

With the special capabilities of the Watch window family, you should have no trouble quickly and efficiently seeing the key data you need at an instant, be it in a DataTip or in the Watch window itself. Make sure to take advantage of the *DebuggerDisplayAttribute* and the Data Visualizers to make it easy for others (and yourself!) to see your data with a minimum of fuss. Finally, the ability to quickly call and debug a method from the Immediate window is a huge boon to productivity that we've needed for a long time.

Chapter 6
WinDBG, SOS, and ADPlus

After all those pages on Microsoft Visual Studio, you are probably thinking that there can't be any more I could write about debuggers. Judging by the length of this chapter, there's obviously quite a bit more to say as Microsoft produces a second debugger, WinDBG. WinDBG is sometimes affectionately referred to as *Windbag*—the Microsoft Office Word spelling checker suggests *Windbag* when encountering *WinDBG* in documents. The Developer Division at Microsoft produces Visual Studio, but WinDBG development comes from the Microsoft Windows Team. That's because WinDBG is designed to debug the operating system itself, whereas Visual Studio is the commercial product for application developers.

You might be wondering why I'm bothering to cover WinDBG in a book that focuses on .NET debugging. Especially when I tell you that WinDBG does not do any .NET debugging at all; it supports only straight native debugging. There's no way with WinDBG to single-step your C# source code, look at objects, or perform any other of the niceties available in Visual Studio. In fact, as you'll find out, whereas Visual Studio has a well-thought-out user interface, WinDBG's UI comes straight out of the 1980s PC development model. Although it technically does have a graphical user interface, it's a wrapper on a console. Don't let the lack of a hand-holding UI scare you though; it's the ultimate power debugger, and when it comes to the toughest of .NET bugs, it is the only tool that will save the day. To give you an idea of the power, in our consulting work at Wintellect, which as you know works only on the toughest bugs, we use WinDBG nearly 70 percent of the time.

The chapter title gives you a hint that there's more than WinDBG involved for .NET debugging. WinDBG acts as the debugger, but it's the SOS (Son of Strike) extension loaded into WinDBG with the smarts about .NET internals to let you see nearly everything going on in a process. ADPlus, also known as *Autodump+*, is the world's largest VBScript program, which can take snapshots of your .NET applications, called *minidumps*, that you'll use on your production servers.

If that last hint about getting minidumps on your production servers doesn't seem that exciting, and you're still not convinced that WinDBG and friends are worth dealing with, I have a few more morsels to drop that should definitely convince you. As all .NET developers should know, the .NET runtime is a garbage-collected system with three heaps. The big question everyone wants answered is, "what heap is this particular object in?" That's exactly what you can see with these tools. If that's not enough to convince you, think about how many times you wish you could see your application at the exact instance it goes down in a production environment. Again, these tools will make that dream a complete reality.

Be prepared: using WinDBG and friends is not always a pleasant experience. I'll do my best to help you over as many hurdles as possible. However, it will take practice using real-world problems. I can't stress enough that these tools are the real secret to hard-core .NET debugging. If you master them, I guarantee you'll be the complete Alpha Geek in your development shop. How's that for motivation?

Some of you may have heard that SOS can be loaded into Visual Studio. That's true, and I'll show you how in this chapter. However, there are some limitations to that support. In my opinion, WinDBG is a far superior platform for minidump analysis, so I've never used SOS inside Visual Studio.

For this chapter, I'll assume that you've never used WinDBG before. WinDBG is extremely powerful, but I'll concentrate solely on using it for .NET applications. Because WinDBG is strictly a native debugger, I'll first cover the native debugging parts that you'll need in order to look at your .NET applications, no matter the type. Once you have a handle on looking at the native side, we'll turn to using SOS to dig all the way through the .NET pieces of your applications. Using ADPlus is straightforward, but I'll show you the ropes there.

My goal for the chapter is to get you fully prepared to start debugging your applications with WinDBG, SOS, and ADPlus. There are some excellent advanced resources, which I will point you to in the Summary section at the end of the chapter. Sadly, much of what you find on WinDBG, SOS, and ADPlus already assume that you know all the basics. I want to spend this chapter getting you sufficiently conversant in the language of WinDBG, SOS, and ADPlus so you can use those resources even more effectively. Between this chapter and the resources I'll cite for you to continue your studies, you'll be a super expert in .NET internals.

Before You Begin

Before we get into using WinDBG, I have to talk about getting everything installed and getting it properly configured. Even if you have experience with WinDBG, I suggest that you read this section to ensure that you have the best WinDBG setup possible.

Installation

Those of you with .NET 2.0 installed already have the SOS extension DLL; it's part of the Framework installation. WinDBG and ADPlus are part of the *Debugging Tools for Windows* package, which is freely downloadable from *http://www.microsoft.com/whdc/devtools /debugging/default.mspx.* At the time I wrote this, I'm using version 6.6.7.5. When you download WinDBG, make sure to download the appropriate Win32 or Win64 flavor.

As I mentioned back in the "Set Up a Source Server" section of Chapter 2, "Preparing for Debugging," to get the source server support, you'll need to install WinDBG with the custom options and include the SDK in the installation. Figure 6-1 shows the correct settings for a complete custom installation of the Debugging Tools for Windows. In addition to the source server support, the SDK includes all the documentation, headers, and libraries necessary to build your own WinDBG extensions to provide any advanced debugging support you could desire. You'll have to do so in native C++. If you're looking for an excellent article idea to start your writing career, you may want to consider writing WinDBG extensions that analyze the output of various SOS commands.

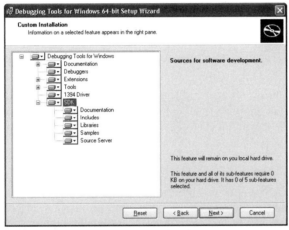

Figure 6-1   SDK installation selected during the Debugging Tools for Windows installation

The Debugging Tools for Windows installation gives you far more than just WinDBG and ADPlus; you get numerous tools for assisting with native user mode and device driver debugging. Whereas I'm going to use WinDBG in this chapter, you may have a burning desire to see your SOS debugging inside a console-based application. The main reason for that is when you pull up a hard-core console-based tool, I can guarantee that you'll scare managers and weaker coworkers out of your office so you can get your work done.

WinDBG is a simple GUI front end on top of a debugging engine, Dbgeng.dll, that does all the heavy lifting. If you want to use a console UI instead, use either NTSD.exe or CDB.exe console-based debuggers that are also installed as part of the Debugging Tools for Windows. The only difference between console-based debuggers is that CDB will use the existing console window for output, whereas NTSD will start a new console window. Everything I discuss in the WinDBG Command window works identically in NTSD.exe and CDB.exe.

Some other tools of note that are also installed are Tlist.exe, which is a console application that reports the currently running processes with detailed information much as Mark

Russinovich's Process Explorer discussed in Chapter 4, "Process Explorer." The Kill.exe program is a terminator program that will rip any type of user-mode process out of memory, even Windows Services, if you have the security permissions. As mentioned previously in this book, all the symbol-management tools are also part of the installation. You may want to poke around the installation directory because the WinDBG Team, as it is known inside Microsoft, is always dropping interesting tools in the Debugging Tools for Windows installation without ever mentioning them.

Additional Reading

Before you even think about starting WinDBG, you have to read the documentation in Debugger.chm in the Debugging Tools for Windows installation directory. I'll be covering WinDBG, SOS, and ADPlus solely from the standpoint of using them to handle .NET applications. Consequently, I won't be able to cover everything that the tools do. The Debugger Tools for Windows documentation is getting better with each release and is some of the best technical documentation I've seen from Microsoft.

The first part you'll want to read is "Debuggers\Debugger Operation" to give you an overview of all the debugging tools. For all the information about symbol handling, read the "Debuggers\Symbols" section. You'll spend a lot of time in the "Debuggers\Debugger Reference" section because that goes into detail about all the commands and their options that you'll execute in the Command window. Finally, read the "Extra Tools\ADPlus" section. If you have the time, the more you read of the WinDBG documentation, the more alpha geek–like you'll become.

By the way, if you look through the help file, you'll notice that there's zero documentation on SOS. The closest thing we have to documentation on SOS is the command help dump from the debugger extension itself. The good news is that help dump has gotten much better and is now usable. We no longer have to poke at the output and guess what we're looking at!

You're probably wondering why, if the WinDBG documentation is so good, I even need to write this chapter. The weakness of the documentation is that it assumes that you have either a coworker sitting there showing you how to use WinDBG or have access to the internal Microsoft mailing lists where the debugger developers respond to questions. I don't think that's an intentional slight, but given that Microsoft developed WinDBG with the operating system developers primarily in mind, it's understandable.

Basics

Once you have the Debugging Tools for Windows installed, there's still some work to do before you can effectively use WinDBG and friends. In this section, I'll talk about getting WinDBG to use your Symbol Server, setting a few options to make your life a little easier, and dealing with the WinDBG window idiosyncrasies.

Symbol Server Setup

Back in Chapter 2's "Set Up a Symbol Store" section, I discussed the steps necessary to set up the two symbol-related environment variables, _NT_SYMBOL_PATH and _NT_EXECUTABLE_ IMAGE_PATH, so you can get symbols loaded. In the "Debugging with Source Servers" section of Chapter 2, I showed how to set the _NT_SOURCE_PATH environment variable to enable the source server for WinDBG. I'm assuming that you've performed those steps to ensure symbol and source happiness. As I stated in that section, WinDBG doesn't give you much information about when it's encountering symbol load problems. In order to ensure that you have the best symbols possible, I will go through the exact steps to get the Symbol Server set up correctly, which can be done with a simple test. I'm going to take you through the steps here but not completely explain the commands you're executing until later in the chapter.

Testing the Symbol Settings

Once you've set the _NT_SYMBOL_PATH environment variable, make sure to start WinDBG either with Microsoft Windows Explorer or a new Command window started from Explorer so the environment variable gets picked up. Here are the exact steps to follow:

1. Ensure you have a live connection to the Internet.

2. Start WinDBG.

3. On the File menu, select Open Executable.

4. Navigate to your Windows directory and double-click Notepad.exe.

5. If you get a "Save information for workspace?" message, click Yes.

6. The Command window will open up and start dumping a bunch of information.

7. If you do not see the Command window, select Command from the View menu.

8. At the bottom of the Command window is the area where you enter commands. Figure 6-2 shows the Command window entry area.

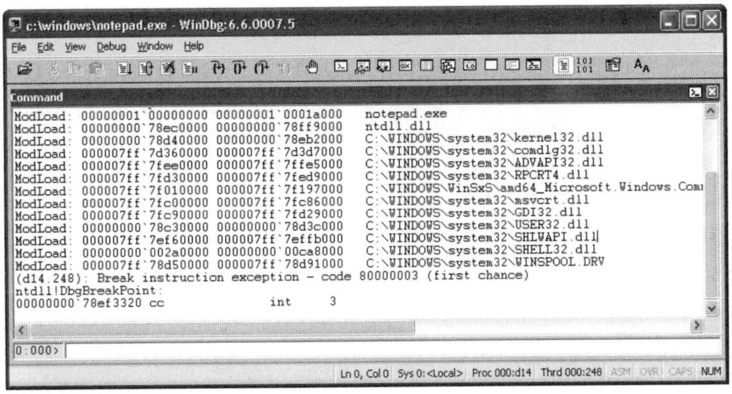

Figure 6-2   The Command window command entry location

9. Type the command *lm* and press Enter (this will list the loaded DLLs in the process).

10. Look for ntdll, and if the string to the right is "(pdb symbols)," your environment variable is set correctly. A good output looks like (the line is wrapped to fit in the book):

```
7c900000 7c9b0000   ntdll    (pdb symbols)   \\Symbols\OSSymbols\ntdll.pdb\
36515FB5D04345E491F672FA2E2878C02\ntdll.pdb
```

11. If the string next to ntdll says "(export symbols)," your _NT_SYMBOL_PATH is incorrect. An incorrect setup will have a line similar to the following (wrapped):

```
7c900000 7c9b0000   ntdll    (export symbols)
C:\WINDOWS\system32\ntdll.dll
```

12. If you have an error, double-check your environment variable carefully and make sure you didn't swap the R and V characters in the SRV string. If you change the environment variable, you'll have to restart WinDBG and proceed through these steps again. For more information about fixing symbol problems, see the section "Ensuring That Correct Symbols Are Loaded" later in this chapter.

13. If you changed your _NT_SYMBOL_PATH environment variable, remember to update the _NT_EXECUTABLE_PATH environment variable to have the same string.

WinDBG Options and Windows

WinDBG works on a *workspace* metaphor where settings are stored based on the main EXE binary name. Every time you change anything on a workspace, which includes set breakpoints; symbol, source, and binary paths; and window layout, WinDBG prompts you to save the workspace whenever the workspace is about to close. It's probably in your best interest to always save the workspace. You can delete unused workspaces or clear specific items saved with a workspace by selecting any of the workspace management items from the File menu.

When you don't have any binary or minidump open, any settings you make are to the *base* workspace, which all subsequent workspaces inherit. Before you start using WinDBG, you'll want to set a few options in the base workspace to make your life a little easier.

Colors Are Cool

When doing the test to check your symbol setup, you probably noticed that WinDBG is verbose to the extreme. Everything goes to the Command window, and you can easily lose track of anything important. Simply loading a large process can result in over 100 lines of output before you execute any WinDBG commands. Fortunately, WinDBG now allows you to color various reasons for the output so that you can separate the wheat from the chaff. The color selections appear at the bottom of the Options dialog box, which you can access by selecting Options from the View menu.

The bad news is that the meaning of all the various color items is not quite documented. Some of the items that you can color, such as Enabled Breakpoint Background, are self-explanatory, but others, such as Error Level Command Window Text, only appear to be self-explanatory—I never have seen my chosen color. In reality, the most important highlighting you'll want is on any *Trace.Write** method calls that your programs make. (Remember, the *DefaultTraceListener* calls the Windows native *OutputDebugString* API function internally.) You can get these important values displayed in a different color by setting Debuggee Level Command Window Text to a different color. I personally always choose green because that indicates goodness to me.

Another color item you'll want to change is the User-selected command window line text. Often I am looking through a very long set of output in the Command window, and I want to mark key data in a different color. That way, when I am scrolling through the Command window, I can find the key areas based on color. Personally, I use red.

Although setting the color is easy, the steps required to change the color are not apparent. In the Command window, you'll highlight the text you want to change. In nearly every other application in the world, you'd right-click and select a menu option, such as Set Selection To User Colors. If you right-click selected text in the WinDBG Command window, that will put the selected text on the clipboard.

However, if you right-click the title bar of the Command window, you'll see the shortcut menu you would have expected inside the window. On that menu, you'll see the real Set Selection To User Colors command that will change the color. There are other items on the title bar shortcut menu, but the most important other than Set Selection To User Colors are Go To Mark (known in the rest of the world as a bookmark) and Help.

As is typical of WinDBG, although you can now set the selected text to your user colors, there's no way to quickly set it back to the default colors. To reset the colors, select Choose Color Text And Recolor Selection, and then manually set the color in the Color dialog box that pops up. I warned you that WinDBG was going to be interesting to learn!

Working with Windows

Before I dive into various WinDBG commands and SOS, I need to spend a few moments preparing you for what you're going to see with WinDBG. The WinDBG UI certainly reflects the fact that true debugger developers worked on it. It's functional, but it may not function as any Windows application you've ever seen.

The various WinDBG windows, which are all accessible on the View menu, are somewhat like tool windows in Visual Studio. When first opened, they default to being undocked from the main frame window and can be moved anywhere on your screen or multi-monitor system. If you double click a window's title bar, it will dock in the main frame. Dragging a window to the main frame will allow you dock the window in various positions in the main frame. Unlike Visual Studio's, the WinDBG windows will dock where they want to dock and not exactly where you want them to be.

The default docking options are to split up the main frame with multiple windows. If you're patient when dragging a window around the main frame, you'll eventually see the black frame fill up the entire main frame instead of just a portion. A window docked in the full frame will show up as a tab at the bottom on the main frame so you can quickly switch between each window. Figure 6-3 shows WinDBG set up with all the open windows docked in the same frame. It's a little odd to get the windows set with the stack at the bottom, which is how I like to set up WinDBG. The trick is to drag the window you want to dock completely away from WinDBG and drag it back to the middle of the WinDBG window. When the drag highlight frame surrounds the complete dock area, release the mouse button.

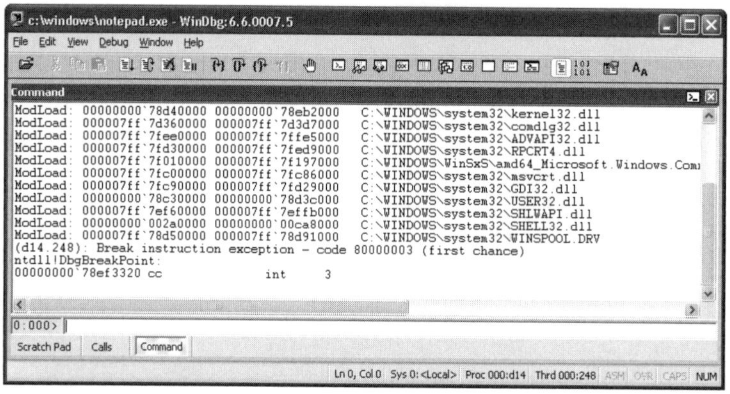

Figure 6-3   WinDBG windows showing tabbed docking

I go through the pain of getting my windows tab docked for two reasons: The first is that with the windows tiled inside the main window, it takes up a huge amount of screen real estate and you find yourself scrolling all the time. The second reason is due to a fundamental problem with WinDBG's floating windows: they have a serious *z-order* problem. If you have a floating window above the main frame, the floating window is always on top, so it blocks access to WinDBG menus and other windows. Some day, the WinDBG team will fix this glaring flaw.

If you have multiple monitors with plenty of screen real estate, you may just want to position the various WinDBG windows on your second monitor and avoid docking in the main frame all together. If you are really into window docking, you can open up multiple dock locations to anchor WinDBG windows where you want on your screen by selecting Open Dock from the Window menu. When you save a WinDBG workspace, you can save all the docks in addition to the window layouts.

The last two things I want to mention about WinDBG windows are tips to make your life easier. The first is that WinDBG always wants to show you the Disassembly window every time you do anything in WinDBG. To prevent the Disassembly window from appearing, on the Window menu, clear the check mark next to Automatically Open Disassembly.

The other window tip is if you look closely at Figure 6-3, you'll see that one of the tabs is titled *Scratch Pad*. As the name implies, WinDBG has a nice little scratch pad where you can copy and paste interesting data any time you want or if you're too lazy to Alt+Tab to Notepad. In order to save the data in the Scratch Pad window, you'll need to associate the Scratch Pad with a file by right-clicking the window's title bar and selecting Associate With File on the shortcut menu.

Dealing with Debuggees

Now that you have a good idea of some of the WinDBG basics, its time to turn to getting debuggees loaded into WinDBG so you can actually do some debugging. For your Windows and console applications, you can start them easily either by passing the file name of the executable on the WinDBG command line or selecting Open Executable on the File menu. If you're starting debugging on your application by passing it on the WinDBG command line, WinDBG treats any command-line arguments passed after the name of your process as such. The Open Executable dialog box, shown in Figure 6-4, shows the Arguments and Start Directory edit controls where you can specify either.

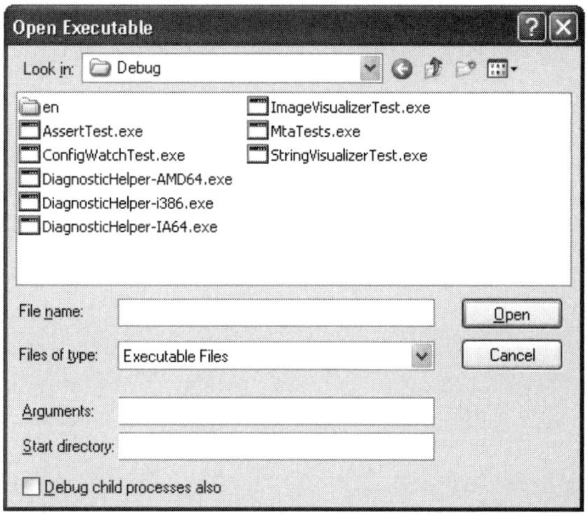

Figure 6-4   The WinDBG Open Executable dialog box

One major recent improvement to WinDBG is that it remembers the command line and starting directory you typed into the Open Executable dialog box when you restart debugging from the same instance of WinDBG. However, if you stop debugging in WinDBG and want to restart your program with a different set of command-line arguments, you'll search the Help in vain for any way to change the command line. You'll need either to end the current instance and restart a new instance of WinDBG or select Stop Debugging from the Debug menu to close the current instance. In both cases, you'll go back to the Open Executable dialog box to set command-line arguments and working directory. No one ever said WinDBG was the most user-friendly application in the world.

If your process is already running, you can also attach to that process by starting WinDBG and selecting Attach To A Process from the File menu. That menu will bring up the Attach To Process dialog box, in which you simply select the process you're interested in debugging and press OK. An extra treat in the Attach To Process dialog shows you the Terminal Services session for the process, the user account, and command line. If the process is running as a Windows Service, you'll see the name of the services running in the process.

No matter if you start or attach to a process, WinDBG will stop immediately in the debugger. This is different from Visual Studio, which has the started or attached process continue executing until it hits a breakpoint, has an unhandled exception, or you manually break into the process. If you don't want to stop when you start or attach to processes, you can change the Create Process event in selecting Event Filters from the Debug menu. This stop on start or attach is called the *loader* or *initial breakpoint* because in native debugging, the first instruction executed is a CPU-specific breakpoint so that debuggers can initialize their states and load items such as symbol tables. Alternatively, if you start WinDBG with the -g command-line option, it will skip the loader breakpoint so you immediately start your application.

There's one other debuggee type to discuss: minidumps. To open a minidump from the command line, pass -z followed by the name of the minidump file. Alternatively, select Open Crash Dump on the File menu. Once you have the minidump loaded, you can issue commands just as if you were sitting at the actual process.

When you're finished debugging, you can click the WinDBG main window Close button (X) at any time. If you're at the command prompt, the Q (Quit) command does the same thing. Both ways to quit will terminate the debuggee. If you want to leave the debuggee running but stop debugging, use the QD (Quit and Detach) command. The WinDBG default is to ask you to save the workspace every time you quit WinDBG. There's an option in the prompt dialog box that pops up when you stop debugging that asks if you want to turn off the dialog box permanently so that WinDBG doesn't ask you to save a workspace again. Personally, I want WinDBG to prompt me because I'm sure I'll forget to manually save the workspace the one time I really need it.

The Command Window

Although there are numerous windows in WinDBG, such as the call stack window, which show you specific information, nearly all the work you'll do when it comes to debugging .NET applications will be in the Command window. In this section, I will cover the types of commands, how to get help, and commands to view all modules and symbols currently loaded. Regardless if you're looking at minidumps or doing the wildest live debugging, you'll always need to get help and look at modules.

WinDBG has three types of commands: regular commands, meta commands (also called *dot* commands), and extension commands. These commands are generally described in the following ways. *Regular commands* control the debuggee. For example, walking the native stack, viewing thread information, and viewing memory are regular commands. *Meta commands* mostly control the debugger and the act of debugging. For example, creating log files, attaching to processes, and writing dump files are meta commands. *Extension commands* are where the action is; they are commands that dig into the debuggee and perform analysis on situations or states. Examples of extension commands include handle dumping, critical section analysis, and crash analysis. All the commands in the SOS are extension commands.

The regular and meta commands are case insensitive, whereas extension commands are traditionally all lowercase. To keep consistent in this chapter, I will show all commands in their lowercase form when discussing them.

Getting Help

When you're staring at the blinking cursor in the bottom of the Command window wondering what command you'll need, you need to turn to the Help. If you just need a tip on what a regular command name is or what its syntax is, the *?* (Command Help) command will bring up a couple of pages of listings so that you can see information about the various regular commands. Some of the regular commands do support passing -? as a parameter, so you can get quick help on their parameters. You'll have to use trial and error to find out which ones support -?. For meta commands, use *.help* (Meta-command Help) to see the quick listing. Help for extension commands is reliant on the order extensions are loaded, which I'll discuss later. However, because all your .NET debugging will be with the SOS extension, use *!help* to see help on SOS. Also, for regular and meta commands, the commands are case-insensitive, but for extension commands, the commands are all lowercase.

Probably the most important command is the *.hh* (Open HTML Help File) meta command. Passing any command type as a parameter to *.hh* will open the Debugger.chm help file to the Index tab with the specified command highlighted. Simply press Enter to see the help information for that command. I hope that in a future version of WinDBG, the development team will fix the *.hh* command so that it opens to the help topic of the specified command automatically.

When looking at the Help for a command in Debugger.chm, pay careful attention to the Environment section that appears with each command. The table in that section tells you the situations in which WinDBG can run the command. Obviously, for user-mode debugging, the *Modes* field will need to identify user mode. Nearly all the user-mode commands work during live debugging in addition to while looking at minidumps.

One thing that's not very clear in the help for any of the commands is why there is a complete lack of consistency when it comes to parameters you can pass to commands. Some commands take parameters you delimit with a hyphen, some take parameters that you delimit with a slash, and others take parameters that have no delimiters at all. Pay close attention to the documentation for how to specify parameters for any given command.

Ensuring That Correct Symbols Are Loaded

As I mentioned in Chapter 2, Visual Studio 2005 has drastically improved the symbol reporting so you can fix symbol loading problems more easily. WinDBG has similar support for symbol problems but requires a little more manual work to make it happen. One thing that makes WinDBG unique is that it employs lazy symbol loading. Visual Studio always loads symbols when a module comes into the address space. This makes sense if you remember that WinDBG is designed to debug the complete 40+ million lines of code of the Windows operating systems. If WinDBG loaded all the symbols, you'd quickly run out of memory in the address space!

Whenever the Command window is active, in other words, you're stopped in the debugger, the *lm* (List Loaded Modules) command will display the list of modules and their corresponding symbol files. As an example, I loaded a console program called SimpleConsoleApp.exe that called *Trace.WriteLine* and stopped after the trace statement completed. In the "Exceptions and Events" section later in the chapter, you'll see exactly how I was able to stop inside my .NET application running on the Windows XP Professional Tablet PC Edition 32-bit version. WinDBG stopped at the trace statement. Issuing the *lm* command shows the following output:

```
0:000> lm
start    end        module name
00400000 00408000   SimpleConsoleApp   (deferred)
5d090000 5d127000   comct132_5d090000    (deferred)
69c30000 6a1d2000   System_Xml_ni    (deferred)
76390000 763ad000   IMM32      (deferred)
773d0000 774d2000   comct132    (deferred)
774e0000 7761d000   ole32      (deferred)
77c10000 77c68000   msvcrt     (deferred)
77d40000 77dd0000   USER32     (deferred)
77dd0000 77e6b000   ADVAPI32    (deferred)
77e70000 77f01000   RPCRT4     (deferred)
77f10000 77f56000   GDI32      (deferred)
77f60000 77fd6000   SHLWAPI    (deferred)
78800000 78840000   mscoree    (deferred)
78850000 788a2000   mscorjit    (deferred)
788b0000 79336000   mscorlib_ni    (deferred)
796c0000 79c01000   mscorwks    (deferred)
7a430000 7a50a000   System_Configuration_ni    (deferred)
7a560000 7ac76000   System_ni    (deferred)
7c370000 7c409000   MSVCR80    (deferred)
7c800000 7c8f4000   KERNEL32    (pdb symbols)
             \\Symbols\OSSymbols\kernel32.pdb\FB3...DF2\kernel32.pdb
7c900000 7c9b0000   ntdll      (pdb symbols)
              \\\Symbols\OSSymbols\ntdll.pdb\365...C02\ntdll.pdb
7c9c0000 7d1d4000   shell32    (deferred)

Unloaded modules:
60340000 60348000   culture.dll
```

Note that I trimmed down the two GUID values in the PDB file locations for Kernel32.pdb and Ntdll.pdb.

The output just shown shows I have symbols loaded for Kernel32.dll and Ntdll.dll; the rest are marked as "(deferred)" because WinDBG hasn't had a reason to load them. If I were to attempt to walk the native call stack at this point, WinDBG would load the symbols for the modules with addresses on the stack.

You can probably guess what the output of the *lm* command tells you, but I wanted to mention just two quick tidbits. The first is that the images that end in "_ni" are .NET binaries that have been NGen'd and compiled to native images. You'll generally see only the Common Language Runtime (CLR) and Common Language Framework (CLF) assemblies NGen'd. If you're thinking that running NGen across your binaries sounds like a great idea to speed up your application, it won't unless your application fits into certain requirements, mainly that your assemblies in the Global Assembly Cache (GAC) and you're sharing code across App Domains. See the MSDN Magazine February 2006 CLR Inside Out column by Claudio Caldato (*http://msdn.microsoft.com/msdnmag/issues/06/02/CLRInsideOut/*).

The unloaded modules report from the *lm* command is a list of modules that have been loaded through the Windows native API function *LoadLibrary* and freed with a call to *FreeLibrary*. In my simple example, you can see that Culture.dll, which is a DLL that's in the Framework directory, has been loaded and unloaded once.

To force a symbol load, the *ld* (Load Symbols) command does the trick. *LD* takes only a module name on the command line, so to force the loading of symbols for SimpleConsoleApp.exe, I'd issue *ld SimpleConsoleApp* and get the following output:

```
0:000> ld SimpleConsoleApp
*** WARNING: Unable to verify checksum for SimpleConsoleApp.exe
Symbols loaded for SimpleConsoleApp
```

WinDBG is very particular about symbols and tells you about anything that could potentially be wrong with the symbols. .NET binaries do not set the native Portable Executable (PE) checksum header field at all. Before the debuggers started relying on GUID values to uniquely identify symbol files, they used timestamps along with the checksum value. WinDBG is being a little old-school with the checksum warning, and because there's no way to set it in .NET applications, train yourself to ignore it.

The *.reload* (Reload Module) command tells WinDBG to reload all symbols. You'll always want to use the */f* option with *.reload* so you ensure that WinDBG reloads the symbols. If you want to reload just a single module, specify that module after the */f*. For example, to load Kernel32.dll, you'd issue the command *.reload /f kernel32.dll*. If you are working with an application that has many modules, *.reload /f* can run for a long while. WinDBG has gotten better about indicating that it's working instead of appearing that it's hung; the Command window entry area will show *BUSY* in the left active process and thread area. To abort the symbol loading or any other long-running command, press Ctrl+Break. You might have to press it numerous times, but WinDBG will eventually stop the command.

You can also verify proper symbol loading through the *lm* command. After forcing all symbols to load, the output of the *lm* command shows the following (I folded the last item on each line to fit the width of the page and truncated the GUID values. I also clipped out the middle portion of the output to avoid repetitive duplication and thus boredom on your part.):

```
0:000> lm
start    end        module name
00400000 00408000   SimpleConsoleApp C (private pdb symbols)
  c:\Dev\3Book\Disk\SimpleConsoleApp\bin\Debug\SimpleConsoleApp.pdb
5d090000 5d127000   comctl32_5d090000   (pdb symbols)
  \\Symbols\OSSymbols\comctl32.pdb\738...CB2\comctl32.pdb
69c30000 6a1d2000   System_Xml_ni C (pdb symbols)
  \\Symbols\OSSymbols\System.Xml.pdb\A6B...C61\System.Xml.pdb
76390000 763ad000   IMM32       (pdb symbols)
  \\Symbols\OSSymbols\imm32.pdb\2C1...162\imm32.pdb
773d0000 774d2000   comctl32    (pdb symbols)
    \\Symbols\OSSymbols\MicrosoftWindowsCommon-Controls-6.0.2600.2180-
       comctl32.pdb\C45...401\MicrosoftWindowsCommon-Controls-
       6.0.2600.2180-comctl32.pdb
...
7c900000 7c9b0000   ntdll       (pdb symbols)
  \\Symbols\OSSymbols\ntdll.pdb\365...C02\ntdll.pdb
7c9c0000 7d1d4000   shell32     (pdb symbols)
  \\Symbols\OSSymbols\shell32.pdb\290...6D2\shell32.pdb

Unloaded modules:
60340000 60348000   culture.dll
```

Those module names followed by a "C" indicate symbols that don't have the checksums set in the module, which as I explained, is any .NET assembly that is loaded. An octothorpe (#) following a module indicates symbols that don't match between the symbol file and the executable. (Yes, you can use the *.symopt* command to set WinDBG to load the closest symbols, even if they're not correct.) In the preceding example, life is good and all the symbols match.

Those symbols listed as having a type of "(pdb symbols)" indicate that they are stripped symbols that are loaded. Because all the native symbols from the operating system are stripped of their private type information and source and line tables, seeing "(pdb symbols)" means you have correct symbols. If you look at the output closely, you'll see another symbol type, "(private pdb symbols)" next to the SimpleConsoleApp module. For the modules you build, both managed and native, you'll see "(private pdb symbols)" indicating that you have all the private data accessible in the PDB file. As I mentioned earlier, just because WinDBG shows that your .NET assembly has all the private info doesn't mean that you can single-step through your .NET source code. If you have native DLLs that you built with full PDB symbols, you will see "(private pdb symbols)" reported for those DLL symbol loads also.

If after loading symbols and issuing the *lm* command, you see anything other than "(pdb symbols)" or "(private pdb symbols)" after the module, symbols for that module were not loaded. Keep in mind that some modules loaded in your process may be from third parties, so you may not have symbols for them. To get a closer look at exactly which modules you have loaded, pass the *v* option to *lm* to see the detailed version information for all modules loaded.

If you want to narrow down the verbose display to a single module, combine the *v* option with *m* to match a single module.

```
0:000> lm v m mscoree
start     end         module name
79000000 79045000   mscoree     (deferred)
    Image path: C:\WINDOWS\system32\mscoree.dll
    Image name: mscoree.dll
    Timestamp:        Fri Sep 23 07:30:38 2005 (4333E75E)
    CheckSum:         00045512
    ImageSize:        00045000
    File version:     2.0.50727.42
    Product version:  2.0.50727.42
    File flags:       0 (Mask 3F)
    File OS:          4 Unknown Win32
    File type:        2.0 Dll
    File date:        00000000.00000000
    Translations:     0409.04b0
    CompanyName:      Microsoft Corporation
    ProductName:      Microsoft® .NET Framework
    InternalName:     mscoree.dll
    OriginalFilename: mscoree.dll
    ProductVersion:   2.0.50727.42
    FileVersion:      2.0.50727.42 (RTM.050727-4200)
    FileDescription:  Microsoft .NET Runtime Execution Engine
    LegalCopyright:   © Microsoft Corporation.  All rights reserved.
    Comments:         Flavor=Retail
```

To see exactly where WinDBG is loading symbols and why, the extension command *!sym* from Dbghelp.dll, which is automatically loaded into WinDBG, offers the *noisy* option. To look at all your symbol loading issues, run the following commands in order:

```
.reload
!sym noisy
ld *
```

The *.reload* command will unload all unused symbols first before you attempt to reload them. The output in the Command windows shows you exactly what process the WinDBG symbol engine goes through to find and load the symbols. Armed with the output, you should be able to solve any possible symbol-loading problem that you'll encounter. To turn off the noisy output, issue the *!sym quiet* command.

Processes and Threads

With the symbol story behind us, I can now turn to the various means of getting processes running under WinDBG. As can Visual Studio, WinDBG can debug any number of disparate processes at a time. What makes WinDBG a little more interesting is that you have better control over debugging processes spawned from a process being debugged.

Debugging Child Processes

If you look back at the Open Executable dialog box in Figure 6-4, you'll notice that the very bottom of the dialog box has a Debug Child Processes Also check box. By selecting it, you're telling WinDBG that you also want to debug any processes started by debuggees. If you forget to select that check box when opening a process, you can use the *.childdbg* (Debug Child Processes) command to change the option on the fly. By itself, *.childdbg* will tell you the current state. Issuing a *.childdbg 1* command will turn on debugging child processes. Issue *.childdbg 0* to turn it off.

To show you some of the multiple process and thread options, in the next section, I'll provide some of the output resulting from debugging the command prompt, Cmd.exe, and choosing to debug child processes also. After I get Cmd.exe loaded up and executing, I'll start Notepad.exe. If you follow the same steps and have child debugging enabled, as soon as you start Notepad.exe, WinDBG will stop at the loader breakpoint for Notepad.exe. It makes sense that WinDBG stopped Notepad.exe, but that also stops Cmd.exe because both processes are now sharing the debugger loop. The *debugger loop* is the thread in the debugger looping between the *WaitForDebugEvent* and *ContinueDebugEvent* APIs as events happen in the debugger.

To see in the UI the processes that are currently running, choose Processes And Threads from the View menu. You'll see a layout similar to that in Figure 6-5. In the Processes And Threads window, the processes are all the root nodes with each process's thread as their children. The numbers next to Cmd.exe, 000:C1C, are the WinDBG process number followed by the Win32 process ID. In Cmd.exe, the thread 000:E04 indicates the WinDBG thread ID and the Win32 thread ID. The WinDBG process and thread numbers are unique the entire time WinDBG is running. That means there can never be another process number 1 until I restart WinDBG. The WinDBG process and thread numbers are important because they are used to set per-process and native per-thread breakpoints and can be used as modifiers to various commands.

Figure 6-5   The Process and Threads window

Viewing Processes and Native Threads in the Command Window

As with anything in WinDBG, if WinDBG displays it in a window, there's a Command window command to get the same information. To view the processes being debugged, the | (Process Status) command does the trick. The output for the two processes shown in Figure 6-5 is as follows:

```
1:001> |
   0  id: c1c   create   name: cmd.exe
.  1  id: ff4   child    name: notepad.exe
```

The dot in the far left column indicates the active process, meaning that any commands you execute will be working on that process. The other interesting field is the one that tells how the process came to run under the debugger. "Create" means WinDBG created the process, and "child" indicates a process that was spawned by a parent process.

The overloaded s command—|s for Set Current Process and ~s for Set Current Thread—does the work to change which process is active. You can also use the Processes And Threads window and double-click the process you'd like to make active. The bold font indicates the active process. When using the s command, you need to specify the process as a prefix to the command. For example, to switch from the second process to the first, you'd issue |0s. To quickly see which process is active, look at the numbers to the left of the Command window input line. As you swap between the processes, you'll see the numbers update. When I switched to the first process using the Cmd.exe and Notepad.exe examples and issued the | command again, the output looked a little different:

```
0:000> |
.  0   id: c1c   create    name: cmd.exe
#  1   id: ff4   child     name: notepad.exe
```

The difference is the octothorpe in front of the Notepad.exe process. The octothorpe indicates the process that caused the exception to stop in WinDBG. Because Notepad.exe is sitting at its loader breakpoint, the exception was a breakpoint. If the active process is the one that had the exception, the dot overrides the octothorpe display.

Viewing native threads is almost identical to viewing processes. I'm going to let Notepad.exe start, so I'll press F5 in WinDBG (alternatively, I could issue the g (Go) command in the Command window). When Notepad.exe appears, I'll open the Open dialog box by choosing Open from the File menu because it creates a bunch of threads, and in WinDBG, I'll press Ctrl+Break to break into the debugger. If you do the same and have the Processes And Threads window open, you should see that Notepad.exe has multiple threads in it and Cmd.exe has two threads.

The ~ (Thread Status) command shows the active threads in the current process. Switching to the Notepad.exe process and issuing the ~ command creates the following output on Windows XP Tablet PC Edition:

```
1:001> ~
.  1  Id: ff4.b10  Suspend: 1  Teb: 7ffdd000  Unfrozen
   2  Id: ff4.fc0  Suspend: 1  Teb: 7ffdc000  Unfrozen
   3  Id: ff4.eec  Suspend: 1  Teb: 7ffdb000  Unfrozen
   4  Id: ff4.e48  Suspend: 1  Teb: 7ffda000  Unfrozen
   5  Id: ff4.d58  Suspend: 1  Teb: 7ffd9000  Unfrozen
   6  Id: ff4.f0c  Suspend: 1  Teb: 7ffd8000  Unfrozen
   7  Id: ff4.b78  Suspend: 1  Teb: 7ffd7000  Unfrozen
   8  Id: ff4.e34  Suspend: 1  Teb: 7ffd6000  Unfrozen
```

As with the | command, the ~ command uses a dot to indicate the current thread and an octothorpe to signify the thread that either caused the exception or was active when the debugger attached. The WinDBG thread number is the next displayed item. As with process numbers, there will be only one thread number 2 for the life of the WinDBG instance. Next come the ID values, which are the Win32 process ID followed by the thread ID. The suspend count is a little confusing. A suspend count of 1 indicates the thread is suspended because you are doing live debugging and are stopped in the debugger. A suspend count of 0 will be shown if you are doing noninvasive debugging, which I'll talk about later in the chapter. If the suspend count is greater than 1, that means there have been multiple calls to the *SuspendThread* API done on that thread. After the suspend count is the linear address of the Thread Environment Block (TEB) for the thread. The TEB is the same as the Thread Information Block (TIB), where the Windows operating systems store the state of the native thread in memory. Finally, Unfrozen indicates whether you've used the ~*f* (Freeze Thread) command to freeze a thread. (Freezing a thread from the debugger is akin to calling *SuspendThread* on that thread from your program. You'll stop that thread from executing until it is unfrozen.)

A command will work on the current thread by default, but sometimes you'll want to see information about a different thread. For example, to see the registers of a different thread, you use the thread modifier in front of the *r* (Registers) command: ~2*r*. If you have multiple processes open, you can also apply the process modifier to the commands. The command |0~0*r* shows the registers for the first process and first thread no matter which process and thread are active.

One trick with the ~ command that is not documented is that if you issue ~ followed by a thread number, WinDBG will display the thread's starting address, the priority, and the priority class. If you issue ~*, you'll see the detailed data for all threads.

```
0:002> ~0
   0  Id: f84.a0c Suspend: 1 Teb: 000007ff`fffde000 Unfrozen
      Start: 11000000`00016a3e
      Priority: 0  Priority class: 32
```

Creating Processes from the Command Window

Now that you know how to view processes and threads, I can move into some of the more advanced tricks that you can perform to get processes started under WinDBG. When stopped in WinDBG, the *.create* (Create Process) command lets you start up any arbitrary processes on the machine. This is extremely helpful when you need to debug multiple sides of a COM+ or other cross-process application. The main parameters to *.create* are the complete path to the process to start and any command-line parameters to that process. As when you start any processes, it's best to put the path and process name in quotation marks to avoid issues with spaces. The following code shows the use of the *.create* command to start Solitaire on one of my development machines:

```
.create "c:\windows\system32\sol.exe"
```

After pressing Enter, WinDBG indicates that the process will be created on the next execution. What that means is that WinDBG must allow the native debugger loop to spin over in order to handle the process creation notification. WinDBG has already made the *CreateProcess* API call, but the debugger hasn't seen it yet. By pressing F5, you will release the debug loop. The create process notification comes through, and WinDBG will stop on the loader breakpoint. If you use the | command to view the processes, WinDBG shows any processes started with .*create* marked as "create" as if you started the session with that process.

Attaching to and Detaching from Processes in the Command Window

If a process is already running on the machine and you want to debug it, the .*attach* (Attach to Process) command does the trick. The .*attach* command requires the process ID in order to perform the attach. If you have physical access to the machine the process is running on, you can look up the process ID with Task Manager, but for remote debugging, that's a little hard to do. Fortunately, the WinDBG developers thought of everything and added the .*tlist* (List Process IDs) command to list the running processes on the machine. If you're debugging Win32 services, use the -*v* parameter to .*tlist* to see which services are running in which processes. The output of the .*tlist* command looks like the following:

```
0n3364 C:\WINDOWS\system32\sol.exe
 0n496 C:\Program Files\Windows NT\Pinball\PINBALL.EXE
0n3348 C:\WINDOWS\system32\inkball.exe
```

When I first saw the output, I thought there was a bug in the command and somebody accidentally typed "0n" instead of "0x." However, I've since learned that 0n as a prefix is the ANSI standard for decimal in the same way 0x is for hexadecimal.

Once you have the decimal process ID for the process, you'll pass it as the parameter to .*attach* (ensuring that you use the 0n prefix or it won't work). As it does when creating processes, WinDBG will say something about the attach occurring on the next execution, so you'll need to press F5 to let the debugger loop spin. From that point on, you're debugging the process you attached to. The only difference is that the | command will report the process as "attach" in its output.

To allow a process you're debugging to run outside the debugger, the .*detach* (Detach from Process) command is available to allow debuggees the ability to run free once again. Because it works only on the current process, you'll need to switch to the process you want to detach from before you execute the .*detach* command. At any point, you can reattach to the process to do full debugging.

If you looked at the help for the .*attach* command or carefully at the Attach to Process dialog box when you start WinDBG, you'll see a reference to a noninvasive attach. This type of attach was originally put in for supporting operating systems older than Windows XP and Microsoft Windows Server 2003. On prior operating systems, once you had a debugger attached to a process, that debugger was attached to that process for life. If the debugger shut down, so did the debuggee.

The noninvasive attach called the *SuspendThread* API on the target process threads and WinDBG just reads memory from the suspended process. You aren't debugging the process, you are examining it. Now that we are on later operating systems that support true detaching while debugging, the need for the noninvasive attach has lessened. However, when we get to the ADPlus discussion later in this chapter, you'll see that the noninvasive attach is used when ADPlus is doing a hang mode configuration. That's so ADPlus runs on Microsoft Windows 2000 and prior operating systems.

The WinDBG noninvasive attach allows me to discuss one of my favorite debugging tricks. If you're doing pure managed debugging in Visual Studio and you reach a point at which you want to load SOS and look at the heap an object is in, you're completely out of luck. If you run into that scenario, you can break into the process in the Visual Studio debugger. With the debuggee stopped in the debugger start WinDBG and noninvasively attach to the suspended debuggee. Then you can perform any informational command that WinDBG offers, such as *!handle*, and even load SOS. Now you have the best of both worlds even if you forgot to start mixed mode debugging from the beginning. When you want to get back to debugging the process with Visual Studio, you'll need to use the *Q* (Quit) command in WinDBG to end the noninvasive attach.

Walking the Native Stack

Because WinDBG is a native-only debugger, it's important to look at the native stack so you have a fighting chance of seeing how your .NET application is working with the operating system. To get that native call stack, the *k* (Display Stack Backtrace) command with one of its modifiers does the trick. The most useful modifier is *P*, which will show any native function parameters and their types for those modules for which you have private .pdb files. Because parameter information is part of the private native data in a .pdb file, you'll see them only for your native DLLs, but that can be a lifesaver for seeing what's going on with your interop code.

In the following example, I stopped a very simple .NET program on the 64-bit version of Windows XP as it made a call to the Windows API function, *OutputDebugString*, which *Default-TraceListener* calls whenever you use *Trace.Write**. You will see slightly different output if you try the same operation on a 32-bit operating system.

```
0:000> kP
Child-SP          RetAddr           Call Site
00000000 0012e990 00000000 78d9fb19 KERNEL32!RaiseException+0x5c
00000000 0012ea60 00000000 78d9f743 KERNEL32!OutputDebugStringA+0x76
00000000 0012ed60 00000000 75ecce24 KERNEL32!OutputDebugStringW+0x42
00000000 0012edb0 00000000 794769e5 mscorwks!DoNDirectCall__PatchGetThreadCall+0x78
00000000 0012ee50 00000000 79476b75 System_ni+0x2269e5
00000000 0012ef20 00000000 79476c11 System_ni+0x226b75
00000000 0012ef80 00000000 79467089 System_ni+0x226c11
00000000 0012efc0 00000000 1a7501cd System_ni+0x217089
00000000 0012f050 00000000 75ecf422 0x1a7501cd
00000000 0012f080 00000000 75d9cb5a mscorwks!CallDescrWorker+0x82
00000000 0012f0d0 00000000 75d9afd3 mscorwks!CallDescrWorkerWithHandler+0xca
00000000 0012f170 00000000 75cf099a mscorwks!MethodDesc::CallDescr+0x1b3
00000000 0012f3b0 00000000 75e56775 mscorwks!ClassLoader::RunMain+0x22e
00000000 0012f610 00000000 75e2ebe8 mscorwks!Assembly::ExecuteMainMethod+0xb9
00000000 0012f900 00000000 75e6a523 mscorwks!SystemDomain::ExecuteMainMethod+0x3f0
```

```
00000000 0012feb0 00000000 75e78205 mscorwks!ExecuteEXE+0x47
00000000 0012ff00 00000000 7401a726 mscorwks!CorExeMain+0xb1
00000000 0012ff50 00000000 78d5965c mscoree!CorExeMain+0x46
00000000 0012ff80 00000000 00000000 KERNEL32!BaseProcessStart+0x29
```

When reading the output, the *k* command shows the module and function separated by an exclamation point. The line "KERNEL32!OutputDebugStringA+0x76" indicates that the module is Kernel32.dll, and the function is *OutputDebugStringA*. The "+0x76" is the offset into the function where the address lies. Since the native code needs either the .pdb files from Microsoft or your native .pdb files to correctly walk the native stack, you should always see offsets generally less than 0x100 (though there may be few larger offsets that are still correct). The native stack walk simply looks for the closest symbols, and if .pdb files are missing for a particular module, you may see extremely large offsets on the functions. I just wanted to give you some advance warning of what happens when you look at your own native stack walks.

If you have good symbols for both your application and the operating system, which you had better have after reading this book, you'll get good call stacks out of the *k* command. However, you will see lines in the call stack output that says, "WARNING: Frame IP not in any known module. Following frames may be wrong." That means that the *k* command is forced to take some guesses at the stack and may be incorrect because the native stack walking code knows nothing of .NET. Other warnings notes, such as "WARNING: Unable to verify checksum for *module_name*," are benign and are output by the symbol loading portions of WinDBG. You'll also see lines that start with "ERROR: Module load completed but symbols could not be loaded for *module_name*." If the module is one of the native image modules (its module name ends with "_ni"), you can ignore that message. As we've seen, WinDBG knows how to deal with those.

The good news is that the *k* command does go to heroic lengths to attempt the stack walk. In the previous example, you can see that it picks up somewhere in a module called MScorwks.dll, which is the main Common Language Runtime (CLR) DLL.

At the very bottom of the stack walk is *BaseProcessStart* in Kernel32.dll. For the main thread of the application, this is the equivalent to going back to the beginning of time. If this happened to be a call stack for a thread other than the main thread, the call stack would go back to *BaseThreadStart*. If you have a call stack all the way to *BaseProcessStart* or *BaseThreadStart*, the odds are excellent that the native call stack is perfect. Unfortunately, on x86, it's relatively rare that you'll see your mixed managed and native call stacks going back that far because of the various native calling conventions and the requirement of Frame Pointer Omission data from the .pdb file. On x64, the call stacks will always walk back to *Base*Start* because there's only a single calling convention. If you do have cases in which your call stacks don't go back to *Base*Start*, keep in mind that WinDBG stops at 50 calls, so if you have a deeper stack, pass a number after the *kP* command to indicate how far you want to go. It's rare that you have more than 250 items on the stack, so I'm in the habit of issuing the command *kP 250* to ensure that I get the full stack. Although we can't always walk native stacks back to the beginning of time, the good news is that all your managed stacks will walk correctly even if you don't have symbols. Such is the beauty of full metadata in the .NET world.

Before moving on to exceptions and events, you should know two additional tricks for looking at native stacks. The first is that if you want to look at the call stack for a particular thread that is not the current thread, you can prefix the *k* command with the thread. For example, to see the native stack for the fifth thread, you'd issue the *~4kP* command. (Remember, the thread numbers start at zero.) Finally, instead of typing each thread manually to see their stacks, you can use the special prefix *~*e*, which tells the debugger to execute the command following the e on each thread. Thus, issuing the *~*ekP* command walks all the threads call stacks in one fell swoop.

In discussing the *k* command, I've been assuming that you do not have a corrupted stack register—otherwise, stack walking could not occur. The native stack can also be wrong if you don't have the .pdb file for some of the binaries also. If you're dealing with bad native stack issues, the secret killer debugging trick is to use the *dps* (Display Words and Symbols) command with the stack register as the memory to analyze. For all CPUs, you'll pass the pseudo register, *$csp*, which will use the appropriate stack register for the operating "bitness." The command, *dps $csp*, will treat the values on the stack as addresses to look up in the native symbol tables. It's similar to dumping memory, but instead, it will attempt the symbol lookup for every address found. The *dps* command remembers the last address it displayed, so to continue up the stack, issue the *dps* command with no parameters.

The '*p*' in *dps* stands for *pointer* and uses the architecture-specific pointer size when looking up values. The cousin commands, *dds* and *dqs*, treat pointers as double word and quad word size respectively.

If the stack pointer register is pointing to 0, *dps* obviously won't do you much good, but if you think you know where the stack lies for the thread, it can be a lifesaver to get you going. The following shows the *dps $csp* command output when I randomly stopped in an application:

```
0:004> dps $csp
00000000 042bec28  00000000 77d6cfbb
                             KERNEL32!WaitForMultipleObjectsEx+0x1cf
00000000 042bec30  00000000 02770b10
00000000 042bec38  00000642 7f4d530e mscorwks!ClrFlsGetValue+0xe
00000000 042bec40  00000642 787af1d0 mscorlib_ni+0x7af1d0
00000000 042bec48  00000000 042bee40
00000000 042bec50  00000000 00000000
00000000 042bec58  00000642 7f4f4874
                             mscorwks!EETypeHashTable::FindItem+0x44
00000000 042bec60  00000642 78826dd8 mscorlib_ni+0x826dd8
00000000 042bec68  00000000 042becd0
00000000 042bec70  00000000 00000001
00000000 042bec78  00000000 00000000
```

Exceptions and Events

The operating system knows when a debuggee is running under a debugger, and whenever the debuggee performs a specific set of actions, the operating system suspends all the threads in the debuggee and notifies the debugger that a debugging event occurred. Without knowing anything about debuggers, you can probably guess that the set of the debugging events are: *process create, process exit, thread create, thread exit, module load, module unload,* a call to the OutputDebugString API, and *an exception occurred.* By the way, the exceptions are Windows exceptions and are reported through Structured Exception Handling (SEH). .NET 2.0 implements exceptions internally with SEH, but that's not to say that the internals may not change in future releases.

Most debuggers, including Visual Studio, allow you to perform actions only when various exceptions occur; WinDBG gives you much more control. For example, if you're doing live debugging, and you want to stop when a particular module is first loaded into memory, you can do so. Where WinDBG gets even more interesting is that it allows you to associate any WinDBG commands, including SOS commands, with events so that you can do extremely powerful live debugging.

Although you may not be doing a lot of live debugging of your .NET applications with WinDBG, the extra event and exception handling will pay for themselves many times over. In the last chapter, I discussed the improved Exceptions dialog box in Visual Studio, in which you could have the debugger stop each time your application throws an exception. The one problem is that, as you saw, Visual Studio reports the exceptions with a debugger dialog box, and you have to physically click the OK button to continue the execution.

What would be a lot better, especially when testing your code, is if you could have the debugger see that you had an exception, automatically perform common operations, and continue execution with no input required. That's exactly what you can do with WinDBG's exception and event handling. For example, if you assigned the command *kP;gc* to .NET exceptions, you'd get the native call stack in the Command window. The semicolon is a command separator, so it acts as press of an Enter key. The *gc* command continues execution based on how you were executing, such as native code single stepping.

In the Command window, the *sx, sxd, sxe, sxi, sxn* (Set Exceptions) commands do all the work, and I'll talk about them more in a minute. However, the easy way to set how you want debugging event handling is through the Event Filters dialog box, which you can get to by choosing Event Filters in the Debug menu and is shown in Figure 6-6. To access the Event Filters dialog box, the debuggee will need to be stopped in WinDBG.

Even with a dialog box to help you, it's still a little confusing to figure out what happens with an exception because WinDBG uses some odd terminology in the *sx** commands and the Event Filters dialog box. The Execution section near the lower right corner of the dialog box indicates how you want WinDBG to handle the exception when it is first thrown. Table 6-1 explains the meanings of the values in the Execution group box.

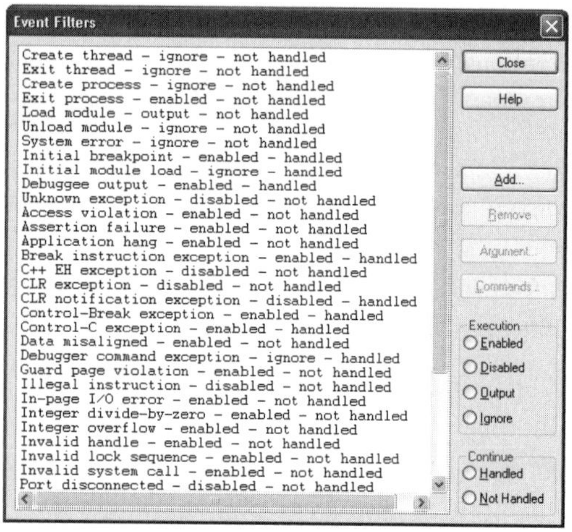

Figure 6-6   The Event Filters dialog box

Table 6-1   Exception Break Status

Status	Description
Enabled	When the exception or event occurs, the target breaks into the debugger.
Disabled	The first time the exception or event occurs, the debugger ignores it (but reports it in the Command window). The second time it occurs, execution halts and the target breaks into the debugger.
Output	When the exception or event occurs, it doesn't break into the debugger. However, a message informing the user of this exception is displayed.
Ignore	When the exception or event occurs, the debugger ignores it. No message is displayed.

You can ignore the Continue section in the lower right corner. It's important only when you want different handling on breakpoint, single-step, and invalid-handle exceptions. If you add your own structured exception handling (SEH) errors to the list, leave the Continue option at the default, Not Handled. That way, any time the exception comes through WinDBG, WinDBG will properly pass the exception directly back to the debuggee. You don't want the debugger "eating" exceptions other than those it caused, such as a breakpoint or a single step.

After selecting a particular exception, the most important button in the dialog box is the Commands button. The name alone should give you a hint about what it does. Clicking the Commands button brings up the Filter Command dialog box shown in Figure 6-7. The first edit control is misnamed and should be labeled *First-Chance Exception*.

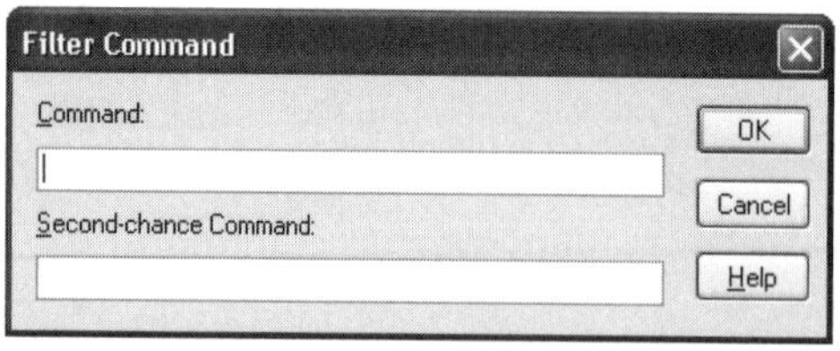

Figure 6-7   Filter Command dialog box

The terms *first chance* and *second chance* are from the native debugging side of the house, but they still apply to .NET debugging. The difference between these two terms has to do with when a debugger sees the exception and what happens to that exception.

If your application is running along and it encounters an exception, the operating system debugging API suspends the debuggee (your application) at the instruction that caused the exception. The debugger is notified that an exception has occurred in the debuggee and that it's the first chance the debugger has to look at it—hence the name *first chance*. The other way to think about this is that the first chance exception is when your code throws the exception.

The debugger looks at the exception and has two decision paths. If the debugger caused the exception in the debuggee, it has to undo the changes it made to the debuggee's state so it doesn't corrupt the debuggee. If you're wondering why a debugger would be messing with the debuggee's state, it's actually quite common; the canonical example is a native breakpoint. When handed the first chance exception, the debugger looks at the address and type of the exception. If the address matches the location where the debugger sets a breakpoint, and the exception is a breakpoint, the debugger does its magic to make the breakpoint disappear and stops in the debugger for the developer. Because the debugger is "eating" the exception, there's no way the debuggee can ever see that a breakpoint occurred.

The other option the debugger has with the first chance exception is after looking at it to proclaim, "This isn't mine" and hand it back to the debuggee. The operating system restarts the debuggee to let the exception be treated normally in the context of the debuggee's exception-handling code. If the debuggee has exception handling, and a catch block handles the exception, the debuggee continues execution from that catch block. The debugger reports that it saw the exception so you'll know a handled exception occurred.

If the exception handed back to the debuggee causes the exception handling to unwind to the final protecting exception handler set by Windows, it's an unhandled exception and the application crashes. At that point, the operating system again suspends the debuggee process and notifies the debugger that the exception is the second chance the debugger has had to see the exception. With the application crashed, the debugger will stop and show the origin location of the exception.

To set up WinDBG to execute a command whenever a .NET exception occurs, open the Event Filters dialog box and look for the CLR exception about halfway down the list. Select CLR Exception, and then click Commands button to specify what will be executed whenever any CLR exception occurs.

When a CLR exception does occur, you will see a message like the following in the Command window:

```
(d20.c1c): CLR exception - code e0434f4d (first chance)
```

The string in parentheses is the Windows process and thread ID of the process and thread having the CLR exception. The value 0xE0434F4D is the SEH exception for .NET exceptions.

If you stare at that value long enough, you may see an interesting value encoded in it. I'll leave it as an exercise for the reader to use WinDBG's *.formats* (Show Number Formats) command to see the hidden secret meaning.

If you want to stop on each .NET exception in WinDBG, you've seen how you can use the Event Filters dialog box to set the Execution to Enabled for CLR Exception to stop in the debugger whenever they are triggered. To do the same in the Command window, you'll use the *sxe* variant of the *sx* command, which enables the exception, and pass the exception value as the parameter to the command: *sxe clr.* The *sx* family of commands has predefined values for the common exceptions, which is why you can use *clr.* If you wanted to be hard-core, you could use the equivalent command *sxe e0434f4d.*

If you're really feeling hard-core and looking at the Event Filter dialog box will take up too much of your precious time, you can also specify the command string you want to execute when the exception occurs. To do the same action at the command line we did earlier by telling WinDBG to walk the stack and continue when any CLR exception occurs, you can use the command *sxe -c"kp;gc" clr.*

If you've looked closely at the Event Filters dialog box in Figure 6-6, you may have caught a glimpse of an event type called CLR Notification Exception nestled under the CLR Exception event. The name sounds interesting, and my first thought was that it had something to do with the Managed Debugging Assistants (MDA) I talked about in Chapter 4. My assumption was wrong—it has nothing to do with MDA. It turns out that the CLR notifications are undocumented, and I've never gotten them to work. However, the SOS *!bpmd* command uses them to assist in setting breakpoints.

Stopping on Trace Statements

One other exception type that comes in extremely handy when doing live debugging is the strangely named *Debuggee output.* That's an odd way of saying *trace statement.* The previous "Walking the Native Stack" section used examples where I stopped on a trace statement, and what I want to show you now is how I did that. The debuggee output has a predefined event code of *out,* so if you simply issue an *sxe out* command, you'll stop whenever your managed application calls *Trace.Write** and the *DefaultTraceListener* calls the native *OutputDebugString* API function. As you'll see when we get deep into SOS, it is possible to set breakpoints, but it's quite painful. Cheating and using *sxe out* to stop in WinDBG on your trace statements makes life much easier.

Those of you working on large projects are probably shaking your head right now at the thought of stopping in WinDBG every 1.5 seconds as a trace statement whizzes by. One of the super advanced tricks in my debugging bag is to take advantage of a little known feature of *sxe out* that lets you specify the trace statement string you want WinDBG to break on when it sees that string from one of your trace statements. If, for example, you wanted to stop on the trace statement when you open a database, you can specify the string to stop on after the *sxe out.*

There are some limitations to what WinDBG can take as the string to monitor. It can't contain any spaces, nor can it have any colons in it. The good news is that they do support enough of regular expression matching that you should be able to piece together a string that will be an exact match.

If the trace statement you want to stop on is something like "Opening database: {0}" (the {0} indicates the position where you'd put in the database name). In that case, your command in WinDBG would look like the following: *sxe out:Opening?database**. The first question mark (?) takes care of the space, and the trailing asterisk (*) indicates that you'll take zero or more characters on the end of the string. For exact details, search for "String Wildcard Syntax" in the WinDBG Help.

Commands for Controlling WinDBG

Since I've talked about controlling what happens on exceptions in your application, it's a good time to talk about some of the useful commands you can use to control WinDBG itself. I've already covered some of the important meta commands (also known as *dot* commands) in discussing how to get help (*.hh*) and symbol handling (*.reload*). What I want to talk about now are a few of the meta commands that will come in handy in your day-to-day debugging battles.

The simplest, yet extremely useful command is *.cls* (Clear Screen). This allows you to clear the Command window so that you can start fresh. Because WinDBG can fill the Command window with a tremendous amount of information, which takes memory to store, it's good to clean the slate occasionally.

If you want to clear just a portion of the Command window, you can highlight the portion you want to delete and select Clear Command Output from the Edit menu. If nothing is selected, the effect is the same as issuing the *.cls* command. Right-clicking the Command window title bar brings up a shortcut menu that also has the Clear Command Output item. No matter how you decide you want to clear the Command window, make sure it is what you want to do because there's no undo capability, so once the output is gone, it's gone forever.

Another extremely useful command is *.shell* (Command Shell), which allows you to start up a Command Prompt console window from the debugger and redirect output to the Command window. Debugging on the same machine the debuggee is running on and pressing Alt+Tab might be an easier approach, but the beauty of *.shell* is that you get the output in the debugger even when doing remote debugging with the Command Prompt console running on the remote machine. You can also use the *.shell* command to run a single external program, redirect its output, and return to the Command window. After issuing a *.shell* command, the Command window input line says *INPUT>*, indicating that the Command Prompt console window is waiting for input. To close the Command Prompt and return to the Command window, use either the MS-DOS *exit* command, or preferably, the *.shell_quit* (Quit Command Prompt) command because it will terminate the Command Prompt even when the window is frozen.

The *.shell* command has a couple of very interesting options. The first is -x, which spawns the process you want to start completely detached from WinDBG. For example, if you issue the command *.shell notepad*, WinDBG assumes that the program is a console-based program, so the Command window switches to the >*Input* prompt ready to display the standard IO. Because Notepad.exe is a GUI program, the only action you can perform is *.shell_quit*.

If you specify the *-x* option before the command to execute (*.shell -x notepad*), WinDBG will just do a normal *CreateProcess* API call on the command to start so it runs cleanly and stays running even after you quit WinDBG. For those of you who want to be true alpha geeks, the fact that WinDBG now easily supports process creation means that you no longer have to use Explorer as your Windows shell; WinDBG will work perfectly well.

The second option to the *.shell* command, *-ci*, allows you to execute a series of WinDBG commands and redirect their output to a program. For example, if you whip up a Perl script to parse the output of the *k* command, you can pass the output like so: *.shell -ci "~*ekp" perl.exe parseKcommand.pl*.

In the Exceptions and Events section, I talked about how you could have WinDBG execute commands when exceptions occurred in your program. If you have a long-running process, and there are numerous exceptions triggering, you can easily lose yourself in a ton of text in the Command window. This is especially important if you are chaining many commands together. To make your life easier, the *.echo* (Echo Comment) command will output a string of your choosing into the Command window when executed. That way it will be much easier to find key locations in the execution transcript.

The *.wtitle* (Set Window Title) command is one of those commands that at first glance does not seem that useful, but it turns out to be a command you use all the time. When you are dealing with multiple dump files from the same application, you end up opening many of them at the same time to compare states and values. However, unless you are a master at divining the exact location of each WinDBG instance location on the screen, it can get confusing extremely quickly which window you are looking at or about to Alt+Tab to. By using *.wtitle* to set the WinDBG title, you'll speed up your multiple instance usage tremendously.

Keeping a log of your trials and tribulations inside WinDBG especially so you can look at data after the fact or send the transcript to someone else is a major key to getting great help from others on your team. WinDBG can log everything that goes to its Command window in a myriad of ways. To open a log file, use the *.logopen* (Open Log File) command. If you want to have the date and time appended on the name of the log file, pass the */t* option before the file name passed to *.logopen*. To have WinDBG automatically name the file for you based on the name of the process you're debugging, pass */d* as the only parameter to *.logopen*.

If you want to append to an existing log file instead of opening a new one, use the *.logappend* (Append Log File) command. Of course, to close a log file at any time, use the *.logclose* (Close Log File) command. A new feature of WinDBG is that you can also select Open/Close Log File on the Edit menu to do the same operations.

The last meta command I'll share with you is one that's part of my secret debugging tricks. When writing error handling, you usually know that by the time you're executing the error handling, your process is in serious trouble. You also know that if you hit a particular piece of error handling, 9 times out of 10, you're probably going to look at specific variable values or the call stack, or you will want to record specific information. What I've always wanted was a way to code the debugger commands I would normally execute directly into my error handling. By doing that, the commands would execute, enabling the maintenance programmers and me to debug a problem faster. My idea was that since trace statements calls go through the debugger, you could embed the commands into a trace statement. You'd tell the debugger what to look for at the front of the trace statement text, and anything after it would be the commands to execute.

What I've just described is exactly how WinDBG's *.ocommand* (Expect Commands from Target) command works. You call *.ocommand*, identifying the string prefix to look for, at the front of any trace statement calls. If the command is present, WinDBG will execute the rest of the text as a command string. Obviously, you'll want to be careful with the string you use, or WinDBG could go nuts trying to execute trace statement calls all through your programs. I like to use WINDBGCMD: as my string. I love this command and sprinkle WinDBG command strings all over my programs!

When using *.ocommand*, if you don't follow the command string with ";*gc*", WinDBG stops when the command ends. In the following function, I ensure that the commands all end with ";*gc*" so that execution continues. To get the commands to execute, I issue *.ocommand WINDBGCMD:* before the program starts. Note that in the trace statement, you can use any commands you would enter at the command line. The following shows a quick example of a trace statement passing a command to WinDBG. I'll discuss the full usage of the *.dump* (Create Dump File) in the next section.

```
// Some work takes place...
catch ( FileNotFoundException ex )
{
    Trace.WriteLine ( "WINDBGCMD: .dump /ma /u FNFE.dmp;kP;gc" );
}
```

Dump File Handling

We've been discussing the meta commands you'll be using while running WinDBG, but the most important meta command is *.dump* (Create Dump File). Because dump files, mainly known as minidumps, are so vital to tracking down those production-only problems, I want to spend some time discussing what they are and exactly what you'll need to do to get the best dumps for .NET development.

In the previous chapter, I discussed how to create and load minidumps from Visual Studio. You're probably wondering why I'm recommending in this chapter that you use a much tougher-to-use tool rather than the nice-and-easy Visual Studio. If you're dealing with minidumps created on your development machine during coding and testing, Visual Studio is absolutely easier to use, and in fact, that's what I use in those situations. However, for dumps from production systems, WinDBG, though more painful to use, offers the power and flexibility you need to look at the toughest problems. This will become much more apparent when we get to loading and using SOS.

What Is a Minidump?

A minidump is a snapshot of the application at a point in time and is akin to core dumps from other operating systems. There are kernel-mode minidumps that the operating system writes when a device driver or other kernel-mode component has an unhandled exception. For more information about kernel-mode debugging and minidumps, see the excellent document *kernel_debugging_tutorial.doc* that's in the WinDBG installation directory.

A user-mode minidump contains the state of the application at a particular point in time. That point can be at the instant of a crash or at any time you used ADPlus to create a minidump of a running process. For those of you who have seen minidumps in the wild, you know the term *minidump* is somewhat of an oxymoron. It's normal to have a usable minidump of a large ASP.NET system to be more than 500 MB. Minidumps that size are a little tough to send as an e-mail attachment.

You're probably scratching your head and wondering why a "mini" dump can be so big and why isn't there a format called *full dump* that captures everything? There actually is a format for a dump called *full dump*, and the Help on the *.dump* command mentions that you can still create them. The full dump format is an older format and has less information than the minidump format. Consequently, it's far better to use the minidump format and put all information into it, even though that makes the created minidump file actually larger than a full dump.

For our purposes, there are only two types of minidumps: a basic minidump and a full-memory minidump. A basic minidump contains essentially only two pieces of information. The first is the version information for each of the loaded modules. The second set of data consists of all the pages of memory necessary to walk the native call stack of each thread in the system.

Given the small amount of data collected, the corresponding file size of a basic minidump is quite small. For a C# console program that does nothing but call *Trace.WriteLine*, the basic minidump on Windows XP Professional x64 Edition is 80 KB. In the native debugging world, a basic minidump is nearly all you need.

A full-memory minidump starts out with the same information as a basic memory minidump but adds every allocated and committed virtual page of memory. That means that you're not only including the current working set, which consists of pages currently in memory, but also all the pages that are swapped out. That's how the numbers add up big in full-memory minidumps. Saving a full memory minidump of the same C# console program now yields 88.9 MB.

When it comes to .NET applications, SOS needs the full-memory minidump to be fully effective. If you step back and think about why, it makes sense. A .NET application is Just in Time (JIT) compiled, and data is in the garbage-collected heap. Without those chunks of memory available in the minidump, there's nothing for SOS to process to tell you about the .NET portions of the process. If all you can get is a basic minidump, you should use a new feature of SOS for .NET 2.0–it can at least walk the call stack and show you the managed methods on the stack.

Creating Minidumps in WinDBG

When doing live debugging with WinDBG, you can create a minidump at any time with the *.dump* command. All options you pass to the *.dump* command are passed before the file name for the dump. To specify creating a full-memory minidump, you'll pass the */ma* option. If the output file already exists, as a safety precaution, the *.dump* command will not overwrite an existing file. To overwrite an existing file, use the */o* option. To ensure a unique file name, add the */u* option to have the date, time, and process ID of the specified file name so you can reexecute the command and keep a consistent first part of the output file name.

If you're going to be saving off numerous minidumps from a single debugging session, you'll want to make sure to use the comment option, */c*, to have your comment printed to the Command window when you open the minidump. The last *.dump* command option worth mentioning is the */b* switch, which compresses the minidump into a .cab file. If space is an issue on a machine, it could be helpful. However, WinDBG writes the minidump to temporary storage before compressing into a .cab file. When using */b*, you see the message "Creating a cab file can take a VERY VERY long time" (sic) in the Command window, so it may be a good excuse for a stretch break.

Opening Minidumps in WinDBG

Creating minidumps is nice; opening them is even more important. Before I discuss how to open, I need to remind you to ensure that you have the _NT_IMAGE_PATH environment variable set to the same value as your _NT_SYMBOL_PATH environment variable. Because the minidumps do not have the actual binary files in them, WinDBG will need to know where it can find the exact versions of the files referenced in the minidump so it can load the appropriate symbols. Hence, you need to tell WinDBG that they are in your Symbol Server.

The easy way to open a minidump is to start WinDBG and on the File menu, click Open Crash Dump or press the keyboard accelerator key (Ctrl+D). If you want to start WinDBG and have it open a minidump immediately, add the WinDBG -*z* option to WinDBG's command line followed by the name of the minidump file. In an ode to ease of use, WinDBG amazingly supports drag and drop from Windows Explorer.

Once you have the minidump open, look immediately at the dump type information, which is output to the Command window right after the WinDBG version and copyright:

```
Loading Dump File [C:\Dev\MyDump.dmp]
User Mini Dump File with Full Memory: Only application data is available
```

You can see from the output that the dump opened above is a full memory minidump, so it's completely usable by SOS. If the minidump type string says anything else, your minidump does not have sufficient information in it for full SOS usage. As I mentioned earlier, the SOS stack walking command will work with .NET 2.0, so if the minidump is the only one you have, at least try the SOS commands to see if you can get any information from the dump.

If you've opened a dump that was written as the result of a Windows SEH crash, in other words, a native code crash, the first command you may want to execute is *.ecxr* (Display Exception Context Record), which reports the state of the application at the time of the crash. This command tells WinDBG to use the *exception record* context, which is the data structure that contains the state of the application at the time of the crash. If the minidump was written from inside the crashing application, always issue the *.ecxr* command. If an external process, such as a debugger, wrote the minidump, the exception record context and the context record are one and the same, and you don't need to use *.ecxr*.

It never hurts to issue the *.ecxr* command when opening a minidump because the debugger will ignore the command if it's not needed. If you do run the *.ecxr* command, you'll see a new register set and call stack appear if you have the Call stack window open. Additionally, the *k* command will report on each use that it's starting at the exception record context for stack walking.

Once the minidump file is open, it's as if you've stopped the application at that location, so you can issue all the WinDBG and SOS commands you could want. Obviously, because you're looking at a snapshot of the application in time, you can't run any debugging actions, such as native breakpoints and single stepping. The great news is that all the wonderful informational commands are right there for you to figure out exactly what went wrong in the application.

The last trick I want to mention about opening minidumps helps in a situation in which you have multiple minidumps to look at. After you've opened the first minidump as described earlier, you can open other minidumps in the same instance of the debugger by using the *.opendump* (Open Dump Files) command. This command is extremely helpful when you have minidumps of two related processes, such as Internet Information Server (IIS) and one of the Microsoft ASP.NET worker processes. It's also nice to look at similar dumps of the same process at the same time.

Extremely Useful Extension Commands

You would think that after this many pages I would *finally* be up to discussing SOS in all its glory. If I jumped into SOS now, I'd be cheating you out of some extraordinarily powerful commands that WinDBG offers. These commands can truly make the difference between having full-memory minidumps simply chewing up tons of disk space and actually fixing the bug.

Even though this is a whole book on .NET debugging, none of you are writing pure managed applications. You have to interact with Windows somehow to communicate with the user, access files, or touch the network. Additionally, many of you are in environments where you have a significant investment in COM components or native DLLs that you'll be using until you retire. In this section, I want to cover some WinDBG commands that make seeing the interaction with the native side of your application much easier.

All of the commands I'm going to mention here are extension commands, which, like SOS, are DLLs that provide additional functionality to WinDBG. WinDBG comes with a standard set of extensions so you don't need to download or install anything else to take advantage of these commands, which you can see by running the *.chain* (List Debugger Extensions) command. Because the WinDBG team is responsible for supporting these commands, they've even gone to the trouble of automatically loading them so they are always at the ready.

The *!analyze* Command

The first command, *!analyze*, has almost mystical capabilities. If you're thinking: "Hey, with a name like that, could *!analyze* just tell me where my bugs are?" you're going down the right track. It has its limitations, but it's the first command you need to run when you open a mini-dump of an application that crashed or experienced deadlocks on the native side. You can use *!analyze* with live debugging, but it's not nearly as useful.

The *!analyze* command takes several parameters, but you'll use only three. Always pass the first one, *-v*, because it sets the output to verbose mode. Without the *-v*, the output is not worthwhile. The second option, *-hang*, will attempt to perform deadlock analysis. Before using *-hang*, switch to one of the threads that you think is deadlocked, and run *!analyze -hang -v* from that thread. The final option, *-f*, is one that you'll rarely use. Its purpose is to force the *!analyze* analysis to run even if there's not a crash. When doing live debugging, it can come in handy every once in awhile.

To show the power of the *!analyze* command, I whipped up a very simple managed application that crashes inside a native C++ DLL function. Of course, with .NET 2.0, you'll see the new *AccessViolationException* exception in your exception handler, but before the exception handler runs, you'll get the ubiquitous Windows crash message. When the crash message appeared, I attached to the crashed program with WinDBG and created a full-memory mini-dump. Instead of showing you all the output at once, I'll display the output and provide a running commentary on what you're looking at so it makes more sense:

```
0:000> !analyze -v
*******************************************************************************
*                                                                             *
*                            Exception Analysis                               *
*                                                                             *
*******************************************************************************

FAULTING_IP:
CrashinDll!BigMistakeToCallMe+1c [c:\junk\cruft\crashme\crashindll\crashindll.cpp @ 40]
00000000 1b0b108c 66c7005000      mov     word ptr [rax],0x50
```

The first part of the *!analyze -v* output is the big banner indicating that exception analysis is running, which is something I wish the WinDBG team would take out. The first piece of information displayed is the address information about the crash itself. Because *!analyze* will load the necessary symbols, you may see symbol loading information between the banner and the FAULTING_IP text. As you can see from the example above, good symbols were loaded, and the analysis is pointing directly to the C++ native source line that crashed:

```
EXCEPTION_RECORD:  ffffffffffffffff -- (.exr ffffffffffffffff)
ExceptionAddress: 000000001b0b108c (CrashinDll!BigMistakeToCallMe+0x000000000000001c)
   ExceptionCode: c0000005 (Access violation)
  ExceptionFlags: 00000000
NumberParameters: 2
   Parameter[0]: 0000000000000001
   Parameter[1]: 0000000000000000
Attempt to write to address 0000000000000000
```

The exception record is the data structure filled in by the operating system SEH when an application has an unhandled native exception. The *!analyze -v* displays the data structure so you can see the exact cause of the crash. If the exception code does not have the textual representation of the exception code, you can look the code up in WINNT.H. If the exception code does not exist, it may be a software exception by a direct call to the Windows API *RaiseException*, which you'll see at the top of the stack walk:

```
DEFAULT_BUCKET_ID:  APPLICATION_FAULT
PROCESS_NAME:  CrashMe.exe
ERROR_CODE: (NTSTATUS) 0xc0000005 - The instruction at "0x%08lx" referenced
memory at "0x%08lx". The memory could not be "%s".
WRITE_ADDRESS:  0000000000000000
BUGCHECK_STR:  ACCESS_VIOLATION
```

The next section shows more detailed information about the crash. If you were to write a quick tool that would parse the output of the *!analyze* command, this output would contain general descriptions of the crash.

```
MANAGED_STACK:
(TransitionMU)
000000000023EDF0 000000001AF6076C CrashMe!DomainBoundILStubClass.IL_STUB(Int32)+0x9c
(TransitionMU)
000000000023EED0 000000001AF608A8 CrashMe!SecurityILStubClass.IL_STUB(Int32)+0x58
(TransitionMU)
000000000023EF80 000000001AF6060F CrashMe!CrashMe.DoSomeWork.Fum(Int32)+0x2f
(TransitionMU)
000000000023EFC0 000000001AF605A4 CrashMe!CrashMe.DoSomeWork.Fo(Int32)+0x34
(TransitionMU)
000000000023EFF0 000000001AF60534 CrashMe!CrashMe.DoSomeWork.Fi(Int32)+0x34
(TransitionMU)
000000000023F020 000000001AF604C4 CrashMe!CrashMe.DoSomeWork.Fee(Int32)+0x34
(TransitionMU)
000000000023F050 000000001AF603DE CrashMe!CrashMe.Program.Main(System.String[])+0xfe
(TransitionUM)
```

Wow! The MANAGED_STACK output is certainly a very nice surprise from the *!analyze -v* command. Whereas the stack walk *k* command lacks any knowledge about managed code, the *!analyze -v* command seems to have some nice smarts built in to give us more information about what's going on in our applications. SOS has a command to walk the call stack, but the *!analyze* command is not using SOS and has the logic built in. We can all keep our fingers crossed that Microsoft will put these same smarts into the *k* command in future versions of WinDBG.

```
LAST_CONTROL_TRANSFER:  from 0000000075ecce24 to 000000001b0b108c
```

This indicates the last call on the stack.

```
(Note: For wrapping, the upper DWORD on the 64-bit addresses was removed.)
STACK_TEXT:
0023ed40 75ecce24 : 0000000a 00000000 74968000 00000000 : CrashinDll!BigMistakeToCallMe+0x1c
[c:\junk\cruft\crashme\crashindll\crashindll.cpp @ 40]
0023ed50 1af6076c : 0000000a 1a960fd0 7c897ef6 00000000 : mscorwks!DoNDirectCall__PatchGetTh
readCall+0x78
0023edf0 1af608a8 : 0000000a 75c746a0 00226ae8 00000001 : 0x1af6076c
0023eed0 1af6060f : 0000000a 0000000a 0023ef0e 0023ef80 : 0x1af608a8
0023ef80 1af605a4 : 02071f48 0000000a 0023ef0e 0023ef80 : 0x1af6060f
0023efc0 1af60534 : 02071f48 0000000a 0023ef0e 0023ef80 : 0x1af605a4
0023eff0 1af604c4 : 02071f48 0000000a 0023ef0e 0023ef80 : 0x1af60534
0023f020 1af603de : 02071f48 0000000a 0023ef0e 0023ef80 : 0x1af604c4
0023f050 75ecf422 : 02071e00 00000003 fffffffe 00285fc8 : 0x1af603de
0023f0b0 75d9cb5a : 0000001d fffffffe 00000000 00000000 : mscorwks!CallDescrWorker+0x82
0023f100 75d9afd3 : 0023f238 00000001 00000001 00000000 : mscorwks!CallDescrWorkerWithHandle
r+0xca
0023f1a0 75cf099a : 00000001 1a960e90 00000000 749dd912 : mscorwks!MethodDesc::CallDescr+0x1b3
0023f3e0 75e56775 : 00000000 00000000 fffffffe 75d409bc : mscorwks!ClassLoader::RunMain+0x22e
0023f640 75e2ebe8 : 0023fc80 0023fc98 0027d918 0025ec40 : mscorwks!Assembly::ExecuteMainMeth
od+0xb9
0023f930 75e6a523 : 00000000 00000000 00000000 75eabc4a : mscorwks!SystemDomain::ExecuteMain
Method+0x3f0
0023fee0 75e78205 : 00000000 0023e060 00000000 00000000 : mscorwks!ExecuteEXE+0x47
0023ff30 7401a726 : ffffffff 00270ba0 00000000 00000000 : mscorwks!CorExeMain+0xb1
0023ff80 78d5965c : 75be0000 00000000 00000000 0023ffd8 : mscoree!CorExeMain+0x46
0023ffb0 00000000 : 7401a6e0 00000000 00000000 00000000 : kernel32!BaseProcessStart+0x29
```

The STACK_TEXT section shows the usual stack trace. The output is identical to the *kb* command, which shows the stack trace and the first four parameters to the function for x64 versions and the first three for x86 versions. If you compare the addresses in the stack trace that don't show function names to the managed stack shown in the MANAGED_STACK section, you'll see that they match up. You'll see this matching only on x64 versions because there is only a single native calling convention, so it's much easier to walk the stack on x64 versions than on x86:

```
FOLLOWUP_IP:
CrashinDll!BigMistakeToCallMe+1c [c:\junk\cruft\crashme\crashindll\crashindll.cpp @ 40]
00000000 1b0b108c 66c7005000        mov     word ptr [rax],0x50
```

```
SYMBOL_STACK_INDEX:  0
FOLLOWUP_NAME:  MachineOwner
SYMBOL_NAME:  CrashinDll!BigMistakeToCallMe+1c
MODULE_NAME:  CrashinDll
IMAGE_NAME:  CrashinDll.dll
DEBUG_FLR_IMAGE_TIMESTAMP:  42c31c8a
STACK_COMMAND:  .ecxr ; kb
```

The FOLLOWUP_IP section is always the same value as the address that crashed. The rest of the fields are there to identify the crashing module, symbol, and the image timestamp of the crashing module. The STACK_COMMAND section shows the command used to produce the STACK_TEXT section, and as the WinDBG documentation says, you can use the same command on your own exploration of the crash.

```
FAILURE_BUCKET_ID:  X64_ACCESS_VIOLATION_CrashinDll!BigMistakeToCallMe+1c
BUCKET_ID:  X64_ACCESS_VIOLATION_CrashinDll!BigMistakeToCallMe+1c
Followup: MachineOwner
```

The last part of the *!analyze -v* output shows the bucket information. A bucket is the unique identifier calculated by the *!analyze -v* command to uniquely identify the fault for the crash. Using these buckets, you can build up a database of all the crashes reported in order to determine which crashes you're seeing more than others so you can apply your fixing effort to the more common crashes.

The Followup and the earlier FOLLOWUP_NAME fields are for using the *!analyze* command with a special file called Triage.ini. With this file, you assign ownership to modules and functions so you'll know whom to yell at when your application crashes. The *!analyze* documentation discusses how to use the Triage.ini file.

The *!handle* Command

Those of us from native Windows backgrounds are paranoid about ensuring that our handles are closed. Since a handle from an API such as *CreateEvent* is an opaque reference to an actual chunk of real memory, you have to be extremely cognizant of ensuring that you appropriately close handles you've opened. If you don't close that handle, you leak memory and system resources.

In .NET, classes such as *EventWaitHandle* do a good job of hiding the actual handle from the developer. However, if you're passing handles from .NET code to native code, there is potential to leak them. Fortunately, WinDBG supports a great command to let you see exactly which handles are open in your process at any given time: *!handle*.

Issuing *!handle* with no parameters will produce the following output:

```
0:000> !handle
Handle 254
  Type          File
Handle 2a8
  Type          Section
  . . .
```

```
Handle 3c0
   Type          Directory
Handle 3c4
   Type          Desktop
Handle 3c8
   Type          Event
. . .
87 Handles
Type            Count
Event           41
Section         4
File            11
Port            1
Directory       2
Mutant          2
WindowStation   2
Semaphore       2
Key             7
Thread          4
Desktop         1
IoCompletion    9
KeyedEvent      1
```

The first part of the output shows the value of each handle and its type. The final portion shows the number of handles currently open in the process and the number of each type. If you suspect that you have a native handle leak, you can keep an eye on the handle count. If you see the overall count going up, you'll also see the count for the leaking type increasing as well.

The wonderful book, *Microsoft Window Internals, Fourth Edition: Microsoft Windows Server 2003, Windows XP, and Windows 2000* by David Solomon and Mark Russinovich (Microsoft Press, 2004) explains all the different handle types that you'll see with the *!handle* command. Most are self-explanatory, but I need to mention that a *Directory* is a kernel-mode Windows Object directory entry, and a *Mutant* is a mutex.

To dig into more information about a specific handle, pass two additional values to *!handle*. The first is the handle value itself, and the second is *f*. The second parameter is a bit field indicating the additional fields you want to see, but you'll always pass *f* to see everything.

If you want to see detailed information about all the handles of a specific type, pass zero for the handle value, *f* for all data, and the handle type as the third parameter. For example, *!handle 0 f Event* will show the detailed information for all Event handles in the process.

The following example shows the display of the detailed data for two handle values: the first is for an event, and the second is for a registry key.

```
0:003> !handle 2b4 f
Handle 2b4
   Type          Event
   Attributes    0
   GrantedAccess 0x1f0003:
        Delete,ReadControl,WriteDac,WriteOwner,Synch
        QueryState,ModifyState
```

```
HandleCount      2
PointerCount     5
Name             \BaseNamedObjects\EventerUniqueID_3504
Object Specific Information
  Event Type Manual Reset
  Event is Waiting

0:003> !handle 2f8 f
Handle 2f8
  Type           Key
  Attributes     0
  GrantedAccess  0x20019:
        ReadControl
        QueryValue,EnumSubKey,Notify
  HandleCount    2
  PointerCount   3
  Name           \REGISTRY\MACHINE\SOFTWARE\MICROSOFT\Fusion\PublisherPolicy\Default
  Object Specific Information
    Key last write time:  21:07:38. 6/20/2005
    Key name Default
```

As you looked through the output, you probably saw some very interesting items related to those handles. The name of the object is the most important field because it's what allows you to easily identify the handle as it relates to your code. By seeing the name of a specific event in addition to its signal state, you now have a fighting chance to see if that's the event you are deadlocking on.

Of course, you won't see the handle name unless you named the specific handle value. If you issue a *!handle 0 f Event* in your application, you'll see that nearly all the events in your process have the completely descriptive name of *<none>*, which indicates that they have no name. By the way, only mutexes, semaphores, and events have optional names. Other handle types, such as registry keys and Windows Stations, have the name of the opened key or station.

An unnamed handle is not a bug—the handle name is an optional value passed to the constructors of *EventWaitHandle*, *Mutex*, and *Semaphore* classes. The reason the name is optional is that if you don't specify the name, the scope of the handle is limited to the process. If you name the handle, it becomes global to the machine in scope.

If you don't think that's a problem, consider the following scenario: You have a process in which you name an event handle *Foo* that you use to block one thread execution until another thread is finished with some work. Everything runs great if only one process is running. If two of the same processes are running and both happen to have threads waiting for the *Foo* event, when that event is signaled, *both* threads in the two separate processes will stop waiting. That's one serious bug!

If you're going to name your handles, and you need to keep them unique to the process, you'll need to add a unique identifier to the name if you want the handle to have just process scope. Because the process ID is guaranteed to be unique as long as the process is running, I always append the current value to the name string to ensure different values for multiple running applications.

The following truncated output shows the unique name I gave to a *Semaphore* class my application created:

```
0:003> !handle 0 f Semaphore
Handle 270
  Type            Semaphore
  Attributes      0
  GrantedAccess   0x1f0003:
        Delete,ReadControl,WriteDac,WriteOwner,Synch
        QueryState,ModifyState
  HandleCount     2
  PointerCount    4
  Name            \BaseNamedObjects\SemaphoreUniqueID_3504
  Object Specific Information
    Semaphore Count 0
    Semaphore Limit 1
```

Because naming an event exposes the event outside the process, I must also mention that tools such as Process Explorer, which I discussed in Chapter 4, can see those values. Depending on your application's security requirements, that could expose data you may not want others to see. At a minimum, you'll want to at least name your handles in Debug builds so you can track down problems easier.

If you're looking for a project that will make your debugging life easier, what we need is a quick tool that will allow us to search for a named handle value so we don't have to read through thousands of lines of *!handle* output. You could write the tool as a WinDBG extension, but you'd have to do that in native C++, and it's certainly an adventure to get extensions working and debugged. A better approach would be to write a .NET console application that reads the standard output so you could pump the output of *!handle 0 f* into the tool with the previously mentioned *.shell -ci* command.

Other Extension Commands

With the big commands *!analyze* and *!handle* out of the way, I want to mention a few other extension commands that you have at your disposal to look at various items in your application or how you're interacting with the system.

The *!runaway* command isn't what you do when faced with debugging a nasty problem with WinDBG; it's the command that will show you the thread times for a process. If your application is chewing up more CPU time than you expect, *!runaway* will show you the thread that's doing the chewing. If you pass *f* as the parameter to *!runaway*, you'll see User Mode Time, Kernel Mode Time, and Elapsed Time, which is the amount of time elapsed since the thread was created. The following shows the *!runaway* output for a simple application:

```
0:003> !runaway f
 User Mode Time
  Thread       Time
   0:8d0       0 days 0:00:00.015
   3:d58       0 days 0:00:00.000
   2:db4       0 days 0:00:00.000
   1:9d8       0 days 0:00:00.000
```

```
Kernel Mode Time
  Thread        Time
    0:8d0       0 days 0:00:00.015
    3:d58       0 days 0:00:00.000
    2:db4       0 days 0:00:00.000
    1:9d8       0 days 0:00:00.000
Elapsed Time
  Thread        Time
    0:8d0       0 days 1:28:21.642
    1:9d8       0 days 1:28:16.673
    2:db4       0 days 1:28:16.658
    3:d58       0 days 0:17:20.285
```

The *!token* command displays the detailed information about a security token to make your security programming easier. Always use the *-n* option to *!token* to see the friendly names for security groups, unless you have values such as S-1-5-21-603047887-89138312-1407646538-1004 memorized.

To find all the Token handles in your process, first issue the *!handle 0 f Token* command to list them. That will show you output like the following, which you can see does not show you much at all about the token:

```
Handle 490
  Type            Token
  Attributes      0
  GrantedAccess   0xc:
        None
        Impersonate,Query
  HandleCount     2
  PointerCount    3
  Name            <none>
  Object Specific Information
    Auth Id    0 : 0x3e4
    Type          Impersonation
    Imp Level  Identification
1 handles of type Token
```

Pass the Token handle value you're interested in to the *!token* command, and you'll see output like that that follows. One very nice feature of *!token* is if you don't specify a Token handle to display, it defaults to the thread token so you can see the impersonation state of the thread.

```
1:013> !token -n 490
TS Session ID: 0
User: S-1-5-20 (Well Known Group: NT AUTHORITY\NETWORK SERVICE)
Groups:
 00 S-1-5-20 (Well Known Group: NT AUTHORITY\NETWORK SERVICE)
    Attributes - Mandatory Default Enabled
 01 S-1-1-0 (Well Known Group: localhost\Everyone)
    Attributes - Mandatory Default Enabled
 02 S-1-5-21-603047887-89138312-1407646538-1004 (Alias: TIMON\IIS_WPG)
    Attributes - Mandatory Default Enabled
 03 S-1-5-32-559 (Alias: BUILTIN\Performance Log Users)
    Attributes - Mandatory Default Enabled
```

```
04 S-1-5-32-545 (Alias: BUILTIN\Users)
   Attributes - Mandatory Default Enabled
05 S-1-5-6 (Well Known Group: NT AUTHORITY\SERVICE)
   Attributes - Mandatory Default Enabled
06 S-1-5-11 (Well Known Group: NT AUTHORITY\Authenticated Users)
   Attributes - Mandatory Default Enabled
07 S-1-5-15 (Well Known Group: NT AUTHORITY\This Organization)
   Attributes - Mandatory Default Enabled
08 S-1-2-0 (Well Known Group: localhost\LOCAL)
   Attributes - Mandatory Default Enabled
09 S-1-5-5-0-54414 (no name mapped)
   Attributes - Mandatory Default Enabled LogonId
10 S-1-5-32-545 (Alias: BUILTIN\Users)
   Attributes - Mandatory Default Enabled
Primary Group: S-1-5-20 (Well Known Group: NT AUTHORITY\NETWORK SERVICE)
Privs:
00 0x00000001e Unknown Privilege         Attributes - Enabled Default
01 0x00000001d SeImpersonatePrivilege    Attributes - Enabled Default
02 0x000000017 SeChangeNotifyPrivilege   Attributes - Enabled Default
Auth ID: 0:3e4
Impersonation Level: Identification
TokenType: Impersonation
```

Before I leave the cool extension commands and the native side of WinDBG as a whole, I need to mention that although I've covered a good deal of interesting features and tricks in WinDBG, I have certainly not covered everything. The more you read the WinDBG documentation, the better you'll be able to learn WinDBG and SOS. You were probably wondering if I was ever going to get to SOS, but with the background on WinDBG under your belt, we can finally start looking at the managed pieces of your application with SOS!

SOS

Now we can shift our attention to the in-depth look of our managed processes running under WinDBG with SOS. Before we jump in, I just want to mention what SOS is doing under the hood to make its magic. SOS takes the metadata from a .NET binary and maps it onto the live addresses in memory so you can see a live application (or minidump) as you expect to see it.

When you start looking at output from various SOS commands, you'll see references to the metadata throughout. It's not a bad idea to keep an eye on the metadata for an assembly when using SOS with ILDASM, the round trip disassembler that comes with the .NET Framework SDK. It's as simple as opening the assembly with ILDASM and pressing Ctrl+M. In the .NET 1.1 days, you needed to run Ildasm.exe with the /ADV switch to see the metadata for an assembly, but for .NET 2.0, the metadata is on by default.

Manually walking the metadata tables gives new meaning to the term *tedious*. The good news is that you don't spend a great deal of time in SOS doing that. I will mention the commands that will let you do the manual metadata walking in due course. Before we can get there, you do need to know how to load SOS.

Loading SOS into WinDBG

As I mentioned back in the beginning of this chapter, everyone already has SOS for .NET 2.0 installed on their systems as its part of the actual .NET Framework installation. The whole trick to SOS is ensuring that you load the exact version of SOS to match the version of the .NET Framework loaded into the process. The good news is that there's a new command in WinDBG, *.loadby* (Load Extension DLL), which makes getting the proper version trivial.

Before using *.loadby*, you'll need to ensure that you have MScorwks.dll loaded in your live process or minidump. Unlike .NET 1.1, which had separate DLLs that implemented the garbage-collected heap for workstations and servers, .NET 2.0 has both heap types in MScorwks.dll. Issue the *lm v m mscorwks* command to see the full version information for the loaded MScorwks.dll. The following shows the output if MScorwks.dll is loaded. If there's no module listed, MScorwks.dll is not loaded.

```
0:012> lm v m mscorwks
start             end               module name
00000642 7f330000 00000642 7fd1d000   mscorwks   (deferred)
    Image path:
 C:\WINDOWS\Microsoft.NET\Framework64\v2.0.50727\mscorwks.dll
    Image name: mscorwks.dll
    Timestamp:        Fri Sep 23 05:17:48 2005 (4333C83C)
    CheckSum:         009E1495
    ImageSize:        009ED000
    File version:     2.0.50727.42
    Product version:  2.0.50727.42
    File flags:       0 (Mask 3F)
    File OS:          4 Unknown Win32
    File type:        2.0 Dll
    File date:        00000000.00000000
    Translations:     0409.04b0
    CompanyName:      Microsoft Corporation
    ProductName:      Microsoft® .NET Framework
    InternalName:     mscorwks.dll
    OriginalFilename: mscorwks.dll
    ProductVersion:   2.0.50727.42
    FileVersion:      2.0.50727.42 (RTM.050727-4200)
    FileDescription:  Microsoft .NET Runtime Common Language Runtime - WorkStation
    LegalCopyright:   © Microsoft Corporation.  All rights reserved.
    Comments:         Flavor=Retail
```

If MScorwks.dll is loaded, pass two parameters to the *.loadby* command. The first is the extension DLL itself, SOS, and the second is the module name of the DLL you want WinDBG to use as the path to the extension to load. In other words, the second DLL is there just to provide the path. The full command is: *.loadby sos mscorwks*.

If you don't see any output after the *.loadby sos mscorwks* command, that means that the SOS extension DLL was loaded just fine. You can double-check that SOS loaded by issuing the *.chain* (List Debugger Extensions) command. If you see SOS as the first DLL listed after the extension DLL search path, you are in great shape.

Those of you paying close attention may be wondering about the requirement to have MScorwks.dll loaded before you can get SOS loaded. This leads to some interesting problems. The first is handling the case in which you are debugging a minidump that uses a different version of the .NET Framework than you have on your machine. The second involves the case in which you want SOS loaded so you can debug your startup code.

In the case of the minidump with a different version of the .NET Framework, ideally, you'll have the different versions of the .NET Framework either installed on other machines or possibly stored on a server. If you do, use the traditional *.load* (Load Extension DLL) command to tell WinDBG to load a particular extension by specifying the complete name and path to the extension DLL as follows:

```
0:000> .load C:\WINDOWS\Microsoft.NET\Framework64\v2.0.50727\sos.dll
```

If you want to load the correct version of SOS, but .NET is not loaded in the debugging session, you can set a native breakpoint on the part of MScorwks.dll that does the first initialization of .NET. Once that breakpoint triggers, you'll have MScorwks.dll loaded and the bare minimum of .NET initialized so the commands in SOS will work.

The trick is to use the *bu* (Set Unresolved Breakpoint) command. With *bu*, you're telling WinDBG to set a breakpoint so that every time a module comes into the address space, the debugger will look to see if that module contains the specified breakpoint, and if it does, WinDBG will set an active breakpoint on that location.

The command you'll use to set the breakpoint on .NET initialization is:

```
bu mscorwks!EEStartup "gu;.loadby sos mscorwks"
```

After the *bu* command are two parameters. The first is the method to break on. In this case, it's the *EEStartup* native method in MScorwks.dll. Obviously, you need the symbols to the .NET Framework in your symbol server in order for this address to work.

The second command to *bu*, delineated by the double quotes, contains the commands we want run when the breakpoint triggers. Inside the quotes are two commands. The first is the *gu* (Go Up) command, which is similar to the g command I discussed earlier. The *gu* command sets a breakpoint on the return address of the current function so execution will stop after the current function executes. For our needs, that will stop execution in the function that called *EEStartup*. If you've been around WinDBG for a while, you might remember the g @$ra command, which is identical.

We're taking advantage of the power of WinDBG because the address in MScorwks.dll that makes the call to *EEStartup* will change with every build. The *gu* allows us to generalize no matter what version of MScorwks.dll you'll be running in the future.

The second command executed at the breakpoint is the familiar command to load SOS.dll. It's safe to do the load as part of the breakpoint because the breakpoint executes only when

MScorwks.dll is already loaded in the address space so the *.loadby* command can use the path where MScorwks.dll resides.

The last item I wanted to mention about the breakpoint approach to loading SOS is that some documentation shows a similar command to the one I presented but uses the *bp* (Set Breakpoint) command. The differences between the *bp* and *bu* commands are minimal except for one: *bu* commands are saved with WinDBG workspace, whereas *bp* commands are not. I like WinDBG to behave as Visual Studio and save my breakpoints across debugging sessions.

Loading SOS into Visual Studio

Loading SOS into Visual Studio is supported on x86 platforms only much as mixed-mode debugging is supported only on x86. Although the 32-bit Visual Studio runs fine on x64, it's essentially doing remote debugging to debug the 64-bit version of the runtime. As a 32-bit process, the debugger can't load the 64-bit version of the SOS DLL.

The other limitation for loading SOS is that you have to be doing either native-only or mixed-mode debugging in order for SOS to load. I discussed how to set up for mixed-mode debugging in the "Mixed-Mode Debugging" section of Chapter 5, "Advanced Debugger Usage with Visual Studio," so I won't repeat it here. Also, note that when you open a minidump file in Visual Studio, by selecting Open Solution on the File menu, the minidump is treated as a native minidump, so you can load SOS into Visual Studio in order to look at the .NET portions.

SOS can be loaded only once you've started debugging, so either single-step into the application or break into the debugger. Once stopped, switch to the Immediate window because that's the only place where SOS can be loaded. In the Immediate window, type the command *.load sos*. Visual Studio's *.load* command is equivalent to the *.loadby* in WinDBG, so it properly loads the version of SOS for the currently loaded framework. If you want to force SOS.dll to load out of a different directory, you can also pass the complete file name to the *.load* command. If SOS loads correctly, the output will be the file path where SOS was loaded from.

As with WinDBG, you'll have to load SOS each time you start debugging. Once it's loaded, you have full access to all the SOS commands just as I'll discuss through the rest of the chapter. If you're more comfortable with the Immediate pane of Visual Studio, you can use it to issue all your SOS commands, but you'll find that all the extra commands available in WinDBG are well worth the effort. You'll find that the more SOS debugging you do, the more you'll use WinDBG.

Getting Help and Using Commands

If you did a search in the WinDBG documentation, you ran into only a single page that discusses SOS and managed debugging. At the time of this writing, the page consists of the briefest overviews of what managed code is and a paragraph on how to load SOS for .NET 1.1.

The first command you'll want to run (and run and run and run) after loading SOS is *!help*. It's the only documentation on SOS, and it's actually not too bad. Running *!help* will show you the list of documented commands supported by WinDBG. For more information on a specific command, type the particular command after *!help*, and you'll get more information about that command. There's an option in the SOS help command output called *FAQ*, and if you pass that to *!help*, you'll see that it's a list of frequently asked questions.

The *!help* command shows the SOS commands in a mixed-case mode, that is, *!ClrStack*. Traditionally, WinDBG extension commands are all lowercase. SOS supports both the mixed case as shown by the Help and the all lowercase.

Some of the old WinDBG hands out there might remember that other extensions provide their own *!help* commands. When you issue an extension command, WinDBG looks down the list of loaded extensions as reported by the *.chain* command. The first matching export command is the one that's run.

To tell WinDBG to run a particular command out of a specific extension DLL, use the format: *!dll name.command*. To get the help out of the default loaded Ext.dll, the command would be *!ext.help*. It's rare that extensions overload commands, but *!help* always is overloaded.

A moment ago, I mentioned that *!help* shows you the documented commands. Some of you may be wondering if there are any undocumented commands in your particular version of SOS. WinDBG extensions are native DLLs that expose their commands as standard exported functions, so it's easy to take a peek.

If you installed the C++ compiler as part of your Visual Studio installation, the default installation includes Dependency Walker (Depends.exe), which you can use to view exported functions from a native binary. If you haven't installed the tools, you can download Dependency Walker from *http://www.dependencywalker.com*. After you open SOS.dll, highlight SOS.dll, and the exported functions list of the Dependency Walker display will show all the functions exported from SOS.

You can easily look through the exported functions list and compare what's exported to what's listed by the *!help* command. In the version I'm currently using, there's an exported function called *!tst*. Executing *!tst* does the same thing as the *!clrstack* command we'll talk about in a moment.

Of course, at this point I need to issue the official "Hacker Warning." Microsoft may have meant to document the command but just forgot. In that case, it's our gain. However, don't hold me responsible if executing the command reformats your hard disk, ruins the paint on your car, or causes your dog to run away from home. If the command does turn out to do something worthwhile, please let others know about it.

Now that I've gotten the most important SOS command, *!help*, out of the way, it's time to turn to the real commands. I'll discuss the various commands in the general order you'll run them on minidumps you'll get from customers.

Program State and Managed Threads

The first command you'll run will be *!eeversion*, which tells you the version of the .NET run-time currently loaded in the process or minidump. You can get the same information from the *lm v m mscorwks* command, but *!eeversion* will tell you if the CLR is in workstation mode, in which all CPUs on the system share a garbage-collected thread, or server mode, in which there's one garbage-collected heap for each CPU.

When doing live debugging with SOS loaded, and you want to take a quick look at the process memory usage, kernel times, and environment variables, you can use the *!procinfo* command. Although there are other commands inside WinDBG to show those pieces of information, you have to wade through the output of three separate commands. With *!procinfo*, you get all that data in one place. If you want to see just one piece of information from *!procinfo*, pass *-mem*, *-time*, or *-env* as the parameter to the command.

If you're doing interop with COM components that are single-threaded apartments, you can use the *!comstate* command to see information about the apartments running on each thread. The important piece of information is the thread ID of the thread calling into a particular apartment so you can track down potential deadlocks. Although you might be wishing that COM would just go away, it will be with us until the end of time.

!threads Command

Seeing the threads that are running managed code is as simple as issuing the *!threads* command. As it stands today, .NET is implemented with each managed thread corresponding to a native thread. Future versions of .NET may implement threads as fibers or some other threading mechanism. The *!threads* command is also one of the few commands that will also work when you're looking at a basic memory minidump.

Using an application that calls only *Trace.WriteLine* and is stopped in WinDBG with an *sxe out*, the thread command looks like the following:

```
0:000> !threads
ThreadCount: 2
UnstartedThread: 0
BackgroundThread: 1
PendingThread: 0
DeadThread: 0
Hosted Runtime: no
                           PreEmptive        GC Alloc      Lock
     ID OSID ThreadOBJ State     GC      Context  Domain   Count APT Exception
0    1  e88  001b4a40   a020 Enabled 01d39400:01d3a350 00157940  1  MTA
2    2  a94  001b5be0   b220 Enabled 00000000:00000000 00157940  0  MTA (Finalizer)
```

The first part of the output shows statistics about the managed threads in the process. UnstartedThread lists the number of threads created, but the application has not called the *Start* method yet.

The *BackgroundThread* field indicates the number of threads that have the *IsBackground* property set to true. You will always see a minimum of one background thread because the finalizer thread is always a background thread. If you know you are setting *IsBackground* to true, it's a good idea to compare the number you see in this field to what you expect in the source code.

The DeadThread field should be zero in all cases. A dead thread, not to be confused with a follower of the band *Grateful Dead*, is a managed thread object that has not been garbage collected and the backing native thread has ended. You may stop in the debugger or minidump and see one or two dead threads if your timing is right.

However, if you have more than a couple of threads listed in the DeadThread field, you have a serious problem. That means you have finalizer threads that have blocked, so the runtime killed them. Because there are references to those thread objects in memory, the garbage collector can never clean them up.

After the statistics comes the data for each managed thread. The first column that is not labeled corresponds to the WinDBG native thread ID reported by the ~ command. For any .NET application, there will always be one pure native thread running: the garbage collector thread.

If the value in the first column is XXXX, it means one of two things. If there is a number in the UnstartedThread statistics, the XXXX indicates those *Thread* objects whose *Start* method hasn't been called. If there are no threads waiting to start, the XXXX indicates the dead threads of blocked finalizers.

The ID column is the ID for the managed thread, which is the same value returned by the *Thread.ManagedThreadId* property. You'll never use the managed thread ID anywhere when using SOS. The OSID column indicates the operating system thread ID. A value of 0 next to an XXX thread because there's no native thread associated with the managed portion. The ThreadOBJ column is the actual *Thread* object in memory.

The State column contains a bit field that describes the state of the thread at a given time. Table 6-2 shows the bit field meanings that come from the Rotor source code. If you're not familiar with Rotor, it's the code name for the Shared Source Common Language Infrastructure project, which Microsoft released to show a European Computer Manufacturers Association (ECMA) implementation of C# and the Common Language Runtime (CLR). You can download the code at *http://www.microsoft.com/downloads/details.aspx?FamilyId=8C09FD61-3F26-4555-AE17-3121B4F51D4D&displaylang=en*. Because the code for Rotor is very close to the real CLR on your computer, it's an excellent place to look for implementation details.

Not all the values in the State are useful, but overall, the number can tell you some very interesting information about the thread. If you're looking for a nice project, a tool or WinDBG extension that would take the thread state and display all the actual values would be useful.

Table 6-2   *!Threads* State Bit Definitions

Flag	Bit Value	Definition
TS_Unknown	0x00000000	Uninitialized thread.
TS_StopRequested	0x00000001	Process stop at next opportunity.
TS_GCSuspendPending	0x00000002	Waiting to get to safe spot for GC.
TS_UserSuspendPending	0x00000004	User suspension at next opportunity.
TS_DebugSuspendPending	0x00000008	Is the debugger suspending threads?
TS_GCOnTransitions	0x00000010	Force a GC on stub transitions (GCStress only).
TS_LegalToJoin	0x00000020	Is it now legal to attempt a *Join()*?
TS_Hijacked	0x00000080	Return address has been hijacked.
TS_Background	0x00000200	Thread is a background thread.
TS_Unstarted	0x00000400	Thread has never been started.
TS_Dead	0x00000800	Thread is dead.
TS_WeOwn	0x00001000	Exposed object initiated this thread.
TS_CoInitialized	0x00002000	*CoInitialize* has been called for this thread.
TS_InSTA	0x00004000	Thread hosts an STA.
TS_InMTA	0x00008000	Thread is part of the MTA.
TS_ReportDead	0x00010000	In *WaitForOtherThreads()*.
TS_SyncSuspended	0x00080000	Suspended via *WaitSuspendEvent*.
TS_DebugWillSync	0x00100000	Debugger will wait for this thread to sync.
TS_RedirectingEntryPoint	0x00200000	Redirecting entry point. Do not call managed entry point when set.
TS_SuspendUnstarted	0x00400000	Latch a user suspension on an unstarted thread.
TS_ThreadPoolThread	0x00800000	Is this a threadpool thread?
TS_TPWorkerThread	0x01000000	Is this a threadpool worker thread? (If not, it is a threadpool completion port thread?)
TS_Interruptible	0x02000000	Sitting in a *Sleep() Wait() Join()*.
TS_Interrupted	0x04000000	Was awakened by an interrupt APC.
TS_AbortRequested	0x08000000	Same as *TS_StopRequested* in order to trip the thread.
TS_AbortInitiated	0x10000000	Set when abort is begun.
TS_UserStopRequested	0x20000000	Set when a user stop is requested. This is different from *TS_StopRequested*.
TS_GuardPageGone	0x40000000	Stack overflow not yet reset.
TS_Detached	0x80000000	Thread was detached by *DllMain*.

The PreEmptive GC column indicates if the thread is interruptible for a garbage collection. The *GC Alloc Context* field reports the synchronization object used by the garbage collector to synchronize access. If the values reported are something other than zero, you're running on a multiprocessor machine. The finalizer thread, unstarted threads, and dead threads will always have zero in this field. The Domain column shows the application domain that owns the thread in the process. You can use the *!dumpdomain* command, which I'll discuss later, to look at the domain itself.

The Lock Count column is extremely important because it shows the locks the thread has acquired. In the example I used, thread 0 has a lock because of the call to *Trace.WriteLine* where we are stopped on because of *sxe out*. You may not realize that the *Trace* object serializes execution to call all the *TraceListeners* in the *Listeners* collection one at a time. If you are tracking down a deadlock in your code, this is the first column you want to look at for potential problems.

The penultimate column, APT, shows the COM apartment-threading model. This is the same data displayed in the *!comstate* command. The final column lists the exception that the thread is currently processing. The column displays more information in parenthesis to help you identify a thread. As you can guess, the (Finalizer) string indicates the finalizer thread, and the other values are self-explanatory. If you see (GC), that shows that the thread has requested a garbage collection.

!ThreadPool Command

If you are using thread pools in your application, you can use the *!threadpool* command to take a look at its state. The following shows a program that has 63 threads in the thread pool:

```
0:018> !threadpool
CPU utilization 0%
Worker Thread: Total: 63 Running: 32 Idle: 31 MaxLimit: 100 MinLimit: 63
Work Request in Queue: 4
QueueUserWorkItemCallback DelegateInfo@000000001a65c070
QueueUserWorkItemCallback DelegateInfo@000000001a6d69f0
QueueUserWorkItemCallback DelegateInfo@000000001a65df50
QueueUserWorkItemCallback DelegateInfo@000000001a65ed40
--------------------------------------
Number of Timers: 0
--------------------------------------
Completion Port Thread:Total: 0 Free: 0 MaxFree: 8 CurrentLimit: 0
                                       MaxLimit: 1000 MinLimit: 63
```

The *CPU utilization* field shows the machine CPU utilization, not the process. The Worker Thread row shows totals for the threads in the pool. In the output, four items on the work queue have yet to be processed. If there are no items to queue or callback timers to complete, you won't see any output there. The final line shows the I/O completion port threads currently running. In ASP.NET applications, you can change the number of I/O completion port threads by setting the *maxIoThreads* and *minIOThreads* attributes in the *processModel* element of Machine.Config.

Managed Call Stacks

As any programmer will tell you, knowing what's on the stack is all important. Whereas looking at the values of locals and parameters on the stack is trivial with Visual Studio, it's a bit of an adventure with SOS.

!ClrStack Command

The primary command for looking at a managed stack is *!clrstack*. All it takes is switching to the thread you want to walk and issuing the command.

```
0:000> !clrstack
OS Thread Id: 0x49c (0)
ESP       EIP
0012f2f8 7c81eb33 [NDirectMethodFrameStandalone: 0012f2f8]
   Microsoft.Win32.SafeNativeMethods.OutputDebugString(System.String)
0012f308 7a61413b
   System.Diagnostics.DefaultTraceListener.internalWrite(System.String)
0012f310 7a61408c
   System.Diagnostics.DefaultTraceListener.Write(System.String, Boolean)
0012f328 7a614172
   System.Diagnostics.DefaultTraceListener.WriteLine(System.String)
0012f334 7a61aa95 System.Diagnostics.TraceInternal.WriteLine(System.String)
0012f370 7a618125 System.Diagnostics.Trace.WriteLine(System.String)
0012f374 02e109fb ArgParser..ctor(System.String[], Boolean, System.String[])
0012f388 02e10998 ArgParser..ctor(System.String[])
0012f398 02e10921 WordCountArgParser..ctor()
0012f3ac 02e100fd App.Main(System.String[])
0012f6b8 796cfabb [GCFrame: 0012f6b8]
```

The above output is from an x86 system and is nearly identical to what you would see with an x64 call stack. The top of the stack on an x64 system does not show the call through interop to *OutputDebugString*, but it will show the following instead indicating the interop function call: *DomainBoundILStubClass.IL_STUB(System.String)*.

Whereas, especially on native x86 code, you may not get the complete stack because you're missing symbol files, you will always get the complete managed call stack with *!clrstack* as long as some native code has not corrupted the stack itself. Seeing the parameter types makes a nice bonus.

To look at the parameter names and values, use the *-p* switch. Locals are displayed with *-l*, and both can be retrieved at the same time with the *-a* switch. In general, displaying parameters works, but occasionally, you'll see *<no data>* where you'd expect to see values. Local variables names are not displayed, but their memory locations and values are. When we get to the "Displaying Object Data" section later in this chapter, you'll see how to get even those items that the *!clrstack* command does not show. The following shows a portion of a *!clrstack -a* output:

```
0012f360 7a618125 System.Diagnostics.Trace.WriteLine(System.String)
    PARAMETERS:
        message = <no data>
```

```
0012f364 03020a50 ArgParser..ctor(System.String[], Boolean, System.String[])
    PARAMETERS:
        this = 0x00b01e5c
        switchSymbols = 0x00b01f50
        caseSensitiveSwitches = 0x00000000
        switchChars = 0x00b01f9c
    LOCALS:
        0x0012f364 = 0x00000002
        0x0012f368 = 0x00000000

0012f388 03020998 ArgParser..ctor(System.String[])
    PARAMETERS:
        this = 0x00b01e5c
        switchSymbols = 0x00b01f50
    LOCALS:
        <CLR reg> = 0x00b01f9c
```

The first item displayed shows the parameter name to the *Trace.WriteLine* method but does not display the data. The second item, *ArgParser..ctor*, properly shows the parameter names and values. The value after the *this* parameter is the object instance in memory and the address you'll need to dump the value. The parameters are shown in the order they are passed to the method. Therefore, the *caseSensitiveSwitches* is a *Boolean*, and you can see that its value is *false*. The local variables are shown at their stack addresses. The first address, 0x0012f364, has the value 0x2, which you can conclude is a value type instead of a memory location. The last item method shown, the one parameter version of *ArgParser..ctor,* shows a local variable that's in a register (enregistered) and not on the stack.

Back in the "Walking the Native Stack" section, I mentioned the nice trick of using the ~*e prefix on a command to execute the command for all threads in the process. I like to use ~*e!clrstack to get all the stacks walked at once so I can see a picture of the application in a few keystrokes.

!DumpStack Command

As we've already seen, there's not a complete way to get a mixed managed and native call stack. However, the *!dumpstack* command can come close. The command runs through the stack register and reports anything that looks like a return address for both native and managed methods. If you want to see just the managed stack output from *!dumpstack*, you can pass *-ee* to limit the output.

On x86 platforms, the output is quite verbose—there can be quite a bit of extraneous information on the stack, so you're going to have to carefully pick your way through. But you should be able to see the proper flow of the stack. If you're lucky enough to be running on an x64 platform, the fact that there's only a single calling convention for both native and managed means that the result of *!dumpstack* is the exact mixed stack. Feel free to use this as justification to your boss to get that dual-processor, dual-core Opteron you've always wanted. The output from *!dumpstack* on x64 for the call stack I showed with *!clrstack* is as follows:

```
0:000> !dumpstack
OS Thread Id: 0x98c (0)
Child-SP          RetAddr           Call Site
000000000012e550 0000000078d9fb19 KERNEL32!RaiseException+0x5c
000000000012e620 0000000078d9f743 KERNEL32!OutputDebugStringA+0x76
000000000012e920 0000000075ecce24 KERNEL32!OutputDebugStringW+0x42
000000000012e970 00000000794769e5 mscorwks!DoNDirectCall__PatchGetThreadCall+0x78
000000000012ea10 0000000079476b75 System_ni!DomainBoundILStubClass.IL_STUB(System.String)+0x65
000000000012eae0 0000000079476c11 System_ni!System.Diagnostics.DefaultTraceListener
.Write(System.String, Boolean)+0xb5
000000000012eb40 0000000079467089 System_ni!System.Diagnostics.DefaultTraceListener
.WriteLine(System.String, Boolean)+0x51
000000000012eb80 000000001a751469 System_ni!System.Diagnostics.TraceInternal
.WriteLine(System.String)+0xe9
000000000012ec10 000000001a751327 WordCount!ArgParser..ctor(System.String[], Boolean,
System.String[])+0xf9
000000000012ec60 000000001a751236 WordCount!ArgParser..ctor(System.String[])+0xa7
000000000012ecb0 000000001a750535 WordCount!WordCountArgParser..ctor()+0x146
000000000012ed10 0000000075ecf422 WordCount!App.Main(System.String[])+0xc5
000000000012f080 0000000075d9cb5a mscorwks!CallDescrWorker+0x82
000000000012f0d0 0000000075d9afd3 mscorwks!CallDescrWorkerWithHandler+0xca
000000000012f170 0000000075cf09f3 mscorwks!MethodDesc::CallDescr+0x1b3
000000000012f3b0 0000000075e56775 mscorwks!ClassLoader::RunMain+0x287
000000000012f610 0000000075e2ebe8 mscorwks!Assembly::ExecuteMainMethod+0xb9
000000000012f900 0000000075e6a523 mscorwks!SystemDomain::ExecuteMainMethod+0x3f0
000000000012feb0 0000000075e78205 mscorwks!ExecuteEXE+0x47
000000000012ff00 000000007401a726 mscorwks!CorExeMain+0xb1
000000000012ff50 0000000078d5965c mscoree!CorExeMain+0x46
000000000012ff80 0000000000000000 KERNEL32!BaseProcessStart+0x29
```

!EEStack Command

I hope you are not tired of walking the stacks yet, but there is one more command, *!eestack*, you can use to see where you are. *!eestack* is identical to the command *~*e!dumpstack*. As you can probably guess, if you pass *-ee* to *!eestack*, that parameter will be passed in turn to each *!dumpstack* call executed on each thread.

Probably the main reason you'll be using *!eestack* is the interesting *-short* option. If specified, that tells *!eestack* to walk only threads that are interesting. In SOS's world, *interesting* threads are those that have acquired a lock, been hijacked in order to allow garbage collection to run, and are currently executing native code.

Displaying Object Data

As you've seen with the *!clrstack* command, SOS will tell you the location of an object in memory. You're going to spend the bulk of your time with SOS looking at those objects so you can see the state of your objects. The good news is that SOS comes with numerous commands that let you look at any object you want. The bad news is that unlike the wonderful Watch window in Visual Studio, in which you can drill deep down into an object with a few clicks, when it comes to SOS, you have to type the dumping commands repeatedly.

!DumpStackObjects (!dso) Command

A surprisingly useful command to get a quick look at what objects are used on the stack is *!dso*. In the following snippet of output, I've stopped on a CLR exception using the command *sxe clr* as discussed earlier.

```
0:000> !dso
OS Thread Id: 0x878 (0)
RSP/REG         Object          Name
000000000012d988 0000000001da49f0 System.ArgumentNullException
000000000012d9c0 0000000001da49f0 System.ArgumentNullException
000000000012d9e8 0000000001da49f0 System.ArgumentNullException
000000000012da78 0000000001da4b30 System.String
000000000012db98 0000000001da49f0 System.ArgumentNullException
000000000012dba0 0000000001da2b28 System.Windows.Forms.MouseEventArgs
000000000012dbb0 0000000001da49f0 System.ArgumentNullException
000000000012dc60 0000000001da49f0 System.ArgumentNullException
000000000012dc68 0000000001da2b28 System.Windows.Forms.MouseEventArgs
000000000012dc70 0000000001da49d0 System.String
000000000012dca0 0000000001da2b28 System.Windows.Forms.MouseEventArgs
000000000012dcc8 0000000001da2b28 System.Windows.Forms.MouseEventArgs
000000000012dcd0 0000000001da49f0 System.ArgumentNullException
000000000012dd08 0000000001d39630 System.Windows.Forms.Button
000000000012dd10 0000000001da49d0 System.String
000000000012dd20 0000000001d36c20 System.ComponentModel.EventHandlerList
```

As you look down the Object column, you're looking at the in-memory instances of your classes. Because this is dumping values that are parameters and locals all the way down the current thread stack, you're going to see object addresses that are the same, such as the *ArgumentNullException*, because that object is passed around from method to method.

You're probably wondering about the value of *!dso* because *!clrstack* will pinpoint the actual parameters and locals in their correct locations. *!clrstack* shows you the specifically referenced objects, but it doesn't show you all the objects. In the output for the *!dso* command, I mentioned that the application is stopped in WinDBG on an exception. Look carefully at the first part of the output from the *!clrstack* command issued at that same location:

```
0:000> !clrstack -a
OS Thread Id: 0x878 (0)
Child-SP         RetAddr          Call Site
000000000012dd20 000000001abf2322 ExceptionMaker.MainForm.DoSomethingQuick(System.String)
    PARAMETERS:
        this = 0x0000000001d02130
        msg = 0x0000000000000000
    LOCALS:
        0x000000000012dd40 = 0x0000000000000000
```

```
000000000012dd60 000000007a682ff6 ExceptionMaker.MainForm.buttonArgNull_Click(System.Object,
  System.EventArgs)
    PARAMETERS:
        this = 0x0000000001d02130
        sender = 0x0000000001d39630
        e = 0x0000000001da2b28
    LOCALS:
        0x000000000012dd88 = 0x0000000000000000

000000000012ddd0 000000007a8d5717 System.Windows.Forms.Control.OnClick(System.EventArgs)
    PARAMETERS:
        this = <no data>
        e = <no data>
    LOCALS:
        <no data>
```

Did you notice any objects that you saw in the *!dso* output that are not in the *!clrstack -a* output? If you realized there was no *ArgumentNullException*, you get a gold star. The *!clrstack* command shows you only the managed stack, but the CLR itself can create objects in its native side that you work with, and you'll see them with *!dso*. In my example, a *!dumpstack* command shows that the item up the stack from *MainForm.DoSomethingQuick* is *mscorwks!JIT_Throw*, which, as you can tell by the name, is the native method that allocates the throw.

As does the *!dumpstack* command, *!dso* grinds through the stack pointer for the current thread and can potentially report false positive values. You can pass the *-verify* option to *!dso* so it will look at each potential object it finds and double-check the objects in any of its instance fields to ensure that those references are valid. However, in most cases, seeing corrupted objects dumped is good because you can look through the displayed objects for bad data.

There are two things that I've found odd about *!dso* on different platforms: On x86, it will show you the string value of a *System.String*, but not on x64. That's quite a time-saving option, so I hope that Microsoft will eventually add that to the x64 version of SOS. The other is that I end up using *!dso* quite a bit because it's faster than *!clrstack -a*, and when you are looking for a particular type instance, it's very convenient.

!DumpObj (*!do*) Command

Once you have an object instance address from *!clrstack* or *!dso*, you'll use *!do* to look at that object. Familiarize yourself with *!do* because you're going to be using it all the time. In the following example, I stopped in a catch block handling a *FileNotFoundException*. Using *!dso*, I got the instance address of the *FileNotFoundException* to dump it out:

```
0:000> !do 00b46080
Name: System.IO.FileNotFoundException
MethodTable: 78c991a4
EEClass: 78c99124
Size: 84(0x54) bytes

(C:\WINDOWS\assembly\GAC_32\mscorlib\2.0.0.0__b7a5c561934e089\mscorlib.dll)
```

```
Fields:
      MT      Field   Offset              Type VT      Attr   Value Name
78c74cd4   40000b4       4        System.String  0 instance 00000000 _className
78c7bd50   40000b5       8  ...ection.MethodBase  0 instance 00000000 _exceptionMethod
78c74cd4   40000b6       c        System.String  0 instance 00000000 _exceptionMethodString
78c74cd4   40000b7      10        System.String  0 instance 00b462b0 _message
78c71c48   40000b8      14  ...tions.IDictionary  0 instance 00000000 _data
78c7538c   40000b9      18     System.Exception  0 instance 00000000 _innerException
78c74cd4   40000ba      1c        System.String  0 instance 00000000 _helpURL
78c746a0   40000bb      20        System.Object  0 instance 00b46580 _stackTrace
78c74cd4   40000bc      24        System.String  0 instance 00000000 _stackTraceString
78c74cd4   40000bd      28        System.String  0 instance 00000000 _remoteStackTraceString
78c78d60   40000be      34         System.Int32  0 instance        0 _remoteStackIndex
78c746a0   40000bf      2c        System.Object  0 instance 00000000 _dynamicMethods
78c78d60   40000c0      38         System.Int32  0 instance -2147024894 _HResult
78c74cd4   40000c1      30        System.String  0 instance 00000000 _source
78c78208   40000c2      3c        System.IntPtr  0 instance        0 _xptrs
78c78d60   40000c3      40         System.Int32  0 instance -532459699 _xcode
78c74cd4   4001b78      44        System.String  0 instance 00000000 _maybeFullPath
78c74cd4   4001b94      48        System.String  0 instance 00b38cfc _fileName
78c74cd4   4001b95      4c        System.String  0 instance 00000000 _fusionLog
```

The header part of the *!do* starts with the fully qualified name of the object. The *MethodTable* field is the address for the metadata description for this object. You can think of *MethodTable* as the behavior of an object, while the instance data is the state. Another analogy for the MethodTable, in C++ terms, is that it's similar to a v-table. After the MethodTable comes the EEClass, which is the data structure that describes a type in terms of jitting and other internal data. In the "Meta Dumping Commands" section later in the chapter, I'll describe the commands you can use to look at these data structures, which you will rarely use.

The *Size* field is important from *!do*, but a little misleading. The size reported is the amount of memory for the object itself, exclusive of what is referenced by the object. In essence, the size reported is that of the C# *sizeof* operator or a Microsoft Visual Basic *LenB* function. However, the actual memory used by the object, which would account for objects the class contains, such as strings, is reported by the *!objsize* command as 1008 bytes. I'll talk much more about the *!objsize* command in the "Looking At the GC Heaps" section after this one.

After the module where this type is loaded comes all the field data. There is a parameter to *!do*, *-nofields*, which will turn off the field display. This is most useful for *String* types. As you look at the field output and you're wondering where the properties are, know that SOS doesn't display them because properties are syntactic sugar for methods. The Visual Studio debugger actually uses the CLR Debugging API's *Eval* method to execute the property methods in your object. SOS cannot execute anything on your object; it's just a display mechanism.

Each displayed field starts with the MT column, which is the MethodTable for the field type. Although the Type column in the *!dumpobj* output shows the .NET type name for the field, the column will display only the last 17 characters of the name. To see the full name, you'll pass the value of the MethodTable column to the *!dumpmt* command, which shows the type metadata. The Field column lists the metadata value for the individual field, which you can see using ILDASM as I described earlier.

The first slightly interesting column is the Offset column. You can probably guess from the name that these are memory offsets from the beginning of the object where the field appears in memory. SOS does not support the option of entering *object address.field_name*, but if you know the offset of the field name you want to always look at, you can add the offset to the address to look at that individual field. For example, if you wanted to be extremely hard core and look at the *_message* field, which is at offset 0x10 in the *FileNotFoundException*, you could issue the command *!do poi(00b46080+10)*. The *poi* option in the command stands for *pointer to integer* and is the WinDBG way of doing a (DWORD_PTR)(*(DWORD_PTR*)(00b46080+10) as you would in C++. Don't worry, I just wanted to show you how the offsets worked; there are much easier ways to look at fields!

After the Offset column is the Type column. This column is much improved in .NET 2.0's version of SOS compared to previous versions. As you can see, it shows the actual type of the field. Previous instances of SOS showed either the value type name or the word CLASS, which indicated an object. The VT column, which stands for Value Type, is related to the Type column. If the value in the VT column is 1 (one), the field is an instance of a value type structure. That information becomes important in order to dump the fields, as we'll discuss in a moment.

The Attr column is the type of storage for the field. In the example shown earlier, all the values were *instance*, which means they are instance data attributed to the class in memory. The value *CLStatic* indicates a field that has the *ContextStaticAttribute* class applied to it so the value is unique per context, which you can define by applying the *ContextStaticAttribute* to a field. I doubt any of you are using *ContextStaticAttribute*, but if you are, know that SOS does not support showing the values of those fields. A value of *TLstatic* indicates that the *ThreadStaticAttribute* is applied to the field so the field has thread local storage for all threads across all domains. The following is the partial output of a *!do* command on a *TLStatic* field:

```
      MT    Field    Offset              Type VT    Attr     Value Name
749e0320  4000005       0     System.String  0 TLstatic  threadLocalField
    >> Thread:Value 808:01d0d260 da0:01d0d260 <<
```

Below the field line are the different object instances for the threads in the system. In the example output, two different threads have instantiated this class, and the values after *Thread:Value* are the Windows native thread ID to the left of the colon and the memory address for the thread instance. If you wanted to look at the instance data for thread 0xDA0, you'd issue the command *!do 01d0d260*.

You can guess that a value of *static* in the Attr column is a field marked as static in C# (or Shared in Visual Basic). There's another type of static value you'll see in the Attr column: *shared*. The *shared* display means that the field has the *readonly/ReadOnly* keyword specified. A read-only static means that the value is unique across application domains. Thus, those fields, as does *TLStatic*, appear differently in the *!do* output:

```
      MT    Field    Offset              Type VT    Attr     Value Name
749e0320  4000098      20     System.String  0    shared         static Empty
                >> Domain:Value   00157950:74989600 1a632320:74989600 <<
```

In the output, two application domains have instances of this field. The first domain instance is at 00157950, and the second is at 1a632320. We'll discuss it more in a little bit, but you can use the *!dumpdomain* command to look at individual domain instances. The number following the domain is the instance in memory for that shared field, which you'll use the *!do* command on if you want to look at them.

One issue I've found with seeing shared static fields is that SOS seems to display the *shared* value in the Attr column only if the assembly is in the GAC. If you are looking at an object instance that's not in the GAC, you'll see only *static* in the Attr column. In order to see the individual instances for each domain, you have to look for the type in the heap, dump each value in turn, and look for the different instance data for each domain. I'll discuss how to find and dump memory in the "Looking at the GC Heaps" section later in this chapter.

The last column, Name, is the field name as you probably guessed, but the second-to-last column, Value, is the most interesting. If the field is a value type instance such as an Int32, you'll see the actual value of the field. In the *FileNotFoundException* I dumped out many pages ago, the _HResult field has a value of −2,147,024,894. Whereas the rest of WinDBG displays everything in hexadecimal by default, SOS shows all value types as decimal. If you are good at number base conversions in your head, you'd see that value is 0x80070002. If you have a photographic memory, you may remember that this Windows error code translates into "The system cannot find the file specified" and certainly fits with a *FileNotFoundException*.

Because I certainly don't have any of those characteristics, I used the WinDBG extension command, *!error*, which converts a number into the error string with the command *!error −0n2147024894*. The 0n is necessary because the number is decimal, and as I mentioned back in the "Attaching to and Detaching from Processes in the Command Window" section, 0n is the ANSI numeric code for decimal.

If the field is a reference type object, the number displayed in the Value column is the in-memory instance referenced by the field. Do you have any guess as to how you'll look at that value? It's with another call to *!do*, of course. Welcome to the fun world of viewing data in SOS. Previous versions of SOS had a wonderful -r option to *!do* that allowed you to set the recursion level so you could dump out multiple levels with minimal typing. If you're looking for a great project that will win you many plaudits in the development community, a WinDBG extension called *!RecursiveDumpObject* would be greatly appreciated.

!DumpVC Command

In your poking at instances with *!do*, you're going to run into a couple things that *!do* doesn't handle. The first I've already hinted at when I mentioned the VT column in the *!do* output. In the following dump, the VT column is set to one, which means that the field is a value type structure:

```
0:000> !do 01d01ab0
Name: ArraysAndValues.Program+DataCoordinate
MethodTable: 1a5f1040
```

```
EEClass: 1a7235a0
Size: 32(0x20) bytes
 (C:\dev\Program\bin\Debug\ArraysAndValues.exe)
Fields:
      MT    Field Offset                 Type VT     Attr     Value Name
1a5f0fc0  4000004       8 ...rogram+Coordinate  1 instance 01d01ab8 coords
```

The command *!do 01d01ab8* spits out that the object is invalid. To see value types, you need to use the *!dumpvc* command. *vc* stands for *value class*.

The *!dumpvc* command needs a little more information beyond the value instance in order to function. It also needs the MethodTable address before the instance address. The following shows the correct execution to dump the *DataCoordinate* instance. In the *Type* field, you see the + sign in the string ...rogram+Coordinate. That indicates that *Coordinate* is a nested structure or class in *ArraysAndValues.Program*.

```
0:000> !dumpvc 1a5f0fc0  01d01ab8
Name: ArraysAndValues.Program+Coordinate
MethodTable 1a5f0fc0
EEClass: 1a723648
Size: 32(0x20) bytes
(C:\dev\Program\bin\Debug\ArraysAndValues.exe)
Fields:
      MT    Field   Offset          Type VT      Attr        Value Name
749ec9a0  4000001        0   System.Int32  0 instance        101 x
749ec9a0  4000002        4   System.Int32  0 instance        505 y
749ec9a0  4000003        8   System.Int32  0 instance         98 z
```

!DumpArray Command

If you're looking at a *Generic.Dictionary* instance, the private field, *entries*, contains the actual values in the *Dictionary*. Dumping an *entries* field instance shows the following:

```
0:000> !do 00b01e7c
Name: System.Collections.Generic.Dictionary`2+Entry[[System.String,
                            mscorlib],[System.String, mscorlib]][]
MethodTable: 78cab650
EEClass: 78cab708
Size: 124(0x7c) bytes
Array: Rank 1, Number of elements 7, Type VALUETYPE
Element Type: System.Collections.Generic.Dictionary`2+Entry[[System.String,
                            mscorlib],[System.String, mscorlib]]
Fields:
None
```

The output tells us that this is an array and the type is of *Dictionary.Entry<String, String>* and there are seven elements in the array. That's nice, but it doesn't show us the elements. When confronted with an array, the *!dumparray* command saves us from manually having to look at memory to piece together what's in it:

```
0:000> !dumparray 00b01e7c
Name: System.Collections.Generic.Dictionary`2+Entry[[System.String,
                            mscorlib],[System.String, mscorlib]][]
```

```
MethodTable: 78cab650
EEClass: 78cab708
Size: 124(0x7c) bytes
Array: Rank 1, Number of elements 7, Type VALUETYPE
Element Methodtable: 78cab788
[0] 00b01e84
[1] 00b01e94
[2] 00b01ea4
[3] 00b01eb4
[4] 00b01ec4
[5] 00b01ed4
[6] 00b01ee4
```

There are three very nice options to the *!dumparray* command. If you want to display the values of the array entries, specify *-detail* before the object address that will use the *!do* or *!dumpvc* commands as appropriate to show the elements. As with *!do*, *!dumparray* supports the *-nofields* switch to skip object field display. Also very useful are the *-start* and *-length* options, which take the index to start dumping at and the number of elements to dump, respectively. One word of caution is that the *-start* and *-length* options must be before *-detail* on the *!dumparray* command line or the values are ignored. The following shows dumping the detailed information from the third element in the array:

```
0:000> !dumparray -start 3 -length 1 -detail 00b01e7c
Name: System.Collections.Generic.Dictionary`2+Entry[[System.String, mscorlib],[System.String,
mscorlib]][]
MethodTable: 78cab650
EEClass: 78cab708
Size: 124(0x7c) bytes
Array: Rank 1, Number of elements 7, Type VALUETYPE
Element Methodtable: 78cab788
[3] 00b01eb4
    Name: System.Collections.Generic.Dictionary`2+Entry[[System.String, mscorlib],
[System.String, mscorlib]]
    MethodTable 78cab788
    EEClass: 78c9ee30
    Size: 24(0x18) bytes
    (C:\WINDOWS\assembly\GAC_32\mscorlib\2.0.0.0__b77a54e89\mscorlib.dll)
    Fields:
          MT    Field  Offset         Type VT     Attr     Value Name
    78c78d60  400097b       8  System.Int32  0 instance 256449012 hashCode
    78c78d60  400097c       c  System.Int32  0 instance         1 next
    78c746a0  400097d       0 System.Object  0 instance  00b01bf8 key
    78c746a0  400097e       4 System.Object  0 instance  00b01c14 value
```

Looking at the GC Heaps

After what seems like a million pages, we are finally up to the key reason for all the fun with WinDBG and SOS: getting information about what's where in the different GC heaps. For those of you who have used the version of SOS that comes with WinDBG for .NET 1.0 or 1.1 debugging, the bad news is that some of the commands have lost functionality in the .NET 2.0 version. You can still get at the same information, but you'll have to do more quick analysis and typing than before.

Before you dive headfirst into SOS and the garbage-collected heap, I'm assuming that you have a good understanding of all the generations, finalization, and how .NET manages the heap. The best discussion is in Chapter 20 in Jeffrey Richter's *CLR via C#*, Second Edition (Microsoft Press, 2005). If you don't have Jeffrey's book, which you should, you can also read his articles "Garbage Collection: Automatic Memory Management in the Microsoft .NET Framework" and "Garbage Collection Part 2: Automatic Memory Management in the Microsoft .NET Framework" in the November and December 2000 issues respectively of MSDN Magazine (*http://msdn.microsoft.com/msdnmag/issues/1100/gci/* and *http://msdn.microsoft.com/msdnmag/issues/1200/gci2/*).

!FinalizeQueue

The first of the GC Heap functions I want to look at, *!finalizequeue*, helps you keep an eye on the objects that implement one of the most misused items in .NET: finalizers. The basic rule of finalizer usage is "don't, except to wrap only a native resource." Adding a finalizer to your class means that on a GC sweep, if there are no references to the object with a finalizer, the object is moved to the freachable queue and will be cleaned up on the next GC sweep. In essence, an object that has a finalizer and is not disposed of manually by the programmer is promoted to the next GC level automatically.

Finalization is a normal part of .NET life, so it's normally not a problem. However, if you're misusing finalizable objects, say continually creating them in a tight loop without manually calling their *Dispose* or *Close* method when you're finished with them, you're putting pressure on the garbage collector. With all of .NET, every time a garbage collection triggers, all your .NET threads are suspended so you are getting less work done. Another problem you can encounter with finalizers is if your code is hanging the finalization thread. Keeping an eye on the objects in the finalize queue is extremely important.

There's a lot of nice information produced by *!finalizequeue*. The key values are how many finalizable objects there are in each GC generation and how many objects are ready to be finalized. You also get a nice listing of all the finalizable types sorted in size order in all the garbage-collected generations. The following shows the output with some of the types removed for clarity:

```
0:007> !finalizequeue
SyncBlocks to be cleaned up: 0
MTA Interfaces to be released: 0
STA Interfaces to be released: 0
----------------------------------
generation 0 has 129 finalizable objects (002038b0->00203ab4)
generation 1 has 50 finalizable objects (002037e8->002038b0)
generation 2 has 0 finalizable objects (002037e8->002037e8)
Ready for finalization 0 objects (00203ab4->00203ab4)
Statistics:
      MT    Count TotalSize Class Name
7b4946e0        1        16 System.Windows.Forms.Control+FontHandleWrapper
78c96338        1        16 System.LocalDataStoreSlot
```

```
7b48d344        1        20 System.Windows.Forms.ApplicationContext
7aeb317c        1        20 System.Drawing.FontFamily
. . .
7aeb32a0       11       396 System.Drawing.Graphics
7b493be8       18       504 System.Windows.Forms.Internal.WindowsGraphics
7b494c68       15       600 System.Windows.Forms.PaintEventArgs
7b4f1504       15      1080 System.Windows.Forms.MenuItem
Total 179 objects
```

If you want to look at the particular objects in a generation that are finalizable or ready for finalization, you can use the WinDBG *dd* (*Display DWORD*) or *dq* (*Display QWORD*) commands for x86 or x64 respectively. In the example, there are 50 objects with finalizers in the Gen 1 heap, and the array containing those objects is (002037e8->002038b0). Because the output above is for x86, I'll use the command *dd 002038b0 l 0n50*. The lower case "l," which indicates the number of elements to dump, and since the *!finalizequeue* reports 50 items, I pass *0n50* to indicate the decimal number that I want. Remember, WinDBG assumes that all numbers are hexadecimal so specifying the 0n has WinDBG dump the length you expect.

```
0:007> dd 002037e8 l 0n50
002037e8  00b111e8 00af2118 00b11228 00b11380
. . .
```

The first column displayed is the address, and the next four double words list the address in memory where instances of these objects are stored. Based on the last section, your Pavlovian response to seeing an object instance is to run *!do* on the address.

!EEHeap Command

Even though the idea of .NET is to let developers stop worrying about memory, the number one concern of .NET developers is their memory usage. If you have a process whose memory usage is spiking, you want to know at a glance if it's the .NET side of your application or some of the native code you're using. Fortunately, the *!eeheap* command makes finding your .NET usage trivial.

If you run *!eeheap* without any command-line options, you'll see the private heaps for each domain, the JIT compiler, modules, and the garbage-collected heaps. For developers working on the internals of .NET inside Microsoft, all of that information is valuable. The rest of us care only about the garbage-collected heap information. Fortunately, you can pass the *-gc* option to *!eeheap* to limit the output.

```
0:001> !eeheap -gc
Number of GC Heaps: 1
generation 0 starts at 0x00b5c3f0
generation 1 starts at 0x00b1f87c
generation 2 starts at 0x00af1000
ephemeral segment allocation context: (0x00bcdf24, 0x00bce3fc)
 segment    begin allocated      size
001b7b48 7a80b84c  7a82d1cc 0x00021980(137600)
001b7488 7b4729cc  7b4889c4 0x00015ff8(90104)
0018cc10 78c50df4  78c70520 0x0001f72c(128812)
```

```
00af0000 00af1000  00bce3fc 0x000dd3fc(906236)
Large object heap starts at 0x01af1000
 segment    begin allocated    size
01af0000 01af1000  01af6db0 0x00005db0(23984)
Total Size  0x13a250(1286736)
---------------------------
GC Heap Size  0x13a250(1286736)
```

There's a huge amount of information in that compact output. The most important is the very last line, which is the total size of all garbage-collected heaps in the process. In the example I've shown, there's only a single heap because the process is running with the workstation-optimized heap. If your process is running using the server heap, which you can enable by setting *<gcServer enabled="true" />* in the *<runtime>* element of App.Config or Machine.Config, you'll see a heap listed for each processor on the machine. The GC Heap Size field will show the totals for all the heaps in the process.

For each generational heap in the system, the *!eeheap* output shows you where generations 0, 1, and 2 all start in memory. A heap itself is broken up into various segments of memory that contain the actual objects themselves. As you'll see when we get to dumping the heap with *!dumpheap*, those addresses become critical to seeing very important information.

After the generational heap segments comes the location of this heap's large object heap. When you allocate objects large than 85,000 bytes, instead of putting them in the regular garbage-collected heaps, they are put in the large object heap. That way you don't pay the cost of moving those large chunks of memory on memory coalescing. Although adjacent free blocks in this heap are coalesced, the runtime does not pack memory in the large object heap because it is in the generational heaps.

Not packing the large object heap means that you can have situations in which your application is ending with an *OutOfMemoryException*, even though it looks as if you have plenty of memory left in the process address space. If given the right conditions for your large allocations, you can end up fragmenting the large object heap. In those cases, the *OutOfMemoryException* means that there's not a big enough free block in the large object heap. As with the generational heaps, the *!dumpheap* command lets you look at what's in the large object heap.

!DumpHeap Command

While you might spend more time typing the *!do* command to look at objects, you'll spend much more time staring at the output of *!dumpheap* than any other command in SOS. As you can guess from the name, *!dumpheap* is all heap inspection. Unfortunately, the command has taken a step backwards from previous versions of .NET, and as you'll see, it takes much more work to get different pieces of information.

You'll almost never want to run *!dumpheap* without a command-line option. If run by itself, *!dumpheap* will walk the entire garbage-collected heap dumping out the method table, the address, and size of each object. The final part of the output is the summary statistics showing the method table, count, total memory size, and name of each type. If you're looking at a minidump of a decent-sized ASP.NET application, *!dumpheap* might run long enough for you to go out for that cup of coffee and stay for a second or third cup.

If you do accidentally issue a *!dumpheap* command or any other long-running command in WinDBG, pressing Ctrl+Break in WinDBG is supposed to stop the command as I explained earlier on. Unfortunately, the extension command architecture in WinDBG says that it's up to the command writer to occasionally ask if the user has asked for the command to abort. Although it might take awhile, *!dumpheap* will eventually respond to the Ctrl+Break key sequence.

When first looking at a .NET heap, you'll want to use the *-stat* option with *!dumpheap* so you can see just the statistics about the heap. That will not dump each object, but you'll get the big picture of the minidump or live debugging session. Initially, you'll want to keep an eye on your classes and the types they contain when looking at the statistics. Don't be surprised that the largest objects reported by *-stat* are *String* instances or *Object* arrays. You're looking at the whole heap, so you are also looking at things created by the FCL or CLR in the heap.

To get a look at just the strings on the heap, you can pass the *-strings* option to *!dumpheap*. This option is great because it shows the first 63 characters of each string so you can easily see what strings you're dealing with. The count column is undocumented, but it seems to show the number of string objects that are string interned. *String interning* is when multiple *String* objects point to the same actual value in memory, which helps save memory.

```
0:007> !dumpheap -strings
total 10521 objects
Statistics:
   Count TotalSize String Value
       1         32 "||"
       1         32 "|2|"
 . . .
       1       5544 "??     value    : The object must be serialized into a
                    byte array"
       2       6288 "<PermissionSet class="System.Security.
                    NamedPermissionSet"versio"
       1       9648 "<NamedPermissionSets><PermissionSet
                    class="System.Security.Name"
Total 10521 objects
```

If you were ambitious enough to write a WinDBG extension that processed objects in the garbage-collected heap, the *-short* option to *!dumpheap* will save you a lot of parsing. All *-short* does is dump the address of the objects on the heap—it dumps no other data.

If you're in a job in which you're paid by the hour, what you'll want to do is dump out the entire heap and manually dump each address to find the individual large objects. The rest of us will want to use the *-min* switch to *!dumpheap*, which allows you to ask for the objects that meet a minimum size. In the following dump, I've asked for the objects of over 6,000 bytes. If you're interested only in the statistics, you can also add the *-stat* switch.

```
0:010> !dumpheap -min 6000
 Address        MT     Size
78c54bdc 78c74cd4     9640
00af39c4 78c9b180     8208
01af3250 78c9b180     6960
total 3 objects
Statistics:
      MT     Count TotalSize Class Name
78c74cd4        1      9640 System.String
78c9b180        2     15168 System.Object[]
Total 3 objects
```

There's also a *-max* switch where you can tell *!dumpheap* to dump all objects up to a specific size. In reality, you won't be using *-max* by itself because you'll be wading through a ton of output. You can combine *-min* and *-max* to look at all objects that are between specific sizes.

Although it would be trivial to dump the three objects in the last example, many times you'll get many objects no matter how you try to narrow the output with the *-min* and *-max* switches. The first column in the *!dumpheap* output shows the nearly ubiquitous method table for the object. The *-mt* switch takes the method table for an object so you can look just for specific values. Even more important, you can combine the *-mt* switch with the *-min* and *-max* switches to display just the key objects you're interested in seeing.

```
0:011> !dumpheap -min 6000 -mt 78c74cd4
 Address        MT     Size
78c54bdc 78c74cd4     9640
total 1 objects
Statistics:
      MT     Count TotalSize Class Name
78c74cd4        1      9640 System.String
Total 1 objects
```

If all we had was the *-mt* option, that would be nice, but you have to admit that manually hunting down a type's method table can be tedious. Fortunately, the *-type* switch makes *!dumpheap* drastically easier to use. The *-type* switch takes a partial string that appears in the fully qualified type name of the objects you are interested in finding in the heap. If the name of one of your classes is *ScatterGraph*, you'd add *-type ScatterGraph* to see just those classes. The comparison is a case-sensitive *String.Contains*, so there are no wildcard lookups. However, because it's just a string comparison, you can take advantage of tricks such as *-type []* to look for all the arrays in the process.

The last two *!dumpheap* options are the starting and ending addresses of a particular segment of the heap to dump. A perfect use for these options is to look at the large object heap. As I mentioned in the *!eeheap* discussion, the last part of the display shows the beginning and ending addresses of each segment in the heap. In the following partial output, the only segment of the large object heap begins at 0x01af1000 and ends at 0x01af6db0:

```
0:11> !eeheap -gc
. . .
Large object heap starts at 0x01af1000
 segment    begin allocated    size
01af0000 01af1000  01af6db0 0x00005db0(23984)
. . .
```

But wait! I've just explained that only objects larger than 85,000 bytes are stored in the large objects heap, and you see that the size of the segment is even less than that. In this example, because the program has not explicitly allocated any large objects on the heap, we need to use the *!dumpheap 01af1000 01af6db0* command to see by ourselves all the weird objects stored in this large object heap.

```
0:011> !dumpheap 01af1000  01af6db0
 Address       MT     Size
01af1000 001514f8       16 Free
01af1010 78c9b180     4096
01af2010 001514f8       16 Free
01af2020 78c9b180     4096
01af3020 001514f8       16 Free
01af3030 78c9b180      528
01af3240 001514f8       16 Free
01af3250 78c9b180     6960
01af4d80 001514f8       16 Free
01af4d90 78c9b180     4096
01af5d90 001514f8       16 Free
01af5da0 78c9b180     4096
01af6da0 001514f8       16 Free
total 13 objects
Statistics:
     MT    Count TotalSize Class Name
001514f8      7       112      Free
78c9b180      6     23872 System.Object[]
Total 13 objects
```

The first part of the large object heap always looks like the output above because the CLR needs to ensure that some key objects, such as the *OutOfMemoryException*, exist prior to usage. If a CLR allocation fails and the CLR has to then allocate garbage-collected space for the actual exception, some interesting and nasty things could happen. The most likely scenario if this were true is that the *OutOfMemoryException* allocation would fail, triggering another out-of-memory exception. At that point, depending on the implementation, the application would go into an infinite loop or simply disappear from memory. Neither scenario is very developer (or user) friendly.

The other reason to put these must-have objects in the large object heap is that to allocate them in the normal garbage-collected heaps would mean they would start out in generation 0 but be promoted over time to generation 2. This would cause more work for the CLR and negatively affect the overall performance of your application.

If you were paying attention during the discussion of *!eeheap*, you may be wondering why you see those small 16-byte free blocks when the smallest object that you are supposed to see in the large object heap is at least 85,000 bytes in size. Obviously, there's nothing you can poke in there that's ever going to fill those holes. Again, the start of the large object heap is a special area where the CLR tries to optimize. You'll notice that nearly all the object sizes are 4K, which is conveniently the page size for x86 and x64 versions of Windows. Your first large object appears after the last free block set up by the CLR.

Since we're talking about free blocks, I wanted to mention that when looking at the normal garbage-collected heaps, you may see a few when you dump the full garbage-collected heap depending where you stop in the debugger. If you have numerous free blocks because of memory problems, especially pinned memory, which we'll talk about in the *"!GCHandles Command"* section later in this chapter, running *!dumpheap* will report the problem after the statistics section.

In the example I've just shown, it was easy to see the complete large object heap because it was in a single segment. Depending on how many giant memory blobs you're allocating you will see situations, especially on computers running x64-based Windows versions, in which the large object heap will be spread across multiple segments as the following *!eeheap -gc* command shows. Since you can't specify multiple ranges to *!dumpheap*, you'll have to dump segments of the large object heap separately to see everything that's there.

```
0:005> !eeheap -gc
Number of GC Heaps: 1
generation 0 starts at 0x0000000001db9558
generation 1 starts at 0x0000000001da2068
. . .
Large object heap starts at 0x0000000011d01000
         segment          begin         allocated              size
0000000011d00000 0000000011d01000  0000000019c3e310 0x0000000007f3d310(133419792)
000000001bae0000 000000001bae1000  00000000232e13a8 0x00000000078003a8(125830056)
0000000024870000 0000000024871000  000000002c071180 0x0000000007800180(125829504)
000000002c870000 000000002c871000  000000002d771030 0x0000000000f00030(15728688)
Total Size         0x17ff3a08(402602504)
------------------------------
GC Heap Size       0x17ff3a08(402602504)
```

It's relatively easy to look at the large object heap, but that's not the number-one question that any developer that's looking at a minidump with SOS is going to ask. The real question is what's in my Gen 2 heap.

The garbage-collected heap is great, but if you hold on to objects too long, they make their way up to the part of the heap containing generation 2 objects, and your application starts chewing up more memory than necessary. As anyone who's looked at the # Gen *x* Collections performance counter (where *x* is 0, 1, or 2) from the .NET CLR Memory object knows, there are many order-of-magnitude generation 0 collections compared to generation 2 collections. If you have objects up in generation 2 that are ready to be collected because there are no more references in the application, they might be sitting there taking up space for quite a while before the CLR gets around to cleaning them up. It's vital that you have a solid idea of what's in your generation 2 memory so you can start looking at these memory-consumption problems.

My biggest complaint about the .NET 2.0 SOS is that we lost a killer feature compared to previous versions. It used to be a simple matter of using the *-gen* switch to *!dumpheap* to ask it to display the objects that belongs into a particular generation in the heap. Now, we have to grind through memory manually. We should all be filing bugs against the CLR team to bring the *-gen* switch back, because as you'll see, to do the analysis manually is extremely tedious and error prone.

To show you how to get at the generation 2 objects, I'll need to describe how the garbage collector lays out the generations in memory. Fortunately, our good friend, the *!eeheap* command, still shows us the key information:

```
0:011> !eeheap -gc
Number of GC Heaps: 1
generation 0 starts at 0x00b3e664
generation 1 starts at 0x00b20034
generation 2 starts at 0x00af1000
ephemeral segment allocation context: (0x00b83f94, 0x00b84670)
 segment    begin allocated    size
001b7b48 7a80b84c  7a82d1cc 0x00021980(137600)
001b7488 7b4729cc  7b4889c4 0x00015ff8(90104)
0018cc30 78c50df4  78c70520 0x0001f72c(128812)
00af0000 00af1000  00b84670 0x00093670(603760)
Large object heap starts at 0x01af1000
 segment    begin allocated    size
01af0000 01af1000  01af6db0 0x00005db0(23984)
Total Size   0xf04c4(984260)
-----------------------------
GC Heap Size   0xf04c4(984260)
```

It's easy to see where the actual generations start in memory simply by looking at the first part of the *!eeheap* output. As you'll see in a moment, that's where you'll start dumping memory to look at objects in the particular heaps. However, when you look down in the ephemeral segment section, things look a little odder. In the example output, there are four separate segments utilized, though there can be any number of ephemeral segments. A segment is simply a chunk of memory. In a perfect world, the entire garbage-collected heap would be one contiguous piece of memory from generation 0 through to the large object heap. The reality is that other assemblies and allocated memory from native code get in the way. Consequently, the .NET runtime allocates the garbage-collected heap in segments and strings them together to make up the whole.

The address ranges under the *begin* and *allocated* columns for each segment show each segment size. It's also interesting that the address ranges specified by the segments are diverse. The first three segments start at 0x7a80b84c, 0x7b4729cc, and 0x78c50df4, but the fourth starts at 0x00af1000. Only the last one seems to make sense because that's the starting address of generation 2.

Before dissecting the generational heap at 0x00af1000, let's explore the content of the first three heaps by using *!dumpheap*. Since we have address ranges for the pieces of the heap, we can pass those ranges to *!dumpheap* to see what's in each of them. The first three heaps all show the same basic information, a single object type followed by a slew of strings:

```
0:011> !dumpheap -stat 78c50df4  78c70520
total 2020 objects
Statistics:
      MT     Count TotalSize Class Name
78c746a0         1        12 System.Object
78c74cd4      2019    128800 System.String
Total 2020 objects
```

There's obviously something special about these three segments in the heaps. To list the objects larger than 400 bytes stored into the heaps, I ran the command *!dumpheap -min 400 78c50df4 78c70520* so I could dump a few of the strings to see what's in them. As I continued to look at a representative sampling of the strings on the heap, it shows that the strings on the heap are all the hard-coded strings used by the runtime itself. A perfect example is the full name of the System.Drawing assembly:

```
System.Drawing.Imaging.Metafile, System.Drawing, Culture=neutral, PublicKeyToken=
b03f5f7f11d50a3a
```

That leaves the last segment as the interesting one. If you have a great spatial mind, you can probably picture exactly what the heap looks like, but the rest of us challenged folks can view Figure 6-8 to see what the heap looks like in memory.

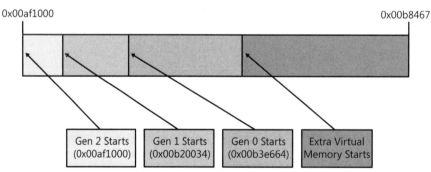

Figure 6-8   Last segment heap memory layout (not to scale)

The fact that the last segment of the heap starts at the same address as the generation 2 part of the heap makes it easy to find because it ends at the start of generation 1. Thus to see what objects are in the generation 2, the command is *!dumpheap -stat 0x00af1000 0x00b20034* using the values we've used all along. Using the values from the last heap segment to dump the content of the generation 2 does not show you all the objects in generation 2. All those string values needed by the CLR in the other segments reported by *!eeheap* are included in the generation 2 dump. However, for practical purposes, the part of the heap that you'll dump from the last segment for generation 2 contains all your objects in generation 2.

The content of generation 1 is easy to see also because it starts at 0x00b20034 and runs up to the start of the generation 0 at 0x00b3e664. Unfortunately, there's no way to tell where the generation 0 part ends, but dumping out the address range from the start of the generation 0 to the end of the heap will show everything that's in there. The problem is that the object in the extra virtual memory area could be reported also but it's already freed memory. Fortunately, you'd look at generation 0 relatively rarely.

What we've been looking at up to this point is a case in which you're running with the workstation heap, which has one heap for the whole process. If you're using the server implementation of heap management, which is anyone doing ASP.NET, and you're running on a multiple-CPU computer, your life just got much more interesting. Because there's one heap per CPU, your generation 2 heap is scattered across all the individual CPU heaps. The following partial output is from a four-CPU system, and you can get an idea of the work you'll have to do to get the content of generation 2:

```
0:011> !eeheap -gc
Number of GC Heaps: 4
------------------------------
Heap 0 (00000000001bc290)
generation 0 starts at 0x0000000080018688
generation 1 starts at 0x0000000080018670
generation 2 starts at 0x000000007fff0068
ephemeral segment allocation context: none
         segment           begin        allocated            size
000000000919b9f0 0000000079777868  00000000797ad410 0x0000000000035ba8(220072)
00000000091904c0 000000007adf52b8  000000007ae1f4d0 0x000000000002a218(172568)
000000000915a200 00000000749890a8  00000000749caf18 0x0000000000041e70(269936)
000000007fff0000 000000007fff0068  00000000800686a0 0x0000000000078638(493112)
Large object heap starts at 0x000000017fff0068
         segment           begin        allocated            size
000000017fff0000 000000017fff0068  000000017fffd758 0x000000000000d6f0(55024)
Heap Size           0x127958(1210712)
------------------------------
Heap 1 (00000000001bda50)
generation 0 starts at 0x00000000bfff4ca0
generation 1 starts at 0x00000000bfff4ba0
generation 2 starts at 0x00000000bfff0068
ephemeral segment allocation context: none
         segment           begin        allocated            size
00000000bfff0000 00000000bfff0068  00000000c004ecb8 0x000000000005ec50(388176)
Large object heap starts at 0x000000018fff0068
         segment           begin        allocated            size
000000018fff0000 000000018fff0068  000000018fff0080 0x0000000000000018(24)
Heap Size           0x5ec68(388200)
------------------------------
 . . .
------------------------------
GC Heap Size        0x2d7930(2980144)
```

For each heap in the system, you can use *!dumpheap* to look at each of the ranges, and you'll have to manually piece together the overall generation 2 heap. It's certainly doable; it's just very tedious. This is the one time you'll be sad about having that 16-CPU monster server.

!GCRoot Command

After you've gotten a good idea as to what lies where in the various heaps, you'll want to look at individual objects to see what other objects are holding on to references to the key object. The term *rooted* is a synonym for *referencing*. If object A has a field of class B, the instance of B is said to be rooted to A, and A is rooted to the garbage-collected heap because you have a reference to the instance of A. That means that because A and B are rooted, neither object can be garbage collected. If you nulled the variable that held on to A, both A and B are available for garbage collection.

The *!gcroot* command takes as its parameter the object address you want to check. The command first looks through all the objects in the garbage-collected heap to see if anything has a reference to that object. Second, it looks through handle references in the *GCHandle* table. When I get to the *!GCHandles* command, we'll discuss the *GCHandle* table in detail. Finally, it looks through the pointers on each of the stacks.

One word of caution with the *!gcroot* command is that it can report false positives on the stack checking. For example, if you have an old address for an object, *!gcroot* can report what looks like valid data. If you suspect the output from *!gcroot* does not make sense because of potential stack issues, pass the *!gcroot* parameter *-nostacks* before the object address to see if that clears up the output. Otherwise, use *!clrstack* and *!dumpheap* to verify that the object truly exists.

If an item on the stack references the object, you'll see output showing you the reference with the chain from the highest level down to the object itself. You'll also see the references to some of the intermediate values. I find it best to search for the object address in the output to skip over the partial chains by using Ctrl+F to bring up the Find dialog box in the Command window.

```
0:009> !gcroot 00b1f690
Note: Roots found on stacks may be false positives. Run "!help gcroot" for
more info.
ebx:Root:00b01c28(System.Windows.Forms.Application+ThreadContext)
    ->00b00b48(AnimatedAlgorithm.AnimatedAlgorithmForm)
    ->00b0e6c4(Bugslayer.SortDisplayControl.SorterControl)
    ->00b119dc(System.Collections.Hashtable)
    ->00b11b48(System.Collections.Hashtable+bucket[])
    ->00b11a3c(NSort.BubbleSorter)
    ->00b1f6b4(Bugslayer.SortDisplayGraph.GraphSwapper)
    ->00b1f690(Bugslayer.SortDisplayGraph.SwapStateArgs)
Scan Thread 0 OSTHread f5c
Scan Thread 2 OSTHread 934
```

The output of *!gcroot* will end with the handle table references for domains in the process. If the display does not contain any references to handles, the object will be eligible for collection when the stack references go away. If the output shows the handle references, like the following output, the object has references that transcend stacks. The handle type displayed indicates the type of rooted memory. Table 6-3 shows the different codes and descriptions of the types of handles you'll see in the output.

```
0:009> !gcroot 00af1144
Note: Roots found on stacks may be false positives. Run "!help gcroot" for
more info.
Scan Thread 0 OSTHread f5
Scan Thread 2 OSTHread 934
Scan Thread 9 OSTHread ef0
DOMAIN(00147EE0):HANDLE(Strong):8d11e0:Root:
        00af1144(System.Threading.ThreadAbortException)
    ->00b11a3c(NSort.BubbleSorter)
```

Table 6-3   Handle Meanings

Code	Meaning	Description
WeakLn	Long-lived weak handle	A tracked handle until reclaimed. Tracking occurs through finalization and across resurrections.
WeakSh	Short-lived short handle	Tracks the object until the first time it is unreachable.
Strong	Strong handle	A normal object reference. Strong handle references are promoted when garbage collection occurs.
Pinned	Pinned handle	A strong handle that is prevented from moving around during garbage collection. Pinned handles occur when objects are passed outside the CLR through interop.
RefCnt	Referenced counted handle	A handle that behaves as a strong handle when the reference count is greater than zero. When the reference goes to zero, the handle becomes a weak handle.
AsyncPinned	Asynchronous pinned handle	A handle type for the CLR internals.
Unknwn	Unknown handle	A handle type that can't be reported.

!ObjSize Command

When I talked about the size reported by the *!dumpheap* command, the size displayed is the size of the object itself and not the total size of everything the particular object contains. To see all the memory held by an object, *!objsize* is your tool of choice. In the following output, the size of the main form itself is only 384 bytes, but the size of everything the form holds is 19,768 bytes:

```
0:011> !dumpheap -type Animated
 Address      MT       Size
00b00b48 02ca37bc      384
total 1 objects
Statistics:
     MT    Count TotalSize Class Name
02ca37bc       1       384 AnimatedAlgorithm.AnimatedAlgorithmForm
Total 1 objects
0:011> !objsize 00b00b48
sizeof(00b00b48) =    19768 (  0x4d38) bytes (AnimatedAlgorithm.AnimatedAlgorithmForm)
```

What makes *!objsize* interesting is that if you execute the command without any parameter, you'll see the complete output of all the rooted objects in the process space. It's an incredibly convenient way to see the entire heap in one output.

!GCHandles Command

Many developers are surprised to find out that you can leak .NET memory. In reality, it's not .NET leaking the memory. When you pass .NET memory to the native side of your application, the garbage collector has to keep track of the memory being passed through interop, thus holding a reference to the memory, like an internal root. If the native code fails to notify the .NET code that it's done with the memory, the reference to the managed memory means it will never be collected. Thus, you've got a memory leak in .NET.

When .NET memory makes the journey over to the native side of your application, the internal reference to the memory is stored in a *GCHandle* structure from the *System.Runtime.InteropServices* namespace. The *GCHandle* structure is simply a wrapper around an *IntPtr* that holds the memory address.

As you expect, the *GCHandle* structures are stored in a table, and if you could look through that table, you could see the types of interop memory you are using in your application. What would be even better is if there were a way to look through the addresses stored in each *GCHandle* structure to see if the memory referenced is still in use.

What I've just described is exactly what the *!gchandles* command is all about. It walks that *GCHandles* table and tells you exactly what types of handles you have outstanding in addition to the current objects in the *GCHandles* tables. The default is show all the *GCHandles* for the entire process. If you're doing multiple domain development, you can pass the *-perdomain* handle to see the handles occurring from each domain.

```
0:011> !gchandles
GC Handle Statistics:
Strong Handles: 68
Pinned Handles: 7
Async Pinned Handles: 0
Ref Count Handles: 0
Weak Long Handles: 22
Weak Short Handles: 43
Other Handles: 0
Statistics:
      MT    Count TotalSize Class Name
78c8e2c4        1        12 System.Security.Permissions.ReflectionPermission
78c77b9c        1        12 System.Security.Permissions.SecurityPermission
78c746a0        1        12 System.Object
. . .
7b4f1504       15      1080 System.Windows.Forms.MenuItem
78c7ac68       34      1224 System.Security.PermissionSet
78c9b180        6     23872 System.Object[]
Total 140 objects
```

The first part of the *!gchandles* output is the most important because it shows you exactly what types of handles are outstanding. As you saw back in Table 6-3, different types of memory handles can put radically different pressure on the garbage collector. The most important handle type to notice is the pinned handles.

Pinned handles are memory locations locked into physical locations in the garbage-collected heap. Because those locations are locked, the garbage collector must move around those locations when coalescing freed memory. This slows down the garbage collector tremendously, so it's extremely important to keep an eye on those pinned handles.

!GCHandleLeaks Command

Seeing the dump of the GCHandles table is nice, but what's even nicer is seeing if any of the handle values stored in the table are missing in action. This is especially true if you're leaking pinned or strong handles. As you can see from the title of this section, the *!gchandleleaks* command takes care of that for you.

To show you how a handle leak could occur, the following code snippet shows code that calls a native method that requires a pinned array in memory. At the bottom of the code, I don't call *GCHandle.Free*, and thus leak the array wrapped by the *GCHandle* variable. Granted, this is a contrived code, but I wanted to show you what a leaked *GCHandle* reference looks like in as short a sample as possible.

```
// Allocate the managed array.
int [] buffer = new int [ 1000 ];
// Pin the buffer in memory in preparation for passing it to native
// code.
GCHandle gch = GCHandle.Alloc ( buffer , GCHandleType.Pinned );
// Get the pinned buffer.
IntPtr ptrToBuffer = Marshal.
                    UnsafeAddrOfPinnedArrayElement ( buffer , 0 );
// Do the native enumeration.
NativeMethods.FillAttachedDevices ( 1000 , (IntPtr)ptrToBuffer );

// Here I forget to remove the root that references the pinned buffer
// with a call to gch.Free
```

Before I get into the command itself, it's worth discussing how you could manually do the equivalent with just the existing WinDBG commands and if we had a command that would output the GCHandles table. Because each handle stored in the GCHandles table is a memory address, we could use the address with the WinDBG *S (Search Memory)* command to search all the memory in the process for that address. If the search does not find the address value, the odds are that the memory has been leaked.

Instead of us doing all that manual typing until our fingers wear off to little nubs, the *!gchandleleaks* command does all the heavy lifting for us. As the output of *!gchandleleaks* warns you, the command's output can possibly be incorrect. The address you're looking for could possibly match junk or data in the address space, so the actual leaked reference wrapped by

GCHandle won't be reported. Additionally, in the rare case when the native code is masking or changing the memory address values passed in by managed code, you can have false reports of leaked handles. The good news is that those two caveats are quite rare, so if you're seeing leaks reported by *!gchandleleaks*, you're almost certainly seeing real problems in your application.

The first part of the *!gchandleleaks* output is the dump of the actual *GCHandles* table itself. Don't be alarmed if the number of handles reported by *!gchandles* and *!gchandleleaks* are different. The *!gchandles* command lists all types of handles, and the *!gchandleleaks* command reports only strong and pinned handle types.

After the strong and pinned handle dump, the command starts showing you all the locations in memory where it found various handle values. Fortunately, *!gchandleleaks* properly listens for Ctrl+Break keystrokes to abort the command. If you do abort the command, ignore the leaked handle output because the command mistakenly reports all unfound handles as leaks.

The last part of the *!gchandles* command is where all the action resides. That's the list of *GCHandle* structures referencing memory that wasn't found in the full memory scan:

```
Didn't find 43 handles:
0000000001ac1678    0000000001ac1680    0000000001ac1688    0000000001ac1690
. . . .
```

Each of the numbers listed is a leaked *GCHandle* structure. Because the *GCHandle* is a value type, you can be hard core and use the *!name2ee* command to look up the method table of the *GCHandle* structure. The easiest way to use the *!name2ee* command is to use the WinDBG syntax for module and address. You'll pass * as the module, the ubiquitous exclamation point (*!*), and the fully qualified class name:

```
0:000> !name2ee *!System.Runtime.InteropServices.GCHandle
Module: 0000000074968000 (mscorlib.dll)
Token: 0x00000000020004f8
MethodTable: 0000000074a322c8
EEClass: 0000000074b38cb8
Name: System.Runtime.InteropServices.GCHandle
. . .
```

With the method table in hand, the previously discussed *!dumpvc* will show you the data for the value type:

```
0:000> !dumpvc 0000000074a322c8 0000000001ac1678
Name: System.Runtime.InteropServices.GCHandle
MethodTable 0000000074a322c8
EEClass: 0000000074b38cb8
Size: 24(0x18) bytes
(C:\WINDOWS\assembly\GAC_64\mscorlib\2.0.0.0__b775c561934e089\mscorlib.dll)
Fields:
        MT    Field Offset          Type VT      Attr        Value Name
749ece80  400195f        0    System.IntPtr  0 instance      285543080 m_handle
. . .
```

With the value of the *m_handle* field is the address of the object. Keep in mind that the *!dumpvc* and *!dumpobj* commands display their data in decimal form. Therefore, to dump the object held by the *GCHandle* structure, I need to prefix the value with 0n to indicate that it's a decimal number:

```
0:000> !do 0n285543080
Name: System.String
MethodTable: 00000000749e0320
EEClass: 0000000074adf000
Size: 90(0x5a) bytes
. . .
```

If your eyes are starting to roll back in your head thinking about how tedious it will be to look at leaked *GCHandle* structures, you're not alone. Put on your native C++ thinking cap for a moment. Because the *GCHandle* structure just contains a single instance field, the object memory, we can reach directly into the *GCHandle* structure to see the wrapped object.

The *D (Display Memory)* command lets us dump a memory address and display the data in any format known to humankind. Because my examples in this section were done on an x64 machine, I'll use *DQ* to display the data in quad words. On a 32-bit machine, you'd use *DD* to display in double word form. Because each value reported as leaked by *!gchandleleaks* is a single *GCHandle* structure, I'll use *l 1* to display only the one object.

```
0:000> dq 0000000001ac1678 l 1
00000000 01ac1678  00000000 11050aa8
```

The first address that appears is the address I dumped, and the second is the value at that location. With the second address, I can pass it to *!do* to display the data.

If you've leaked more than two handles, even this quicker way of looking at the objects is going to take you hours to get through looking at the actual objects. Way back in the "*!DumpObj (!do)* Command" section, I showed the hard way of looking at an individual field in an object by using the *poi* expression, which stands for *pointer to integer*. Because the *GCHandle* structure simply wraps the address, you can achieve the same thing by passing the address of the *GCHandle* structure in the *poi* wrapper to dereference the .NET object.

```
0:000> !do poi(0000000001ac1678)
Name: System.String
MethodTable: 00000000749e0320
EEClass: 0000000074adf000
Size: 90(0x5a) bytes
```

Although I went through a bit of discussion tangential to the *!gchandleleaks* command, I thought it was a good chance to poke around at a few other commands and techniques that you'll need to know. The key point to remember when it comes to memory leaks in .NET is that if you are seeing the Private Bytes performance counter rising at the same rate as the # Bytes in All Heaps performance counter, you're most likely looking at managed memory being leaked by the native side of your application.

!VerifyHeap Command

Although .NET 2.0 has added quite a bit of magic pixie dust to help detect heap corruptions when passing managed data to native code, there's still plenty of opportunity for the ugly head of a native code wild write to a pointer to ruin your day. If you're doing a good deal of interop and you suspect a problem in the managed heap, use *!verifyheap* to ensure that all the objects are in good shape.

The *!verifyheap* command looks at each object on the heap and validates that its fields point to valid objects. If there are no problems on the heap, you'll see no output. If there are problems, you'll see output like the following:

```
0:007> !verifyheap
-verify will only produce output if there are errors in the heap
object 000000001105a7c0: bad member baadd00ddeadbeef at 000000001105a7c8
Object baadd00ddeadbeef has no generation
object 000000001105a7c0: missing card_table entry for 000000001105a7c8
curr_object : 000000001105a7c0
Last good object: 000000001105a790
----------------
```

The mention of *-verify* in the output got me a little curious. It seemed to me that any SOS operations dealing with the heap should be part of *!dumpheap*, so I passed the *-verify* option to *!dumpheap* and got the exact same output.

Exceptions and Breakpoints

Now that I've beaten the heap to death, let's turn to some commands that you'll use during live debugging. Although it will be rare that you'll be doing live debugging of production systems, it's nice to know these commands are available if you need them. What's even better is that these commands are drastically easier to use than what we had to do in .NET 1.1 to stop on exceptions or breakpoints.

!StopOnException (!soe) and !PrintException (!pe) Commands

Back in the "Exceptions and Events" section, I discussed using *sxe clr* to stop on any .NET exception. Although that might be good enough for some general poking around, for faster debugging, you'll probably want more control over exactly what exception you stop on. Happily, the *!soe* command makes stopping on a specific exception trivial.

When using *!soe*, you have to at least specify if the exception you want to stop on is a first-chance or second-chance exception. To specify that you'll want to stop on first-chance exceptions, you'll specify the wildly misnamed *-create* option before the fully qualified name of the exception. For second-chance exceptions, you'll specify *-create2*.

After specifying the option and the fully qualified exception name, you'll need to specify a debugger pseudo register value. The documentation for *!soe* states that you can omit specifying the pseudo register, but I've found that *!soe* doesn't work correctly without the pseudo register specified.

I've already mentioned two pseudo registers in this chapter, *$csp*, the call stack pointer, and *$ra*, the return address. WinDBG has many other pseudo registers that allow you to get specific information, such as *$tid* (Thread ID) without resorting to machine-dependent hacking. In addition to the special values, WinDBG offers twenty user-defined pseudo registers, *$t0* to *$t19*, in which you can store any values you'd like. The *r* command allows you to store values into the pseudo registers.

The following shows use of the *!soe* command to stop whenever an *ArgumentNullException* is thrown and use of pseudo register $t1 internally:

```
0:004> !soe -create System.ArgumentNullException 1
Breakpoint set
```

My first reaction when I saw the text *Breakpoint set* was to execute a *bl (Breakpoint List)* command to view the breakpoint *!soe* set. If you do the same, you'll see that there's no actual breakpoint in the list. That had me wondering because if the *!soe* command wasn't setting a breakpoint, the only other way to cause a debuggee to stop in the debugger is through an event or exception. Running the *sx* command showed exactly how *!soe* did its magic:

```
0:000> sx
  ct - Create thread - ignore
. . .
clr - CLR exception - break - not handled
    Command: "!soe  System.ArgumentNullException 1;
                   .if(@$t1==0) {g}
                   .else {.echo 'System.ArgumentNullException hit'}"
. . .
```

The *!soe* magic turns out to be quite elegant. When you issue the *!soe* command, it executes the following command:

```
sxe -c "!soe  System.ArgumentNullException 1;
           .if(@$t1==0) {g}
           .else {.echo 'System.ArgumentNullException hit'}" clr
```

Every time a .NET exception occurs, the specified command executes. First, *!soe* looks to see if the exception is of the specified type. If so, it will set the user-defined pseudo register to 1. The *.if* and *.else* tokens are part of the Debugger Command Programs functionality in which you can write rudimentary programs. See the WinDBG documentation for more information on how to use them.

If you're thinking that there might be some limitations with the *!soe* command because it takes over the .NET exception event with a single conditional, you're right. If you want to stop on multiple exceptions that are derived from a common base class, you can use the *!soe* command, which handles that with the *-derived* option. For example, if you wanted to stop on any exceptions derived from *System.TypeLoadException*, which is the base class for both *System.DllNotFound-Exception* and *System.EntryPointNotFoundException*, you'd type the command:

```
!soe -derived -create System.TypeLoadException 2
```

For stopping on multiple exceptions that are not related through inheritance, you need to spend quality time with the *sxe* command. Fortunately, as you can see from the example I showed earlier, it's mainly an exercise in getting the conditional command worked out. The following command has two *!soe* commands monitoring exceptions and reporting the results into pseudo registers $t5 and $t6. The two extra @ signs at the beginning of the *.if* conditional force WinDBG to use the C++ expression evaluator for the condition. The default expression evaluator is the MASM (Microsoft Assembler), so I need to do this to force the correct evaluation. Note that I broke the following command for readability. When you type it into the WinDBG Command window, you'd type it on one line.

```
sxe -c "!soe System.IO.FileNotFoundException 5;
      !soe System.NotImplementedException 6;
      .if @@((@$t5==0) && (@$t6==0))
          {g}
      .else {.echo 'My exception hit!' }"
  clr
```

If you've stopped on an exception or are debugging a minidump, you can turn to the *!pe* command to take a look at the detail of the exception. Run by itself, *!pe* shows the last exception in the current thread, just as the *!threads* command does. If you have the address of an exception object, you can pass that to *!pe*. In order to see inner exceptions also, use the *-nested* option.

The most important piece of information that *!pe* shows you is the call stack. Because the call stack inside an exception is a byte array, without the *!pe* command, there's no way of figuring out where the exception originated. This new functionality is a huge boost to quickly finding problems.

```
0:000> !pe
Exception object: 01d04030
Exception type: System.NullReferenceException
Message: Object reference not set to an instance of an object.
InnerException: <none>
StackTrace (generated):
    SP       IP               Function
    0012EF50 1A7503EE DieAway.Program.Fum(System.Text.StringBuilder)
    0012EFB0 1A75034B DieAway.Program.Fo(System.Text.StringBuilder)
    0012EFE0 1A7502DB DieAway.Program.Fi(System.Text.StringBuilder)
    0012F010 1A75026B DieAway.Program.Fee(System.Text.StringBuilder)
    0012F040 1A7501FC DieAway.Program.Main(System.String[])

StackTraceString: <none>
HResult: 80004003
```

!BPMD Command

Compared to prior versions of SOS, the .NET 2.0 version offers drastically easier support for setting breakpoints. Now there's a single command, *!bpmd*, that does all the work and doesn't require you to worry about whether the method is jitted or not. The command relies on the method descriptor of the particular method, but you don't have to worry about hunting it down; the *!bpmd* command even takes care of that for you if you know the module name that contains the method and the name of the method itself.

```
0:006> !bpmd nsort.dll NSort.QuickSorter.Sort
Found 2 methods...
MethodDesc = 00000000025eada0
MethodDesc = 00000000025eadb0
Adding pending breakpoints...

0:006> !bpmd nsort.dll NSort.HeapSort.Sort
Found 1 methods...
MethodDesc = 00000000025ea830
Method is jitted, placing breakpoint at code addr 0000000002b5cc60
```

Both of the commands executed above set breakpoints; the difference to the output depends on if the method is jitted or not. If the method(s) are not jitted, you'll see output like the first part where *!bpmd* will be monitoring when jitting occurs, and when the particular method is jitted, the *!bpmd* command will set a *ba* (*Break on Acccess*) command on the first instruction of the method. If the method is already jitted, the *ba* breakpoint will be directly set on the method's jitted location.

The *!bpmd* command is somewhat of a sledgehammer approach. In the output above, you see that setting a breakpoint on my *NSort.QuickSort.Sort* method results in two methods found. The *!bpmd* command simply does a string lookup, and if there are overloads, it sets breakpoints on all overloaded methods.

As does the *!soe* command, *!bpmd* works its magic through the debugger events–the CLR Notification Exception in particular. As I mentioned earlier, the CLR Notification exceptions are undocumented and don't work when used directly, but *!bpmd* must have the special secret to make them work.

```
0:006> sx
. . .
clrn - CLR notification exception - break - handled
      Command: "!bpmd -notification;g"
. . .
```

Running the application and executing a method that's not jitted will result in output like the following:

```
(f3c.bc0): CLR notification exception - code e0444143 (first chance)
JITTED NSort!NSort.QuickSorter.Sort(System.Collections.IList)
Setting breakpoint: bp 02B5A9E0
```

This is where the *!bpmd* command is making the *ba* breakpoints on the method's jitted location so that you'll stop whenever the method is executed. You can verify that the breakpoints are set by using the *bl* command:

```
0:009> bl
 0 e 00000000 02b5a9e0     0001 (0001)  0:****
 1 e 00000000 02b5aab0     0001 (0001)  0:****
 2 e 00000000 02b5cc60     0001 (0001)  0:****
```

Knowing the module and qualified method name make *!bpmd* a snap to use, but most of the time developers are lucky to have a vague notion of the name. One of these days there will be a pill to give us all photographic memories. Until them, I'll show you the easy trick for finding the method you want to break on.

To start, run the *!dumpheap* command to get the method tables of the particular class you want. A method table, along with the class data structure, are what describe an object in memory. Once you have the method table, it's easy to look up the method descriptor for the method. Let's look at a case in which I want to set a breakpoint on another of the sorting algorithms I've been using in this section:

```
0:009> !dumpheap -stat -type NSort
total 43 objects
Statistics:
            MT    Count TotalSize Class Name
00000000025eb500      1        32 NSort.ShellSort
00000000025eb240      1        32 NSort.ShakerSort
00000000025eb100      1        32 NSort.SelectionSort
00000000025eafc0      1        32 NSort.QuickSortWithBubbleSort
00000000025eae40      1        32 NSort.QuickSorter
00000000025eacc0      1        32 NSort.OddEvenTransportSorter
00000000025eab80      1        32 NSort.InsertionSort
00000000025eaa40      1        32 NSort.InPlaceMergeSort
00000000025ea8c0      1        32 NSort.HeapSort
00000000025ea740      1        32 NSort.FastQuickSorter
00000000025ea5c0      1        32 NSort.DoubleStorageMergeSort
00000000025ea480      1        32 NSort.ComboSort11
00000000025ea340      1        32 NSort.BubbleSorter
00000000025ea200      1        32 NSort.BiDirectionalBubbleSort
00000000025eb3c0      1        48 NSort.ShearSorter
00000000025ec000     13       312 NSort.DefaultSwap
00000000025ebd80     15       360 NSort.ComparableComparer
Total 43 objects
```

Taking advantage of the *!dumpheap -stat* and *-type* options quickly gets me the method tables for all classes that have NSort in the name. Armed with a method table, I can use the SOS metadata walking command *!dumpmt* to display the information about the particular method table. In order to get the method descriptors, which are the metadata information about an individual method, I'll make sure to pass the *-md* option to *!dumpmt* because they are not shown by default:

```
0:009> !dumpmt -md 00000000025eaa40
EEClass: 000000000261e378
```

```
Module: 00000000026c6a60
Name: NSort.InPlaceMergeSort
mdToken: 0200000d
(C:\dev\3Book\Disk\Chapter Examples\Chapter 6\Debug\NSort.DLL)
BaseSize: 0x20
ComponentSize: 0x0
Number of IFaces in IFaceMap: 1
Slots in VTable: 8
---------------------------------------
MethodDesc Table
          Entry        MethodDesc      JIT Name
00000000744a03c0  0000000074c24300   PreJIT System.Object.ToString()
0000000074574460  0000000074c24310   PreJIT System.Object.
                                                  Equals(System.Object)
000000007438cec0  0000000074c24340   PreJIT System.Object.GetHashCode()
0000000074234130  0000000074c24350   PreJIT System.Object.Finalize()
0000000002b53d30  00000000025ea9b0    NONE NSort.InPlaceMergeSort.
                                            Sort(System.Collections.IList)
0000000002b56a00  00000000025ea990     JIT NSort.InPlaceMergeSort..ctor()
0000000002b53d28  00000000025ea9a0    NONE NSort.InPlaceMergeSort.
                                           .ctor(System.Collections.IComparer,
                                               NSort.ISwap)
0000000002b53d38  00000000025ea9c0    NONE NSort.InPlaceMergeSort.Sort
                                              (System.Collections.IList,
                                                  Int32, Int32)
```

The key column in the output above is the MethodDesc. If you know the method descriptor, you can use the *-md* option to the *!bpmd* command to bypass the module and qualified name completely. In the following example, I'm setting the breakpoint, but the method has not been jitted yet. If the method had been jitted, the *!bpmd* command would report that it was setting the actual breakpoints.

```
0:006> !bpmd -md 00000000025ea9b0
Adding pending breakpoints...
```

Deadlocks

Overall, the .NET Framework makes handling synchronization issues very easy with the *Thread.Monitor* class as sync blocks. Of course, there's no protection against you screwing up your synchronization and deadlocking your application completely. If the Framework had foolproof synchronization, you certainly wouldn't be reading this book nor would we all have jobs.

!SyncBlk Command

The critical section of the managed world is a SyncBlock. Any time you're using the *lock/ SyncLock* keyword or *Monitor.Enter*, you're using a SyncBlock. If you suspect that you're dead-locked on a SyncBlock, you simply need to run the *!syncblk* command to see which ones are being held.

```
0:021> !syncblk
Index SyncBlock MonitorHeld Recursion Owning Thread Info  SyncBlock Owner
   23 001b8bec           3         1 001f8298   d88   9   00b33eb0 System.Object
   24 001b8c1c          21         1 001fb130   330  15   00b33fbc System.Byte[]
-----------------------------
Total           34
CCW             0
RCW             0
ComClassFactory 0
Free            0
```

The data displayed by the *!synblk* command is a little convoluted, so let me discuss exactly what's in each field. The *Index* field is the particular SyncBlock index field for the object indicating the particular SyncBlock from the SyncBlock cache in use. You can see all the values in the SyncBlock cache by adding the *-all* parameter to *!syncblk*. If you want to look at a particular index, you can pass that integer value as a parameter to *!syncblk* also.

The SyncBlock field is the address of the actual SyncBlock in the SyncBlock cache. Because a SyncBlock is not a .NET object, you can't use *!do* to dump it. If you're really curious, you can use *dd* or *dq* to look at the address, and you'll be looking at the next three fields, so it's not so exciting.

The MonitorHeld field is undocumented. The Recursion field indicates how many times the thread has acquired the particular SyncBlock. Keeping an eye on this field can help you when doing the code inspection to match up acquisitions and releases. The *Owning Thread Info* field shows three different pieces of information. The first is the thread object itself and is the same value shown in the ThreadOBJ field in the *!threads* command. The hexadecimal second number is the Windows thread ID, and the last number is the WinDBG thread number.

The final column is the most important because it shows the object address and type being used for synchronization. As with any time you have an object address, you can pass the address to *!do* to look at it. The key to remember is that this is not the object that the thread is deadlocked on but the object that is owned by the thread. The thread is deadlocked because it's trying to acquire a different object.

It's great that the *!syncblk* command can show you which threads are currently holding SyncBlocks, but you're going to have to do a little exploration to figure out exactly which objects are being held by each thread. The digging isn't too hard and ties together various SOS commands.

My program has run and seems to have encountered a deadlock—the application isn't responding. After attaching WinDBG and loading SOS, the first command to run is *!syncblk* to take a look to see if there are any potential blockages:

```
0:021> !syncblk
Index SyncBlock MonitorHeld Recursion Owning Thread Info  SyncBlock Owner
   33 001b75a4          21         1 001f3dc0   204  10   012b7810 System.Byte[]
   34 001b75d4           3         1 001dfee0   9c4   9   012b7704 System.Object
-----------------------------
. . .
```

Threads 9 and 10 are both holding locks, so I'll switch over to thread 9 with ~9s and issue !clrstack to see where the managed code is sitting:

```
0:009> !clrstack
OS Thread Id: 0x9c4 (9)
ESP        EIP
03f7f6c0 7c90eb94 [GCFrame: 03f7f6c0]
03f7f7f8 7c90eb94 [HelperMethodFrame: 03f7f7f8]
                    System.Threading.Monitor.Enter(System.Object)
03f7f84c 00d91538 ThreadsDemo.MonitorBad.WriterFunc()
03f7f8b4 793d7a7b System.Threading.ThreadHelper.
                            ThreadStart_Context(System.Object)
03f7f8bc 793683dd System.Threading.ExecutionContext.
                        Run(System.Threading.ExecutionContext,
                            System.Threading.ContextCallback,
                            System.Object)
03f7f8d4 793d7b5c System.Threading.ThreadHelper.ThreadStart()
03f7faf8 79e88f63 [GCFrame: 03f7faf8]
```

The x86 !clrstack command shows that the last managed method called is Monitor.Enter, so the odds are good that this thread is waiting for a SyncBlock. However, the thread could have just made the call to Monitor.Enter and may not have processed the actual blocking code, so to verify that I'm in a lock, the native stack walk command, kP, will show that there are WaitForMultipleObject-type native methods on the top of the stack. Further up the stack, you see MScorwks.dll methods that have *lock* and *wait* in their names, so it's easy to see what's going on:

```
0:009> kP
ChildEBP RetAddr
03f7f430 7c90e9ab ntdll!KiFastSystemCallRet
03f7f434 7c8094e2 ntdll!ZwWaitForMultipleObjects+0xc
03f7f4d0 79f8ead4 KERNEL32!WaitForMultipleObjectsEx+0x12c
03f7f538 79f17522 mscorwks!WaitForMultipleObjectsEx_SO_TOLERANT+0x6f
03f7f558 79f17493 mscorwks!Thread::DoAppropriateAptStateWait+0x3c
03f7f5dc 79f1732f mscorwks!Thread::DoAppropriateWaitWorker+0x144
03f7f62c 79f8ea4d mscorwks!Thread::DoAppropriateWait+0x40
03f7f688 79e77f50 mscorwks!CLREvent::WaitEx+0xf7
03f7f698 7a0fd9c3 mscorwks!CLREvent::Wait+0x17
03f7f724 7a0fdbbf mscorwks!AwareLock::EnterEpilog+0x94
03f7f740 7a0fdd2a mscorwks!AwareLock::Enter+0x61
03f7f7a4 7a094352 mscorwks!AwareLock::Contention+0x16c
03f7f844 00d91538 mscorwks!JITutil_MonContention+0xa3
WARNING: Frame IP not in any known module. Following frames may be wrong.
03f7f8ac 793d7a7b 0xd91538
. . .
```

I do like the name *WaitForMultipleObjectsEx_SO_TOLERANT*. The !syncblk output told us that thread 9 is waiting on a *System.Object*. From the managed stack, the *MonitorBad.WriterFunc* method is the one that's currently acquired a particular *System.Object*. That doesn't tell us the exact object the thread has deadlocked on. With a simple example like this one, you can probably deduce through simple code inspection the deadlock reason; it's much more difficult if you have many threads and synchronization objects in use.

What we need to now look for is the exact object address being passed to *Monitor.Enter* so we can see what this thread is attempting to acquire. If you try the *!clrstack* command with the *-a* option, as I described earlier, you'll see that you won't get the object address that way. To see the objects on the stack, run the *!dso* command. The good news is that because the thread is blocked in the call to *Monitor.Enter*, the last object on the managed stack will be the actual parameter passed.

```
0:009> !dso
OS Thread Id: 0x9c4 (9)
ESP/REG  Object    Name
ecx      012bc940 System.Globalization.GregorianCalendar
03f7f6f8 012b7810 System.Byte[]
03f7f790 012b7810 System.Byte[]
03f7f7bc 012b83c0 System.Threading.ContextCallback
03f7f84c 012b7810 System.Byte[]
03f7f850 012b7704 System.Object
03f7f854 012b76e4 ThreadsDemo.MonitorBad
03f7f88c 012b7e10 System.Threading.ThreadHelper
03f7f898 012b7e10 System.Threading.ThreadHelper
```

As you can see, the *System.Byte[]* at 0x012b7810 is at the top of the stack, so that's the object passed to *Monitor.Enter*. By running the *!syncblk* command again, you can see that that's the object held by thread 10:

```
0:009> !syncblk
Index SyncBlock MonitorHeld Recursion Owning Thread Info  SyncBlock Owner
   33 001b75a4          21         1 001f3dc0   204  10  012b7810 System.Byte[]
   34 001b75d4           3         1 001dfee0    9c4   9  012b7704 System.Object
-----------------------------
. . .
```

We've established that thread 9 is waiting for the SyncBlock for the *System.Byte[]* that thread 10 owns, so we know what one side of the deadlock is. If I repeated the same steps for thread 10, we'd see that thread 9 owns the SyncBlock thread 10 is waiting for. If you haven't guessed, I contrived this example by having thread 9 acquire the SyncBlocks in A and B order, whereas thread 10 acquires them in B and A order.

If the SyncBlock deadlock is occurring from objects in the same class, it's easy enough to see that the managed call stacks on each thread will have different methods from the class making the call to *Monitor.Enter*. A code inspection at that point will probably show you the problem. If the deadlocks are happening because of different classes, you may want to look up the particular field names to make it easier for the code inspection.

In that case, you'll need to find the object of the class holding the field, which is what the *!gcroot* command is for. To see what class is referencing the object at 0x012b7810, I'll issue the following command:

```
0:009> !gcroot -nostacks 012b7810
DOMAIN(0014BD98):HANDLE(WeakLn):8e1028:Root:012b7cb4(
                     System.Windows.Forms.NativeMethods+WndProc)->
012b7a3c(System.Windows.Forms.Timer+TimerNativeWindow)->
```

```
01281b88(System.Windows.Forms.Timer)->
0128a408(System.EventHandler)->
0128079c(ThreadsDemo.MainForm)->
012b76e4(ThreadsDemo.MonitorBad)->
012b7810(System.Byte[])
```

As you can see, the object at address 0x012b7810 is held by the class instance *Threads-Demo.MonitorBad* at 012b76e4. Our good friend, the *!do* command, will dump out that instance and give us the field name for *System.Byte[]*.

```
0:009> !do 012b76e4
Name: ThreadsDemo.MonitorBad
MethodTable: 00907974
EEClass: 00da1878
Size: 32(0x20) bytes
 (C:\Dev\Presentations\MSFT\DotNet\Demos-2005\Debug\ThreadsDemo.exe)
Fields:
      MT    Field Offset                 Type VT    Attr    Value Name
7910f73c 4000012     4        System.Random  0 instance 012b7710 rng
79124418 4000013     8        System.Byte[]  0 instance 012b7810 buffer
790fb238 4000014     c ....Threading.Thread  0 instance 012b7ddc writer
79124228 4000015    10      System.Object[]  0 instance 012b7880 readers
0090704c 4000016    14 ...adsDemo.Signaller  0 instance 012b76b8 sig
790f9c18 4000017    18        System.Object  0 instance 012b7704 synchObj
```

To look for SyncBlock deadlocks on an x64 machine is nearly as simple, but there's a small twist. In some cases, the x64 *!clrstack* command won't always show you the *Monitor.Enter* call at the top of the stack as it does in the x86 *!clrstack* version. The following shows the same deadlocked thread I demonstrated, but on an x64 machine:

```
0:004> !clrstack
OS Thread Id: 0x84c (4)
Child-SP         RetAddr          Call Site
00000000042bf3e0 00000642782e595e ThreadsDemo.MonitorBad.WriterFunc()
00000000042bf4c0 00000642782e91af System.Threading.ExecutionContext.Run(
                                   System.Threading.ExecutionContext,
                                   System.Threading.ContextCallback,
                                   System.Object)
00000000042bf510 000006427f6688d2 System.Threading.ThreadHelper.
                                                     ThreadStart()
```

To double-check that the thread is blocked, use the *kP* command to see if the top of the stack contains calls to the native *Wait** functions.

```
0:004> kP
Child-SP         RetAddr          Call Site
00000000 042bec28 00000000 77d6cfbb ntdll!ZwWaitForMultipleObjects+0xa
00000000 042bec30 00000642 7f587fb1 KERNEL32!WaitForMultipleObjectsEx+0x1cf
00000000 042bed50 00000642 7f584e61 mscorwks!
                                 WaitForMultipleObjectsEx_SO_TOLERANT+0xc1
00000000 042bedf0 00000642 7f46b449 mscorwks!
                                 Thread::DoAppropriateAptStateWait+0x41
```

```
00000000 042bee50 00000642 7f56beb4 mscorwks!
                                     Thread::DoAppropriateWaitWorker+0x195
00000000 042bef50 00000642 7f496ab7 mscorwks!Thread::DoAppropriateWait+0x5c
00000000 042befc0 00000642 7f5977dd mscorwks!CLREvent::WaitEx+0xbf
00000000 042bf070 00000642 7f5d02ce mscorwks!AwareLock::EnterEpilog+0xc9
00000000 042bf140 00000642 7f548857 mscorwks!AwareLock::Enter+0x72
00000000 042bf170 00000642 7f5b7d35 mscorwks!AwareLock::Contention+0x1e7
00000000 042bf230 00000642 80154765 mscorwks!JITutil_MonContention+0xf1
00000000 042bf3e0 00000642 782e595e 0x642 80154765
00000000 042bf4c0 00000642 782e91af mscorlib_ni+0x2e595e
00000000 042bf510 00000642 7f6688d2 mscorlib_ni+0x2e91af
. . .
```

I'm please to see that *WaitForMultipleObjectsEx_SO_TOLERANT* is cross platform. Since I'm talking about deadlocks, I should show you the quick tricks to finding deadlocks on Windows handle-based objects, such as mutexes and events.

Windows Kernel Handle Deadlocks

As you've seen, poking at SyncBlock deadlocks isn't too bad at all. Fortunately, looking for deadlocks on window handles is not that much more difficult. If you believe you're looking at a handle-based deadlock, the first thing you'll want to run is *!eestack -ee*. You might remember from the "Managed Call Stacks" section that it is the single command that will walk all the managed stacks in your application. After the output is done, search for any threads containing *WaitHandle.Wait** at the top of the stack. Those threads are the ones that are blocked while attempting to acquire a handle-based Windows kernel resource.

If you have only two or three threads waiting for an object, you can switch to each of those threads and use *!dso* command to look at the objects on the stack for the particular threads. For those many threaded reader/writer situations, you can run *~*e!dso* to execute *!dso* on all the threads in the application. You're looking for the first item listed to be a *SafeHandles .SafeWaitHandle* object because that contains the Windows kernel handle you're blocking on. Looking up the list of objects will show the particular *WaitHandle*-derived object your code is accessing.

If you followed the advice I gave back in the *!handle* section of always naming your handle values, you can take either the *SafeHandle*-derived or *WaitHandle*-derived object and dump it with *!do*. Either one will show the handle field, which is the native Windows kernel handle that's blocked. As shown next, you can pass the handle value to *!handle* to see exactly which handle it is. Note the *0n* on the handle value passed to *!handle*. That's there because the *!do* shows the values as decimal, and the default radix is hexadecimal, so I have to be specific.

```
0:021> !do 00b40d58
Name: Microsoft.Win32.SafeHandles.SafeWaitHandle
MethodTable: 78c8725c
EEClass: 78c871f8
Size: 20(0x14) bytes
(C:\WINDOWS\assembly\GAC_32\mscorlib\2.0.0.0__b77a5c56194e089\mscorlib.dll)
```

```
Fields:
      MT    Field   Offset           Type VT     Attr   Value Name
78c78208  40005b2       4   System.IntPtr  0 instance    1208 handle
78c78d60  40005b3       8   System.Int32   0 instance      44 _state
78c81164  40005b4       c   System.Boolean 0 instance       1 _ownsHandle
78c81164  40005b5       d   System.Boolean 0 instance       1 _fullyInitialized
0:021> !handle 0n1208 f
Handle 4b8
  Type          Mutant
  Attributes    0
  GrantedAccess 0x1f0001:
        Delete,ReadControl,WriteDac,WriteOwner,Synch
        QueryState
  HandleCount   2
  PointerCount  14
  Name                  \BaseNamedObjects\Mutex Numero Dos
  Object Specific Information
    Mutex is Owned
```

Other SOS Commands

In this section, I want to cover a few of the other commands that you'll find useful in some situations. As I discussed at the beginning of the SOS section, you'll want to keep an eye on the exports for SOS.dll to see if other interesting commands show up. Some will probably be documented in various Microsoft employee blogs, but finding them on your own is always a great first step.

!DumpIL Command

For those of you having a party with the *System.Reflection.Emit* and doing dynamic intermediate language (IL) on the fly, seeing what exactly is happening in your generated code is sometimes impossible. Although you can grind through the byte codes, manually decoding each one with the ECMA specification document, you probably have better things to do with your time. Of course, if you're paid by the hour, that's an excellent exercise to make quite a bit of money.

To see the IL at a glance, you need just to pass either the address of the *DynamicMethod* object or the method descriptor of the object. *!dumpil* was added by the SOS team for viewing dynamic IL, but it also works perfectly well on any method descriptor. The following example shows a dynamic method that calls *Console.WriteLine* and returns the value of the second parameter passed in:

```
0:000> !dumpheap -type DynamicMethod
  Address       MT    Size
012843e0  79183fa8      52
012846ac  791841b0      32
total 2 objects
Statistics:
      MT    Count   TotalSize Class Name
791841b0        1          32 System.Reflection.Emit.
                               DynamicMethod+RTDynamicMethod
79183fa8        1          52 System.Reflection.Emit.DynamicMethod
Total 2 objects
```

```
0:000> !dumpil 012843e0
This is dynamic IL. Exception info is not reported at this time.
If a token is unresolved, run "!do <addr>" on the addr given
in parenthesis. You can also look at the token table yourself, by
running "!DumpArray 012864a0".

IL_0000: ldarg.0
IL_0001: call a000002 (01286520)
IL_0006: ldarg.1
IL_0007: ret
0:000> !do 01286520
Name: System.Reflection.Emit.VarArgMethod
MethodTable: 79183f58
EEClass: 79221bfc
Size: 16(0x10) bytes
 (C:\WINDOWS\assembly\GAC_32\mscorlib\. . .\mscorlib.dll)
Fields:
      MT    Field   Offset                 Type VT     Attr    Value Name
79101a20  40024f2        4 ...ection.MethodInfo  0 instance 01284c60 m_method
79119b10  40024f3        8 ...t.SignatureHelper  0 instance 012864d4 m_signature
```

!SaveModule Command

The *!dumpil* command is great for looking at the IL itself, but sometimes you need a little more. One of my favorite commands in SOS is the *!savemodule* command. From the name, you can guess that it has something to do with saving and modules. In other words, the *!savemodule* command will write the complete assembly out from debugger. What's even better is that *!savemodule* works with live debugging in addition to minidumps.

The command takes two parameters: the base address of the module, and the file name to save to. The extra special part of *!savemodule* is that it works for both .NET binaries and native binaries. In the following example, I'm showing the two modules I'm going to save. The first is a .NET module, and the second is the all important Kernel32.dll. After the *lm* commands, I'm executing the *!savemodules* for each one:

```
0:000> lm a 11000000
start    end        module name
11000000 11010000   AnimatedAlgorithm C (private pdb symbols)
C:\Dev\Debug\AnimatedAlgorithm.pdb
0:000> lm a 7c800000
start    end        module name
7c800000 7c8f4000   KERNEL32   (private pdb symbols)  c:\Symbols\
\kernel32.pdb\BCE87...542\kernel32.pdb
0:000> !savemodule 11000000 foo.exe
3 sections in file
section 0 - VA=2000, VASize=8aa4, FileAddr=1000, FileSize=9000
section 1 - VA=c000, VASize=3c8, FileAddr=a000, FileSize=1000
section 2 - VA=e000, VASize=c, FileAddr=b000, FileSize=1000
0:000> !savemodule 7c800000 x.dll
4 sections in file
section 0 - VA=1000, VASize=81fb5, FileAddr=400, FileSize=82000
section 1 - VA=83000, VASize=43a0, FileAddr=82400, FileSize=2400
section 2 - VA=88000, VASize=65ee8, FileAddr=84800, FileSize=66000
section 3 - VA=ee000, VASize=5bdc, FileAddr=ea800, FileSize=5c00
```

Although that output is surely thrilling, the real excitement begins when you look at the files on disk, which are written to the directory where you started WinDBG from. The file size for my AnimatedAlgorithm.exe is 49,152 bytes, and the Foo.exe I saved with the *!savemodule* command is the exact same size. Of course, my immediate thought the first time I ever executed the *!savemodule* command was to run the saved module. Unfortunately, on Win64 systems, the error is "foo.exe is not a valid Win32 application", and on Win32 systems, the error is "The application failed to initialize properly (0xc000007b). Click on OK to terminate the application." The same errors occur if you try to load the native saved binary as well.

At this point, you're probably wondering what all the excitement is about the *!savemodule* command. Although you can't run the .NET saved module, you can load it into Lutz Roeder's amazing .NET Reflector, which I discussed earlier in the book. Since .NET Reflector has the amazing decompiler, you can look at the decompilation of that module. This is a huge boon to debugging if you have a minidump from a client site that's using a different version of a third-party component that you tested against and you don't have that component's source code. It also can save your job if you've shipped a binary and you've lost the source code to that version.

Although there aren't any decompilers for native code, you can disassemble native modules written by the *!savemodules* command. If you installed the C++ parts of Visual Studio, you have a decent disassembler built right into Link.exe. The undocumented command line is *link -dump -disasm <module>*. If you don't want to see the code bytes in the disassembly, run the command line *link -dump -disasm:nobytes <module>*. The Link.exe disassembler will also take advantage of your Symbol Server, so you'll at least see where the functions start in the large sea of instructions. If you really want to get serious about the native disassembly, download Russ Osterland's excellent PEBrowse Professional Windows Disassembler at *http://www.smidgeonsoft.com/*. Make sure to check out Russ's excellent PEBrowse Interactive Debugger and other utilities, which work with both native and managed applications.

Metadata Dumping Commands

When I discussed using the *-md* option to *!bpmd*, I used one of the metadata dumping commands, *!dumpmt*, to figure out the method descriptor required to use *-md*. That's one of the few metadata dumping commands you'll use. Another command to quickly get a method descriptor is *!ip2md*, which takes an executable address and reports the method descriptor that's executing. In nearly all cases, you'll be looking at addresses reported by *!clrstack*.

There are numerous other commands you can use to wind your way through all the metadata in the process address space. From commands such as *!dumpdomain* to show you which modules belong to which app domain, to *!dumpmodule* to dump everything in a module, to *!dumpclass* to display the EEClass information, you can spend days using SOS to look at metadata. The good news is that you rarely have to look at the metadata information. In all the debugging I've done with SOS, my concern has been the heap, the whole heap, and nothing but the heap.

However, if you truly want to understand .NET from the ground up, you will spend some time gyrating through the metadata in memory. There's a great article on using the SOS metadata commands by Hanu Kommalapati and Tom Christian in MSDN Magazine, with the wonderful title: "JIT and Run: Drill Into .NET Framework Internals to See How the CLR Creates Runtime Objects" (*http://msdn.microsoft.com/msdnmag/issues/05/05/JITCompiler/default.aspx*). That article will show you exactly what's happening under the hood of .NET and how to use the metadata dumping commands in SOS. I'll refer you there for more information on the metadata dumping commands.

ADPlus

Now that I've discussed WinDBG and SOS, we can finally turn to ADPlus. For some strange reason, your network administrators are never too keen on letting you install Visual Studio on a production server and single-stepping that mission-critical application. In those cases, the best you are going to get is a minidump, which ADPlus does with aplomb.

By installing the Debugging Tools for Windows, you not only get the trinity of WinDBG, CDB, and NTSD debuggers, you also get ADPlus.vbs, which is the Visual Basic Script file that is ADPlus. The good news is that once you've installed the Debugging Tools for Windows on one machine, to install ADPlus on a production server is simply a matter of using XCOPY to copy the entire Debugging Tools for Windows directory tree. That's extremely helpful because when you tell a network administrator that you want to install software on a production server, they look at you as if you had just told them that you were outlawing all caffeinated drinks and donuts from the office.

What ADPlus does is build a script file containing all the commands you want to execute and passes that script file to the debugger on the command line. As you can imagine, this makes your life much easier because ADPlus can abstract the grunt work for you. More importantly, ADPlus offers a consistent configuration scheme so you can easily reuse the configurations for other projects. Once you get used to the ADPlus way of operating, it's quite easy to take it into directions you didn't think possible. By the way, by default, ADPlus uses CDB as the debugger, but you can specify WinDBG or NTSD with the *-dbg* command-line switch to ADPlus.

ADPlus has two execution modes you can use for snapping managed minidumps. Running ADPlus in *hang mode* means that the CDB debugger will do a noninvasive attach to the target process and write a minidump of the process. When run in *crash mode*, ADPlus will configure CDB to attach as a normal native debugger, and you'll have specific actions, such as running specific SOS commands or creating minidumps, when the configured exception or breakpoint is hit. There's an undocumented third mode, called Quick. However, that mode produces only basic minidumps, so you can't process them with SOS.

Before I jump into techniques for configuring ADPlus, you should look at the ADPlus documentation in the Debugging Tools for Windows help file, Debugger.chm. You'll find the documentation in Debugging Tools for Windows\Extra Tools\ADPlus. If you really want to see how ADPlus works, it's also not a bad idea to read the ADPlus.vbs file. It's surprisingly well commented, and you'll learn even more tricks on how to use it. As with nearly every thing else in this book, I'm assuming that you've at least scanned the ADPlus documentation.

One major issue with ADPlus is that the documentation does not discuss at all the correct way to use command-line parameters with ADPlus. Simple switches are fine, but if you pass an option that takes a file or directory, make sure to pass the complete path to the item. ADPlus has a small problem in that it assumes that the current directory is where ADPlus.vbs is located, so any relative paths to directories or files in command line switches will be incorrect.

Hang Mode

Having the ability to get vital information out of your application automatically is a huge boon for debugging. In most cases, your production application debugging will revolve around using ADPlus hang mode to get the information so you can look at the live data. If you read the ADPlus documentation, you saw that the ADPlus command line alone is sufficient for you to grab a minidump of a process at any time.

However, it's far better to set up a configuration file that contains all the options you'll want so you can reuse it. Listing 6-1 shows my standard configuration file that I use for all .NET applications to get a minidump and a few other key pieces of information. You can also find this file in the .\ADPlus directory in the code.

Listing 6-1   DNHANG.XML ADPlus Configuration File

```
<!-- Default ADPlus HANG mode configuration for all process types. -->
<ADPlus>
  <Settings>
    <!-- Set the mode to HANG -->
    <RunMode>HANG</RunMode>
    <!-- Snap the dumps, don't tell me about it -->
    <Option>Quiet</Option>
  </Settings>
  <HangActions>
    <!-- For custom actions, I want to see all      -->
    <!-- the handle info, the managed CLR version,  -->
    <!-- managed threads, managed call stacks, and  -->
    <!-- bigger objects.                            -->
    <CustomActions>
      !handle 0 f;
      .loadby sos mscorwks;
      !eeversion;
      !threads;
      ~*e!clrstack;
      !dumpheap -stat -min 100;
    </CustomActions>
  </HangActions>
</ADPlus>
```

The *<Settings>* element contains the global options for the whole configuration file, and you can see that I'm specifying hang mode. The *Quiet* in the *<Option>* element is extremely important to set. By default, ADPlus wants to pop up a message box and let you know where it's writing files. As we all know, any extraneous message boxes are not a great idea, so I tell ADPlus to shut up and just do its job. The *Quiet* option is especially important if you are going to use

ADPlus on a test machine and you have a script set up to call ADPlus at specific intervals. With the message box up, the VBScript file will never end.

The *<HangActions>* element, pardon the bad pun, is where the action occurs. In nearly all cases, the default actions for hangs, defined in the *<Options>* element, are very worthwhile to run. I've listed all the commands run by default in Table 6-4 because the documentation does not report what's run. The first column of the table lists the ADPlus keyword for the command. To keep you from typing a long command string every time for each command, ADPlus allows text substitution from the configuration file. Additionally, these keywords expand to include any appropriate directories for the current run, which has a timestamp in the name, so you won't know the names beforehand. Note that I have not discussed some of the commands in this chapter because they are geared toward native development.

Table 6-4   Standard Commands in ADPlus Hang Mode

ADPlus Keyword	Actual Command	Meaning
FullDump	.dump /ma /c <comment> <filename>	Creates an SOS-compatible minidump.
Stacks	~*kb250	Walk the first 250 items on the call stacks for each thread.
LoadedModules	lm v	Display all the version information for loaded modules.
MatchingSymbols	lm l	Show all modules that had symbols loaded.
Heap	!heap 0 -k	Displays all operating system heap information, and on x86 systems, shows the stack back trace associated with each entry.
Handle	!handle 0 0	Displays the statistics table from the !handle command.
Dlls	!dlls	Show the table entries of all loaded modules.
Locks	!ntsdexts.locks	Display all acquired critical sections.
ThreadUsage	!runaway	Show how much time is used by each thread.

The *<CustomActions>* element is where even more action occurs. It allows you to specify any custom commands you want to execute after those specified in the *<Options>* element. As you can see from the comments in Listing 6-1, I'm running numerous SOS commands to get more information about the state of the application. If you've read the chapter to this point, the commands should be self-explanatory.

One issue with ADPlus configuration files that the documentation does not make clear is that you must explicitly separate all keywords and commands with semicolons. That's why I like to line up the items under the elements so I can scan down the list and ensure that the semicolon is present. Nothing is worse than building up a complicated ADPlus configuration file and having the debugger not report any data because ADPlus generates an invalid command.

Fortunately, ADPlus properly parses the separate lines, so it's no trouble. Of course, there would have to be one special case to the rule of semicolons on each line: the *Clear* keyword. In the *<HangAction><Option>* element, you can tell ADPlus not to do any of the default commands with *Clear*. If a semicolon follows *Clear*, ADPlus will report an invalid command error.

Because the configuration file in Listing 6-1 does not include a *<ProcessID>* or *<ProcessName>* element under the *<Settings>* element, you need to specify the process to run against on the ADPlus command line. To specify a process ID, use the *-p* switch, and to specify the process by name, use the *-pn* switch. What most people don't realize about ADPlus is that it will happily script the debugger to attach to multiple processes so you can specify multiple *-p* or *-pn* switches as required.

If you are working with IIS 6.0 and want to snap only a minidump of a particular application pool, the command *Tlist.exe -v* will show you all running processes and their command lines. (Tlist.exe comes as part of the Debugging Tools for Windows.) Look through the list for the different W3wp.exe instances and their *-ap* command-line options to identify the application pool in which each instance is running. You'll then have the process ID of the exact W3wp.exe instance you can use with ADPlus's *-p* switch.

The two other ADPlus switches you'll need to specify if you are using my DNHANG.xml file are *−c*, which tells ADPlus the full path to the configuration file, and *−o*, which is the output directory for all files. As part of the debugger script buildup, ADPlus will create a directory in the output location called Hang_Mode__Date_*month-day-year*__Time_*hour-minute-seconds*. This is great because that means you can continue to run the same ADPlus command line repeatedly without losing your data.

In the run's output directory are two key files: the minidump file and the log from the debugger. You could open the minidump and execute all the debugger commands again, but it's best to first open the log file and read the output. That way you save a great deal of time because you can see the results of the common commands, and if there are any anomalies, you can open up the dump and poke at it until your heart is content looking for the problem. By the way, if you want to see the script ADPlus generated for the debugger, look in the CDBScripts directory.

The one drawback of the default options in the hang configuration file is that it's writing a full-memory minidump. Although that minidump is invaluable, because the noninvasive attach is suspending your process, it can take too long to create the dump. With a large ASP.NET application, the minidump creation can easily take five to ten minutes to create. While the worker process is stopped in the debugger, all the connection requests are bouncing off and falling on the floor.

Listing 6-2 shows my DNHANG-Quick.xml file, which does a minimal amount of work to tell you what's going on in a .NET application. By turning off all the default operations that ADPlus wants to do, we avoid the full-memory minidump time and native call stack walks, which require symbol-loading time but still get useful .NET information. Since you can execute any commands in the *<CustomActions>* element, you have complete control of the information you want to see at any time.

Listing 6-2   DNHANG-Quick.xml ADPlus Configuration File

```
<!-- Quick HANG mode configuration for all process types. -->
<ADPlus>
  <Settings>
    <!-- Set the mode to HANG -->
    <RunMode>HANG</RunMode>
    <!-- Snap the dumps, don't tell me about it -->
    <Option>Quiet</Option>
  </Settings>
  <HangActions>
    <!-- Clear out all the default options that ADPlus wants to run. -->
    <Option>
      Clear
    </Option>
    <!-- For custom actions, I want to see all     -->
    <!-- the handle info, the managed CLR version, -->
    <!-- managed threads, and managed call stacks. -->
    <CustomActions>
      .loadby sos mscorwks;
      !eeversion;
      !threads;
      ~*e!clrstack;
    </CustomActions>
  </HangActions>
</ADPlus>
```

Crash Mode

Whereas hang mode simply gathers some information and jumps off the process, crash mode means that ADPlus configures the debugger to attach as a native debugger and perform specific commands on an exception or breakpoint. Although we can't yet set those breakpoints on our C# source code, there's still a tremendous amount of power available in the ADPlus crash mode.

Crash Mode Exceptions

The *<Exceptions>* element in the configuration file defines the actions you want to perform for all exceptions or a specific exception. There's one issue with the *<Exceptions>* element that may cause you some grief, and I want to show you how to work around it. Under *<Exceptions>*, the *<Options>* element can take a very neat keyword, *FullDumpOnFirstChance*. The documentation implies that you'll get a full-memory minidump each time your code throws any native SEH exception. Because .NET's exceptions are implemented internally with SEH, getting a minidump on each throw is a wonderful way of seeing what's happening in your application when running under testing scenarios. Listing 6-3 shows the configuration file that looks as if it would work.

Listing 6-3   Incorrect ADPlus configuration for a minidump for each exception

```
<ADPlus>
  <Settings>
    <!-- Only CRASH mode supports attaching and looking at exceptions. -->
    <RunMode>CRASH</RunMode>
    <!-- Be quiet and don't show any message boxes. -->
    <Option>Quiet</Option>
    <!-- Exception options. -->
  </Settings>
  <Exceptions>
    <!-- *Doesn't work!* *Doesn't work!* *Doesn't work!* *Doesn't work!*-->
    <Option>FullDumpOnFirstChance</Option>
  </Exceptions>
</ADPlus>
```

Although Listing 6-3's code will produce a minidump for each type of SEH exception, it over-writes the particular exception's minidump file each time one is thrown. In other words, you get a minidump of only the last exception thrown instead of all previous exceptions.

Fortunately, it's not too hard to come up with a workaround. The ADPlus documentation discusses the *<Config>* element under the *<Exceptions>* element in which you can configure the action you want for a specific exception or all exceptions. In reality, the *<Config>* element is where you're specifying the *sx* operations, which I discussed in the "Exceptions and Events" section earlier in the chapter. The configuration file in Listing 6-4 shows how to get a unique dump on each SEH thrown in your application.

Listing 6-4   DNCRASH-DumpOnAllFirstChance.xml ADPlus Configuration File

```
<!-- Write a minidump on all SEH exceptions ADPlus configuration file. -->
<ADPlus>
  <Settings>
    <!-- Only CRASH mode supports attaching and looking at exceptions. -->
    <RunMode>CRASH</RunMode>
    <!-- Don't pop up any modal dialogs. -->
    <Option>Quiet</Option>
    <!-- Exception options. -->
  </Settings>
  <Exceptions>
    <!-- Configure all exceptions to write a new dump every time there's a
         first chance exception. -->
    <Config>
      <!-- Set the configuration for all exceptions. -->
      <Code>AllExceptions</Code>
      <!-- Write the dump on first chance exceptions.-->
      <Actions1>FullDump</Actions1>
      <!-- Note that you can't use the ReturnAction1 element because it causes
           an error in ADPlus if you use AllExceptions. The documentation does
           not make clear that the ReturnActions1 applies only if you are
           setting specific exceptions values. -->
    </Config>
  </Exceptions>
</ADPlus>
```

When it comes to .NET, what you really want to get are minidumps only when a specific .NET exception type is thrown. Having a production application writing a minidump on every exception is completely impractical. With SOS giving us the *!soe* command, we might have something we can use to write that minidump only on a nasty *OutOfMemoryException*. Toward the bottom of the "*!StopOnException* (*!soe*) *and* *!PrintException* (*!pe*) Command" section earlier in this chapter, I discussed how the *!soe* command did its work by invoking the *sxe* command. If you didn't read that section carefully, I would encourage you to read it because that gives us a hint on how to get a minidump only when a specific .NET exception is thrown.

Listing 6-5 shows an ADPlus configuration file that writes a minidump only if there's been an *OutOfMemoryException*. *OutOfMemoryException* bugs are extremely hard to track down, but you can now use ADPlus to get the debugger attached and when the horrible occurs, you'll have the exact state of the application at the instance the problem happened.

Listing 6-5   DNCRASH-DumpOnOutOfMemoryException.xml ADPlus Configuration File

```xml
<!-- Write a minidump only when an OutOfMemoryException occurs ADPlus
     configuration file. -->
<ADPlus>
  <Settings>
    <!-- Only CRASH mode supports attaching and looking at exceptions. -->
    <RunMode>CRASH</RunMode>
    <!-- Don't pop up any modal dialogs. -->
    <Option>Quiet</Option>
    <!-- Exception options. -->
  </Settings>
  <Exceptions>
    <!-- Default to not doing any dumps on first chance exceptions. -->
    <Option>
      NoDumpOnFirstChance
    </Option>
    <Config>
      <!-- For all exceptions, turn off the stack walking for first chance
           exceptions. In production environments, you don't want to pay the
           performance hit for initial symbol loading and stack walking. -->
      <Code>
        AllExceptions
      </Code>
      <!-- At least log the message to the log file.-->
      <Actions1>
        Log
      </Actions1>
      <!-- If we're falling over on an unhandled exception, log it and write
           a minidump.-->
      <Actions2>
        Log;
        MiniDump;
      </Actions2>
      <!-- For first chance exceptions, say the debugger didn't handle it so
           the normal unwinding code gets it. -->
      <ReturnAction1>
```

```
        GN;
      </ReturnAction1>
      <!-- For unhandled exceptions just quit. -->
      <ReturnAction2>
        Q;
      </ReturnAction2>
    </Config>
    <Config>
      <!-- Set the configuration for CLR first chance exceptions. -->
      <Code>
        clr
      </Code>
      <!-- Turn off all the defaults from ADPlus.-->
      <Actions1>
        Void
      </Actions1>
      <!-- Execute the cool command to do the dump on the specific exception. -->
      <!-- Here's how to read the command:
          .loadby sos mscorwks
          // Load SOS based on the MScorwks.dll path.
          !stoponexception System.OutOfMemoryException 3
          // Tell SOS to set pseudo register 3 to 1 if the exception thrown is
          // a System.OutOfMemoryException.
          .if(@$t3==1){...}
          // Using the debugger command program, execute the expression in the
          // curly braces if pseudo register 3 is 1.
          .dump /ma /u c:\\x\\y\\foo.dmp
          // Write out a minidump. There's no way to get the full path to
          // where ADPlus is writing out the rest of the dumps.
          // Note that the command program code has a bug in it in which it
          // doesn't properly handle single \ characters. You probably don't
          // want spaces in the output directories either.
      -->
      <CustomActions1>
        .loadby sos mscorwks;
        !stoponexception System.OutOfMemoryException 3;
        .if @@(@$t3==1){.dump /ma /u C:\\DumpDirectory\\OOM.dmp}
      </CustomActions1>
      <!-- After taking the dump, let the application have it. -->
      <ReturnAction1>
        GN
      </ReturnAction1>
    </Config>
  </Exceptions>
</ADPlus>
```

There are two interesting points about the configuration file in Listing 6-5. The first is that the ADPlus default is to write a call stack out each time you have a first-chance exception. Because the idea of my configuration file is to run on production environments, having the symbol loading and stack walking occurring every time causes a performance hit that you don't need. Consequently, I turn off the stack walking but leave the logging on, which writes to the output log that a specific exception happened.

The second item is how I go about determining the exact CLR exception that occurred. As I mentioned, I take advantage of the *!soe* command to write one in a specific pseudo register if the exception type matches. If that's the case, I use the cool debugger command language to do a conditional command that will write the dump on that exception. Unfortunately, there's no way in your custom commands sections in ADPlus to get the current output directory name, so I have to manually declare exactly where the particular dump file will be written. With the */u* switch to *.dump*, I can ensure that the name is unique so as not to overwrite files. In addition, as you can see from the comments in the configuration file itself, you have to use double slashes (\\) for each path item because the debugger engine parses the string wrong.

The ADPlus configuration file's exception-handling prowess is an outstanding addition to your debugging tool chest. I showed an example of writing a minidump whenever a specific .NET exception is thrown, but a good exercise would be to extend DNCRASH-DumpOnOut-OfMemoryException.xml to write minidumps on several specific .NET exceptions. Take a look at the "*!StopOnException (!soe) and !PrintException (!pe)* Commands" section earlier in this chapter to get some ideas.

Before I move to ideas for handling breakpoints by using ADPlus configuration files, I do need to mention one last item concerning using ADPlus to configure the debugger in a production environment. If your architecture has you throwing thousands of exceptions in normal operation, you're going to have performance problems with the debugger attached to your application. When running under a native debugger, any SEH exception causes the operating system to suspend all the threads in the debuggee and report the exception into the debugger.

The heavy cross-process communication overhead can make your application unresponsive because of the volume of exceptions. As many bugs I work on for clients occur only in production environments, if you can't run ADPlus because of the volumes of exceptions being thrown, you've destroyed the last best hope of finding those problems. If you are throwing exceptions just because you can, you'll want to think long and hard about your architecture and fix it if you can. Finally, if you have an exception type called *GoodReturn-Exception* in which you report success, trust me—you need to rearchitect your application immediately!

Crash Mode Breakpoints

Configuring a breakpoint is very much like configuring an exception, except that you use the *<Breakpoints>* element. A very common scenario in which you'd want to get a minidump at a particular breakpoint is if your ASP.NET worker process is mysteriously ending. That means at some point in its operation, something is calling the Windows *ExitProcess* API from Kernel32.dll to end the application. The configuration file in Listing 6-6 shows setting a breakpoint on *ExitProcess* and writing a minidump.

Listing 6-6   DNCRASH-BreakOnExitProcess.xml ADPlus Configuration File

```
<!-- Break on ExitProcess ADPlus configuration file. -->
<ADPlus>
  <Settings>
    <!-- Set the mode to CRASH. -->
    <RunMode>CRASH</RunMode>
    <!-- Do the work, don't tell me about it. -->
    <Option>Quiet</Option>
  </Settings>
  <Exceptions>
    <!-- Don't dump on first chance exceptions. -->
    <Option>
      NoDumpOnFirstChance
    </Option>
  </Exceptions>
  <Breakpoints>
    <NewBP>
      <!-- Set the breakpoint on ExitProcess. -->
      <Address>
        kernel32!ExitProcess
      </Address>
      <!-- A normal breakpoint. -->
      <Type>
        BP
      </Type>
      <!-- When hit, do a full memory minidump and walk the call stacks. -->
      <Actions>
        FullDump;
        Stacks;
      </Actions>
      <!-- After doing the actions, continue on and let the application end. -->
      <ReturnAction>
        G
      </ReturnAction>
    </NewBP>
  </Breakpoints>
</ADPlus>
```

The main interesting point in Listing 6-6 is that because *ExitProcess* is an exported function from Kernel32.dll, I can use the *module!exported function* syntax to specify the native address to set. Once you have the minidump created on the call to *ExitProcess*, you'll need just to open up the minidump and look at the call stack of the current thread to see what led up to the call.

Snapping at the Right Time

As you've seen, getting the minidump written on a specific exception or when executing a native location isn't too difficult. However, it is a different story for other types of issues when you'd want to get the minidump, such as when memory usage grows past a certain point, or you suspect you're throwing an excessive number of exceptions. Fortunately, with all the performance counters available in Windows, there's data available for you to analyze and determine if this is the right time to create the minidump.

You could write your own performance counter monitor program that would spawn ADPlus when your specific condition was met, but the performance alerts built into Windows will do everything you need. You simply have to click a few buttons to tell the operating system what performance counters you want to monitor, the condition when the error occurs, and how to execute the program to write the dump. It's so simple, even a manager could handle it.

For example, if you suspect that there may be a kernel mode handle leak in your ASP.NET application, you could set up a performance alert to write a minidump whenever the handle count was greater than 5,000. To create this performance alert, from Control Panel\Administrative Tools, start the Computer Management console with administrator privileges. Under the System Tools, Performance Logs and Alerts tree control node, right-click Alerts, and from the shortcut menu, select New Alert Settings. After naming your alert in the New Alert Settings dialog box and clicking OK, the property page for the alert will open.

On the General tab of the alert property page, click Add, and the Add Counters dialog box will appear. Set the Performance Object to Process, select Handle Count in the counters list box, and in the instances list box, select your ASP.NET worker process. Clicking the Add button will add the performance counter but be sure to click the Close button to go back to the alert property page where you can set the Alert When Value Is combo box to Over and type 5000 in the Limit edit control. Figure 6-9 shows the filled-out General page.

Figure 6-9   Performance alert General property page

In the Sample Data Every section of the General property page, you'll want to pick an appropriate sampling interval for the performance alert. For the example I'm showing, a sampling value of once per hour is probably good. Since minidumps take several minutes to write out, you want to pick an interval that doesn't cause your performance alert to hang the machine by constantly writing out dumps of the target process. It's also a good idea to set the account to use in the Run As edit control. That way, if your batch file does more than just call ADPlus, you'll have the appropriate rights to network shares and other resources.

On the Action tab, select the Run This Program check box, and in the now-enabled edit control, type the program to run. It's best to use a batch file to start ADPlus from Performance Alerts so you don't have to mess with the long command-line options necessary for ADPlus inside the property page. Additionally, that gives you more processing options, such as restarting the worker process or anything else you would need to do to recover from the issue. In addition, you'll want to include the complete path to the batch file to ensure that it runs correctly. Figure 6-10 shows the completed Action tab.

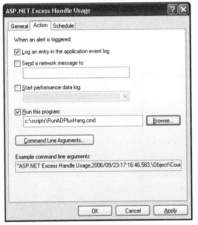

Figure 6-10   Performance Alert Action tab

The default Performance Alert behavior is to run the scan continually. However, if you want to have more control over the starting and stopping, the Schedule tab lets you control the exact starting and stopping times. You can also choose to start and stop the scans manually from the Management Console.

After you've clicked OK to create your performance alert, you still have one more step to allow it to run correctly. Still staying in Computer Management, you need to go to the Services and Applications, Services node in the tree control. In the Services view, double-click Performance Logs and Alerts to bring up the property pages for the service. Click the Log On tab, and select the Allow Service To Interact With Desktop check box. If the user is not set to the Local System account, you may need to enable that first.

Performance alerts are a wonderful tool, but if you're going to use them on a production server, you'll want to carefully think through what will occur when the performance alert triggers. While you're trying to solve a nasty bug, you could cause very nasty problems for your server if you accidentally leave the sampling interval at 5 seconds, causing the server to end up in a minidump-writing frenzy. However, at least with performance alerts, you'll stand a fighting chance of getting that dump right when you need it.

Summary

Just when you were beginning to wonder if this chapter would ever end, you finally have enough information to begin mastering WinDBG, SOS, and ADPlus effectively. These are complicated tools, and my mission was to provide you the background and tricks for utilizing them to start making sense of the toughest production-only problems you encounter.

After surviving this chapter, you're prepared to fully understand and utilize two of the best resources in the world about advanced debugging. The first is a bit dated, but it's still one of the best references around, *Production Debugging for .NET Framework Applications*, from the Patterns and Practices Group at Microsoft (*http://msdn.microsoft.com/library /default.asp?url=/library/en-us/dnbda/html/DBGrm.asp*). The guide will take you systematically through ASP.NET deadlocks and memory leaks. There's nothing I can do to improve on anything that Aaron Barth and Jackie Richards wrote.

The final WinDBG, SOS, and ADPlus resource is simply a blog, but oh, what a blog it is! Tess Ferrandez's "If broken it is, fix it you should" (*http://blogs.msdn.com/tess/default.aspx*) blog must become your home page. Tess is an Escalation Engineer at Microsoft and lives day in and day out in SOS debugging the problems that no one else can at Microsoft. She's a far better writer than I could ever hope to be, and I always learn something every time I read one of her posts. To take your SOS knowledge to the next level, start with her first post and read forward. I'm just thankful that I was able to get the Bugslayer column in MSDN Magazine before Tess started developing software.

Part III
Power Tools

In this part:

Chapter 7
Extending the Visual Studio IDE

As Microsoft Visual Studio has progressed over the years, more and more of a developer's day is spent inside one window frame. In the ancient past of Microsoft Visual C++ 6.0, many of us used only basic editing, building, and debugging. For bug tracking, design diagrams, and advanced editing, we were using other tools. With the advent of Visual Studio 2005, it's almost possible to spend your entire working day inside the same application. From the Visual Studio Team System version control and bug tracking, to the class designer, to Web deployment, it's all right there. We even have a Web browser included so you can "research" while still looking productive. As far as I can tell, all that's lacking are three key add-ins for Visual Studio to truly keep us there all day: e-mail integration, Internet messaging integration, and Halo integration. If those three add-ins get written, you can let your Alt+Tab fingers atrophy.

Without a doubt, the extensibility story for Visual Studio is a very strong one. Sadly, very few developers consider how much power they have at their fingertips. Countless developers have said if only Visual Studio would do "X," it would be the greatest development environment on the planet. In nearly all cases, what they were asking for was relatively easy to do given the extensibility we have in Visual Studio. Many developers complain that end users don't take the time to learn about computers. I always counter that argument with "I can't believe how many developers know almost nothing about their development environments." Developers don't need to know all the registry keys used by Visual Studio, but they do need to know what it takes to extend the environment so they can solve problems once or add a missing feature required by their development shop.

There are four elements to the extensibility functionality: macros, add-ins, wizards, and Visual Studio Industry Partner (VSIP). Visual Studio allows you to create macros with the built-in Visual Studio Macros IDE editor. This editor looks and behaves just as the Visual Studio environment does, so your investment in learning about that environment pays off when writing macros. This environment is called Visual Studio for Applications (VSA) and is something you can integrate into your products.

The one limitation of VSA is that you can write macros only in Microsoft Visual Basic. Since Microsoft .NET is supposed to be language-agnostic, I can't see why Microsoft limited the environment by not supporting C#. Basically, this limitation means that it doesn't matter that you had decided to stick to C#—maybe because you have a thing for semicolons—you'll still need to learn Visual Basic to write macros.

The second option is through add-ins and wizards. Whereas macros are nice for small, non-UI–related tasks, add-ins are COM components that allow you to write true extensions to the IDE. For example, you can create tool windows (your own windows), add property pages to the Options dialog box, and respond to menu commands from add-ins. Anyone you give a macro to can see your macro source code, but add-ins are distributed in binary form, and you can use any language that supports COM to write them.

Wizards are most useful for tasks that require you to lead the user through the steps necessary for accomplishing a task. A perfect example is the Smart Device Application Wizard that walks you through creating a smart device application. With the advent of Visual Studio Templates, there's much less need for wizards.

The final extensibility options are Visual Studio Industry Partner (VSIP) packages. Almost any of the ideas you've had for extending Visual Studio can be handled with a macro or an add-in. However if you wanted to create a completely new project type, create an editor that handles a new language, or create a debugger that can debug binaries running on a different operating system, you would need to turn to VSIP. For more information on VSIP, visit the extensibility Web site at *http://msdn.microsoft.com/vstudio/partners*. The great news about VSIP is that it no longer requires a license fee to get the VSIP SDK. Now you can get the SDK free by filling out a legal agreement.

As you can imagine, VSIP is a huge topic and one worthy of an entire book on its own, so I won't be covering it here. My goal for this chapter is to give you an idea of what macros and add-ins can do by presenting real-world tools that have helped speed up my development. By seeing what these tools do, you'll get a good overview of the trials and tribulations you'll run into when writing your particular "tool that no one can live without." Given the fact that very few developers do wizards, I won't discuss those. When it comes to macros and add-ins, I won't be taking you through the usual "click this wizard button to make an add-in pop out" steps that other books will. I'm assuming that you've read the Visual Studio documentation, so I'll spend my time pointing out the holes and problems I ran into in order to save you all the time I wasted getting things to work.

I'll first cover some tricks for macros that aren't in the documentation and lead up to CommenTater, a cool macro that ensures that your XML documentation comments are included and up to date. The first add-in, WhoAmI, is an extremely simple tool to show the user account and permissions that an instance of Visual Studio is running under. As I discussed extensively in the introduction, if you are developing software with administrator privileges, you are absolutely and completely wrong. The second add-in, Hidden Settings, shows how to create custom property pages in the Options dialog box with new Visual Studio 2005 managed code registration. Hidden Settings provides a way to access various hidden and undocumented settings for Visual Studio.

The final add-in, SettingsMaster, is the most ambitious. The mission of SettingsMaster is to provide .NET batch project settings so you can change a single project or all the projects in a solution without having to manually change each project. For example, with SettingsMaster, changing a define on all projects is as simple as clicking a button. Additionally, SettingsMaster comes with settings configurations to change your build settings to those I recommended in the section "Schedule Time for Building Debugging Systems" of Chapter 2. Armed with SettingsMaster, keeping your team projects coordinated should be trivial.

Extending with Macros

Before I discuss the CommenTater macro and the other macros in the Wintellect.VSMacros project (which you can find in the .\Macros directory with the book's source code), you'll need to load it into the Macro Explorer window in Visual Studio. Macros are a per-user setting, so the WintellectToolsInstall.MSI does not install them. To add the Wintellect.VSMacros file to your IDE, first open the Macro Explorer (on the View menu, select Other Windows, and then select Macro Explorer, or press Alt+F8 with the default keyboard settings), right-click the Macros item in the tree list, select Load Macro Project from the context menu, and then select .\Macros\Wintellect.VSMacros.

I also want to spend a little bit of time discussing a few key things about macros and some of the issues you'll encounter. The biggest point I want to make is that even if you think you have the coolest add-in idea in the world and can't wait to get started, you need to spend a lot of time writing macros before you jump into building add-ins. Because macros access all the same objects and properties as add-ins, they provide the best opportunity to learn about the ins and outs of the Visual Studio object model. As you'll see later in the chapter, the object model has numerous quirks, and getting add-ins working is sometimes problematic. Macros are much easier to write and debug, so you'll want to use them first to prototype.

Before finding the Macro option on the Tools menu, you should spend some time reading the documentation about macros and the object model. Macros themselves are discussed in the Visual Studio 2005 documentation by searching for Visual Studio Macros. You can find the all-important object model by searching for Automation Object Model Chart in the Help.

After perusing the documentation for a while to see what the various objects are, start recording macros so that you can see some of the objects in action. Keep in mind that recording works primarily on the code editors (including the Find/Replace dialog boxes), Solution Explorer, and window activation. You won't be able to record things such as building up a Web form or Windows form with controls. Also make sure to take a look at the macro samples provided by Microsoft, which are automatically loaded into the Macro Explorer as part of the Samples macro project. The macro samples are good examples of how to use the object model to solve problems. The MakeAddinFromMacroProj macro (in the MakeAddin macro project) is one of my personal favorites because it takes a macro and converts it to an add-in. It shows the power we now have at our fingertips with Visual Studio.

Another favorite module is the Debugger module because it shows you almost everything you can do with the *Debugger* object. For more tricks with the Debugger object, go to Jim Griesmer's blog entry at *http://blogs.msdn.com/jimgries/archive/2005/12/12/501492.aspx*. He's a developer on the debugger team at Microsoft, and he shows you his favorite debugger macros, which are worth adding to your collection.

There are two ways to execute macros: by double-clicking the macro function name in the Macro Explorer and by using the Command window. If you start typing macro, the Command window's IntelliSense pop-up window, shown in Figure 7-1, will allow you to choose the macro to run.

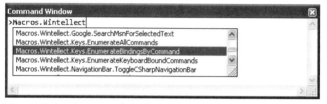

Figure 7-1   Command window's IntelliSense pop-up window executing a macro

If you're really into using the Command window to run macros or any of the other built-in commands, the built-in alias command allows you to redefine shorter text commands so that you don't have to type something like this every time you want to run a macro:

```
Macros.Wintellect.CommenTater.AddNoCommentTasksForSolution
```

To alias the previous example to something shorter, use the following command in the Command window:

```
alias CTforSLN Macros.Wintellect.CommenTater.AddNoCommentTasksForSolution
```

You also can remove aliases by passing a /d in front of the defined alias.

Macro Parameters

One fact that's not very clear from the Macro Explorer window and the Command window's IntelliSense pop-up window is that the only macros shown in both windows are macros that don't take any parameters. That makes sense in Macro Explorer because it would be pretty difficult to pass parameters when you're double-clicking an item. However, if you're using the Command window, you probably do want to pass some form of parameter. The trick is to declare the macro subroutine as taking a single optional string parameter, as in the following:

```
Sub ParamMacro(Optional ByVal theParam As String = "")
```

While looking at this declaration, you're probably wondering how you'd pass multiple parameters to the macro. It turns out that when you pass parameters, the macro environment in

Visual Studio treats parameters as a single string, and it's up to you to chop up the string to extract individual parameters. The good news is that it takes a simple bit of regular expression knowledge to do your own parsing. Even better news is that I've already done the work, so you need just to copy my code.

In Wintellect.VSMacros, the Utilities module contains a function, *SplitParameters*, which treats commas as parameter delimiters and returns the individual parameters as a string array. When you look at the function, you'll see that a regular expression, written by Michael Ash, does all the heavy lifting. I found that regular expression at the wonderful RegExLib.com Web site, which is a great resource for anything related to regular expressions.

In the Utilities module, you'll also find some convenient wrappers I created around the Command window and Output window objects. These make showing the results of macros much easier than manually manipulating those windows. As you look through the macros in Wintellect.VSMacros, you'll see them used all over the place.

Debugging Macros

Since VSA is just Visual Studio in a slightly different form, all the debugging tricks except the C#-specific items I talked about in Chapter 5, "Power Debugging," also apply to debugging macros. However, one of the first things you'll notice about both macro and add-in development is that the Visual Studio IDE swallows exceptions like crazy. Although it makes sense for the IDE not to allow any exceptions to percolate up and crash the IDE, the IDE swallows so many unhandled exceptions, you might not even realize you're causing exceptions. When I developed my first macros, I sat for 20 minutes wondering why I could never seem to hit a breakpoint I set.

What I end up doing to ensure that there are no surprises is to open the Exceptions dialog box in the Macro IDE, select the Common Language Runtime Exceptions node in the Exceptions tree control, and then select the Thrown check box. This will set the macro debugger to stop on any exception. Figure 7-2 shows the proper settings. This will probably cause you to stop in the debugger a lot more, but at least you won't have any surprises when it comes to your code.

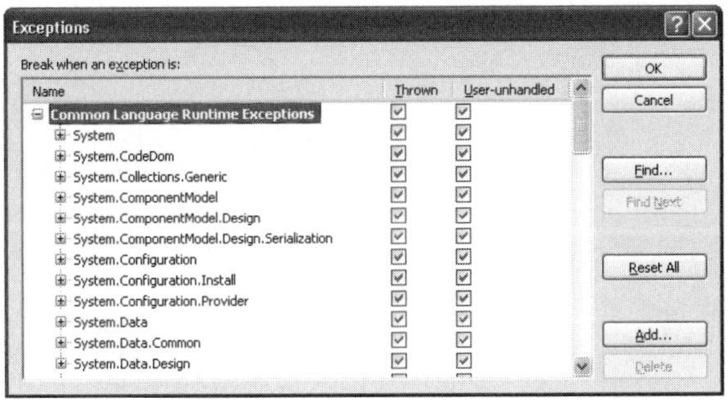

Figure 7-2   Setting the Exceptions dialog box to stop on all exceptions

One thing I've also noticed about debugging macros is that even when you set the Exceptions dialog box to stop on all exceptions, it might not. The trick to getting the macro debugger to start working correctly is to set a breakpoint somewhere in your code after you've set the Exceptions dialog box settings.

Code Elements

One of the most amazing aspects of Visual Studio is that all the programming constructs for source files can be accessed easily through the object model. The fact that we can now simply add, change, or remove items such as methods in all languages supported by Visual Studio without having to do the parsing ourselves opens up huge opportunities for all sorts of unique tools that might never have been created because parsing is so hard. Every time I use the code elements to manipulate the code in a file, I'm amazed at how cool this capability really is.

To show you how easy it is to access and utilize the code elements, I created a macro, shown in Listing 7-1, that dumps the code elements out of the active document. What's not obvious is that the code works for any language supported by Visual Studio. The output reports the name of the code element along with its code element type. The type indicates if the code element is a method, variable, et cetera. You can find this macro with this book's sample code in the Wintellect.VSMacros, Examples module along with its supporting module, Utilities.

Listing 7-1 DumpActiveDocCodeElements macro

```
' Dumps all the code elements for the open document of a project.
Public Sub DumpActiveDocCodeElements()
    ' Where the output goes. Note that the OutputPane class comes
    ' from the Utilities macro project.
    Dim ow As OutputPane = New OutputPane("Open Doc Code Elements")
    ' Clear the output pane.
    ow.Clear()

    ' See if there's a document open.
    Dim doc As Document = DTE.ActiveDocument
    If (doc Is Nothing) Then
        ow.WriteLine("No open document")
        Exit Sub
    End If

    ' Get the code model for the doc. You have to get the project
    ' item to diddle down to the code elements
    Dim fileMod As FileCodeModel = Doc.ProjectItem.FileCodeModel

    If (fileMod IsNot Nothing) Then
        DumpElements(ow, fileMod.CodeElements, 0)
    Else
        ow.WriteLine("Unable to get the FileCodeModel!")
    End If
End Sub

Private Sub DumpElements(ByVal ow As OutputPane, _
                         ByVal elements As CodeElements, _
                         ByVal indentLevel As Integer)
```

```
    Dim currentElement As CodeElement2
    For Each currentElement In elements

        Dim i As Integer = 0

        While (i < indentLevel)
            ow.OutPane.OutputString("  ")
            i = i + 1
        End While

        ' If there's an exception accessing the FullName property,
        ' it's probably an unnamed parameter.
        Dim name As String
        Try
            name = currentElement.FullName
        Catch e As COMException
            name = "'Empty Name'"
        End Try
        Dim kind As vsCMElement2 = CType(currentElement.Kind, vsCMElement2)
        ow.WriteLine(Name + "(" + currentElement.Kind.ToString() + ")")

        Dim childElements As CodeElements = Nothing

        childElements = currentElement.Children

        If (Not (childElements Is Nothing)) Then
            If (childElements.Count > 0) Then
                DumpElements(ow, childElements, indentLevel + 1)
            End If
        End If
    Next
End Sub
```

CommenTater: The Cure for the Common Potato?

As you could tell from discussion of the custom Code Analysis/FxCop rules I provide as part of the book's source code, I have a fetish about making sure my XML documentation comments are on all public items in an assembly and are up to date. One of my favorite features in Visual Studio is that typing /// or '" above a construct automatically inserts the appropriate documentation comments for an item, depending on the language. There are two very important reasons you should always fill out XML documentation comments. The first is that doing so enforces a consistent commenting standard across teams and, well, the .NET programming universe. The second is that the IDE IntelliSense automatically picks up any specified <summary> and <param> tags, which is a great help to others using your code because it gives them much more valuable information about the item. If the code is in the project, you don't have to do anything to get the benefits of using documentation comments. If you're providing a binary-only solution, the documentation comments can be gathered into an XML file at compile time, so you can still provide the cool summary tips to users. All you need to do is have the resultant XML file in the same directory as the binary, and Visual Studio automatically picks up the comments to show in the IntelliSense tips. By the way, the Object Browser will also use the XML file for its display.

I encourage you to read about all the XML documentation comment tags in the Visual Studio documentation so that you can do the best job possible documenting your code. It's very easy to create the files by setting the /DOC option to the C# and Visual Basic .NET compilers, and you'll want to do so for every configuration you build. To manually turn on the /DOC switch for non-ASP.NET C# projects, select the Build tab in the project properties, and then in the Output section, select the XML documentation file check box. The default is to put the file in your Output path, which is hard-coded initially. That means if you change your Output path, Visual Studio will continue writing your XML documentation file to the original directory. Fortunately, all you need to do is clear and reselect the XML documentation file check box to apply the latest output path. Figure 7-3 shows the Output section filled out.

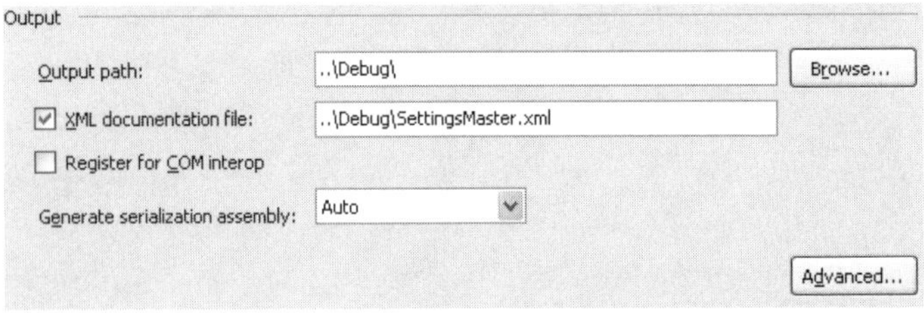

Figure 7-3   Setting the XML documentation file for C# projects

As usual, Visual Basic non-ASP.NET projects are slightly different. In the project properties, click the Compile tab and select the Generate XML Documentation File check box. Visual Basic does the right thing and always puts the XML documentation file in the same directory where the assembly builds. If the prospect of manually setting the documentation file for every configuration in your projects sounds tedious, you'll want to use SettingsMaster to do all the work for you.

Since documentation comments are so important, I wanted some way of automatically adding them to my C# and Visual Basic .NET code. While Roland Weigelt's outstanding GhostDoc add-in (*http://www.roland-weigelt.de/ghostdoc/*) is excellent for automating one method's comments at a time, I wanted a tool that would look for all methods I'd forgotten to document and add comments so I could find where they were missing. As I was thinking about how I would show the user all the missing comments, I stumbled across a very nice feature of the Task List window in the IDE. If you set the Task List window combo box to Comments, any comments in your code that contain "TODO" automatically show up in the window. In fact, if you go to the Options dialog box from the Tools menu, select Environment, and then select the Task List property page, you'll see that HACK, MISSING, and UNDONE are other tokens that the IDE will look for in your comments. You can also add your own tokens, such as FIX, UPDATE, and WHO_IS_THE_IDIOT_THAT_WROTE_THIS (spaces cannot be used in the tokens). My idea was to have either a macro or an add-in that would add any missing documentation comments and use "TODO" in the comments so that I could easily go through and ensure that all the documentation comments were properly filled out. The result was CommenTater. The following shows a method that's been processed by CommenTater:

```
/// <summary>
/// TODO - Add Test function summary comment
/// </summary>
/// <remarks>
/// TODO - Add Test function remarks comment
/// </remarks>
/// <param name="x">
/// TODO - Add x parameter comment
/// </param>
/// <param name="y">
/// TODO - Add y parameter comment
/// </param>
/// <returns>
/// TODO - Add return comment
/// </returns>
public static int Test ( Int32 x , Int32 y )
{
    return ( x ) ;
}
```

While the idea of showing the TODO items in the Task List is an excellent one, there's a small problem with C# with Visual Studio 2005: the TODO items don't show up. Prior versions of Visual Studio had this working with C#, and it works with Visual Basic in Visual Studio 2005. I hope that this will be fixed in a service pack release because it's a very useful feature.

Visual Studio makes iterating the code elements in a source file trivial, so I was pretty excited because I thought that all I'd have to do was wind through the code elements, grab any lines above the method or property, and if the documentation comment wasn't present, poke in the documentation comment for that method or property. That's when I discovered that the code elements all come with a property named *DocComment* that returns the actual documentation comment for the item. I immediately tipped my hat to the developers for thinking ahead and really making the code elements useful. Now all I needed to do was set the *DocComment* property to the value I wanted, and life was good.

Once you have the book's macros open, double click Wintellect, right-click the Comment-Tater module, and then select Edit to bring it up in the macro editor. The source code for the macro is too large to include in the book pages, but consider looking at the file as I discuss the ideas behind its implementation. My main idea was to create two functions, *AddNoComment-TasksForSelectedProjects* and *CurrentSourceFileAddNoCommentTasks*. You can tell from the names what level the functions were to work on. For the most part, the basic algorithm looks relatively similar to the examples in Listing 7-1 in that I just iterate through all the code elements and manipulate the *DocComment* property for each code element type.

The first issue I ran into was what I considered a design flaw in the code element object model. The *DocComment* property is not a common property on the *CodeElement* class, which can be substituted as a base for any general code element. So I had to jump through the hoops necessary to convert the generic *CodeElement* object into the actual type based on the *Kind* property. That's why the *RecurseCodeElements* function has the big *Select...Case* statement in it.

The second problem I ran into was completely self-inflicted. For some reason, it never dawned on me that the *DocComment* property for a code construct needed to be treated as a fully formed XML fragment. I'd build up the documentation comment string I wanted, and when I'd try to assign it to the *DocComment* property, an *ArgumentException* would be thrown. I was quite confused because it looked like the *DocComment* property was both readable and writable, but it was acting as if it were only readable. For some bizarre reason, I had a brain cramp and didn't realize that the reason for the exception was that I wasn't properly bracketing my documentation comment XML with the necessary *<doc></doc>* element. Of course, thinking that the *DocComment* property was read-only, I implemented all doc comment updating using text insertion. After my brain cramp fixed itself, I realized that I needed just to set a properly formed XML string into the *DocComment* and let Visual Studio take care of all insertions. The last oddity I want to mention about *DocComment* properties is that C# *DocComment* properties always show the *<doc></doc>* root when you look at the string, but Visual Basic .NET *DocComment* properties do not.

Listing 7-2 shows the *ProcessFunctionComment*, and you can see that I take advantage of the XML classes in the Microsoft .NET Framework library to do the hard work required to get the information out of the existing documentation comment string, allowing me to build up a new version. The *ProcessFunctionComment* function might reorder your documentation comments; I had to pick an order for putting the individual nodes in the file. Additionally, I format the comments as I like to see them, so CommenTater might change your careful formatting of your documentation comments, but it won't lose any information.

Listing 7-2   ProcessFunctionComment from CommenTater

```
' Does all the work to take an existing function comment and ensure
' that everything in it is correct. This might reorder your
' comments, so you might want to change it.
Private Sub ProcessFunctionComment(ByVal func As CodeFunction)

    Debug.Assert("" <> func.DocComment, """""" <> Func.DocComment")

    ' Holds the original doc comment.
    Dim xmlDocOrig As New XmlDocument
    ' I LOVE THIS!  By setting PreserveWhitespace to true, the
    ' XmlDocument class will keep most of the formatting...
    xmlDocOrig.PreserveWhitespace = True

    ' This is annoying. Since Visual Basic does not properly put on
    ' the <doc> root element, I've got to add it so LoadXml works.
    Dim xmlString As String = func.DocComment
```

```vb
If (func.Language = CodeModelLanguageConstants.vsCMLanguageVB) Then
    Dim sb As StringBuilder = New StringBuilder()
    sb.AppendFormat("<doc>{0}</doc>", xmlString)
    xmlString = sb.ToString()
End If


' Speaking of inconsistencies... Even though I keep all formatting
' of any inner XML, setting a C# DocComment property will strip out
' empty CRLF lines. Visual Basic preserves all formatting.


xmlDocOrig.LoadXml(xmlString)

Dim rawXML As New StringBuilder

' The function name properly formatted for XML.
Dim FName As String = ProperlyXMLizeFuncName(func.Name)

' Get the summary node.
Dim node As XmlNode
Dim nodes As XmlNodeList = xmlDocOrig.GetElementsByTagName("summary")

If (0 = nodes.Count) Then
    rawXML.Append(SimpleSummaryComment(func, FName, "function"))
Else
    rawXML.AppendFormat("<summary>{0}", vbCrLf)
    For Each node In nodes
        rawXML.AppendFormat("{0}{1}", node.InnerXml.Trim(), vbCrLf)
    Next
    rawXML.AppendFormat("</summary>{0}", vbCrLf)
End If

' Get the remarks node.
nodes = xmlDocOrig.GetElementsByTagName("remarks")
If (nodes.Count > 0) Then
    rawXML.AppendFormat("<remarks>{0}", vbCrLf)
    For Each node In nodes
        rawXML.AppendFormat("{0}{1}", node.InnerXml.Trim(), vbCrLf)
    Next
    rawXML.AppendFormat("</remarks>{0}", vbCrLf)
ElseIf (True = addRemarksToFunctions) Then
    rawXML.AppendFormat("<remarks>{0}TODO - Add {1} function " + _
                        "remarks comment{0}</remarks>", _
                        vbCrLf, FName)
End If

' Get any parameters described in the doc comments.
nodes = xmlDocOrig.GetElementsByTagName("param")

' Does the function have parameters?
If (0 <> func.Parameters.Count) Then

    ' Slap any existing doc comment params into a hash table with
    ' the parameter name as the key.
    Dim existHash As New Hashtable
```

```
For Each node In nodes
    Dim paramName As String
    Dim paramText As String
    paramName = node.Attributes("name").InnerXml
    paramText = node.InnerText.Trim()
    existHash.Add(paramName, paramText)
Next

' Loop through the parameters.
Dim elem As CodeElement
For Each elem In func.Parameters
    ' Is this one in the hash of previous filled-in params?
    If (True = existHash.ContainsKey(elem.Name)) Then
        rawXML.AppendFormat("<param name=""{0}"">{1}{2}{1}" + _
                                            "</param>{1}", _
                            elem.Name, _
                            vbCrLf, _
                            existHash(elem.Name))
        ' Get rid of this key.
        existHash.Remove(elem.Name)
    Else
        ' A new parameter was added.
        rawXML.AppendFormat("<param name=""{0}"">{1}TODO - Add " + _
                            "{0} parameter comment{1}</param>{1}", _
                            elem.Name, vbCrLf)
    End If
Next

' If there is anything left in the hash table, a param
' was either removed or renamed. I'll add the remaining
' with TODOs so the user can do the manual deletion.
If (existHash.Count > 0) Then
    Dim keyStr As String
    For Each keyStr In existHash.Keys
        Dim desc As Object = existHash(keyStr)
        rawXML.AppendFormat("<param name=""{0}"">{1}{2}{1}{3}" + _
                                            "{1}</param>{1}", _
                            keyStr, _
                            vbCrLf, _
                            desc, _
                            "TODO - Remove param tag")
    Next
End If
End If

' Take care of returns if necessary.
If ("" <> func.Type.AsFullName) Then
    nodes = xmlDocOrig.GetElementsByTagName("returns")
    ' Do any returns nodes, but only if there's an actual return value.
    If (0 = nodes.Count) Then
        If (String.IsNullOrEmpty(func.Type.AsFullName) = False) And _
           (String.Compare(func.Type.AsFullName, "System.Void") <> 0) Then
            rawXML.AppendFormat("<returns>{0}TODO - Add return comment" + _
                                            "{0}</returns>", _
                        vbCrLf)
```

```
                End If
            Else
                rawXML.AppendFormat("<returns>{0}", vbCrLf)

                For Each node In nodes
                    rawXML.AppendFormat("{0}{1}", node.InnerXml.Trim(), vbCrLf)
                Next

                rawXML.Append("</returns>")
            End If
        End If

        ' Copy existing examples nodes, if any.
        nodes = xmlDocOrig.GetElementsByTagName("example")
        If (nodes.Count > 0) Then
            rawXML.AppendFormat("<example>{0}", vbCrLf)
            For Each node In nodes
                rawXML.AppendFormat("{0}{1}", node.InnerXml.Trim(), vbCrLf)
            Next
            rawXML.AppendFormat("</example>{0}", vbCrLf)
        End If

        ' Copy existing permission nodes, if any.
        nodes = xmlDocOrig.GetElementsByTagName("permission")
        If (nodes.Count > 0) Then
            For Each node In nodes
                rawXML.AppendFormat("<permission cref=""{0}"">{1}", _
                                node.Attributes("cref").InnerText, _
                                vbCrLf)
                rawXML.AppendFormat("{0}{1}", node.InnerXml.Trim(), vbCrLf)
                rawXML.AppendFormat("</permission>{0}", vbCrLf)
            Next
        End If

        ' Finally exceptions.
        nodes = xmlDocOrig.GetElementsByTagName("exception")

        If (nodes.Count > 0) Then
            For Each node In nodes
                rawXML.AppendFormat("<exception cref=""{0}"">{1}", _
                                node.Attributes("cref").InnerText, _
                                vbCrLf)
                rawXML.AppendFormat("{0}{1}", node.InnerXml.Trim(), vbCrLf)
                rawXML.AppendFormat("</exception>{0}", vbCrLf)
            Next
        End If
        func.DocComment = FinishOffDocComment(func, rawXML.ToString())
    End Sub
```

Once I had everything working with documentation comment updating, I thought it'd be a good idea to go ahead and implement the code necessary to handle an undo context. That way you could do a single Ctrl+Z and restore all changes to CommenTater in case of a bug. In prior versions of Visual Studio, there was a bug in the undo contexts if I sent them globally, so all changes the macro made could be undone in a single operation. Fortunately, the developers fixed that bug so that I can offer a global undo. If you like the idea of having the individual change undo, you can set the *individualUndo* field near the top of the file to True.

Another tweak I had to make to the macro moving from Visual Studio .NET 2003 to Visual Studio 2005 was to revamp the project enumeration. Prior versions of Visual Studio did not allow project folders, so my macro was finding files only that were at the top level. Since there's an arbitrary number of folder levels, I needed just to do the recursion looking for all project items that have a non-empty *FileCodeModel* property. If you do have to enumerate project items, make sure to look at the *ListProj* macro in the Samples.VSMacros file because that will show you exactly what you'll need to do.

In addition to the *individualUndo* field I mentioned earlier, there are two other option fields that you may want to change. By default, the CommenTater macros put comments only on those items that are public in an assembly. If you want to have missing documentation comments applied to all methods, set the *visibleOnly* field at the top of the file to *False*. The final option field to change the output is the *addRemarksToFunctions* field. As you can see from the name, if it's set to *True*, all methods will be checked for a *<remarks>...</remarks>* section in the comment, and if one is not there, the macro will add it with a TODO.

CommenTater is a macro I use all the time, and I think you'll find it useful for your development. As with any code, there's always room for improvement. One feature I'd like to integrate into the code is automatic *<exception>...</exception>* documentation generation. Since the *CodeElements* don't go into methods, you'd have to do some parsing on the actual text of the method or property. That sounds like a job for a regular expression and the good news is that Tony Chow already produced them in an MSDN Magazine article (*http://msdn.microsoft.com /msdnmag/issues/05/07/XMLComments/default.aspx*). Another feature that may take a little more work would be one that allows users to specify the formatting they want for their XML documentation comments. Whereas I like mine with the element markers and inner text all on separate lines, others may not like that. If you have any other feature suggestions, don't hesitate to send them to me because I will definitely consider them.

More Macros for You

As you look through Wintellect.VSMacros, you'll see numerous other modules, which contain macros you'll find useful in your daily development. In Chapter 5's "Advanced Breakpoints and How to Use Them" section, I mentioned the *BreakPointHelper* module, which contains two macros, *SetBreakpointsOnDocMethods* and *RemoveBreakpointsOnDocMethods*. Those macros run though the code elements in the active document, set a breakpoint at the entry point for each method and property in the file, and remove them, respectively. These macros take advantage of the *BreakPoint.Tag* property to identify the breakpoints set by the *SetBreakpointsOnDocMethods* macro so that the *RemoveBreakpointsOnDocMethods* macro removes only those breakpoints. That way none of your existing breakpoints are removed by using these macros.

Also in Chapter 5, I discussed the TracePointMacros module in the "Tracepoints" section. The macros in that module show you how to work around the major limitation of Tracepoint breakpoints by faking out the IDE to think it is stopping on a breakpoint but using another thread to tell the debugger to continue execution.

The revision marks in the Visual Studio editor are wonderful because a small yellow bar next to a line indicates a line that's changed but that you haven't saved. A small green bar is a line that's changed but you have saved. Unfortunately, there's no way for you to have the editor clear out those bars so you can see changes between two points. What you have to do is close the editor window and reopen it. The problem there is that when you reopen the window, the cursor does not go back to the last place you were editing in the document but to the first line and column. Because there are many times when you want to look at code changes in isolation, The RevMarks module contains a single macro, *ClearRevMarks*, which saves your current location and selection in the file, closes the source window, reopens it, and puts the cursor and selection back. When I initially started to write the macro, I thought it would be a ten-line quickie, but things are not always so simple in Visual Studio. You can see the trials and tribulations I went through by looking at the macro's code.

The Keys module was born out of my frustration looking for the keystroke bound to a particular command. The Options dialog box, Environment node, Keyboard property page is fine for binding a command to a keystroke, but it's worthless for easily finding keystrokes that perform different commands in different editors or contexts. The first macro, *EnumerateAllCommands*, lists all the commands in the IDE in alphabetical order along with the keystrokes that are bound to them. Because various tools in the IDE may implement identically named commands, such as *Edit.Breakline*, the keystroke bindings are shown prefixed with the tool they are bound to. For example, the following shows that the *Edit.Breakline* command has four different bindings as the tool is shown to the left of the :: characters.

```
Edit.BreakLine (Windows Forms Designer::Enter |
               Text Editor::Shift+Enter |
               Text Editor::Enter |
               Report Designer::Enter)
```

The two other macros in the Keys module, *EnumerateBindingsByCommand* and *EnumerateKeyboardBoundCommands* are similar in that they show only commands bound to keystrokes. The *EnumerateBindingsByCommand* dumps out the list sorted by keystrokes, and *EnumerateKeyboardBoundCommands* shows the output sorted by command. As a real keyboard maven, I've learned a huge number of new keystrokes by looking at the output of these two macros. In my case, my carpel tunnel syndrome is exacerbated by mouse usage, so the more I can keep my fingers on the keyboard in Visual Studio, the healthier I am.

We all want Visual Studio to run as fast as possible, and a blog entry by Roland Weigelt at *http://weblogs.asp.net/rweigelt/archive/2006/05/16/446536.aspx* showed a macro, *ToggleCSharpNavigationBar*, that toggles the navigation bar on top of the C# editor on and off. Roland mentioned that he's discovered that turning off the navigation bar, which are the two combo boxes on top of the editor window that allow you to navigate classes and methods in a file, speed up the editor for him. Although I haven't done any actual performance tests, it feels faster for me. Because I never use the navigation bars, turning them off was no big deal for me. Roland graciously allowed me to include his macro in the NavigationBar module.

Two other modules, SelectedSearch and FormatToHtml, are courtesy of Jeff Atwood, of the outstanding CodingHorror.com blog fame, which is mandatory to add to your blog subscription list. In his Google Search VS.NET macro entry (*http://www.codinghorror.com/blog /archives/000428.html*) is a great macro that uses Google to search for the selected text in a source code window or in the Output window. Because the MSDN Library for Visual Studio 2005 search is extremely slow and not very good, Jeff's excellent macro, *SearchGoogleFor-SelectedText*, makes looking up something much more bearable. I added two macros to the SelectedSearch module, *SearchGoogleMicrosoftForSelectedText*, which searches the Microsoft-related section of Google for the selected text, and *SearchMsnForSelectedText*, which searches MSN for the selected text. I've bound these to my Alt+G and Alt+M for instant search happiness.

If you've ever pasted code from the Visual Studio editor into Microsoft Word, an HTML editor, or your blog, you know that instead of getting HTML as you would expect, you get some ugly Rich Text Format. Jeff wanted nice clean HTML, so he wrote some excellent macros to put pristine HTML on the clipboard (*http://www.codinghorror.com/blog/archives/000429.html*). For most code, you'll use the *Modern* and *ModernText* macros because those produce HTML with *<div>* and *<span>* elements. If you're working with an environment that doesn't have those codes, use the *Legacy* and *LegacyText* macros. To someone like me who puts tons of code into documents, these macros are worth their weight in gold. I also appreciate Jeff's permission to allow me to include them with the book's source code.

While I use Jeff's macros, I should also mention that many people are very happy with Colin Coller's CopySourceAsHtml (CSAH) add-in, which you can download from *http://www.jtleigh.com/people/colin/software/CopySourceAsHtml/*. The CSAH add-in offers support for background colors, line numbering settings, and syntax highlighting. It also comes with full source code and is an excellent example of how to write a good add-in.

Visual Studio Add-Ins

Macros are excellent for those smaller, isolated tasks, but if you have more advanced UI or input needs or you want to protect your source code, you're going to have to turn to writing add-ins. Although writing a macro is much easier, add-ins allow you to handle the following tasks, which you can't handle in macros:

- Add your own tool windows and dialog boxes to the IDE.
- Add your own command bars (that is, menus and toolbars) to the IDE.
- Add custom property pages to the Options dialog box.

As you'll see in a moment, developing and debugging is more difficult with add-ins than it is with macros, so I'd highly recommend trying to do all you can in macros if possible before tackling an add-in.

Basically, add-ins are COM objects that plug into the IDE. If you were worried about losing all that COM knowledge you've learned over the last few years, don't be—you'll still need some of it in the add-in world. What's interesting is that because managed languages support COM, you can write your add-ins using Visual Basic or C#. Although I like C++ as much as the next developer, I like the productivity enhancement of .NET even more, so in this chapter I'll concentrate on those issues related to writing add-ins in managed languages.

As usual, you should start your add-in journey by reading the documentation. Second, you need to visit *http://go.microsoft.com/fwlink/?linkid=57538*, which is the page that contains the Visual Studio 2005 Automation Samples download. There are many excellent examples to show you how to accomplish many common add-in and wizard tasks.

For those of us who have paid our dues writing add-ins with previous versions of Visual Studio, there are some very welcome changes to the Visual Studio 2005 model. The best change in my opinion is the wonderful new registration model. We no longer have to deal with the registry to let Visual Studio know about your add-in. You simply drop the registration file, which ends in .AddIn, in the appropriate directory, and Visual Studio is ready to use your add-in. For the current user, the .AddIn file goes into C:\Documents and Settings*user_name*\My Documents\Visual Studio 2005\Addins. For all users, the location is C:\Documents and Settings\All Users\Application Data\Microsoft\MSEnvShared\Addins.

The second best change is that Option pages can be created directly from .NET and no longer require a custom shim COM component. Another area that no longer requires shim COM components is .NET tool windows, which allow you to add your own windows to the IDE. In fact, creating tool windows is so trivial that I'll refer you to the Visual Studio documentation at *http://msdn2.microsoft.com/en-us/library/envdte80.windows2.createtoolwindow2.aspx*. Other improvements include better internationalization support and slightly better toolbars.

Tricks of Add-In Development

As with any development, the documentation covers the basics but does not show you the trials and tribulations you'll run into during your own add-in development battles. Instead of having you overloading Google's servers with search queries trying to find the real tricks to add-in development, I wanted to give you the answers to obstacles that I ran into developing the add-ins that are in the book's source code. In this section, I'm assuming that you've already read the documentation on add-ins at *http://msdn2.microsoft.com/en-us/library/5abkeks7.aspx*.

To focus on the add-in development process, I'll introduce the first add-in I developed: WhoAmI. As I discussed extensively in the "Why must you always develop as a non-admin?" section in Chapter 4, "Common .NET Debugging Questions," there's absolutely no reason you should ever log in with administrator rights to develop software. The only time you need administrator rights is when you are debugging across user accounts. In those cases, you'll start only the debugger with administrator rights while you're logged in as a member of the Users group. Because you'll be running multiple instances of Visual Studio, it can get a bit confusing as to which instance is running in which account. The WhoAmI add-in does nothing more than create a toolbar with a button that displays both a graphic and the user account for the instance of the IDE.

The only interesting detail in the WhoAmI add-in is that the one command added to the IDE, *WhoAmI.Rights*, is re-created each time the IDE is started because the IDE does not handle dynamic buttons on toolbars. If I didn't handle my own dynamic button updating, the WhoAmI add-in could display the wrong graphic if you changed the rights granted to the account. You might not be moving your account in and out of the Administrator's group manually, but it's perfectly reasonable to assume that you might be using Aaron Margosis's fantastic MakeMeAdmin command file to temporarily boost your User-level account to Administrator rights. For more information on MakeMeAdmin, see Aaron's blog at *http://blogs.msdn.com/aaron_margosis/archive/2004/07/24/193721.aspx*.

Even though WhoAmI isn't that interesting from the standpoint of other add-ins, it does suffice to show nearly all the pieces of add-ins you'll implement in yours. It does the work to create a toolbar and supports full internationalization. It's also small enough to completely understand at a glance. As you work your way through the hints in this section, you should open the .\WhoAmI\WhoAmI.sln file so you can follow along.

After you've gone through the Add-In Wizard to create the skeleton for your masterpiece, you may want to change the name of your add-in main class. The wizard-generated code treats the name you specified as the namespace name for everything in the add-in. It also names the class that implements the *IDTExtensibility2* and the optional *IDTCommandTarget* interfaces, *Connect*. The only problem is that the IDE needs the complete name of the class to load it out of your add-in assembly. Thus, any commands you add have the full name *MyAddIn.Connect .MyCommand.*

Personally, I don't like seeing that "Connect" in the middle of all of my commands. I want any commands my add-in supports to be the add-in name and the command. To me it looks more professional and makes it much easier to access them from the Command window. As my coworkers can tell you, I can sometimes be a perfectionist. Fixing this little oversight is relatively easy.

The trick is to name the class that implements the *IDTExtensibility2* and the optional *IDT-CommandTarget* interfaces the name of your add-in and put it outside of any namespaces. Because a type outside of a namespace will trigger a Code Analysis Design warning, "Declare types in namespaces," you'll need to suppress that error in your code. If you look at .\WhoAmI\Connect.cs, you'll see an example of how I used the *SuppressMessage* attribute to solve it.

For add-ins that are more complicated and for which you'll be creating numerous code files, you'll want to change the default namespace for the add-in to something other than the default, which is the add-in name, and thus it will conflict with the class now exposed outside namespaces. For the SettingsMaster add-in, I renamed the default namespace to *Settings-MasterWorker*.

Although it's your decision as to what you name your commands, everyone will want to fix how your commands and toolbars are registered and created, respectively, from the wizard-generated code. The registration is in the *IDTExtensibility.OnConnection*–derived method, and you'll want to engage in the good refactoring practice to pull all command registration and toolbar creation out into its own methods. This makes it much easier when you need to add commands to your add-in because they are handled in one place in the code.

The debates have raged back and forth about whether you should attempt to delete your commands before you add them when the add-in's *IDTExtensibility.OnConnection*–derived method is called with *ext_ConnectMode.ext_cm_UISetup* value. I always delete and re-create my commands to ensure that I know the exact state of the commands when they are added. When it comes to toolbars, they can be added only once, so you'll want your initialization code to first look for the toolbar in the *CommandBars* collection, and if that generates an *ArgumentException*, you'll need to create the toolbar. You can see an example of how I do that in the *AddButtonTo-CommandBar* method in *Book_Code_Install_Directory* \WhoAmI\Connect.cs.

Because internationalization is an area of major improvement in the add-ins in Visual Studio 2005, I was quite surprised that the documentation for handling satellite assemblies, described in the "Walkthrough: Creating Managed Satellite DLLs" section of the documentation, has you start a command prompt and manually run Resgen.exe to compile a .resx file to .resources and use the Assembly Linker, AL.exe, to create the satellite. Although you might be able to finagle those steps into build events, it's definitely a major pain and certainly not scalable.

My guess is that the extensibility team wasn't talking to other parts of the IDE team because if you want internationalized satellite assemblies in any other .NET project, you simply have to add a new resources file to your project and specify the culture as part of the name. For example, if you want to add French Canadian resources, you'd add a resources file named Resources.fr-ca.resx to your project. The IDE will build the culture resources and automatically put them in the appropriate directory where the main assembly is built. Ignore the add-in discussion of internationalization in the add-in documentation, and use the standard .NET internationalization support in the IDE to internationalize your add-ins. You can read about the IDE support at *http://msdn.microsoft.com/library/default.asp?url=/library/en-us/vbcon /html/vbwlkwalkthroughlocalizingwindowsforms.asp.*

In developing WhoAmI, I wanted to show full internationalization and ran across three bugs. The first is that any bitmaps you want to use on a toolbar can have only integer values as the name when passed to *Commands2.AddNamedCommand2*, the method that sets your toolbar bitmap. However, the resources editor in Visual Studio will report that all bitmaps with integer names you add to the .resx file have invalid names. Fortunately, the .resx file still compiles.

The second problem I found with internationalization is related to how your add-in appears in the IDE About Box and the Add-In Manager dialog box. The add-in documentation discusses how to internationalize items in the .AddIn file, which is the add-in registration file, by specifying the string resource file prefixed with the @ symbol. What's not clear from the documentation is that the *<Assembly>* element in the .AddIn file must have the full path to the assembly specified or none of your strings or icons will be loaded correctly in the About box. Oddly, the Add-In Manager dialog box does correctly display your internationalized data even if you do not specify the full path in the *<Assembly>* node.

While developing add-ins, specifying the full path to the assembly in the .AddIn file is easy, but it is a little more complicated in installations. Because I'm using the excellent Windows Installer XML (WiX) Toolset, the solution turned out to be relatively easy. Since the .AddIn file is an XML file, I could use the built-in WiX XML custom actions to write the full path as part of the install. You can see how I included the updating in the *Book_Code_Install_Directory* \Install\WintellectTools\AddIns.wxs file.

The last internationalization bug I found isn't shown in the WhoAmI add-in, but you'll see it in the next add-in, HiddenSettings. In a major improvement, the IDE now reads your add-in's option pages out of the .AddIn file. You list the top-level category, which appears in the root of the Options dialog box tree, and any subcategories, which appear as child nodes in the tree that shows your add-in option pages. Unfortunately, there's no way to specify the internationalized name of the category and subcategory values. Your installation will have to either install a different .AddIn file based on the user interface language or write the appropriate values as part of the installation. I hope that Microsoft will fix this bug in the next version of Visual Studio.

The last part of this list of tricks involves the toolbars. As with previous version of Visual Studio, the toolbars are a problematic area of add-in development. You would think that after fifteen years of Visual C++ and Visual Studio, we would have a toolbar solution that would not have so many rough edges. We're still limited to basic buttons and combo boxes on toolbars from add-ins, thus forcing you to design around the limitations instead of thinking about the best user interface for solving your particular problem. Although Microsoft has finally made it easier to remove an add-in with Devenv.exe's /ResetAddin command-line switch, none of the toolbars created by the add-in are removed. Therefore, the users will be left with empty toolbars littering up their IDE, which can be deleted only by using a Visual Studio macro or a JavaScript/VBScript script file that accesses the IDE programmatically.

Since littering is bad, my first attempt to solve this problem was to use an interesting feature called temporary toolbars. My hope was that the IDE saved off the temporary toolbar location in order to restore it to the same location. After coding up temporary toolbar support in the WhoAmI add-in, I found that there was no location saving, and even worse, the temporary toolbar appeared in random places.

Because having toolbars randomly bouncing around is not a preferred user interface practice, I used the permanent toolbar solution. That put the onus on my installation code to remove the toolbar on the uninstall. If you're doing per-user installations of your add-in into the C:\Documents and Settings*user_name*\My Documents\Visual Studio 2005\Addins directory, you can use a JavaScript file that uses the Visual Studio automation model to do the work.

However, an add-in such as WhoAmI is one that should be installed into the global add-in location (C:\Documents and Settings\All Users\Application Data\Microsoft\MSEnvShared \Addins) because it's one you'll want in all instances of Visual Studio. When I changed my installation to install into the global location, I realized that having the install do the custom action to remove the toolbar was going to work only for the user account doing the uninstall. The issue is that toolbar locations are stored on a per-user basis.

As it turns out, I have found no good solutions to this bug. My add-ins that create toolbars install JavaScript files that are left behind after uninstalling that you'll need to run in each user account to remove the toolbar. You can see these files in the .\Install\WintellectTools directory.

Option Pages and the HiddenSettings Add-In

As I mentioned in the introduction to this section, the Visual Studio team has greatly improved the option page support in Visual Studio 2005. We no longer have to create a separate native C++ DLL for pages we want to display in the Options dialog box. Now option pages are nearly as simple as a standard Windows Forms control.

You don't even need to write code; everything happens in the .AddIn file. For each option page, you simply add a *<ToolsOptionsPage>* element containing a *Category* and *SubCategory* element to describe where the page should appear in the Option dialog box. From the *SubCategory* element, Visual Studio knows what type to load for creating the option page by using its *FullClassName* element. Last but not least, the Assembly element specifies where this type can be found. The following snippet of a .AddIn file shows setting an option page:

```
<ToolsOptionsPage>
  <Category Name="HiddenSettings">
    <SubCategory Name="Debugger">
      <Assembly>.\HiddenSettings\HiddenSettings.dll</Assembly>
      <FullClassName>HiddenSettings.DebuggerOptionsPage</FullClassName>
    </SubCategory>
  </Category>
</ToolsOptionsPage>
```

To show an example of option pages, I created a whole add-in, HiddenSettings, that does nothing more than provide two option pages in the Options dialog box under the HiddenSettings node called Debugger and Text Editor Guidelines, as shown in Figures 7-4 and 7-5, respectively.

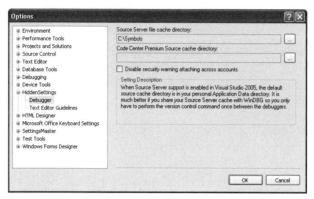

Figure 7-4   HiddenSettings Debugger option page

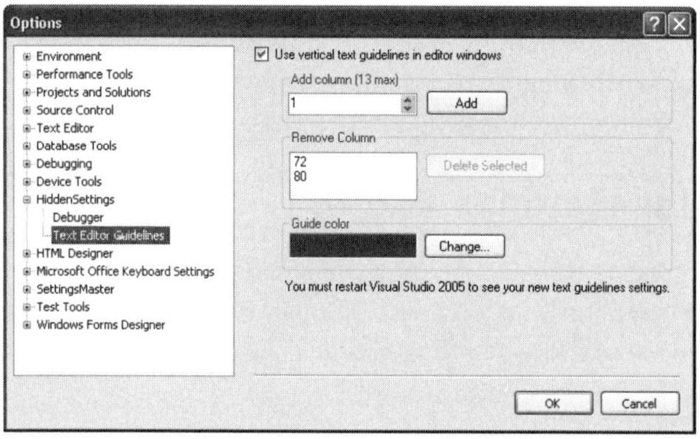

Figure 7-5   HiddenSettings Text Editor Guidelines option page

As you can probably guess, the Debugger option page exposes hidden settings used by the debugger. The first allows you to set the cache directory for source files extracted through the debugger's Source Server support. For more information about Source Servers, see the "Set Up a Source Store" section in Chapter 2. The second setting on the page allows you to set the download directory for Code Center Premium (CCP) source code if you have access to the Windows source code. See *http://www.microsoft.com/resources/sharedsource/ccp/pre-mium.mspx* for more information about CCP. The final option on the Debugger option page disables the security warning that pops up every time you attach to a process running in another user account.

The Text Editor Guidelines option page exposes a wonderful undocumented feature in the Visual Studio editor windows. Many programming editors, such as SlickEdit's outstanding Visual SlickEdit, have a simple bit of functionality that's a huge godsend: a vertical line down specific columns. If you're restricted to a line limit, as I am in any code shown in the book, it's great to know at a glance when you're getting close to that limit. Sara Ford, one of the developers on Visual Studio, blogged about this at *http://blogs.msdn.com/saraford/archive/2004/11/15/257953.aspx*, and I immediately had to write a UI to make the key easier to use. The values in the key are a little tricky to set, and now you don't have to worry about it.

As I mentioned in the previous section, there's the internationalization bug that forces you to hard-code the option page category and sub-category values of the corresponding *Name* attribute of the *<ToolsOptionsPage> <Category* and *SubCategory>* sub-elements in the .AddIn file. Another bug with option pages is that you won't receive proper notifications when the user moves to another control. That makes it rather difficult to perform data validation, so you'll have to find other ways to ensure that the data the user has entered is valid. For example, in the Debugger option page, I don't allow you to enter the Source Server file cache directory into the edit control because it is read-only. To ensure that the directory is a valid directory, I use a *FolderBrowserDialog*.

SettingsMaster

At this point, you've been reading about quite simple add-ins, and it's time to turn to a more involved add-in that I think you'll find quite useful: SettingsMaster. As I discussed in the introduction, SettingsMaster's purpose is making it trivial to update your build settings across projects and solutions. Now if you need to change items, such as the output directory or add a new define to the compilation, you can do it with a single button click instead of driving yourself insane manually updating 37 different projects.

If you purchased the previous edition of this book, you have a version of SettingsMaster that worked with Visual Studio .NET 2003. SettingsMaster proved quite popular, and the most common request I got about this version when I was asking for feedback was that Settings-Master absolutely had to be updated for Visual Studio 2005. What I originally thought was going to be a basic port of the code turned out to be a complete rewrite from scratch because of changes in the Visual Studio project models and to make the implementation drastically simpler.

One major change with the new version is that SettingsMaster works only with Visual Basic and C# projects. The previous edition also worked with native C++ projects, but with the excellent new Visual C++ property inheritance through .vsprops property sheets, there was no need for me to reproduce a feature of the IDE.

Using SettingsMaster

After you've installed SettingsMaster with the WintellectToolsInstall.MSI file, you'll see that it adds a toolbar with two buttons to the IDE. Although the user interface is simple, there's a lot that happens behind the scenes when you click one of those buttons. No matter if you're working with a normal .NET project or one of those slightly odd Microsoft ASP.NET 2.0 projects, you can change at will any settings exposed through the automation model. All settings are stored in .SettingsMaster files, which are just XML files.

The first button on the SettingsMaster toolbar maps to the *SettingsMaster.CorrectCurrentSolution* command. This command applies the default settings file to all the updatable projects in the solution. Updatable projects are those that are .NET projects and are not read-only. If the project is read only from the version control system, SettingsMaster does not check it out because I felt it would be too easy to accidentally change the build settings and cause havoc with your master build.

You can change the .SettingsMaster file that this button will apply in the SettingsMaster section of the Options dialog box. The initial default is, appropriately enough, SettingsMasterDefaults.SettingsMaster, which the install put beside the SettingsMaster add-in and sets all your build settings for all projects and configurations to those I recommended in Chapter 2.

The second button maps to the *SettingsMaster.CustomProjectUpdate* command, which allows you to multiple-select the projects you want to update and prompts you for the .SettingsMaster file to apply to those projects. As with the *SettingsMaster.CorrectCurrentSolution*, you can update only .NET and read-only projects. In case you were not aware, you can select multiple projects in Solution Explorer by holding the Ctrl key and clicking each project you want to change.

One additional feature of *SettingsMaster.CustomProjectUpdate* is if you execute it from the Command window, you can pass in the full path to the configuration file after the command. That allows you to more quickly execute custom settings. In fact, you could write a micro command for all the custom .SettingsMaster files you would like. The following macro shows just how simple that is:

```
Public Sub ApplyFavorites()
    DTE.ExecuteCommand("SettingsMaster.CustomProjectUpdate", _
                        "C:\Settings\Favorites.SettingsMaster")
End Sub
```

For your custom project-updating enjoyment, the WintellectToolsInstall.msi installation includes three other .SettingsMaster files. The CodeAnalysisOnAndAllErrors.SettingsMaster and CodeAnalysisOff.SettingsMaster files turn on and off Code Analysis for all configurations. The EnableDocComments.SettingsMaster file turns on the XML documentation file creation for all configurations. In the source code for SettingsMaster are a few other .SettingsMaster files I used to help with project setup for the book's source code and debugging add-ins.

Creating your own .SettingsMaster files is quite easy. When you create a new .SettingsMaster file, set the schema property to SettingsMaster.xsd from either the installation directory or the .\SettingsMaster code directory. The SettingsMaster.xsd has <xs:documentation> tags all through it, so you should have no trouble understanding which element goes where. Listing 7-3 shows an example .SettingsMaster file. The main trick to remember with .SettingsMaster files is that all the individual setting elements for a project or a configuration map directly to a project or configuration automation name. In the "Implementation Highlights" section later in this chapter, I'll discuss more about the decisions I made in setting up the .SettingsMaster files. You'll want to read Listing 7-3 because it discusses some of the special processing I do on particular nodes to make things a bit easier for you when creating your own custom .SettingsMaster files.

Listing 7-3   Example .SettingsMaster file

```xml
<?xml version="1.0" encoding="utf-8"?>
<!-- ************************************************************************
* Debugging Microsoft .NET 2.0 Applications
* Copyright © 1997-2006 John Robbins All rights reserved.
************************************************************************ -->
<!-- An example settings file. -->
<SettingsMasterConfiguration
    xmlns="http://schemas.wintellect.com/SettingsMaster/2006/02">
  <NormalProject>

    <!-- Setting common project properties for all languages. -->
    <CommonProjectProperties>
      <Company>Wintellect</Company>
    </CommonProjectProperties>

    <VBProjectProperties>
      <!-- VB specific properties, 0 = off, 1 = on. -->
      <OptionExplicit>1</OptionExplicit>
      <OptionStrict>1</OptionStrict>
    </VBProjectProperties>

    <ConfigurationProperties Name="All" Platform="Any CPU">
      <!-- Set the start action to 1, which means start the program
           specified in the <StartProgram> element. -->
      <StartAction>1</StartAction>
      <!-- The StartProgram element has special processing which expands
           environment variables. In this example, I'm setting Visual
           Studio 2005 as the program to debug and taking advantage of
           the fact that the Visual Studio installation sets the
           %VS80COMNTOOLS% on all machines. There's no checking in the
           processing for empty environment variables. -->
      <StartProgram>%VS80COMNTOOLS%..\IDE\devenv.exe</StartProgram>
      <!-- The XML Doc Comments file. If this has the string $(OutputPath) in
           it, the OutputPath property will be substituted as appropriate. If
           $(AssemblyName) is used, the current assembly name will be
           substituted. SettingsMaster ignores $(OutputPath) for
           Visual Basic projects as it's not needed. -->
<DocumentationFile>$(OutputPath)\$(AssemblyName).xml</DocumentationFile>
      <!-- Treats all warnings as errors. -->
      <TreatWarningsAsErrors>true</TreatWarningsAsErrors>
    </ConfigurationProperties>

    <!-- Configuration for C# debug builds. -->
    <CSharpConfigurationProperties Name="Debug" Platform="Any CPU">
      <!-- The compilation constants are all separated with ';'. Note that
           the DefineDebug and DefineTrace properties are ignored on the
           configuration but are picked up by setting DEBUG;TRACE into the
           DefineConstants property. -->
      <DefineConstants>DEBUG;TRACE</DefineConstants>
    </CSharpConfigurationProperties>
```

```
<!-- Configuration for C# release builds. -->
<CSharpConfigurationProperties Name="Release" Platform="Any CPU">
  <DefineConstants>TRACE</DefineConstants>
</CSharpConfigurationProperties>

<!-- Configuration for VB debug builds. -->
<VBConfigurationProperties Name="Debug" Platform="Any CPU">
  <!-- Sets the Debug conditional compilation. -->
  <DefineDebug>true</DefineDebug>
  <!-- Sets the Trace conditional compilation. -->
  <DefineTrace>true</DefineTrace>
</VBConfigurationProperties>

<!-- Configuration for VB release builds. -->
<VBConfigurationProperties Name="Release" Platform="Any CPU">
  <!-- Sets the Trace conditional compilation. -->
  <DefineTrace>true</DefineTrace>
</VBConfigurationProperties>
</NormalProject>
<AspNetProject>
  <AspNetProjectProperties>
    <!-- Turns on Code Analysis. -->
    <EnableFxCop>true</EnableFxCop>
    <!-- Enable unmanaged debugging. -->
    <EnableUnmanagedDebugging>1</EnableUnmanagedDebugging>
  </AspNetProjectProperties>
</AspNetProject>
</SettingsMasterConfiguration>
```

Initial Explorations

When I first looked at porting over the Visual Studio .NET 2003 version of SettingsMaster, I almost immediately realized that it wasn't simply going to be a recompile. I'd designed the system around setting properties in configurations, which was perfectly reasonable at the time. That way I could have a collection of XML nodes that specified "Debug," and I'd know what configuration it applied. Now configurations also include the CPU type because .NET 2.0 can specify Itanium, x64, x86, and the platform-independent Any CPU. Although I couldn't have anticipated how Microsoft would have implemented the CPU scheme, one thing I should have handled in the previous edition was setting properties on the projects themselves. Those properties are like those in the *<CommonProjectProperties>* and *<VBProject-Properties>* elements shown in Listing 7-3.

Finally, one consistent problem with the previous version was that I didn't include a schema file to perform validation and to assist users in creating their own files. By implementing a good schema file, I could let the magic of XML do the main work of verifying that the data in the file was good instead of trying to do it manually in my code.

Because the default ASP.NET 2.0 projects are not really projects at all, I had to look at how those would impact the SettingsMaster design. As I suspected, ASP.NET projects are radically different compared to "normal" .NET projects. I don't mean to imply that ASP.NET is "abnormal," but the only thing that ASP.NET projects have in common with class library projects is that they allow editing in a code window.

In exploring the different project types, I whipped up numerous macros to dump all the properties on projects and configurations. Although normal projects and configurations showed all the values you can change from their property pages, ASP.NET projects showed only a few.

I was disappointed because I was hoping that values in the MSBuild Options, available in the Web Site Properties dialog box, would be exposed so you could set items, such as the strong name key and fixed named assemblies. Basically, the only items you can set are the types of debugging (.NET, SQL, or native) and if you want Code Analysis to run. That's better than nothing, but it limits the usefulness of the SettingsMaster for ASP.NET projects. In doing the research on ASP.NET projects, I noticed that the various settings are saved in both the solution and in the hidden .suo file.

Turning to normal .NET projects, my first worry was that there was going to be a major difference between a Smart Device project and a Windows project. The good news is that the only real differences are in the language-specific properties, not the platform type. The differences based on the languages are not that major, so it wasn't a big deal to handle.

In the previous version of SettingsMaster, a major part of the work was handling the huge differences between .NET and C++ projects. As I've mentioned, there's been a major addition to the C++ system in the form of property sheets. The idea is that you'll put common macros and build definitions in a .vsprops file and add that file to your project so you can inherit its values. There's a UI for controlling property sheets in your C++ projects–the Property Manager window. In a C++ project, to open this window, in the View menu, select Property Manager. Now you can set up common build settings, add those files in the Property Manager window, and change your C++ project settings without wading through hundreds of property pages. Peter Huene has an excellent discussion on using the Property Manager window at *http://blogs.msdn.com/peterhu/archive/2004/06/07/150488.aspx*. Since Visual Studio already had a feature to provide project settings for C++ projects, I wasn't going to reimplement the feature in SettingsMaster.

Implementation Highlights

After establishing the research, my major task was to come up with the .SettingsMaster file format. Because property setting for a project or configuration is easy, I knew I wanted the actual property elements to be the property names. That way I could have, for example, a line like the following to set any configuration property:

```
configuration.Properties.Item ( currProperty.Name ).Value = value;
```

The *Value* property is an object, so it turns out that I simply treat the value of the element as a string, and .NET will take care of the conversion for me.

By going with this mapping of element names to property names, the .SettingsMaster file is defining the individual items, and combined with some careful schema work I could add properties without changing the code. It turned out that I spent one-third of the development time working on SettingsMaster.xsd to ensure that I got it right.

There was obviously going to have to be some a priori knowledge about the schema in the SettingsMaster source code, and Table 7-1 lists the main nodes for a normal project that appear under the *<NormalProject>* elements. Because there are so few properties to set for ASP.NET projects, Table 7-2 lists all the actual settable property values under the *<AspNetProject­Properties>* elements.

Table 7-1   NormalProject Child Elements

Node Name	Description
CommonProjectProperties	Contains all the project properties that are common between Visual Basic and C# projects, such as *ApplicationIcon*, *Company*, and *PostBuildEvent*.
VBProjectProperties	Contains the Visual Basic–specific project properties *OptionCompare*, *OptionExplicit*, and *OptionStrict*.
ConfigurationProperties	The main node that defines all the common properties for a configuration, such as *CheckForOverflowUnderflow*, *DocumentationFile*, and *TreatWarningsAsErrors*. This node takes two required attributes. The *Platform* is a string that identifies the CPU type and can be "x86", "x64", "Itanium", and "Any CPU". The *Name* attribute is the configuration name. A special case of the *Name* attribute is "All" that has SettingsMaster apply that this nodes settings to all configurations of that *Platform*. This allows you to set common settings for Debug and Release builds, such as the *DocumentationFile* and *RunCodeAnalysis*.
CSharpConfigurationProperties	Contains the C# specific setting, *DefineConstants*. The *Name* and *Platform* attributes apply here also.
VBConfigurationProperties	Contains the Visual Basic–specific settings *DefineConstants*, *DefineDebug*, and *DefineTrace*. The *Name* and *Platform* Attributes apply here also.

Table 7-2   The AspNetProjectProperties Child Elements

Node Name	Description
EnableFxCop	Set to 1 to enable Code Analysis to be run on the project.
EnableNTLMAuthentication	Set to 1 to enable NT Lan Manager Authentication.
EnableSQLServerDebugging	Set to 1 to enable Microsoft SQL Server Debugging. You must be a sysadmin in SQL Server to debug stored procedures.
EnableUnmanagedDebugging	Set to 1 to enable native debugging.
FxCopRules	The string containing the Code Analysis rules you want enabled, disabled, and treated as warnings. Look at CodeAnalysisOnAndAllErrors.SettingsMaster for an example how this string needs to be specified.

Once I had the core logic for the .SettingsMaster files and their processing, I turned to handling the enable state for the commands. My main concern was having the commands enable and disable appropriately, so I didn't allow the user to change the settings on read-only projects or while debugging. The *SettingsMaster.CorrectCurrentSolution* command logic was simple in that the button would be enabled only if a solution was open, it contained at least one Visual Basic or C# project, and that project was not read-only. For the *SettingsMaster .CustomProjectUpdate* command, at least one of the selected projects must be writable.

During development, I ran into only two problems worth mentioning. All of my initial development took place with SettingsMaster.dll loading from the C:\Documents and Settings*user_name*\My Documents\Visual Studio 2005\Addins local directory. Life was going along great when it was time to do testing with SettingsMaster.dll loading from the C:\Documents and Settings\All Users\Application Data\Microsoft\MSEnvShared\Addins, which is the global add-in location. SettingsMaster has two persisted options, a Boolean to indicate if you want any changed projects automatically saved and a string that is the complete path to the default .SettingsMaster file used when *SettingsMaster.CorrectCurrentSolution* executes. My first runs from the global location were causing serialization exceptions as soon as I tried to read the data out of the settings file stored in the C:\Documents and Settings *user_name*\Local Settings\Application Data\Wintellect\SettingsMaster directory. The exception information was saying that the code in SettingsMaster.dll could not load SettingsMaster.dll.

That one had me scratching my head for a few seconds until it dawned on me that Visual Studio is probably not checking the global location when it's resolving assemblies. Fortunately, it's a very easy fix because all you need to do is handle the *CurrentDomain.AssemblyResolve* event handler and return the right SettingsMaster.dll assembly when requested.

The second small issue I ran into was when I wanted to do some tweaking on SettingsMaster and moved the assembly loading from the global location back to the C:\Documents and Settings*user_name*\My Documents\Visual Studio 2005\Addins. No matter what I tweaked, I could not get the *IDTExtensibility.OnConnection* derived method called with *ext_ConnectMode.ext_cm_UISetup* value so I could reset the toolbars and commands. It turns out that when you use Devenv.exe's excellent /ResetAddIn switch, there's one more thing besides the toolbar that the IDE forgets to delete. In the HKEY_CURRENT_USER\Software\Microsoft\VisualStudio\8.0\PreloadAddinStateManaged registry key, Visual Studio stores a key name made up of the add-in name and the path to the .AddIn file. If that value is set to 0x2, Visual Studio assumes that it's already initialized the UI and won't pass the *ext_ConnectMode.ext_cm_UISetup* value again. If you delete the key or set its value to 0x1, you'll get the chance to reinitialize your add-in.

Possible Future Enhancements

SettingsMaster is very useful as is, but if you're looking for a project, there are plenty of enhancements you could add to SettingsMaster to make it even better:

- There is no configuration editor for the XML configuration files. Since the property grids are fairly easy to program, you might want to consider writing a configuration file editor so that you don't have to edit the configuration files by hand. This configuration editor should be accessible from the SettingsMaster command bar in addition to the Options dialog box property page.

■ One feature that would be relatively easy to add would be an event handler that watches when projects load and automatically updates the project settings.

■ A nice feature would be to add a command to write out the current project settings to a SettingsMaster configuration file so that you could apply those settings to other projects.

■ To provide additional user feedback, you could also write out changes made by Settings-Master to the Output window.

■ SettingsMaster supports only the ASP.NET projects that come standard with Visual Studio 2005. If you're porting an ASP.NET 1.1 project to ASP.NET, the new model is completely different and makes porting harder. Additionally, if you want a real build for your ASP.NET 2.0 projects, you're out of luck. Fortunately, Scott Guthrie, the Product Unit Manager at Microsoft for ASP.NET, Internet Information Server, and Windows Forms, had his team develop the Visual Studio 2005 Web Application Project Model (*http://webproject.scottgu.com/*) to solve those problems. If you like the Web Application Project Model, you may want to enhance SettingsMaster to support it.

Summary

With the new macro and add-in capabilities present in the Visual Studio 2005 IDE, developers now have the ultimate power to make the environment do exactly what they need to do to help solve their problems faster. In this chapter I wanted to show some of the gyrations necessary to build real-world–level macros and add-ins. Although there are still some quirks in the IDE, the overall picture more than makes up for it. I hope the holes I stumbled into and discussed will save you some time in developing your extensions to the Visual Studio 2005 IDE.

Developers have been asking for the full power of Visual Studio 2005 for a long time. We now have it, and I encourage you to implement the tools you've always dreamed about. The rest of us could use them!

Chapter 8
Writing Code Analysis Rules

If you couldn't tell from my excitement in discussing the Code Analysis applications in the "Always Build with Code Analysis Turned On" section of Chapter 2, "Preparing for Debugging," I think Code Analysis, and the stand-alone version, FxCop, are two of the most exciting parts of .NET development. As soon as I saw the original version of FxCop, I immediately had to know how to add my own rules to the mix. Fortunately, it's not as hard as you might think, as you'll learn in this chapter.

If you skipped over the discussion of Code Analysis in Chapter 2, I strongly suggest that you read it before reading this chapter. That section discusses the reasons why Code Analysis is so important and why you'll want to turn it on for all your builds. Additionally, it discusses all the custom rules that I provided from a usage standpoint. This chapter is all about gory details necessary to writing the rules, and I assume that you've already read that section in Chapter 2.

Before we jump into the details of writing rules, I have to make a major hacking alert. Microsoft has never documented how to write rules, so I've had to perform the magic of reverse engineering to figure out how to create rules. Fortunately, given Reflector's amazing decompiling abilities, it's mainly a matter of just reading through all the rules provided with Code Analysis. Also, the FxCop Team, who's responsible for Code Analysis and provides the stand-alone version, FxCop, has stated publicly multiple times that they are working on a complete new engine for static analysis for future versions of Microsoft Visual Studio. That engine will be bigger and better, and will break backwards compatibility with the existing engine. The good news is that the FxCop team has said that they will finally document the new engine for rule writers.

Even with those warnings, the good news is that Visual Studio 2005 will be around awhile, so investing in any custom rules will definitely pay for themselves the first time they find a bug. Because I use all of these rules every day, I have a stake in keeping them up to date with any changes Microsoft makes to the rules engine. Check the book's update site, *http://dtt.wintellect.com*, for the latest information about all the Code Analysis rules discussed in this chapter and in the book's source code.

The rules I discuss in this chapter work both with Code Analysis built into the Visual Studio 2005 Team Suite Edition and Team Developer Edition in addition to the stand-alone FxCop available at (*http://www.gotdotnet.com/team/FxCop/*). That way you can benefit no matter which version of Visual Studio you are using. Because Code Analysis and FxCop are two different versions, there's no way to use a single rule with both. All of my rules are built to run with FxCop 1.35, which was the latest version available when I wrote this book.

One other point I need to make before we jump into rule development is that some of the rules I developed in this chapter rely on analyzing the Intermediate Language (IL) code generated by the compiler. Since virtually all of .NET development is done with either C# or Visual Basic, I worried only about those two compilers. If other languages start becoming more popular, I'll update the rules to account for those languages.

Thinking About Rule Development

Back in the old .NET 1.0 days, the original version of FxCop used standard Reflection to open the assembly under analysis and walk through the data in the assembly. Although that worked, we all know that Reflection is quite slow and locks the assembly, so you had to shut down FxCop every time you wanted to rebuild the assembly. The Reflection engine did a decent job of letting you access all parts of the compiled code, but all the IL code for a method was returned as a giant text string. That meant that to do deep analysis on code constructs, you had to write extreme regular expressions or possibly a full-blown IL parser. That severely limited rule development to essentially the FxCop team at Microsoft, who was being paid to write the rules.

After a few FxCop releases, the team rewrote the tool from scratch to remove the Reflection engine and switched to a new analysis engine called *Introspection*. The new engine did everything the Reflection engine did but didn't lock the assembly and was much, much faster. Additionally, it provided fantastic access to the underlying IL, so you no longer had to parse text buffers. The access is interesting in that either you can access the opcodes directly, or you can have the Introspection engine walk the IL for you.

Even better is that you get very cool support from the Introspection engine to access the call graph for callers and callees. You'll need just to make sure that the rule that you want makes sense from the standpoint of analyzing the binary. For example, if you are thinking about considering a performance analysis rule, unless you can look for an exact IL or call pattern, it might be better to use source analysis for that type of rule. A good example of a performance rule that works because you're looking for a fixed pattern is the TestForEmptyStringsUsing-StringLength rule you'll find in PerformanceRules.dll.

When I first started looking at rule development, I couldn't quite get my head around what the Introspection engine was doing. After a while, it finally dawned on me that the way to think about it was that Introspection is just manual reflection. Whereas reflection loads up the assembly and calls the types and other information in the assembly, the Introspection engine maps the assembly into memory and goes through the grind of walking all the internal tables by hand. Interestingly, if you start looking hard at the Introspection engine with the

Reflector tool, you'll see that through Introspection, it also supports creating code, much like the *Reflection.Emit* namespace.

The assemblies that provide the hooks for your rules to load into the Introspection engine are Microsoft.Cci.dll and FxCopSdk.dll, respectively. For building your rules with Code Analysis, you need to use the version in the *Visual_Studio_2005_Install_Directory*\Team Tools\Static Analysis Tools\FxCop, and for FxCop, you'll use the versions from the FxCop installation directory. If you're building your rules primarily for Code Analysis, you can fix your builds so your rules will compile no matter where the user has installed Visual Studio 2005. After you've added the references to the two assemblies, close the project and open the .VBProj /.CSProj file with either the XML editor or Notepad. Search for the Reference elements for Microsoft.Cci.dll and FxCopSdk.dll. In the *HintPath* element, replace the hard-coded path with the property *$(FxCopDir)*, which MSBuild will expand to the appropriate path on the machine. The following shows a fixed-up *Reference* element:

```
<Reference Include="FxCopSdk, Version=8.0.0.0, Culture=neutral,
          PublicKeyToken=b03f5f7f11d50a3a,
          processorArchitecture=MSIL">
  <SpecificVersion>False</SpecificVersion>
  <HintPath>$(FxCopDir)\FxCopSdk.dll</HintPath>
  <Private>False</Private>
</Reference>
```

For more tricks about building for both Code Analysis and FxCop, see the FxCop team's blog at *http://blogs.msdn.com/fxcop/*.

Once you've built your rules, you need to load them. If you're using Code Analysis, the only place where rules are loaded from is *Visual_Studio_2005_Install_Directory*\Team Tools\Static Analysis Tools\FxCop\Rules. If you install the Code Analysis rules with WintellectToolsInstall.msi, my install takes care of putting the rules in the right location so they automatically show up as part of the Code Analysis page in Visual Studio 2005. For the stand-alone FxCop program, you add rules to the project by selecting Add Rules from the Project menu. The rules I built for FxCop are in the .\FxCop directory where you installed the book's source code. If you attempt to load the rules from the .\Debug or .\Release directory, which are built for Visual Studio 2005 Code Analysis, you will get exception error reports from FxCop.

Basics of Rule Development

Getting started with rule development is relatively straightforward. In Listing 8-1, I combine the three files of an example EmptyFxCopRule project so you could follow along with me. The simple base class, *BaseEmptyFxCopRule*, exists solely to derive from the required abstract *BaseIntrospectionRule* class from the *Microsoft.FxCop.Sdk.Introspection* namespace in FxCopSdk.dll. *BaseIntrospectionRule* assumes that the description text and related data reside in an embedded resource. Consequently, the three parameters required by the *BaseIntrospectionRule* constructor are the type name of the rule, the embedded resource file name that contains the rule descriptions, and the assembly that contains the embedded resource file. Because you'll most likely have more than one rule per assembly, having a simple base class, such as *BaseEmpty-FxCopRule*, means that you can hide the common resource information manipulation in the base class and require derived classes to specify the type name in calling the base class constructor.

The second file, EmptyAssemblyRule.cs, shows a minimal rule that looks at assemblies. I'll talk more about the *Check* method later. The *TargetVisibiliy* property is where you specify the type of items you want to see. For example, if you wanted your rule limited to only public items, you'd return *TargetVisibilities. ExternallyVisible*. The main point to notice in EmptyAssemblyRule.cs is that the name of the class is *EmptyAssemblyRule*. You can see that in its constructor, *EmptyAssembly-Rule* passed that string into the base class.

The final file in Listing 8-1 is the embedded resource XML file. I did a little format tweaking so you could see the individual elements more easily. The key text is the *Rule* element *TypeName* attribute at the top, because that's how the engine matches up the data about the rule with the code for the rule. Whereas there's only one rule shown in the XML file, you will have one *Rule* element for each rule you develop in an assembly. If you've used Code Analysis, you're probably wondering why all of the elements are required, but the only ones you see are the *Rule* element, *CheckId* attribute, and *Name* element. Whereas the stand-alone FxCop shows you all the elements when you double click a rule, Microsoft simply didn't provide that user interface in the integrated Code Analysis.

The name of the embedded resource XML file must end in "Rules.xml" for the integrated Code Analysis to load and show your rules. The FxCop stand-alone version can handle any named file. If Code Analysis cannot load the rules out of your assembly, in the Code Analysis view, the tree control will not show any child items under your rule assembly name.

Listing 8-1   Minimal Code Analysis Rule Source Files

```
************** BaseEmptyFxCopRule.CS **************
using System ;
using Microsoft.Cci;
using Microsoft.FxCop.Sdk;
using Microsoft.FxCop.Sdk.Introspection;

namespace EmptyFxCopRule
{
    [CLSCompliant(false)]
    abstract public class BaseEmptyFxCopRule : BaseIntrospectionRule
    {
        protected  BaseEmptyFxCopRule ( String name )
            : base ( name                           ,
                    "EmptyFxCopRule.RuleData"       ,
                    typeof(BaseEmptyFxCopRule).Assembly  )
        {
        }
    }
}
************** EmptyAssemblyRule.CS **************
namespace EmptyFxCopRule
{
    /// <summary>
```

```
    /// Summary description for EmptyRule.
    /// </summary>
    [CLSCompliant ( false )]
    public class EmptyAssemblyRule : BaseEmptyFxCopRule
    {
        public EmptyAssemblyRule ( )
            : base ( "EmptyAssemblyRule" )
        {
        }

        public override TargetVisibilities TargetVisibility
        {
            get
            {
                return ( TargetVisibilities.All );
            }
        }

        public override ProblemCollection Check ( Module module )
        {
            return ( null );
        }
    }
}
************** EmptyRules.XML **************
<?xml version="1.0" encoding="utf-8" ?>
<Rules FriendlyName="Example Empty Rule">
  <Rule TypeName="EmptyAssemblyRule"
        Category="EmptyRule.Simple"
        CheckId="ER0000">
    <Name>
      EmptyAssemblyRule: The prose name of the rule goes here.
    </Name>
    <Description>
      EmptyAssemblyRule: Add your description here.
    </Description>
    <Owner>
      EmptyAssemblyRule: This is optional, but is generally the developer.
    </Owner>
    <Url>
      EmptyAssemblyRule: The URL for help containing the rule.
    </Url>
    <Resolution>
      EmptyAssemblyRule: The string that points out the error to the user.
    </Resolution>
    <Email>
      EmptyAssemblyRule: The optional e-mail address of the rule author.
    </Email>
    <MessageLevel Certainty="99">
      Warning
    </MessageLevel>
    <FixCategories>
      NonBreaking
    </FixCategories>
  </Rule>
</Rules>
```

Before you even consider writing the code for your rule, I need to point out a few development tricks. First, note that adding an XML file to the project does not add it as an embedded resource. Consequently, after adding the XML resource file that describes the rule, make sure you set the Build Action to Embedded Resource instead of Content. When creating new rules, even if they are additional rules in an existing assembly, always test to make sure it's set up correctly by loading it into your target environment to see if you have the rule names and descriptions from the XML file displayed. Both Code Analysis and FxCop are not too forgiving if there are issues with your rules XML file. If the environment shows you the appropriate data when you load your rule, you're in good shape. One other hint is to get in the habit of ensuring that the *CheckId* attribute is always unique across all assemblies. Code Analysis uses that value to save the rule state to the project file. If you have duplicate errors, Code Analysis looks only for the first rule with that number and ignores the others.

The last hint with the XML file concerns the *MessageLevel* and *FixCategories* elements. Those must both conform to the *MessageLevel* and *FixCategories* enumerations, respectively. Just so you have them, here are the definitions from Reflector:

```
public enum MessageLevel
{
    CriticalError = 1,
    CriticalWarning = 4,
    Error = 2,
    Information = 0x10,
    None = 0,
    Warning = 8
}

public enum FixCategories
{
    Breaking = 1,
    DependsOnFix = 2,
    NonBreaking = 4,
    None = 0
}
```

The *MessageLevel* element has a required attribute, *Certainty*, which seems to be the confidence, measured as a percentage, you have in diagnosing the error. Nearly all the Microsoft rules are 95 percent or higher, but only FxCop shows you the value. If you're going to the trouble of writing a rule and you have a confidence level of only 5 percent in the rule being correct, you may want to reconsider what you're doing.

The All-Important *Check* Method

As you've probably guessed, the *Check* method is where all the action is. The *BaseIntrospectionRule* class defines six different virtual *Check* methods you can override in your rules, though you'll use the following four almost exclusively:

```
ProblemCollection Check ( Member member );
ProblemCollection Check ( Module module );
ProblemCollection Check ( Parameter parameter );
ProblemCollection Check ( Resource resource );
```

As you scan down the list of *Check* methods, you can see, for example, that if you want a rule that works on embedded resources, you simply override the version *Check* that takes the *Resource* type as a parameter. It's a little harder to see, but if you want to check classes and methods, you'd use the version that takes a *Member* as the parameter. Inside that *Check* method, you'd use the C# *as* or Visual Basic *TryCast* statement to convert the *Member* type into the specific type you're interested in working with. When I started to write Code Analysis rules, the first ones I wanted to add involved assemblies, and fortunately, those are the easiest to get started with. Consequently, I used the *Check* method that takes a *Module* as the parameter.

As I discussed back in Chapter 2, I find it quite odd that the Design Guidelines do not make it mandatory to include an XML documentation file with your assemblies. This is especially annoying when all .NET languages now support creating the file directly from the source code comments. Therefore, I wanted a rule that would check that an assembly always has documentation associated with it.

This very important rule, AssembliesHaveXmlDocCommentFiles, turns out to be extremely simple to write. You can find the code in the eponymous .cs file in the .\Wintellect.FxCop.DesignRules directory. To show you how simple the rule is, Listing 8-2 shows the *Check* method that does all the work. As you can see, if you return *null/Nothing* in the *Check* method, that tells Code Analysis that you didn't find any errors. Returning an allocated *Problems* array signals that there are errors and tells you the text of the error. In Listing 8-2, I use the *BaseIntrospectionRule.GetResolution* method to get the Resolution element out of the AssembliesHaveXmlDocCommentFiles rule's XML file. In this case, the string is: "'{0}' is missing or has an invalid XML Doc Comments file." The format item allows me to put the name of the assembly in the error text. The *BaseIntrospectionRule.GetResolution* method takes variable-length arguments, so you can get as much detail as you need into the error message. What's nice about the *Problems* property in the *BaseIntrospectionRule* is that if you have a rule that is recursive, you can add all the problems you've found in the code to it and take care of getting them all at the end. With most rules returning only a single error string, you'll usually use code like that specified in the error portion of Listing 8-2 to do the work.

Listing 8-2   Check Method for AssembliesHaveXmlDocCommentFiles Rule

```
public override ProblemCollection Check ( Module module )
{
    if ( null == module )
    {
        throw new ArgumentNullException ( Constants.InvalidModule );
    }
    // Is this module an assembly?
    if ( NodeType.Assembly != module.NodeType )
    {
        return ( null );
    }

    // First, check if this is a DLL library.
    if ( false == IsLibraryAssembly ( module.Location ) )
```

```
    {
        // It's not a DLL, so there's no need for an XML file.
        return ( null );
    }

    // Build up the name to the XML file, which should be in the same
    // directory as the DLL.
    String XmlFile = Path.ChangeExtension ( module.Location ,
                                            XMLExtension );

    bool failedTests = false;

    if ( true == File.Exists ( XmlFile ) )
    {
        // The file exists, so lets see if it's a proper and happy XML
        // file.
        try
        {
            XmlDocCommentsFileDictionary tempFile =
                    new XmlDocCommentsFileDictionary ( XmlFile );

            tempFile = null;
            // I guess you could optionally check that the timestamps
            // are close here, but there are no guarantees that the .XML
            // file has been edited or even produced by a different
            // tool such as Innovasys Document! X.
        }
        catch ( XmlException )
        {
            failedTests = true;
        }
    }
    else
    {
        failedTests = true;
    }

    if ( true == failedTests )
    {
        // Build up the error string to return.
        String fileName = Path.GetFileName ( module.Location );
        Resolution res = GetResolution ( fileName );
        Problem prob = new Problem ( res );
        Problems.Add ( prob );
    }
    return ( Problems );
}
```

Although AssembliesHaveXmlDocCommentFiles is relatively easy, I wanted to create other rules that would look to see if an assembly had the *AssemblyTitleAttribute*, *AssemblyCompany-Attribute*, *AssemblyDescriptionAttribute*, and *AssemblyCopyrightAttribute* all applied and not set to empty strings. At first, I thought it was going to be pretty easy to do this because I had just to decompile the Microsoft rule MarkAssembliesWithAssemblyVersion in DesignRules.dll. A quick peek at the rule showed that the *Module* passed to the *Check* method had a *Version* property on it. My hope was that there were either properties to get the attributes I wanted or a simple way to get attributes for an assembly. Of course, life wasn't so easy, but it turned out to be a good way to learn about the Introspection engine usage.

In a previous Reflector exploration mission, I saw that the *Microsoft.FxCop.Sdk.Introspection.RuleUtilities* class had several *GetCustomAttributes* methods that pointed out an *Attributes* property on the various *Microsoft.Cci* namespace types. With Reflector's wonderful Analyzer, I just had to click on the Used By node to see who called the method I was interested in using. Looking through the various rules files supplied with Code Analysis, you'll see that all the calls to any *RuleUtilities.GetCustomAttributes* method were using a set of predetermined attribute types defined in the *Microsoft.Cci.SystemTypes* class as static public fields of type *Microsoft.Cci.Class*. The *Microsoft.Cci.SystemTypes* class is the class that represents types in the *System.** namespaces. Poking through the *Microsoft.Cci.SystemTypes* class, I saw that the FxCop team had already done the work I needed because they already had fields that returned the *TypeNode* class for the attribute classes I wanted. That saved a huge amount of work on my part.

The second parameter expected by *GetCustomAttributes* is of type *Microsoft.Cci.TypeNode*, which is perfect because it is the base class for all type items, such as *Microsoft.Cci.Class* (yes, the same as the fields of *SystemTypes* representing the attributes I'm interested in), *Microsoft.Cci.EnumNode*, and *Microsoft.Cci.Reference*. Therefore, my next mission was to find an example of getting a type out of a *Module* class to see what method to call.

To tie everything together, Listing 8-3 shows the *Check* method that implements the actual rule and the *AttributeType* method to get the type for the AssembliesHaveCopyrightAttributesRule. Because all the assembly attributes rules I wrote (AssembliesHaveCompanyAttributesRule, AssembliesHaveCopyrightAttributesRule, AssembliesHaveDescriptionAttributesRule, and AssembliesHaveTitleAttributesRule) are almost identical, they all share a base class, *BaseAssemblyAttributeRule*, and they simply define the abstract *AttributeType* property to return the particular method to look up. You can see all the action in full in the Wintellect.FxCop.DesignRules project.

Listing 8-3   Checking if an assembly attribute exists

```
/// <summary>
/// The property all derived classes use to return the attribute type
/// they are looking for.
/// </summary>
abstract public TypeNode AttributeType
{
    get;
}

/// <summary>
/// Does the actual rule validation.
/// </summary>
/// <param name="module">
/// The assembly to check for a specific attribute.
/// </param>
```

```
/// <returns>
/// null means the attribute is present.
/// </returns>
/// <exception cref="ArgumentNullException">
/// Thrown if <paramref name="module"/> is null or Nothing.
/// </exception>
public override ProblemCollection Check ( Module module )
{
    if ( null == module )
    {
        throw new ArgumentNullException ( Constants.InvalidModule );
    }
    // Is this module an assembly?
    if ( NodeType.Assembly != module.NodeType )
    {
        return ( null );
    }


    // Get the custom attribute type.
    AttributeList attribList =
            RuleUtilities.GetCustomAttributes ( module ,
                                                AttributeType );
    if ( 1 == attribList.Length )
    {
        // Get the value of the attribute because it does exist. Since
        // I've found one attribute, that means there's an
        // ExpressionList with one item in it. Converting that to a
        // string, we get the value of the attribute. I figured this out
        // by looking at all the attributes on a module and looking at how
        // their values were determined. Thank goodness for the Watch
        // window when it comes to some serious spelunking!
        String strValue = attribList [ 0 ].Expressions [ 0 ].
                                                        ToString ( );
        if ( 0 == strValue.Length )
        {
            // Build up the error string to return.
            Problem prob = CreateModuleProblem ( module.Name );
            Problems.Add ( prob );
        }
    }
    else
    {
        // Build up the error string to return.
        Problem prob = CreateModuleProblem ( module.Name );
        Problems.Add ( prob );
    }
    return ( Problems );
}
```

Before jumping into the advanced rule development, I want to point out two hints that will help speed your rule development. The first is that you should definitely spend some quality time in Reflector looking at the Microsoft *FxCop.Sdk.Introspection.RuleUtilities* so you can see more examples of using the *Microsoft.Cci* classes in your own rules.

The second hint is about debugging your rules. If you're building your rules to use the stand-alone FxCop program, you need just to set the Start action in the Debug property tab to Start External Program and set the program to FxCop.exe. Whenever you load your rule into FxCop.exe, your breakpoints will revert from unresolved to resolved, and you'll be able to debug as you would any normal class library.

If you are building your rules to use the internal Visual Studio 2005 Code Analysis version, it gets a little more interesting to do your debugging. The actual analysis is not done inside Visual Studio 2005, it's done in a program called FxCopCmd.exe located in the *Visual_Studio_2005_Install_Directory*\Team Tools\Static Analysis Tools\FxCop directory. If you were super fast on the keyboard, you could try to attach to the FxCopCmd.exe process when it starts, but you'd probably miss it. You could also add a *Debugger.Break* call inside your rule, but the odds are quite high that you'd accidentally leave that call in when you check your code in. Fortunately, you can specify command-line parameters to FxCopCmd.exe to specify the module to analyze and the rule assembly you want to run.

After you set the Start action in the Debug property tab to Start External Program and the program to FxCopCmd.exe, you'll need to set the command-line options. You have to specify /console to indicate that you want error output to go to the screen. The /file: option allows you to specify the assembly to analyze, and /rule: is what you use to set the rule assembly to use. Now you can easily debug your Code Analysis rules. If this sounds tedious to set repeatedly, look at the FxCopCmdDebug.SettingsMaster file in the Wintellect.FxCop.UsageRules directory. You can use that file with the Settings Master add-in presented in Chapter 7, "Extending the Visual Studio IDE," to update all configurations to debug a specific program repeatedly.

Advanced Rule Development

As it turns out with rule development, you can approach your rule in several different ways. In this section, I'll show you those ways. What's amazed me about rule development is how little code you end up writing to produce some very complicated rules.

DoNotUseTraceAssertRule and CallAssertMethodsWithMessageParametersRule Rules

The two easiest-to-understand rules are the DoNotUseTraceAssertRule and CallAssertMethods-WithMessageParametersRule from the Wintellect.FxCop.UsageRules.dll assembly. As I discussed in the section "Assertions in .NET", in Chapter 3, you never want to call *Trace.Assert* in your application because it will remain in release builds, and having a customer staring at an assertion is a recipe for disaster. I also mentioned in that chapter how you should always use *Debug. Assert* with the message parameters so you can get more information in the assertion reporting than just that the assertion failed. Because those are on my list of rules that should be added to the Design Guidelines, I wanted a Code Analysis rule to ensure that you didn't violate them.

I started with the CallAssertMethodsWithMessageParametersRule because I thought it might be the easiest to develop. When you override the *Check* method that takes a *Member* parameter, you can convert the parameter into a *Method*, which has an *Instructions* property containing all the IL instructions as an array through the *InstructionList* class. As I was prototyping up the rule, I saw that each *Instruction* has a *Value* property defined as an *Object*. Using the great feature in the Watch window that shows the real type for anything in an *Object* value, for CALL and CALLVIRT instructions, the *Value* field was a *Method*. That turns out to be the method being called, and just as viewing the disassembly in ILDASM, its *FullName* property contains the complete name of the method. In about five minutes, I had the *Check* method implementing the rule as shown here:

```
public override ProblemCollection Check ( Member member )
{
    // Safely convert the member into a method.
    Method method = member as Method;
    if ( null != method )
    {
        // It's simple enough to walk the instructions.
        for ( int i = 0 ; i < method.Instructions.Length ; i++ )
        {
            OpCode currOp = method.Instructions [ i ].OpCode;
            // Is this a call?
            if ( ( currOp == OpCode.Call ) ||
                 ( currOp == OpCode.Callvirt ) )
            {
                Method callee = method.Instructions [ i ].
                                                    Value as Method;
                if ( null != callee )
                {
                    // Is this a call to Debug.Assert with a single
                    // parameter?
                    if ( callee.FullName ==
                      "System.Diagnostics.Debug.Assert(System.Boolean)" )
                    {
                        // Yep. Report the error.
                        Resolution res = GetResolution (
                                RuleUtilities.Format ( method ) );
                        Problem prob = new Problem ( res );
                        Problems.Add ( prob );
                    }
                }
            }
        }
    }
    return ( Problems );
}
```

When I turned to the DoNotUseTraceAssertRule, it was obvious that the nearly identical approach would work. In fact, the only difference is that instead of looking for just a single overload, I needed to look for all *System.Diagnostics.Trace.Assert* methods. Fortunately, the *Method* type inherits from *Member*, which has a *DeclaringType* field, which will give you the namespace, and the *Name* field, which is an *Identifier*, will give you just the name of the method. This rule took all of two minutes to develop.

DoNotLockOnPublicFields, DoNotLockOnThisOrMe, DoNotLockOnTypes, and DoNotUseMethodImplAttributeWithSynchronized Rules

If you read my good friend Jeffrey Richter's seminal book, *CLR via C#, Second Edition* (Microsoft Press, 2005), you'd probably agree that his discussion in the section "The *Monitor* class and SyncBlocks" in Chapter 24, "Thread Synchronization," is both funny and sad at the same time. He discusses the "Great Idea" the CLR team had for how the designers thought SyncBlocks should work. Unfortunately, the way they were implemented was botched, and Jeffrey exposes all sorts of problems if you use the SyncBlocks as Microsoft intended. The way Jeffrey recommends to fix these issues is to do your SyncBlock locking with a private instance field in the class. When I read that section of the chapter, I immediately saw that all the problems Jeffrey mentioned should be Code Analysis rules to ensure that you don't accidentally expose those issues with your synchronization.

I first tackled the DoNotUseMethodImplAttributeWithSynchronized rule to look for the bad case of using *MethodImplAttribute* with the *MethodImplAttributes.Synchronized*. That's bad because static methods cause you to lock on all instances of that type, and instance methods will lock on the *this/Me* pointer. I coded up the rule to look for *MethodImplAttribute* attributes on the method using the techniques I used in the AssembliesHave*AttributesRules, but it didn't work. Poking around a bit with Reflector and ILDASM, I realized that there's something special about how *MethodImplAttribute* is handled by the compiler and the CLR because it is not through standard attributes. Fortunately, I also found that the *Method* type has a property, *ImplFlags*, which holds the *Microsof.Cci.MethodImplFlags*, which map directly to the real *Method-ImplAttribute*. I simply ANDed the *Method.ImplFlags* with *MethodImplFlags.Synchronized* and would know if the invalid attribute was used so I could report the error.

When I turned to testing the rule on as much code as I could find, it turned out that there was a major problem with the rule. There was no bug in my code, but there's a problem in some automatically generated code. When you declare an event handler in your class, under the covers, you're actually generating two methods, *add* and *remove*, for your event that allow callers to hook up their event handlers. That's what makes it trivial to use the C# += operator on an event.

Sadly, that automatically generated code has the *MethodImplFlags.Synchronized* value plastered on both of those methods to do the synchronization. In an ideal world, everyone would implement their own *add* and *remove* methods for events and properly handle their synchronization. Alas, that's not going to happen in reality. Even though the auto-generated code is an error, seeing several dozen events always being flagged will cause people to turn off the rule, which is the worst thing that can happen in a diagnostic tool.

To make the rule more usable, I had to add code that specifically looked for the automati-cally generated event *add* and *remove* methods. The pattern is a simple regular expression: (*add_*|*remove_*).+\(.+*EventHandler*. If I see that pattern in the method's full name, I won't flag the method as an error. If you want more background information on why you want to explicitly do your own event add and remove methods, see the section "Explicitly Controlling Event Registration and Unregistration" in Chapter 10 of *CLR via C#, Second Edition*.

Whereas looking for an attribute is relatively easy, I figured that because the other three rules would require figuring out the parameter to *Monitor.Enter*, they would take a little more work, which they certainly did. My first thought was to look at the possibilities of "visiting" the appropriate methods. The *BaseIntrospectionRule* derives from the *Microsoft.Cci.StandardVisitor*, which has methods that enable you to ask the Introspection engine to walk the IL instructions for you. For example, if you were interested only in binary expressions, you'd override the virtual *VisitBinaryExpression* method, and your code gets called back when encountering them. With the *Visit** methods, you can save yourself a huge amount of code because you don't have to do the manual analysis of every single instruction.

I coded up a prototype that overrode *VisitMethodCall* to see if I could tease out the parameter passed to *Monitor.Enter* in order to do the analysis on it. Unfortunately, the parameter data showed only that the data was an *Object*, which is the exact parameter that *Monitor.Enter* takes. When I looked at the IL in Reflector, I realized that the *VisitMethodCall* was working as it should because the code prior to the call had already done whatever conversion was necessary to force the data into an *Object* type. That's when I realized that I was going to have to do some IL analysis all on my own to determine the exact parameter types.

I whipped up some code in C# and Visual Basic that did all the synchronization wrong to see if I could find a pattern to the IL generation so I could look for that to produce the errors. After compiling the code every possible way to ensure that there weren't any optimization differences, I found the patterns. For example, if you your code makes a call to *lock(this)*, the following code is produced:

```
The C# IL that indicates the this/Me pointer is passed is the following:
1. ldarg.0
2. dup
3. stloc.0
4. call  void [mscorlib]System.Threading.Monitor::Enter(object)
For Visual Basic, the IL looks like the following:
1. ldarg.0
2. stloc.0
3. ldloc.0
4. call void [mscorlib]System.Threading.Monitor::Enter(object)
```

The actual instruction that puts the *this* pointer on the stack is *LDARG.0*. It turns out that in the case of *lock(this)* and *lock(<public field>)*, three instructions before the CALL to *Monitor.Enter* is the key data about what's being passed to the *Monitor.Enter* call. A call to *lock(<type>)* was slightly different code in that the third instruction before is the CALL to *Type.GetTypeFrom-Handle*, and the fourth instruction before the CALL to *Monitor.Enter* is loading the token to the actual class on the stack.

Because these patterns are so similar, I developed a base class, *BaseLockAnalysisRule*, in .\Wintellect.FxCop.UsageRules\UsageRules.cs that does all the work to look for calls to *Monitor .Enter*, and if found, calls an abstract method, *RuleLogic*, which does the particular rule's problem reporting. In Listing 8-4, I extracted the *BaseLockAnalysisRule.Check* method so you could see the common work. Also in the listing is the *DoNotLockOnPublicFields.RuleLogic* method as an example. The *RuleLogic* method for *DoNotLockOnThisOrMe* and *DoNotLockOnTypes* are self-explanatory.

Listing 8-4 *BaseLockAnalysis.Check* and *DoNotLockOnPublicFields.RuleLogic* Methods

```
/////////////////////////////////////////////////////////////////
// BaseLockAnalysis.Check method (and helpers) shared by
// DoNotLockOnPublicFields, DoNotLockOnThisOrMe, and DoNotLockOnTypes
/////////////////////////////////////////////////////////////////
public override ProblemCollection Check ( Member member )
{
    // Safely convert the member to a method.
    Method method = member as Method;
    if ( null != method )
    {
        // Save off if this is a Visual Basic module.
        Boolean isVisualBasic = RuleUtilities.IsVisualBasicModule (
                            method.DeclaringType.DeclaringModule );
        // It turns out that calling the VisitMethodCall does not give
        // sufficient information about the parameter. I'll look through
        // the IL so I can extract the actual item being passed. This
        // is a little messy and works for C# and Visual Basic. It may
        // not work for other languages.
        for ( int i = 0 ; i < method.Instructions.Length ; i++ )
        {
            OpCode currOp = method.Instructions [ i ].OpCode;
            // Is this a call?
            if ( ( currOp == OpCode.Call ) ||
               ( currOp == OpCode.Callvirt ) )
            {
                Method callee = method.Instructions [ i ].
                                                Value as Method;
                if ( null != callee )
                {
                    // Is this a call to Monitor.Enter?
                    if ( callee.FullName ==
                        "System.Threading.Monitor.Enter(System.Object)" )
                    {
                        // Get the location of the call to Monitor.Enter
                        // so it can be output in any error message.
                        SourceContext ctx = method.Instructions [ i ].
                                                SourceContext;
                        if ( true == isVisualBasic )
                        {
                            HandleVisualBasicCode ( method , i , ctx );
                        }
                        else
                        {
                            HandleCSharpCode ( method , i , ctx );
                        }
                    }
                }
            }
        }
    }
    return ( Problems );
}
```

```csharp
private void HandleVisualBasicCode ( Method method ,
                                     int callToEnter ,
                                     SourceContext sourceContext )
{
    // If two instructions above the call to Monitor.Enter is a call
    // to Microsoft.VisualBasic.CompilerServices.ObjectFlowControl::
    // CheckForSyncLockOnValueType(object), the actual parameter is
    // passed to that item.
    // Here's an example of the IL from a Visual Basic method:
    // L_0002: ldarg.0
    // L_0003: ldfld object VBErrors.VBErrors.Class1::obj
    // L_0008: stloc.0
    // L_0009: ldloc.0
    // L_000a: call void [Microsoft.VisualBasic]Microsoft.VisualBasic.
    //                    CompilerServices.ObjectFlowControl::
    //                    CheckForSyncLockOnValueType(object)
    // L_000f: nop
    // L_0010: ldloc.0
    // L_0011: call void [mscorlib]System.Threading.Monitor::
    //                    Enter(object)
    int callIndex = 2;
    Instruction callCheck = method.Instructions [ callToEnter -
                                                  callIndex ];
    // If it's an NOP, it's a debug build, so go back one more
    // instruction.
    if ( callCheck.OpCode == OpCode.Nop )
    {
        callIndex++;
        callCheck = method.Instructions [ callToEnter - callIndex ];
    }
    Method callCheckMethod = callCheck.Value as Method;
    if ( null != callCheckMethod )
    {
        if ( true == callCheckMethod.FullName.
                         Contains ( "CheckForSyncLockOnValueType" ) )
        {
            // The actual parameter is what's passed to
            // CheckForSyncLockOnValueType, which I can handle in the
            // C# code logic.
            HandleCSharpCode ( method ,
                               callToEnter - callIndex ,
                               sourceContext );
        }
        else
        {
            // There's no CheckForSyncLockOnValueType call, so the
            // code is generated like C#.
            HandleCSharpCode ( method , callToEnter , sourceContext );
        }
    }
    else
    {
        // If it's not a call instruction, treat the code as normal.
        HandleCSharpCode ( method , callToEnter , sourceContext );
    }
}
```

```
private void HandleCSharpCode ( Method method ,
                                int callToEnter ,
                                SourceContext sourceContext )
{
    Instruction fourthBack = null;
    if ( ( callToEnter - 4 ) >= 0 )
    {
        fourthBack = method.Instructions [ callToEnter - 4 ];
    }
    Instruction thirdBack = method.Instructions [ callToEnter - 3 ];
    // Let the derived class do its magic.
    RuleLogic ( fourthBack , thirdBack , method , sourceContext );
}
/////////////////////////////////////////////////////////////////////
// DoNotLockOnPublicFields.RuleLogic Method
/////////////////////////////////////////////////////////////////////
protected override void RuleLogic ( Instruction lockParameterOne ,
                                    Instruction lockParameterTwo ,
                                    Method method ,
                                    SourceContext sourceContext )
{
    // This rule relies only on lockParameterTwo.
    Debug.Assert ( null != lockParameterTwo ,
                   "null != lockParameterTwo" );
    if ( null == lockParameterTwo )
    {
        throw new ArgumentNullException ( Resources.LockParamTwoNull );
    }
    // The C# IL looks like the following:
    // 1. ldarg.0
    // 2. ldfld object UsageRulesLockTests.Class1::obj
    // 3. dup
    // 4. stloc.0
    // 5. call void [mscorlib]System.Threading.Monitor::Enter(object)
    // The Visual Basic IL looks like the following. The caller takes
    // care of getting the ldfld value from CheckForSyncLockOnValueType
    // before calling this method.
    // 1. ldarg.0
    // 2. ldfld object VBErrors.VBErrors.Class1::obj
    // 3. stloc.0
    // 4. ldloc.0
    // 5. call void [Microsoft.VisualBasic]Microsoft.VisualBasic.
    //               CompilerServices.ObjectFlowControl::
    //                       CheckForSyncLockOnValueType(object)
    // 6. nop <-- Only there in a debug build!
    // 7. ldloc.0
    // 8. call void [mscorlib]System.Threading.Monitor::Enter(object)
    Field field = null;
    // Is this a ldfld instruction?
    if ( lockParameterTwo.OpCode == OpCode.Ldfld )
    {
        // Grab the value out of the instruction.
        field = lockParameterTwo.Value as Field;
        if ( null != field )
        {
```

```
                    // If the field is visible outside the assembly, it's a
                    // public, so flag the error.
                    if ( true == field.IsVisibleOutsideAssembly )
                    {
                        // Yep. Report the error.
                        String fmt = RuleUtilities.Format ( method );
                        Resolution res = GetResolution ( fmt , field.FullName );
                        Problem prob = new Problem ( res , sourceContext );
                        Problems.Add ( prob );
                    }
                }
            }
        }
    }
}
```

When I first developed the *DoNotLockOnPublicFields.RuleLogic* method, I missed the *IsVisible-OutsideAssembly* property, so I went through a huge amount of work to look up the assembly containing the type so I could get the *TypeNode* for the field to determine if it was public. After struggling through some very tough crashes from deep inside the Introspection engine, I was wondering if I would be able to get the rule working. Following my own advice in "The Debugging Process" section of Chapter 1, "Bugs: Where They Come From and How You Solve Them," I thought creatively and walked away for a while. While working on another rule, I stumbled on the *IsVisibleOutsideAssembly* property in Reflector and realized that solved all the problems.

Such is the fun of working completely without documentation. When the future version of Visual Studio that comes with the new analysis engine and full documentation is released, it won't be as challenging to develop rules. The good news is that today you have rules that work to find very nasty SyncBlock issues so you can make sure that your code avoids them.

AvoidBoxingAndUnboxingInLoops Rule

As has been beaten into the head of nearly every developer using .NET, converting from value types to objects (boxing) and objects to value types (unboxing) is a bad thing to do frequently because it can kill your performance. However, unless you are disassembling your binary to text and manually searching for the BOX and UNBOX instructions after every build, it's hard to know exactly when boxing and unboxing happen. An occasional BOX instruction is unavoidable, such as when you pass an integer as a parameter to *String.Format*, but having that BOX or UNBOX instruction inside a loop can be a major performance killer.

When I first developed AvoidBoxingAndUnboxingInLoops from the Wintellect.FxCop.PerformanceRules.dll assembly, I thought that all I would have to do was look through the instructions for the method, and if I found any BOX or UNBOX instructions, I'd report the error. I liked that approach, because it turned out that implementing the rule was as simple as the following code snippet:

```
private void WalkInstructionsManually ( Method memberMethod )
{
    // Look at each instruction in the method.
    for ( int branchIndex = 0 ;
```

```
        branchIndex < memberMethod.Instructions.Length ;
        branchIndex++ )
{
    switch ( memberMethod.Instructions [ branchIndex ].OpCode )
    {
        // Is it a box?
        case OpCode.Box:
            boxInstuctCount++;
            break;
        // Is it any kind of unbox?
        case OpCode.Unbox:
        case OpCode.Unbox_Any:
            unboxInstructCount++;
            break;
    }
}
}
```

The only problem with simply looking for the raw instructions is that you end up with more false positives than I felt you should. When talking to people who used the rule written with the above loop, they found it rather annoying and had a tendency to ignore it. My next thought was to report an error only if there were three BOX instructions and one UNBOX instruction. That eliminated many of the false positive warnings, but it came back to bite me on a big performance-tuning job.

The client had slow code, and one of my standard tricks is to run Code Analysis or the stand-alone FxCop across the code with my rules enabled. The analysis reported nothing out of the ordinary, so we rolled up our sleeves and started digging like crazy through performance counters in PerfMon and other performance tools. After several days of hard digging, we found that the problem was a single BOX instruction inside a critical loop. Changing a structure, which is a value type, into a class gave us the performance boost the client needed. I felt horrible that the client had to wait several days for me to fix the problem when a smarter rule would have narrowed this problem down in minutes. I immediately started looking at how I could report only when I saw BOX or UNBOX instructions that occurred in any looping construct.

Handling all the looping constructs (*do, for, foreach,* and *while*) was going to be a big job. However, I saw that the *Microsoft.Cci.StandardVisitor* from the Code Analysis Microsoft.Cci.dll had very cool methods called *VisitDoWhile, VisitFor, VisitForEach,* and *VisitWhile,* so I immediately overrode each of them and ran through a quick test to see what I would have to do to find the BOX and UNBOX instructions. Sadly, it turns out that those sexy methods are never called. In fact, when I looked at FxCop 1.35, which was released after Visual Studio 2005, those methods no longer appear on the *Microsoft.Cci.StandardVisitor* class. That meant that I was going to have to do the instruction stream analysis myself.

After hours of writing small methods and disassembling everything in sight, I found the patterns in IL generation that indicate a loop versus a conditional. Conditionals will move to offsets forward in the IL stream, whereas branches move backwards in the stream. Now that I had the patterns, it was possible to look for the BOX and UNBOX instructions that occur inside just the loops. Listing 8-5 shows all the code for the AvoidBoxingAndUnboxingInLoops rule. In the code are the comments that describe every action I performed.

The main item to notice in the code is that I took a bit of the easy way out in the algorithm in which I analyze loops. I don't do any special processing for nested loops, so if you have a BOX in an inner loop, it will be reported as an error for both the inner and outer loops. When I sketched out what it would take to handle all the recursion to account for them, I felt that it was easiest to look through each loop even though I might be looking through various instruction sections multiple times.

Listing 8-5 AvoidBoxingAndUnboxingInLoops Rule Code

```
/*-----------------------------------------------------------------------------
 * Debugging Microsoft .NET 2.0 Applications
 * Copyright © 1997-2006 John Robbins -- All rights reserved.
 -----------------------------------------------------------------------------*/
using System;
using System.Collections;
using System.Globalization;
using System.Xml;
using Microsoft.Cci;
using Microsoft.FxCop.Sdk;
using Microsoft.FxCop.Sdk.Introspection;
using System.Diagnostics;
using System.Diagnostics.CodeAnalysis;

namespace Wintellect.FxCop.PerformanceRules
{
    /// <summary>
    /// The rule to check for box and unbox instructions inside loops.
    /// </summary>
    [CLSCompliant ( false )]
    public class AvoidBoxingAndUnboxingInLoops : BasePerformanceRule
    {
        /// <summary>
        /// Gets the base class hooked up.
        /// </summary>
        public AvoidBoxingAndUnboxingInLoops ( )
            : base ( "AvoidBoxingAndUnboxingInLoops" )
        {
        }

        /// <summary>
        /// Sets the visibility to all methods.
        /// </summary>
        public override TargetVisibilities TargetVisibility
        {
            get { return ( TargetVisibilities.All ); }
        }

        /// <summary>
        /// Checks for excessive box and unbox instructions inside loops.
        /// </summary>
```

```
/// <param name="member">
/// The method to check.
/// </param>
/// <returns>
/// null  - The assembly has a box/unbox problem in loops.
/// !null - The error message to report.
/// </returns>
public override ProblemCollection Check ( Member member )
{
    // Safely convert the member to a method.
    Method method = member as Method;
    if ( null != method )
    {
        // Look at each instruction in the method.
        for ( int iCurr = 0 ;
              iCurr < method.Instructions.Length ;
              iCurr++ )
        {
            // Get the current instruction.
            Instruction ins = method.Instructions [ iCurr ];
            // Is this a looping branch?
            if ( true == IsLoopingBranch ( ins ) )
            {
                // Calculate the index into this array of instructions
                // where the branch goes.
                int branchToIndex = FindBranchOffsetIndex ( iCurr ,
                                              method.Instructions );
                // Now I've got the starting and ending indexes of the
                // loop range. Run through and look for all BOX and
                // UNBOX instructions. In case you're wondering, my
                // algorithm here does not pay attention to nested loops.
                // In other words, if there are two nested loops, I'll
                // be looking through the inner loop code twice. I
                // looked at trying to handle nested loops, but it
                // quickly degenerates into a nasty situation in which
                // I'd have to create numerous data structures to track
                // which indexes in the instruction array I've already
                // looked at and processed. In the big scheme of things,
                // I thought this simpler route was more than sufficient
                // to do the work.
                if ( true == HasBoxOrUnboxInLoop ( branchToIndex ,
                                                   iCurr ,
                                                   method.Instructions ) )
                {
                    // Got an error.
                    // Put the name in the same format as FxCop does.
                    String typeName = RuleUtilities.Format ( method );
                    // Get the one resolution.
                    Resolution res = GetResolution ( typeName );
                    Problem prob = new Problem ( res );
                    Problems.Add ( prob );
                }
            }
        }
    }
}
```

```
        return ( Problems );
}

private static bool HasBoxOrUnboxInLoop ( int branchToIndex ,
                                          int branchIndex ,
                                          InstructionList instructionList )
{
    for ( int i = branchToIndex ; i < branchIndex ; i++ )
    {
        switch ( instructionList [ i ].OpCode )
        {
            // Is it a box?
            case OpCode.Box:
            // Is it any kind of unbox?
            case OpCode.Unbox:
            case OpCode.Unbox_Any:
                // Just one of these is bad enough to trigger the error.
                return ( true );
            //break;
            default:
                break;
        }
    }
    return ( false );
}

private static int FindBranchOffsetIndex ( int branchIndex ,
                                           InstructionList instructionList )
{
    // Get the offset we're looking for.
    int branchToOffset = (int)instructionList [ branchIndex ].Value;
    int iCurr = branchIndex - 1;
    // Loop backwards until we find the top offset for the loop.
    while ( iCurr > 0 )
    {
        if ( branchToOffset == instructionList [ iCurr ].Offset )
        {
            return ( iCurr );
        }
        iCurr--;
    }
    Debug.Assert ( iCurr != 0 , "iCurr != 0" );
    return ( 0 );
}

// I can't really help the complexity here. The switch statement in the
// method is the problem.
[SuppressMessage ( "Microsoft.Maintainability" ,
                   "CA1502:AvoidExcessiveComplexity" )]
private static Boolean IsLoopingBranch ( Instruction ins )
{
    Boolean retValue = false;
    switch ( ins.OpCode )
    {
        // Is this a branching instruction?
        case OpCode.Bge:
        case OpCode.Bge_Un:
```

```
                    case OpCode.Bgt:
                    case OpCode.Bgt_Un:
                    case OpCode.Ble:
                    case OpCode.Ble_Un:
                    case OpCode.Blt:
                    case OpCode.Blt_Un:
                    case OpCode.Bne_Un:
                    case OpCode.Brfalse:
                    case OpCode.Brfalse_S:
                    case OpCode.Brtrue:
                    case OpCode.Brtrue_S:
                        {
                            // From *lots* of staring at all sorts of IL code
                            // generation, the pattern is that conditionals (if
                            // statements jump forward in the IL stream), whereas
                            // loops (for, do, while, foreach) move backwards.
                            // Therefore, if the Value field, which is the branch
                            // to offset, is less than this instruction's offset,
                            // we're looking at a loop.
                            int branchToOffset = (int)ins.Value;
                            if ( branchToOffset < ins.Offset )
                            {
                                retValue = true;
                            }
                        }
                        break;
                }
                return ( retValue );
            }
        }
    }
```

ExceptionDocumentationInvalidRule and ExceptionDocumentationMissingRule Rules

The final rules I want to discuss are the most important in my opinion. As you could tell from Chapter 2, I'm a huge believer in XML documentation, especially the *<exception>* tag. I wanted rules that would tell you when you were missing that tag in your documentation for your direct throws and if you documented an exception but didn't actually throw the exception.

Poking through the *Visit** methods, I saw that the *VisitThrow* method looked as if it fit the bill, but I wasn't so sure it would work because every other time I tried to use the *Visit** methods, they didn't work. Fortunately, in this case, they do work. As you've seen, the *Node* class, which is the base type for all parameters to the *Visit** methods, contains lots of descriptive information about operands, values, and other important items you'll need to build great analysis rules.

The *Throw* class, which is passed to the *VisitThrow* method, has an *Expression* property that can access the *TypeNode* that's being thrown in the *Type* property. Consequently, the statement *Throw.Expression.Type.FullName* is all that it takes to get the type being thrown, regardless of whether it's a throw followed by a new exception type or a throw of a local variable.

Of course, there was no way developing this rule was going to be straightforward. When I started the work to process the RETHROW instructions, the *Expression* property was *null*, so I had a problem finding the type. I could have given up, deciding not to handle rethrows, but I really felt they were important to document. After a good bit of poking around, I realized that I needed to look at the catch blocks in the method, which contain information on the exception type to be rethrown, to see if I could match up the rethrow to its actual block.

Getting the exception handlers for a method is trivial because the Introspection engine hands them to you right in the *Method.ExceptionHandlers* property. One thing I should tell you at this point about the Introspection engine metadata reader is that it's rather lazy—it won't read in the metadata until it is absolutely necessary—so I accessed only *Method.ExceptionHandlers* in the *VisitThrow* method. The act of visiting gets the metadata all read in.

Although having all the catch blocks was great, I wasn't sure how I was going to exactly match a RETHROW instruction to the catch block where it occurred. After some poking around, I found a very interesting property, *UniqueKey*, that all *Node* values contain. *Node* is the root base class of most of the types in *Microsoft.Cci* namespace. I wondered how unique it was because if everything provided by the Introspection engine (from individual instructions through higher constructs) had a unique value, I could look for the particular RETHROW instruction inside each catch block's instructions so I could match them up. Sure enough, that's exactly how everything works out.

Of course, there was one last trip-up. The *ExceptionHandler* contains the first basic block of the entire catch statement and the block after the catch block ends. It does not have any of the blocks between those two points. To make things even more bizarre, there's no way that I found to loop through the instructions starting at an arbitrary place in the stream. This means that unless the *UniqueKey* property for the rethrow was in the first basic block of the catch statement, I wasn't going to be able to figure out the type. Therefore, it was going to make the rule almost worthless in my opinion.

After nearly rubbing my head bald trying to figure out how to get the blocks between the start of the catch and the end, I finally realized that sometimes the only way is the brute-force way. What I needed to do was save the method being processed, and when looking for the rethrow *UniqueKey*, start at the first statement in the method and then skip to the start of the catch block. Once there, I could look for the *UniqueKey* value indicating the rethrow. It's not very pretty, but it certainly works. Considering that the entire rule-writing system is undocumented, I'm quite happy about how the solution turned out. Listing 8-6 shows the *Check*, *VisitThrow*, and *IsRethrowInCatchBlock* methods from the *BaseExceptionDocumentationRule* class, which is the base class for ExceptionDocumentationInvalidRule and ExceptionDocumentationMissingRule.

Listing 8-6 *BaseExceptionDocumentationRule.Check, BaseExceptionDocumentationRule.VisitThrow,* and *BaseExceptionDocumentationRule.IsRethrowInCatchBlock* methods

```
/////////////////////////////////////////////////////////////////////
// BaseExceptionDocumentationRule.Check Method
/////////////////////////////////////////////////////////////////////
public override ProblemCollection Check ( Member member )
```

```
{
    if ( null == member )
    {
        throw new ArgumentNullException ( Constants.InvalidMember );
    }
    Method memberMethod = member as Method ;
    if ( null == memberMethod )
    {
        return ( null ) ;
    }

    // Start by saving off the method under evaluation.
    currentMethod = memberMethod ;

    // Allocate a new array list to fill with exceptions for this
    // method.
    methodExceptions = new ArrayList ( ) ;

    // Get the declaring module so I can look up the XML Documentation
    // file.
    String mod = memberMethod.DeclaringType.DeclaringModule.Location ;

    // Get the XML Doc Comment file for this module.
    XmlDocCommentsFileDictionary currXmlDocs =
                                        OpenModuleXmlDocFile ( mod ) ;

    // Start the walking of this method's code. I'm interested only in
    // the body of the method, not all the attributes and such, so I'll
    // walk just the method body instead of the whole thing.
    VisitBlock ( memberMethod.Body ) ;

    // Now that pounding through the IL is done, get the documented
    // exception tags for this method into an array list.
    ArrayList docdExceptions = null ;
    if ( null == currXmlDocs )
    {
        docdExceptions = new ArrayList ( ) ;
    }
    else
    {
        // Get the documented exceptions for this method. Notice
        // that Method.DocumentationId.Name contains the XML Doc
        // Comment decorated name. However, the name returned by
        // Cci is correct for straight methods but not for properties,
        // indexers, or nested items, so I need to correct it.
        String xmlName = FixCciDocumentationName (
                                memberMethod.DocumentationId.Name);
        docdExceptions = currXmlDocs.GetExceptionTypesThrown(xmlName);
    }

    // Because the RuleLogic methods could use ArrayList.BinarySearch, I
    // need to sort the elements in both arrays before passing them on.
    methodExceptions.Sort ( ) ;
    docdExceptions.Sort ( ) ;
```

```
        // Ask the derived type to do its logic. If there are any items in
        // the problemExceptTypes array, those are the ones with problems.
        ArrayList problemExceptTypes = RuleLogic ( methodExceptions ,
                                                   docdExceptions   ) ;

        // Were there any problems to report?
        if ( problemExceptTypes.Count > 0 )
        {
            // Yep, create the Problem report.
            foreach ( String exVal in problemExceptTypes )
            {
                Resolution res =
                    GetResolution ( RuleUtilities.Format ( memberMethod ),
                                    exVal                                 );
                Problem prob = new Problem ( res ) ;
                Problems.Add ( prob ) ;
            }
        }
        return ( Problems ) ;
}
//////////////////////////////////////////////////////////////////////
// BaseExceptionDocumentationRule.VisitThrow Method
//////////////////////////////////////////////////////////////////////
public override Statement VisitThrow ( Throw Throw )
{
    if ( null == Throw )
    {
        throw new ArgumentNullException ( Constants.InvalidThrowType );
    }
    // Nothing like a check that's a palindrome! Here I'm checking if
    // the Throw parameter is a THROW or a RETHROW instruction.
    if ( Throw.NodeType == NodeType.Throw )
    {
        // The easy case! Grab the Expression.Type field, and I've got
        // the type being thrown.
        methodExceptions.Add ( Throw.Expression.Type.FullName ) ;
    }
    else if ( Throw.NodeType == NodeType.Rethrow )
    {
        // A little harder case. There's no type associated with the
        // rethrow instruction, so I need to grind through the
        // exception handlers and match up this instruction to the
        // appropriate handle and extract the type that way.

        // Get the ExceptionHandlerList from the method. The reason I
        // don't do this in the Check method is that the FxCOP metadata
        // reader is lazy and won't read the metadata unless necessary.
        // If I save off the ExceptionHandlerList *BEFORE* calling
        // VisitBlock, *AND* this is the only rule run, the metadata
        // reader hasn't filled it out yet. By grabbing the
        // ExceptionHandler list here, I'm assured that it's always
        // filled in.
        ExceptionHandlerList exceptionHandlerList =
                                    currentMethod.ExceptionHandlers;
```

```
                // Just to make sure....
                Debug.Assert ( exceptionHandlerList.Length > 0 ,
                               "exceptionHandlerList.Length > 0" );

                // Signals I've found the appropriate block.
                bool foundType = false;

                // Loop through the exception handlers.
                for ( int i = 0 ; i < exceptionHandlerList.Length ; i++ )
                {
                    ExceptionHandler exh = exceptionHandlerList [ i ];
                    // I care only if it's a catch block.
                    if ( NodeType.Catch == exh.HandlerType )
                    {
                        // Do the hard work of looking through the whole catch
                        // block.
                        foundType = IsRethrowInCatchBlock ( Throw.UniqueKey ,
                                                            exh );

                        if ( true == foundType )
                        {
                            methodExceptions.Add ( exh.FilterType.FullName );
                            break;
                        }
                    }
                }
                Debug.Assert ( true == foundType , "true == foundType" );
            }
#if DEBUG
            // Just because I'm paranoid...
            else
            {
                Debug.Assert ( false , "Invalid Throw type!!" );
            }
#endif
            return ( base.VisitThrow ( Throw ) ) ;
}
//////////////////////////////////////////////////////////////////
// BaseExceptionDocumentationRule.IsRethrowInCatchBlock Method
//////////////////////////////////////////////////////////////////
private Boolean IsRethrowInCatchBlock ( int rethrowId ,
                                        ExceptionHandler exh )
{
    // Here's the deal: The ExceptionHandler has just the *start* block
    // in it, not all the blocks. Fortunately, it also has the block
    // that occurs after the catch. This method will get all the blocks
    // between those ranges (excluding the start) and look to see if
    // rethrow's unique ID appears between those ranges. If so, it
    // returns true.
    // This whole gyration is necessary because there's no way to ask
    // for the next block.
    // The big assumption here is that the code blocks are in logical
    // order. I feel that's a pretty safe assumption to make. ;)

    // For a bit of an optimization, I'll go ahead and look through the
    // exh.HandlerStartBlock for the rethrow. This will find those
```

```
// simple cases [catch(...){ throw; }] and avoid grinding through
// the big list of Statements looking for the particular catch.
StatementList startBlockStatements =
                    exh.HandlerStartBlock.Statements;
for ( int quickLookStatement = 0 ;
     quickLookStatement < startBlockStatements.Length ;
     quickLookStatement++ )
{
   if ( rethrowId ==
           startBlockStatements [ quickLookStatement ].UniqueKey )
   {
      // Got it!
      return ( true );
   }
}
// The throw is not in the first basic block, so grind through all
// the blocks in the catch.

// Save off the unique ids for the starting block and the after the
// catch block.
int startBlockKey = exh.HandlerStartBlock.UniqueKey;
int afterBlockKey = exh.BlockAfterHandlerEnd.UniqueKey;

// We have to start at the beginning statement in the method and
// grind all the way through.
int currentMethodStatement = 0 ;

// Run through until we find the starting block.
for ( ;
     currentMethodStatement < currentMethod.Body.Statements.Length ;
     currentMethodStatement++ )
{
   if ( startBlockKey ==currentMethod.Body.
                   Statements [ currentMethodStatement ].UniqueKey )
   {
      break;
   }
}
// I've already looked at the current block above, so I'll just bump
// right on past it here.
currentMethodStatement++;
// Loop through all the blocks in the catch statement until I find
// the block after the catch.
for ( ;
     currentMethodStatement < currentMethod.Body.Statements.Length ;
     currentMethodStatement++ )
{
   Block currBlock = (Block)
         currentMethod.Body.Statements [ currentMethodStatement ];
   // Have I reached the end?
   if ( currBlock.UniqueKey == afterBlockKey )
   {
      // Yep, leave.
      return ( false );
   }
```

```
            // Run through the instructions in this block looking for my
            // matching rethrow.
            int currInstruction = 0;
            for ( ;
                    currInstruction < currBlock.Statements.Length ;
                    currInstruction++ )
            {
                if ( currBlock.Statements [ currInstruction ].UniqueKey ==
                                                            rethrowId )
                {
                    return ( true );
                }
            }
        }
        // This is pretty serious!
        return ( false );
    }
```

Once I figured out the secret to getting all the information I needed, the actual work on the rules was easy. I wrote a class, .\Wintellect.FxCop.DesignRules\XmlDocCommentsFileDictionary.cs, which makes handling the XML documentation file for an assembly quite easy. For the Exception-DocumentationMissingRule, after I've found all throw and rethrow types, I build another list of all the documented throws from the XML documentation file. I remove all the items documented from the throw list, and any left over are the missing documentation items. Since Exception-DocumentationInvalidRule is the opposite action, I put all the core logic in the *BaseException-DocumentationRule* class so the work in the actual rule classes is quite simple.

Summary

Even though the FxCop team is feverishly working on a completely new rules engine and will not be documenting the Introspection engine, I still feel that writing your own rules is worth exploring. I hope I was able to show you some nice tricks to get started and how to write any rule you think possible with the wonderful binary analysis tools in Code Analysis/FxCop. If you're interested in writing rules but don't have an idea of one you could write, I'll leave you with a few I'd love to see:

- **Permission Documentation Check**   Much like the ExceptionDocumention*Rules I presented in this chapter, the *<permission>* tag is just as important. Write a rule that looks for permission attributes on methods or *Assert.Demand* calls inline, and verify that the appropriate value is documented.

- **Add *DebuggerDisplayAttribute* to public classes**   In Chapter 5, "Advanced Debugger Usage with Visual Studio," I showed how important the *DebuggerDisplayAttribute* class is to getting quick help in DataTips and the Watch window. Write a rule that looks for public classes, and if a *DebuggerDisplayAttribute* or *DebuggerTypeProxyAttribute* are not present, flag it as an error.

- **Incorrect *DebuggerDisplayAttribute* string**   Also in regards to the *DebuggerDisplay-Attribute*, the different expression evaluators in the debugger have varying capabilities. For example, the C# expression evaluator can handle calling methods, but Microsoft Visual Basic cannot. Write a rule that looks for invalid constructs in a *DebuggerDisplayAttribute* string, and flag an error if one occurs. Extra credit will be given if you also validate all the values to be displayed in braces as existing properties or fields.

- **Naming handles**   As I discussed in Chapter 6, "WinDBG, SOS, and ADPlus," the !handle command in WinDBG is wonderful for showing the state of all open handles in a process. However, if the handles aren't named, it's almost impossible to figure out what handle is what. Write a rule that verifies that all handle classes are called with the constructor that sets a name and that the name is not the empty string or *null/Nothing*.

Index

Symbols & Numbers

John Robbins

John is a cofounder of Wintellect (*http://www.wintellect.com*), a consulting, debugging, and education company dedicated to helping companies produce better software faster. At Wintellect, John heads the consulting and debugging services side of the business and has helped debug and tune applications for companies such as eBay, Microsoft, and AutoDesk, as well as many other corporate development shops. He also travels the world teaching his "Mastering .NET Debugging" and "Mastering Windows Debugging" courses so developers everywhere can learn the techniques he uses to solve the nastiest software problems known to man. As one of the world's recognized authorities on debugging, John takes an evil delight in finding and fixing impossible bugs in other people's programs.

John is based in New Hampshire, United States, where he lives with his wife, Pam, and the world famous debugging cats, Chloe and Gracie. In addition to being the author of the books *Debugging Microsoft .NET 2.0 Applications* (Microsoft Press, 2006), *Debugging Applications for Microsoft .NET and Microsoft Windows* (Microsoft Press, 2003), and *Debugging Applications* (Microsoft Press, 2000), John is a contributing editor for *MSDN Magazine*, in which he writes the "Bugslayer" column. He regularly speaks at conferences such as Devscovery, Tech-Ed, and DevWeek.

Prior to founding Wintellect, John was one of the early engineers at NuMega Technologies (now Compuware),where he played key roles in designing, developing, and managing such products as BoundsChecker, TrueTime, TrueCoverage, SoftICE, and TrueCoverage for Device Drivers.

Before he stumbled into software development in his late twenties, John was a paratrooper and Green Beret in the United States Army. Since he can no longer get adrenaline highs by jumping out of airplanes in the middle of the night onto unlit, postage-stamp-size drop zones carrying full combat loads, he is very happy to still be able to get out and hike up mountains under his own power.

Additional Resources for Visual Basic Developers

Published and Forthcoming Titles from Microsoft Press

Microsoft® Visual Basic® 2005 Express Edition: Build a Program Now!

Patrice Pelland • ISBN 0-7356-2213-2

Featuring a full working edition of the software, this fun and highly visual guide walks you through a complete programming project—a desktop weather-reporting application—from start to finish. You'll get an introduction to the Microsoft Visual Studio® development environment and learn how to put the lightweight, easy-to-use tools in Visual Basic Express to work right away—creating, compiling, testing, and delivering your first ready-to-use program. You'll get expert tips, coaching, and visual examples each step of the way, along with pointers to additional learning resources.

Microsoft Visual Basic 2005 *Step by Step*

Michael Halvorson • ISBN 0-7356-2131-4

With enhancements across its visual designers, code editor, language, and debugger that help accelerate the development and deployment of robust, elegant applications across the Web, a business group, or an enterprise, Visual Basic 2005 focuses on enabling developers to rapidly build applications. Now you can teach yourself the essentials of working with Visual Studio 2005 and the new features of the Visual

Basic language—one step at a time. Each chapter puts you to work, showing you how, when, and why to use specific features of Visual Basic and guiding as you create actual components and working applications for Microsoft Windows®. You'll also explore data management and Web-based development topics.

Programming Microsoft Visual Basic 2005 *Core Reference*

Francesco Balena • ISBN 0-7356-2183-7

Get the expert insights, indispensable reference, and practical instruction needed to exploit the core language features and capabilities in Visual Basic 2005. Well-known Visual Basic programming author Francesco Balena expertly guides you through the fundamentals, including modules, keywords, and inheritance, and builds your mastery of more advanced topics such as delegates, assemblies, and My Namespace. Combining

in-depth reference with extensive, hands-on code examples and best-practices advice, this *Core Reference* delivers the key resources that you need to develop professional-level programming skills for smart clients and the Web.

Programming Microsoft Visual Basic 2005 Framework Reference

Francesco Balena • ISBN 0-7356-2175-6

Complementing *Programming Microsoft Visual Basic 2005 Core Reference*, this book covers a wide range of additional topics and information critical to Visual Basic developers, including Windows Forms, working with Microsoft ADO.NET 2.0 and ASP.NET 2.0, Web services, security, remoting, and much more. Packed with sample code and real-world examples, this book will help developers move from understanding to mastery.

Programming Microsoft Windows Forms
Charles Petzold • ISBN 0-7356-2153-5

Programming Microsoft Web Forms
Douglas J. Reilly • ISBN 0-7356-2179-9

Debugging, Tuning, and Testing Microsoft .NET 2.0 Applications
John Robbins • ISBN 0-7356-2202-7

Microsoft ASP.NET 2.0 *Step by Step*
George Shepherd • ISBN 0-7356-2201-9

Microsoft ADO.NET 2.0 *Step by Step*
Rebecca Riordan • ISBN 0-7356-2164-0

Programming Microsoft ASP.NET 2.0 *Core Reference*
Dino Esposito • ISBN 0-7356-2176-4

For more information about Microsoft Press® books and other learning products,
visit: **www.microsoft.com/books** *and* **www.microsoft.com/learning**

Additional Resources for Developers: Advanced Topics and Best Practices

Published and Forthcoming Titles from Microsoft Press

Code Complete, Second Edition
Steve McConnell • ISBN 0-7356-1967-0

For more than a decade, Steve McConnell, one of the premier authors and voices in the software community, has helped change the way developers write code—and produce better software. Now his classic book, *Code Complete*, has been fully updated and revised with best practices in the art and science of constructing software. Topics include design, applying good techniques to construction, eliminating errors, planning, managing construction activities, and relating personal character to superior software. This new edition features fully updated information on programming techniques, including the emergence of Web-style programming, and integrated coverage of object-oriented design. You'll also find new code examples—both good and bad—in C++, Microsoft® Visual Basic®, C#, and Java, although the focus is squarely on techniques and practices.

More About Software Requirements: Thorny Issues and Practical Advice
Karl E. Wiegers • ISBN 0-7356-2267-1

Have you ever delivered software that satisfied all of the project specifications, but failed to meet any of the customers expectations? Without formal, verifiable requirements—and a system for managing them—the result is often a gap between what developers think they're supposed to build and what customers think they're going to get. Too often, lessons about software requirements engineering processes are formal or academic, and not of value to real-world, professional development teams. In this follow-up guide to *Software Requirements*, Second Edition, you will discover even more practical techniques for gathering and managing software requirements that help you deliver software that meets project and customer specifications. Succinct and immediately useful, this book is a must-have for developers and architects.

Software Estimation: Demystifying the Black Art
Steve McConnell • ISBN 0-7356-0535-1

Often referred to as the "black art" because of its complexity and uncertainty, software estimation is not as hard or mysterious as people think. However, the art of how to create effective cost and schedule estimates has not been very well publicized. *Software Estimation* provides a proven set of procedures and heuristics that software developers, technical leads, and project managers can apply to their projects. Instead of arcane treatises and rigid modeling techniques, award-winning author Steve McConnell gives practical guidance to help organizations achieve basic estimation proficiency and lay the groundwork to continue improving project cost estimates. This book does not avoid the more complex mathematical estimation approaches, but the non-mathematical reader will find plenty of useful guidelines without getting bogged down in complex formulas.

Debugging, Tuning, and Testing Microsoft .NET 2.0 Applications
John Robbins • ISBN 0-7356-2202-7

Making an application the best it can be has long been a time-consuming task best accomplished with specialized and costly tools. With Microsoft Visual Studio® 2005, developers have available a new range of built-in functionality that enables them to debug their code quickly and efficiently, tune it to optimum performance, and test applications to ensure compatibility and trouble-free operation. In this accessible and hands-on book, debugging expert John Robbins shows developers how to use the tools and functions in Visual Studio to their full advantage to ensure high-quality applications.

The Security Development Lifecycle
Michael Howard and Steve Lipner • ISBN 0-7356-2214-0

Adapted from Microsoft's standard development process, the Security Development Lifecycle (SDL) is a methodology that helps reduce the number of security defects in code at every stage of the development process, from design to release. This book details each stage of the SDL methodology and discusses its implementation across a range of Microsoft software, including Microsoft Windows Server™ 2003, Microsoft SQL Server™ 2000 Service Pack 3, and Microsoft Exchange Server 2003 Service Pack 1, to help measurably improve security features. You get direct access to insights from Microsoft's security team and lessons that are applicable to software development processes worldwide, whether on a small-scale or a large-scale. This book includes a CD featuring videos of developer training classes.

Software Requirements, Second Edition
Karl E. Wiegers • ISBN 0-7356-1879-8

Writing Secure Code, Second Edition
Michael Howard and David LeBlanc • ISBN 0-7356-1722-8

CLR via C#, Second Edition
Jeffrey Richter • ISBN 0-7356-2163-2

For more information about Microsoft Press® books and other learning products, visit: **www.microsoft.com/mspress** *and* **www.microsoft.com/learning**

Additional Resources for Web Developers

Published and Forthcoming Titles from Microsoft Press

Microsoft® Visual Web Developer™ 2005 Express Edition: Build a Web Site Now!
Jim Buyens ● ISBN 0-7356-2212-4

With this lively, eye-opening, and hands-on book, all you need is a computer and the desire to learn how to create Web pages now using Visual Web Developer Express Edition! Featuring a full working edition of the software, this fun and highly visual guide walks you through a complete Web page project from set-up to launch. You'll get an introduction to the Microsoft Visual Studio® environment and learn how to put the light-weight, easy-to-use tools in Visual Web Developer Express to work right away—building your first, dynamic Web pages with Microsoft ASP.NET 2.0. You'll get expert tips, coaching, and visual examples at each step of the way, along with pointers to additional learning resources.

Microsoft ASP.NET 2.0 Programming
Step by Step
George Shepherd ● ISBN 0-7356-2201-9

With dramatic improvements in performance, productivity, and security features, Visual Studio 2005 and ASP.NET 2.0 deliver a simplified, high-performance, and powerful Web development experience. ASP.NET 2.0 features a new set of controls and infrastructure that simplify Web-based data access and include functionality that facilitates code reuse, visual consistency, and aesthetic appeal. Now you can teach yourself the essentials of working with ASP.NET 2.0 in the Visual Studio environment—one step at a time. With *Step by Step*, you work at your own pace through hands-on, learn-by-doing exercises. Whether you're a beginning programmer or new to this version of the technology, you'll understand the core capabilities and fundamental techniques for ASP.NET 2.0. Each chapter puts you to work, showing you how, when, and why to use specific features of the ASP.NET 2.0 rapid application development environment and guiding you as you create actual components and working applications for the Web, including advanced features such as personalization.

Programming Microsoft ASP.NET 2.0
Core Reference
Dino Esposito ● ISBN 0-7356-2176-4

Delve into the core topics for ASP.NET 2.0 programming, mastering the essential skills and capabilities needed to build high-performance Web applications successfully. Well-known ASP.NET author Dino Esposito deftly builds your expertise with Web forms, Visual Studio, core controls, master pages, data access, data binding, state management, security services, and other must-know topics—combining definitive reference with practical, hands-on programming instruction. Packed with expert guidance and pragmatic examples, this *Core Reference* delivers the key resources that you need to develop professional-level Web programming skills.

Programming Microsoft ASP.NET 2.0
Applications: *Advanced Topics*
Dino Esposito ● ISBN 0-7356-2177-2

Master advanced topics in ASP.NET 2.0 programming—gaining the essential insights and in-depth understanding that you need to build sophisticated, highly functional Web applications successfully. Topics include Web forms, Visual Studio 2005, core controls, master pages, data access, data binding, state management, and security considerations. Developers often discover that the more they use ASP.NET, the more they need to know. With expert guidance from ASP.NET authority Dino Esposito, you get the in-depth, comprehensive information that leads to full mastery of the technology.

Programming Microsoft Windows® Forms
Charles Petzold ● ISBN 0-7356-2153-5

Programming Microsoft Web Forms
Douglas J. Reilly ● ISBN 0-7356-2179-9

CLR via C++
Jeffrey Richter with Stanley B. Lippman
ISBN 0-7356-2248-5

Debugging, Tuning, and Testing Microsoft .NET 2.0 Applications
John Robbins ● ISBN 0-7356-2202-7

CLR via C#, Second Edition
Jeffrey Richter ● ISBN 0-7356-2163-2

For more information about Microsoft Press® books and other learning products,
visit: **www.microsoft.com/books** *and* **www.microsoft.com/learning**

Additional Resources for C# Developers

Published and Forthcoming Titles from Microsoft Press

Microsoft® Visual C#® 2005 Express Edition: Build a Program Now!
Patrice Pelland • ISBN 0-7356-2229-9

In this lively, eye-opening, and hands-on book, all you need is a computer and the desire to learn how to program with Visual C# 2005 Express Edition. Featuring a full working edition of the software, this fun and highly visual guide walks you through a complete programming project—a desktop weather-reporting application—from start to finish. You'll get an unintimidating introduction to the Microsoft Visual Studio® development environment and learn how to put the lightweight, easy-to-use tools in Visual C# Express to work right away—creating, compiling, testing, and delivering your first, ready-to-use program. You'll get expert tips, coaching, and visual examples at each step of the way, along with pointers to additional learning resources.

Microsoft Visual C# 2005 *Step by Step*
John Sharp • ISBN 0-7356-2129-2

Visual C#, a feature of Visual Studio 2005, is a modern programming language designed to deliver a productive environment for creating business frameworks and reusable object-oriented components. Now you can teach yourself essential techniques with Visual C#—and start building components and Microsoft Windows®–based applications—one step at a time. With *Step by Step*, you work at your own pace through hands-on, learn-by-doing exercises. Whether you're a beginning programmer or new to this particular language, you'll learn how, when, and why to use specific features of Visual C# 2005. Each chapter puts you to work, building your knowledge of core capabilities and guiding you as you create your first C#-based applications for Windows, data management, and the Web.

Programming Microsoft Visual C# 2005 Framework Reference
Francesco Balena • ISBN 0-7356-2182-9

Complementing *Programming Microsoft Visual C# 2005 Core Reference*, this book covers a wide range of additional topics and information critical to Visual C# developers, including Windows Forms, working with Microsoft ADO.NET 2.0 and Microsoft ASP.NET 2.0, Web services, security, remoting, and much more. Packed with sample code and real-world examples, this book will help developers move from understanding to mastery.

Programming Microsoft Visual C# 2005 *Core Reference*
Donis Marshall • ISBN 0-7356-2181-0

Get the in-depth reference and pragmatic, real-world insights you need to exploit the enhanced language features and core capabilities in Visual C# 2005. Programming expert Donis Marshall deftly builds your proficiency with classes, structs, and other fundamentals, and advances your expertise with more advanced topics such as debugging, threading, and memory management. Combining incisive reference with hands-on coding examples and best practices, this *Core Reference* focuses on mastering the C# skills you need to build innovative solutions for smart clients and the Web.

CLR via C#, Second Edition
Jeffrey Richter • ISBN 0-7356-2163-2

In this new edition of Jeffrey Richter's popular book, you get focused, pragmatic guidance on how to exploit the common language runtime (CLR) functionality in Microsoft .NET Framework 2.0 for applications of all types—from Web Forms, Windows Forms, and Web services to solutions for Microsoft SQL Server™, Microsoft code names "Avalon" and "Indigo," consoles, Microsoft Windows NT® Service, and more. Targeted to advanced developers and software designers, this book takes you under the covers of .NET for an in-depth understanding of its structure, functions, and operational components, demonstrating the most practical ways to apply this knowledge to your own development efforts. You'll master fundamental design tenets for .NET and get hands-on insights for creating high-performance applications more easily and efficiently. The book features extensive code examples in Visual C# 2005.

Programming Microsoft Windows Forms
Charles Petzold • ISBN 0-7356-2153-5

CLR via C++
Jeffrey Richter with Stanley B. Lippman
ISBN 0-7356-2248-5

Programming Microsoft Web Forms
Douglas J. Reilly • ISBN 0-7356-2179-9

Debugging, Tuning, and Testing Microsoft .NET 2.0 Applications
John Robbins • ISBN 0-7356-2202-7

For more information about Microsoft Press® books and other learning products,
visit: **www.microsoft.com/books** *and* **www.microsoft.com/learning**

What do you think of this book?
We want to hear from you!

Do you have a few minutes to participate in a brief online survey? Microsoft is interested in hearing your feedback about this publication so that we can continually improve our books and learning resources for you.

To participate in our survey, please visit:

www.microsoft.com/learning/booksurvey

And enter this book's ISBN, 0-7356-2202-7. As a thank-you to survey participants in the United States and Canada, each month we'll randomly select five respondents to win one of five $100 gift certificates from a leading online merchant.* At the conclusion of the survey, you can enter the drawing by providing your e-mail address, which will be used for prize notification *only*.

Thanks in advance for your input. Your opinion counts!

Sincerely,

Microsoft Learning

Learn More. Go Further.